RE-AWAKENING LANGUAGES

Theory and practice in the revitalisation of Australia's Indigenous languages

Edited by
John Hobson, Kevin Lowe,
Susan Poetsch and Michael Walsh

SYDNEY UNIVERSITY PRESS

Published 2010 by Sydney University Press

SYDNEY UNIVERSITY PRESS
University of Sydney Library
sydney.edu.au/sup

© John Hobson, Kevin Lowe, Susan Poetsch & Michael Walsh 2010
© Individual contributors 2010
© Sydney University Press 2010

Reproduction and Communication for other purposes
Except as permitted under the Act, no part of this edition may be reproduced, stored in a retrieval system, or communicated in any form or by any means without prior written permission. All requests for reproduction or communication should be made to Sydney University Press at the address below:

Sydney University Press
Fisher Library F03
University of Sydney NSW 2006 AUSTRALIA
Email: sup.info@sydney.edu.au

Readers are advised that protocols can exist in Indigenous Australian communities against speaking names and displaying images of the deceased. Please check with local Indigenous Elders before using this publication in their communities.

National Library of Australia Cataloguing-in-Publication entry

Title:	Re-awakening languages : theory and practice in the revitalisation of Australia's Indigenous languages / edited by John Hobson ... [et al.]
ISBN:	9781920899554 (pbk.)
Notes:	Includes bibliographical references and index.
Subjects:	Aboriginal Australians--Languages--Revival.
	Australian languages--Social aspects.
	Language obsolescence--Australia.
	Language revival--Australia.
	Language planning--Australia.
Other Authors/Contributors:	
	Hobson, John Robert, 1958-
	Lowe, Kevin Connolly, 1952-
	Poetsch, Susan Patricia, 1966-
	Walsh, Michael James, 1948-
Dewey Number:	499.15

Cover image: 'Wiradjuri Water Symbols 1', drawing by Lynette Riley.
Water symbols represent a foundation requirement for all to be sustainable in their environment. For Indigenous people traditional languages are a foundation for cultural survival, hence the importance of traditional language revival, resource development and teaching programs for all Indigenous Australians.
Cover design by Miguel Yamin, the University Publishing Service

Contents

Dedication	vii
Acknowledgements	viii
Conventions	ix
Foreword	xi
Jeannie Bell	
About the authors	xiii
Introduction: Re-awakening Australian languages	xxv
John Hobson, Kevin Lowe, Susan Poetsch and Michael Walsh	

Part One: Language policy and planning — 1

Introduction: Language policy and planning — 3
    John Hobson

1. Closing the policy–practice gap: making Indigenous language policy more than empty rhetoric — 6
    Adriano Truscott and Ian Malcolm

2. Why language revitalisation sometimes works — 22
    Michael Walsh

3. Our ways of learning in Aboriginal languages — 37
    Tyson Kaawoppa Yunkaporta

Part Two: Language in communities — 51

Introduction: Language in communities — 53
    Kevin Lowe

4. Monitoring the use of Kaurna — 56
    Rob Amery

5. Introducing Wiradjuri language in Parkes — 67
    Geoff Anderson

6. Going public with language: involving the wider community in language revitalisation — 75
    Knut J. Olawsky

7. Ngapartji Ngapartji: Indigenous language in the arts 84
    Beth Sometimes and Alex Kelly

8. Awakening or awareness: are we being honest about the retrieval
    and revival of Australia's Aboriginal languages? 90
    Trevor Stockley

Part Three: Language centres and programs 101

Introduction: Language centres and programs 103
Michael Walsh

9. *Maam ngawaala: biindu ngaawa nyanggan bindaayili.*
    Language centres: keeping language strong 106
    Anna Ash, Pauline Hooler, Gary Williams and Ken Walker

10. Language centre as language revitalisation strategy:
    a case study from the Pilbara 119
    Sally Dixon and Eleonora Deak

11. Whose language centre is it anyway? 131
    Kimberley Language Resource Centre

12. Revitalisation strategies for Miriwoong 146
    Knut J. Olawsky

Part Four: Language in education 155

Introduction: Language in education 157
Susan Poetsch and Kevin Lowe

13. Using identical resources to teach young and adult
    language learners 162
    Ursula Brown

14. Aboriginal languages programs in TAFE NSW:
    delivery initiatives and strategies 170
    Jackie Cipollone

15. Reclamation process for Dharug in Sydney using song 181
    Richard Green

16. Developing the Dhurga Program at Vincentia High School:
    the language teacher's perspective 188
    Karen Lane

17. So you want to work with the community? Principles and strategies
    for school leaders affecting the establishment of Aboriginal language
    programs 194
    Kevin Lowe and Peter Howard

18. Establishing a school language program: the Parkes High School experience — 210
    Stephen Maier

19. Language revitalisation: community and school programs working together — 216
    Diane McNaboe and Susan Poetsch

20. The importance of understanding language ecologies for revitalisation — 225
    Felicity Meakins

21. The rebirth of Wergaia: a collaborative effort — 240
    Julie Reid

22. Strategies for doing the possible: supporting school Aboriginal language programs in NSW — 253
    Mari Rhydwen

Part Five: Literacy and oracy — 263

Introduction: Literacy and oracy — 265
    Michael Walsh

23. Questions of fluency in Australian languages revitalisation — 267
    John Hobson

24. Sounds, spelling and learning to read an Aboriginal language — 281
    Caroline Jones, Paul Chandler and Kevin Lowe

25. English influence on the pronunciation of re-awakened Aboriginal languages — 293
    Nicholas Reid

Part Six: Language and technology — 307

Introduction: Language and technology — 309
    John Hobson

26. Increasing the accessibility of information on the Indigenous languages of Victoria — 312
    Heather Bowe, Julie Reid and Kathy Lynch

27. Flexible IT resources for community language reclamation: using culturally appropriate contexts — 323
    Cat Kutay, George Fisher and Richard Green

28. Electronic dictionaries for language reclamation — 339
    Aidan Wilson

Part Seven: Language documentation   **349**

Introduction: Language documentation   351
Michael Walsh

29. Libraries, languages and linking up   355
Faith Baisden

30. Yan-nhaŋu language documentation and revitalisation   361
Claire Bowern and Bentley James

31. A house already lived in   372
Christina Eira and Lynnette Solomon-Dent

32. Bringing the language home: the Ngarrindjeri dictionary project   387
Mary-Anne Gale and Syd Sparrow

33. The development of the Gamilaraay, Yuwaalaraay & Yuwaalayaay Dictionary   402
John Giacon

34. Emergency language documentation teams: the Cape York Peninsula experience   418
Clair Hill and Patrick McConvell

Index   433

Dedication

During the course of this volume's preparation two very significant events occurred.

One of the authors, George Fisher, a Wiradjuri man and language revitalisation warrior of long standing, passed from this life. His loss from the fight for revitalisation's front line will be deeply felt by many for a long time to come.

Shyla Maple Madden was born to Nezmia Hay. Nezmia provided invaluable administrative support to the team in the early stages of the editorial process. Shyla's conception and delivery spanned a much shorter time than this volume's and was far more a labour of love for Nezmia and her partner.

We dedicate this volume to George in celebration of a life lived well for his language, and to Shyla in the hope that the world she grows up in will be made richer in opportunities for her to learn and speak hers with its publication.

And so the cycle continues.

Acknowledgements

The editors wish to thank a number of individuals and agencies that assisted in the production of this volume.

To all the authors who entrusted their issue to us and endured our repeated interference with it, we owe great thanks. Without their contribution the volume would not achieve the standard that it does.

To the Office of the Board of Studies NSW we are indebted for supporting community writers – many of whom had never had the opportunity to publish before – for facilitating the concept and much of the process, and affording Kevin Lowe and Susan Poetsch the opportunity to pursue the project in the first place.

To both the Koori Centre and the Department of Linguistics at the University of Sydney for providing John Hobson and Michael Walsh the freedom to undertake this endeavour, we also extend our thanks.

To the Department of Aboriginal Affairs, and particularly the always supportive Anthony Seiver, we wish to express our great appreciation for the generous provision of funds towards publication costs.

To Jeanie Bell thanks are also due for graciously providing the foreword. It is a privilege to carry the endorsement of an Aboriginal academic and community member who has worked so long and tirelessly for Australian languages.

To Lynette Riley we are particularly appreciative for the opportunity to use the cover of the volume to display her most impressive artistry that draws on her Wiradjuri tradition.

And finally, to Nezmia Hay, for nursing the editorial team along through the early stages of her and our confinement we are especially grateful. She showed great patience and tolerance with us no matter how annoying and persistent we became, and is clearly destined to make a wonderful mother.

Conventions

Unless otherwise specified the terms *Aboriginal* and *Indigenous* should be taken to refer specifically to Aboriginal Australians and Australian Aboriginal or Torres Strait Islander people throughout this volume. When used without capitals the terms *aboriginal* and *indigenous* should be taken to refer generally to the native populations of any country. Thus the aboriginal or indigenous populations of Australia are referred to as Aboriginal, Aboriginal and Torres Strait Islander people, or Indigenous Australians.

The term *Dreaming* is capitalised throughout where it refers to Indigenous Australian religious tradition. A number of authors have also chosen to follow a stylistic variation currently common in Australia of referring to senior Indigenous Australians as *Elders*.

In Australian contexts, *language* is frequently used to refer implicitly to Indigenous languages and a number of authors herein follow this practice.

As arrangements for the publication of this volume included that all chapters be individually downloadable via the internet,[1] no universal table of abbreviations or acronyms is provided. Instead these are introduced in each chapter as they arise.

---

1 ses.library.usyd.edu.au/handle/2123/6647.

Foreword

The revival of Aboriginal and Torres Strait Islander languages in Australia has been in progress for several decades, and in this time a lot of methods and strategies for reviving, renewing and maintaining our languages have been tried and tested. There are many success stories that can be told, and many others of attempts to revive language in a community or region which may only last the length of time that government funding sustains them.

When this happens the people involved in the program often lose hope. Interest and motivation drops when there isn't a paid worker keeping the language program alive and relevant to the different age groups and situations where language may be used in a contemporary setting.

What has been successful or unsuccessful in different ways is a matter of debate and also depends largely on what the language community decides is useful and relevant to them. The traditional custodians or speakers of these languages may find it important to reclaim only certain parts of a language in order to achieve short-term goals for their families and their communities, while others may be aiming for more long-term goals of increasing the number of fluent speakers.

What each language or family group does is critical to the bigger picture of what we all are trying to achieve: cultural maintenance and survival as the first people of the land. Each contribution, big or small, is part of an ongoing struggle facing all indigenous people around the world. In the midst of globalisation we strive to maintain and strengthen our identity and connection to country through our language, cultural practices and values for present and future generations.

The contribution of Aboriginal and Torres Strait Islander people in Australia to linguistic and cultural diversity worldwide is essential and is happening through the important work in which we are all involved. The achievements and success of this work are reflected in the papers and case studies presented in this very important book.

This work is sustained in different ways in different places with leadership from the Elders and the knowledge holders in our communities. They provide us with guidance from the Elders who walked before them, and who still watch over us today to give us the strength to endure the challenges we face now and in the future.

This collection of papers reflects the story of different groups and their experiences. They are the voice of the land and the voice of the people breathing life back into the languages that existed on country for thousands of years prior to their more recent decline. Such stories will provide invaluable inspiration to those community people just beginning the journey of reclaiming their language, as well as to those of us who are continually reviewing what we have done so far and continue to do in our efforts to renew, revive and maintain our unique language and culture in this country – our homeland.

Galangoor nguu, dimingali moghwidhaan, djinaang djaan
Good spirit, sacred stories, feet on the ground

Jeanie Bell

Batchelor Institute of Indigenous Tertiary Education

About the authors

Rob Amery completed a PhD at the University of Adelaide in 1998 (published in August 2000) on Kaurna language reclamation. He serves as consultant linguist to Kaurna language programs in schools and community projects and has advised on numerous place-naming initiatives and other Kaurna naming activity. He works closely with members of the Kaurna community to reclaim the language from historical materials and to develop it for use in a range of contemporary contexts. He convenes the Kaurna Warra Pintyandi group which meets monthly to address requests for names and translations, and to work on Kaurna language projects.

Geoff Anderson *Garrama Ngarru Ngarru* (Hunter of Sweet Things) is a Wiradjuri man from Parkes, a proud member of the Wiradjuri Council of Elders, the Eastern States Indigenous Languages Working Group and current president of the local Aboriginal Education Consultative Group. He is not a qualified teacher but teaches Wiradjuri to people of all ages in a voluntary capacity to the best of his ability. His language work has been a healing process for him and he has seen many people finding themselves by learning it. Geoff aims to get the language to as many people as possible, especially young ones, so they can get in touch with their identity and culture.

Anna Ash has worked in Aboriginal language revitalisation in Queensland, the Northern Territory and New South Wales (NSW). She has contributed to the *Lardil dictionary*, *A Lardil learner's guide* and the *Gamilaraay Yuwaalaraay Yuwaalayaay dictionary*. Since 2004 she has been coordinator-linguist with Many Rivers Aboriginal Language Centre under the auspices of Muurrbay in Nambucca Heads, supporting Aboriginal communities in the revitalisation of seven languages through analysing and documenting, publishing resources such as dictionaries, grammars, memoirs, stories and student workbooks, and supporting educational programs. Anna is currently completing a Graduate Certificate in Editing and Publishing.

Faith Baisden has had many years experience working with communities around Australia as they explore project development aimed at the reclamation and preservation of languages. This has included work with her own Yugambeh community, whose country is to the south of Brisbane in south-east Queensland. Faith has maintained a special interest in promoting the work produced by the various communities to ensure that new initiatives and resource concepts are shared to best advantage by all in the national network of committed language supporters. She is a member of the Queensland Indigenous Languages Advisory Committee and the Eastern States Indigenous Languages Working Group.

Heather Bowe is a senior lecturer in linguistics at Monash University and holds a PhD from the University of Southern California. Heather's interest in Aboriginal languages began when she was an advisory teacher for bilingual education in the Pitjantjatjara lands of South Australia. Since 1993 Heather's research has focused on Aboriginal languages of Victoria. She was instrumental, alongside those at Worawa Aboriginal College, in the development of the *Indigenous languages of Victoria, revival and reclamation: Victorian Certificate of Education study design*. Heather leads the Australian Research Council linkage project, 'Reclamation of Victorian Indigenous languages: using ICT to enable effective exchange among academics, educators and the Indigenous community', which is reported on in this volume.

Claire Bowern is assistant professor of linguistics at Yale University. She attended the Australian National University and Harvard, where her PhD was on the verb system of the Bardi language and how it has changed over time. She has been involved in language documentation, description and revitalisation in northern Australia for the last ten years. This has included volunteer work with the Kimberley Language Resource Centre. For the last five years she has been working with Yan-nhaŋu people from Milingimbi on language documentation.

Ursula Brown started working at a school through her local Community Development Employment Projects program in 1996. From 1997 to 2008 she completed 13 courses, from Certificate of Attainment up to Master of Indigenous Languages Education. Ursula has received several awards for dedication to study, and to her community. She has worked with the NSW Department of Education and Training (DET) on a casual basis since 1996 as an Aboriginal education assistant, teacher's aide (special) and a teacher's aide. Since completing her Bachelor of Education Ursula has worked as a casual classroom teacher, a support teacher learning assistance, a librarian and a release from face-to-face teacher.

Paul Chandler started his education career in 1987 teaching science and mathematics in his local community at Matraville High School. After completing a MSc in psychology and a PhD in cognition and learning at the University of New South Wales (UNSW), in 1992 he became the first academic from education to receive an Australian Research Council post-doctoral research fellowship. Paul completed two terms as head of the School of Education at UNSW before being appointed dean of education at the University of Wollongong. In 2008, at a National Press Club event, Paul was awarded as one of Australia's ten most pre-eminent researchers. Paul's real passion is working with young people and, for 25 years, he has been heavily involved in improving Indigenous outcomes in education and health through an array of community-driven projects and initiatives.

Jackie Cipollone is a language educator with 30 years of experience in the secondary school and vocational education and training sectors. Her current role as education programs manager in the Technical and Further Education (TAFE) NSW Social Inclusion and Vocational Access Unit includes collaborating with the Aboriginal Education and Training Directorate in the NSW DET on the implementation of the

TAFE NSW Aboriginal languages qualifications. She would like to acknowledge the many generous contributions of her Aboriginal colleagues in this work.

Eleonora Deak has been a linguist with Wangka Maya Pilbara Aboriginal Language Centre since 2004. She is working with Banyjima and Jurruru speakers and custodians to update the database and dictionary resources for these languages. Eleonora and Wangka Maya language workers updated the resources for Thalanyji, Bayungu, Burduna and Binigura. Eleonora also worked at Diwurruwurru-jaru Katherine Regional Language Centre from 1999 to 2002 as the south-east linguist. She worked with the language teams to continue school programs at Urapunga, Ngukurr and Minyerri and supported other language work in Ngukurr. She finished her honours in linguistics at the University of Queensland.

Sally Dixon worked at Wangka Maya Pilbara Aboriginal Language Centre from 2006 to 2009. In her role as community linguist she helped develop community language resources as well as language documentation and description work. Prior to that she worked in the Philippines in an indigenous education non-government organisation, helping to structure the multilingual curriculum and create resources for schools. She completed undergraduate studies at UNSW and a Graduate Certificate in Language Endangerment Studies at Monash University. She is currently completing her PhD at the University of Sydney, looking at how Aboriginal children acquire code-switching behaviour as part of their multilingual development.

Christina Eira is the community linguist for Victorian Aboriginal Corporation for Languages. This role is focused on Aboriginal communities reviving their languages, based on principles of the reclamation of authority in language. Christina works alongside Koorie people as they develop skills and confidence in language work, and within academic linguistics exploring the ramifications of this work for epistemological, methodological and theoretical concerns. Previously she worked with immigrant communities on language maintenance. For her PhD Christina explored social and political discourses underlying standardisation processes and orthographic development. Christina has co-produced dictionaries in four languages, and a contemporary grammar of Narungga from South Australia.

George Fisher, Wiradjuri and Gadigal Elder, passed away during the writing of this paper. We would like to acknowledge the contribution he made in Sydney to the growth of not only his own language, Wiradjuri, but also language teaching in general. George was one of the first Aboriginal musicians recorded in Australia, playing in The Opals then Mr George, and touring Australia as support for both David Cassidy and the Bee Gees. He used these musical and recording skills in his teaching of language. It is reported that when he found his language, he said that no-one was ever going to take it from him again, and that he now realised why people said he spoke English back to front, as he could now speak in the language in which he was thinking.

Mary-Anne Gale is a research fellow at the University of Adelaide and the University of South Australia. Being a linguist and teacher, she currently works with the Ngarrindjeri community and schools in the revival of the Ngarrindjeri language.

Much of her career has been in Aboriginal teacher training, working with Warlpiri, Yolŋu, Pitjantjatjara and now Ngarrindjeri adults. She has recently written a course for TAFE South Australia to train adults to teach endangered Aboriginal languages. In her spare time she collaborates with Aboriginal Elders in writing and publishing their life stories, and is presently writing the life story of David Unaipon, the man represented on the Australian 50-dollar note.

John Giacon was born in Italy and grew up in Wollongong. He worked in schools in NSW and the Australian Capital Territory, mainly in maths, science, religion and administration. In 1994 he moved to Walgett and shortly after began working on the Yuwaalaraay language, and later Gamilaraay. John has worked in a number of language programs including in Walgett, has been involved in producing language resources, including the *Gamilaraay, Yuwaalayaay and Yuwaalayaay dictionary* and the yuwaalaraay.org website and worked on the *NSW K-10 Aboriginal Language Syllabus*. He is currently doing a PhD on Gamilaraay-Yuwaalaraay at the Australian National University, teaches the languages, and is working on more resources for them.

Richard Green has been involved in learning the Dharug *dalang* (language) since his youth. He has been acknowledged in his community as a songman and a teacher of language. It has been a long road for him to improve his language knowledge, study his language then learn how to teach it. He has been teaching in schools for years, and his program has been acknowledged as having improved school attendance among Aboriginal students.

Clair Hill has worked on north-eastern Cape York languages for seven years, in particular the Umpila-Kuuku Ya'u–Kaanju dialect group. This work has included coordinating and participating in documentation projects funded by the Australian Institute of Aboriginal and Torres Strait Islander Studies (AIATSIS) and the Maintenance of Indigenous Languages and Records program, and a three-year major documentation project funded by the Hans Rausing Endangered Languages Project. She is currently undertaking a PhD at the Max Planck Institute for Psycholinguistics and the University of Leuven. Her current projects include: Language of Perception project, Categories group at the Max Planck Institute for Psycholinguistics; AIATSIS Online Language Community Access Pilot project; and Optional ergative marking and the architecture of case systems, University of Leuven.

John Hobson has over 20 years of experience in Indigenous Australian languages and linguistics, ten of those spent in Central Australia. He has worked on various dictionary projects, trained translators and interpreters, and delivered Aboriginal language and literacy courses at the Institute for Aboriginal Development. He has worked as a linguist and literature production supervisor in four concurrent bilingual programs at Yipirinya School, and trained Indigenous linguists and language workers at Batchelor Institute's Centre for Australian Languages and Linguistics in Alice Springs. Currently he lectures at the Koori Centre, University of Sydney, where he coordinates and teaches in the graduate programs in Indigenous languages education.

Pauline Hooler *ngarri Gumbaynggirr nyami*. Pauline works at the Muurrbay Language Centre as an administration officer and part-time language teacher. She considers language as synonymous with identity, as the language belongs to and connects the people to the land. She feels that learning language is a healing process; it makes you realise that someone is not whole until they know their language. For her, language filled a gap in her life that she did not know she had. She believes that language is also a healing process for Mother Earth as she has not heard the voices of her first children for over a hundred years and all of a sudden she is hearing and recognising them. Pauline says to her students that Mother Earth is hearing the native tongue of her country and all the rain that falls on Australia's north coast is Mother Earth crying tears of happiness and cleansing.

Peter Howard is associate professor at the Institute for Advancing Community Engagement at the Australian Catholic University, Strathfield campus in NSW. He has been involved in academic programs and community development for Aboriginal communities since the 1980s. Peter has a background in engaging with Aboriginal peoples to bring about authentic change within educational programs and in enhancing community capacity.

Bentley James holds a PhD in anthropology from the Australian National University titled 'Time and tide in the Crocodile Islands: change and continuity in Yan-nhangu marine identity'. A social and cultural anthropologist, linguist and educator he has lived and worked with the people of the Crocodile Islands for the past seventeen years recording their history, languages, ritual, social organisation and recent prehistory. In 2003 he published the Yan-nhaŋu dictionary. He presently leads a number of multidisciplinary projects in collabaration with the Yan-nhaŋu people (and institutional partners) linking traditional ecological knowledge, satellite mapping and online (talking) pictorial dictionary technology on the Crocodile Islands.

Caroline Jones has worked in research and education in Aboriginal languages with communities west of Katherine in the Northern Territory since 1993 and in NSW since 2004. She completed a PhD in linguistics in 2003 at the University of Massachusetts on young children's receptive language development in the area of speech sounds. She worked in research at the Macarthur Auditory Research Centre, Sydney laboratories at the University of Western Sydney, then as a lecturer in the School of Education at UNSW, and is currently a senior lecturer in education at the University of Wollongong.

Alex Kelly is a media arts practitioner and producer who has worked on magazines, film installations, documentaries, theatre, large community projects and online media. In 2004 Alex moved to Coober Pedy to support the Irati Wanti (The Poison, Leave It) campaign of the Kupa Piti Kungka Tjuta (Senior Aboriginal Women of Coober Pedy). From Coober Pedy she moved to Alice Springs to produce the acclaimed Ngapartji Ngapartji project from 2005 to 2010, which she conceptualised with Trevor Jamieson and Scott Rankin. She was the 2007 recipient of the Australia Council for the Arts Kirk Robson award and a 2008 YouthActionNet fellow.

The **Kimberley Language and Resource Centre** (KLRC) was the first regional language centre in Australia. Established in 1984, it is the peak representative body for Aboriginal language groups in the Kimberley, Western Australia (WA). The KLRC is a grass-roots organisation informed directly of the needs of the Aboriginal language groups through its community work. For directors, Elders, language speakers and community members – past and present – the organisation stands for the survival of their languages, as represented in its mission statement 'Keeping language strong'.

Cat Kutay has been working with George Fisher and other Wiradjuri people in Sydney for many years setting up computing applications for use in language teaching in schools and with adults. The process has been two-way, studying the culture of the language and its mode of transmission, and exploring open source software to assist the limited tutors available in Sydney for school teaching and adult training. In the last year Cat Kutay has also assisted Richard Green in using IT for song writing in language for school students.

Karen Lane has been teaching Indonesian and French for the past 16 years at Vincentia High School. Since 2004 she has been involved in the planning, program writing, teaching and resource development for the Dhurga language program. She works on the program closely with community member and Dhurga teacher Mitch Martin. Together they have worked with the local community and a linguist to prepare a program suitable for Year 8 Stage 4 students. They are enthusiastic about taking this to the next level and implementing a Stage 5 course.

Kevin Lowe, a Gubbi Gubbi man from south-east Queensland, is Inspector, Aboriginal Education in the NSW Office of the Board of Studies, a key position in the development of Aboriginal syllabuses and curriculum perspectives in NSW. He had extensive experience in schools, TAFE and universities before taking up this position in 2001. He has also been the deputy chairperson of the Federation of Aboriginal and Torres Strait Islander Languages. For many years he has been actively involved in the NSW Aboriginal Education Consultative Group. He is currently working with Aboriginal communities, schools and education systems in establishing programs that centre on the development of school–community learning partnerships.

Kathy Lynch is an associate professor in ICT research and development at the University of the Sunshine Coast and obtained her PhD in education in 2005 from Monash University. She is an honorary research associate at the Faculty of IT at the University of Technology Sydney, the Faculty of Computing and IT at Makerere University (Uganda), and the University of Cape Town. Kathy has been an editor and reviewer for international journals and conferences in the fields of IT and education, published and presented at international and national conferences, received national competitive grants, university grants and industry funding, and is the author of two textbooks.

Diane McNaboe is a Wiradjuri woman from central-western NSW. Her passion for languages began 19 years ago when she was coordinator of the Janggara Dance and

Cultural Group. Diane is currently employed as an Aboriginal education resource teacher at Dubbo West Public School and teaches Wiradjuri at primary and high school levels, as well as adults in the community and the annual languages summer school at the Koori Centre, University of Sydney. She researches the language with Wiradjuri experts in the community and is often called upon to proofread texts that are being created in the language.

Steve Maier completed a Bachelor of Education at Sydney College of Advanced Education and began teaching at Dunheved High School, St Marys in 1990. In 1996 he moved to Parkes in central-west NSW and has been teaching at Parkes High School ever since. He has a particular interest in Aboriginal education, issues and culture, stemming from his training and work in geography, legal studies and Aboriginal studies. Becoming good friends with a number of local Indigenous people from Parkes and Forbes, Steve's interest and appreciation of Aboriginal culture grew and led to his involvement in learning and promoting the Wiradjuri language.

Ian G Malcolm is emeritus professor and honorary professor in the Faculty of Education and Arts at Edith Cowan University where he was, until his retirement in 2003, professor of applied linguistics and co-director of the Centre for Applied Language and Literacy Research. He has carried out research in such areas as classroom discourse analysis, tertiary languages education, cross-cultural communication and Aboriginal English, and has published widely in applied linguistics with international publishers. He has lectured by invitation in the UK, USA, Singapore, China, Thailand, Malaysia, the Netherlands, Germany and Norway, as well as Australia.

Patrick McConvell holds a PhD in African studies and linguistics from the School of Oriental and African Studies in London and has worked on languages in the western Northern Territory, the Kimberleys and Pilbara of Western Australia for over 30 years. Apart from grammar and dictionary work, he is interested in language maintenance, the shift to Kriol, code-switching and language mixing. He has been involved with the setting up of the KLRC, working in bilingual schools, and Indigenous language worker training at Batchelor College. He has held a number of positions including lecturer at the Northern Territory and Griffith Universities, linguistic research fellow at AIATSIS, and principal anthropologist in land and native title claims in the Northern Territory and Queensland.

Felicity Meakins worked as a community linguist at Diwurruwurru-jaru Aboriginal Corporation (DAC) in Katherine from 2001 to 2004, producing language resources and facilitating revitalisation programs with Gurindji, Bilinarra and Ngarinyman people. Felicity joined the Aboriginal Child Language project at the University of Melbourne in 2004 as a PhD student. From 2007 she continued documenting Gurindji, Bilinarra and Gurindji Kriol with a DOBES (*Dokumentation Bedrohter Sprachen*) project at the University of Manchester while she was again based at DAC in Katherine. Felicity created dual-language DVDs and books, and collaborated on two dictionaries. She currently holds a Hans Rausing Endangered Languages Documentation Program grant to produce a Gurindji Kriol grammar and dictionary.

Knut J. Olawsky is a specialist in language documentation, field linguistics and endangered languages and has published grammars of Dagbani (Ghana) and Urarina (Peru). In his role as senior linguist and coordinator of the Mirima Language Centre he is engaged in the revitalisation of the Miriwoong language of the east Kimberley region (north-western Australia). His academic background includes a PhD from Dusseldorf (Germany) as well as postdoctoral positions at the University of California, Berkeley (1999–2000) and at La Trobe University, Melbourne (2000–05), where he was a Hans Rausing Endangered Languages Documentation Program fellow (2003–05). While his commitment to the Miriwoong people involves a range of non-academic tasks, he stays connected to the academic world through casual teaching and presentations on an international level.

Susan Poetsch is currently working as a curriculum officer at the Board of Studies NSW. Her role involves working with Aboriginal community members, linguists and school staff to implement the NSW *Aboriginal Languages K–10 Syllabus* and develop local programs in various locations in the state. She has also worked as a teacher–linguist for the Katherine Regional Language Centre in the Northern Territory, as a research assistant on the Australian National Placenames Survey at Macquarie University and as an English language teacher in China, Korea, Sydney and on Thursday Island in the Torres Strait.

Julie Reid was awarded her PhD in linguistics from La Trobe University in 1998. She began working on Victorian Aboriginal languages with Professor Barry Blake in the early 1990s, and is currently a research fellow at Monash University, where she is developing materials for the Aboriginal Languages of Victoria Web Resource Portal Project, alongside Heather Bowe and Kathy Lynch. Julie has also taught the *Indigenous languages of Victoria, revival and reclamation: Victorian Certificate of Education study design* at the Victorian School of Languages, and is a member of the Victorian Curriculum and Assessment Authority's Implementation Committee for this study design.

Nicholas Reid holds a PhD from the Australian National University and teaches linguistics within the School of Behavioural, Cognitive and Social Sciences at the University of New England, Australia. He has written a grammar and dictionary of the Northern Territory language Ngan'gi. Nicholas is strongly committed to the preservation of linguistic diversity. He is actively involved in various language maintenance initiatives in the Daly River region, including heritage work on endangered song language traditions in the community of Wadeye. He has run workshops for the NSW Board of Studies on developing orthographies for and writing NSW languages, and acts in an advisory capacity for various local language re-awakening projects.

Mari Rhydwen is currently Aboriginal languages consultant with the NSW DET. Following undergraduate studies in linguistics and education in London and Cambridge, Mari undertook a PhD at Sydney University on Kriol, literacy and language change in the Northern Territory. She has held research and teaching posts at a number of

Australian universities, as well as at the School of Australian Linguistics and Batchelor College. She has also coordinated a community language centre.

Lynnette Solomon-Dent is a Monero/Ngarigu woman. She has a Bachelor degree in Education (Monash University) and a Graduate Certificate in LOTE methodologies. She has been teaching Aboriginal languages for over 20 years at university, TAFE, primary and early childhood levels. Lynnette has published books in the Koorie education area to encourage teachers to start teaching Aboriginal studies. Lynnette is also the community linguist and language consultant to the *Yirruk-Tinnor* Gunnai Language program in Gippsland. This work has included major projects such as the development of an extensive storyboard Dreaming trail in Gunnai, and a series of six illustrated books. She is currently developing an encyclopaedic dictionary of Gunnai. Lynnette is also an artist with a number of publicly sold paintings and photographs to her credit.

Beth Sometimes is an artist, musician and writer based in Alice Springs. She has had a six-year collaborative creative relationship with the Pitjantjatjara community at Pukatja in South Australia and has worked with the *Ngapartji Ngapartji* project and theatre show since 2006. She is a semi-fluent Pitjantjatjara speaker. Beth is currently working as musical director for a new theatre work in development by Big hART and Windmill Performing Arts: *Nyuntu Ngali* and preparing her first major publication *'from sometimes love beth'* – a compendium of postcards sent in 2008.

Syd Sparrow is a member of the Ngarrindjeri community and a qualified lawyer, as well as an academic at the University of South Australia. After a long career with legal aid, Syd now lectures in the David Unaipon Centre for Indigenous Education and Research.

Trevor Stockley speaks Gumatj and worked from 1979 to 1992 at Yirrkala and Laynhapuy Homeland Schools, Northern Territory, focusing on Yolŋu control, the inclusion of Yolŋu knowledge in a balanced curriculum, implementing Yolŋu ways of working and community-based teacher training. His work at Cairns TAFE as a curriculum writer and teacher for the Diploma of Indigenous Australian Language Studies, led to his work in north Queensland as a specialist Aboriginal languages teacher and program writer for the Warrgamay and Gudjal language revival programs. Trevor has delivered community-based language awareness workshops for the Warrgamay, Djirrbal, Ngadjan, Girramay, Nyawaygi and Gudjal language groups. He is currently involved in the continuing struggle for language rights and bilingual/multilingual education in the Northern Territory.

Adriano Truscott is an English as a second language teacher-linguist and has been working on language advocacy, revival and community language projects in the mid-west of WA. He has been involved in the development of a range of language projects including multimedia products (online, TV, radio, press, exhibitions), an accredited Aboriginal language course (Wajarri) and training for teachers in linguistics and language teaching. He currently works with the ABC Two-Way Literacy and Learning project for the Department of Education and Training WA in training, the two-way philosophy, and resource development in the classroom, as well as researching Aboriginal English.

Ken Walker is a Gumbaynggirr/Bundjalung man from Nambucca Heads on the north coast of NSW. Ken has worked with the Gumbaynggirr language since joining a language class at Sherwood, west of Kempsey in 1990. Muurrbay Aboriginal Language and Culture Co-operative became incorporated in 1992 and was established in the old church in Bellwood, Nambucca Heads. Ken is now Chairperson of Muurrbay, which in the last five years has grown to include the Many Rivers Aboriginal Language Centre, supporting seven languages of coastal NSW. Ken also runs the Aboriginal languages summer school at the Koori Centre, University of Sydney and liaises with government and education departments and community organisations about language and cultural issues.

Michael Walsh has carried out fieldwork in the top end of the Northern Territory since 1972, mainly in the Darwin-Daly region. This has been a mixture of academic endeavours as well as consultancies since 1979, mainly relating to Aboriginal land issues. From 1999 he has been involved in the revitalisation of Aboriginal languages in NSW. From 1982 up until the end of 2005 he was part of the teaching staff of the Department of Linguistics, University of Sydney. Since then, as an honorary associate, he has continued his research – especially through a large Australian Research Council grant running from 2004 to 2010 and involving a team of linguists and musicologists.

Gary Williams is a Gumbaynggirr/Bundjalung man from Nambucca Heads on the north coast of NSW. Having grown up around language speakers but, for various reasons, not learning how to speak it, he jumped at the chance when Muurrbay Language Centre offered a full-time Gumbaynggirr language course. He has taught language at Muurrbay, in Years 11 and 12 at Nambucca Heads High School and at the annual languages summer school at the Koori Centre, University of Sydney. He now divides his time between Muurrbay and the Many Rivers Aboriginal Language Centre. He finds it very rewarding to talk to other language groups and see how they approach language reclamation.

Aidan Wilson is a PhD candidate in linguistics at the University of Melbourne and an audio engineer at the Pacific and Regional Archive for Digital Sources in Endangered Cultures. He began working with the Wagiman people in 2005 in preparation for an honours project for his bachelor degree at the University of Sydney. Aidan has continued working with the Wagiman people since completing his Honours degree – most recently to update the Wagiman dictionary.

Tyson Kaawoppa Yunkaporta has ancestral ties to Nungar people in South Australia, but, as he grew up in Queensland, his name comes from his mob on Cape York. He holds a Bachelor of Education and Master of Education, and worked in Queensland as a teacher for ten years before moving to western NSW in 2006. Tyson is a carver of traditional weapons and instruments and uses this traditional knowledge to inform his work and research in Aboriginal education. He is currently studying for his doctorate in education and working as an Aboriginal education consultant for western NSW, where he has helped to develop school programs for five Aboriginal languages.

Introduction
Re-awakening Australian languages

John Hobson,[1] Kevin Lowe,[2] Susan Poetsch[3] and Michael Walsh[4]

> Above all, let us permit native children to keep their own languages – those beautiful and expressive tongues, rich in true Australian imagery, charged with poetry and with love for all that is great, ancient, and eternal in the continent. There is no need to fear that continued knowledge of their own languages will interfere with the learning of English as the common medium of expression for all Australians. In most areas of Australia the natives have been bilingual, probably from time immemorial. Today white Australians are among the few remaining civilised people who still think that knowledge of one language is the normal limit of linguistic achievement. (Strehlow 1957, p. 53)

As in other parts of the postcolonial world, the Indigenous languages of Australia have been undergoing a renaissance over recent decades. Many languages that had long ceased to be heard in public and consequently been deemed 'dead' or 'extinct' have begun to emerge from hiding to reveal themselves as only having been dormant, awaiting a world in which it was safe for them to re-awaken. While a tragically large number of languages have undoubtedly succumbed to 200 years of violence and repression, it is an inspiring testament to their speakers' resilience to see how many have resisted and survived to be heard again. This is especially so in the face of Australia's obsessive tradition of English monolingualism that manifests itself even today, half a century after Strehlow's plea, in government policies that mandate daily hours of English-only instruction in bilingual schools and assume that literacy only exists in English (Simpson et al. 2009; Truscott & Malcolm, this volume).

It is in this environment that this volume seeks to provide the first comprehensive snapshot of the courageous actions and determined aspirations of Indigenous people

---

1 Koori Centre, University of Sydney.
2 Aboriginal Curriculum Unit, Office of the Board of Studies NSW.
3 Aboriginal Curriculum Unit, Office of the Board of Studies NSW.
4 Department of Linguistics, University of Sydney.

and their supporters for the revitalisation of Australian languages in the 21st century. Many of the papers convey Indigenous narratives of the efforts of individuals and small groups whose aggregated achievements underpin the long-term revitalisation of many of Australia's Indigenous languages. Language revitalisation is underpinned more fundamentally by notions of cultural sovereignty – Indigenous people asserting their ownership and pride in their heritage – past, present and future. To move from being an act of colonial resistance, to genuine acceptance of the value of Indigenous languages and cultures in Australian society more broadly, the legitimacy of language work can no longer be in question: we know *why* we are doing this work. However, we must continue to ask, *how can we do it better?*

The contributions to this volume describe both the satisfactions and tensions of this ongoing and life-long struggle. They also draw attention to the need for effective planning and strong advocacy at the highest political and administrative levels, if language revitalisation in Australia is to be successful and if people's efforts are to have longevity. Sustained and appropriate support is required to ensure that programs are not just available but that they are sufficiently robust to clearly match linguistic and educational needs across a range of unique contexts.

Geographically and linguistically isolated, revitalisers of Indigenous Australian languages have often struggled to find guidance for their circumstances unaware of the successes and failures of others walking a similar path, whether at home or abroad. Viewed from far across the seas, the possibilities being created by others can appear doubly remote. Even close at hand the inspiring successes of the Māori can sometimes seem disheartening, given the apparent luxury of a single language, single state government and linguistic rights enshrined in a treaty. However, as those of us who have been fortunate enough to witness revitalisation activity in other countries can attest, the practice is often more alike than different, and the theory remains largely the same (Lowe & Walsh 2004).

Notwithstanding these issues, the guiding light for local language revitalisers in the new century has clearly been *The green book of language revitalization in practice* (Hinton & Hale 2001) – so much so that it is sometimes referred to locally as 'the Bible'. Many of the contributions in the Green Book relate specifically to situations in North America, but the intention was to provide a series of case studies of language revitalisation in practice that could inform the activities of practitioners across the rest of the world. At the same time some of the contributions, drawing on wide experience, tackled more general issues and could shape not just the practice but also the theory of language revitalisation.

It cannot be denied that the current volume is an Australian homage to Hinton and Hale. However, rather than simply replicate, we have intentionally sought to supplement it by providing local people with the incentive and opportunity to share the learning from their language journeys. The guidance provided in the Green Book is clear, simple, practical and just as applicable here and now. In this volume our emphasis is simply on Indigenous Australia and we follow the model of the Green Book to the extent that we present case studies and try to meld theory with practice.

Based on the varied experience and imperatives of the different members of the editorial team we have also sought to span distinctions that are sometimes construed as exclusive. Thus we have actively solicited contributions from community-based practitioners, professional linguists and academic theorists, and accorded them equal prestige. We have also particularly invited papers by Indigenous authors and, through the generosity of the Office of the Board of Studies New South Wales, were able to provide grants-in-aid to Indigenous community writers in that state. A central device with this intent was also to invite non-Indigenous writers to partner with community members to co-author their work. We are therefore delighted to report that, of the 47 named authors, one third are Indigenous Australians – itself a notable achievement in Australian linguistics.

Of course we would have liked more, and are acutely conscious of a number of excellent initiatives and practitioners nationally that could have been showcased. But while the call for papers was made through every connection at our disposal, and generated considerable interest, many potential contributors were unable to meet our deadlines due to pressures of other work – including language revitalisation. We are most grateful to those that were able to fit this additional chore into a very busy array of commitments. Notwithstanding, we should confess that our original aspiration was that we *might* be lucky enough to secure a dozen or so contributions, not the 34 we are delighted to present herein. This is an indication of the range of people participating in the revitalisation process, some of whom would now be referred to as language activists (Florey et al. 2009).

Another heartening feature of the volume that emerges is the consistently positive view of the future it offers and the recurrent emphasis on sharing, partnership and moving forward. There is little of the fearful rhetoric of needing to protect the languages from the ravages of insensitive linguists or defend Indigenous intellectual and cultural property from those who would abuse it that has so often characterised the field in the past. Equally there is little of the assertion of assumed academic authority over Indigenous people's knowledge and rights. Perhaps this is an indication that we are coming of age; that the various participants are capable of recognising the value of each other's contributions, needs and interests, and can readily work together if afforded the necessary mutual respect. Let us hope so.

With that in mind we urged authors to ensure their papers were written in accessible language. There is little use in reams of turgid academic prose to community activists who are unused to navigating it; it has given them little assistance to date. We hope we have been largely successful in that aim also.

As editors we preferred to keep a loose rein on content. However we were rather insistent about some terminology, in particular to eschew terms like *moribund*, *dead* and *extinct*. Such terms, as applied to their languages, are most often offensive to

Indigenous people and are avoided in favour of terms like *sleeping* (for example Leonard 2008). In any case it seems absurd to continue with such labels for languages that may now have hundreds of speakers as a result of language revitalisation efforts (Walsh 2009). Even the term *speakers* is potentially problematic as distinctions can be made according to levels of proficiency: partial speakers, semi-speakers, fluent speakers, and so on (Hobson; Reid, this volume). Again our preference has been to simply adopt terminology that reflects the current idiom of Indigenous people who usually would use the term without qualification.

Another terminological issue relates to the process and activities connected with 'bringing languages back'. Among the terms that have been used are *revival, renewal* and *reclamation* (Senior Secondary Assessment Board of South Australia 1996, pp. 21–22). Although we are well aware of these and the desire to bring clarity to the field, we have chosen for the most part to adopt a single term, language *revitalisation* to cover a wide range of situations. This not only creates a resonance with the Green Book but also simplifies the task of applying more fine-grained distinctions to complex, on-the-ground situations that may invite more than one description, and currently be in a process of developmental change. Nevertheless we have sanctioned the innovative terminology adopted by the contribution from the Kimberley Language Resource Centre: language *continuation* – referring to all strategies used to keep languages 'alive'. Also Stockley (this volume) cautions us on the use of terms like *awareness* versus *awakening*. In an evolving field we can expect the terminology to continue to be the subject of debate. There are however some special conventions adopted in this volume, particularly with regard to *Aboriginal, Dreaming, Elders* and *Indigenous*: the reader is referred to the Conventions section.

The papers are presented under a range of sections predetermined by the editors: policy and planning, centres and programs, education, literacy and oracy, technology, and documentation. Of course, as might be expected, the final contributions sometimes defy such simplistic categorisation and could just as easily appear in more than one section. For example there is hardly a chapter that does not make some mention of education or technology. We have responded by assigning them on mixed criteria of best fit and producing relative balance across the volume. If any therefore seem misaligned, the responsibility rests with us rather than the authors.

In the Green Book, Clay Slate, a long-term practitioner in the Navajo language program, outlined attempts to promote advanced Navajo language scholarship as:

> badly needed work that might be considered too technical, pedagogical, 'applied,' or politically aggressive for academia. For instance, there is a need for coinage and elaboration work in election terminology, medical interpreting, courtroom, interpreting, and other professional areas. Such direct work on the Navajo lexicon must be collaborative and thus based in extensive oral critical interplay. (2001, p. 402)

Such elaboration has also been in progress for languages in the Asia-Pacific region for some time. For instance since mid-2004 the Māori language has had an Institute of Excellence in the Māori Language (Te Panekiretanga o te Reo Māori) and, in the Australian context, ARDS (Aboriginal Resource Development Services)[5] have been pivotal in advancing various domains including law, government, the economy, health and so forth, among the Yolŋu of north-east Arnhem Land. We look forward to this kind of extension of Indigenous languages to engage with the wider community becoming a part of language revitalisation.

We also hope that this volume will not only suggest new possibilities for language revitalisation practitioners but also inform policy development for Indigenous languages in this country and the position of Australian languages generally (Liddicoat 2008; McKay 2007, 2009a, b; Walsh, forthcoming; Truscott & Malcolm, this volume).

Ultimately we are greatly pleased by the breadth, depth and diversity of the papers offered. They represent a detailed profile of the current status of Indigenous Australian languages revitalisation and provide many examples and much guidance for others to follow. Most importantly they clearly demonstrate that we have achieved much and should look positively to the future.

References

Florey M, Penfield S & Tucker BV (2009). *Towards a framework for language activism*. Paper presented at the 1st International Conference on Language Documentation and Conservation (ICLDC), 14 March 2009, Honolulu, Hawaii [Online]. Available: hdl.handle.net/10125/5014 [Accessed 25 December 2009].

Hinton L & Hale K (2001). *The green book of language revitalization in practice*. San Diego: Academic Press.

Leonard W (2008). When is an 'extinct language' not extinct? Miami, a formerly sleeping language. In K King, N Schilling-Estes, LW Fogle, JJ Lou & B Soukup (Eds). *Sustaining linguistic diversity: endangered and minority languages and language varieties* (pp. 23–33). Georgetown University Round Table on Languages and Linguistics Proceedings. Georgetown: Georgetown University Press.

Liddicoat AJ (2008). Models of national government language-in-education policy for indigenous minority language groups. In TJ Curnow (Ed) *Selected papers from the 2007 Conference of the Australian Linguistic Society*, Adelaide [Online]. Available: www.als.asn.au/proceedings/als2007/liddicoat.pdf [Accessed 20 January 2010].

Lowe K & Walsh M (2004). California down under: Indigenous language revitalization in New South Wales, Australia. In WY Leonard & EB Stelómethet Gardner (Eds). *Language is life*. Proceedings of the 11th Annual Stabilizing Languages Conference. Survey Report 14. Berkeley CA: Survey of California and Other Indian Languages [Online]. Available: linguistics.berkeley.edu/~survey/resources/publications.php [Accessed 25 December 2009].

---

5 See www.ards.com.au.

McKay G (2007). Language maintenance, shift and planning. In G Leitner & I Malcolm (Eds). *The habitat of Australia's Aboriginal languages: past, present and future* (pp. 101–29). Berlin: Mouton de Gruyter.

McKay G (2009a). Developing an Aboriginal languages policy for Western Australia: some issues. In A Mahboob & C Lipovsky (Eds). *Studies in applied linguistics and language learning* (pp. 108–23). Newcastle on Tyne: Cambridge Scholars Press.

McKay G (2009b). English and Indigenous languages in the Australian language policy environment. In H Chen & K Cruickshank (Eds). *Making a difference: challenges for applied linguistics* (pp. 283–97). Newcastle upon Tyne: Cambridge Scholars Press.

Senior Secondary Assessment Board of South Australia (1996). *Australia's Indigenous languages framework.* Wayville, SA: Senior Secondary Assessment Board of South Australia.

Simpson J, Caffery J & McConvell P (2009). Gaps in Australia's Indigenous language policy: dismantling bilingual education in the Northern Territory. Australian Institute of Aboriginal & Torres Strait Islander Studies Research Discussion Paper 23. Canberra: Aboriginal Studies Press [Online]. Available: www.aiatsis.gov.au/research/docs/dp/DP24.pdf [Accessed 20 January 2010].

Slate C (2001). Promoting advanced Navajo language scholarship. In L Hinton & K Hale (Eds). *The green book of language revitalization in practice* (pp. 389–410). San Diego: Academic Press.

Strehlow TGH (1957). *Dark and white Australians.* Melbourne: Riall Bros.

Walsh M (2009). The rise and fall of GIDS in accounts of language endangerment. In H Elnazarov & N Ostler (Eds). *Endangered languages and history* (pp. 134–41). Proceedings of FEL XIII, Khorog, Tajikistan, 24–26 September 2009. Bath: Foundation for Endangered Languages.

Walsh M (forthcoming). 'The language was sleeping, it was not lost': an overview of the state of Indigenous languages in Australia and ongoing strategies for revitalisation. In *Proceedings of the Aboriginal Policy Research Conference*, Ottawa, 9–13 March 2009.

Part One
Language policy and planning

Introduction
Language policy and planning

John Hobson[1]

As the proverb suggests: those who fail to plan, plan to fail. This is no less applicable in language revitalisation, particularly in the Indigenous Australian context where the current dearth of governmental policy and planning is little short of alarming. When we look to similar postcolonial, English-speaking societies the absence of Australian legislation guaranteeing Indigenous language rights is starkly obvious. The Canadian Assembly of First Nations developed its first policy on language and culture in 1972 and in 2004 presented the government with draft legislation (Assembly of First Nations, n.d.). The Māori Language Act was passed in 1987 (Māori Language Commission, n.d.) and, in 1990, President Bush signed the Native American Languages Act (Rehyner 1993, p. 31). Of course the lack of a treaty history underpinning the recognition of Indigenous populations, their cultural and linguistic rights in Australia cannot be overlooked in this regard.

What minimal Indigenous languages policy that does exist across Australian jurisdictions often seems more honoured in the breach than the observance,[2] or languishes for want of meaningful implementation; lots of good words, but not much action. The lack of broadly-based planning and coordination for language revitalisation in many parts of Indigenous Australia can also make it very difficult to build on the achievements of others and advance the process beyond first steps.

While the existence of a robust policy framework for government informed by community ambitions can undoubtedly be of great value, it is still not sufficient to ensure that languages will survive and flourish. Governments will not save your language – only you can do that – and the task may need to be accomplished without, or even in spite of, the implementation of any official policy.

One recently productive area of policy and planning by Australian governments for Indigenous languages has been the development of syllabuses and curricula for languages education in schools, and this is encouraging. However communities must

---

1 Koori Centre, University of Sydney.

2 Witness for example the Northern Territory Department of Education and Training's directive that the first four hours of instruction in bilingual schools must be in English (2009).

be mindful that positive outcomes in classrooms alone are not enough to revitalise languages. The effort must be broader than just schools, and language communities must be vigilant to retain control of their languages, not allowing departments of education to fill the policy gaps for themselves.

Government policy almost always privileges government interests over those of its constituents and seeks to establish limitations on what is deemed appropriate or relevant. The more cynical might even suggest that policy is habitually tied to the electoral cycle, so that what funding is meted out attracts primarily to short-term, fixed-cost, tangible outcomes; a CD, website or book that the minister can launch in front of the media, or sets goals that will not be evaluated until well after the next election.

But policy and planning for language revitalisation do not have to be the sole province of government, or necessarily be beholden to government funds. In fact it is probably essential for success that Indigenous organisations, communities, families and individuals take control of the issue for themselves and develop and implement their own strategies. There are many revitalisation strategies that do not require money; talk is cheap.

I have had the great pleasure of spending the night in the households of indigenous language activists in both New Zealand and Canada where the family plan to ensure the children retain their language includes a policy of no English at mealtimes. I am also aware of activists locally who have a policy of only speaking to their new baby in their heritage language to fulfil their family plan to produce the first new native speaker in a generation. Then there are others implementing a personal policy of saying everything in their own language first wherever possible, relegating the dominant language to second place.

The movement to institute a new tradition of giving Indigenous Welcome to Country speeches (ideally in language) has been highly successful across Australia with only modest support from governments but a strong groundswell of enthusiasm from within communities. There is no reason why a similar movement for wider application of Indigenous languages could not take place. The boards of many community organisations, for example, could conduct voting in a local language without significant preparation or cost. It would take little more than a declaration of policy and a plan to implement it.

Of course there is already one very strong locus of language policy and planning across Indigenous Australian communities – the language centre movement. This function alone validates their existence and suggests that the goal of establishing a language centre should be firmly embedded in language communities' long-term revitalisation plans. In the interim such organisations as land councils, native title groups and Elders' councils have the potential to foster language policy development and planning for their constituent communities without necessarily having to take on practical language work as part of that initial step.

There is a lot that can be done. It just takes some planning.

The three papers in this section offer us substantially different but equally significant perspectives from which to approach Indigenous languages revitalisation in Australia, and establish three useful lenses through which the remainder of the volume can be viewed.

The paper by Truscott and Malcolm gives a comprehensive and insightful overview of the history of Indigenous languages policy in Australia, the failure to implement it successfully and the apparently entrenched custom of either ignoring it completely, or subverting it in practice, which they term *invisible* policy. Their discussion illuminates the underlying political landscape of Australian languages policy that makes redundant any need to engage in a broader discussion of the issues here.

Walsh, on the other hand, offers us the considerable benefit of several decades spent in the documentation, analysis and revitalisation of Australian languages in addition to a detailed familiarity with the literature internationally. From this he distils the essential elements of 'Why language revitalisation sometimes works'. While clearly not proffered as a checklist, those engaged in language revitalisation planning could do worse than compare both past and proposed strategies to assess how these factors might be implicated in their success or failure.

Finally, Yunkaporta provides an eloquent expression of an essential ingredient in the revitalisation process, the Indigenist perspective. Although principally concerned with planning for Indigenous languages education his discussion of the importance of story sharing, learning maps, non-verbal learning, symbols and images, land links, non-linear processes, deconstruction and reconstruction, and community links serves to ground consideration of the issues outside the Western academic realm and firmly within the perspective of language-owning communities.

References

Assembly of First Nations (n.d.). *Chronology of language and culture activities and events* [Online]. Available: www.afn.ca/article.asp?id=833 [Accessed 24 November 2009].

Maori Language Commission (n.d.). *A history of the Maori language* [Online]. Available: www.tetaurawhiri.govt.nz/english/issues_e/hist/index.shtml [Accessed 24 November 2009].

Nothern Territory Department of Education & Training (2009). Policy: compulsory teaching in English for the first four hours of each school day [Online]. Available: www.det.nt.gov.au/teachers-educators/literacy-numeracy/literacy/teaching-in-english [Accessed 31 December 2009].

Reyhner J (1993). American Indian language policy and school success. *The Journal of Educational Issues of Language Minority Students*, 12(3): 35–59.

1
Closing the policy–practice gap: making Indigenous language policy more than empty rhetoric

Adriano Truscott[1] and Ian Malcolm[2]

Abstract

Though there have been significant advances in some states and territories in reviving Indigenous languages, there are language mechanisms that constantly work throughout society to perpetuate the elevated status of the language of the dominant group – standard Australian English. These language mechanisms include language testing, education curricula and the media. They serve to – intentionally or otherwise – undermine the legitimacy of and discriminate against certain non-dominant groups, such as speakers of Aboriginal English, creoles and traditional languages. Consequently a de facto or invisible form of language policy exists that is not explicitly written but is implicitly created: it privileges monolingualism over multilingualism and impedes full revitalisation and maintenance of Indigenous languages. The elevated status of English encourages a shift away from these languages and encourages speaker communities to accept – automatically, unconsciously and therefore without resistance – the hegemonic ideologies of the dominant socio-political group. This shift goes against certain human rights and has significant implications in the fields of health, education, law and social justice.

This paper looks at the dominance of Standard Australian English (SAE) and its impact on Indigenous languages. Though the acquisition of English is important it does not need to work against the maintenance of languages as it is doing today. In fact building academic understanding using the home language can help develop competency in English. So the aim here is to raise awareness about the language ideologies that form the invisible language policy experienced in Australia today. An understanding of these invisible linguistic forces can provide language professionals and educators a means to deconstruct and decolonise the discriminatory processes that foster linguistic and cultural assimilation.

---

[1] Department of Education and Training, Western Australia.
[2] Faculty of Education and Arts, Edith Cowan University.

The endangered state of Indigenous languages in Australia has been well documented (McConvell & Thieberger 2001; Australian Institute of Aboriginal & Torres Strait Islander Studies 2005) as has the need for a coherent and consistent language policy (Ozolins 1993; Erebus Consulting Partners 2002) to help reverse language decline and restore a sense of linguistic identity to Indigenous communities (Fishman 1991). This decline has been made more severe through aggressive assimilatory policies towards Indigenous people carried out over the past 200 years (Moran 2005). Today, policies and practices continue to undermine Indigenous language revival, but these are less visible as they are indirect in their effect.

In spite of these pressures language revitalisation in Australia is strong in certain areas. Communities, through language centres and programs in schools, local halls and homes, have brought language and language-related knowledge back into people's lives in the face of great challenges. Language revitalisation and maintenance is, therefore, part of a bigger picture – the recognition of the rights and identity of Indigenous peoples. Australia is a signatory of several international human rights declarations that acknowledge these rights.[3] There are also official policies and documents that recognise:

- the value of Australia's Aboriginal language diversity and its importance in education (Department of Education, Science & Training 2000)
- the social dysfunction caused by decline in language (Human Rights and Equal Opportunity Commission 1997)
- the importance of teaching Aboriginal and Torres Strait Islander studies, cultures and languages to all Indigenous and non-Indigenous students (Ministerial Council on Education, Employment, Training & Youth Affairs [MCEETYA] 1995, p. 1)
- the importance of the use by teachers of culturally inclusive methodologies and the provision of education which will strengthen Indigenous students' identity and cultural values (MCEETYA 1995, p. 5)
- the importance of bilingual and bicultural education (Australian Labor Party 2007, p. 215).

One factor working against the success of these policies that are supportive of Indigenous languages, is the invisible, or de facto, language policy which puts the objective of Standard Australian English (SAE) literacy above all other language objectives (such as language maintenance). Indeed the effect of the way in which the objective of SAE literacy is pursued can be to deny the essential place of Indigenous languages in people's lives and in the continuance of their cultures. It is not so much

---

3 Australia is a signatory to human rights declarations that specifically address children's right to education in their first language. These declarations include: the Universal Declaration of Human Rights (Article 27), the Universal Declaration on Cultural Diversity (Articles 5 and 6), the International Covenant on Civil and Political Rights (Articles 26 and 27), Convention on the Rights of the Child (Articles 14.1 and 29.1) and the International Covenant on Economic, Social and Cultural Rights (Article 13).

the goal of SAE literacy for all Australians (which indeed has near universal approval) that is being contested here, but the subordination of other language objectives to this end. This subordination can be labelled *invisible*, since its overriding of other linguistic goals such as revitalisation is not stated, but assumed. Invisible language policy, then, can seriously and adversely affect not only language revitalisation and Indigenous education as a whole but how multilingualism and language rights are seen in the mainstream society.

This paper looks at some of the effects of invisible language policy on language revitalisation and education. We, as educators and applied linguists, will examine three questions: What is language policy? What does invisible language policy look like? How can we counteract the negative effects of it?

Ideologies of language planning

To understand what can drive language planning we need to consider ideologies of language. These ideologies can be defined as the 'socioculturally motivated ideas, perceptions and expectations of language, manifested in all sorts of language use' (Blommaert 1999, p. 1). The ideologies of language planning are therefore the assumptions, attitudes and perceptions of languages and their speakers that are involved in putting language policy into practice. An example of language ideology can be seen in the Australian Language and Literacy Policy (Department of Employment, Education & Training [DEET] 1991, p. 32), which says the following:

> Australian English is integral to Australian identity. It is the vehicle for mainstream Australian culture. Being proficient in Australian English is essential for effective functioning in the community and the workplace. A key message of this policy is that Australian English must be accessible to and accessed by all Australians.

Here we can see a particular perception or ideology of Australian English having an elevated political, social, cultural and economic status by associating it directly with Australian identity, the carrying of Australian culture, the community and the workplace. It is worth noting that the *National Policy on Languages* was not claimed to be rescinded by government with the introduction of this language and literacy policy, yet the binding of English, and only English, to Australian identity effectively undermines the policy's recognition of the 'linguistic diversity of Australia' (Lo Bianco 1987, p. 9).

Policy-makers form decisions based on issues such as the readiness or instinct to use one language variety over another, the status of that language variety, the symbolic quality of a language in relation to nationhood, as well as cultural authenticity, modernity, equality and other values (Blommaert 1999). Consider these values in the following example. In an Australian Liberal Party article entitled 'Fighting terrorism', one of the ways listed to fight the war on terror was by 'establishing *citizenship tests* that will help ensure a *modern* Australia maintains sentiments of *nationhood* and attachment to a *common language, distinct heritage* and *shared values.*' (Liberal Party 2007 [emphasis added])

Here we can see a clear ideology of nationalism. The text gives a symbolic quality to a 'common language' – Australian English – representing one nation and therefore strength in unity against a common enemy. This article even suggests a way of ensuring how the nation will stay safe in the face of terrorism – a citizenship test. This test is written in English which shows us the de facto priority of one language over all others (Shohamy 2006). This government document contradicts one of the principles of the *National Policy on Languages*, as we shall see later.

Ideologies of society

Viewing English in symbolic and political terms is particularly noticeable in education and immigration discourse. Indeed Blommaert (1999) notes that these attitudes are related to broader social, political and historical concepts including power relationships among groups in societies, discrimination, nation-building and social engineering. The results of these issues often involve different groups, dominant and non-dominant, either directly or indirectly; and relate to factors such as:

- the stigmatising of certain languages/varieties, for example Aboriginal English being generally stigmatised by white Australian society (McArthur 1998)
- restrictions on the use of certain languages/varieties: for example banning Indigenous languages in schools; the exclusive use of SAE as the medium of education in schools; current repression of bilingual programs in the Northern Territory.

These factors help maintain SAE monolingualism by promoting ideologies of the dominant group and by marginalising or excluding minorities. Overt language policies can afford to pay lip service to inclusive language, diversity and democratic processes as long as covert mechanisms are functioning to execute policies with contrary aims. Of course, popular policies are often supported by more widespread assumptions about human life and development. In the Australian setting it could be argued (adapted from Malcolm 2009) that at least five such assumptions have been behind some of the kinds of policies advocated in relation to Indigenous education in the past two centuries:

- assumptions of *social Darwinism*, leading to low expectations of Indigenous students and consequent policies with minimal educational objectives for them
- assumptions of *cultural imperialism*, leading to low estimation of Indigenous languages and cultures and policies of education aiming at assimilation
- assumptions of *cultural deprivation*, leading to policies which count the Indigenous linguistic and cultural inheritance as a handicap and seek to rectify it
- assumptions of *cultural relativism*, leading to policies embracing Indigenous languages and cultures within an inclusive multicultural society

- assumptions of *global imperatives*, leading to policies which subordinate lesser objectives, including supporting home languages, to that of equipping citizens for a marketplace of global competitiveness.

While the earlier assumptions on this list may be less current and even discredited today, they still may underlie unreflected practice in some education areas (see below), though the fifth assumption probably has the most overt influence on current policy developments.

What are language planning and policy?

Language policy is the 'decision-making process, formally stated or implicit, used to decide which languages will be taught to (or learned by) whom and for what purposes' (Cooper 1989, p. 31). It depends on the language culture of a society, meaning 'the set of behaviours, assumptions, cultural forms, prejudices, folk belief systems, attitudes, stereotypes, ways of thinking about language, and religio-historical circumstances associated with a particular language' (Schiffman 1996, p. 5). How we speak, make sentences and use any language is influenced by many social, cultural, political and environmental factors: home, school, the media, the courts, and so on. This influence can be intended or unintended, written and explicit or unwritten and implicit. All these factors can be planned for many reasons (Baldauf 1993) and on many levels: at the home, community, state, national and even international level. Language planning therefore is how you put language policy into practice.

When all this planning is written down we can say it is an overt language policy, like the *National Policy on Languages* (Lo Bianco 1987). An invisible language policy can coexist with such a policy by endorsing practices which deny the overtly stated principles. Take for example the principle that:

> No Australian resident ought to be denied … equal, appropriate and fair treatment by the law including representation and other rights commonly associated with equality or deriving from citizenship, because of language disabilities, or lack of adequate, or any, competence in English. (p. 8)

This principle is effectively denied by the introduction of a citizenship test which implicitly requires competence in SAE (see above).

Language planning in Australia

English has become the de facto official language of Australia but does not carry legal status (Lo Bianco 1987). Australia's main aim in language policy has been achieving English monolingualism (Lo Bianco 2000) and this has been achieved in explicit and implicit ways. After a period of positive language activism and consultation starting in the 1970s, in 1984 the Senate Committee on Education and the Arts released the Report on a National Language Policy. The aim of this very inclusive report was to create a coordinated language policy for Australia. While it has been argued that the dominance of English remained unchallenged (Tollefson 1991), this report nevertheless marked a unique recognition of the aspirations and rights of Australians of all language backgrounds and, as such, is of enduring significance, despite the fact that its information and resulting recommendations have been conveniently ignored. Senate recommendations based on submissions from Indigenous organisations made sure that Indigenous language maintenance and revival was explicitly covered.

As a result of the report, in 1986 the minister of education commissioned the *National Policy on Languages* (NPL), which saw Australia become the first English-speaking country with a policy on languages (Centenary of Federation Committee 1994, p. 29, cited in Lo Bianco 1995). In general the policy looked at short- and long-term Indigenous language maintenance and revival based on three main notions: consultation and shared decision making; the national importance of Aboriginal languages; and prioritising the educational and social role of languages currently in use. In the 1990s, however, Australia moved from community considerations to national economic and internationally strategic intentions, as reflected in the changed emphasis of the Australian Language and Literacy Policy (1991). Among other things this new and narrowly focused policy 'contradicted and sought to undermine the core multicultural and multilingual basis of the NPL' (Lo Bianco 2000, p. 53). The main role was to 'eliminate the inclusiveness of the NPL by targeting "literacy", assessment and foreign languages' (Moore 1996, p. 481). Today, exclusive SAE literacy, assessment and foreign languages are still being heavily targeted.

Despite Australia having an earlier and explicit overall language policy – the NPL – it now mainly follows a de facto policy of non-intervention, meaning that Indigenous language development is left to happen on its own without any direct strategic assistance from the government. This approach to language planning and policy favours the dominant group. What happens as a result is that language planning becomes heavily influenced by decisions taken in a range of areas that affect language use and perceptions. These areas include education, immigration selection and foreign trade patterns and priorities (Lo Bianco 2000), the media, language in the public space (see Figure 1), citizenship tests and rules and regulations (Shohamy 2006). Over time the sometimes subtle effects and consequences of these areas on language use become readily accepted everyday practices.

What does visible language policy currently look like?

Australia has many statements of policy and intention that give due regard to Indigenous people, their languages and their aspirations. These statements address language education and revitalisation as important factors for ensuring the identity of Indigenous peoples and their access to equal opportunities in work and education. The Australian Labor Party's ALP National Platform and Constitution, for example, is very positive about Indigenous language revitalisation:

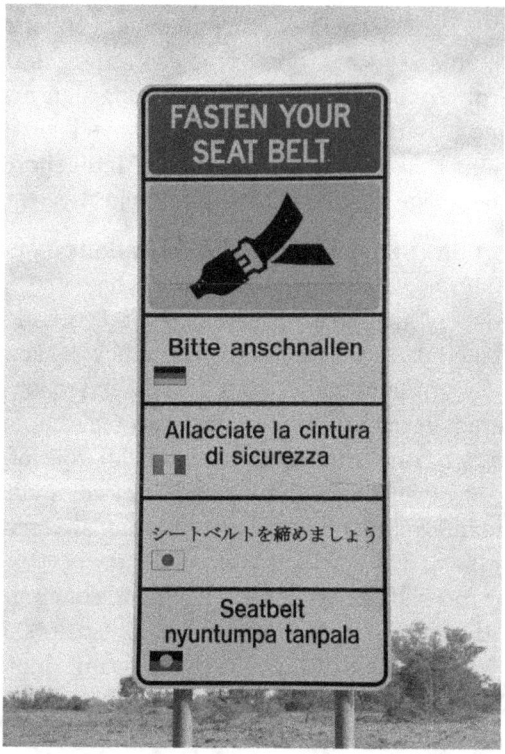

Figure 1. A wonderful sight: a multilingual road sign on the Ernest Giles Road, Nothern Territory – a popular spot for tourists; but notice the order of languages (English, German, Italian, Japanese and Western Desert).

> Labor will make the protection, preservation and revitalisation of Indigenous languages a major priority. The urgency of this is underscored by the probability that 90 per cent of Indigenous languages will disappear over the next generation. (Australian Labor Party 2007, Chapter 13, Principle 105)

The main visible language policy embodying this principle is the Maintenance of Indigenous Languages and Records program (MILR). In the 2007–08 period this federal program spent 9.3 million Australian dollars on 72 projects that worked on about 160 languages (Hansard 2008).

These projects are mainly carried out by short-term (annually funded), Indigenous-run regional language centres and community programs which play 'a central and invaluable role' in language maintenance and revival (Tsunoda 2005, p. 21). However language centres are highly vulnerable, as their survival and operation is at the whim of the federal government (Sussex 2004) and there is no long-term Indigenous language continuance strategy currently in place.

In education, the main vehicle for language policy implementation, there are many more statements of good intent, such as the National Aboriginal and Torres Strait

Islander Education Policy (DEET 1989) and the Ministerial Council on Education, Employment and Youth Affairs' Australian Directions in Indigenous Education 2005-08 (MCEETYA 2006). The Labor Party constitution chapter on 'Respecting Human Rights and a Fair Go for All' (ALP 2007, p. 125) states, among other things, that the party will:

- value 'Indigenous decision making in education and promote community leadership on the importance of education'
- support 'quality teaching environments and institutions that are culturally inclusive and will encourage Indigenous knowledge and perspectives in education curriculum'
- support 'bi-lingual and bi-cultural education [which] ... have value for both Indigenous and non-Indigenous Australians'.[4]

The MCEETYA Taskforce 2000 explicitly states the principle that schooling should acknowledge the 'capacity of all young Indigenous people to learn by expecting all Indigenous children to be fluent in SAE and at the same time being inclusive of the student's home language' (MCEETYA 2000, p. 20). There is, then, a stated commitment to being inclusive with respect to the home languages of Indigenous people, recognition of the importance of the maintenance of Indigenous languages and of the role of Indigenous people in educational decision-making. Moreover there is an acknowledgement of the role of bilingual/bicultural education. All this suggests that education poses no threat to the home languages of Indigenous people. Yet these assurances are always overshadowed by the co-existent commitment to use education to make all Indigenous people fluent in SAE. It is interesting to note the wording of the press release coming from the office of the former Minister for Education, Employment and Workplace Relations, Julia Gillard, in releasing the report 'Indigenous language programs in Australian schools: a way forward', in December 2008. After a brief reference to the 260 schools with Indigenous language programs, the release quickly and irrelevantly introduces the subject of '[SAE] literacy and numeracy outcomes':

> The Australian Government is committed to supporting [all] languages education in Australian schools. The School Languages Program provides funding of $112 million from 2005 to 2008 to support the learning of all languages, including Indigenous languages.
>
> The Australian Government has also committed $540 million to improve literacy and numeracy outcomes and close the gap in educational attainment for Indigenous Australians.
>
> The Government firmly believes that all Australian students need to be proficient

---

4 Despite the last principle former Federal Education Minister and Deputy Leader of the Labor Party, Julia Gillard has voiced support of four hours compulsory English in bilingual schools (Robinson, 2008). This paper was also written before the release of the 2009 ALP National Platform and Constitution, which no longer recognises these statements.

> in English to be able to fully participate in the world of work and further study.
> (Gillard 2008)

The only reference to what the government firmly believes relates to English, despite the fact that the subject of the report being released is Indigenous languages. Thus no real commitment is shown to Indigenous languages. The government's primary concern is with English; and this brings us to invisible language policy.

What does invisible language policy look like?

Invisible language policy is the effect, intended or otherwise, direct or indirect, of government policies on language use. It is seen as the allocation of priorities – that is to say, funding – whatever the rhetoric of visible language policy. If 'language policies are mostly manifestations of intentions' (Shohamy 2006, p. 51) then what happens on the ground tells us what the policy is really doing. Invisible language policy has been documented worldwide[5] and is associated with the promotion of the language and interests of a linguistically and politically dominant group while giving lip service through visible language policy to the languages and interests of non-dominant groups within the society. This unwritten and indirect form of policy is informed by ideologies which favour social and linguistic mainstreaming and centralised control.

The ideologies mentioned above can actually reverse the positive principles of policies by the way they are put into practice, and these reversals can often violate democratic principles and personal rights (Shohamy 2006).

Let us take, for example, the principle of language maintenance. It is possible to endorse this principle at the policy level with the MILR, but to implement it in a way that brings limited benefit to the speakers, or future speakers, of the language – as language work has no community required development dimension and language risks being maintained as a museum piece rather than as part of living culture: if funding were given, for example, to language documentation projects and not to long-term projects of community-led language revitalisation.

Similarly it is possible to endorse the principle of community control but, at the same time, not to give communities the continuity of resources required to exercise that control over their language maintenance in an effective way. Again, with the MILR, funding is short-term and not guaranteed to communities – although it may be more secure for some more established language centres. The Reference Group of the National Review of Education for Aboriginal and Torres Strait Islander Peoples made the following comment about education (including language maintenance) for Indigenous students:

> The Joint Policy [the National Aboriginal and Torres Strait Islander Education
> Policy] is criticised for its perceived concern about Aboriginal and Torres Strait

---

5 Schiffman (1996) examines the US, France and India. Shohamy (2006) mainly looks at the UK, Israel and the US.

Islander people's access to, and participation in, 'mainstream' education and its silence about supporting alternative and community controlled education initiatives (this leads some authors to brand the joint policy as assimilationist). (Commonwealth of Australia 1994, p. 6).

The principle of inclusivity may be subverted by being interpreted in a subjective way, as simply a way of bringing everybody together, rather than as a means of achieving social justice for groups that experience exclusion because other groups are being privileged (as discussed more fully in Malcolm 1999).

The principle of equal opportunity, when applied without adequate reference to the differing prerequisites for different groups to benefit from it, may actually worsen disadvantage. For example, Indigenous students unfamiliar with SAE will be disadvantaged when they are exposed to the same SAE immersion and literacy testing programs as other learners.

These violations happen when policies are enforced from above without appropriate and transparent consultation with communities, Indigenous representative bodies, Indigenous and, if appropriate, non-Indigenous language professionals and when following ideologies of the dominant group. These ideologies run the risk of perpetuating negative stereotypes, misunderstandings about education and misleading representations of Indigenous people, often children. For example the Western Australian Aboriginal Child Health Survey Report implied that low academic performance and attendance among Indigenous students were greatest where they spoke Aboriginal English or an Aboriginal language (Sharifian 2008). The report recommended explicit SAE teaching throughout all years of school. This view of the student's home language devalues the identity of the child through devaluing the home languages; and it wrongly implies that the students' home languages are an obstacle to SAE development.

Skutnabb-Kangas (2000, p. 571) has observed a general change from *old* (overt, physically punitive and direct) to *new* (covert, psychologically punitive and structural) forms of language control and oppression used by those in power to exert their ideology. In Australia the results of the old forms of discrimination on the lives of Aboriginal and Torres Strait Islander people are officially documented. However the newer forms of control exist, deliberately or not, in invisible language policy.

In the next section we will focus on two areas in which Indigenous education has suffered as a result of invisible language policy: the areas of bilingual education and national testing. Two issues will become clear:

- mechanisms that create invisible language policy may comprise influence from diverse fields (for example media, education, legal practice, and so on) (See Schiffman 1996; Shohamy 2006)
- though intentions are good, control is exerted on groups such as students, schools and language speaker communities through financial reward and incentive, psychological punitiveness, ideological rhetoric and often passive acceptance.

Bilingual education

Indigenous people are being documented by government and the media as failing to achieve policy objectives either in their own languages or in SAE. For example, despite the positive policy statements mentioned above in the introduction, the documented improved learning outcomes of bilingual education (NT DEET 2005), the positive involvement of local communities, the rights associated with language and the overwhelming research on the benefits of bilingual education, the Northern Territory government has decided to put an emphasis on English learning in schools. The explicit intention of the Territory government was to 'improve attendance rates and lift the literacy and numeracy results of remote schools' (Toohey 2008). The decision, however, effectively reduces bilingual education to monolingual education; this is the implicit effect of the decision and is therefore an example of invisible language policy. It is based on the ideology that English is more important in the lives of children and teachers than their own languages, regardless of the wishes of communities. The community reaction to this decision – which goes against the human rights principles of the government as well as international human rights declarations of which Australia is a signatory – was expressed in *The Australian* newspaper:

> It's like spitting on the bilingual program and devaluing the Indigenous children's first language without any respect. Language is our living treasure and our survival, we nurture our language just like a child. (Robinson 2008)

Some schools have already started to enforce English and ban Indigenous teachers from speaking their languages, which is having negative effects on the schools (Australian Broadcasting Corporation 2009). Serious consideration is required by policy-makers with regards to democratic principles and their violation, as well as the ideologies upon which these principles are grounded.

One size fits all: The National Assessment Program

This decision to end bilingual programs was encouraged by the results of the national, standardised SAE literacy and numeracy test, the National Assessment Program – Literacy and Numeracy (NAPLaN), which began in 2008. NAPLaN is just one part of the Australian federal government's two-billion dollar 'Education Revolution'. This is a high-stakes test for schools and, ultimately, state education departments as they will be either rewarded or penalised depending on results. Though the tests are for all students, regardless of their language background, they have been designed for students who speak SAE as their home language or dialect of English.[6] More specifically the tests do not account for the progression of English language learning that the students follow, as well as learning the subject content. Therefore Indigenous students who speak an Aboriginal language, creole or Aboriginal English

---

6 This is not to say that designing the tests in this way has been intentional; the test writers may simply not have considered the needs of the minority students because of a lack of awareness of additional language and dialect learning issues.

are immediately disadvantaged. While the intention to improve SAE literacy is noble, the consequences for Indigenous languages maintenance and education efforts are disastrous. Following the NAPLaN results of the nine bilingual education schools in the Northern Territory, the Territory government, with the support of the federal government, has moved to effectively end all bilingual programs. It should be noted that this justification of closure has not been based on second language acquisition research (Krashen 1982; Cummins 1981); rather it can only be assumed that such decisions, like those of the past, are based on ideology and instinct.

How can we counteract the effects of invisible language policy?

Language teachers, language centres, language workers, linguists – Indigenous and non-Indigenous – schools and some government departments together have long been working hard to overcome the enormous challenges described in this paper. To counteract the effects of these de facto practices and policies, these groups need more support. Those who wish to support Indigenous language education and maintenance, as well as Indigenous education by Indigenous people more generally can take action to:

- reassert the rights of Indigenous people to the maintenance of the languages that are important to their lives and culture, as equal members of a wider society which acknowledges plurality and equity
- expose the use of public language which can promote exclusivist and invisible language policy at the expense of the interests of Indigenous and other non-dominant groups
- question the practices which are supported in whole or in part by invisible language policy and which undermine the interests of Indigenous and other non-dominant groups
- promote the Aboriginal idea of two-way bicultural education and insist on the resourcing of language education programs which realise it
- engage cross-sector support from local government and government departments – particularly from the health and justice areas, among others – professional education organisations, community providers and the media.

Language centres have the experience, contacts and expertise to continue these actions in their regions through their government and private networks. This work could be supported by a national and independent Indigenous body which could also provide the necessary political strength to ensure governments, at all levels, are kept in check. Universities can interrogate government practice and distribute knowledge to raise awareness wherever their networks allow them. Indigenous and non-Indigenous people, working two-way (Malcolm & Konigsberg 2007, pp. 267–97) where possible and appropriate, can create a positive change for languages and their speakers.

Conclusion

The range of government statements and policies present a mix of opportunities and obstacles. One obstacle is the gap between policy and practice that we have called invisible language policy. We live in a country that despite the best of intentions, actively, as well as unconsciously, reinforces monolingualism. Governments continue to deploy a range of tactics to improve the western ethnocentric educational outcomes of Indigenous students. While the goal of SAE proficiency is necessary and widely accepted, this goal is pursued in such a way that what happens in practice directly and indirectly undermines the Indigenous languages of Australia, their speakers, people and cultures. What is happening to bilingual schools is a shocking example of this policy–practice gap. Even when there are written policies to maintain and revive languages, the opportunities to achieve this are limited by political decisions based on ideology rather than knowledge gained through consultation or research. Such decisions do not help resolve urgent issues of education, health and social justice. Nor do they enable reconciliation. They prevent it.

However an awareness of issues that hold back equal cultural prosperity can create new possibilities to take language maintenance and revival to the next level. Governments need to be held accountable for the often vaguely worded and poorly respected policies they make – and the well-worded policies they forget about – as well as the language they choose to use. The success of language revitalisation requires more than language-specific funding and initiatives. The complexity of the social, cultural, economic and political issues behind language use and rights needs a broad strategy to confront it. Those involved in Indigenous languages, education, health, media and social justice can work together to ensure structural change, so that these invisible and visible language policies are monitored and questioned and that words like *inclusivity* and *equality* are used only with transparent and agreed meanings.

References

Australian Broadcasting Corporation (2009). Education union warns of 'Nazi' language ban [Online]. Available: www.abc.net.au/news/stories/2009/03/09/2510919.htm [Accessed 25 March 2009].

Australian Institute of Aboriginal & Torres Strait Islander Studies (2005). National Indigenous Languages Survey report 2005. Canberra: Department of Communication, Information Technology and the Arts.

Australian Labor Party (2007). ALP national platform and constitution 2007 [Online]. Available: www.alp.org.au/platform/index.php [Accessed 25 March 2009].

Baldauf RB (1993–94). 'Unplanned' language policy and planning. *Annual Review of Applied Linguistics*, 14: 82–89 [Online]. Available: library.uq.edu.au/eserv/UQ:7746/UnPlannedLPP.pdf [Accessed 25 March 2009].

Blommaert J (Ed) (1999). *Language ideological debates*. Berlin: Mouton de Gruyter.

Commonwealth of Australia (1994). National review of education for Aboriginal and Torres Strait Islander people. Canberra: Australian Government Publishing Service.

Cooper RL (1989). *Language planning and social change*. New York: Cambridge University Press.

Cummins J (1981). The role of primary language development in promoting educational success for language minority students. In California State Department of Education (Ed). *Schooling and language minority students: a theoretical framework* (pp. 3–49). Los Angeles: Evaluation, Dissemination and Assessment Center, California State University.

Department of Education, Employment & Workplace Relations (2008). Media release: new report on Indigenous language in schools [Online]. Available: mediacentre.dewr.gov.au/mediacentre/gillard/releases/newreportonindigenouslanguageinschools.htm [Accessed 5 December 2009].

Department of Education, Science & Training (2000). National Indigenous English literacy and numeracy strategy [Online]. Available: www.dest.gov.au/schools/publications/2000/LNS.pdf [Accessed 20 March 2009].

Department of Employment, Education & Training (1989). National Aboriginal & Torres Strait Islander education policy: summary and implementation. Canberra: Commonwealth of Australia.

Department of Employment, Education & Training (1991). Australia's language: the Australian language and literacy policy: Companion volume to the policy information paper. Canberra: Australian Government Publishing Service.

Erebus Consulting Partners (2002). Review of the Commonwealth languages other than English programme: a report to the Department of Education, Science and Training [Online]. Available: www.detya.gov.au/schools/publications/2003/lote/reviewreport.pdf [Accessed 25 March 2009].

Fishman J (1991). *Reversing language shift*. Clevedon: Multilingual Matters.

Hansard (2008). Senate questions on notice. Question 290, Tuesday May 13, 2008 [Online]. Available: www.aph.gov.au/hansard/senate/dailys/ds130508.pdf [Accessed 25 March 2009].

Human Rights & Equal Opportunity Commission (1997). Bringing them home: report of the national inquiry into the separation of Aboriginal and Torres Strait Islander children from their families. Sydney: Commonwealth of Australia.

Krashen S (1982). *Principles of first and second language acquisition*. Oxford: Pergamon.

Liberal Party of Australia (2007). Fighting terrorism [Online]. Available: www.liberal.org.au/about/documents/FIGHTINGTERRORISM.pdf [Accessed 25 March 2009].

Lo Bianco J (1987). *National policy on languages*. Commonwealth Department of Education. Canberra: Australian Government Publishing Service.

Lo Bianco J (1995). Pluralist nations: pluralist language policies? Paper presented at Global Cultural Diversity Conference, Sydney Convention and Exhibition Centre, Darling Harbour, April 26–28. Department of Immigration & Citizenship. [Online]. Available: www.immi.gov.au/media/publications/multicultural/confer/04/speech18a.htm [Accessed 25 March 2009].

Lo Bianco J (2000). Making languages an object of public policy. *Agenda*, 7(1): 47–62.

Malcolm I (1999). English and inclusivity in education for Indigenous students. *Australian Review of Applied Linguistics*, 22(2): 51–66.

Malcolm I (2009). Indigenous speakers of ES(A)D: practices, ideas and issues affecting assessment. Presentation to the National Symposium on Assessing English as a Second/Additional Language in the Australian Context, University of New South Wales, February 20–21, 2009.

Malcolm I & Konigsberg P (2007). Bridging the language gap in education. In Leitner G & Malcolm IG (Eds). *The habitat of Australia's Aboriginal languages – past, present and future*. Berlin: Mouton de Gruyter.

McArthur T (Ed) (1998). *Concise Oxford companion to the English language*. Oxford: Oxford University Press.

McConvell P & Thieberger N (2001). State of Indigenous languages in Australia. Australia State of the Environment Technical Paper Series (Natural and Cultural Heritage) Series 2, Department of the Environment and Heritage [Online]. Available: www.environment.gov.au/soe/2001/publications/technical/indigenous-languages.html [Accessed 25 March 2009].

Ministerial Council on Education, Employment, Training & Youth Affairs (1995). A national strategy for the education of Aboriginal and Torres Strait Islander peoples, 1996–2002. Canberra: Department of Education, Employment, Training & Youth Affairs.

Ministerial Council on Education, Employment, Training & Youth Affairs (2000). Report of MCEETYA Task Force on Indigenous Education: March 2000. Canberra: Ministerial Council on Education, Employment, Training & Youth Affairs.

Ministerial Council on Education, Employment, Training & Youth Affairs (2006). Australian directions in Indigenous education 2005–08. Canberra: Ministerial Council on Education, Employment, Training & Youth Affairs.

Moran A (2005). White Australia, settler nationalism and Aboriginal assimilation. *Australian Journal of Politics & History*, 51(2): 168–93.

Northern Territory Department of Employment, Education & Training (2005). Indigenous languages and culture in Northern Territory schools. Report 2004–2005. Darwin: Northern Territory Department of Employment, Education & Training.

Ozolins U (1993). *The politics of language in Australia*. Cambridge: Cambridge University Press.

Robinson N (2008). Push for English causes Aboriginal backlash. *The Australian*, 20 November [Online]. Available: www.theaustralian.news.com.au/story/0,,24678230-12149,00.html [Accessed 25 March 2009].

Schiffman H (1996). *Linguistic culture and language policy: the politics of language*. London: Routledge.

Sharifian F (2008). Aboriginal English in the classroom: an asset or liability. *Language Awareness,* 17(2): 131–38.

Shohamy E (2006). *Language policy: hidden agendas and new approaches*. London: Routledge.

Skutnabb-Kangas T (2000). *Linguistic genocide in education or worldwide diversity and human rights?* Mahwah, New Jersey: Lawrence Erlbaum Associates.

Sussex R (2004). The repositioning of language centres: an appreciation of David Ingram's language centres: their roles, functions and management. *Current Issues in Language Planning,* 5(4): 457–71.

Tollefson JW (1991). *Planning language, planning inequality*. Harlow: Longman.

Toohey P (2008). Northern Territory kids get four hours a day in English. *The Australian*, 15 October [Online]. Available: www.theaustralian.news.com.au/story/0,,24498933-13881,00.html [Accessed 25 March 2009].

Tsunoda T (2005). *Language endangerment and language revitalisation*. Berlin: Mouton de Gruyter.

2
Why language revitalisation sometimes works

Michael Walsh[1]

Abstract

The last 20 years have seen a global upsurge in language revitalisation but some of these efforts prosper while others falter. Focusing mainly on language revitalisation initiatives in south-eastern Australia an attempt is made to consider what sort of factors contribute to successful language revitalisation. Among these are some that are relatively obvious, like a sizeable knowledge base, access to linguistic expertise and sustained commitment from Elders. However there are other factors perhaps less often considered, such as cultural awareness (Spindler 1999; Spindler & Spindler 1994). These and other factors will be described and then applied to a number of language revitalisation initiatives in south-eastern Australia. Hopefully this will trigger discussion and debate about the prerequisites for more effective language revitalisation as well as its sustainability.

Preamble: from the general to the particular

To consider some of the factors that contribute to the success of language revitalisation initiatives I will review some general ideas drawn from commentators from around the world and then focus on some of the efforts undertaken in recent years in south-eastern Australia. Obviously these remarks should only be thought of as general guidelines rather than as definitive answers. As Ash, Fermino and Hale point out:

> local conditions are very particular and, in the final analysis, unique. Programs in support of local languages necessarily address local conditions. The sharing of materials and ideas among language projects and the use of consultants in relevant fields (for example, linguistics, education, and computers) are good and often absolutely necessary, of course, but the structure of a local language program is determined by local considerations. We have seen no exceptions to

---

[1] Department of Linguistics, University of Sydney.

this, neither in places we have worked – Australia, Central America, and North America – nor in places we have visited or read about, including Europe, China, Northern Ireland, North Africa, and Polynesia. Realism is no less essential in this regard than in relation to the challenges confronting the movement as a whole. (2001, p. 20)

This particularistic approach is in contrast to the forthright pronouncements of the Blackfeet language activist, Darrell R. Kipp (2000):

> Rule 1: Never Ask Permission, Never Beg to Save the Language. Go ahead and get started, don't wait even five minutes. Don't wait for a grant ...
>
> Rule 2: Don't Debate the Issues
>
> Rule 3: Be Very Action-Oriented: Just act
>
> Rule 4: Show, Don't Tell. Don't talk about what you will do. Do it and show it. (cited in Reyhner 2003, p. 3)

While it's possible that this approach has been effective for the Blackfeet, I doubt that it could be applied to situations with which I am familiar in Australia. There are situations which require some adjustment before there can be much hope for success in language revitalisation. For instance Fettes (1997, pp. 307–08) observes:

> The first strand of language renewal does not depend on the indigenous language itself at all. It is the task of confronting, marginalizing, and dismantling the secondary discourses of alienation carried by the invading language. Critical illness, here, is the state of a community whose members see themselves as powerless to change their lives; whose families are being destroyed by abuse; and whose leadership, whether in the fields of politics, health, education, social welfare, or whatever, is locked into distant, impersonal structures and meaning systems.
>
> ... an Apache, Bernadette Adley-SantaMaria, told us that some tribal members view the language as evil, as contrary to the teachings of the Bible. Such a discourse will doom a language in the long run, unless you can either marginalize it or replace it with a different, language-friendly one.

Self-respect and empowerment

The literature on endangered languages, however, does throw up some themes that fall somewhere between the highly particular and highly general ends of the spectrum. A number of commentators for instance (see also Amery 2000; Dauenhauer & Dauenhauer 1998) have emphasised the need for self-respect and empowerment:

> revitalization is not about recreating a community of native speakers; it is rather about issues of self-respect and empowerment, and about reclaiming one's ethnic identity – issues of human value which cannot necessarily be measured in number of words or phrases learned. (Craig 1992, p. 23)

Consistent with these sentiments one group of New South Wales Aboriginal people (in some areas referred to as Goories, also known as Koories), the Gumbaynggirr, presented an eloquent manifesto in 1991:

> We believe
> - that we Goories are our culture
> - that home is the place where our culture is passed on. We have learnt that schools are only good as back-ups; they are not the first place where culture is taught
> - that we and our culture have been invaded and hurt over the last 203 years.
> - that we need to talk about the way we are now, and about our roots, so that we can be clear about what we want to pass on to our kids
>
> If we are confident about our Goorie culture, it will help us not just to cope with the society around us, but to stand strong in our identity and share this strength with our kids. (Muurrbay cited in McKay 1996, p. 48)

Indigenous control

Another recurring issue is the need for Indigenous control of the process. Too often language revitalisation attempts to focus excessively on educational institutions that are usually not under the control of the Indigenous community. The Gumbaynggirr manifesto stresses 'that schools are only good as back-ups; they are not the first place where culture is taught'. A more strident rejection of schools as a primary focus is provided by Johnson (1987, p. 56):

> the school is usually the major non-Aboriginal organization in a community [referring especially to northern Australia], and its ways of working are alien to Aboriginal society. It is probably the major instrument of assimilation at work, and as such acts as an agent of the outside government and society. Any language maintenance project should be very wary of working directly with and through the non-Aboriginal education system. The fate of language is very closely bound up with that of local control and understanding of educational goals, and language maintenance must include this as one of its basic aims.

Some examples of what is needed for 'successful' language revitalisation

Yamamoto (1998, p. 114) sets out nine factors 'that help maintain and promote the small languages':

- the existence of a dominant culture in favour of linguistic diversity
- a strong sense of ethnic identity within the endangered community
- the promotion of educational programmes about the endangered language and culture
- the creation of bilingual/bicultural school programmes
- the training of native speakers as teachers
- the involvement of the speech community as a whole

- the creation of language materials that are easy to use
- the development of written literature, both traditional and new
- the creation and strengthening of the environments in which the language must be used.

These are all worthy ingredients and should be considered when assessing an existing language revitalisation effort or planning a proposed one. But there are other approaches which, in my view, overreach what is needed – at least in Aboriginal Australia. One such approach has been advanced by David Crystal (2000, pp. 130–41):

> [six] postulates for a theory of language revitalization (i.e. prerequisites for progress towards the goal of language being used in the home and the neighbourhood as a tool of inter-generational communication):
>
> 1. An endangered language will progress if its speakers increase their prestige within the dominant community
> 2. An endangered language will progress if its speakers increase their wealth relative to the dominant community
> 3. An endangered language will progress if its speakers increase their legitimate power in the eyes of the dominant community
> 4. An endangered language will progress if its speakers have a strong presence in the educational system
> 5. An endangered language will progress if its speakers can write their language down
> 6. An endangered language will progress if its speakers can make use of electronic technology.

Most of these I would see as possibly desirable but not necessary for success, and indeed most of them are not achievable in Aboriginal Australia. For instance in the near future it's neither likely that speakers will increase their wealth relative to the dominant community nor that they will increase their prestige within the dominant community. Literacy in one's own language and use of electronic technology might be desirable but are by no means necessary for an endangered language to progress.

There are now sets of guidelines available (for example Assembly of Alaska Native Educators 2001; Grenoble & Whaley 2006, especially pp. 202–04; Ignace 1998; Linn et al. 2002; Paton et al., forthcoming). There is also program-specific advice like Hinton (2002, pp. 91–105) on the master–apprentice system. Reyhner (1999, p. vi) sets out suggested interventions based on different stages of language endangerment. Hinton (1994, pp. 243–44) presents eight points of language learning in terms of what the teacher should do with a counterpart activity for the learner.

An example of success in an Australian school-based program

This case study of St Mary's Primary School in Bowraville, NSW will present some of the features that I regard as contributing to a general wish list for successful language revitalisation programs:

Three key features contribute to the success of the language program at St Mary's.

First, the support provided by the Muurrbay and the MRALC [Many Rivers Aboriginal Language Centre] enhances program quality by providing appropriately trained teaching staff.

Second, the Gumbaynggirr language program at St Mary's fits within the context of the school's social justice vision. In particular, the vision, energy, and commitment of the principal to make a difference in the lives of the students and their families – to break the cycle of poverty and powerlessness experienced by many of the schools' students and their families – has created a context in which the Gumbaynggirr language program can thrive. The principal has fostered this commitment among her staff.

Third, there is a clear understanding of the necessary components of a successful language program. For instance, in 2005 when several local schools expressed an interest in introducing Gumbaynggirr language classes they did not proceed because of the lack of Gumbaynggirr language teachers. In response to this need, Muurrbay developed a course that not only helps students learn Gumbaynggirr, but that also assists them in developing skills in *how to teach language*. Muurrbay staff recognise that simply knowing some Language is not enough; people need to develop their teaching skills before they can work successfully with children in classrooms. (Purdie et al. 2008, pp. 174–75)

A wishlist for successful language revitalisation programs

The language-culture connection and cultural awareness

Particularly in south-eastern Australia there are Aboriginal individuals and groups who assert that they have lost their language and therefore their culture. I witnessed statements of this kind many times during a survey of NSW Aboriginal languages undertaken with two Aboriginal co-researchers in 1999–2000 (Palmer 2000). Sometimes it was followed up with remarks such as: 'We've got nothing!' Such comments were around before that survey and still persist. One reaction is for some Aboriginal people – usually youngish men, in my experience – to undertake what I have referred to as the cultural 'grand tour' (Walsh 2009). This is a reference to the practice undertaken by the young elites of England during the 17th and 18th centuries where they would spend two to four years travelling across Europe experiencing its languages and cultures. The modern Aboriginal practitioners of the cultural grand tour are in search of 'culture' and roam mainly across northern Australia looking for 'real Aborigines' with 'real culture'. Sometimes they encounter Aboriginal people in a town like Darwin who tell them that in fact real culture is not there but thousands of kilometres to the south in the desert country or hundreds of kilometres to the east in north-east Arnhem Land. Some may realise that they had culture all the time and, while it may be interesting to observe cultural practices at the other end of Australia, one should accept that culture is inside a person and their group. As the

Gumbaynggirr expressed it: 'We believe that we Goories are our culture ... that we need to talk about the way we are now' (Muurrbay, cited in McKay 1996, p. 48).

It seems to me that this kind of cultural awareness is absolutely critical for success in a language revitalisation initiative. One must acknowledge that there is a deep connection between one's language and culture, that they are legitimate as they are now and that the culture and language of other groups is not somehow better than one's own. To that end the Spindlers, specialists in the anthropology of education (for example Spindler & Spindler 1994; Spindler 1999), have identified different kinds of cultural knowledge and see *cultural therapy* as a means to improving the cultural awareness of students and teachers. In particular, *submerged cultural knowledge* (Spindler 1999, pp. 468–70) is especially relevant for a significant number of Aboriginal people. In my view Aboriginal people who are comfortable using the word culture will also be more accepting of practices that will assist the delivery of a language revitalisation program (Walsh 2009). This acceptance of culture can also allow a people to get over some of the wrongs they have experienced in the past.

Stebbins (2003, pp. 10–11), referring to the Tsimshian people of British Columbia, comments on the link between language and social justice. The renewal of their language has the potential to be a source of strength for the community. This is important as these and other First Nations peoples are frequently looked down upon by other Canadians, but:

> Even within the Tsimshian community there is a dearth of positive ways of expressing and elaborating on Tsimshian identity. For example, in making statements about themselves or their community to me, Tsimshian people regularly said things like: 'We have to argue,' 'There's a lot of jealousy in our community,' 'You won't want to come back to us dumb Indians.' I am unable to recall an example in which a Tsimshian person made a positive statement about their community. (Stebbins 2003, p. 11)

The very act of promoting the language assists potential speakers to confront some of the negative attitudes towards the language that they have acquired after a long period of discrimination. For example consider the Tlingit people of south-east Alaska:

> In reality, many people are afraid of the traditional language. It is alien, unknown, and difficult to learn. It can be a constant reminder of a deficiency and a nagging threat to one's image of cultural competence.
>
> ...
>
> It is not easy to overcome this pain. Many potential language teachers have commented with bitterness, 'They beat the languages out of us in school, and now the schools want to teach it.' (Dauenhauer & Dauenhauer 1998, p. 65)

Community cohesion

Assuming that a group or at least most of its members have achieved cultural awareness, an important prerequisite for effective language revitalisation is community cohesion. Without a degree of consensus, it is difficult to resolve language issues – such as the practice of dual naming in New South Wales. Dual naming is a minimal form of language revitalisation in which pre-existing Aboriginal names are reinstated for places already commonly known by a non-Aboriginal name, and is an initiative of the Geographical Names Board of NSW (GNB). Dawes Point, for example, is the non-Aboriginal placename for the southern foot of the Sydney Harbour Bridge that has had the Dharug name *Tar-ra* re-instated.

I have participated in quite a few meetings with Aboriginal groups on dual naming, at which it has been pointed out that the GNB has no intention to coerce Aboriginal people into reaching a decision. If there is a division of opinion about how to proceed then the GNB will withdraw until a consensus has been reached (see also Troy & Walsh 2009). This is an instance of divided community opinion in miniature; in the delivery of a full-language revitalisation program there will be numerous decisions to make, most of them much more pressing than a dual naming exercise. If the community cannot reach consensus often enough on even small issues, then the success of language revitalisation programs will be put in jeopardy.

Community control

Another recurring theme is that the process of language revitalisation needs to be under Indigenous community control. This is sufficiently obvious that little more needs to be said. However as the Indigenous community becomes enmeshed in a network of non-Aboriginal organisations there need to be constant reminders to these other agencies that community control must be respected and genuinely embraced in their negotiations (see also Penfield et al. 2008).

More than language

Numerous language revitalisation programs have stressed that language is just one part of the process and that other cultural activities need to be integrated into that process.

Sizeable knowledge base and access to information on endangered languages

If the knowledge base for an endangered language is minimal then there are limits on what can be achieved in a language revitalisation program. For instance the Yitha-Yitha/Dadi-Dadi language, traditionally spoken along one part of the NSW-Victoria border, is one example of insufficient data to allow a major language revitalisation initiative, with just 150 items of vocabulary and five pages of grammar (Blake 2002, p. 164). Nevertheless significant progress has been made for a number of Victorian Aboriginal languages in spite of their relatively meagre documentation (see also J. Reid; Eira & Solomon-Dent, this volume).

Another issue is access to information on endangered languages. In the past some Aboriginal groups were barely aware of the recordings of their ancestral languages held in libraries and archives. Even when they have been aware of such resources there can be a considerable amount of processing required before they can be converted into a form suitable for language revitalisation. This processing often requires expertise in linguistics. In some instances a community may wish to restrict access to their information (see, for instance, Newry & Palmer 2003). This is a matter that must be addressed on a case by case basis.

Access to linguistic expertise

Having surveyed numerous language revitalisation programs in Australia and around the world (Walsh 2005) I do not know of any that have been successful and have not had the sustained input of expertise in linguistics. Input from a linguist may be necessary but it can cause disquiet in an Aboriginal community. Increasingly linguists have questioned their role in the process (see also Dobrin 2005, 2008; Grenoble 2009; Kroskrity 2009; Musgrave & Thieberger 2007). For example Rice (2009, p. 38) poses these among other questions:

> Putting language activists and linguists together, we can then ask questions such as the following: How do the goals of linguists and the goals of language activists mesh with one another? Can they contribute to each other's enterprises? Importantly, in a situation where the linguists tend to be outsiders to a language community, what do linguists have to offer?

In an article tellingly titled 'What I didn't know about working in an endangered language community' Nagy (2000) presents the linguist as wearing five hats: being involved in general social science, theoretical linguistics, sociolinguistics, applied linguistics, and technology. So the multifaceted nature of this work places high demands on the next generation of scholars. They will need appropriate training in the first instance and a reward structure that will advance rather than retard their careers. The linguist also needs to explore ways in which the community can be better integrated into their process as Grinevald (2007, p. 43) observes:

> A future perspective in terms of the community also means considering the sustainability of the work done on the language, through empowerment of members of the community, particularly in the form of continued training of speakers and semi-speakers capable and interested, and participation and support to the production of language materials, with a view to producing material that is actually usable in the field and by the community.

In addition, Eira (2008) explores some of the ways in which linguists may be unaware of how some of their underlying discursive practices impede collaborative efforts (see also Eira 2007).

Overcoming the genetic fallacy

Frequently members of an Aboriginal community will claim that the best (or even the only) people who should teach the language are the Elders and the only people who should learn it are descendants of speakers of the ancestral language. It is also sometimes claimed that it will be easier for those descendants to learn that language because it is part of them. These views can have disastrous consequences for a successful language revitalisation program, particularly when the Elders have little or no knowledge of the language and may be ashamed and, at the same time, younger people find learning the language not at all an easy process but a highly demanding and demoralising one. The Dauenhauers (1998, p. 84) have dubbed this the *genetic fallacy*, that is the 'assumption that the ancestral or heritage language will be easier for a person of the same ethnic background ... [and] teachers must also be of the ethnic group'. This genetic fallacy needs to be acknowledged and people need to accept that regaining a language is not easy for anyone – indeed it is a formidable task requiring long-term commitment and continuing support.

The need to foreground oracy rather than fall back on the 'easier' option: literacy

For Aboriginal languages which have not been spoken much in recent decades it can be tempting for members of the community to rely on literacy, and the same is true of teachers whether they be community members or not (see also Dauenhauer & Dauenhauer 1998, pp. 86–91). This is not a matter of all or nothing: both oracy and literacy should have a place but, in my view, regaining oral skills should be the primary goal. One means of foregrounding oracy is through technology.

Technology

It needs to be emphasised that the use of technology in a language revitalisation program needs to be appropriate. Sometimes it can amount to an avoidance strategy, a technical fix (Dauenhauer & Dauenhauer 1998, pp. 70–71) which actually impedes genuine training and interaction. However there are uses which can be beneficial, such as talking dictionaries, where a resource that is otherwise predominately literate gains an oral dimension through audio-clips. An example is the very substantial materials developed for South Australian languages like Arabana (Wilson & Hercus 2004) and Adnyamathanha (Tunstill 2004). This is particularly valuable for Aboriginal people who may be less than comfortable with the orthography developed for their language (see also N. Reid, this volume). The talking dictionary gives them direct access to the voices of their ancestors or older community members. Interestingly, computer technology can also be used to improve literacy as Auld (2002) reports on the use of talking books in Ndjébbana, a language with around 200 speakers in central Arnhem Land. In their case oracy is not really the problem but the talking books assist people to become print-literate. In some instances technological solutions may have particular appeal to younger people as with the deployment of dictionaries into mobile phones (Wilson, this volume).

Trained teachers of languages

One of the more significant ingredients for success in language revitalisation is having trained teachers of languages (Hobson 2006). As indicated earlier in discussing the genetic fallacy, it is not enough just to be a member of the community; teaching languages effectively requires targeted training. Sometimes in the past, teachers of Aboriginal languages have had no teacher training of any kind – let alone specific training in languages pedagogy. This shortfall is now being addressed by such targeted programs as the Master of Indigenous Languages Education based at the Koori Centre at the University of Sydney.

Sustained commitment from Elders

This is another factor that may seem so obvious as to be not worth raising. However I believe it is something that needs to be kept in the foreground as other essential factors like community cohesion and community control crucially hinge on a sustained commitment from Elders.

Regional support network

To sustain a language revitalisation effort it is essential that there be a regional support network. It cannot be over-emphasised how herculean a task such efforts can be. Particularly when there are just a few people working in isolated centres, the constant difficulties can prove overwhelming. Opportunities to share experiences with others engaged in similar activities is necessary on a fairly regular basis not just to learn from others but to recharge one's batteries.

Willingness to draw on existing resources from elsewhere and adapt them to the local situation

There is now a wealth of resources developed elsewhere which have the potential to be adapted. For instance the Yup'ik of Alaska have made their bilingual curriculum available (Norris-Tull 2000) and there are online resources for various languages including Hawaiian,[2] Māori,[3] and Comanche.[4] Within Australia the NSW Department of Education and Training has produced an online guide entitled 'Introducing an Aboriginal languages program'.[5]

Funding

Finally it is worth mentioning funding. I have left it until last because, in my view, while financial support is very useful it is not what I would see as a primary ingredient for success. One can think of programs operating side by side: one relatively well

---

2 See www.ahapunanaleo.org/eng/.

3 See www.rakaumanga.school.nz.

4 See www.comanchelanguage.org.

5 See www.curriculumsupport.education.nsw.gov.au/primary/languages/aboriginal/.

resourced and achieving very little, the other not well resourced at all but making significant progress. Indeed one commentator has given advice on 'What to do before the grants come through' (Ahlers 2009).

Addressing problems but not being overwhelmed by them

As a postscript to this wish list it is appropriate to acknowledge that there are numerous problems in the delivery of a successful language revitalisation program – Tsunoda (2005, pp. 179–200) presents a comprehensive account of them – but one should not become overwhelmed by them.

A wishlist in relation to a successful language revitalisation program

While it is unlikely that any one program will have all of these, those that are working better will probably have most of them. For example we can apply these factors to the Gumbaynggirr (see also Walsh 2001). Given the previously mentioned Gumbaynggirr manifesto it is clear that cultural awareness has underpinned this program from its earliest days. Whatever the internal issues that may have been going on in the background, the Gumbaynggirr appear to have maintained unity in their language revitalisation efforts. It is also clear they have maintained community control of the process. It is no accident that the Gumbaynggirr organisation responsible for language revitalisation, the Muurrbay Aboriginal Language and Culture Co-operative, contains the word culture: it is apparent in their publications and activities that they see language as being grounded in a broader cultural context. Regarding the knowledge base, the Gumbaynggirr have been fortunate to be able to draw on fairly substantial materials, not just written but audio recordings. They have also had the long-term commitment from Brother Steve Morelli who made a point of gaining expertise in linguistics so that he could better assist the process. More recently members of the Gumbaynggirr community have been gaining skills in linguistics as well. The Gumbaynggirr clearly have a preference for sourcing teachers from their own community but they have allowed outsiders to be involved in the process, and these teachers have gained the appropriate level of training. They have maintained a good balance between oracy and literacy and have embraced technology in appropriate ways. There is little doubt that there has been a sustained commitment from Elders and they have been part of a regional support network. They have shown a willingness to draw on existing resources from elsewhere and adapt them to the local situation, and have been fortunate enough to gain a certain amount of funding.

While they have been one of the more successful language revitalisation programs it has not been easy for the Gumbaynggirr and remains a struggle. But their progress shows it can be possible and provides a ready example for others to follow.

References

Ahlers JC (2009). Language restoration before funding: or, what to do before the grants come through. In WY Leonard & SEB Gardner (Eds). *Language is life* (pp. 48–59). Proceedings of the 11th Annual Stabilizing Indigenous Languages Conference. Berkeley: Survey of California and Other Indian Languages.

Amery R (2000). *Warrabarna Kaurna! reclaiming an Australian language*. Lisse: Swets & Zeitlinger.

Ash A, Fermino J & Hale K (2001). Diversity in local language maintenance and restoration: a reason for optimism. In L Hinton & K Hale (Eds). *The green book of language revitalization in practice* (pp. 19–35). San Diego: Academic Press.

Assembly of Alaska Native Educators (2001). *Guidelines for strengthening indigenous languages*. Anchorage: Alaska Native Knowledge Network [Online]. Available: www.ankn.uaf.edu/ Publications/language.html [Accessed 26 March 2009].

Auld G (2002). The role of the computer in learning Ndjébbana. *Language Learning & Technology*, 6(2): 41–58 [Online]. Available: llt.msu.edu/vol6num2/auld/ [Accessed 25 March 2009].

Blake B (2002). Reclaiming languages in Aboriginal Victoria. In D Bradley & M Bradley (Eds). *Language endangerment and language maintenance* (pp. 156–66). London: Routledge Curzon.

Craig C (1992). A constitutional response to language endangerment: the case of Nicaragua. *Language*, 68(1): 17–24.

Crystal D (2000). *Language death*. Cambridge: Cambridge University Press.

Dauenhauer NM & Dauenhauer R (1998). Technical, emotional, and ideological issues in reversing language shift: examples from southeast Alaska. In L Grenoble & L Whaley (Eds). *Endangered languages: language loss and community response* (pp. 57–98). Cambridge: Cambridge University Press.

Dobrin L (2005). When our values conflict with theirs: linguists and community empowerment in Melanesia. In P Austin (Ed). *Language documentation and description*. Vol 3 (pp. 42–52). London: School of Oriental & African Studies.

Dobrin L (2008). From linguistic elicitation to eliciting the linguist: lessons in community empowerment from Melanesia. *Language*, 84(2): 300–24.

Eira C (2007). Addressing the ground of language endangerment. In MK David, N Ostler & C Dealwis (Eds). *Working together for endangered languages: research challenges and social impacts* (pp. 82–98). Proceedings of the Foundation for Endangered Languages Conference XI, Kuala Lumpur, 26–28 October 2007. Bath: Foundation for Endangered Languages.

Eira C (2008). Linguists and communities: discursive practice and the status of collaborative language work in Indigenous communities. *Language and Intercultural Communication*, 8(4): 278–97.

Fettes M (1997). Stabilizing what? An ecological approach to language renewal. In J Reyhner (Ed). *Teaching Indigenous languages* (pp. 301–18). Flagstaff, Arizona: Center for Excellence in Education.

Grenoble L & Whaley D (2006). *Saving languages: an introduction to language revitalization.* Cambridge: Cambridge University Press.

Grenoble L (2009). Linguistic cages and the limits of linguists. In J Reyhner & L Lockard (Eds). *Indigenous language revitalization: encouragement, guidance & lessons learned* (pp. 61–69). Flagstaff, Arizona: Northern Arizona University.

Grinevald C (2007). Linguistic fieldwork among speakers of endangered languages. In O Miyaoka, O Sakiyama & ME Krauss (Eds). *The vanishing languages of the Pacific rim* (pp. 35–76). Oxford: Oxford University Press.

Hinton L (1994). *Flutes of fire*. Berkeley: Heyday Books.

Hinton L (2002). *How to keep your language alive: a commonsense approach to one-on-one language*. Berkeley: Heyday Books.

Hobson J (2006). Who will teach our languages? In N Parbury & R Craven (Eds). *Aboriginal studies: making the connections* (pp. 166–74). Collected Papers of the 12th national Aboriginal Studies Association Conference; Bankstown, 2–3 November 2006. Sydney: Aboriginal Studies Association.

Ignace MB (1998). *Handbook for Aboriginal language program planning in British Columbia*. North Vancouver: First Nations Education Steering Committee [Online]. Available: www.fnesc.ca/publications/pdf/language.pdf [Accesssed 25 March 2009].

Johnson S (1987). The philosophy and politics of Aboriginal language maintenance. *Australian Aboriginal Studies*, 1987(2): 54–58.

Kipp DR (2000). *Encouragement, guidance, insights, and lessons learned for native language activists developing their own tribal language program*. St Paul, Minnesota: Grotto Foundation.

Kroskrity P (2009). Language renewal as sites of language ideological struggle. The need for 'ideological clarification'. In J Reyhner & L Lockard (Eds). *Indigenous language revitalization: encouragement, guidance & lessons learned* (pp. 61–69). Flagstaff, Arizona: Northern Arizona University.

Linn MS, Naranjo T, Nicholas S, Slaughter I, Yamamoto A & Zepeda O (2002). Awakening the languages. Challenges of enduring language programs: field reports from 15 programs from Arizona, New Mexico and Oklahoma. In B Burnaby & J Reyhner (Eds). *Indigenous languages across the community* (pp. 105–26). Flagstaff, Arizona: Northern Arizona University.

McKay G (1996). *The land still speaks: review of Aboriginal and Torres Strait Islander language maintenance and development needs and activities*. Canberra: Australian Government Publishing Service.

Musgrave S & Thieberger N (2007). Who pays the piper? In MK David, N Ostler & C Dealwis (Eds). *Working together for endangered languages: research challenges and social impacts* (pp. 47–

55).Proceedings of the Foundation for Endangered Languages conference XI, Kuala Lumpur, 26–28 October 2007. Bath: Foundation for Endangered Languages.

Nagy N (2000). What I didn't know about working in an endangered language community. *International Journal of the Sociology of Language*, 144: 143–60.

Newry D & Palmer K (2003). 'Whose language is it anyway?' Rights to restrict access to endangered languages: a north-east Kimberley example. In J Blythe & RM Brown (Eds). *Maintaining the links: language, identity and the land* (pp. 101–06). Proceedings of the 7th Foundation for Endangered Languages conference; Broome, Western Australia, 22–24 September 2003. Bath: Foundation for Endangered Languages.

Norris-Tull D (2000). *Our language our souls. The Yup'ik bilingual curriculum of the Lower Kuskokwim school district: a continuing success story*. Fairbanks: Alaska Native Knowledge Network [Online]. Available: ankn.uaf.edu/curriculum/Yupiaq/DelenaNorrisTull/bLower%20 Kuskokwim%20bilingual.htm [Accessed 26 March 2009].

Palmer K (Ed) (2000). *Strong language, strong culture: New South Wales strategic language study. Final report and strategy action plan* [compiled by DF Hosking, TJ Lonsdale, JF Troy, & MJ Walsh]. Canberra: Australian Institute for Aboriginal & Torres Strait Islander Studies.

Paton D, Pascoe B & Eira C (forthcoming). Peetyawan weeyn: a guide for community language programs. Melbourne: Victorian Aboriginal Corporation for Languages.

Penfield SD, Serratos A, Tucker BV, Flores A, Harper G, Hill J Jr & Vasquez N (2008). Community collaborations: best practices for North American indigenous language documentation. Small languages and small language communities. *International Journal of the Sociology of Language*, 191: 187–202.

Purdie N, Frigo T, Ozolins C, Noblett G, Thieberger N & Sharp J (2008). *Indigenous languages programmes in Australian schools: a way forward*. Camberwell: Australian Council for Educational Research [Online]. Available: www.dest.gov.au/NR/rdonlyres/FBEAC65B-3A11-41F0-B836-1A480FDD82F9/25487/LPfinal130109NP.pdf [Accessed 25 March 2009].

Reyhner J (1999). Some basics of indigenous language revitalization. In J Reyhner, G Cantoni, RN St Clair & E Parsons Yazzie (Eds). *Revitalizing indigenous languages* (pp. v–xx). Flagstaff, Arizona: Northern Arizona University.

Reyhner J (2003). Native language immersion. In J Reyhner, O Trujillo, RL Carrasco & L Lockard (Eds). *Nurturing native languages* (pp. 1–6). Flagstaff, Arizona: Northern Arizona University.

Rice K (2009). Must there be two solitudes? Language activists and linguists working together. In J Reyhner & L Lockard (Eds). *Indigenous language revitalization: encouragement, guidance & lessons learned* (pp. 37–59). Flagstaff, Arizona: Northern Arizona University.

Spindler G & Spindler L (Eds) (1994). *Pathways to cultural awareness: cultural therapy with teachers and students*. Thousand Oaks, California: Corwin Press.

Spindler G (1999). Three categories of cultural knowledge useful in doing cultural therapy. *Anthropology and Education Quarterly*, 30(4): 466–72.

Stebbins T (2003). *Fighting language endangerment: community directed research on Sm'algyax (Coast Tsimshian)*. Osaka, Japan: Osaka Gakuin University.

Troy J & Walsh M (2009). Reinstating Aboriginal placenames around Port Jackson and Botany Bay. In H Koch & L Hercus (Eds). *Aboriginal placenames: naming and re-naming the Australian landscape* (pp. 55–69). Aboriginal History Monograph 19. Canberra: Aboriginal History Inc and ANU E Press.

Tsunoda T (2005). *Language endangerment and language revitalization*. Berlin: Mouton de Gruyter.

Tunstill G (2004). *Adnyamathanha years R-10: a teaching framework for revival and second language learning in years reception to ten*. Hindmarsh, South Australia: Department of Education & Children's Services Publishing.

Walsh M (2001). A case study of language revitalisation in 'settled' Australia. *Current Issues in Language Planning*, 2(2–3): 251–58.

Walsh M (2005). Will indigenous languages survive? *Annual Review of Anthropology*, 34: 293–315.

Walsh M (2009). Losing the plot in Aboriginal Australia? Loss of culture, loss of language. Paper presented at the Aboriginal Policy Research Conference, Ottawa, Ontario, 12 March 2009.

Wilson G & Hercus L (2004). *Arabana, years R to 10: an Arabana teaching framework for reception to year ten: language revitalisation and second language learning*. Hindmarsh, South Australia: Department of Education & Children's Services Publishing.

Yamamoto A (1998). Linguists and endangered language communities: issues and approaches. In K Matsumura (Ed). *Studies in endangered languages* (pp. 231–52). International Clearing House for Endangered Languages, Linguistic Studies Vol 1. Tokyo: Hituji Syobo.

3
Our ways of learning in Aboriginal languages

Tyson Kaawoppa Yunkaporta[1]

Abstract

Aboriginal culture has not been lost – just disrupted. Our ways of knowing, being, doing, valuing and learning remain in an ancestral framework of knowledge that is still strong. Through Indigenous research in western New South Wales that explores these knowledge systems in land, language, people and the relationships among them, eight ways of learning have been identified. This chapter makes recommendations for using the eight ways in the teaching of Aboriginal languages in schools.

Tracking the pedagogy in our language

There is deep knowledge in our languages. There is a spirit of learning in our words. This is more than just knowledge of what to learn, but knowledge of how we learn it. This is our pedagogy, our way of learning. We find it in words about thinking and communicating. We find it in the language structure, in the way things are repeated and come around in a circle, showing us how we think and use information. The patterns in stories, phrases, songs, kinship and even in the land can show us the spirit of learning that lives in our cultures.

If your language has just one word for speak, tell, say and talk, then it is telling you something about the role of speech in learning – particularly if that same word carries the negative meaning of forcing somebody to do something against their will. You will go softly with the way you instruct, keeping in mind that the word for thinking and knowing in that language is also the word for loving. The language itself is giving you a picture of how to approach language education in your place. It might be telling you to give students a healthy balance of supportive discipline and independence. This is strong pedagogy.

---

1 Department of Education & Training, New South Wales.

It is true that all Aboriginal languages are different and carry their own ways and values, but we also have many things in common. That Aboriginal idea of balance between social support and self-direction is one of them. To use the Aboriginal concept of balance – if that is a part of our way – then it makes sense for us to find what pedagogy we have in common with non-Aboriginal ways too, balancing the two worlds. If we find the overlap between our best ways of learning and the mainstream's best ways of learning then we will have an equal balance.

From our language and our land knowledge we know there are always connections among all things, places where different elements are no longer separate but mix together and become something else. This way of working gives us new innovations as well as bringing us together. There are eight ways of learning that have been found at this interface of two worlds. This chapter not only shows those eight ways but also follows them in the way it is written. First we see how each of the eight ways came out of a research project and then we see how to use the eight ways in your Aboriginal language classroom.

The story

Story takes you up, and then down, leaving you in a place that is higher than before. It runs through everything in land, body, mind and spirit, tying together the shape of learning for all peoples. So this narrative about a western New South Wales (NSW) research project continues through these next eight sections, tying all of the elements together.

The eight ways came from Indigenous research, which is research done by and for Aboriginal people within Aboriginal communities, drawing on knowledge and protocol from communities, Elders, land, language, ancestors and spirit. These things formed the methodology – the ways and rules for working in research. As the research took place across western NSW and the researcher was a man with kinship ties in the far north and ancestral ties in the far south of Australia, that methodology had to work in the middle ground among different Aboriginal nations. It also had to work in the middle ground between Aboriginal knowledge systems and western learning systems.

Messages from land and spirit gave shape to the methodology, the way of working. Work was done with river junctions and interconnecting songlines that brought together different cultural knowledges. The work of Indigenous researchers who had gone before was also followed, bringing to the centre the idea of the *cultural interface* of Dr Martin Nakata from the Torres Strait, the idea of a dynamic overlap of knowledges from different peoples. This idea of the interface was found not only in research literature, but in Indigenous law and stories from all around Australia and the world.

The map

Following the model of a local river junction, the Aboriginal researcher and a local Ngemba mentor worked with non-Aboriginal education experts at a place between Bourke and Brewarrina where three rivers meet to become one. This river gave the shape for a map of the project, a way to bring together the ways of learning from different cultures and find what they had in common, then follow those common ways. The interface among three Aboriginal and western learning frameworks was found and the eight ways were born from that, carrying the best of both worlds down the river.

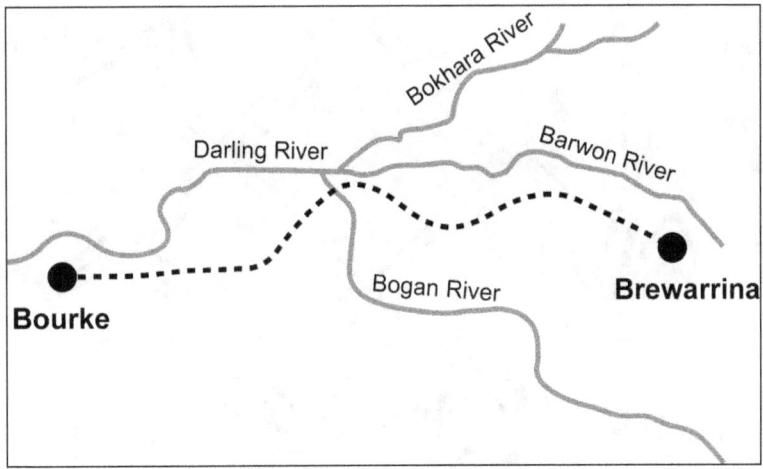

Figure 1. The map.

The silence

In our world the deepest knowledge is not in words. It is in the meaning behind the words, in the spaces between them, in gestures or looks, in meaningful silences, in the work of hands, in learning from journeys, in quiet reflection, in the Dreaming. The eight ways were tested on journeys following the river along a codfish songline linking to the Murray River, tested in ceremony, tested in the carving and use of tools to represent them. This silent knowledge was explored with the hands and the feet. A lot of this knowledge can't be shown with words in a book like this – but in our way it would be up to the Aboriginal listener, and in this case the reader, to fill in those gaps themselves – to fill it with their own cultural knowledge and teaching experience.

The signs

That same silent knowledge was also explored with the eyes, through the signs and images we all see – our way of visualising and sharing ideas that has been with us forever, the things that make up our mental landscape. These were not only signs from the land and animals, but also signs made by people. This became a way of finding, working with and sharing the eight ways through images. The images of the eight ways were brought together in one picture that was modelled on a kinship system to show they are not steps to follow, but dynamic and interactive processes.

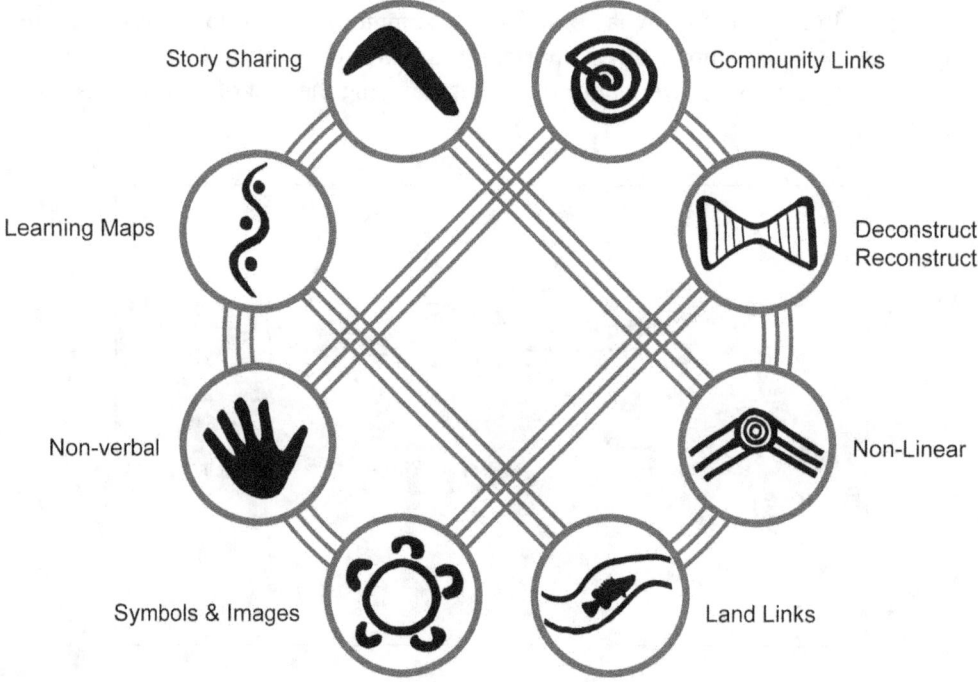

Figure 2. The eight ways as symbols.

The land

Entities in the land like stones, animals, plants and rivers all provided knowledge through the research to uncover and share the eight ways. The languages and stories of the land were a part of this too. For example language and Dreaming stories from one language group showed that learning, thinking and all other journeys take a winding path, suggesting that there are no straight lines to knowledge or outcomes. This knowledge was tracked further into the land, walking and talking with local people down winding rivers and in the winding tracks of blue-tongue lizards. This winding path became the symbol for one of the eight ways and provided a map for thinking about and working with the other seven ways.

The shape

The winding path provided a shape for thinking outside of the straight line, that Western linear logic. But there were other shapes as well, particularly circular ways of thinking found in kinship systems, land knowledge, art and language structures. There was also a two-way shape, a balance and symmetry where opposites meet. That way of thinking brought home the cultural interface, allowing an understanding of the shapes of logic from different cultural viewpoints. For example it became clear that not all western thinking was in a straight line. It was also non-linear, in the way they think about cycles in science and in the recent tradition of lateral thinking that zig-zags in a similar way to the winding path mentioned above. All eight ways came to be developed in this way, finding the best ways of thinking in common across cultures, coming from two sides and meeting in the middle.

The back-tracking

One shape that came from the best thinking in both ways was from the idea of back-tracking through knowledge, a process with a shape like two funnels coming together at a centre point. In this way of learning you always give a model of the end product of any learning right at the start. This model can then be broken down into increasingly smaller parts then put back together – deconstructed and reconstructed. At the same time each piece must be seen as part of the whole, and as part of a purposeful activity in the real world. This way was seen in the mainstream practice of scaffolded literacy as well as in the Aboriginal learning of traditional cultural practices.

This was used in the research to help develop the eight ways by examining other models and research projects done by Indigenous people from around the world. It gave a vision of the end product, then a way of back-tracking through the process before attempting to go forward. This story you are reading now is starting that deconstructing–reconstructing process – giving an example of the eight ways in action, a model that will be broken down in more detail then put back together with the reader later in the chapter.

The home-world

In the research to find the eight ways, knowledge was always centred on the local communities in the region. It began with local knowledge then spiralled out to national and international literature and practice. It spiralled because no matter where knowledge came from in the world it was always found while orbiting out around the local centre, grounded in the question, 'What does this mean to local people and how will it benefit the local community?'

The researcher not only worked with local knowledge and contexts but also left the product of the research with the local community. This meant passing on these eight ways to be used by local schools for connecting with the community through the curriculum, and to be used by community people in developing language or cultural programs that have integrity and intellectual rigour in our own ways of knowing. The researcher does not own this way of working, nor does the Department of Education or a university. The eight ways came from this western region and belong to this place. At the same time this way of working also links to other contributing regions and peoples around the world, but its centre is here.

Detail of the eight ways

The first way is story sharing

The killer boomerang symbol is our narrative model (see Figure 2, top left). Your story starts with normal life (handle end) then builds to a climax (boomerang elbow), but at the end (boomerang tip) when things calm down and return to 'normal', life is never the same. It's at a higher place than before because new knowledge has come.

This is a powerful tool in the Aboriginal language classroom. You tell your personal stories about any topic right at the start, and make sure you give the students a chance to share their stories as well. That way you are drawing on everybody's home culture and knowledge for the lesson. You can build units of work around stories too. You draw culture, vocabulary and grammar items from the story itself, rather than teaching isolated cultural lessons, lists of words and language structures.

The way in action

In one Stage 4 Aboriginal language program in western NSW each unit was based on a story. They didn't want to teach body parts first, then family words, then animals and so forth, so instead they took their lessons from the story. They learned some body parts, animals and family names that were mentioned in the story, not as lists of words, but as parts of whole sentences in language that combined these things in a culturally meaningful way. In this way they were living Aboriginal language and culture, not just remembering some Aboriginal words.

The second way is learning maps

The winding path symbol represents a journey. Learning journeys can be drawn as a map with points of understanding indicated along the way rather than at the end. Learning journeys never take a straight path but wind, zig-zag, or go around. It is best to base these maps on the land where your language is from.

In the Aboriginal language classroom these learning maps help students to see where they are and where they are going in their journey of language learning. You can have whole units or even the whole scope and sequence for the year mapped out in this way. This can be based on the local landscape with local seasonal changes worked in. For example students might know they are about to begin their Term 1 assessment piece when the nights start getting cooler, when they see a seasonal indicator on the map in their classroom. Criteria for quality work, vocabulary lists and even attendance data can be added to this visual map.

The way in action

In one Stage 4 Aboriginal language program in western NSW the teacher mapped out the scope and sequence for the year based on a road that runs through her country. Hills at the start of the journey represented early challenges like getting pronunciation right. Each bend in the road represented quarterly assessment tasks, while other landmarks indicated changes to new topics and units of work. A significant totemic animal from that language group was shown on the map, along with its tracks, to indicate that this map showed the journey of that animal.

The third way is non-verbal learning

The symbol of the hand represents all knowledge that can be understood or acquired without words, including gestures, inference, expressions, eye movement, kinaesthetic learning, images and revealed knowledge (for example dreams, insight, inspiration, reflection).

In the Aboriginal language classroom this is a key element of culture and pedagogy. It is important to use total physical response activities where physical actions are used together with the words and ideas students are learning. The Aboriginal teacher uses facial expressions, body position, mime and gestures to communicate the meaning of language words and phrases, and this ensures that students are linking their language not to an English translation, but to their own cultural and personal meanings. We also use observation, watching people for the real meaning behind their words, and this skill can even be used with print – reading between the lines to find implied meanings. This is useful if you have to use an English text written by a non-Aboriginal person about culture, as it helps us to be critical and keep our own standpoint, to defend against colonising influences. With listening, as well as reading, a lot of information in our traditions comes from the learner filling in the blanks of speech or text. Finally, as Aboriginal language teachers we also need to facilitate that sense of personal spiritual connection where non-verbal learning comes from land, ancestors, the Dreaming and even our own bodies.

The way in action

In one Aboriginal language program in western NSW a traditional song about a process in the land was taught to students, but the focus was not on a word-for-word translation. The deeper knowledge of the song was unspoken, but conveyed through gestures to accompany the song, as well as through tone and expression. The tone was serious business and had to be done just right. There was meaning in the rhythm of the song associated with the land process that the song helps to bring about. Deeper layers of meaning came from repetition and performance of the song in different contexts. When they got it right, evidence of the learning came when the land did what the song was asking it to do – a natural event that had not happened in a long time – it rained.

The fourth way is symbols and images

This symbol represents people sitting at a meeting place yarning. It is an example of a simple symbol that contains a lot of deeper information and understandings.

Aboriginal thinking is often done in images or shapes rather than words. Concepts can be shown this way.

In the Aboriginal language classroom this can give the same outcomes as the non-verbal way of learning – students linking language to their own cultural meanings rather than to English translations. For example, if a student has a picture of their mum labelled *Gunhi*, instead of writing in their books, '*Gunhi* – Mother', this is linking the language to their own reality rather than to an English translation. Symbols and pictures can be used to represent words and concepts, or even learning processes. You can see this way at work in the learning maps as well.

The way in action

In one school in western NSW some students created a sand painting using Aboriginal symbols taught by a local Elder. Another group made a story map from a local Dreaming story, using both pictures and words to show where the main incidents in the story occurred on country. Later a group of Stage 4 Aboriginal language students studied these images, linking them to the appropriate words and story in language. They then made message sticks about a common theme using those images and others to represent language words and cultural concepts based on the theme of the unit. For oral assessment they were expected to 'read' the symbols on the message sticks to the class using only the language words they had learnt.

The fifth way is land links

The symbol represents a river. All the animals, plants and geographic forms in land and water contain deep knowledge. They also provide metaphors for concepts. Knowledge of local land and place is central to Indigenous ways of knowing.

In the Aboriginal language classroom this way is crucial as we are teaching *the languages of the land.* This link to land and country should always be present as it ensures cultural integrity. For example we know that often our Dreaming stories are misrepresented as fables or children's tales, and we can tell when this is happening because land and place are left out when people tell our stories in this way. An indication of cultural integrity in storytelling is that land and place are central to the story. There's no story without place, and no place without story. So linking your lesson content to land is one way of maintaining cultural integrity in your language program.

The way in action

In a Stage 4 Aboriginal language course in western NSW a unit of work was planned in which the class mapped out the events of a local Dreaming story on a geographical map of the area, following the river system. Different kinds of country such as redsoil and blacksoil were to be labelled in language along with landmarks, animals and the main sites of the story events. Other stories that intersected with this one at certain places were also mapped showing the way stories from other country connected with this one at special places. This leads into a comparative study of regional languages and cultures.

The sixth way is non-linear processes

The symbol represents circular logic at the centre, and the lines either side show the interface between opposites. In Aboriginal worldviews opposites meet to create something new, with symmetry and balance concepts valued above oppositional thinking. This sign has been carved into a boomerang (Figure 3). In this way we can also see that learning doesn't go straight from one side to the other. It bends out to the side, bringing in knowledge that might seem to be off topic but that creates deeper understandings and richer learnings. This also shows that at low levels of knowledge there is a wide gap in cross-cultural understanding, but when you find the higher knowledge from both ways they come together with many things in common.

In the Aboriginal language classroom this way is a hard thing for which to plan. It is the most difficult of the eight ways to understand. It is best to think of it as how you move and think in hunting, gathering or fishing. You don't go straight and you don't think of just one thing you want to collect at the end. You think of a thousand things in the landscape and your experience that help you to find what you're looking for, and you seldom walk in a straight line to find it. For us this way is about giving ourselves permission to follow our own ways of approaching a topic, without feeling like we have to change culture to fit Western ideas of a learning progression from A to Z.

The way in action

In the planning of a Stage 4 Aboriginal language course in western NSW we were looking at how to teach a continuous tense that was part of a story for study. Should we just say, 'Here is the suffix and you use it this way. Now, do some practice sentences'? No. That's not how we learn. So we looked at the connection between this suffix and the body function to which it is linked. We told funny stories about that and made a lot of rude jokes. Then we looked at a song about this, and the way a sense of striving comes through that body function and through a continuous action. We decided to use humour and song to teach the students the deeper meaning behind the way you use that continuous tense suffix. What was a grammar item before became a cultural lesson. The students would come to it from that different angle and in doing this they would find a deeper meaning and retain the knowledge better.

The seventh way is deconstruct/reconstruct

The symbol of the Torres Strait Islander drum represents the way knowledge can be learned by back-tracking through the context and the whole form in supported stages, then reproduced independently. The shape shows a balance between independence and support. This can be seen in literacy scaffolding programs as well as in traditional activities like learning corroboree.

In the Aboriginal language classroom this way gives a supportive structure to what you teach. Pronunciation, spelling and memorising words doesn't come at the start but in the middle. You start with a whole text as a model – like a dialogue, a Welcome to Country, a song or a story. You look at the social and cultural context of this, give it a purpose, and model how it is used. You look at the structure of it; teach the cultural codes you see there, unpack it and work through the stages of learning you find in the language text. Only then, in the middle, do you get to what Western education refers to as 'the basics' – the pronunciation and spelling and so on. From there, our students use their strengths as independent learners and we support them in putting the language back together to create their own meaningful texts and yarns.

The way in action

In a Stage 3 Aboriginal language class in western NSW students were supposed to be memorising the names of body parts. But they seemed to be more interested in teasing each other. So the teachers presented a dialogue of two students teasing each other in language. The insults were made up of body parts combined with pronouns and adjectives. The teachers performed the dialogue several times with gestures and expression getting the meaning across to the students. They discussed cultural ways of dealing with conflicts from past and present. They performed the dialogue several times, with students later following the text on a written handout, joining in and mimicking the funnier parts. They examined each line and looked at how the structure was repeated. They sorted the words into pronouns, adjectives and nouns and practised pronunciation. They kept these lists in the same order as the sentence structure and then expanded those lists with new vocabulary. They used these lists to create their own insults, then in pairs built these into a funny dialogue that they practised and performed for the class.

The eighth way is community links

This symbol is Brad Steadman's knowledge spiral from Brewarrina. It shows how, in the Ngemba way, creation patterns at the local level are repeated at the non-local level throughout the universe. It also shows how non-local information is viewed and used from local standpoints for community benefit, with all learning returned to the community.

In the Aboriginal language classroom this is important because, while you are drawing on local traditional knowledge in your school program, you are also promoting and maintaining this knowledge in the community. There is a give and take here. Another aspect of this is respecting the diverse group identities of students in your language class and school community, making sure they bring their unique cultural standpoint to the learning of this language. Our peoples have always been multilingual, learning the languages of other groups but always with the cultural protection of maintaining a home identity at the centre. When there are students from other language groups in your class their culture must be respected, and they must see the relevance of learning this different language with a view to developing the skills to learn and promote their own language. With every bit of knowledge you teach, students should clearly see the answer to the question, 'What does this mean for me and my mob?' This includes your non-Aboriginal students. Then that knowledge should be returned to the community in useful ways. The most obvious way to do this is through performances and displays, but community development and awareness projects are also possible.

The way in action

In a Stage 4 Aboriginal language course in western NSW students organised family language days to promote language revival, teach language to the community and showcase their work and skills for community evaluation. They performed songs and put on plays in language that were based on Dreaming stories, set up language activities for community members and held competitions. This gave a purpose to all the work the students did in class, as they knew every piece would end up being judged by their families. Community engagement and attendance at these days has been strongest when they have been held outside the school grounds, in a community space.

How to use all eight ways in a unit of work

It is best to start with community knowledge and a story related to the content. Share your stories and hear the students' stories to find out what they know already about the topic or related topics. Whatever you want the students to be able to do by the end of the unit, model it first. Get them to work with those models in ways that don't need words, like watching or copying your body language and gestures for meaning, total physical response activities, cutting up written and visual texts and sequencing them, looking for the unspoken meaning behind the words or just quietly reflecting. Question outsider knowledge sources and test for truth and integrity. Find the deeper knowledge of craft work, such as women's business in weaving, and always link these to language use. Create a visual map of the learning and make maps of the land to show the places and connecting paths of stories. Make mind maps of ideas. Always link content back to land and place. Use images, colours and symbols to teach new vocabulary and concepts like grammar and structure. Don't build to final outcomes, but rather find the outcomes along the way and don't be afraid to go off the straight track to find them. Support students in the first half of the unit by backtracking though the modelled work then guide them towards working independently in the second half. Finally return the learning to community for community benefit and for them to evaluate. Allow Elders and other keepers of knowledge to have a say in the criteria for success.

We already do this!

The truth is these eight ways are not even needed if curriculum developers work with cultural integrity in a balanced partnership between the community and the school. The eight ways will be strong in a program then, even if the participants have never heard of them. An example of this is the Dubbo Wiradjuri program which was written before the eight ways were developed, but still covered all eight elements (see McNaboe & Poetsch, this volume). This occurred because the programming team was working with cultural integrity and there was community knowledge at the centre of everything with Aboriginal people leading the project:

1. Story was embedded in each unit as a source of knowledge, themes and vocabulary, rather than having isolated lists of body parts, animals, greetings and so forth
2. Story-mapping activities put these stories into the context of country. Genealogy mapping and visual maps of historic events were also planned
3. Gestures, total physical response and craft activities were included to enhance non-verbal knowledge skills. Deeper unspoken meanings and values behind cultural activities, texts and vocabulary were explored
4. Images were to be used in story work, artwork and the learning of vocabulary
5. Most concepts were related back to land and place, particularly the river
6. Structures like family trees and timelines were redrawn in familiar non-linear ways, for example family forests. Local concepts of balance were introduced, such as in health and diet
7. Creating products for assessment always began with examining model texts
8. Units were grounded in local knowledge through Elders with each unit being centred around a rule written in Wiradjuri from a list of Elders' instructions for living on country. Assessment focused on ways to promote those rules in the community.

Cultural integrity in language instruction

These eight ways are a call for cultural integrity, for an end to culture as a tokenistic add-on. Johnny cakes are good, but if we're not using language when we make them, then why are we doing this with our class? We need to learn *through* culture, not just *about* culture. Painting some dots on a cardboard boomerang and singing Humpty Dumpty in Aboriginal language is no longer good enough. These eight ways of working are for using cultural knowledge not just in *what* we teach, but in *how* we teach. Doing that puts us on an equal intellectual level with the education business of pedagogy; allows us to make partnerships as teachers of language courses that are on an equal academic footing with mainstream subjects.

This partnership needs to create an equal dialogue: an interface between our ancestrally-perfected ways of learning and departmental policies and frameworks for teaching. At that high level of knowledge we find more common ground than differences across cultures. This gives rise to respect and an empowerment of community. When our ways become part of planning at that higher level our values can also gain a place in the organisational structure of the school, giving us a true voice and true agency in education. Our culture and language is currently in the curriculum at the level of extra content. This has opened the door for us to bring it up to the next level.

Language and culture is the first step, the key. Aboriginal language teachers have the power to lead change in education, but there must be integrity in this as well as high intellectual standards. Rather than reproducing tokenistic souvenirs of culture we must put forward our deep knowledges to set the standard and demand quality from the best that mainstream learning has to offer. Remember that at low levels of knowledge there is only difference across cultures but at high levels there is common ground. Every one of the eight ways of learning shown in this paper is present in western and other cultures as well as our own. Our higher-order thinking processes need to be revealed in cultural items that are currently seen as primitive, simple or exotic. We need to bring the deep knowledges from different cultures alongside each other and find that common ground for a true act of reconciliation.

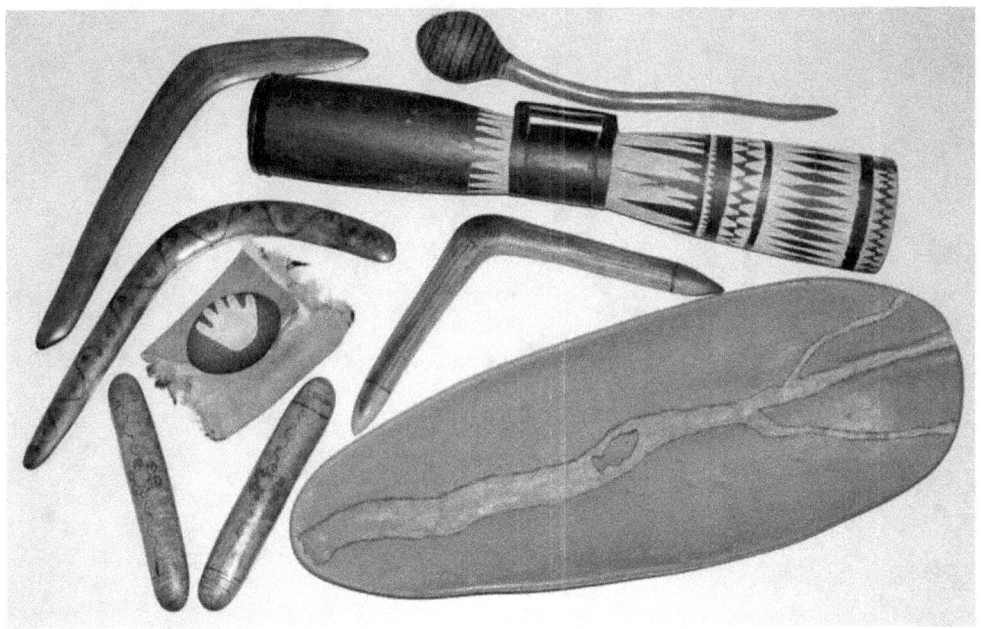

Figure 3. Not just 'artefacts', but eight tools for learning.

Part Two
Language in communities

Introduction
Language in communities

Kevin Lowe[1]

There is wide agreement on the centrality of the revitalisation of Indigenous languages to the sovereign aspirations of Aboriginal communities. Aboriginal and Torres Strait Islander peoples in Australia, along with other decolonising peoples in the world, see their languages as providing a window through which they can view their past and envision their future.

When respected Gamilaraay Elder Auntie Rose Fernando said, 'Language is our soul' (Board of Studies 1998) she articulated a view that both knowledge of and access to language is a key to the long-term survival of Indigenous people's own unique place and identity within Australia. Indigenous people have been overwhelmed by the pressure to adopt the coloniser's tongue as their own first language. Attempts to bring about the restoration of local languages and dialects are not only hampered by the number and diversity of languages, but also by complex histories of massacres, dispersal, tribal relocations, and inter-marriages that have stretched to breaking point the links to local language and cultural knowledge. The work of individuals and small groups within communities, however, has kept tenuous links to Indigenous ontology and epistemologies open, with their activities forming the basis of the renaissance of traditional languages across Australia.

This work is not without deep tensions, as those working in the area of language revitalisation will attest. Questions regarding who is capable, let alone entitled, to teach language are bandied around communities, often masking broader issues such as which language will be privileged in which location. These questions, coupled with the potentially divisive issues of authority, language ownership and fluency have often been the focus of community concerns as they commence work on revitalising their languages. Yet, as is attested elsewhere, the nurturing of language within families and communities has provided an avenue for engendering real and sustained interest in language and cultural reclamation. This nurturing gives form and substance to the long-held community aspirations for language revitalisation (for example Palmer 2000). Along these lines, Walsh (this volume) provides an outline of the range of

---

1 Aboriginal Curriculum Unit, Office of the Board of Studies NSW.

potential factors that maximise the chance of success for the revitalisation of any given language. These authors make the point that foundational strength comes from being able to assert a direct link between cultural connectedness and the uniqueness of Indigenous identity. The revitalisation of Indigenous languages is part of the larger renaissance of indigeneity where a community's involvement is an act of reasserting their sovereignty in their own country and maintaining it, even when living elsewhere.

There are many realities, theoretical and practical, associated with successfully establishing these programs as community driven and controlled. They include such questions as: what is the role of linguistic support? How are the differing partial remembrances of language to be incorporated? Can Indigenous people living off country be taught language, especially if it is not their own? What access can non-Indigenous people have to languages? The capacity to resolve these and other questions will test the mettle of Indigenous communities, community language workers, and the agencies which employ them in successfully negotiating solutions. There are immense tasks facing communities in the challenge to make the transition from language slumber to awakening.

The papers in this section of the volume consider the importance and value of language revitalisation both to communities themselves and to wider public understanding.

Amery's paper on the Kaurna community – represented by the key individuals in Kaurna Warra Pintyandi (KWP) – highlights the importance of self-assertion as the authority on language, as well as the means that the KWP developed to control requests to use Kaurna in the public domain. Amery outlines some of the methods that the KWP working group used to protect the integrity of their language and also make it accessible to the general public in the form that they want. The development of the *Kaurna Placenames* website has been one means by which this has been achieved. The paper also foregrounds how the establishment of a long-term relationship between a non-Indigenous linguist and an Aboriginal community has enhanced the quality and quantity of resources and training that the community has been able to access over the life of the larger language revitalisation project.

Anderson's paper is a personal journey of reconnecting with language and sharing it for his own and the community's health and pride. He looks directly through the lens of community to show the extraordinary redemptive power of language learning. Anderson focuses on the enormously positive impact of language work on the whole community, the willingness of schools and others to support community projects and the growing pride with which the local Aboriginal community has sought to engage themselves and the non-Aboriginal community in the building of belonging within their own country.

Olawsky describes a range of strategies to increase the profile, value and recognition of the Miriwoong language. He argues that even in the early stages of revitalisation, these efforts play a positive role in supporting community pride by providing the language with legitimacy in the speech community itself as well as in the broader public view. Olawsky suggests that current thinking on language revitalisation strategies needs to be more inclusive of activities that engender pride and linguistic identity, particularly through seeing language privileged by diverse usage across the community.

Sometimes & Kelly further the argument for the importance of the wider use of language by discussing its use in public theatre. Using the *Ngapartji Ngapartji* Pitjantjatjara community arts project the authors discuss how reconnection to language has been embedded in the theatre production, linking language to Dreaming, kin, community and place, and, through the theatre-goer, to a wider Australian audience. Sometimes & Kelly argue that Indigenous languages need the efforts of all Australians to nurture and protect them as they are icons for the whole nation.

Stockley's paper challenges any notion that language revitalisation is an easy project. He shows that community-driven language revitalisation is fraught with deep local and regional tensions. While Stockley argues cogently that language work is a lifelong project, he also clearly illustrates the enormous community benefits that are to be had through community members coming together, picking up challenges, having fun, and reconnecting through the deeper cultural domain of community cohesion and connectedness.

References

New South Wales Board of Studies (1998). *New South Wales Aboriginal languages interim framework K–10*. Sydney: New South Wales Board of Studies.

Palmer K (Ed) (2000). Strong language, strong culture: New South Wales strategic language study. Final report and strategy action plan [compiled by DF Hosking, TJ Lonsdale, JF Troy & MJ Walsh]. Canberra: Australian Institute for Aboriginal & Torres Strait Islander Studies.

4
Monitoring the use of Kaurna

Rob Amery[1]

Abstract

Kaurna, the language of the Adelaide Plains in South Australia, was probably last spoken on an everyday basis in the 1860s. Fortunately, reasonable documentation has enabled its revival some 130 years later (see Amery 2000). The use of Kaurna in the public domain has now emerged as the dominant function of the language. Kaurna is used for a variety of naming purposes, the giving of speeches of Welcome to Country, acknowledgement of Kaurna land or for public performance. Requests for names, translations and information about the Kaurna language were initially dealt with on an ad hoc basis. The establishment of Kaurna Warra Pintyandi in 2002 allowed for these requests to be dealt with in a more orderly fashion. Currently six to ten requests are addressed in the regular monthly meetings. This article analyses how protocols and processes for dealing with the myriad of requests has evolved. A database has been established which is being mapped on Google Earth. This helps us to monitor and plan for the use of Kaurna in the public domain. There are lessons here for others starting out on the long journey of getting their language back.

Kaurna was probably last spoken on an everyday basis in the 1860s, though the 'last speaker', Ivaritji, died in 1929.[2] Fortunately the language was reasonably well documented by German missionaries, Clamor Schürmann and Christian Teichelmann, who arrived in Adelaide in October 1838. In total about 3000 to 3500 words were recorded together with hundreds of sentences and their English translations. A 24-page sketch grammar was written (Teichelmann & Schürmann 1840) but very few texts exist. As no sound recordings of the original language remain, pronunciation has

---

[1] School of Humanities, University of Adelaide, Kaurna Warra Pintyandi.
[2] Whilst it seems likely that Ivaritji was a first language speaker of Kaurna as a child in the 1840s, the only material recorded from her later in life by Daisy Bates (1919) and John McConnell Black (1920) are short wordlists of 26 and 66 words respectively.

been determined through detailed comparison of written records of the language with reference to closely related neighbouring languages, Nukunu and Adnyamathanha, for which sound recordings do exist. Efforts to revive Kaurna as a spoken language commenced in 1989. The language is now taught to relatively small numbers of students in programs offered at all levels of education from kindergarten to university. Less than 100 Kaurna people have participated in Kaurna courses or workshops over the last two decades, though some expressions have spread beyond this core group. The majority of students in most courses are non-Aboriginal. Aboriginal persons from other language groups are often also participants.

We are still at a relatively early stage in the revival of Kaurna, even though it has been taught now for nearly 20 years. The language is spoken to a minimal extent in Kaurna households and in the community, principally a handful of speech formulas and some salient vocabulary. However there has been an explosion of naming activity and its use in public ceremony, and it has been incorporated into a number of public artworks.

Kaurna in the public arena

Following efforts to reclaim and re-introduce the Kaurna language, its use in the public arena has now emerged as the dominant function of the language. One of the main reasons for Kaurna people learning the language is to be able to give speeches of Welcome to Kaurna Country. The first speech was delivered by Kauwanu (Uncle) Lewis O'Brien in 1991 and speech-giving has since increased exponentially. I documented 104 speeches given in 1997, the final year of my PhD research. There are now several Kaurna individuals who give more than 100 speeches each per year. However, use of Kaurna for public speech-giving is not new. Upon his arrival in the new colony of South Australia Governor Gawler gave a speech to the assembled Indigenous inhabitants and had it translated into Kaurna by then Protector of Aborigines, William Wyatt, and early colonist James Cronk. Gawler also appealed to colonists to inform the colonial administration of Indigenous names so that they might be recognised and placed on the map. A number of Kaurna placenames, such as Yankalilla and Onkaparinga, appear on the earliest maps and remain in use today. Kaurna hymns were sung in public by the Kaurna children who attended the school run by the German missionaries at Piltawodli, the 'Native Location'. Singing Kaurna songs in public is a practice that is continued by the Kaurna Plains School choir and Alberton Primary School choir today. A government schooner built at Port Adelaide in 1848 was named the *Yatala*. And there has been sporadic use of Kaurna words over the intervening years; for instance, the Adelaide Bushwalkers club named their newsletter *Tarndanya* with the first issue published in January 1948.

Kaurna people themselves first turned to the archives in 1980 with the naming of Warriappendi Alternative School and have since named numerous organisations, programs and other entities, as well as themselves, their children and their pets. In recent years Kaurna naming activity, largely as a result of raised awareness of

Adelaide's Aboriginal past, has greatly increased. This naming activity has very often been initiated by Kaurna people, or other Aboriginal people, working within community organisations, schools, universities, government departments and so forth. But, increasingly, many non-Indigenous people want to acknowledge Kaurna land through naming activity. Sometimes these are individual, private requests such as naming a property or a boat. On other occasions it might be through a business for a business name, product name, or name for a boardroom and so on. But on most occasions it is effected through a public institution.

Since 1995 Kaurna language has been incorporated into a number of public artworks beginning with the *Yerrakartarta* installation by Daryl Milika Pfitzner and Muriel Van der Byll, outside the Hyatt Hotel on North Terrace in the heart of the city of Adelaide. In 2001–02, with the redevelopment of the Festival Theatre concourse, Kaurna text was also incorporated into the *Kaurna Yerta Kaurna Meyunna Tampendi* installation. Kaurna naming activity has increased so much, in fact, that it has been difficult to keep track of it.

Dealing with Kaurna requests

Through my involvement in Kaurna language programs and Kaurna language research since 1989, I have often been approached for information about Kaurna language, culture, history and placenames, as well as for advice regarding Kaurna naming, inclusion of text in works of art and for translations of various kinds. These requests have come from members of the Kaurna community; have been referred by the Department of Education and Children's Services (DECS) Aboriginal Education Unit, Tandanya National Aboriginal Cultural Institute, the South Australian Museum, Australian Institute of Aboriginal and Torres Strait Islander Studies; or have come directly from schools, government departments, businesses, artists or members of the public. During the 1990s I would give technical advice but would make it clear to the person making the request that, as a non-Kaurna person, I was not able to authorise or endorse its use and referred them to Kaurna people for approval. Often I copied the request and my response to Kauwanu Lewis O'Brien who had an email account at the University of South Australia. Most other Kaurna people were more difficult to contact. At the same time Kauwanu Lewis was dealing with many similar requests that he was receiving directly.[3] Sometimes he sought my advice on spelling or points of grammar and assistance with translation. On other occasions he dealt with requests himself without reference to me.

While I did give advice to members of the public I always felt somewhat uncomfortable about this as a non-Aboriginal person, and wondered whether these many requestors did actually follow my advice and seek approval from a Kaurna person. I hoped to establish some kind of forum whereby these requests could be discussed and approved by Kaurna people. At that time there was one representative Kaurna body, the Kaurna

---

3 The public also sought advice from other Kaurna people, though much of this activity was beyond my knowledge or awareness. Some has since come to my attention.

Aboriginal Community and Heritage Association Inc (KACHA). Kaurna language was included in KACHA's constitution but the organisation was always preoccupied with protection of heritage sites, internal politics and more pressing matters, so that Kaurna language matters were never discussed and I never received a reply to letters I wrote to the committee. However two matters were addressed by the Chair of KACHA, Fred Warrior, in 1996–97. These were the *Ruins of the Future* installation during the Festival of Adelaide in 1996 and the Adelaide City Council Kaurna naming initiative. A message in Kaurna language was recorded by Cherie Watkins and myself in the presence of Fred for the installation, whilst Kaurna park names were discussed and approved on a map spread out on Fred's kitchen table.

The formation of Kaurna Warra Pintyandi

The Kaurna Warra Pintyandi (KWP)[4] group formed without fanfare in 2002. At the conclusion of a series of workshops on Kaurna funeral protocols (see Amery and Rigney 2006) we decided to continue meeting on a monthly basis to work on projects and consider requests related to the Kaurna language. An agenda was set and comprehensive minutes recorded for each meeting. The need for a name for the group became apparent after some months of coming together to meet. The name, Kaurna Warra Pintyandi (creating/constructing Kaurna language) was adopted. It had been used previously for workshops associated with a project whereby new expressions were developed for use by mothers, fathers and other caregivers for use with babies and young children (see Amery & Gale 2000) was adopted. KWP meetings have been attended by a small number of regulars, notably Ngarpadla (Auntie) Alitya Wallara Rigney, Kauwanu Lewis Yerloburka O'Brien, Cherie Warrara Watkins and myself since its inception in 2002. Several early regulars no longer attend but have been replaced by others. Some Kaurna people attend occasionally when an issue arises that is of particular relevance to them. Meetings are also often attended by guests who include overseas visitors, researchers and individuals making a request to the committee. See Amery & Rigney (2007) for a more extensive discussion of the role of KWP, its history and relationship to the Kaurna community.

Monitoring the use of Kaurna in the public arena

Whilst we had some record of the many names that had been discussed by the KWP committee in the minutes and in my PhD thesis (Amery 1998), prior to that we did not have a detailed record. We had not kept all details of phone calls, phone messages, emails, letters and face-to-face conversations over the years, though some emails and phone messages were retrievable. I and some members of the Kaurna community had notes, sometimes cryptic, scattered in our diaries or on scraps of paper.

We were also often unsure of whether people actually used the name or whether they had followed the advice of the committee. We were also aware of Kaurna naming

---

4 See www.adelaide.edu.au/kwp/.

activity occurring without reference to the KWP committee, both by Kaurna people and by others. Sometimes use of Kaurna names was approved by Kaurna people but there was no central record of this approval and on many occasions KWP members had no idea of what was happening.

Requests for names were often repetitive with many people seeking names meaning wellbeing, healing, partnership, together, meeting together, working together, unity and so on, and we were finding it hard to remember what names had already been used and by whom. We were a little concerned that we were doubling up on the same names for similar purposes. We wanted some mechanism whereby we could monitor the use of Kaurna language in public in a more systematic way.

Many requests being put to the committee were exceedingly vague and we often had little information on which to go. We were also often unclear about the nature of the request and had no indication about where and how the name or translation would be used and by whom. As a result we designed a questionnaire to collect more specific information. The increasing number of requests had also become a massive burden on our time, both on the KWP meeting itself and on my time before and after the meeting, so we suggested that people consider making a donation to the committee. In December 2006 we established a schedule of fees and began issuing invoices for our services. The questionnaire was redesigned in 2008 by University of Adelaide lawyers together with Amery and the KWP committee to include statements relating to indemnity and liability and the schedule of fees was added. The collated questionnaires now form a kind of register of requests.

In December 2005 we filed an application to register the KWP logo as a certified trademark, so that users could identify that correct protocols had been observed for names, translations and so forth which had been approved by the KWP committee. Unfortunately the proposed KWP trademark has still not been registered, as KWP is not an incorporated body and the University of Adelaide has not been prepared to own the trademark on behalf of the KWP group. The KWP group still asks that the KWP logo be used for these purposes, though this would be much stronger if the logo was officially registered as a certified trademark in the same way that the Australian Made or Woolmark logos are used.

The Kaurna Requests database

The Kaurna requests database was established in November 2005 when a visiting French student, Virginie Leonce, who had studied my Australian Indigenous Languages course at the University of Adelaide, volunteered to undertake some work for the Kaurna cause. I set about designing a database on FileMaker Pro so that she could go through my records and enter data into relevant fields. We compiled information about the nature of the Kaurna names and translations, linguistic issues and information about the approval process. We established ten numbered categories for the kind of entity (placename, personal name, business name/organisation, program/ forum/conference, building, room, publication/brochure, simple translation, art-project, festival) and letter-coded categories (A-H) for the different kinds of people or organisation making the request (individual/private, organisation, education, government, business, reconciliation movement, environment group, other). These were further colour-coded according to whether the name was permanent or temporary or whether the requestor was Aboriginal or non-Indigenous (Figure 1).

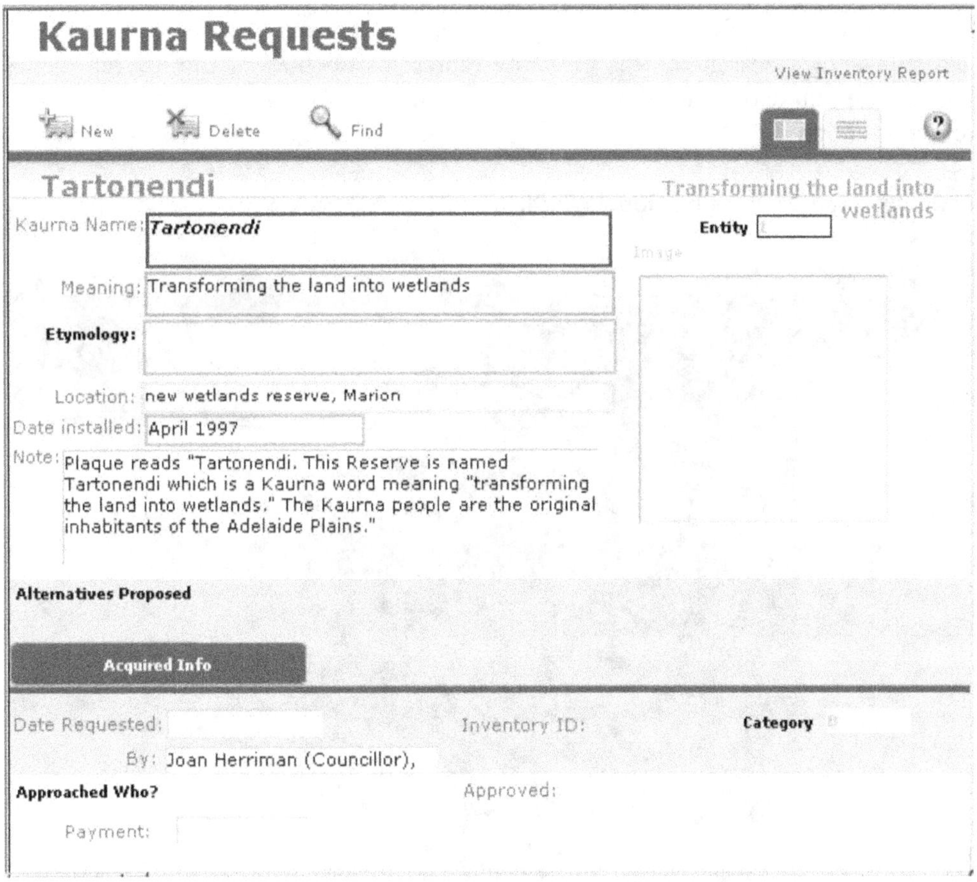

Figure 1. Kaurna requests database.

In 2006 we sought funding from the Department of Communications, Information Technology and the Arts to continue the project and publish the requests database on the web. With the establishment of the *Kaurna Placenames* website,[5] where information entered into a Microsoft Access database was displayed on Google Earth maps, the Kaurna requests database was transformed into a sister database in Access to sit alongside the placenames database. Four separate pages were established for each item in the database: name, linguistic information, request process and geographic information system data.

---

5 See www.kaurnaplacenames.com.

62 Re-awakening languages

The letter-coded categories used initially were replaced with more transparent names on drop-down menus, thus facilitating data entry and interpretation. A number of entities such as walking trail and reserve, and categories such as health were added. A new field, requestor identity (Kaurna, other Aboriginal, Aboriginal/non-Aboriginal collaboration, and non-Aboriginal), was also added to allow us to know who was driving the request agenda.

There are now over 700 entries in the database, though many of these are incomplete and still being researched. This probably represents 80–90% of the Kaurna names used in the public domain, though previously unknown usage is constantly coming to our attention.

Mapping Kaurna names on Google Earth

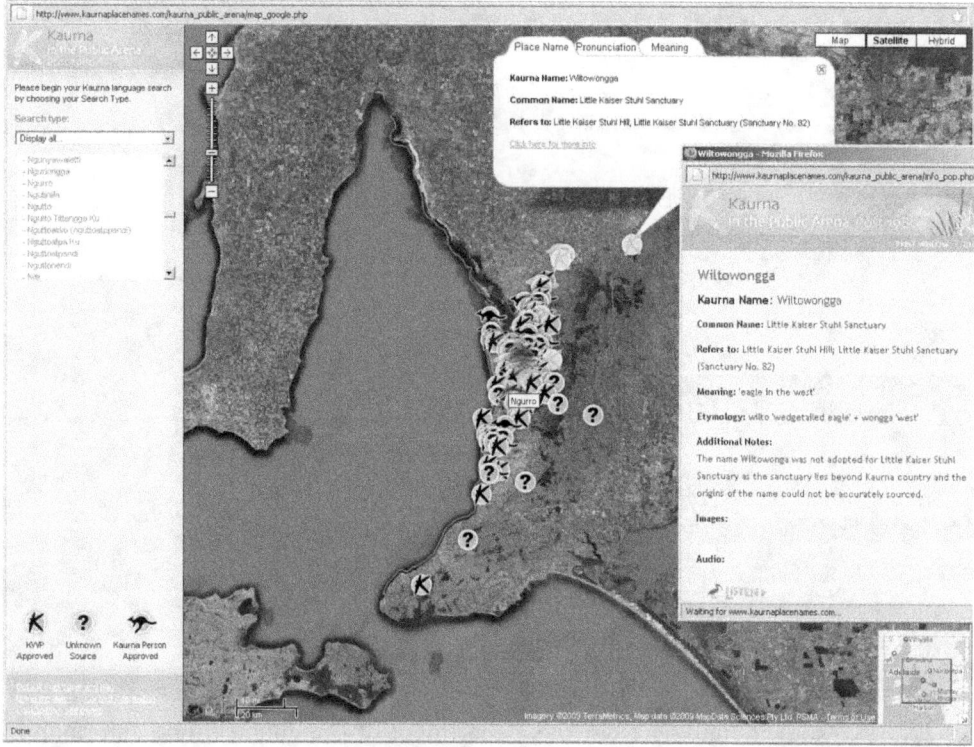

Figure 2. All Kaurna entries displayed on satellite view, with pop-up boxes showing for Wiltowonga.

In 2008–09 KWP contracted Beanstalk Creative and Production, who had developed the website for the Kaurna placenames project, to develop a set of pages to display Kaurna language used in the public domain. Clicking on an item brings up additional information in a window, including a picture and sound file for pronunciation purposes (Figure 2). The location is pinpointed with a precise latitude and longitude reading unless we need to disguise the precise location, as in the case of a women's refuge or sacred site. In this case the name appears in a list to the side of the maps. Clicking on the names brings up information as before.

The 'Kaurna in the Public Arena Post 1980' web pages were designed so that names assigned to a particular category such as business names, trails or buildings and so forth could be displayed at the same time. Alternatively we can see all the names being used by businesses, health providers, Indigenous organisations or non-Indigenous individuals and so on. In this way we can tell at a glance which names are being used where for a particular set of purposes. Whilst we could easily search the database for a particular name or category and generate a report, the visual display on Google Earth provides a far more user-friendly way of keeping track of this activity.

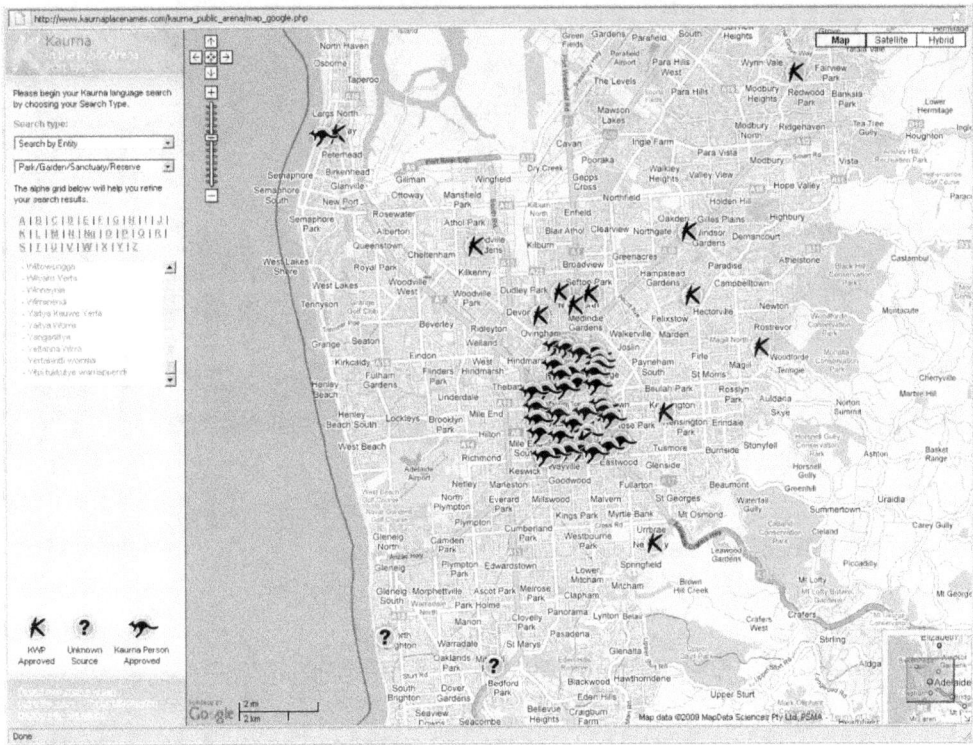

Figure 3. Parks, gardens, sanctuaries and reserves displayed within the inner Adelaide metropolitan area (map view).

Symbols are used to quickly identify information that relates to the approval process. A KWP logo indicates names and words that have been approved by the KWP committee. A *tarnda* (male red kangaroo) marks names that are being used by Kaurna people or where it is known that a Kaurna person has approved of its use. A question mark is used where we have no information about the approval process or where we know that no Kaurna person was consulted (Figures 2 and 3).

Whilst the *Kaurna Placenames* website is available to the public, for now the 'Kaurna in the Public Arena Post 1980' pages will be password-protected, accessible only to KWP members and others to whom they choose to grant access. This restricted access is intended to be temporary and will eventually be lifted.

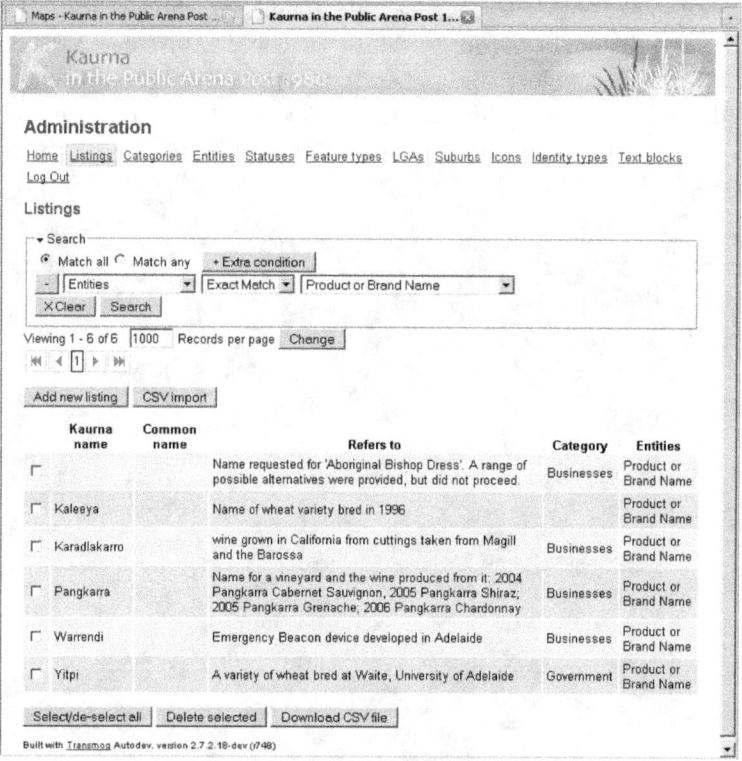

Figure 4. List of product or brand names selected from the database underpinning the maps.

Discussion

We now have a mechanism established to compile information on the use of Kaurna in the public domain and keep track of its usage. We will soon have a website that displays the information in various ways that the user can choose. We are also able to enter data directly into the database online where it is taken up immediately on the Google Earth maps (Figure 4). But we have a backlog of names and requests to research and data to enter.

Of course it would have been preferable to establish processes for monitoring the use of Kaurna language 20 years ago. We did not foresee the importance of monitoring use of the language at that stage. We did not anticipate the extent to which the language would be taken up. Nor did we have time to maintain a detailed record.

Now that the database has been established it will be much easier to keep a comprehensive record of naming activity as it takes place. This will give Kaurna people much greater control. Knowledge is power. The database and web pages are powerful tools whereby we can plan for the development and use of the language. See Amery (2001) for a detailed discussion of language planning in relation to Kaurna.

We use both the *Kaurna Placenames* website and the 'Kaurna in the Public Arena Post 1980' web pages to establish norms of spelling and pronunciation by posting downloadable sound files on them. We also use these pages to establish authoritative meanings and derivations of the names and texts, thereby assisting in the planning of the Kaurna language corpus. And the pages significantly enhance the status of the language through the posting of accurate information and display of Kaurna language activity in user-friendly ways.

Conclusion

The Kaurna requests database, *Kaurna Placenames* website and the 'Kaurna in the Public Arena Post 1980' web pages with Google Earth images provide a useful model for other groups to monitor use of their own languages. However it is strongly advisable to set up a mechanism for recording names, translations and their use sooner rather than later in the revitalisation process in order to capture as much of a language as possible. Beginning earlier also minimises the effort in attempting to include offline work already collected.

The database needs to be fashioned in a way that records information about the words themselves, their reference and location, together with information about who is using them and for what purpose. The database can be tailored to the needs of both the language group and other users. The precise structure will depend in large part upon the purposes for which the language is used. In the Kaurna situation it has been important to document the approval process as well as the usage itself.

The process of documenting names and translation in the public domain also serves to celebrate language revitalisation efforts thereby further motivating and spurring on the language movement.

References

Amery R (1998). Warrabarna Kaurna! Reclaiming Aboriginal languages from written historical sources: Kaurna case study. Unpublished PhD thesis (2 vols). Linguistics, School of Humanities: University of Adelaide.

Amery R (2000). *Warrabarna Kaurna! Reclaiming an Australian language*. Lisse, Netherlands: Swets & Zeitlinger.

Amery R (2001). Language planning and language revival. *Current Issues in Language Planning*, 2(2&3): 141–221.

Amery R, Buckskin V & Watt B (2008). Mapping Kaurna names on Google Earth. Paper presented at the Aboriginal and Torres Strait Islander Spatial Information (ATSISI) workshop. University of South Australia, Adelaide, November 2008.

Amery R & Gale M (2000). Kaurna warra pintyandi. Ngadluko perko. Kaurna language workshop report. Kaurna warra yellakaitya – developing the Kaurna language for contemporary situations. Interim report. Enfield, South Australia: Aboriginal Education Unit, November 2000.

Amery R & Rigney AW with Varcoe N, Schultz C & Kaurna Warra Pintyandi (2006). *Kaurna palti wonga – Kaurna funeral protocols*. [book, CD and sympathy cards]. Adelaide: Kaurna Warra Pintyandi.

Amery R with Kaurna Warra Pintyandi. (2007). Kulluru marni ngattaitya! Sounds good to me! A Kaurna learner's guide [Draft prototype version]. Adelaide: Kaurna Warra Pintyandi.

Amery R & Rigney AW (2007). Collaborative language revival – the work of Kaurna Warra Pintyandi. In MK David, N Ostler & C Dealwis (Eds). *Working together for endangered languages: research challenges and social impacts* (pp. 21–28). Proceedings of the Foundation for Endangered Languages Conference XI, Kuala Lumpur 26–28 October 2007. Bath: Foundation for Endangered Languages.

Bates D (1919). Typescripts, correspondence, photographs etc (11 vols). Folio 6/III/5k, Barr Smith Library, University of Adelaide, South Australia.

Black JM (1920). Vocabularies of four South Australian languages, Adelaide, Narrunga, Kukata, and Narrinyeri with special reference to their speech sounds. *Transactions of the Royal Society of South Australia*, 44: 76–93.

Teichelmann CG (1857). Dictionary of the Adelaide dialect. ms Number 59. Bleek's catalogue of Sir George Grey's library dealing with Australian languages, South African Public Library.

Teichelmann CG & Schürmann CW (1840/1962). *Outlines of a grammar, vocabulary, and phraseology, of the Aboriginal language of South Australia, spoken by the natives in and for some distance around Adelaide*. Adelaide: Published by the authors at the native location. Facsimile edition 1962, State Library of South Australia. Facsimile edition 1982, Adelaide: Tjintu Books.

5
Introducing Wiradjuri language in Parkes

Geoff Anderson[1]

Abstract

This is a personal account of the introduction of Wiradjuri language to schools and school communities in Parkes in central New South Wales. It discusses the need for language, culture and heritage, including the personal healing required, that can contribute to recovery from the loss of language and identity for Indigenous people. The introduction of Wiradjuri language, culture and local heritage in Parkes raised awareness and pride to the point where racism was significantly reduced in the schools. Further, the children's proactive, anti-racist attitude has had a positive impact on parents and the wider community. It is also evident in the political acceptance of Indigenous identity by the erection of Welcome to Wiradjuri Country signs by the Parkes Shire Council. The inclusion of Welcome to Country ceremonial sections for school assemblies has now expanded into civic ceremonial activities. Acceptance of this identity and growth in self-esteem can also be recognised by the enrolment of parents and community members in Wiradjuri language classes conducted in the evenings.

Murrugay barra (First steps)

People ask me when did I first get interested in the Wiradjuri language. My truthful answer would be, 'The language found me.' I also believe the Elders of the past who own the language realised that it was safe to come out again through the children, and we who learn and teach it now are only teaching new caretakers for the language and its future.

In 2004 I was invited to go to a language class at a school in the nearby town of Forbes. The class was organised by the deputy principal who had discovered the wonderful work that Wiradjuri Elder, Stan Grant Snr, and Dr John Rudder had done in getting Wiradjuri language revitalisation going. The deputy principal had made

---

1 Wiradjuri Council of Elders.

the classes free to the public in the school holidays, all on her own time. She had introduced Wiradjuri to the students in her school and had been getting great results with it. From that point on I was feeling as if I belonged. I then knew this was me and I knew I had to help get the culture of the language out to the community. I don't know how I knew; I just did. I still think the Elders of years gone by had whispered in my ear and told me.

Yindhamarru-gu Mudyigang-gu (Respect to the Elders)

To establish any Aboriginal language within your community you need the support of the Elders who will speak from their souls. It is their culture; it is alive within them, and it *is* them. They must be shown the respect they deserve and be informed about any language programs or projects you wish to begin. You need Elders who will let the past be released and decide that it is time to let the language be spoken again.

I knew of one Elder in town who was very concerned at what we were going to be teaching in the schools. I had the opportunity to show her. I gave a Wiradjuri welcome at a friendly barbecue at the high school, just to let this Elder hear the language being spoken again and as an introduction to the school. At the end of the barbecue she asked me to sit down and I was told that that was the first time she had heard Wiradjuri language being spoken since she was a child. This woman was viewed with great respect in the town so I knew at that point I was allowed to go ahead and, the more I sat and listened, the more words she started to say. She felt safe.

It is important to find out if your Elders wish to be involved. Sit down and listen to what they want spoken about and taught, like the Elder I just spoke of. I sat and listened to her and what she had to say about the language, what she would like it to achieve, and what I could speak of.

I showed her respect and she gave me respect back. Without that from her we couldn't do the language. So just because they can't speak language fluently doesn't mean they don't deserve the respect of being involved. Find out what they want to be taught and given away. Some topics, ideas and concepts they won't let you teach, so remember; you need Elders' approval to move on. As one Elder said to me, 'You must give it away to keep it.' and I still go by that theory today. The more we can tell people the more it will stay. The more language we teach, the more people will hear – and it's your language and you are entitled to learn it and speak it. On this journey I've learnt that Elders are essential as they are the knowledge-keepers, and school teachers are the knowledge-givers. Once a teacher learns some words they have ways of making it fit into a curriculum to suit a classroom situation. They are trained to teach and both will show you as many things as they can to help you.

Yalmambirra mayiny (Teach the people)

In 2005 a community meeting was held for anyone who wanted the language taught in the schools here in Parkes. From that meeting we found we had the community's backing and principals' support. But, most of all, we had the teachers who wanted to help to get the language back through the classroom. You need teachers who themselves want to learn some of the language and can guide you in the direction needed to work together to get things going. Listen to the teachers from the schools. Don't dig your heels in and think, 'This is my language, not yours.' Don't ever think anything like that. The teachers want to learn language just as much as you do and they know how to teach. They have skills in using syllabuses and teaching programs and they are a vital support for Aboriginal community language teachers. They may not feel the language inside like you do, but they are needed. Believe me; they have a vital role in the whole way of getting things going and I have found any advice from teachers to be helpful.

To get things going in Parkes we had to sit down and do some real hard yards and work out time factors of when we thought the language could be started. We had to work many hours with the NSW Office of the Board of Studies (OBOS). We also formed a language group in the early days and it worked extremely well. OBOS supported the tutors and teachers to bring the language into the classrooms in the way of workshops and some resources. OBOS is essential to the goal you are trying to reach and they will bring the way of getting it into the schools.

It seems too coincidental that we had me learning the basics of the language at workshops in Forbes, OBOS supporting us to get the language going in schools in town, and teachers from the schools in town learning the basics of the language at workshops in Dubbo. To me there was a force at work, trying to get everyone together to teach language that was hidden and had not been spoken for two generations by the Wiradjuri people. I personally believe that the Elders of the past were working at getting things to fall into place. I can't explain it any other way.

The local or regional Aboriginal Education Consultative Group (AECG) is vital for starting any Aboriginal language program in any school. Informing them of what you are hoping to achieve in the community is a step that must be made. They are needed to sign off for funding and letting them know gets the word out to the community that this is happening. If you get involved with the AECG it will make work easier for yourself. As soon as you mention that by doing this you can create employment, you will always be helped.

Bubay barra (Small steps)

Remember; take small steps to start off with. Don't expect things to happen in the first meeting, because they won't. It will take sometimes years to get a project like this off the ground. Remember that you are revitalising a language and it will take an enormous amount of time and energy. The Elders of the past are talking to you and you're in charge of sharing the language and getting it out to the public. I had a personal fear that I was taking things too quickly and the whole language reclamation would implode on me. I would deliberately walk away from it for a few weeks, up to a few months, until I felt it was okay to go ahead again.

You will know when you are going too fast; you will feel uncomfortable. Take small steps but, at the same time, don't ignore people who really want to help you like principals and teachers. These people want to learn a new language as well, so let them, remembering that you have to give it away to keep it. Wiradjuri language in some areas has not been spoken for two generations but in some areas has just been hidden. I feel I am now trying to bridge the gap and fill in a void – a void within myself and also other people. I have been trying to bring back unspoken words and I have met people who will want nothing to do with it, but also people like me, wanting more and more of filling the black hole within the soul.

I have met Elders who were ostracised for speaking language so they will need reassurance it's okay to speak again. You must have the drive to keep up the spirit and keep telling people it will work, because it will work and the results will astound you.

Yarrandhu ngiyang (Speak your words)

Keep listening to your heart and at the same time keep learning your language – just a few words to start with – then work those words into a small phrase. You will make mistakes. Learn from them, but have a go and don't worry. You must teach yourself the language and improve your fluency because no-one else can. You need to commit to the learning, the language. Most of all I personally have a commitment to the Elders of the past who have had the language taken from them. Remember this is your spirit and soul you're trying to share with people. You are trying to reclaim your ancestors' footprints, so don't rush it and be a good ambassador for the Elders of the past. They deserve it.

In my experience an effective way of getting the language into the ears of the community and accepted was to learn the Wiradjuri Welcome to Country. By doing so I found people were hearing those hidden words for the first time and, by doing it on a voluntary basis, I gave a better public impression. I can remember doing the welcome speech for a group of Wiradjuri healthcare workers and to see their faces glow, with me saying a few words, was just beyond belief. Some said later that day that they had never heard Wiradjuri words spoken since their grandparents spoke it, and comments like that will make you feel very proud.

I have had the honour of welcoming everyone from the premier of the state to Olympians and I had the chance to do the welcome when the cross for World Youth Day came through town. So, just by learning the welcome in your language, you will give a great public impression and you're letting words be heard. Remember that the adults you're speaking to are the parents of the children you want to teach it to; so make a good presentation.

Yalmambirra (Teaching will start)

I shared my enthusiasm for the language with teachers from the Parkes High School. They had begun a trial of the language and I joined them in a few workshops in 2006.

They were all as keen as I was and, by doing this, we were able to get more of an idea of what was involved in getting a program up and running. From this we actually held a meeting once a month for ourselves. We would meet at each other's houses and discuss language, what we could do with it, and how we can teach it. But, most of all, we started to teach ourselves some language. OBOS then asked Parkes High School to be a part of a pilot program and the school leapt at the chance. The language is now being taught in the school and each year gets stronger and stronger.

I was at Parkes East Public School one day and I had to see a teacher. I went into the library and she was teaching a class of Stage 1 and 2 students and they were singing 'Heads, Shoulders, Knees and Toes'. A teacher asked me did I know how to sing this in Wiradjuri and, fortunately, I did. This was my big chance. I had never stood in front of a class of children in my life and taught anything, and at no point of my life did I think I would be in this situation. I wrote the translation up on the board and taught them how to say the words and then to sing the song. The teacher was amazed at how the kids wanted to know more and, after a few short and very nervous lessons, we had the base set for the language to be placed into another Parkes school.

We had children asking their parents if they were Aboriginal and, in some cases, we had several students saying to Wiradjuri children, 'I wish I was Aboriginal'. The teacher and I would listen with amazement. We both thought, 'This is too good to pass up.' With what we had heard from the mouths of children in such a short time, we had to get it into the school more regularly. The teacher approached the principal and from there on we were teaching Wiradjuri in Parkes East Public School from Term 3, 2006, unfunded.

The staff met it with open arms and, with the little bit of what I knew, I had children saying hello in the playground and the school using some Wiradjuri words. But, most of all, the staff were trying to say some words. The teacher got me to translate the school assembly into Wiradjuri and the school still uses it today. We were educating the next generation of Australians on how to accept and learn about Wiradjuri culture, and the children wanted more.

Then the principal decided this was so good he applied for funding for it to be taught in the school, because he was starting to hear it spoken in parts of the playground. He noticed that the Koori kids' attendance and pride was rising. The principal applied for funding, knowing that I would help out in the school and basically make sure it was being taught properly. So he had no problems with it starting, as he knew he had someone to be there from the beginning and help it get off the ground. That makes a huge difference. The less work you make for the school the better they will like the idea, and by creating employment for someone to come and teach language you take the pressure off yourself.

Just remember that children are like sponges; they will absorb all the knowledge you give them and want more. What you give them they will see as neutral and without any political views at all. Whether they are Aboriginal or non-Aboriginal children, they all want to learn equally. I am not a teacher of any sort and I just let my thoughts flow from my heart with the students. You will be amazed just how much you do know. So give yourself credit and keep yourself one step ahead of them, even if that one step is one word.

The thing we learnt from this was that we needed resources for the students, so I then started making PowerPoint presentations for the children and searching for more language. This pushed me forward in the drive for knowing more words, thus improving myself. My biggest fear was being asked a question I didn't know the answer to. I would just simply tell the student, 'I will find out for you what that word is'. It really wasn't anything to be worried about at all. I thought I was saying words slow and clear but I realised I was too fast and I needed practice on pronunciation. So, remember that when you are teaching a class not everyone speaks a language and they don't hear it like you.

Ngurrigal guwalanha (Surprise happenings)

The language has turned out to be a wonderful thing in Parkes. And, with the schoolchildren in Parkes East Public School speaking some language, we have a school boasting zero racism. The parents have accepted the language and we find that it's breaking down the invisible wall of racism within the community. The student representative council of the Parkes East Public School approached the Parkes Shire Council for Welcome to Wiradjuri Country signs to be placed on the road north and south of Parkes. The Council agreed to this request from the school and the signs that are 4.5 metres high and 1.5 metres wide are seen by 5500 cars per day. So from the humble beginnings of 'Heads, Shoulders, Knees and Toes', the children of Parkes are now showing the Wiradjuri Elders and people respect. And they are returning the respect.

From getting the language in the school we have had something happen that I was not expecting. We have formed a community language class for adults. Aboriginal and non-Aboriginal adults are invited. Anyone who wants to know some language or just have some personal healing; the doors are open. With the rapport we have built we are allowed to use the Parkes East Public School's classroom free of charge. It never ceases to amaze me that people come to a class, and they know words already that were being used by their parents or grandparents, and they didn't realise it was Wiradjuri. You will be told with great happiness that they know that word you just said because their grandmother said that. I know how they feel, as the more words I learnt the more words I realised I had heard from older family members. The principal met us with open arms and helped promote the classes with the school newsletters. Now we get between six and 11 people per week and we have trained two of our language tutors in the school programs through it. But I think to see an adult learn something that is missing from their childhood is amazing and the best way to learn something is to teach it. We make sure that someone is available every week for class to teach the language.

Once the language is in the schools you then create employment. We needed community teachers and we are lucky that we have three young people in Parkes who want to learn language and teach language. If you spread the word out that you are trying to get language going in your community, here is some advice; don't at any point turn anyone away from it. If someone asks you a word for something, tell them and if they keep wanting to know, tell them. This shows they want to know something about the language. Work on them and encourage them and these people can be your community teachers.

I personally have seen social healing begin to happen. When a parent comes to the community class I will tell them the first night they are there, they will feel a difference inside themselves in a few weeks. And in a few weeks they have all said to me they knew what I meant. I know what happened to me and what strength it has given me, so I was talking from personal experience. Learning the language that belongs inside will heal you. Learning your native language will make you feel more complete. As one Elder said to me, 'All our children are on a dreaming; they are lost. Teach them their language and they will find themselves'.

On a more personal note I have now created such rapport with the schools that I am one of the few people that can walk in off the street and be seen as nearly a member of staff. School students will yell out, 'Hello!' or, '*Yamandhu marang*?' And some Wiradjuri people in town call me the Language Man, a tag I will wear with honour. I have also been honoured by being put on the Wiradjuri Council of Elders and being asked to be a part of the Eastern States Language Group, with only two representatives from each state being asked.

Giyira (The future)

In the long term I know deep down that the language will stay in the school. It has more right than any other language in the education system and than anything else being taught. We are told we are a multicultural country and now we are beginning to study and learn about the first culture that was here. I have taken this challenge on, to get the language in the schools in Parkes as a community member. And at no point have I been paid for all the work I have done. People say, 'You should be paid.' and I just reply, 'No!'

I love it, that's why I do it. The word community means just that, community. You must keep positive with all the hard work you do. But, if you're coming from the heart, then it's not hard work because you love every minute of it. I have had the chance to meet some wonderful people and made many incredible friends from all walks of life and socio-economic backgrounds, but remembering at the same time I can ask favours from these people and they know I am there for them as well. You need friends like that; you can't do it without them.

We will face racial confrontations in the future; I know because people are always scared of something they know nothing of. But if we can teach the children we will then have an entire generation of the future who will see Aboriginal culture as a part of this country. And it's alive, not something to be hidden away for museums or archives or as a painting to hang on a wall.

I think one young Parkes East Public School student's words sum it all up; 'I learn Wiradjuri language and culture so I can go home and teach my parents.' I don't think I could say anymore than what that young girl said to me.

6
Going public with language: involving the wider community in language revitalisation

Knut J. Olawsky[1]

Abstract

This article investigates the representative use of language in public life during initial stages of revitalisation. Based on experience with the Miriwoong revitalisation program the public use of language during the earliest revival stages, along with other strategies, is shown to play a supportive role.

Fishman (1991) introduces a Graded Intergenerational Disruption Scale for Threatened Languages which postulates a continuum of eight stages to define different levels of language loss. Stage 8 correlates to a language close to extinction and Stage 1 describes a surviving language. Based on this model one can stipulate a typical process of language revitalisation, starting with language acquisition by individuals progressing to groups of learners in the first two steps, which reflects the situation of the Miriwoong language. While Fishman's scale positions the use of a threatened language in the dominant community at the later stages of revitalisation, the Miriwoong case demonstrates that this strategy can be useful at any point of the process. Though it is acknowledged that a community-based approach leading to diglossia is indispensable for language revitalisation, the symbolic use of a language close to extinction is vital, not only in order to lift its status in the wider community and to strengthen the linguistic identity of its traditional speakers, but also to stimulate active language use in the community.

To illustrate this approach the public use of language as a component of the Miriwoong revitalisation program is characterised. It is demonstrated that, compared to other strategies, the public relations component is the one with the highest cost-efficiency ratio. This contradicts the hypothesis that the inclusion of such activities at an early stage represents a waste of efforts. In conclusion

---

1 Mirima Dawang Woorlab-gerring Language and Culture Centre.

the addition of this component is recommended for application in revitalisation programs on a wider scale.

Public language use in Miriwoong revitalisation

Miriwoong, a non-Pama-Nyungan language of the Jarrakan family, can be classified as severely to critically endangered with all fluent first language speakers being aged over 60 years. Of the middle-aged speakers only a handful have a sound knowledge of the language but generally lack grammatical proficiency. The reasons for the gradual loss of Miriwoong can be found in history, including the Stolen Generations period, where people were actively discouraged from using their traditional language by official Australian government policies that were directed towards assimilation. This has led to a massive degradation of the language's status, resulting in a loss of linguistic identity in following generations. With the dominance of English in all domains of daily life and the rise of Kriol, whatever is left of this identity has been suffocated in most speakers to a level where people feel embarrassed to use Miriwoong in public. Members of the younger generation merely know isolated words which also occur in Kriol. Kriol and Aboriginal English nowadays are the first languages for most Miriwoong.

Efforts to preserve and revitalise the Miriwoong language have been made for over two decades and some of these activities have had visible success. Among the projects which have been part of the language program are language documentation, classroom lessons, bush trips, and the creation of employment as an incentive to learn the language. As discussed elsewhere in this volume (Olawsky) one of the more successful initiatives is the organisation of bush trips with elders and young people to enhance language and cultural skills through an experience-based approach.

Because these activities form the backbone of a successful revitalisation program, they consume considerable resources – naturally requiring substantial involvement of human labour and materials that are not always available. Other activities of the Mirima Dawang Woorlab-gerring Language and Culture Centre (MDWg)[2] were traditionally considered sidelines to its main work, such as the casual inclusion of Miriwoong placenames on a map of the Ord River. In past years, however, the use of Miriwoong terms in public – especially in relation to signage – has gained more significance. What started out as an instance of loose cooperation between MDWg and the Western Australian Department of Water has now grown into partnerships with a variety of agencies and organisations.

As a long-term outcome it is hoped that the wider community will progressively recognise the status of Miriwoong as the legitimate traditional language of the area, one that still plays a fundamental role today. Subsequently the Indigenous community

---

2 The Miriwoong language revitalisation program is conducted by Mirima Dawang Woorlab-gerring Language and Culture Centre in Kununurra. Other details of this program are described in a separate article in this volume (Olawsky).

will be encouraged to exhibit their language, not only in public, but on more basic levels such as at home. The following sections describe how a strategy that I will call *language publicity* is being implemented in the revitalisation process for Miriwoong.

Interpretive signage and bilingual signs in Miriwoong and English

Since 2005 work has been in progress to introduce public signage to relevant areas of Miriwoong country. One example is the erection of interpretative signage at six popular locations in the wider Kununurra area. These signs explain the traditional usage of the respective area in English and provide the Miriwoong placename as well as the Miriwoong words for relevant plants found in the vicinity. Other examples are the development of similar signs for an interpretative walking trail at Mirima National Park, as well as the placement of bilingual 'Don't Litter' signs at various locations around town. Another signage project involves a partnership with the Western Australian Department of Water to create a map of the Ord River system on which placenames are printed in Miriwoong and English.

Welcome speeches

For special public or semi-public events, agencies and organisations have developed a sense of 'political correctness' in that they request a traditional owner of the land to open the event with a short speech, sometimes followed by a cultural performance. The use of Miriwoong language at these openings, even though usually kept very short, helps create public awareness about the traditional language of the area and gives speakers increasing confidence that their use of Miriwoong is sought and acknowledged.

Joint ventures

The involvement in joint ventures between MDWg and government departments or related agencies gives all people involved insight into the traditional values and the efforts made to revive these. By providing assistance to agencies such as Workbase, and similar organisations which may request assistance in implementing initiatives targeting local Indigenous people, awareness about language issues is easily raised. Sometimes this is achieved by suggesting a Miriwoong name or slogan for a new project, scheme, or building. The selection process for a certain name can be rather comprehensive and would often involve a range of language speakers, thereby stimulating the search for specific terms and strategies to combine these in grammatically correct structures.

Language and culture awareness training

Regular one-day language and culture orientation seminars for staff of relevant organisations and other individuals working with Miriwoong people aim to raise awareness about some of the issues associated with the coexistence of Indigenous and non-Indigenous people. These seminars also give an overview of the Miriwoong sound system and orthography and shed some light on language-related issues. In 2008 over 130 key personnel from a range of organisations were part of the training. By involving younger community members as facilitators a transfer of linguistic knowledge occurs through the training.

Media contact

Ethnic divisions and misunderstandings are still prevalent in major parts of the population. Representatives of the revitalisation program liaise with the local media whenever there are positive events to report. Focusing on language- and culture-related achievements by Miriwoong people helps the wider public understand both sides. Language is usually perceived as a positive theme by both media and the wider population and tends to be welcomed by editors and journalists. One of the latest initiatives, due to start this year, is a regular language section in the local newspaper which will feature basic, media-relevant aspects of Miriwoong lexicon and grammar.

Internal language policy

While the above initiatives are examples showing how language is carried into *higher* domains, the open interaction with the general public is a relatively new development in the Miriwoong revitalisation process. Over a decade ago Miriwoong elders concluded that the use of their language should focus exclusively on the native community. In effect, sharing of Miriwoong words and other parts of speech would only be allowed in a limited context. Outsiders would not have indiscriminate access to language materials developed by MDWg but would be required to adhere to predefined protocols in order to obtain access to language materials. In some cases access would not be granted at all, depending on the intended usage.

In essence the issue is one of exercising control over the language, which is understandable from a historic point of view. In a situation where the language is the last thing which has not been taken away from a community, a strong sense of protectionism can easily emerge. Where the reasons for such restrictions are directly related to a cultural perspective of language, such as the link between land and language, a sensitive approach is required so as to avoid breaches of cultural protocol.

At first sight a language policy such as the one described here would appear to be in direct opposition to the otherwise publicity-based approach practised in the revitalisation of Miriwoong. However it must be understood that language publicity exercised by the appropriate speakers is regarded as valuable and important. Appropriate use here implies that the bottom-up model à la Fishman is recognised, in the sense that the Indigenous community receives priority in language learning and language transfer. The community is committed to making their language public in a controlled manner and in ways determined by the traditional authorities. This does not automatically exclude outsiders from learning the language. In recent years the Miriwoong community has become more open to an increased level of language sharing which is reflected by initiatives such as publishing selected language items through the media. This approach is supported by the community as they are given a sense of ownership by controlling how and where their language is used (see also Kimberley Language Resource Centre, this volume).[3]

Reversing Language Shift (RLS) and language publicity under review

A notable aspect of Fishman's RLS model is the claim that revitalisation must always proceed from the bottom up, beginning at the grass roots level, as is described by Romaine (2006, p. 451): 'One of the most frequent mistakes activists make is to attempt to reverse the diglossic hierarchy by promoting the minority language in the domains now dominated by the majority language.' In other words, if a minority language (X in Fishman's model) is promoted for use in a high domain (H, that is the domain of the dominant language Y) that would be viewed as a waste of resources and efforts. In this study I will not question the general order of the steps in Fishman's model, however it will be suggested that language publicity is a useful element at any stage of the revitalisation process. I further define this term as an application of any form of the use of X outside the Indigenous community, specifically in public domains. This use does not necessarily coincide with active use on the highest levels, such as in education and government, but includes the promotion of X in less prominent areas of H, such as in public signage and during specific community events. By employing this strategy, X will not pose any threat to the dominant language Y, which would not be expected from a language ranking at Fishman's Stage 7–8 anyway.

One may distinguish direct and indirect strategies aimed at enhancing language use. Direct strategies include typical language-centre activities such as documentation and formal teaching, as well as master–apprentice-style methods that are based on direct language transfer. Language publicity is an indirect method in that it targets marginal domains and audiences but does not involve language teaching at first sight. However the active involvement of language learners in the process indirectly supports the transfer process. In fact all media-prone activities require the organised involvement of language speakers. In this context older and younger speakers work together as they prepare a desired output for a specific project.

Of the numerous strategies and methods used in language revitalisation programs many have some positive effect, especially when applied as part of a structured program tailored to suit an individual language community. However most direct strategies aimed at enhancing language transfer also face serious challenges which can result in a loss of efficiency. To take the Miriwoong case as an example, language lessons in a classroom situation, for instance, strongly depend on the motivation factor. Where learner motivation is poor, this leads to truancy and discontinuity of lessons. Bush trips involving language learning have a high success rate, however they represent a

---

3 While the restrictions mentioned make an interesting topic to elaborate on, space does not permit their discussion here. At present the revitalisation process is not being affected by these constraints.

very expensive component of revitalisation. The innovative language revival through employment approach (see Olawsky, this volume) is even more costly. In reality most efficient revitalisation strategies require large amounts of funding, an ever-present challenge to any program. In comparison, introducing the endangered language into public life is an exceptionally economical method to promote the language. The question, naturally, is how useful is language publicity?

Is it really a waste of effort?

The RLS model suggests that the use of a critically endangered language in a high domain is a waste of energy and resources. In reality language publicity does not appear to waste any resources. The development of signage, for example, serves as a stimulus to elders contributing their knowledge as they spend time discussing the relevant terms to be used. At the same time young people learn from their input. The result is a series of signs paid for by the shire council or national park management. The community not only gains pride in their contribution but also increases their active engagement with the language.

Media coverage, to name another example, will primarily strengthen the community's linguistic identity as well as raise public awareness. However any media report will have to be based on actual linguistic activity before it goes public. If an activity is worth documenting, why not showcase it? After all, it takes little effort and even less money to produce a newspaper article or conduct a simple interview.

Revitalisation strategies should also pay attention to the status level of a language; what is required at Stage 7–8 may differ from what is required at higher stages of Fishman's Graded Intergenerational Disruption Scale (GIDS). Arguably, for a language on the verge of extinction, almost anything will do as long as it is part of a structured revitalisation program. Community-based activities remain the backbone of revitalisation but these should be complemented by additional strategies.

Most experts will admit that Australian language revitalisation attempts, whether they follow the bottom-up model or not, have had limited success. After all, families cannot be forced to use a specific language at home. One among many reasons for this is that Indigenous languages do not have the prestige or status they deserve, neither in the Indigenous community nor in the wider public. Where people have given up on reviving their language would it do any harm to implement a single component that aims at strengthening a language from the top down? It is reasonable to assume that if a language receives recognition in the public domain this will also reflect on its status within the (potential) speaker community. Language publicity is bound to increase the motivation of Indigenous people to revitalise and actively use their language. This could be viewed as a reversion of McConvell's (1992, p. 219) conclusion that 'removing Aboriginal languages from public domains like education reduces their status and ultimately threatens their survival'.

Is it accepted?

One has to consider that certain changes have occurred in Australian society making language publicity more feasible. In large parts of the general public, and especially in government circles, it is now regarded as politically correct to acknowledge Aboriginal languages as a matter of national significance (see also Truscott & Malcolm, this volume). As our daily lives are exposed to the ever-present media, and as opinions are shaped and influenced by newspapers and television programs, it becomes almost obligatory to incorporate issues related to endangered languages as well as words from these languages in this domain. Anyone who finds themselves or their activities showcased in the media gains pride and status in the eyes of the wider community – and so does the language. While this opportunity may not have been available previously, the media of our time generally show a greater openness to embracing the issues of minorities. It is a chance not to be missed.

In the Miriwoong case the readiness of organisations and agencies to involve members of the Indigenous community in public events further contributes to lifting the linguistic profile. Though it must be conceded that the motivation behind this is, in some cases, based on a sense of political correctness rather than a genuine understanding of language revitalisation, such events still support the just cause. On most occasions the actual welcome speech would only consist of a simple greeting or a few short sentences in the traditional language, often followed by a translation or explanation in English. The inclusion of Indigenous language is in fact even expected by event organisers. More complex speeches may follow at a later stage of revitalisation where the opportunity arises. Even if at present this component has a predominantly symbolic character rather than being instructive, its value is to be seen in encouraging language identity and to strengthen the active use of the language (see also Amery, this volume).

What is the goal?

Most Aboriginal languages find themselves somewhere near Stage 8 of the GIDS scale (Lo Bianco & Rhydwen 2001). Where are these languages going? If the alternative is between using a language in the public domain and not using it at all, the choice is obvious. Revitalisation can be understood as a relative process. Realistically the goal, for most if not all languages now at Stage 7 or 8, is not to reach Level 1 or 2 where a language such as Miriwoong would rule side by side with English (Lo Bianco & Rhydwen 2001); it would be overambitious to expect this to happen in any society otherwise dominated by a single strong language. As Romaine (2006, p. 456) puts it, domains occupied by H cannot ' … replace the home as the primary site and agency of language transmission'. A realistic goal is to achieve diglossia where the language is stabilised in lower domains such as home and informal education, but supported by other domains such as the media and other public levels as a tool to promote the lower ones. Eventually these could function as a tool for the language to gradually penetrate lower domains as well.

The goals that publicity may have within a language planning framework include:

- Enhance linguistic identity within the community by raising the profile of the language
- Increase the motivation to learn the language
- Offer innovative, attractive domains of language use to younger speakers
- Increase active language use
- Contribute to language awareness in the wider community
- Lift the status of the language to gain local control of language policies
- Strengthen the general reconciliation process.

Outlook, opportunities and recommendations

The exhibition of Miriwoong language in public life has been progressing over the last few years and has been found supportive of language revitalisation. While Indigenous people have accepted many aspects of modern life they are determined to preserve their traditional values. Language as the core of these values has been carried into parts of the western-dominated environment by creating awareness and displaying language on signs noticed and read by everybody. The development of partnerships between Indigenous people and government agencies is invaluable in lifting the profile of traditional languages in Western society.

Given the current situation in the process of Miriwoong language revitalisation it appears that an additional component – the use of language in public life – should be considered when using Fishman's GIDS in order to structure the revitalisation of threatened languages. The Miriwoong example demonstrates that this can occur even at the early stages of revitalisation. Crystal (2000) lists a number of factors which are designed to strengthen an endangered language. The first factor in this regard is that a language will progress if its speakers increase their esteem within the dominant community. Another factor mentioned relates to the increase of legitimate power of a language community in the eyes of the dominant one. Both factors directly reflect the approach adopted as a component of the Miriwoong language revitalisation program.

The process of revitalisation operates differently in each language community and recommendations should be given based on the individual situation. Differences may apply when contrasting a demographic environment such as a town to an isolated remote community.[4] For communities that wish to implement the language publicity approach into their existing strategies the following options may be considered:

- newspaper articles reporting about language work
- newspaper or magazine contributions with instructive language content
- language guides

---

4 Miriwoong is a special case as it reflects an outback community in a small-town setting dominated economically and politically by a non-Indigenous population.

- short radio spots
- signage
- interviews
- maps
- working with partners
- welcome speeches at events
- crash course for outsiders and community members (even mixed classes)
- website with language content.

The above can be understood as an open list, as revitalisation programs for other languages may supply further creative ideas related to language publicity. All of the above strategies represent inexpensive and time-efficient ways of promoting the language. Applied as icing on the well-structured revitalisation program cake, these strategies are hardly a waste of effort. The experience of going public in the Miriwoong case casts serious doubts on the claim that a minority language should not be promoted in high domains. Language publicity may not be a major revitalisation strategy but it can play a supporting role for languages which have little to lose.

References

Crystal D (2000). *Language death*. Cambridge: Cambridge University Press.

Fishman JA (1991). *Reversing language shift: theory and practice of assistance to threatened languages*. Clevedon: Multilingual Matters.

Hinton L (1997). Survival of endangered languages: the Californian master–apprentice program. *International Journal of the Sociology of Language*, 123: 177–91.

Kofod F (1978). The Miriwung language (East Kimberley): a phonological and morphological study. Unpublished masters thesis, University of New England.

Lo Bianco J & Rhydwen M (2001). Is the extinction of Australia's Indigenous languages inevitable? In J Fishman (Ed). *Can threatened languages be saved? reversing language shift, revisited: a 21st century perspective* (pp. 391–422). Clevedon: Multilingual Matters.

McConvell P (1992). Review of Fishman (1991). *Australian Journal of Linguistics*, 12(1): 209–20.

McConvell P & Thieberger N (2001). *State of Indigenous languages in Australia – 2001*. State of the environment Australia technical papers, Series 2. Canberra: Department of the Environment and Heritage.

Romaine S (Ed). (1991). *Language in Australia*. Cambridge: Cambridge University Press.

Romaine S (2006). Planning for the survival of linguistic diversity. *Language Policy*, 5(4): 443–75.

7
Ngapartji Ngapartji: Indigenous language in the arts

Beth Sometimes and Alex Kelly[1]

Abstract

Ngapartji Ngapartji is a high-profile arts, theatre and language maintenance and revitalisation promotion project produced by social-change company Big hART. Since 2005 Ngapartji Ngapartji has been operating an innovative and experimental program which includes: the creation of an online interactive language and culture learning website, working with Pitjantjatjara-speaking young people, Elders and linguists; an arts-based community development program; a highly successful touring theatre work which is performed bilingually and a media campaign promoting the development of a national Indigenous languages policy. Ngapartji Ngapartji demonstrates the role the arts can play in the reversal and prevention of further loss of Australia's Indigenous languages. While Ngapartji works primarily with Pitjantjatjara, a relatively vital language, we believe that the key processes and outcomes of the project have practical applications to other language revitalisation contexts.

What is the project?

Ngapartji Ngapartji is a long-term community development Pitjantjatjara language and arts program based on Arrernte country in Mparntwe (Alice Springs). Since 2005 the project has delivered a broad variety of arts workshops in Pitjantjatjara communities, created an online language and culture website, nationally toured an award-winning theatre production and recently produced a documentary.

Arts mentors and producers work alongside Pitjantjatjara linguists, Elders and young language speakers in the spirit of *ngapartji-ngapartji*, which describes a concept of reciprocal exchange. The incredibly diverse range of skills contributed by participants and team – both Indigenous and non-Indigenous – has created a culture of respect and

---

[1] Both authors are from Ngapartji Ngapartji.

a rich ground for creative, collaborative relationships founded in language exchange. This is the culture into which audiences of the website and theatre show are invited.

How does it work?

As well as maintaining an office space in Alice Springs and conducting town-based activities with young participants, every few months various members of the Ngapartji Ngapartji team bundle into the old blue Toyota and travel to remote communities such as Pukatja (Ernabella), Pipalyatjara and Kaltukatjarra (Docker River) to run workshops. These workshops are energetic bursts of activity exploring a range of art forms – filmmaking, performance, music – which are structured to be responsive to community requirements and flexible when working with people dealing with difficult circumstances. Within these workshops, communities create their own content in their own language.

The content that is created feeds back into the website and the theatre show, and is made accessible to communities through the distribution of DVDs and CDs and broadcast on local channels. Within this long-term process Ngapartji Ngapartji has negotiated and crafted its role as an organisation in order to respond to the needs of participants. The role that has emerged is that of an agent in storytelling. In the process of expressing stories of place and identity the essence of what makes art and what makes community is developed and augmented. Ngapartji Ngapartji's role is to facilitate a process driven by participants. One of the most important issues identified by those participants from the beginning is that of language revitalisation among Pitjantjatjara speakers.

About Pitjantjatjara

Pitjantjatjara can be seen as a strong language with over 2500 speakers across northern South Australia, the south of the Northern Territory and into Western Australia. However Pitjantjatjara is still regarded as endangered as it is changing substantially among generations with classical Pitjantjatjara being spoken less and less by young people. The domains of the language are shrinking, especially among young people, and particularly those young people that no longer live on traditional Pitjantjatjara country, but in towns such as Alice Springs, Port Augusta, Coober Pedy and Adelaide where they speak a mix of Pitjantjatjara, English and other Indigenous languages such as Luritja and Arrernte.

As a language project Ngapartji Ngapartji becomes a forum within the community for discussion concerning language and language transmission:

> Kuwari tjitji tjuta ninti wiya tjukurpa pulka tjutaku. Kuwari Pitjantjatjara uti tjuta kutju wangkanyi. Ninti wiya. Mungatu nyangangku katjangku wangkangu, Ngunytjimalu wangkangu, 'Malu anytjapiri mantjila', ka tjitji kutju kunyu putu kuliningi, 'Nyaa, Nyaa?' Putu alatjitu kuliningi anytjapiri. Tjana ninti wiya, nyanga tjana tjutaku,

> *Pitjantjatjara alatjitu. Malu anytjapiri wangkanyi, tangka panya, malu tangka munu winki katinyi, palyantja wiyangku katinyi – anytjapiri – whole.*
>
> These days children do not understand complex words. These days they are only speaking really basic Pitjantjatjara. They lack knowledge. Recently this person's son was saying, 'Go and get *malu anytjapiri*' and the child he was speaking to apparently couldn't understand and was saying, 'What? What?' He couldn't understand it at all, *anytjapiri*. They don't understand these kinds of words, real Pitjantjatjara. If you say *malu anytjapiri*, it means, you know, cooked kangaroo that you would carry together, not yet divided up – *anytjapiri* – whole. (Milyika Carroll, pers comm., 2008)

Ngapartji Ngapartji participants include young people from Alice Springs town camps such as Abbott's Camp, Anangu Pitjantjatjara Yankunytjatjara (APY) land residents who have shifted to Alice because they or their partners are in need of renal dialysis, and both young people and Elders from remote communities – in particular Ernabella, on the APY lands. The project has worked with around 300 participants since 2005 and about 25 of those have come on one or more of the nine national tours of Ngapartji Ngapartji.

By developing activities that are driven by an engagement with Indigenous language such as music recording, filmmaking and travelling to cities to deliver a bilingual theatre show, the domains in which the language is used are increased. Both younger and older Pitjantjatjara participants engage with broader dialogue concerning language, and in discussion around emerging conceptual realms regarding the experiences that are being shared. By conducting dialogue concerning project development bilingually, the language is revitalised through broader contextual relevance and increased use.

Focused translation and interpretation through the process of creating art, theatre and film leads to detailed examination of classical language use and the documentation of words, ideas, phrases, grammar, story and song. Through producing work that engages multiple age groups from the community, an intergenerational exchange occurs with a language focus. *Ninti Mulapa* translates as highly knowledgeable and is the name given to the language reference group made up of senior Pitjantjatjara people who advise and consult on aspects of Ngapartji Ngapartji, in particular the Ninti website, created as a language and culture learning forum. Through the process of reviewing film and other content created by young people both in town and out bush, these senior people are able to re-engage with communities from which they are separated, consult on subject matter and monitor language use. Ninti Mulapa combines traditional knowledge with contemporary creative processes.

This activity-based reciprocal approach has been an effective means to resist language shift. Instead of simply preserving the language (in dictionaries, footage of classical speakers, and so on), speakers themselves are revitalising it, and at the same time participating in a discourse about the importance of language which extends across generations. The project therefore does not see language in isolation but recognises the relationship between language and cultural continuity at every level.

Language pride not language shame

Community ownership over the project is high and reflected in changing attitudes to the Pitjantjatjara language, especially among younger project particpants. The Ngapartji Ngapartji touring show, especially the popularity of its recent tour to Ernabella, has strengthened the sense of pride in the language among native speakers. Aspects of the show make it popular and significant for younger generations, not least in their capacity to build content. In particular the use of theatre and new media together are targeted to enhance and develop traditional storytelling and contemporary media skills among participants.

Lead actor Trevor Jamieson's energetic demonstration of a capacity to walk two ways – to uphold pride in his language and culture, fighting its loss through displacement, while also sparring skilfully with the English-speaking world – inspires young people to reposition their language in the framework of cultural power. Within the Ngapartji Ngapartji model of exchange, the conflict between 'traditional' and 'mainstream' life choices may be negotiated, if not averted.

Young people

Engagement with the mainstream or Western ways is often seen by senior Pitjantjatjara people and observers as a cause of language loss. However this engagement is both necessary for the survival of communities and in changing the attitudes of young people toward their language. Young people's fascination with and participation in popular culture is inevitable and desirable. Using the forms of popular culture to produce language-related content therefore creates a high level of credibility for language material. Young people become proud of producing content in Pitjantjatjara because of the status associated with the project and the content that has been made to date. This content goes on to gain recognition for the importance of Pitjantjatjara from the exposure to theatre and language-learning audiences. The popularisation of language content in partnership with multigenerational engagement in this way has applications across the field of language revitalisation.

Follwing the Big hART model, Ngapartji Ngapartji has used the profile of the touring theatre work to generate interest in the maintenance of Indigenous languages among non-language speakers. The project also campaigns for the development of a national Indigenous languages policy. In this way it hopes to create a legacy for all Indigenous languages, not just Pitjantjatjara.

The idea to push for a policy emerged after discussions with many language workers, linguists and the Federation of Aboriginal and Torres Strait Islander Languages. Over the last three years the Ngapartji Ngapartji team have researched the status of language support in each state and put together a position paper on language policy. Every touring season politicians, advisors, language workers, academics, linguists and other influential people are invited to watch the show and encouraged to consider the importance of Indigenous languages. This has resulted in substantial national media coverage on television programs such as *SBS News*, *ABC News*, *Sunday Arts* and *Living Black*, as well as on ABC Radio National and in newspapers such as *The Age* and *The Australian* – all of which have highlighted the importance of Indigenous languages.

Broader applications

While Ngapartji works with Pitjantjatjara, a relatively vital language, the innovative approach has had outcomes and involved processes which could be employed in other language revival contexts.

For example: Ngapartji Ngapartji has worked collaboratively with young people to create living language tools. Through embedding the use of Indigenous language in engaging activities such as music recording and filmmaking, popularity is generated in content that is relevant and holds personal interest for participants, thus increasing the currency of the language and the appeal of participation. Creating popular culture content in an Indigenous language, especially film and music that is accessible via the internet and mobile phone, attracts young people – the future generation of language speakers and revivers.

We suggest that the creation of media by young people is a strong identity-building activity which, when linked with language that is being revived or revitalised, results in a reinforcement of participants' association with that language and a relationship between self-worth and their language.

The engagement of young speakers in developing content in their own languages in turn empowers communities. A multigenerational approach enhances language use as a broader part of cultural continuity. Engaging young community members through language-based activities gives access to Elders who have the relevant cultural and life experience to understand the importance of language revitalisation, whilst legitimising the cultural forms to which young people are attracted.

If media content created by young people is of the same high standard as other media with which they engage, then their own language content will always be more popular – we have observed this hands down with Ngapartji Ngapartji.

There is genuine and widespread interest in and concern for Indigenous languages in mainstream Australia. This is evident through the success of Ngapartji Ngapartji (every ticket to every show has been sold, with over 30 000 people seeing the show to date), the huge popularity of singer/song-writer Gurumul Yunipingu, the success of films such as *Ten canoes* and *Samson & Delilah* and the interest shown by non-Indigenous students learning Indigenous languages in schools and adult learning contexts.

Ngapartji Ngapartji has exposed the general public to Indigenous language in an emotive context – theatre – providing a platform for meaningful engagement and giving liberty to understanding. Through the creatively-presented telling of a personal narrative, a level of intimacy is created which is vital to the actual shift towards engagement with the movement.

By integrating recognised cultural forms such as popular music with Indigenous language, as Ngapartji Ngapartji has done by translating the music of Bob Dylan, Talking Heads and others into Pitjantjatjara, accessibility and affinity is engendered (but see also McNaboe & Poetsch, this volume, for the pitfalls of language revitalisation using English song structures). This could be a powerful tool in language re-awakening and applicable to multiple generations.

The Ngapartji Ngapartji project has sought to actively engage the general public in the language maintenance and revitalisation movement via information provided on the website and through events associated with the theatre show, such as panels and letter-writing campaigns. Not every project should necessarily try to replicate the scale of Ngapartji Ngapartji or seek to create a touring theatre work. However, engagement with the mainstream, through media coverage or the web presence of language content that projects have produced, can leverage further interest in revitalisation within communities when they feel that there is wider interest and concern for their language from outside.

The project embraces contemporary technologies at the same time as it revitalises traditions, breaking down dichotomies that can create shame and stymie language preservation. The participant-driven, reciprocal model of working embodied in such a project builds pride and further leverages significant exposure in the mainstream.

The Ngapartji Ngapartji project, which was always designed to be discrete time-wise, is now complete. it ran from 2005 to 2010. A 'memory basket' and a documentary titled *Nothing Rhymes with Ngapartji* have been produced as legacies of the project and these are available at libraries nationally.

8
Awakening or awareness: are we being honest about the retrieval and revival of Australia's Aboriginal languages?

Trevor Stockley[1]

Abstract

This is a report on the process of language retrieval and revival for some Aboriginal languages in north Queensland in recent years. The writer challenges language workers, language centres and government funding bodies to be honest with language learners about their role in the process of language awakening and revitalisation and the anticipated language outcomes.

Reference is made to the importance of doing language work on country, the practicalities of working to awaken a language there, the retrieval and revival process when preparing and conducting Aboriginal language awareness workshops, and the continuing language learning and revitalisation process through language programs on country. The development of the Warrgamay language program and the Gudjal language program is reviewed, noting some of the difficulties due to the lack of language resources. The writer acknowledges the vital need to work with and respect the position of Elders, and the essential training role embedded within all language learning activities.

The conclusion draws attention to the limited funding available for retrieval and revival language work and the narrow views held by many funding bodies in regard to their understanding of the second language learning process as it applies to these Aboriginal languages. Finally, a metaphor from traditional life at Yirrkala, Northern Territory is used to draw an analogy between fire and the process of language re-awakening through awareness, retrieval, revival and revitalisation.

---

1 Indigenous languages teacher and consultant.

Awareness, retrieval, revival, revitalisation

Which is the right word? None of these words helps to fully understand and appreciate the intense feelings of joy, empowerment and pride or the strong want and need in a language learner when first hearing and speaking their ancestral Aboriginal language; nor the enormous difficulty, challenges, dedication, frustration and time which will be involved in learning and using, what is in fact, a new second language.

Australia as the modern world knows it has been here a mere 200-odd years, a blink in time for ancient Aboriginal Australia. But these 200 years have been unequally shared with non-Indigenous Australians, speaking a foreign language and living a very different culture. In this short time the Aboriginal languages of Australia, the languages of the land, have for the most part been silenced. The condition of Aboriginal languages varies from the treasured few in the far north and centre of Australia, which are still spoken right through, used for everyday communication and are being learnt by children as their first language; to those languages which are struggling, not being learnt by children anymore and often only being spoken or partially remembered by a few Elders; and then to those languages which are no longer spoken, where the knowledge of the Elders is scarce. These are the language remnants of Australia's Aboriginal language heritage of around 250 distinct languages (Senior Secondary Assessment Board of South Australia 1996, p. 7).

In the past, colonial, commonwealth and state governments have shown little regard for the languages of Aboriginal people, with these languages depicted as inferior and simple, and the speakers shamed and punished. Survivors of the violence and introduced diseases were often forcibly moved off their lands, breaking the bond between country and language. Later government policies of stealing children, breaking up families and punishment for traditional beliefs and values prevented languages from being passed on. A violent colonial history and its overwhelming consequences have left many Aboriginal languages without speakers and learners, and many who would like to be speakers and learners have been left without languages, right across Australia. Today these Aboriginal languages, which have often been inadequately recorded and sometimes went unrecorded, are being revitalised by community-based Aboriginal language groups.

The challenge is to work together to halt the decline of Aboriginal languages, to create an *awareness* of the language remaining in the community, to *retrieve* any language knowledge which has been recorded, to *revive* the language for the descendants of today and to *revitalise* the language for the children of tomorrow. A further challenge is to assist learners and funding bodies to discard the incorrect, preconceived idea inherited from our colonial past that these languages are simple and will be easy and quick to learn. Australian Aboriginal languages sound different when spoken and are constructed in different ways from the Aboriginal English or Standard Australian English being spoken as a first language by the majority of Aboriginal people today. Language learners will find that, even though it was their own ancestors who were the last speakers, this will not make it easier for them to learn and speak these unique languages (see also Walsh, this volume).

There appears to be a hopeful assumption that Aboriginal languages are still there, sleeping, recumbent, just waiting for a community of speakers to come and make a bit of wake-up noise. In reality the continuing process of culture change and language loss has had enormous effects on Aboriginal people and their languages. We cannot avoid the tough historical reality for Indigenous people arising from the loss of their lands and the denigration of their culture and languages for generations, which has resulted in many Aboriginal languages no longer being spoken in homes. Aboriginal languages in some cases may not have been spoken for a number of years, sometimes generations. As a consequence of this relentless attack on Aboriginal languages their re-awakening involves the processes of language retrieval, revival and revitalisation and will need many years of hard language work and research, and more years of dedicated practice for learners to make new sounds, learn many new words and their meanings, learn new ways to form words and sentences, and to master the different grammar of an Aboriginal language. Language revival, turning the language loss process around, and heading back on the road to language revitalisation, is indeed the process being undertaken but may well only result in partial success. All language learners learn something about their language but only a dedicated few will achieve a strong command of the new sounds and intonation and come to terms with the different grammar and sentence structures involved (see also N. Reid, this volume).

Learning your Aboriginal language can make you feel really good about yourself; it can help you to feel comfortable about the world by understanding the effects of history on your language. Understanding and learning language can make you think differently about your identity and self concept, your place in your family and community. It makes you feel proud. These are tremendous social and emotional results from language work but we must be honest, both with ourselves and language learners, about what can be achieved in bringing back these languages through a revitalisation process. We need to be honest about the daunting and dedicated language work necessary and the long-term view required when anticipating a full return of spoken language. This view requires us to look towards generations of language learners, to a pool of future language speakers, writers and readers. It is a view which includes language-speaking communities with families who are maintaining and passing on their languages in the face of the dominance of English and its overpowering role in Australian society. The unavoidable, fundamental and most difficult feature in this language revitalisation process is the basic need to communicate, the need to use the language you are learning. There is a need for other people to converse with, for someone to share with, others to be in a language group with, friends to joke with or swear at, family to be serious with, to care for and to do all this, in your ancestral Aboriginal language.

We know why this language loss has happened and we also know that even those few remaining, fully-spoken Aboriginal languages in Australia are still seriously threatened by loss due to social upheaval and change of government policy. What we need to know is how to turn this language situation around and find real ways to revitalise languages on country while remaining true to the spirit of the languages, the wishes of the Elders and the hopes of the learners. This leads us to an important question: What do Aboriginal people want to do with their re-awakened languages in the Australian society of today?

Language awareness workshops

In recent years I have worked with the Girringun Aboriginal Corporation and the North Queensland Regional Aboriginal Corporation Language Centre. By using and sharing my teaching skills and the knowledge gained from learning and speaking Gumatj (one of the Yolŋu Matha languages of north-east Arnhemland), I have been able to help in the continuing process of retrieval, revival and revitalisation of some Aboriginal languages in north Queensland. This is a community-based language movement which was started after consultation with Elders in an attempt to try and fulfil their wishes and dreams to re-awaken their languages and to hear them on country again.

The languages chosen to work with in the wet tropics were the rainforest Dyirrbal languages of Djirrbal, Ngadjan and Girramay, the coastal rainforest languages of Warrgamay and Nyawaygi and, in the dry country around Charters Towers, the languages of Gudjal (and Gugu-Badhun). It is important that all the language work happens on country and this is a central element of our activities. On country language work allows us to show respect to the Elders, to the ancestral voices and to give a context to these languages of the land. The public profile of the languages is lifted with people being aware and interested that language business is happening in their community. The very nature of on-country language work ensures that a greater number and broader spectrum of the community have access and the opportunity to attend language workshops. Attendance at on-country language awareness workshops is high, as most participants are local, avoiding the logistics of transporting a select few learners and Elders to a distant centre. We found that many people including parents, teenagers and younger children could all make it for a day or two at the local hall to have a look and a listen about language. This on-country language retrieval and revival work has generally occurred over weekends in venues such as the local town hall, the shire council training room, a church hall, a community keeping place, out of hours access to classrooms, a display pavilion at the showground and a local club committee room. Following is a list of two-day workshops conducted during 2005–06:

- a Warrgamay workshop for the Warrgamaygan at Ingham
- two Ngadjan workshops for the Ngadjandji at Malanda and Atherton
- two Djirrbal workshops for the Djirrbalngan at Ravenshoe and Herberton
- a Girramay workshop for the Girramaygan at Jumbun

- a Nyawaygi workshop for the Nyawaygi people at Mungalla station
- two Gudjal workshops for the Gudjalbara at Charters Towers.

After initial consultation and agreement with Elders to proceed with each workshop, preparation by the language teacher begins in earnest and includes many hours of reading, research, language learning and writing. When preparing I make use of all available language materials including linguistic sources, recordings of speakers, dictionaries, historical accounts and past projects. As I work with these resources, putting them into plain English, I produce a handbook and soundbook for each language to be used in the workshop and for future reference.[2] This is undertaken with the aim of bringing back Aboriginal language knowledge in a suitable place on country and in a more easily accessible, understandable and respectful way, while still incorporating an appropriate level of language difficulty. For the rainforest Dyirrbal and coastal rainforest languages I used the linguistic work of Dixon (1972), Dixon & Blake (1981) and previous language resources by Grant & Reppel (2000). For the dry country languages I used the dictionary work of Santo (2006) and the linguistic work of Sutton (1970, 1973), including recordings of Fred Toombah.

During the workshops we raise the participants' awareness and understanding of their traditional language and its historical relationship with contemporary Australian society. It is vital that learners get the sounds of the language right as we are not learning another kind of English, so we spend considerable time on their language soundbook, to become familiar with the tongue positions of new sounds and getting used to hearing and saying them correctly while starting to learn a bank of vocabulary. The workshops are videorecorded to provide later reference for the group and a resource for future learners. Although we only have two days a lot of Aboriginal language knowledge is discussed in the workshops as we work through the handbook and soundbook, including:

- Aboriginal languages before the invasion
- language change and borrowed words
- writing and spelling the particular Aboriginal language
- sounds and pronunciation of the Aboriginal language
- some grammar and rules of the Aboriginal language
- traditional kinship names and relationships
- local Aboriginal placenames
- useful and useable words, commands, phrases and questions
- time, location and number words
- strategies for learning Aboriginal languages.

It is important to quickly develop positive teaching and learning relationships and

---

2 Locally published materials available from the Australian Institute of Aboriginal & Torres Strait Islander Studies library.

an environment where people feel relaxed and comfortable while still working hard on their language learning. We aim to achieve this by working on country; showing respect to Elders and their language knowledge; working together on language learning; and sitting, eating and talking together in informal settings at tea breaks. We try to create a social feeling in the workshops and utilise the fact that most of the learners are locals, family and kin. The catering for the workshop is organised by a language co-worker with the help of the local community. The workshops conducted so far have been successful and well received by Elders and learners, with all participant evaluations being positive. Below are a few responses from language speakers and workshop participants after the Girramay workshop at Jumbun in 2006:

> I haven't heard this many people speaking my language for 40 years.
>
> I remember when the old people used to talk like this.
>
> Last night I had a dream where my father came to me and talked in our traditional language, telling me to pick it up and speak it properly.
>
> Too deadly. When will we do this again?

By working closely with Elders I ensure that these are the people who are recognised and respected as being the holders of the local Aboriginal language knowledge and traditions. These workshops are an important catalyst for further language revitalisation projects for the community. After the workshops various ideas have been suggested, all involving using and learning more language.

- Take your language knowledge home and share it with family and friends
- Approach the school and gain support for teaching the local Aboriginal language, possibly as a Language Other Than English (LOTE) subject
- Approach the preschool and child care groups in town to encourage language songs, displaying pictures and words for animals in language
- Have more culture days and visits to schools, preschools and childcare centres by Elders and parents
- Continue with the interest and energy of the community language group and run local language meetings
- Develop a language program and hold a series of language classes on country.

The Djirrbal people liked the school LOTE idea which worked well while there was enough supportive staff at the school and language teachers available. The Nyawaygi people decided to continue with local language meetings while the Girramay, Warrgamay and Gudjal people all made the decision to start work on language programs.

Language programs

The next step in the language revitalisation process was the research, writing and appropriate delivery of on-country Aboriginal language programs:

- Warrgamay (Stages 1, 2 and 3): 20 full days of lessons in Ingham
- Gudjal (Stage 1): six full days of lessons in Charters Towers.

A lack of linguistic resources, language materials and records can make revitalisation work difficult and this will be the likely situation for many languages, as it was not until the 1960s that linguists really started working with and recording Aboriginal languages. For some languages this was too late to get the whole linguistic picture, so other language retrieval strategies must be used to find an Aboriginal solution to this dilemma. As I worked to retrieve Gudjal language knowledge, while writing the Gudjal language program, I realised that there were insufficient resources available to make a good attempt. This led to discussions with the Gudjal Elders about how we could find a resolution and continue with the program. The Gudjal Elders negotiated with the Gugu-Badhun Elders, who are traditionally a close family and speak a sister language to Gudjal. The Gugu-Badhun Elders agreed to permit the use of their more complete linguistic resources, such as Sutton (1973).

In another example the Gudjal language group needed to look at ways to 'find' missing words they required. We needed the word for 'name' to be able to ask different Gudjal questions and this word had not been recorded in either language. As I was working on a number of languages in the region I compiled a list of words for name looking for the traditional connections among people, country and language:

- The Gudjal word for tooth is *rirra* (or *riyala* or *wurriya*)
- The Warrungu word for tooth, seed and name is *rirra*
- The Gugu-Badhun word for tooth and seed is *rirra*
- The Djirrbal word for tooth, seed, and name is *dirra*
- The Warrgamay word for tooth, seed and spear point is *yirra*.

We did not have resources for the languages to the west but the language and land connections can be easily seen moving among Djirrbal, Warrungu, Gugu-Badhun, Gudjal and Warrgamay. The question was, that if *dirra* and *rirra* mean tooth, seed and name in all the close languages, could this meaning be stretched and included into the Gudjal meaning of tooth, so that *rirra* (or *riyala* or *wurriya*) means tooth, seed and name in Gudjal? These are language revival issues for Elders and learners that entail many hours of discussions, to make informed decisions by considering language, family, history and linguistic issues all together.

The Elders and learners involved in the Warrgamay language group also had to make decisions about their language. One such decision concerned the orthography to be used when writing and whether to use the International Phonetic Alphabet symbols or the Roman alphabet. The Warrgamay decision was mixed; using ŋ for ng, changing j to dj; aa to aː, ii to iː, and uu to uː, while retaining ny.

The Warrgamay language program consisted of three stages for which the group organised the catering, retaining the important social and relaxed learning environment established at their initial awareness workshop.

Stage 1 (eight days) saw high attendance with many age groups involved. Elders, teenagers, children, sisters, cousins and aunties were all involved or spent a day passing through. Everyone who turned up gained some Warrgamay language knowledge and gave life to the group and their efforts in reviving their language. The first session in the morning was always centred on the soundbook, so all learners could feel comfortable in a structured group activity with sound and word repetition exercises. In the session after morning tea the language learning became more demanding, learning greetings and farewells, body part names, songs and games and simple questions and answers, such as asking the name of people and things. The afternoon session again involved sounds work and usually a point of interest for example, kinship which was an interesting project covering a number of weeks and involved looking at the old Warrgamay skin names and kinship structure, learning to say kinship terms, playing a kinship card game as a group, and developing a family tree for each learner using traditional Warrgamay relationship names. This activity needed the help of Elders and clearly demonstrated to younger learners how family and kin are still connected to each other and country.

Stage 2 (six days) began with nine learners. We continued to use the soundbook sharing the lead role, encouraging learners to self-correct by thinking about where their tongue should be, saying the words out loud and working in pairs. Attendance started to fall off as the language content became more difficult requiring more commitment and some serious language learning strategies. Learners improved their reading and writing skills in Warrgamay and some learners were using their language and practising regularly. Sessions included easy questions and answers, suffixing rules to show movement and location, word order, learning vocabulary for the construction of short sentences, using personal pronouns, fluency and intonation.

Stage 3 (six days) saw the group become a core of three adults and one teenager. These dedicated learners came to every language lesson, putting in long hours reviewing language knowledge and learning vocabulary while keeping word order, fluency and intonation in mind. They did their out loud practice at home and were good at correcting each other. Learners needed to think about, talk about and use their language for a serious amount of time every day. There are great demands in learning a second language but these learners, who all lived on country and had strong family links along with language memories from the past, overcame the difficulties and persevered, being rewarded as language connections were made and their understanding and confidence started to grow. Their language learning has become a part of their life as a Warrgamay person. Topics included extending the work started in Stage 2 and new work such as questions using possessive pronouns and the ownership/purpose suffix, suffixing rules for verb tenses, the ergative rule and learning more vocabulary.

It is integral to the continuing process of revitalisation that language be supported, celebrated and used in the community and by families in everyday life. Since the language awareness workshop and language program, the profile of Warrgamay language in the general community has increased. This is important and the learners foster this regularly when interacting with language learners and non-learners, both Indigenous and non-Indigenous. Remember that question: What do Aboriginal people want to do with their languages in the Australian society of today? Well, some ways which the Warrgamaygan have used their *Warrgamay mayay* include:

- providing names for Warrgamay children
- providing country names for a local walking trail, Wallaman Falls and Girringun National Park
- speaking Warrgamay during Welcomes to Country, public functions and events such as the opening of the Ingham Heritage building and the Tyto Wetlands environment in Ingham
- using Warrgamay body part names and songs at pre-school and youth camps
- organising bush trips to experience and learn Warrgamay flora, fauna and country names
- laying a commemorative plaque in Warrgamay at a local school
- using Warrgamay at the local carols by candlelight
- using Warrgamay greetings and farewells in public and with family
- using Warrgamay placenames
- using Warrgamay words in general conversation
- answering the phone with Warrgamay greetings and farewells
- putting Warrgamay messages on their answering machines
- using Warrgamay words and names in email addresses and correspondence
- using Warrgamay questions and short commands with each other
- putting up Warrgamay signs around the home and office.

The most powerful and positive outcome has to be the increased number of Warrgamay words being spoken and heard on country again. Although this is not a return to full use it is definitely a revival of language, entailing lots of hard work, confidence and pride, and represents a satisfying level of language understanding and use for the learners. These learners, these new speakers, would like to be involved in a full return of language use with others to speak with, listen to, learn from and answer their questions. They are willing to have a go and are brave beacons of Aboriginal language use, often in places where it can still be difficult to use your ancestral language in public.

The language awareness workshops and the graduated language-learning program are two real and successful ways to raise the public profile of the languages and to raise peoples' language abilities. The training of language workers within the program directly reflects the wishes of Elders in their determined struggle to uphold and pass on the unique value and importance of these Aboriginal languages, and is integral to the continuation of the revitalisation process. Being a language teacher doesn't always mean standing at the front of a class. Some people do that kind of teaching well, but all language learners are teachers when they share bits of their knowledge with their family, friends and other learners. Warrgamay language learners need to encourage other Warrgamay people by using and regularly talking about their language learning and by encouraging and participating in community and family language activities.

Conclusion

Government funding bodies must recognise the importance of Indigenous languages and develop strong policies, in collaboration with the people, to support *all* Indigenous languages. Funding bodies must understand that any language revitalisation program, including those described above, are part of an intergenerational language re-awakening, a revival process which needs ongoing and adequately allocated funds to keep the learning cycle continuing. For example Warrgamay Stage 4 has not yet been delivered; Stage 1 should have already been delivered again to bring in more learners; Gudjal Stage 2 has not yet been delivered. The Girramay people, who also decided on a language program, have not yet had any lessons delivered.

No matter how hard learners and teachers try, there is no quick and easy way to learn to speak an Aboriginal language; it takes dedication, time and practice. Knowing a few words of your language may make you feel proud, however it does not constitute speaking or revitalising a language (see also Hobson and, for a contrasting view, Meakins, this volume). Languages will not be revived with respect and understanding in a short period of time, with one-off language programs and unrealistic expectations of fluency. Adopting a short-term attitude towards funding the revitalisation of Aboriginal languages does not do justice to the efforts of the learners and Elders, nor does it give respect and regard to the voices of these important ancestral languages. There is a crucial need for understanding and adequate funding, as well as a need for cooperation and collaboration, to utilise the skills and knowledge of both Aboriginal and non-Aboriginal language teachers, Elders, linguists and language workers in an effort to recognise and achieve community expectations of the revitalisation process.

When I lived at Yirrkala in Arnhemland one of the many things my teacher and mentor, Dhuwanydjika Burarrwaŋa taught me was a Yolŋu idea about fire. Back in the old days a fire was always kept burning, sometimes blazing for warmth and comfort and other times kept as coals for cooking and relaxing around. When Yolŋu were travelling across country a particular wood was used which could be held and carried while the pith inside still smouldered. This fire was carried from place to place to be shared, nurtured and kept alive. It was always ready to use. By blowing on and caring for this smouldering coal you could readily have a fire, warmth, comfort, a hearth and a home wherever you camped. You tried not to let your fire die out as it would mean getting out your firesticks and beginning the process of making fire again or, if you were lucky and family were nearby, you would ask your kin to share their fire.

The lesson tells us that it is always easier to rekindle a fire by blowing on still-smouldering coals, rather than letting the fire go out and starting anew. It also reminds us of the tradition of sharing with kin and that it may now be words which need to be shared. The language fire in many communities today is not a blazing fire but resembles a quiet fire of just warm coals. The time for action is now, while there are still some coals. There is an urgent need to work with Elders who still remember how to blow on those old coals to re-kindle the language fire, to give warmth and comfort to their people, their families and their children and to hear Aboriginal languages on country again.

Acknowledgements

This on-country language work in north Queensland would not be possible or successful without the gift of Gumatj language and cultural understanding from Yolŋu Elders and friends at Yirrkala in the Northern Territory together with the trust of Elders and language learners in north Queensland.

References

Dixon RMW (1972). *The Dyirbal language of North Queensland.* London: Cambridge University Press.

Dixon RMW & Blake BJ (Eds) (1981). *Handbook of Australian languages.* Volume 2: Wargamay language of north Queensland. Canberra: Australian National University Press.

Grant E & Reppel C (2000). *Girramay language kit.* Innisfail, Qld: Innisfail District Education Office.

Santo W (2006). *Gudjal language pocket dictionary: Gudjal to English and English to Gudjal wordlist: a wordlist of the Gudjal language as spoken by the Gudjal people from the Mt Garnet, Cashmere and Herbert areas and upper Clark and east to Charters Towers, Mount Sturgeon, Mount Emu Plains, Lolworth and Reedy Springs.* Thuringowa, Qld.: Black Ink Press.

Senior Secondary Assessment Board of South Australia (1996). *Australia's Indigenous languages framework.* Wayville, SA: Senior Secondary Assessment Board of South Australia.

Sutton P (1970). *Language elicitation, texts, and some songs from Charters Towers and Palm Island, Qld.* [Sound recording 001911-001913]. Canberra: Australian Institute of Aboriginal & Torres Strait Islander Studies.

Sutton P (1973). Gugu-Badhun and its neighbours: a linguistic salvage study. Unpublished Masters thesis. Macquarie University.

Tsunoda T (1974). A provisional Warrungu dictionary. Unpublished manuscript. Townsville, Qld.

Part Three
Language centres and programs

Introduction
Language centres and programs

Michael Walsh[1]

Language centres have been an important component in language revitalisation since they came into being in the mid 1980s. Mostly these centres have been a focus for the linguistic aspirations of a number of languages in a region. This is certainly the case for the Kimberley Language Resource Centre (KLRC), the Many Rivers Aboriginal Language Centre (MRALC) from New South Wales and the Wangka Maya Pilbara Aboriginal Language Centre (Wangka Maya). However this section also describes the activities of two centres whose primary focus is on just one language: Miriwoong in the case of Mirima Dawang Woorlab-gerring, and Gumbaynggirr in the case of the Muurrbay Aboriginal Language and Culture Co-operative.

The Muurrbay Co-operative began in 1986 and has been a significant success story (Walsh 2001; 2009). We know that some initiatives have not been so successful (Walsh, this volume) so it is instructive to look at the details of ongoing activities as presented in this section. In particular, the contribution on the Kimberley Language Resource Centre is quite explicit about the structure of the organisation, its management approach and its strategic planning.

Ash, Hooler, Williams and Walker provide basic accounts of Muurrbay and the Many Rivers Aboriginal Language Centre supplemented with statements from Aboriginal Elders, teachers and linguists. The statement from Muurrbay Chair, Ken Walker, has a general application for language centres anywhere, even though he was particularly referring to one initiative of which he was an early leader:

> It's a hard road to hoe, but you gotta start somewhere, and don't expect miracles first up. It doesn't work. We started in '85 and we're still going, we're still learning. Don't give up, don't lose heart because the rewards at the end are beneficial for you and your community.

This modest call to arms underplays the very significant advances made by Muurrbay and Many Rivers in recent years in terms of resource production, training and language education across the communities.

---

[1] Department of Linguistics, University of Sydney.

Dixon and Deak's chapter on the Wangka Maya centre addresses the important issue of scope in relation to the range of activities undertaken by language centres. They point out that language centres are expected to handle a multitude of different tasks but in the end must make strategic decisions about how to prioritise. To underline the variation in approaches they present five case studies involving different languages: Thalanyji, Ngarluma, Nyangumarta and Bayungu as well as a group of eight Pilbara languages with five different foci and outcomes. The first showcases traditional knowledge of plant names and uses and was partly funded by a local mining company. The second resulted in the production of a range of materials that will eventually underpin a school-based program. These materials have capitalised on new technologies with greater appeal to younger language learners (see also Wilson, this volume). The third, a life-history of a prominent Nyangumarta man, emphasises literacy skills and is illustrated by the narrator, a talented artist. The fourth presents 100 words on DVD in eight Pilbara languages combining audio, visual and written material. The fifth is a Bayungu picture dictionary in which a template for another dictionary is recycled – this being one of the strengths of a regional language centre: materials created for one language can be shared and adapted for another.

The engagement of the Wangka Maya centre with a local mining company for one of its projects raises the issue of autonomy. KLRC reminds us of the need to consider ownership of the language revitalisation process or, in their terms, self-determination in language continuation. They complain that Western academia's views on appropriate measures for language revitalisation take precedence over those of Aboriginal people. This has significant implications, they would argue, for funding and support from grant bodies and puts strain on their quest for self-determination. Does one yield to outside forces in order to be better resourced or go it alone and be under-resourced? Such issues are by no means restricted to the Kimberleys or to Indigenous Australia in general (for example Rice 2009). They form part of an ongoing debate on the interaction between linguists and language activists.

Olawsky's paper deals with another language centre in the Kimberleys: Mirima Dawang Woorlab-gerring but from another point of view. It raises the important issue of employment possibilities in connection with revitalisation and presents evaluations of some of the revitalisation strategies adopted. Interestingly they have attempted to apply a master–apprentice model in the local context but, like some other attempts in Australia (for example Hobson & Laurie 2009; Hill & McConvell, this volume), it has had limited success to date. The Miriwoong centre demonstrates once again how language centres throughout Australia struggle to deliver effective outcomes while seriously under-resourced but have nevertheless achieved significant results. We can also see that the problems encountered and the issues to be addressed show considerable similarities across a varied range of contexts: the Kimberleys, the Pilbara and one portion of New South Wales.

References

Hobson J & Laurie B (2009). *An Australian trial of the master–apprentice method.* Paper presented at the 1st International Conference on Language Documentation and Conservation (ICLDC): Supporting Small Language Together. University of Hawai'i at Manoa, 12–14 March 2009 [Online]. Available: hdl.handle.net/10125/4985 [Accessed 24 November 2009].

Rice K (2009). Must there be two solitudes? language activists & linguists working together. In J Reyhner & L Lockard (Eds) (2009). *Indigenous language revitalization: encouragement, guidance & lessons learned* (pp. 37–59). Flagstaff, Arizona: Northern Arizona University.

Walsh M (2001). A case of language revitalisation in 'settled' Australia. *Current Issues in Language Planning*, 2(2&3): 251–58 [Online]. Available: www.multilingual-matters.net/cilp/002/0251/cilp0020251.pdf [Accessed 24 November 2009].

Walsh M (2009). The rise and fall of GIDS in accounts of language endangerment. In H Elnazarov & N Ostler (Eds). *Endangered languages & history* (pp. 134–41). Proceedings of the Foundation for Endangered Languages Conference, FEL XIII, Khorog, Tajikistan, 24–26 September 2009. Bath: Foundation for Endangered Languages.

9
Maam ngawaala: biindu ngaawa nyanggan bindaayili.
Language centres: keeping language strong

Anna Ash, Pauline Hooler, Gary Williams and Ken Walker[1]

Abstract

We begin by describing the history and main activities of Muurrbay Aboriginal Language and Culture Co-operative and Many Rivers Aboriginal Language Centre. Comments from Elders, language teachers and researchers are included to reflect the opinions of a diverse range of Aboriginal and non-Aboriginal people. We discuss some aspects of research, publishing, language education and information technology. Finally we make some recommendations for groups who are just starting out on this challenging but rewarding road.

This volume was at least partially inspired by *The green book of language revitalization in practice*. There is a chapter in that book called 'Diversity in Local Language Maintenance and Restoration: A Reason for Optimism'. It emphasises that there is a positive future for the revitalisation of Aboriginal languages:

> There is reason for optimism because local language communities all over the world are taking it upon themselves to act on behalf of their imperilled linguistic traditions in full understanding of, and in spite of, the realistic perception that the cards are stacked against them. There is, in effect an international movement in which local communities work in *defiance* of the forces pitted against their embattled languages. It has something of the character of a modern miracle, if you think about it – while they share the goal of promoting a local language, these groups are essentially independent of one another, coming together sometimes to compare notes, but operating in effective separation.

> Two factors in our optimism are the very existence of the movement itself and what is sometimes decried as a flaw in the movement: the feature of

---

[1] All authors are from the Muurrbay Aboriginal Language and Culture Co-operative & Many Rivers Aboriginal Language Centre.

> independence ... but this is a strength, in fact a true reason for optimism. It is the natural consequence of the fact that local conditions are very particular and, in the final analysis, unique ... The sharing of materials and ideas among language projects and the use of consultants in relevant fields (e.g. linguistics, education and computers) are good and often absolutely necessary, of course, but the structure of a local language program is determined by local considerations.
> (Ash et al. 2001, p. 20)

We believe there are still good reasons for optimism. It seems to us that right across New South Wales (NSW) there are more and more Aboriginal communities keeping their languages strong. In some places language centres are helping the process along; in other places communities are getting on with it in their own way, utilising help where it is offered from another type of Aboriginal organisation such as a museum, or radio station, or from some schools. This volume is about sharing ideas and materials. Muurrbay Aboriginal Language and Culture Co-operative (Muurrbay) – Many Rivers Aboriginal Language Centre (MRALC) is all about sharing ideas and materials, without forgetting that every community and language is unique. This diversity is a strength that means that there is a broader knowledge base – different people will have different answers to the same challenges.

Muurrbay and the Many Rivers region

Muurrbay began in 1986 when Gumbaynggirr Elders joined together to revive their language. Muurrbay means white fig tree in the Gumbaynggirr language; the white fig played an important role in the Dreamtime. Muurrbay's purpose is to support Aboriginal people, particularly Gumbaynggirr, in the revival and maintenance of their language and culture, and so strengthen their sense of identity, self-esteem and links to country.

Auntie Maggie Morris, founding member and patron of Muurrbay who passed away in early 2005, passionately wanted to pass down the language and traditions of her Gumbaynggirr people. The Elders worked with linguist Brother Steve Morelli to run the first Gumbaynggirr language course in Sherwood, west of Kempsey. Muurrbay is now based in the old church on Bellwood Road, Nambucca Heads, where Gumbaynggirr language classes began in 1997. There are more Gumbaynggirr speakers in 2009 than there were ten years ago. You could say that the language has had its lowest ebb, but now the tide of speakers is slowly but surely rising. We estimate that there are now several hundred partial speakers of Gumbaynggirr. So Muurrbay continues to grow as a centre for Aboriginal community activities including classes in Gumbaynggirr language, arts and cultural practices; specialised workshops on teaching techniques and information and communication technology (ICT); and community meetings.

In 2003 the Aboriginal and Torres Strait Islander Commission (ATSIC) Many Rivers Regional Council commissioned a report on the Aboriginal languages of the region. Councillors recognised the importance of language and cultural maintenance and wanted to develop a more strategic and long-term plan that made best use of limited funds. The report made ten recommendations, including that a working party investigate establishing a regional Aboriginal language centre, that further training be provided for Indigenous language teachers, and a scholarship be established for an Aboriginal linguistics student to conduct research in the region. In 2004 ATSIC councillors supported the setting up of a regional language centre, and Muurrbay was asked to oversee it. It was hoped that the positive developments in language revitalisation achieved by Gumbaynggirr people could also occur for other language groups of the region. These included language research, publishing a dictionary–grammar and teaching resources, and developing an appropriate adult language course so that adults could then teach the language to children.

The New South Wales context

In 2004 the NSW government was the first state government to launch an Aboriginal languages policy. The NSW Department of Aboriginal Affairs (DAA) through its Community Languages Assistance Program has supported many language programs across NSW, including several of Muurrbay's publishing ventures and the Aboriginal Languages Summer School.[2]

Several reports refer to the important role played by regional language centres. For example, the NSW report *Strong Language: Strong Culture* recommended that NSW ATSIC support the development of regional language and culture centres. Many Aboriginal people were consulted; their feedback included the comment that language centres should 'cater for more than one language in order to service whole communities' (Palmer 2000, p. 39). They could be distributed evenly across the state, one for each of the six ATSIC regions; a prime function would be the nurturing of Indigenous linguists and development of local expertise. As has happened elsewhere in Australia 'the creation of language centres and their support should form a key component to any language strategy in the state' (Palmer 2000, p. 39).

The Australian Institute of Aboriginal and Torres Strait Islander Studies (AIATSIS) *National Indigenous Languages Survey Report 2005* recommends 'Regional Indigenous Language Centres should operate in all areas of need to provide infrastructure and technical support to Community Language Teams', and notes:

> One of the most important initiatives of the 1980s was the creation of Regional Indigenous Language Centres ... to provide good services on a local and face-to-face basis to a variety of locally supported projects ... They employ (or should employ) Indigenous or non-Indigenous trained linguists, and Indigenous language workers who can assist with the production of both applied (community and school) material and language and culture documentation in the sense of 'documentary linguistics'. (AIATSIS 2005, p. 7)

---

2 A community-based language learning fest held annually at the Koori Centre, University of Sydney since 2007, under the auspices of Muurrbay-MRALC.

MRALC shares many features with the well-established regional language centres of the Northern Territory and Western Australia, such as Diwurruwurru-jaru in Katherine and Wangka Maya in Port Hedland (see Olawsky and Dixon & Deak, this volume), conducting research on several Aboriginal languages and supporting people to learn and teach their languages. These language centres were established in the late 1980s–early 1990s when the Aboriginal languages of southern states were being sorely neglected. Thankfully, in the last decade, the Australian government has increasingly recognised the importance of Aboriginal languages to people of southern states, and has funded language centres or smaller language projects in these areas. One main difference is that in NSW and Victoria, most language research relies quite heavily on archival records and audio recorded some time ago, rather than quite recently.

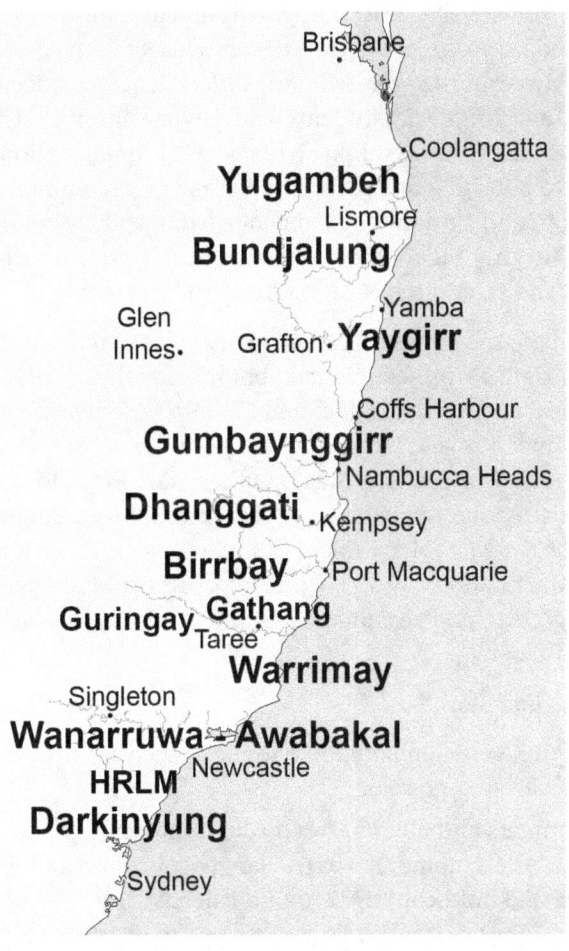

Figure 1. Languages supported by Muurrbay–MRALC

MRALC overview

MRALC provides strategic support for Aboriginal communities of the Many Rivers region who want to revitalise their languages. Seven languages are supported, which cover the NSW coastal strip from the NSW-Queensland border to the Hawkesbury River. From north to south these are the Bundjalung–Yugambeh dialect chain, Yaygirr, Gumbaynggirr, Dhanggati, Gathang (Birrbay, Warrimay and Guringay), Hunter River and Lake Macquarie Language (Awabakal–Wanarruwa), and Darkinyung. Language revitalisation refers to situations in which the language is no longer being fully passed down from one generation to the next. While this applies to all the languages of this region, there are some situations in which individual speakers are passing on their language knowledge.

Muurrbay–MRALC provides technical, linguistic and administrative support for many community initiated language projects. We work closely with Aboriginal people from the Tweed to the Hawkesbury River including Elders, language teachers, professionals, language workers and linguistic students and anyone interested in their language. MRALC has particularly strong links with several organisations having worked closely with them to publish grammar–dictionaries or run community-based language programs; Dhanggati and Darkinyung Language Groups; Bundjalung, Guiwan (Taree) and Ulugundahi (Yaygirr) Elders groups; Thunghutti Tiddas Aboriginal Corporation; Ngarralinyi Radio and Wonnarua Nation Aboriginal Corporation.

MRALC researched the meanings of Yaygirr/Yaegl placenames in the Lower Clarence for an Indigenous signage project, in collaboration with Yaegl Elders, North Coast Institute of Technical and Further Education (TAFE), Clarence Valley Council and the North Coast Computer Project. According to Bernie Francis, the coordinator of the North Coast Computer Project, this 'has breathed new life into our community and regenerated interest for the importance of this community's language program. The first village sign of *Illarwill* [black duck] is already up with others soon to follow!' (pers. comm., 19 March 2009). We have also supported a Dhanggati group to produce illustrated language teaching resources, and are currently supporting a Bundjalung group to record an Elder.

Our main activities include:

- research; compiling written and audio archival records; documenting knowledge of Elders and analysing grammar
- producing grammars and dictionaries through extensive community consultation, for example several community-based language groups have been formed that advise projects and hold copyright of published works
- developing language learning resources and courses for adults and supporting school programs.

Aboriginal Elders, teachers and linguists speak up

Bundjalung Elder and language speaker, Uncle Charles Moran has acknowledged that language centres can be useful:

> I am writing in support of the Muurrbay Language Centre who I have had dealings with. Being a language speaker from the Bundjalung Nation I am very aware just how important it is to teach our Indigenous language in schools and communities. (pers. comm., 16 February 2009)

Uncle Charles stresses the importance of young people learning to pronounce language properly:

> Bugal mulligan – good morning. Jingeewahla wutha behanye – how are you today? Nganyah nyarry Charles Moran. Ngay Bundjalung barry – I am Bundjalung fellow, from the far North Coast of New South Wales. I grew up learning language from two old tribal brothers who hardly spoke English. When they conversed with each other it was only language they spoke, and I was privileged enough to have them teach me. Because I spent time with them they taught me about culture, language and bush skills. These two old brothers were custodians of the Clarence River and the Rocky River at Tabulam. I find language and culture go together, it gives me great pride to be able to speak my language and understand it. It also makes me feel proud to be Aboriginal ... I also find a lot of people speak language but can't pronounce the words properly around here. I would like to see language taught in schools where there maybe teachers come out of it. I think language would give young people something to be proud of, give them an identity, maybe teach them to respect themselves and to respect others. (pers. comm., 16 February 2009)

Uncle Charles also points out that, at times, teaching language has been a problem 'because some linguists don't understand the significance of the language' (pers. comm., 16 February 2009). In the past Bundjalung was taught off country and some Elders disagreed with this. If linguists are operating within an Aboriginal organisation and under the direction of an Aboriginal board or committee, then these sorts of incidents will be avoided. This is reinforced by Diana Eades who recorded Uncle Harry Buchanan speaking Gumbaynggirr in the 1970s: 'The model of Aboriginal leadership and ownership of the languages and cultures of the region, combined with collaboration with non-Aboriginal experts in language and education, is producing outstanding publications and educational programs.' (pers. comm., 12 February 2009). Muurrbay–MRALC is directed by the Muurrbay board which has 23 years experience in language revitalisation.

Several people have acknowledged the role of Muurrbay–MRALC in providing communities with access to well-qualified and experienced staff, namely language workers–researchers, teacher–linguists and ICT experts. Wanarruwa man, Rob Lester states that 'MRALC assists organisations such as ours with the expertise of specialist staff in our journey to revive our language of the Hunter Valley Region ... [it] is invaluable to our communities' (pers. comm., 10 February 2006). Jeremy and Tracy Saunders of the Biripi–Gathang language group emphasise that it is about the language centre supporting community aspirations:

> Muurrbay has provided an invaluable service to the Biripi Nation. Their professionalism and assistance helping us reconstruct our language was amazing, and their continued support and assistance is very much appreciated. Money cannot buy what Muurrbay has given the people of the Biripi Nation. (pers. comm., 10 February 2009)

Deb Brown, then secretary of the Thunghutti Tiddas Aboriginal Corporation, acknowledges that it is also about language centre staff respecting Elders' essential and valuable role in any language work: 'Your willingness to travel to our community to discuss our needs and your preparedness to consult with Elders as intellectuals in the field has been very encouraging and has assisted the promotion of Dhanggati culture for our young people' (pers. comm., 15 February 2006). Dhanggati man Ray Kelly has worked on several projects with MRALC:

> The language centre has assisted in administering a small grant, but more importantly in supporting my language education and in beginning a dialogue about language and how it is used. I am developing my own insights about Dhanggati language that may be of interest to other people. When I first started working on language it seemed such a difficult task when there is so much anxiety in the community. I realised that we can approach language work with good faith and as much research as possible. Now I look forward to an ongoing dialogue about the usefulness and value of Aboriginal languages: how we can use them to make sense of where we are today. (pers. comm., 19 February 2009)

Muurrbay–MRALC advises various organisations including local Aboriginal land councils, schools, TAFEs and universities, NSW Department of Environment and Climate Change, NSW Aboriginal Languages Research and Resource Centre, NSW DAA, local councils, the Office of the Board of Studies NSW and NSW Department of Education and Training (DET). Representatives from government organisations and consultant linguists acknowledge the role played by language centres. Mari Rhydwen is the Aboriginal languages consultant based at the Curriculum K–12 Directorate of the NSW DET since 2005. Her job is to support Aboriginal language programs in NSW schools and she has found benefits in collaborating with language centres such as Muurrbay–MRALC:

> Developing and supporting school programs for Aboriginal languages is a painstaking and challenging task. Unlike other language programs that draw on a substantial range of published resources like textbooks, dictionaries and computer software to use in the classroom, teachers in Aboriginal language classrooms must produce their own. During the year, staff at Many Rivers–Muurrbay have continued to develop teaching resources for Gumbaynggirr as well as advising on resources for other language groups … It is clear that working

with linguists at Muurrbay has enhanced the skills of [Aboriginal language] teachers. This was particularly evident at the Nambucca workshop where a team from Muurrbay, including [Anna Ash] and Julie Long gave a presentation. This included bringing a bus full of children so that Michael Jarrett could do a demonstration class as well as organising for the school principal to participate. In addition the presentation by the Bellbrook Thunghutti Tiddas, in conjunction with Amanda Lissarrague, made very clear the contribution linguists can make. In addition you arranged for Gary Williams to provide a Welcome to Country ... The ongoing work on Bundjalung, Dhanggati, Gathang, HRLM and Wonnarua, Darkinyung and Yaygirr by Many Rivers linguists makes a vital contribution to the school language programs. (pers. comm., 30 November 2005)

Teacher–linguist Andrew Ingram writes that the existence of a language centre enables him to work on language revitalisation in northern NSW:

While work in the field of language revitalisation can be a personally and professionally rich and rewarding experience, it is a daunting prospect for the individual. Many of the factors that make it so can be minimised through the assistance of a well-run language/cultural centre. One of the main issues facing the language worker is sourcing of sufficient funding – for wages for all involved in the project, for equipment, and for developing resources. Funding from a language centre for revitalisation projects can either be direct, where the centre itself provides funds, or indirect, where the language centre assists in applying for funding and auspices a particular community-based project. Language centres also play a strategic role in the language worker developing relationships with community, in terms of introductions to key community members. They are also a good way for communities to access appropriate language workers. Language centres also provide much needed logistical support, organising meetings, workshops and other group activities, allowing the language worker to concentrate on their immediate tasks. They also provide access to library resources, recording equipment, and sometimes access to the publishing process. (pers. comm., 17 March 2005)

Elder Poppy Harry Walker works with teacher Sharon Tucker on the Bundjalung Language Program at Bonalbo Central School. Sharon acknowledges the support that language centres can give a school program:

Muurrbay–MRALC have been crucial to our introduction of Bundjalung as our Year 7 LOTE subject. We have relied on the staff for advice and guidance on orthography, lesson development and community consultation; this needs to be ongoing for us. Muurrbay is also involved in a community language project with our Elder, Poppy Harry Walker, which not only is revitalising the Western Bundjalung language but also is providing the resource basis for our school language program. (pers. comm., 19 March 2009)

The role of language centres in collaborating with many organisations is emphasised by university lecturer Caroline Jones, 'Muurrbay and MRALC ... [have] a wealth of staff talent and commitment, effectively supporting community groups, productively collaborating with government, universities, TAFE and schools, and consistently delivering high quality teaching and landmark teaching resources and reference material.' (pers. comm., 11 February 2009).

Publishing language materials

Muurrbay–MRALC began by focusing on language research and over the last three years has published many language resources including grammar–dictionaries, teaching resources and short stories. Researchers make use of ICT such as Transcriber[3] (for listening to and transcribing CDs), Toolbox[4] (for analysing data, interlinearising and making dictionaries) and Audiamus[5] (for compiling audio CDs together into a library or corpus). It is important that communities have good access to research results and a percentage of all books are distributed free of charge. The books are carefully researched and reviewed with extensive community consultation undertaken before we progress to publication. Desktop publication using Adobe InDesign ensures good quality publications which reinforce the status of these languages and encourage positive attitudes in the general public. Muurrbay–MRALC has produced grammar–dictionaries for the languages from the Hunter River and Lake Macquarie, Darkinyung, Dhanggati, and Gumbaynggirr, with Gathang and Yaygirr to come next. All languages change all the time. After seven years a second edition of the Gumbaynggirr dictionary was published which reflected all the work that had been done since the first, including a slight change in the spelling system, more information about the way the language works – its grammar – and information about new words that had been created to talk about things to do with many areas of modern day life, including office and household goods.

Language centres throughout Australia play an important role in distributing draft documents and publishing language resources. Researcher and author Jim Wafer notes of Muurrbay–MRALC:

> Their brief covers an enormous area, from the Hawkesbury to the Queensland border, and for this region they carry out community consultation, language teaching, research and publication. My interest is particularly in their publication record: four highly professional dictionary/grammars, six books of teaching resources, and a state-wide guide to the languages of NSW, all over a period of about four years. (pers. comm., 20 March 2009)

The authors of *A handbook of Aboriginal languages of NSW and the ACT* approached Muurrbay to publish this excellent resource, as they wanted an experienced Aboriginal publisher and copyright holder and for any profits to go back into language

---

3 See trans.sourceforge.net/

4 See www.sil.org/computing/toolbox/

5 See www.linguistics.unimelb.edu.au/thieberger/audiamus.htm

revitalisation. Several teaching resources have been published including the *Barriyala: Let's Work, Gumbaynggirr Language Student Workbooks* and *Mayalambala: Let's Move It*, a poster-based teaching resource. These teaching resources have been created so that they will be useful for more than one language. *Barriyala* is available electronically in Microsoft Word so other language groups can adapt and use it. *Mayalambala* is based on pictures, so can be used for any language. Story books for children such as *Dulaybam Dunggiir* and *Bamay Possum's Party* are also valuable for children.

Language teaching and other activities

Language learners have varying needs. Muurrbay delivers full-time Certificate II and IV Gumbaynggirr language courses. Other courses have been delivered more informally for those who just want to pick up some lingo and pass it on to their family and friends.

Administrative staff have supported community-based language projects by administering small grants from DAA. In 2005–06 we hosted two regional language conferences that raised a lot of interest in language revitalisation and allowed people to share ideas, get inspired and get started. Since then we have focused on research and delivering workshops for specific languages so that people can learn more about sounds, spelling and grammar, and have input into the research. Language staff have the knowledge and cultural awareness to provide language advice to Aboriginal people in general, as well as those studying language teaching and linguistics. We receive many requests for language advice from Aboriginal people and organisations that are using language in many areas, including educational, ceremonial and in the workplace. We advise on:

- translating speeches such as a Welcome to Country, acknowledging country and Elders, as well as songs, prayers and eulogies
- translations for signage (places, houses and buildings, such as TAFE colleges and medical centres), naming babies and events
- teaching resources and ideas; advice on selecting words when there is more than one word to choose from for any given thing, providing CD recordings that can be used as pronunciation guides, sample lesson plans, teaching activities and worksheets.

Language revitalisation 'three step'

This is a formula that has worked for us in the Many Rivers Region, so it may be worth considering if your group is just starting out.

Step one: language resources

Find out everything that is known about your language:

- Record speakers

- Collect all written records, old wordlists, placenames and grammars
- Collect all language recordings.

Step two: language analysis

Analyse your materials to find out how your language works. You will need people with training in linguistics to do this. Linguists and language researchers should be able to assist.

- Sounds and spelling: work out the sounds of your language and a standard way to spell them. Aboriginal languages and English have some similar sounds such as a, i, u, m, n, l, w, y. Other sounds are quite different, for example most Aboriginal languages have an 'rr' like Scottish Robby Burns (trill/flap), allow 'ng' to start a word, and don't always need to distinguish between pairs like b/p, t/d and k/g in the spelling
- Language is more than just lists of words. So how do we put words together so that we can talk in sentences? This is the grammar or rules of the language. The grammar of Aboriginal languages is very different from English. We want to remain true to the language; we don't want to be influenced by English.

Here is a Gumbaynggirr example showing how to indicate location. English uses a separate word – a preposition of location, such as in, at and on to show where something is positioned, while Aboriginal languages use a *tag ending* or suffix.

> *nguraa-la*
>
> house-in
>
> in the house

Another Gumbaynggirr example shows that word order is used differently:

> *marlamgarl-u*　　*yiinyjan*　　*jumbaal*
>
> dingo-ERG　　bite-PAST　　python
>
> The dingo bit the python.

This same meaning can be shown with a different word order:

> *jumbaal*　　*yiinyjang*　　*marlamgarl-u*
>
> python　　bite-PAST　　dingo-ERG
>
> The dingo bit the python.

Following analysis which utilises software such as Transcriber and Toolbox, and extensive checking, a wordlist or dictionary and grammar can be produced.

Step three: learning language and developing teaching resources

Once the basic language resources of dictionary and grammar have been produced the focus is then for community members to learn more language so they can teach kids in school, community classes, TAFE and at home. Classes can be informal or TAFE-accredited but, in either case, time needs to be spent designing them. Along the way various teaching resources can be developed such as a learner's guide to help explain the grammar, songs, tapes, computer-based resources, games, story books and comics.

You gotta start somewhere

Muurrbay Chairperson, Ken Walker was interviewed for a DVD, *It's a Hard Road to Hoe but You Gotta Start Somewhere: Designing a Community Language Project*. Ken provides advice on all aspects of language revitalisation, from setting up a language program to finding funds, staying with the language and reaping the rewards:

> The benefit of that [research] now, all that process we went through, is shown in the children we teach and in the adults we teach, because it gives them a sense of pride, and esteem in their self and their culture and their language that never existed before. Work for language is never ending, it's always going on, there's something new happening all the time. You've got to modify and move with the times. You've got to be flexible in your language use, so it's a continuous thing … Muurrbay or places like it will never really die out if the people don't want it to. It's a hard road to hoe, but you gotta start somewhere, and don't expect miracles first up. It doesn't work. We started in '85 and we're still going, we're still learning. Don't give up, don't lose heart because the rewards at the end are beneficial for you and your community. (NSW Board of Adult & Community Education, 2006).

References

Ash A, Fermino J & Hale K (2001). Diversity in local language maintenance and restoration: a reason for optimism. In L Hinton & K Hale (Eds). *The green book of language revitalization in practice* (pp. 19–35). San Diego: Academic Press.

Australian Institute of Aboriginal & Torres Strait Islander Studies (2005). *National Indigenous Languages survey report 2005*. Canberra: Department of Communications, Information Technology and the Arts.

Jones C (2008). *Darkinyung grammar and dictionary: revitalising a language from historical sources*. Nambucca Heads, NSW: Muurrbay.

Lissarrague A (2006). *A salvage grammar and wordlist of the language from the Hunter River and Lake Macquarie*. Nambucca Heads, NSW: Muurrbay.

Lissarrague A (2007). *Dhanggati grammar and dictionary with Dhanggati stories*. Nambucca Heads, NSW: Muurrbay.

Lissarrague A (forthcoming). *A grammar and dictionary of Gathang: the language of the Birrbay, Guringay and Warrimay*. Nambucca Heads, NSW: Muurrbay.

Long J (2007). *Barriyala: let's work. Gumbaynggirr language student workbooks 1–3*. Nambucca Heads, NSW: Muurrbay.

Morelli S (2008). *Gumbaynggirr bijaarr jandaygam, Ngaawa gugarrigam: Gumbaynggirr dictionary & learner's grammar*. Nambucca Heads, NSW: Muurrbay.

Morelli S (forthcoming). Yaygirr dictionary and learner's grammar. Nambucca Heads, NSW: Muurrbay.

Muurrbay Aboriginal Language & Cultural Co-op (1994). *Bamay Possum's party*. Sherwood, NSW: Muurrbay.

Muurrbay Aboriginal Language & Cultural Co-op (2001). *A Gumbaynggirr language dictionary: Gumbaynggirr bijaarr jandaygam*. Canberra: Australian Institute of Aboriginal & Torres Strait Islander Studies.

Muurrbay Aboriginal Language & Cultural Co-op (2006). *Dulaybam Dunggiirr: Grey-faced Wallaby and Koala. A Gumbaynggirr Dreaming story told by Phillip Shannon*. Victoria, BC: Trafford First Voices.

Muurrbay Aboriginal Language & Cultural Co-op (2006). *Mayalambala: let's move it. Teaching resource and user's guide*. Nambucca Heads, NSW: Muurrbay.

NSW Board of Adult & Community Education (2006). *It's a hard road to hoe but you gotta start somewhere: designing a community language project*. Sydney: NSW Board of Adult & Community Education.

Palmer K (Ed) (2000). *Strong language, strong culture: New South Wales strategic language study. final report and strategy action plan* [compiled by DF Hosking, TJ Lonsdale, JF Troy & MJ Walsh]. Canberra: Australian Institute for Aboriginal & Torres Strait Islander Studies.

Wafer J & Lissarrague A (2008). *A handbook of the Aboriginal languages of New South Wales and the Australian Capital Territory*. Nambucca Heads, NSW: Muurrbay.

10
Language centre as language revitalisation strategy: a case study from the Pilbara

Sally Dixon and Eleonora Deak[1]

Abstract

Community language centres are a significant feature of the language revitalisation landscape in Australia. In the early imaginings of community groups and language policy planners alike, language centres had vast potential to direct and coordinate language revitalisation efforts on a number of fronts. Over time language centres have evolved a very specific set of functions that constitute their language revitalisation process. This paper will examine several case studies that demonstrate the variety of approaches employed by Wangka Maya Pilbara Aboriginal Language Centre to respond to the different language situations in its region. Common elements emerge across the case studies such as the provision of specialists, training of language workers, coordination of resource production, and maintenance of an accessible archive. These elements form the core of the language centre's own language revitalisation strategy, and determine the nature of the language centre's enduring role within a larger network of partners in the language revitalisation challenge.

Language centres first began to emerge in Australia in the mid-1980s as communities started recognising the need for a coordinated intervention in their radically changing language ecologies. The first centres were grass-roots projects, sometimes involving strategic collaboration with key outsiders such as linguists, language professionals or teachers. Wangka Maya Pilbara Aboriginal Language Centre (Wangka Maya) was one such organisation.

This was also a time of a national linguistic awakening on behalf of the Australian government, following the establishment of both bilingual schooling and the School

---

1 Both authors are from Wangka Maya Pilbara Aboriginal Language Centre.

of Australian Linguistics (now the Centre for Australian Languages and Linguistics at Batchelor Institute of Indigenous Tertiary Education [BIITE]) in the Northern Territory. Australia's Indigenous languages were a key focus of the first national language policy adopted in 1987 (House of Representatives Standing Committee of Aboriginal and Torres Strait Islander Affairs [HRSCATSIA] 1992). This was the first time that the right of Aboriginal people to have equal access to their traditional languages in a range of settings was recognised in federal government policy. Central to this policy was the sustained federal support of regional language centres, as it was recognised quite early on that a language landscape as diverse and rich as Australia's would require a response largely coordinated from the regions. Thus the number of language centres around the country expanded quickly in the following years with the support of federal government funding.

Numerous policy documents, submissions and reviews outlined an ambitious number of roles that language centres were thought to be in an advantageous position to perform (for a good summary see HRSCATSIA 1992). These centred around four main areas. Firstly, providing support for language programs in the schools from initial advocacy on behalf of communities through to providing curriculum support, teacher training and making resources. Secondly, providing support for work on Aboriginal languages at the community level, including employment and training of language speakers, strategic planning, provision of specialists, archive maintenance, and acting as a production centre. Thirdly, continuing the research and documentation of Aboriginal languages via the coordination and management of linguists. And, fourthly, providing coordinated administrative support to the region including the training and development of administrative capacity in other organisations.

For those of us who work in or directly with language centres, at least some of these activities are now common practice and may seem self-evident. But this is quite a broad charter and language centres have never really been funded to achieve all of these objectives. This perhaps explains why language centres currently differ from each other in terms of their main language revitalisation activities. For example the Diwurruwurru-jaru language centre in Katherine has always been instrumental in the coordination of language classes in primary schools, whereas Wangka Maya has largely left this to the education department and instead supported schools through the development of school-appropriate learning materials.

This volume presents a good opportunity for us to reflect on the evolution of the role of language centres in the language revitalisation challenge. We have decided to take a case-study approach outlining a variety of language revitalisation projects. We then examine the common themes running through each of the case studies to highlight the key features of Wangka Maya's underlying strategy. By doing so we hope to highlight how the initially broad range of expectations for language centres have been refined into a continually viable model of language revitalisation.

Ngambunyjarri: Thalanyji plant names and uses

Thalanyji, the traditional language of the Onslow area, would now be categorised as a severely endangered language on the indicators (Australian Institute of Aboriginal & Torres Strait Islander Studies 2005, p. 125). The language is used fluently by six old people while, among the parent generation, there are varying degrees of use, fluency and comprehension. Children are not learning it as their first language but they are sometimes exposed to Thalanyji when they are with their parents or grandparents. Work to document, promote and learn this language has taken various forms over the past 15 or so years: schools programs, formal training programs for language workers (via the Pundulmarra Technical and Further Education campus in South Hedland), recording of oral histories, and the production of various children's resources. The primary linguistic fieldwork was carried out by Peter Austin and included the publication of the first Thalanyji dictionary (1992b).

In recent years two very dedicated language workers, Anne and Shirley Hayes, have been working in partnership with Wangka Maya to document Thalanyji and increase their own knowledge of the language. In late 2005 they approached Wangka Maya with an idea to create an ethnobotanical plant book that would showcase both the depth of traditional knowledge surrounding plant use and the Thalanyji language as the vehicle for transmitting this knowledge. Since there were few full speakers left the need to document this knowledge was felt to be a matter of considerable urgency.

The language workers coordinated all of the documentation of language and traditional knowledge on this project. They spent many hours listening to the Elders talk about the plants in Thalanyji and using the language to elicit specific information. As a result they demonstrated enormous growth as language speakers and writers over the course of the project. By the time the book was launched in July 2008, one language worker who was renowned for her shyness in front of crowds of strangers (in any language) had the confidence to get up at the launch and give part of her speech in Thalanyji. There is also much anecdotal evidence that this increase in Thalanyji language use has spread throughout the community, including among children. Likewise the writing skills of the language workers have increased dramatically with the consistent practice the project afforded.

The language workers and their native title representative body, Buurabalayji-Thalanyji Association, used their royalties from BHP Billiton to fund the publication of the book. The Association also provided logistical support and additional support personnel for the duration of the project. Wangka Maya provided the support of a linguist to help with writing down the language and collating and structuring the information. The linguist also trained the team on the use of various types of recording equipment and methodology, and facilitated access to botanical specialists who helped with plant identification. Wangka Maya also managed the production of the book and took it through the editing, layout, graphic design and printing phases.

The final product, *Ngambunyjarri* (Hayes & Hayes 2008), is a high-quality publication, well placed to showcase the Thalanyji language and traditional knowledge, and guarantee that this knowledge will be available for subsequent generations of Thalanyji people. For many the book has created a sense of pride in Thalanyji language and culture, not only among the Thalanyji people, but also in the broader community. This positive atmosphere will hopefully pave the way for many more future activities to promote the Thalanyji language.

Ngarluma Language Project

Ngarluma is the language of the traditional owners of the coastal Pilbara region, which encompasses the towns of Roebourne and Karratha, and extends inland to the Millstream-Chichester National Park. On the NILS indicators it would be classified as severely endangered, with the approximately 20 full speakers belonging to the grandparental and older adult generations, and varying use throughout the adult and child age groups. There has also been considerable shift towards another dominant Aboriginal language, Yindjibarndi. Over the past century there have been varied and discontinuous efforts to document the language (from wordlists collected by early European settlers, to the fieldwork of linguists Kenneth Hale and Carl von Brandenstein), but only a few projects that were directly aimed at revitalising the language.

The Ngarluma Language Project arose directly out of a renewed interest at the community level in promoting Ngarluma language and culture. A partnership was formed between Wangka Maya and the Ngarluma native title representative body, which was keen to put some staff and resources towards language and culture initiatives. Thus a language team emerged and work began on several different smaller projects, all with the main aim of increasing the amount of Ngarluma used in the community, especially with and among children.

These projects included more traditional language materials such as a dictionary, children's picture dictionary, and sketch grammar. These were deemed important resources in the long term for many people in the community who would hopefully want to learn the language. In addition it was felt that they could form the building blocks of more text-based resources, such as a learners' grammar, which would be needed if Ngarluma were to be eventually taught in the school.

The team's main focus, however, was on the production of resources that would showcase and promote spoken language. So they developed a range of short films and language-learning DVDs based on day trips around Ngarluma country. The results ranged from short film bites that were posted on YouTube and swapped on mobile phones, to short films (on fishing, bush tucker, kinship, and local sites) that were distributed on DVD throughout the community. Film was deemed an excellent vehicle for the Ngarluma community for several reasons:

- it is extremely accessible with most households having a TV, DVD player and mobile phones

- DVDs are a highly valued and traded commodity in the community
- spoken language could be promoted (as well as written via the use of subtitles)
- local kids found the DVD and mobile phone formats familiar and engaging.

The Ngarluma team's success is an exceptional example of a community-driven language project largely founded on their access to and utilisation of the full range of skills and resources at their disposal. For example, media editing skills were provided by a local Ngarluma man who was employed by the native title representative group and seconded to the language project; film equipment was sourced by utilising the representative body's mining connections; and the representative body itself provided a comfortable and welcoming space in which to work as well as access to extra vehicles.

What role was left for the language centre? Wangka Maya provided a linguist throughout the project who helped in several important ways. The linguist coordinated the dictionary and sketch grammar work, which was essential to the team's long-term goals of greater adult learning and inclusion of the language in local schools. The linguist also provided ongoing training in the standard orthography and transcription, and helped structure the language learning components of film resources. Wangka Maya had several templates for language resources, and access to production facilities that allowed resources such as the picture dictionary and 100 Words in Ngarluma DVD (see below) to be made with relative ease and at no expense to the language team.

As the work progressed Wangka Maya agreed to apply for and received funding on behalf of the team. This allowed the team to access funding that otherwise probably wouldn't have been extended to a 'new' group. The language centre's national network of contacts also allowed the team to tap into the exciting new work being done on mobile phone dictionaries (see Wilson, this volume) and the Ngarluma mobile phone dictionary is now in prototype form.

Ngajumili muwarr wanikinyarni partanyja wirtujatinyankanu mirtanyajartinyi: my life story

Nyangumarta is one of the strongest languages of the Pilbara with several hundred speakers, including children who are learning it as their first language at home. It probably approaches the 'safe' degree of endangerment on the NILS indicators. Nyangumarta is commonly spoken in Port Hedland as both a first language and an Aboriginal lingua franca. It also has prestige in the non-Indigenous community and there are regular requests for Wangka Maya to run Nyangumarta courses.

For a number of years there has been considerable support for Nyangumarta within the local government and independent school system. The Strelley Literacy Centre at the independent bilingual school in the Strelley community produced storybooks, encyclopedic books, audiotapes and some videos in the Nyangumarta language. More recently Nyangumarta has been taught at three local primary schools. Considerable documentation has been undertaken by teacher–linguists and through the auspices of the Summer Institute of Linguistics' bible translation work.

William (Nyaparu) Gardiner first approached Wangka Maya wanting to record his life-story (Gardiner 2006). A Wangka Maya linguist recorded him yarning about his life, and he transcribed the recordings himself. A talented artist, Gardiner drew a series of ink illustrations depicting various episodes in his life. A Wangka Maya Nyangumarta language worker translated the stories into English. He then worked together with the language worker and a linguist to structure the book, which was published and launched in May 2006 as one of the activities in the 1946 Pilbara Pastoral Workers' Strike 60th anniversary.

Gardiner is a strong believer in the importance of literacy in maintaining language and knowledge. He takes pride in his own literacy skills, which he learned first through schooling in English and later transferred to Nyangumarta and several other Pilbara languages. Writing down his stories was an opportunity for him to maintain his Nyangumarta literacy skills as well as giving other Nyangumarta speakers something to read and maintain theirs. As it is a relatively strong language Wangka Maya agreed that there would be a demand for developing a higher level of written literature in Nyangumarta and that it would build on the resources already available for children.

In fact this outcome was also achieved through the process that was used to make the book, as the interaction between Gardiner and the much younger language worker gave the language worker an opportunity to use her own Nyangumarta language skills. This process gave her a deeper knowledge of the idiosyncratic variation possible within her language, as well as some of the differences between Nyangumarta and English and the challenges this poses for translation.

Hundred words in ... DVD series

One of the most common requests to the language centre is for resources that will help people pronounce words in Pilbara languages. In response to this Wangka Maya decided to embark on producing some new audio resources to complement our dictionary and text-based productions. DVD was chosen as the format as it allowed the simultaneous presentation of written word, spoken word and image.

Eight languages were chosen to represent a spread of Pilbara language families and levels of endangerment. These languages were also chosen because in most cases there was some language work happening in the Pilbara at the time (for example the Ngarluma Language Project above), so there was the added value of supporting existing activities. The centre then picked 100 words covering a range of semantic domains and word classes, as well as some useful phrases. A Wangka Maya language worker used the centre's dictionary databases to translate the list into each of the eight languages. Language workers and linguists worked with speakers to check the lists and record them being spoken clearly. The images were sourced from the image archive and supplemented by a few new photographs. The Wangka Maya media trainee created the DVD template into which the audio and text for each language was added.

The result is a resource that can be used both by language speakers who want to teach their children or improve their own skills, and by non-Indigenous people who are interested in learning some language.

Payungu picture dictionary

Bayungu[2] is no longer a fully spoken language, although many people use partial Bayungu alongside their English. It is the traditional language belonging to the coastal country between Carnarvon and Exmouth. There has been relatively substantial documentation of the language, mainly by linguists Geoffrey O'Grady (for example O'Grady 1967) and Peter Austin (for example Austin 1978) when the old people were still alive in the 1960s and 70s. Peter Austin helped develop a Bayungu program for Carnarvon Senior High School which was used during the 1980s, and in 1992 he published a dictionary for Bayungu (Austin 1992a). Since that time Wangka Maya has produced a fuller Bayungu dictionary and a sketch grammar (Wangka Maya PALC 2007; 2008).

The development of the Payungu Picture Dictionary (Wangka Maya Pilbara Aboriginal Language Centre 2006) is primarily the story of one Wangka Maya language worker. She is a Bayungu woman herself and is comfortable with speaking and understanding basic Bayungu. When she first approached Wangka Maya for work and training she explained that her primary goal was to create tangible resources for learning the language. These resources would help her improve her own skills in Bayungu, and prompt other adults to do the same. More importantly the resources would allow future generations to have access to their heritage and, in the short term, they would help her teach her own children some Bayungu. A picture dictionary and accompanying audio CD was seen very much as a first step along this path.

The language worker used a picture dictionary that was created by Wangka Maya for another language as a template for her own work. She tapped into the Certificate in Aboriginal Language Work at Pundulmurra College, and supplemented this with the ongoing support of Wangka Maya linguists and language workers to develop her language description and documentation skills. Because the Wangka Maya archive contained the field recordings made by O'Grady and Austin with her family members, she immediately set to work listening to and transcribing these recordings.

As there were no longer speakers with whom to check the material, these recordings and the existing dictionary formed the basis of the picture dictionary. Listening to recordings also proved a useful way to get in touch with the language and dramatically improved the language worker's vocabulary and confidence in constructing a variety of basic sentences. Wangka Maya colleagues provided support in developing a range of auxiliary skills such as the use of a variety of recording equipment and computers.

---

2 Since publication of the *Payungu Picture Dictionary*, the Bayungu people have elected to change the orthography so the sound that was previously written as p is now written as b.

Even before the *Payungu Picture Dictionary* and accompanying audio CD were launched there was growing interest among Bayungu people in the finished product, and Wangka Maya fielded many requests for copies. At the launch many Bayungu people expressed their desire to improve their language skills. The language worker has gone on in subsequent years to produce many additional resources for the language including an information booklet on Bayungu lifestyle and culture, and a phrasebook. She has completed both the Certificate and Advanced Certificate in Aboriginal Language Work at Pundulmurra College and is currently enrolled in the Bachelor of Arts (Language and Linguistics) at BIITE in the Northern Territory.

Common themes and the revitalisation process

The case studies presented above demonstrate some of the wide variety of activities in which Wangka Maya has been involved, from language documentation and dictionary making, to publishing adult literature and multimedia learners' materials that focus on the spoken language. This variety results from the fact that every language situation is different. The case studies, therefore, also demonstrate that language centres are well placed to respond to language situations ranging across the spectrum of language endangerment indicators. Yet, despite the obvious differences among the language situations described in the cases studies, there were several common threads running throughout. These threads, woven together, constitute the Wangka Maya language revitalisation strategy.

Firstly, we identify what our role will be in revitalising a language through a process of consultation. Language centres can either lead projects or take a supporting role, depending on what is appropriate for the situation. Sometimes it is appropriate for Wangka Maya to directly lead projects and this is usually the case for projects aimed at indirectly promoting language revitalisation. An example of this was given in the '100 words in ... ' case study. The desire of non-Indigenous people (such as teachers, nurses and other community workers) to learn a Pilbara language was recognised as having the potential for positive flow-on effects throughout the community, in terms of improved provision of key services (especially in the health and education spheres), as well as increased awareness of Indigenous people's language rights. Both outcomes increase the prestige of Pilbara Aboriginal languages and create space within the broader community for language revitalisation to occur. The project achieved the additional and compatible outcome of producing an excellent resource for the revitalisation of each language by the speakers themselves.

These kinds of language centre-driven activities are undertaken as opportunities arise and are actually a minor aspect of Wangka Maya's work. Language revitalisation cannot happen without speakers and, as such, we are fundamentally led by language speakers. This means that we develop our work plans to complement interest or activity that is emerging from the community. Furthermore, as an institution, Wangka Maya does not see itself as the controlling force of language work in the Pilbara. As testament to this the centre often works in formal partnerships with other community organisations, such as native title representative groups (shown in the Thalanyji and Ngarluma case studies), schools, colleges (*Payungu Picture Dictionary*) and community councils. Such partnerships allow all parties to make the most out of all the opportunities for resourcing, funding, and community energy that exist in the vibrant Pilbara region. They also ensure that the language community always retains control and ownership of the language revitalisation process.

Fundamental to revitalisation partnerships is deciding what specific support the centre will provide. Some key themes emerge from the case studies in this regard. Probably our most important support work is the employment of individual language speakers with the goal of equipping them to lead the revitalisation of their own language. We use mentoring and careful scaffolding of training that allows language workers to develop a range of core and auxiliary skills (the *Payungu Picture Dictionary* is a good example of this). This approach is based on a sustainability principle that sees the direct transfer of specialist skills into the community as the best way of ensuring long-term value from the language centre's activities. This, in turn, increases the likelihood of language revitalisation at the community level.

The employment of such individuals can be part of a broader community attempt to revitalise a language. It can also arise from the fact that there are some situations where language work is more likely to be performed by individual speakers. These individuals are often unlikely to find the financial means or professional support to work on their language outside of a language centre. William Gardiner's biography demonstrated that the production of adult-level literature in a relatively strong language depends on the interest and commitment of individuals to tell, transcribe and translate their stories. The *Payungu Picture Dictionary* demonstrated how, at the opposite end of the language endangerment spectrum, it takes one person to take the first step in order to inspire others to revitalise a language that is no longer fully spoken.

One of the roles we are most consistently asked to fill is as a provider of specialists to help with different aspects of language revitalisation. So it is fair to say that the strategic use of specialists is central to our language revitalisation strategy. Because Wangka Maya is a long-term, stable entity it has been able to build up a vast network of specialists in various fields. When a new specialist is brought into the network for one project they then become a resource for other language groups. The most commonly requested specialists are linguists, and so Wangka Maya retains several in full-time positions and a large network of contractors. Linguists are typically asked to provide support with a wide range of tasks including orthography training, recording and transcribing language, making dictionaries, training language workers, creating learners' materials, and advising on language revitalisation projects.

Wangka Maya usually suggests to speaker groups that, in addition to providing the specific service requested, linguists should work on documenting, describing and analysing the language. This is especially recommended when a high proportion of the activity on a project easily overlaps with the activities of language research. For example, the recordings made for the Ngarluma language DVDs were later analysed for the production of the dictionary. The linguist made efficient use of the time spent with speakers writing subtitles for the DVDs to ask questions about the language that would also help with its description.

This dovetailing of community-driven activities with more research-oriented work is an important part of Wangka Maya's long-term language revitalisation strategy. It gives added value to each project, providing the basis for more in-depth language resources. For example, sketch grammars were developed by the consulting linguists in the Thalanyji and Ngarluma projects, and these will now form the basis of learners' grammars. Our approach ensures that this vital research work continues and that it does so with the full participation and consent of the speaker community.

Other specialist services in our network include anthropologists, ethno-botanists, media personnel, graphic designers, illustrators and printers. Wangka Maya can provide the human resources management of such personnel and ensure that they work to ethical standards, particularly with respect to intellectual property and copyright of traditional Indigenous knowledge. It is worth highlighting that, because Wangka Maya works across multiple projects all the time, it can support some trainee specialist roles such as media and graphic design officers on a permanent basis. This not only means that all projects can make use of these services in-house and at low cost to each project, it also opens up exciting employment paths to local Indigenous youth.

Related to this, Wangka Maya is also frequently asked to oversee the production of specific resources, something that can be daunting for groups unfamiliar with the publication process. We do this through a combination of our in-house publishing capabilities (which we use to print our dictionaries for example), and external printers for the higher end print and multimedia productions (for example the Thalanyji plant book). This provides cost-effective solutions for the production and distribution of language materials.

Importantly, Wangka Maya serves as a repository for language work done in the region. We can advise groups on archiving materials and standards, and actively reproduce or repatriate to the Pilbara copies of pre-Wangka Maya materials held in other archives. Some Pilbara languages are no longer fully spoken and archival materials are the only substantial records of the language. Speakers of such languages rely on having ready access to archived records for their language work to commence in the first place – this was highlighted in the production of the *Payungu Picture Dictionary*. So, for some language groups, the fact that we maintain an accessible archive is a key step in their language revitalisation process.

The final component of our language revitalisation strategy is good administration. The fact that Wangka Maya is able to manage many different sources of grant funding and its own income-generating enterprises, results in a greater capacity for us to achieve our core business of language revitalisation. Key to the present discussion is that the administration is firstly accountable to the community through its committee structure and, secondly, that it is accessible to the wider community. That is, Wangka Maya is able to provide administrative support for language groups so that they may increase their access to various funding pools. This was illustrated in the Ngarluma project case study.

The language centre as model of language revitalisation

All of the features outlined above constitute the underlying basis of Wangka Maya's own language revitalisation strategy. The centre provides a core set of resources, specialists and facilities, from which speakers – whether individuals or groups – can draw to create language revitalisation projects that suit their particular circumstances. In fact, if we take a broader perspective, the funding of language centres itself constitutes an essential component of any national strategy to promote and revitalise Aboriginal and Torres Strait Islander languages. Hence the reason for the title of this paper: the language centre as language revitalisation strategy. For, even at the most basic level, the very presence of a language centre that is active in the community in a variety of ways (including activities that are additional to their core language work such as running cultural awareness training, or providing graphic design and media services) increases the presence and prestige of Aboriginal cultures and languages. At its very best, as we have attempted to show, the language centre is much greater that the sum of its parts.

Compared to the broad range of expectations that made up the vision of those early language centre pioneers and language policy makers, Wangka Maya has developed a strategy of language revitalisation centred around a smaller set of core functions. These restricted functions have evolved to fit the needs of the Pilbara language ecology and, as such, represent only one strategy in an array of potentially valid approaches (see also Kimberley Language Resource Centre, this volume). All voices need to be heard in the process of re-imagining the role of language centres. What is clear is that no language centre has been able to do it all. We would therefore suggest that the future development of language centres should focus on how each language centre fits in as a strategic partner within each language ecology, and how they empower individual language groups to take charge of their own language revitalisation. By doing so, language centres have the potential to be an enduring and central strategy in Australia's response to the diminishing linguistic diversity of this country.

References

Austin P (1978). *Southern Pilbara fieldnotes: Dargari, Dhalandji, Yinggarda, Bayungu, Burduna, Dyiwarli, Binigura, Dyururu.* Australian Institute of Aboriginal & Torres Strait Islander Studies, MS409.

Austin P (1992a). *A dictionary of Payungu, Western Australia*. Bundoora, Vic.: La Trobe University, Department of Linguistics.

Austin P (1992b). *A dictionary of Thalanyji, Western Australia*. Bundoora, Vic.: La Trobe University, Department of Linguistics.

Australian Institute of Aboriginal & Torres Strait Islander Studies (2005). *National Indigenous Languages Survey report 2005*. Canberra: Department of Communications, Information Technology & the Arts.

Gardiner G (2006). *Ngajumili muwarr wanikinyarni partanyja wirtujatinyankanu mirtanyajartinyi: my life story*. Port Hedland, Western Australia: Wangka Maya Pilbara Aboriginal Language Centre.

Hayes A & Hayes S (2008). *Ngambunyjarri: Thalanyji plant names and uses*. Port Hedland, Western Australia: Wangka Maya Pilbara Aboriginal Language Centre.

House of Representatives Standing Committee of Aboriginal and Torres Strait Islander Affairs (1992). *Language and culture – a matter of survival: report of the Inquiry into Aboriginal and Torres Strait Islander Language Maintenance*. Canberra: Australian Government Publishing Service.

O'Grady G (1967). Unpublished field notes: notebook 8. fieldnotes, Western Australia, Vol 8. Elicitation of miscellaneous words, phrases and sentences in Thalanji, Burduna, Bayungu, Wadjeri, Thargari, Yindjibardi, Bangjima and Marduthunira Australian Institute of Aboriginal & Torres Strait Islander Studies, MS 2024.

Wangka Maya Pilbara Aboriginal Language Centre (2006). *Payungu picture dictionary*. Port Hedland, Western Australia: Wangka Maya Pilbara Aboriginal Language Centre.

Wangka Maya Pilbara Aboriginal Language Centre (2007). *Bayungu dictionary*. Port Hedland, Western Australia: Wangka Maya Pilbara Aboriginal Language Centre.

Wangka Maya Pilbara Aboriginal Language Centre (2008). *Bayungu sketch grammar: an introduction to the structure and use of Bayungu*. Port Hedland, Western Australia: Wangka Maya Pilbara Aboriginal Language Centre.

11
Whose language centre is it anyway?

Kimberley Language Resource Centre

Abstract

Typically regional language centres are referred to in the context of supporting documentation, materials production and school programs, and often employ university-trained linguists and other 'experts' to work on individual languages. Despite many successful projects facilitated by the Kimberley Language Resource Centre, this approach did not result in sustainable revival strategies for Kimberley languages and has not dramatically increased language use. We describe how the organisation has in recent years gathered Aboriginal community perspectives on language revival resulting in a revision of the strategic plan and management model. The organisation's focus is now strongly directed towards community-managed revival with emphasis on promoting pre-school language acquisition. After summarising the reasons for changing direction we refer to the strategies being used to support it. We then go on to discuss how this approach struggles to receive support outside the Aboriginal communities the organisation works with. Grant bodies, particularly government ones, are reliant on Western academic perspectives on maintenance and revival when assessing funding submissions. In neither the organisation's context nor the social context do they accept with equal validity Aboriginal people's perspectives on how to revive their own languages. The Kimberley Language Resource Centre was established under a model of self-governance in the early spirit of self-determination. After briefly describing the operational changes and current strategies we conclude by setting out the difficulties of getting support for Aboriginal self-determined strategies. We do this by asking two questions: (a) whose responsbility is language continuation at the community level and why does the answer, the community, pose a problem for the Kimberley Language Resource Centre? and (b) why are Aboriginal revival strategies seen as less valid than the strategies of Western academia and education?

The aim of this paper is to tell a story. The story covers the beginnings of the organisation, a summary of its operational practices past and present, a summary of its project strategies and finally a discussion about where the Kimberley Language Resource Centre (KLRC) is placed in the fight to continue the Aboriginal languages of the Kimberley, a region of great linguistic diversity. It is not possible in such a short paper to go into great detail about differing academic versus community views on endangered languages work. The KLRC has employed and continues to employ a wide variety of Aboriginal and non-Aboriginal administrative and language staff and consultants. Naturally each comes with their own worldviews and their own opinions on what is best.[1]

However it is important to establish clearly that the the KLRC is an Aboriginal organisation which, under its governance model, is directed not by its staff but by its members and the Board of Directors[2] elected from the membership. Successive boards have taken the advice of its staff, particularly linguists, but in recent years directors have begun to take more into consideration what needs are being talked about at the grass roots level. It is the role of both board and staff to find a resolution to those needs in the overall context of language continuation.[3]

Background to the organisation

Aboriginal activist, anthropologist and linguist Gloria Brennan first put forward the idea of Aboriginal, locally controlled 'institutes of Aboriginal languages' (1979, pp. 52–55). Various Kimberley Aboriginal people and linguists working in the area consulted with Aboriginal groups and organisations about similar ideas. In 1984 funding was

---

1 This paper has been written in standard English by a non-Aboriginal staff member who has worked for the organisation since February 2002, with advice and guidance from Aboriginal colleagues and the 2008–10 Board of Directors. Historical and other information about the organisation is based on project reports and administrative paperwork, for example meeting minutes, government reporting documents, staff reports, strategic and business plans. Verbal and anecdotal evidence which has been documented and email communications are also used. The views set out in this paper are not the views of one person but of Aboriginal peoples from a wide range of language and personal backgrounds. It is the goal of this paper that these views will be listened to respectfully within academic and government contexts.

2 The Board of Directors was previously the Executive Committee. Reference to board and directors refers to both past and present governance.

3 The KLRC uses the term *language continuation* to refer to all strategies language groups in the Kimberley are using to keep their languages alive. The goal of any strategy is to have languages spoken into the future in whatever way is appropriate for a group or community. This term avoids others such as revitalisation, reclamation and maintenance. Categorising a language's vitality can limit the type of language activity proposed. For example, for a language with one remaining fluent speaker documentation is argued to be a priority to preserve the language whereas language nests can be equally appropriate for the community to wake up the language.

received to run a pilot study across the region called the Kimberley Language Support Project. The subsequent report *Keeping Language Strong* (Hudson & McConvell 1985) identified a broad range of issues such as concerns about loss of intergenerational language transmission, concerns about the effect of English on the languages and the need for advocacy to government, as well as ideas on orthographies and resource development. All are still current topics.

The KLRC became the first regional language centre, incorporated in 1985. After 24 years the organisation has cemented its status with Aboriginal people as the peak representative body for languages within the region. It services an area of 422 000 square kilometres with six towns, approximately 50 remote Aboriginal communities and numerous outstations. Aboriginal people form almost 48% of the population, a target group of roughly 16 500 people (Kimberley Development Commission 2009).

The KLRC is governed by an elected board of 12 Aboriginal directors under the recently revised Office for Indigenous Corporation rules. The board, elected at an AGM, is chosen from and accountable to a 200 plus membership representative of the 30 or so languages still spoken in the Kimberley (about a fifth of the remaining national languages). Directors sit on the board for two years.[4] The governance factor has an important role in setting an Aboriginal agenda, as will be discussed below.

Setting the direction

The recommendations from *Keeping Language Strong* are wide-ranging and refer to research, school programs, orthographies, repatriating materials and setting up and staffing an office. Recommendation 19 states, 'community adults and schools jointly shoulder the burden of responsibility for keeping Aboriginal languages strong according to their particular expertise' (Hudson & McConvell 1985, p. 89).

However, despite a summary of the issues precipitating the loss of languages in the community (pp. 35–37), proposals on how schools and the research community can work with Aboriginal people to change attitudes to language (pp. 40–44) and a mention of the importance of speaking to children in languages (p. 59), the report does not provide any specific recommendation on how Aboriginal people could overcome barriers to oral language acquisition in children in their community.

In 1993, internal correspondence to a coordinator from a linguist set out in stages a strategy for languages with less than 100 speakers (KLRC 1993). Stage one proposed to document the languages and make resources 'before it's too late'; stage two to use those resources in language classes, which would lead to stage three, the languages becoming first languages again. There is no timeframe set.

This literacy-based approach to language continuation was reaffirmed in a collection of draft policy documents from 1995. One states the 'KLRC considers it important to undertake research work towards a grammar and a dictionary over the production

---

4 The present board was elected in December 2008.

of other kinds of 'applied' materials' (KLRC 1995, p. 1). There was no indication in these policies how stage three above, languages becoming first languages using language teaching materials, could realistically be achieved. Neither is there mention of strategies to revive spoken language in pre-school children or promote community responsibility for that. Applied materials are noted to be impossible to develop without basic research having been done on the language first, that is a grammar or dictionary.

In 1998 a strategic planning process led to the production of the first *Strategic Plan* (KLRC 2000). The stated aims at that time were:

- Ensure the KLRC has the necessary physical and human resources to achieve its vision
- Advocate on behalf of languages at all levels
- Help keep languages strong by ensuring resources and information are accessible
- Keep language strong by undertaking community-driven projects
- Keep language strong by assisting with passing of language on to children
- Keep language strong by helping adults to learn
- Effectively monitor, evaluate and review the performance of the KLRC.

Even though passing on language to children is an aim, only one objective in the strategic plan refers to oral language. This is a reference to *kōhanga reo*[5] that a coordinator in the early 1990s supported. Linguistic discussion of oral learning programs had taken place but within the context of Western education (compare McConvell 1986).

Aboriginal staff members from that time state the language nests were managed by the community because linguists did not appear to be interested. One language nest in particular was anecdotally successful as the participants, now teenagers, are speaking the language with some fluency. However funding from the Western Australian Department of Education was withdrawn in 2001 and lobbying for ongoing funding by the language groups involved did not succeed. Despite the well-documented success of language nests in New Zealand and Hawai'i, a strategy that might have ensured future language speakers was simply stopped.

Setting the management model

The focus of the pilot study recommendations influenced the organisation's management model, since documentation and resource development relied on university-trained linguists. When a language group or community sent a request to the board the submission for funds invariably included wages for a linguist or other specialist to oversee discrete projects. Over the years a symbiotic relationship was created. Many Aboriginal people, particularly non-literate older generations, believed that language work through the KLRC only had a high status if a non-Aboriginal

---

5 Language nests, a language transmission model developed by the Māori in New Zealand

specialist was involved in the work and it resulted in a grammar, dictionary or other written resource.

One elderly language speaker, when asked to become involved in a bush trip for language learning, stated she did not need to teach the children herself because she had given all her language to the linguist who wrote it down in a big book which the children can learn from (pers. comm., 21 September 2006). This person is literate in her language, but the big book she was referring to is a PhD thesis.

An Aboriginal staff member says she too was completely convinced that if she put energy into helping linguists document the languages of the Elders, her language would continue. As a fluent speaker herself, a discussion never took place about orality and literacy, or that the relevance of the community being the managers of the language nests was that humans acquire first language(s) from what is heard before school and not what is written at school.

Even a previous coordinator of the KLRC was quoted as saying:

> We've been tearing our hair out producing resources ... And the producing doesn't make any difference ... If it was me making the decisions ... I'd be putting all my energy into creating the circumstances for languages to be passed down to children. People keep thinking that we, the center, are going to make languages survive. They don't like hearing, 'You've got to do it yourself!' (Abley 2003, p. 38)

Current situation

Reviewing the direction

Several factors prompted an internal review of the KLRC strategic direction in 2004:

- More and more people were questioning why children were not speaking languages despite all the work that had been done for languages.
- Between 2001 and 2004 a great deal of money for discrete language projects was sourced, but linguists or other project managers could not be found to initiate the unformulated projects.
- The backlog of projects had become overwhelming. A great deal of time was being spent chasing non-Aboriginal support with partial outcomes, for example unfinished resources or written materials unusable by the community.
- The assistant coordinator was promoted to become the first Aboriginal coordinator[6] since the first year of the organisation.

A strategic planning specialist sourced through Indigenous Community Volunteers assisted with the development of a framework but the main review was internally managed. Questionnaires were sent out widely to both Aboriginal and non-Aboriginal people and groups. The board reviewed the *Strategic Plan* (KLRC 2000) identifying areas that were becoming unmanageable, unachievable or were not being met

---

6 This position has since been retitled manager.

operationally. Previous projects were reviewed – particularly the incomplete ones – looking at how they were requested, how they were funded, how they were managed and what problems occurred completing them. Staff and consultants asked straightforward questions at meetings and workshops about what people saw as the issues for their particular language group or community, how they learned or did not learn their languages and what they believed would be the most effective way to revive languages and why.

The aims in the revised *Strategic Plan* (KLRC, 2005) and *Business Plan 2008–11* (KLRC 2008) are:

- Encourage the oral transmission of languages and knowledge
- Advocate for Kimberley Aboriginal languages
- Build capacity in Kimberley communities to own and manage language and knowledge continuation
- Engage in partnerships, develop networks and fundraise.
- Strengthen the effective operations, resourcing and governance of the KLRC.

A comparison with the 2000 aims shows the change in direction to focus strongly on oral language transmission. The 2005 strategic plan still incorporates objectives for facilitating documentation and supporting schools, but the focus of how to meet those objectives is now external rather than internal.

The social context

Broader social issues affecting language continuation that the review made explicit were:

- lack of funds for communities to progress their own goals
- lack of information about theory and practice for possible language continuation strategies
- government intervention and top down management reinforcing disempowerment to change the way things are done in general
- a legacy of the colonial worldview continuing to shape beliefs about language and society and creating a barrier to language use
- inappropriate education curricula and lack of respect for cultural and linguistic values leading people to believe they must choose education in English at the expense of their own languages
- lack of knowledge of the right to maintain linguistic and cultural heritage[7]

---

7 Article 30 of the United Nations Convention on the Rights of the Child states, 'In those States in which ethnic, religious or linguistic minorities or persons of indigenous origin exist, a child belonging to such a minority or who is indigenous shall not be denied the right, in community with other members of his or her group, to enjoy his or her own culture, to profess and practise his or her own religion, or to use his or her own language' (United Nations, 1989).

- social and community issues preventing people becoming involved in language continuation strategies
- negative experiences of research influencing people to believe they have no other choices and thus choosing not to do anything rather than work within a documentation model
- lack of recognition of how language continuation happens naturally, for example cultural and ceremonial activities, nurturing of children through language(s) when they are very young, language use during natural resource management (NRM) activities.

Social issues cannot be solved by the KLRC, but they need to be accounted for. Two linguists on separate occasions have told staff that many linguists will not work in Australia because they do not want to be involved in the social and political issues which accompany documentation work in northern areas. Both stated that graduates go to the Pacific in particular where they are 'appreciated' more than in this country (pers. comm. May 2007 & 2 September 2008). The KLRC does not see how it can fix this situation but it can work with the Aboriginal people who live with these problems daily to help them create space for language continuation in their communities.

Reviewing the management model

The results of this review led to the development of a new project management model (Figure 1).

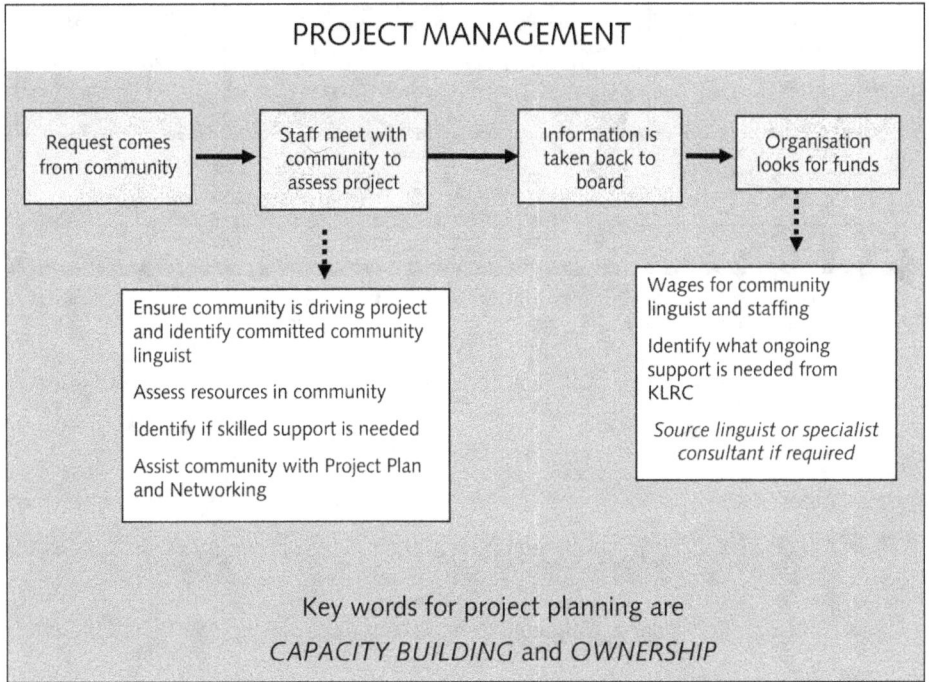

Figure 1. Project management model.

The language continuation continuum

There is an urgent need to forefront the cultural divide between Aboriginal oral cultures and Western literate cultures. The divide is disempowering Aboriginal people because literacy is argued to be a 'passport to success' in the dominant culture (compare Freire & Macedo 1987).

Even in the face of the undisputed need for access to the dominant culture through English, Aboriginal people talk of reviving languages by returning to how the old people passed on the knowledge and the languages, on country and through the spoken word. Many of today's Elders were taught in that way. As they got older they became more concerned about the loss of their languages. They now want to go back to teaching how they learned.

This is intuitive to Aboriginal people but is actually an articulation of academic research on language acquisition and language learning (compare Newport, Gleitman & Gleitman 1977; Krashen 1981; Chomsky 1986; Richards & Rodgers 1986; Johnson & Newport 1989; Cook 1993; Foster-Cohen 1999). These works inform aspects of what Aboriginal people are observing about both first language(s) acquisition and additional language(s) learning for both children and adults in the Kimberley context.

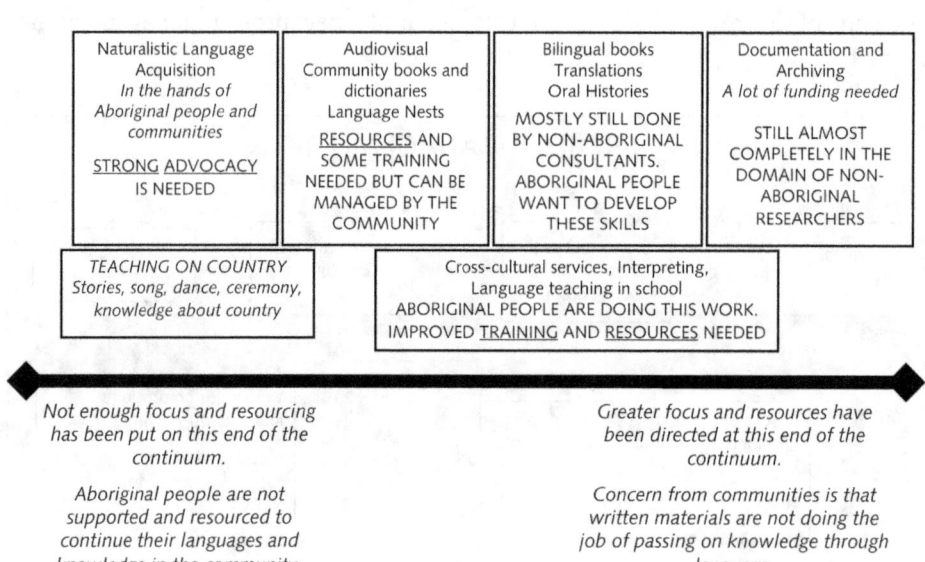

Figure 2. Language Continuation Continuum.

The KLRC captures the complexity of this situation by referring to Teaching On Country (TOC) and placing that in the context of the Language Continuation Continuum (LCC). The LCC visually sets out the range of possible language continuation activities (Figure 2). Within this context TOC does not just refer to the act of oral language transmission on country as an activity, but captures the unbroken links of knowledge and country to languages. The desire to return to this way of passing on languages reflects feelings of great loss about what is no longer being taught about country and culture. Nettle & Romaine capture this by linking loss of indigenous linguistic diversity to loss of biodiversity (2000, p. 51).

Strategies and projects

In order to support the LCC and TOC the language centre staff is using the following strategies:

- *creating greater awareness by increasing metalinguistic and sociolinguistic knowledge among Aboriginal community linguists.*[8] Through workshops delivered and meetings held we have identified that lack of understanding of the real purpose of linguistic documentation prevented Aboriginal people initiating or supporting appropriate community-level continuation strategies. We also identified that despite the intuitive understanding of language nests and the need to teach primarily through the spoken word, Aboriginal people are not aware that there is evidence to back this up in international research on how humans acquire their first language(s) and how humans best learn or are taught second language(s).
- *empowering Aboriginal community linguists to develop and manage projects.* Often the type of projects Aboriginal people want to carry out are based on the principles of TOC, but accessing sustainable funding for what is essentially the maintenance of a cultural lifestyle is pretty near impossible. By empowering Aboriginal groups to argue for cultural and linguistic diversity alongside the Western culture, they can lobby government and the private sector to resource a sustainable lifestyle with sustainable employment, for example NRM, interpreting, education, community development and childcare.
- *directing funding towards community management of continuation strategies.* This improves administrative transparency for the community, and decision-making is centred there.

Some recent projects and activities supporting these strategies are:

- workshops skilling people to use documentation materials
- community dictionaries
- community accessible materials development from ethno-biological resources

---

8 The KLRC uses *community linguist* to refer to Aboriginal people who become involved in language continuation in a variety of ways. It does not refer specifically to linguistic documentation work.

- collaborative development of a communication and consultation strategy with a government department
- audiovisual training for communities to document languages
- an adult education short course incorporating classroom teaching with existing resources and oral immersion activities on country
- mentoring in pre-school language acquisition methods, for example with childcare groups
- promotion of an holistic curriculum model for integrating languages and cultural knowledge with the Western Australian curriculum areas
- development of an early years oral curriculum

Most of this work is achieved without direct project funding. Attempts to gain increased operational funding for additional staff members to support this work are consistently unsuccessful.

Refocusing the worldview

One of the main concerns of Aboriginal people in the Kimberley is the separation of languages from country.

Meek (2007) identifies how the contexts in which indigenous languages are spoken can be changed by a shift of perspective which separates the social use of language from what begins to be thought of as the traditional cultural uses of language. The younger generations begin to see indigenous languages as belonging to the Elders and not as part of their own lives.

In the Kimberley the belief that documentation materials and school programs can take the place of natural language acquisition has possibly been a trigger for the separation of languages from country and consequently daily life. Documentation work with older language speakers was sending a message that the languages belonged to the Elders in very specific contexts. The Elders meanwhile wanted English to become a target language for the younger generations. However many older speakers use a pidgin or dialect of Kriol, which they believe to be a type of English, even on country. Thus children acquire neither traditional languages nor English. In discussions with older generations about getting back to country we often ask the question about their choice of language(s). One answer is that children have to have English for school. The other answer is that children do not understand the languages. Much of our awareness-raising in the community talks about how languages can live beside each other. Traditional languages can be spoken in the community context as well as on country. Doing so will ensure the children *can* understand.

Another recent trigger for the distancing of languages from social use is the national spotlight on improving conditions for Aboriginal people, which the current Australian government refers to as 'closing the gap'. There is a strong focus on the English language as a means of improving Aboriginal social conditions through employment, education and training. The more this message is pushed, the less people believe their own linguistic heritage can be part of the solution for their children (compare Ball & Pence 2006, p. 115) and so Aboriginal languages run the risk of dying out completely.

Self-determination in language continuation: who sets the agenda?

The story to this point says that the KLRC's present strategic direction has a foundation in what Kimberley Aboriginal people want for their languages. The issue for the organisation is that we now operate with a different model of revival and maintenance to funding bodies, academic institutions and Western language teaching models.

There are opponents of what the organisation is doing. Disputing the wisdom of the KLRC's community capacity building focus a linguist stated, 'I believe that it is one of the roles of the KLRC is to turn scientific studies into materials for use in the community. There are many languages in the Kimberley and the KLRC needs to employ well more than a dozen linguists' (pers. comm., 20 March 2006). Another linguist observed that Aboriginal people in the Kimberley are being let down because documentation is not being encouraged (pers. comm., 19 March 2007).

Such views inform government. If the board and membership have set a different agenda for preserving their languages, what evidence is there that their chosen method of language continuation will not work? There is plenty of academic research that suggests that it *will* work. If Aboriginal people believe it will, then that also overcomes another concern of one of the linguists quoted above about lack of interest from young Aboriginal people in Western linguistic study. Caffrey concludes that even for Aboriginal people who have undertaken linguistic studies 'formal linguistic training has made limited contribution to the documentation and maintenance of Australia's Indigenous languages to date' (2008, p. 236).

The concern the KLRC Board of Directors wants addressed is the lack of recognition of the role Aboriginal people not only *want* to but *have* to play in the continuation of their own languages.

This concern can be explored by asking two further questions:

Whose responsbility is language continuation at the community level and why does the answer, the community, pose a problem for the KLRC?

> We must apply an ecological bottom-up approach to language maintenance ... Action needs to begin at the most local level in two senses. First, most of the work will have to be done primarily by small groups themselves ... Second, it is necessary to concentrate on the home front (i.e. intergenerational transmission) ... Without transmission, there can be no long-term maintenance. (Nettle and Romaine 2000, p. 177)

The direct effect of placing responsibility for language continuation within the community is that, if the KLRC does not meet the government criteria for a regional language organisation, we will not be operationally resourced. This means not having the staffing to fill out funding submissions, advocate for the issues, promote the organisation and pursue fee-for-service income. To become sustainable and independent of government, and so fulfil the Aboriginal agenda set by the membership and board, we need in the first instance to be adequately funded operationally. The organisation can then more effectively assist the communities with their bottom-up strategies for language continuation.

Aboriginal activist Noel Pearson (2007) talks passionately about the importance of Aboriginal languages to the reconciliation process and the need to make space at the community level for language continuation. However he also argues for the documentation model of funding:

> There needs to be a generous government funded campaign for the maintenance of each indigenous language employing full-time linguists and other expert staff. Private, not-for-profit and public organisations should work together, but language policy and adequate funding must be provided by the national government.

If language activists and academics continue to fight to resource documentation and school programs but do not also argue for linguistic and cultural diversity to be resourced at the community level, the KLRC will be forced to return to the previous model of language continuation to survive. Since this model did not achieve spoken language revival at the community level, this is potentially a huge loss to the Kimberley and the nation as a whole.

Why are Aboriginal continuation strategies seen as less valid than the strategies of Western academia and education?

> In societies across the world since ancient times, the quest for knowledge has been elevated to a high-level discipline, even an art form. In Yolŋu society, knowledge has always been considered valuable – almost more valuable than life itself ... So why don't Yolŋu learn ... Could it be that the dominant culture education delivered to Yolŋu is so ineffective that almost no education occurs, and Yolŋu are left thinking that the age of knowledge and thinking is at an end? (Trudgeon 2000 pp. 121–22)

There can be no comparison between the transmission of knowledge within literate and oral cultures, but comparison is still sought.

When Aboriginal people express their beliefs on language acquisition in a way that can be conceptually understood by non-Aboriginal people, there may emerge ideas such as language nests which can be understood and accepted by both Aboriginal and non-Aboriginal people.

What about when Aboriginal people are expressing something that cannot be interpreted into the Western worldview so easily, such as the need to protect country and spiritual and social health and wellbeing through continued connection to languages? Does lack of understanding or disagreement on the part of the non-Aboriginal person make Aboriginal decisions about languages *wrong*? Are non-Aboriginal people in the Kimberley asked to explain in such an exposing manner what their cultural background is, why they speak and think the way they do, and then argue for why they should be allowed to continue speaking their language and living their cultural lifestyle?

> There is a lot written about us and the question is how do we get a balance between what others are writing about us and what we think and mean about ourselves? How do we have control and direct the knowledge about us? (Kimberley Land Council & Waringarri Resource Centre 1991 p. 39)

Conclusion

> One of the many criticisms that gets levelled at indigenous intellectuals or activists is that Western education precludes us from writing or speaking from a 'real' and authentic indigenous position. Of course, those who do speak from a more 'traditional' indigenous point of view are criticized because they do not make sense (speak English, what!). Or, our talk is reduced to some 'nativist' discourse, dismissed by colleagues in the academy as naive, contradictory and illogical. (Smith 1999, p. 14)

The KLRC acknowledges the importance of the documentation work done on languages of the region, through the organisation and by independent researchers. It also acknowledges the contribution of both Aboriginal and non-Aboriginal people to sustaining language programs. Both strategies provide resources to support language continuation. They do not, however, result in significantly increased spoken language use or continuation of cultural knowledge through languages.

The KLRC is arguing to get the voices of Kimberley Aboriginal people heard despite top-down government policies and a continued academic approach to language continuation. It is imperative for the languages of the Kimberley that these voices are understood. If the KLRC struggles to get their message heard and consequently cannot do the work it is being asked to do by Aboriginal people, we have to ask not only 'whose languages?', but also, 'whose language centre is it anyway?'

> Among Aboriginal people, to know my world is to speak my language ... I didn't speak English until I went to school. By learning the English language I learned how to deal with the non-Aboriginal world. Now that we can both speak the same language, we would like to ask you to sit down with us, so that we can start talking and listening to one another. (Ivan Kurijinpi McPhee cited in Kimberley Land Council 1998, p. 26)

Acknowledgments

The KLRC would like to acknowledge Newry & Palmer's (2003) paper, 'Whose Language is it Anyway?' in reference to the title of this paper.

References

Abley M (2003). *Spoken here: travels among threatened languages*. London: William Heinemann.

Ball J & Pence A (2006). *Supporting indigenous children's development: community-university partnerships*. Vancouver: University of British Columbia Press.

Brennan G (1979). *The need for interpreting and translation services for Australian Aboriginals, with special reference to the Northern Territory – a research report*. Canberra: Department of Aboriginal Affairs.

Caffrey J (2008). Linguistics training in Indigenous adult education and its effects on endangered languages. Unpublished doctoral thesis, Charles Darwin University, Northern Territory.

Chomsky N (1986). *Knowledge of language*. New York: Praeger.

Cook V (1993). *Linguistics and second language acquisition*. London: Macmillan.

Foster-Cohen SH (1999). *An introduction to child language acquisition*. London: Longman.

Freire P & Macedo D (1987). *Reading the word and the world*. London: Routledge & Kegan Paul.

Hudson J & McConvell P (1985). *Keeping language strong (long version)*. Broome: Kimberley Language Resource Centre.

Johnson J & Newport M (1989). Critical period effects in second language learning: the influence of the maturational state on the acquisition of English as a second language. *Cognitive Psychology*, 21: 60–99.

Kimberley Development Commission (February 2009). *Population structure & characteristics* [Online]. Available: www.kdc.wa.gov.au/kimberley/tk_demo.asp [Accessed 26 March 2009].

Kimberley Land Council & Waringarri Resource Centre (1991). *The Crocodile Hole report*. Broome: Kimberley Land Council.

Kimberley Land Council (1998). *The Kimberley: our place our future: Conference report*. Broome: Kimberley Land Council.

Kimberley Language Resource Centre (1993). Plan for language groups that have less than 50–100 speakers. Unpublished manuscript.

Kimberley Language Resource Centre (1995). A policy for research work at the KLRC. Unpublished manuscript.

Kimberley Language Resource Centre (2000). Strategic plan. Unpublished manuscript.

Kimberley Language Resource Centre (2005). Strategic plan. Unpublished manuscript.

Kimberley Language Resource Centre (2008). Business plan 2008–11. Unpublished manuscript.

Krashen S (1981). *Second language acquisition and second language learning*. London: Pergamon.

Meek B (2007). Respecting the language of elders: ideological shift and linguistic discontinuity in a northern Athapascan community. *Journal of Linguistic Anthropology*, 17(1): 23–43.

McConvell P (1986). Aboriginal language programmes and language maintenance in the Kimberley. *Australian Review of Applied Linguistics.* Series S, 3: 108–22.

Nettle D & Romaine S (2000). *Vanishing voices: the extinction of the world's languages.* Oxford: Oxford University Press.

Newport E, Gleitman L & Gleitman H (1977). Mother I'd rather do it myself: some effects and non-effects of maternal speech style. In C Snow & C Ferguson (Eds). *Talking to children: language input and acquisition* (pp. 109–49). Cambridge: Cambridge University Press.

Newry D & Palmer K (2003). Whose language is it anyway? rights to restrict access to endangered languages: a north-east Kimberley example. In J Blythe & R McKenna Brown (Eds). *Maintaining the links: language, identity and the land* (pp. 101–06). Proceedings of the 7th Foundation for Endangered Languages Conference. Broome, Western Australia, 22–24 September. Bath: Foundation for Endangered Language.

Pearson N (2007). Native tongues imperilled. *The Australian* [Online]. Available: www.theaustralian.news.com.au/story/0,20867,21352767-7583,00.html [Accessed 27 March 2009].

Richards JC & Rodgers TS (1996). *Approaches and methods in language teaching.* Cambridge: Cambridge University Press.

Smith LT (1999). *Decolonizing methodologies.* London: Zed Books.

Trudgeon R (2000). *Why warriors lie down and die.* Darwin: Aboriginal Resource and Development Services Inc.

United Nations (1989). *Convention on the rights of the child* [Online]. Available: www.unhchr.ch/html/menu3/b/k2crc.htm [Accessed 19 May 2009].

12
Revitalisation strategies for Miriwoong

Knut J. Olawsky[1]

Abstract

This chapter discusses details of the language revitalisation program pursued at Mirima Dawang Woorlab-gerring (Mirima place for talking) in Kununurra, Western Australia. Typical strategies employed here include traditional style language lessons as well as the development of an experience-based learning approach. Further activities include a master–apprentice program based on the model introduced by Hinton (1997). Most recently, employment is also used as an additional incentive for young people to touch ground with their traditional language again. Apart from an account of the strategies and activities employed at the language centre, the issues of success and failure are analysed and recommendations made to render the process more successful. This study is supported by the traditional owners of Miriwoong country. It is their desire to learn from others and to pass on their experience so that others may learn from them. *Waniya meljeb-bebe beniyawoon, jirrijib yirriyan berri* (They watch and listen, we show them).

Miriwoong is a non-Pama-Nyungan language and classified as a member of the Jarrakan family. Other Jarrakan languages include Gija (Kija) and Gajirrabeng (Gajirrawoong), a closely related language now nearly extinct. The heart of Miriwoong country is the wider Kununurra area in the East Kimberley region of Western Australia that stretches up to about 100 kilometres eastward across the border into the Northern Territory. Towards the west of Kununurra, Miriwoong land extends for another 20–30 kilometres beyond the Ord River. The northern parts of the former landmass now covered by Lake Argyle are also part of Miriwoong territory.

The first revitalisation efforts go back to the early 1970s when a group of Miriwoong elders formed the Mirima Council and started a number of initiatives, including

---

1 Mirima Dawang Woorlab-gerring Language and Culture Centre.

working with a linguist. When the Miriwoong people started to realise their language was in peril they made arrangements for it to be documented. Eventually a language centre was constructed in 1991. Today Mirima Dawang Woorlab-gerring (MDWg) employs a full-time linguist, a part-time linguist plus a number of support staff. MDWg also has five language workers employed part-time through the National Jobs Package (NJP). They are the backbone of MDWg's work, dealing with a wide range of tasks, most of which are related to language documentation and teaching. They function as teachers in language lessons, plan and prepare classes and engage in activities such as archiving, documentation, consultation, and field trips. As the language workers are partial speakers of Miriwoong they very much depend on the advice from senior language speakers for detailed language-related questions and studies. Elders are engaged as consultants on a regular basis.

Most of the early linguistic work on Miriwoong was done by Frances Kofod, the linguist who initially started work with the Miriwoong people. In 2007 Kofod completed a dictionary of Gajirrabeng with the help of Keeley Palmer who started work at the language centre in the late 1990s. A Miriwoong dictionary was completed in 2009.

Language status

Based on the Language Endangerment Status Indicator from the *National Indigenous Languages Survey Report* (Australian Institute of Aboriginal & Torres Strait Islander Studies 2005), Miriwoong can be classified as severely to critically endangered. According to Fishman's (1991) Graded Intergenerational Disruption Scale for Threatened Languages, Miriwoong would rank somewhere between Stage 7 and 8. All fluent speakers who use Miriwoong as their first language are 60 years of age or older. There are only a handful of moderately fluent speakers in the 40–60 age group but Miriwoong is not their primary language and they do not have comprehensive grammatical proficiency. While many Miriwoong people have a passive understanding of a range of words, they are not in a position to use language structures in context or interact fully in Miriwoong with each other. The knowledge of Miriwoong in children is limited to those words borrowed by the local variety of Kriol.

Most if not all languages traditionally spoken in the Kimberley region are gradually being replaced by the use of Kimberley Kriol. Though Kriol still lacks wider public recognition it has come to dominate as a lingua franca over traditional Aboriginal languages. Many families have also shifted to using Aboriginal English as their first language. While the Kriol variety spoken in Kununurra contains some Miriwoong vocabulary the impact of its use on Miriwoong has been devastating.

One of the most serious challenges faced by MDWg is the fact that the process of revitalisation is a race against time. With only a small number of fluent speakers left, all of whom are elderly, major efforts must be made to gather as much linguistic information as possible and to pass on this knowledge to learners of other age groups. As this requires the combined efforts of linguists, the community and partners, the provision of financial resources is a crucial factor. Most government-based funding programs are not flexible enough to meet the specific needs of individually tailored revitalisation programs. While government agencies increasingly see the need to support Indigenous communities, language work is often regarded a luxury given the urgent need for other crucial services such as health, housing, or general education. As a result language centres throughout Australia are struggling to get their modest share of a limited national budget put aside for language revitalisation.

Some revitalisation activities and strategies

Similar to other Australian language centres MDWg pursues a variety of strategies aimed at the revitalisation of Indigenous languages. The situation at MDWg slightly differs from the one at regional language centres in that the main focus is on one language, Miriwoong, with marginal support for nearby or related languages such as Gajirrabeng, Ngarinyman and Jaminjung where the need arises.

The traditional focus of language centres towards revitalisation is the promotion of documentation, literacy and oracy, as well as the encouragement of cultural activities. In addition to the classic task of organising language classes a new initiative involving specially structured excursions has become an important part of MDWg's activities. Employment is another factor that has become relevant for the revitalisation program. Furthermore the development of bilingual public signage represents an important role for MDWg's revitalisation strategy (see Olawsky, this volume). The following pages characterise details of these activities.

Documentation

Documentation and archiving occur on an ongoing basis and are designed to provide the necessary data for the development of teaching materials, as well as creating the theoretical foundation for language teaching. A Miriwoong dictionary is one important project in this area currently in progress, and it is designed to function as a major resource for semi-speakers. The structure of the dictionary puts the use of Miriwoong in a learner's context as most entries show examples of how a word is used in a sentence and relevant cross-references are listed throughout. A possible further development will be the production of a digital version with images and sound recordings. The use of technology seems a feasible approach as most young Miriwoong are becoming increasingly familiar with the use of computers. The development of a digital dictionary will also provide increased user-friendliness, since the use of the print version depends on the acquisition of literacy skills.

Literacy and oracy

Most literacy- and oracy-related activities involve school-aged children and young adults between eight and 16 years. Among the typical regular activities are some that promote literacy and oracy in a classroom situation, and others which focus on the transfer of language skills in a cultural setting.

The spelling system developed for Miriwoong is entirely consistent as it mostly reflects a one-to-one match between writing and sound. Literacy is promoted by conducting weekly language classes with groups from the Aboriginal learning programs of the local school. MDWg also offers young Miriwoong adult classes on a voluntary basis. Cultural protocol prescribes that male and female learners be taught separately.

Formal language lessons focus on transferring literacy and oracy skills in Miriwoong. The majority of participants are of Miriwoong descent with a minority of learners from other Aboriginal groups. The level of literacy in English varies considerably among individual students.

The language course begins with an overview of the Miriwoong sound inventory and alphabet. Subsequent lessons typically involve a general theme for one or two sessions in sequence, such as trees, birds, water animals, things around the house. The most popular teaching method involves a multimedia-based approach using slide shows, which include single words in writing, image, and sound. After introducing a series of new words, exercises follow in order to encourage the interactive use of materials by learners. Examples include word sleuths, word puzzles, memory games, and a variety of exercises aimed at strengthening phonological, orthographic, and semantic recognition and production.

The classes are taught by language workers who are partial speakers of the language themselves, but are also exposed to various kinds of language input including tasks such as revising and adding dictionary entries, data entry, or the development of new language lessons and exercises.

Bush trips

Lessons also focus on the simultaneous teaching of language and culture. As part of this project MDWg organises bush trips with elders and young people. Some of these excursions are overnight trips, usually to a remote area away from distractions that are prevalent in town. Activities include hunting and fishing skills, making of artefacts and the practice of traditional music. Each component is accompanied by oral presentations of the vocabulary related to the respective theme.

Master–apprentice program

In the second half of 2009, MDWg started a Master–Apprentice Language Learning Program (MALLP) based on the model developed by Hinton (1997). The project involves six teams each composed of a senior, fluent speaker and a partial speaker. The one-on-one immersion takes place on a part-time basis as speakers spend an average of two hours per day together. While this activity is still at its initial stages, the potential outcomes are promising: most of the junior participants are language workers at MDWg and also engage in language teaching for non-speakers. The input they receive through their work with the elders is expected to have a strong impact on their language proficiency, which will further enhance their role as language trainers and role models inside and outside the classroom.

Creation of employment opportunities

Recent governments have focused on the creation of employment for Indigenous people. This has become crucial for obtaining funding, and language centres are encouraged to work towards creating employment opportunities where resources can be made available. In addition, employment related to language and cultural work represents an incentive for young people to connect with traditional values rather than working in the mining or agricultural sectors.

MDWg has been developing training and employment opportunities on a small scale with some success. At this stage several young people aged 18–24 are employed as assistants on the bush trips described above. They not only function as practical assistants to the elders but are also viewed as role models for younger participants. They have obtained training in a variety of activities and have acquired a basic vocabulary related to each theme. In the longer term these assistants could enter into more regular employment with the possible expansion of the project.

Another initiative has been developed in collaboration with the Western Australian Department of Environment and Conservation (DEC). This project aims at training a group of young people (aged 18–26) as interpretive officers at the local Mirima National Park and several other jointly managed conservation areas. In this capacity they will conduct regular guided tours for visitors and provide Miriwoong names of the fauna and flora of the park as well as explain selected traditional customs related to the area. Trainees undergo a 40-hour program that provides them with the relevant linguistic and other theoretical knowledge required for this task, supplemented by a series of on-site sessions. Most participants have very limited knowledge of Miriwoong as they start the training, and the prospect of obtaining paid employment functions as an incentive to acquire language proficiency to some extent.

Public language use

A further revitalisation strategy used at MDWg is the promotion of Miriwoong language on a public platform. This includes the development of public signage and several other forms of relating to the wider community (see Olawsky, this volume).

Successes and challenges

The activities and efforts made by MDWg have had varying degrees of success over the past years. In this section the impact of MDWg's various activities is evaluated as challenges and achievements are singled out.

Evaluation of documentation efforts

So far the grammar of Miriwoong has been scarcely documented. A sketch grammar by Kofod (1978) describes some aspects of the language but additional research is necessary to provide more comprehensive documentation. The absence of grammatical components in language teaching must also be perceived as a major obstacle in the revitalisation process. In order to improve this situation more linguistic research needs to be conducted to produce a pedagogical grammar, and the overall number of language classes must be increased. A project that commenced in July 2009 aims at engaging linguists in grammatical research as well as training a larger number of language teachers.

Evaluation of classroom teaching

Language teaching in a formalised environment, such as lessons taught in school, plays a vital role in MDWg's revitalisation program in that it provides the setting for a regular, sustained transfer of language. Students experience the lessons as an integral part of their education and see members of their own community using and teaching the language. However weekly lessons tend to suffer from irregular attendance, which is a general problem also occurring within the public school system. As a result a different group of learners may be present each week which disrupts the sequential progression of lessons. The worst-case scenario is of a learner who keeps attending the first lesson over and over again and subsequently loses interest in the language. Due to truancy issues discontinuous teaching of language sessions has become a challenge. As a general result the level of language competency taught so far is at a relatively low level, mainly comprising lexical knowledge – single words or short phrases.

Evaluation of bush trips

Obviously, low attendance numbers are related to motivational issues, which are a general challenge for the revitalisation of Miriwoong. Under the influence of a western lifestyle, traditional culture has become less appealing for many young people, and this affects their choice of language. This is being addressed by offering a more attractive learning environment – bush trips. While the costs for these excursions are relatively high, involving one-off investments such as 4WD vehicles and camping equipment, as well as recurring expenses such as fuel, consultant salaries and food, the outcome is exceptional. The knowledge transferred during these trips clearly exceeds the classroom transfer of purely lexical knowledge and literacy. Joint trips of elders with young people offer possibilities that cannot be achieved in the classroom:

- Language is intertwined with the knowledge of country and nature. Displaying an image of a specific area matches in no way the experience of being in touch with the land and simultaneously learning about the words related to it.
- Miriwoong elders feel more at ease using the language in full sentences when moving around freely rather than sitting behind a desk in a classroom atmosphere.
- The educational value experienced by young participants is longer lasting than the one resulting from classroom teaching as a larger number of senses are involved in an outdoor experience.
- Concepts that are hard to explain on a whiteboard can be demonstrated through active involvement of the learners.

- Distractions such as telephones, people walking by or other interruptions do not affect the gatherings out bush, as there is no mobile phone coverage after travelling more than ten kilometres out of town.

Teachers and supervisors have to ensure that such trips are carefully organised and the desired outcome is planned beforehand. Generally the vocabulary most likely to be used during such a trip is introduced a few days before during a preparatory language lesson.

Challenges to this strategy mainly concern the time, effort and costs required to organise this project. While the motivation for attendance is much higher compared to the classroom approach, individual trips with an appropriate selection of elders and learners are not easy to coordinate and a lot of time is spent on logistics such as transport, food and the selection of participants. The climate in this part of Australia has a further impact on the organisation of a successful trip as most roads become impassable during the wet season.

While the strength of this strategy lies in the quality of teaching, it probably suffers on the side of quantity. In order to achieve a measurable outcome the frequency and length of language and culture learning trips need to be increased.

Evaluation of employment approach

While the creation of employment is a useful component of the overall revitalisation approach at MDWg, it is also an initiative utterly dependent on the availability of funding. As long as funding can be sourced this strategy can be pursued. However the number of people involved in training employment programs is expected to be relatively low in the short and mid-term. From a longer-term perspective employment opportunities arising from tourism-related business could become self-sustaining and possibly help fund other revitalisation activities. While these will probably have limited impact on the use of Miriwoong in the community, ongoing linguistic training of young motivated Miriwoong individuals has the potential of generating role models.

Outlook, opportunities and recommendations

Despite the challenges described in the previous section there is a chance to revitalise the Miriwoong language, if at least some of these difficulties can be mastered. The reason for this optimism is not only based on the successful components of the revival program but also on the fact that the Miriwoong people have preserved a strong sense of cultural identity. The task of language activists, elders, partial speakers, and the language centre is to ensure that this sense of identity be inseparably linked with the use of the Miriwoong language. As the number and intensity of activities that assist learners in recognising the value of traditional language correlates to increased language awareness in young people, it is critical that these efforts be multiplied.

Stronger short-term efforts will be required to fight the battle against time. It must be understood that once the language is no longer spoken, revival efforts would be much more costly and less likely to succeed.

The lack of motivation in students and subsequent discontinuous learning are very persistent challenges. These are the areas that need most attention and concepts must be developed outside the linguistic field to make the language learning experience more appealing. Given the difficult general environment in which most learners grow up, combined efforts of social services, the education system and language experts will be required.

Bush trips that involve a strong component of language and cultural learning have proven to be an efficient way of skills and knowledge transfer. While these represent an expensive strategy for language revitalisation the results suggest that this method be consistently applied.

Language-related employment is another avenue to ensure young people are continuously exposed to Indigenous language use. While this approach is also cost-intensive, there is the possibility of it developing into self-sustaining activities by engaging in high-growth sectors such as the tourism industry.

Recent expansion of MDWg's work is promising in this regard; funding has been made available for a building extension to accommodate the increased level of language-related activities. While the language centre has started to independently generate income from some of its activities, further funding has been approved for an Action Plan for Miriwoong Language Survival, which will encourage an expansion of the master–apprentice-style program.

The use of Miriwoong language as the primary means of communication inside the family, and the subsequent development of diglossia, remains a long-term goal. The circumstances that have led to the shift from Miriwoong to Kriol and English cannot be simply reversed. Therefore other strategies must be sought in order to re-introduce the traditional language to the heart of Miriwoong communities. These include informal learning approaches such as community-internal activities or family-oriented excursions that implement the use of Miriwoong. These efforts will have to be accompanied by a formal language education program, initially through the language centre and followed, ideally, through the public education system. While the latter remains on the wish list of linguists and language activists at this stage, other avenues as discussed herein will continue to be pursued.

References

Australian Institute of Aboriginal & Torres Strait Islander Studies (2005). *National Indigenous Languages Survey report 2005*. Canberra: Department of Communications, Information Technology and the Arts.

Fishman JA (1991). *Reversing language shift: theory and practice of assistance to threatened languages*. Clevedon: Multilingual Matters.

Hinton L (1997). Survival of endangered languages: the Californian master–apprentice program. *International Journal of the Sociology of Language*, 123: 177–91.

Kofod F (1978). The Miriwung language (East Kimberley): a phonological and morphological study. Unpublished masters thesis, University of New England.

Kofod F & Palmer K (2007). *Gajirrabeng-English dictionary*. Kununurra: Mirima Dawang Woorlab-gerring.

Part Four
Language in education

Introduction
Language in education

Susan Poetsch and Kevin Lowe[1]

Indigenous communities often express a degree of reservation about language programs in educational institutions. They question the capacity and sustained commitment of those institutions to offer the kinds of programs they value. Schools are recalled or experienced as places where their languages are actively discouraged and devalued. Community mistrust also stems from the perceived power of the institution, with its seemingly innate tendency to take ownership and control in a range of ways – including restrictive timeframes and lesson locations, set pedagogical approaches, differing notions of the role of a teacher and unreliable sources of funding. Community wariness is further heightened because culture is embedded in language, and so the risk of losing control of both is greater. When community members become dissatisfied with a language program they often resist by using the main option available to them: choosing to disengage.

Another risk is that communities can simply leave the responsibility for revitalising and maintaining their languages to educational institutions alone. As McCarty argues, schools cannot have the impact that the primary language institutions of family and community can (cited in Hornberger 2008, p. 161). People's homes are where languages need to live. Ultimately, if the aims for any given community include considerable reinstatement of fluency and language use by community members, then educational institutions can only ever be an adjunct to the broader goals and tasks.

At the same time, however, educational institutions have the potential to be powerful sites for language learning and can have a positive synergy with community language revitalisation efforts. For example, as McCarty goes on to argue: schools are potential sites of resistance and opportunity; schools can become strategic platforms for more broad-based language planning (including orthographic standardisation, preparing teachers, elevating the status of oppressed and marginalised languages); and there are few instances of successful language revitalisation in which schools have not played a crucial role.

---

1 Both authors are from the Aboriginal Curriculum Unit, Office of the Board of Studies NSW.

Formal curriculum (including curriculum suitable for re-awakening Indigenous languages) has been developed for schools and post-compulsory educational contexts in several Australian states and territories.[2] However these are only documents; their value lies in effective implementation in local contexts. Educational institutions can offer a continuum of language teaching and learning, based on curriculum that sequences content and facilitates effective methodologies. They have the potential to offer support structures within their own respective systems, as well as develop links among sectors and providers. In this way language-learning pathways can be available from preschool through to primary, secondary, post-compulsory schooling and higher education.

For language programs to be successful in educational institutions, communities need to own and drive the programs; and institutions need to critically analyse the range of justified reservations held by communities, be flexible in course delivery, open real channels of communication and cooperation with communities, and establish programs which are genuinely responsive to Indigenous people's needs and aspirations for the revitalisation of their languages. Given the significant challenges of working in the context of re-awakening languages, planning cannot be piecemeal or ad hoc. There is a need to build a team that has members with relevant skills and capacities that can also take a strong advocacy role in the institution and in the community. The team needs to be strongly supported in its efforts to learn and develop the language, make teaching materials, and build the human resources and skills base.

The potential contribution of educational institutions to the re-awakening of languages, and the optimism of successful and effective partnerships between them and communities, are captured in the chapters that follow. The papers not only exemplify successful program development in a range of educational contexts, but also describe obstacles encountered in local situations and how these were, or could be, overcome.

Brown is committed to the journey of the revitalisation of Dhurga in her own community on the south coast of New South Wales (NSW). Her chapter deals with the challenge of the lack of resources for awakening languages, the importance of building up the store of teaching and learning materials and being efficient with those that are available. Her research with beginner learners clearly shows that resources and materials can have multiple uses and applications.

Through three adult language-learning case studies, Cipollone describes how the nationally-accredited Aboriginal languages qualifications – recently developed by Technical and Further Education (TAFE) NSW – are being successfully adapted for courses in Dhurga, Gamilaraay and Dharawal. Each community context has unique

---

2 For example Board of Studies New South Wales (2003), Northern Territory Department of Education & Training (1998), South Australian Department of Education & Children's Services (2003), Technical & Further Education New South Wales (2007), Victorian Curriculum & Assessment Authority (2004, 2009), Western Australian Department of Education & Training (2005, 2007).

local human and other resources, and the paper canvasses the keys to success, the challenges and the future directions for each of the three locations.

Establishing and working on Dharug programs in Sydney, Green emphasises the importance of community links and developing direct and extensive Aboriginal involvement in language development and program implementation. He describes his use of both well known and innovative language teaching and learning activities which are motivating and effective for engaging students in a language program in early secondary school years.

Also working in the context of a high school program, Lane outlines the background research and the steady development of the Dhurga program in Vincentia. Her chapter illustrates the skills that a teacher of languages (in this case Indonesian) can offer an Aboriginal language program development team, including effective pedagogy for language learning, knowledge of the operation of the particular school site and the educational system more broadly. Lane also describes how she too is learning from a number of local community members through their sharing of language and culture with her and the students.

Lowe & Howard explore the critical tension points from community perspectives that underpin the establishment of a learning partnership between the Aboriginal educators and principal in a particular school in NSW. Findings from this case study, based on data collected through interviews, indicate that the long-term viability of the language program was largely dependent on the Aboriginal educators' view of the school leadership. The measure of success the educators applied to the program was the degree to which they believed their language was respected by the school through the privileging of their knowledge and culture.

A teacher at Parkes High School in central western NSW, Maier describes the growing relationship between the school and local community. This relationship provides a strong foundation for the planning and gradual growth of Wiradjuri courses in the school's curriculum. He describes achievements to date and future plans to continue to develop the program, and highlights the key role of the Aboriginal community language tutor in the success and integrity of the program.

McNaboe & Poetsch describe connections between adult learning and school programs, also for Wiradjuri. In recent years school–community partnerships have developed within and across individual school sites, as well as between the school and TAFE sector. These synergies have led to a notable increase in language teaching and learning in towns throughout Wiradjuri country. Community members' take-up of the range of available courses has been strong. In turn, school programs provide stimulus for further development of speakers and teachers. This paper illustrates these points through a description of the development of the teaching program for Dubbo College.

Meakins highlights the importance of considering language ecologies when designing revitalisation programs suitable for specific locations. She describes the mixing practices used by speakers of the Gurindji, Bilinarra and Ngarinyman languages of the Northern Territory. Current language maintenance practices in these communities include code switching between a traditional language and Kriol (a strategy commonly used by older people) and systematic combining of a traditional language and Kriol – a fossilised form of code switching and a strategy commonly used by younger people. In these ways communities *are* maintaining aspects of their traditional languages. In the context of rapid shift Meakins argues for the value of the often-maligned wordlist learning approach to language teaching, together with a staged introduction of aspects of grammar of the traditional languages. Such teaching strategies, she argues, are more suitable than immersion methods to this ecology as they provide a means of increasing the proportion of aspects of the traditional languages in the new mixed varieties of younger generations.

Reid gives an uplifting description of the achievements of a group of Wotjobaluk people of the Wimmera region of Victoria. Through a very challenging course of study based on the *Indigenous languages of Victoria, revival and reclamation: Victorian Certificate of Education study design*, the community members have been playing an active role in an academically rigorous reconstruction of their language, Wergaia. As one of the course participants, Bronwyn Pickford put it, 'I felt pride and greater confidence. I discovered an untapped talent – my linguistic skills'. Through their collaboration with Reid and their strong commitment to the process the class was able to produce a community consultation copy of a Wergaia grammar and dictionary.

Finally, Rhydwen's paper acknowledges the very real and complex challenges involved in revitalising languages in NSW where language loss has been great and where languages typically have incomplete documentation and few resources for teaching and learning. Despite these challenges she provides sound reasons for pursuing language programs in schools and gives an overview of the range of effective strategies currently provided to support the implementation of those programs, including schools working positively with the community, training and careers for Aboriginal languages teachers and tutors, and establishing networks of schools to maximise the use and development of resources. Thus she provides us with an optimistic conclusion to this section.

References

Board of Studies New South Wales (2003). *Aboriginal languages K–10 syllabus*. Sydney: Board of Studies NSW [Online]. Available: www.boardofstudies.nsw.edu.au/syllabus_sc [Accessed 18 December 2009].

McCarty T (2008). Schools as strategic tools for indigenous language revitalization: lessons from Native America. In N Hornberger (Ed). *Can schools save indigenous languages? policy and practice on four continents*. New York: Palgrave Macmillan.

Northern Territory Department of Education & Training (1998). *NT curriculum framework, Indigenous languages and culture* [Online]. Available: www.det.nt.gov.au/education/teaching_and_learning/curriculum/ntcf [Accessed 18 December 2009].

South Australian Department of Education & Children's Services (2003). *South Australian curriculum, standards & accountability framework: Australian Indigenous languages*. South Australia: Hyde Park Press [Online]. Available: www.sacsa.sa.edu.au [Accessed 18 December 2009].

Technical & Further Education New South Wales (2007). *Certificates I, II and III in Aboriginal language/s*. Sydney: Technical & Further Education NSW

Victorian Curriculum & Assessment Authority (2004). *Indigenous languages of Victoria, revival and reclamation: Victorian Certificate of Education study design*. East Melbourne: Victorian Curriculum & Assessment Authority [Online]. Available: www.vcaa.vic.edu.au/vce/studies/lote/ausindigenous/ausindigindex.html [Accessed 18 December 2009].

Victorian Curriculum & Assessment Authority (2009). *Aboriginal languages, cultures and reclamation in Victorian schools: standards P–10 and protocols*. East Melbourne: Victorian Curriculum & Assessment Authority.

Western Australia Curriculum Council (2007). Aboriginal languages of Western Australia study design. Perth: Western Australia Curriculum Council [Online]. Available: www.curriculum.wa.edu.au/internet/Senior_Secondary/Courses_Aboriginal_Languages [Accessed 18 December 2009].

Western Australia Department of Education & Training (2005). *Outcomes and standards framework, languages other than English*. East Perth: Government of Western Australia [Online]. Available: www.det.wa.edu.au [Accessed 18 December 2009].

13
Using identical resources to teach young and adult language learners

Ursula Brown[1]

Abstract

According to the *Report on school-based Aboriginal Language Program activity in NSW During 2006* there are several difficulties that arise when implementing an Aboriginal language program. Those difficulties may include funding availability, staffing, resource production, professional development and programming (Rhydwen, Munro, Parolin & Poetsch 2007, p. 4). Often one or more of these factors can cause discontinuity. This paper investigates the use of identical pedagogical resources to teach an Indigenous language to diverse age groups to ascertain whether they could be reused successfully, thereby reducing the overall costs of pedagogical resource production. During the course of this research project youth from Broulee Public School and adults from the Mogo Public School community were taught lessons in Dhurga, an Indigenous language from the south-east coast of NSW. Each class was taught using the same resources. I conclude that it is possible to use the same resources for various age groups while continuing to cater to the needs of beginning language learners of Dhurga from Stage 1 through to adult. This will enable funding for resources to be used economically allowing more money to be utilised in other vital aspects of Aboriginal language programs, including the employment and training of Aboriginal community language teachers.

As a child I knew words that other kids did not know, but I wasn't taught them at school. I wondered why some people were calling things by different names; were my words made up or were their words wrong? As a teenager I was taught that those words were part of my grandfather's heritage – his traditional language, Dhurga. As an adult I now know that these words are real and an important part of my heritage –

---

1 Dhurga Community.

my Aboriginal language, Dhurga – which I hope to be able to pass on to my children. Today I see these words written and hear them spoken by people in my community, both black and white. As proud as I am of this I sometimes also wonder if this newfound interest in Aboriginal languages will be just another passing phase.

My hope is that research into Aboriginal languages in schools will demonstrate that there are many positive outcomes for all students and the broader community resulting from the revival and introduction of Aboriginal languages. Some positive outcomes may include raised self-esteem, improved retention and attendance rates, and better decoding skills in literacy (see also Jones, Chandler & Lowe, this volume). I believe that introducing an Aboriginal language into any school will not only benefit the students and community, but also help keep Aboriginal languages and cultures from becoming extinct.

Originally this paper was written for a research project I conducted as a component of my 2008 study in the Master of Indigenous Languages Education (MILE) offered by the Koori Centre at the University of Sydney. A module of the MILE required me to complete a research project based on my own teaching. My research question was, 'Is it possible to employ identical pedagogical resources to teach youth and adults Indigenous languages?' I was hoping that the research would show that pedagogical resources could cater to the needs of beginning language learners from Stage 1 through to adult, enabling more money to be used in other aspects of Aboriginal language programs, including the employment and training of Aboriginal community language teachers.

All research for this paper was carried out using Dhurga, a language from the south-east coast of New South Wales (NSW), which belongs to the country among Wandandian to the north, Wallaga Lake to the south, and Braidwood to the west. Dhurga is one of several languages used within the Yuin land boundaries (Eades 1976).

Description of the project

The project was a study that included two groups of participants; one group were primary school-aged students, or Young Dhurga Learners (YDL), and the second group were Adult Dhurga Learners (ADL). While conducting my research project, certain differences in learning Aboriginal languages between these two groups became apparent to me, including the use of metalanguage[2] by each group and how they to responded its use; the influence of the age of a learner on speed of acquisition of sounds, vocabulary and grammar; the importance of writing a program which caters for the varying needs, interests, age and stages of learning; and developing resources to support the program.

Community consultation was based on my own cultural knowledge as part of my obligation to the community that I live in, belong to, and work with. I also attempted to follow the *unwritten protocols* (Smith 1999). I had been raised by my family to

---

2 Language used to talk about language.

be honest and respectful, especially to Elders, use manners at all times, and trust in others. I also referred to the Federation of Aboriginal and Torres Strait Islander Languages (FATSIL) *Guide to Community Protocols for Indigenous Projects* (2004) and the Board of Studies (BOS) NSW *Working with Aboriginal Communities; A Guide to Community Consultation and Protocols* (2001).

I approached Broulee and Mogo Schools about my research project. Both were positive about it, especially seeing that there might be benefits from the findings. I attended two community group meetings where I explained my proposal, which was endorsed through both the local parents and citizens association and Aboriginal education group.

The ADL lessons were delivered at Mogo Public School. The participants were Aboriginal and non-Aboriginal community members. The YDL lessons were carried out at Broulee Public School where each student from Year 1 through to Year 6 participated.

Mogo Public School is small with less than one hundred enrolments and a high Aboriginal population of about 43%. Mogo School was in the first year of their Dhurga language program. There were ten participants from the Mogo community in the ADL class, one of whom was an Aboriginal Elder. Broulee Public is a much bigger school with around three hundred enrolments and around five percent Aboriginal population. This school has been teaching Dhurga for about five years. Each of its 12 classes was observed during this study.

My research project was fundamentally an action research project (Dick & Swepson 1997). Lessons were planned, observations made, modifications employed, and the cycle continued. This seemed the most appropriate method for my investigation.

There were two different methods for collecting data, one being the use of student observation by the action research teacher of both language-learning groups. The other method was shared feedback from the ADL participants, either verbally or in written form.

Writing a program that caters to the needs of learners

The needs of the Mogo ADL class were assessed during the initial lesson. There were several requests made about content by the class. Most participants wanted to learn the same content as their children had – firstly, to understand what they were saying and, secondly, to reinforce their learning. There was a desire to learn local place and plant names and to be able to use Dhurga words in English sentences. I explained that at this point Dhurga is in the process of revitalisation and there are some words known, but the grammar is still being reconstructed, and these limits affect what students can learn. A program and sequence of lesson plans were developed based on the learning needs of this group.

There were six one-hour lessons for the ADL class. These lessons were based on Stage 4, Pathway B of the *NSW Aboriginal Languages K–10 Syllabus*. Pathway B was chosen because it is intended for beginning learners of Aboriginal languages but targets more mature ages, whereas Pathway A targets students from Kindergarten to Stage 3 who will continue with that language through to Stages 4 and 5 (BOS NSW 2003, pp. 11–13). The reasoning for this choice was that the students of this class, although adults, are beginner learners of this language. The participants were attending as an interest group rather than an employment course, so I decided against the use of the Technical and Further Education (TAFE) NSW certificate courses which focus on assessment tasks, employment and resource creation (TAFE NSW, n.d.).

The Broulee lessons consisted of 12 classes of one half hour per week. Broulee was already employing Pathway A of the NSW syllabus, which reflects the learning that will take place for students who begin the study of a language in K–6. Though the same overall language situation applied to Broulee, they had already been teaching and learning Dhurga for the past five years.

The two Dhurga language teachers and I met to discuss what they would like me to teach. Both teachers were open-minded and suggested that they would be happy for me to teach anything that would assist me in my research project. They recognised that whatever I taught would be relevant and either reinforcement or good revision. Therefore the lessons to the YDL group were for the students to practise or revisit past learning and to implement my pedagogical resources to compare their response with the ADL results.

Developing resources to support each program

After the topic matter was planned for the ADL, the development of the resources was the next step. I created resources that I thought would be suitable to both ADL and YDL. Each resource was created for primary school-aged students targeting language syllabus requirements, based on gaining optimal student attention and participation, and included the use of the four macro-skills – listening, speaking reading, and writing.

My concern was that the resources developed might be seen as degrading or belittling to the ADL class. However, class discussion suggested that being beginning learners of any language meant, 'it was almost like being in kindergarten again, so we need to go back to basics' (ADL participant, pers. comm., December 1 2008). The resources included a language map, English and Dhurga pronunciation guides, phoneme charts, booklets, magnetic cutouts, games and stencils. The use of metalanguage was also included within some ADL classes.

I tried to create thematic kits so that all macro-skills would be used within each theme. There were three kits created each containing an A4 big book, board magnets, card games, mini create-your-own booklets and stencils. One kit was based on kin terms, another on *Minja njin?* (What's this?), and the third on *Wanaga?* (Who?).

The ADL students were the first to see and use the resources. This group gave me a combination of oral or written feedback at the end of each lesson, while resources and methodology were still fresh in their minds. I took notes and discussed their ideas within the class. Considering the comments made by the adult group I thought that I could easily use all of the resources in the next stage of the project, the YDL stage.

I was able to teach 12 classes to the YDL group. Most of those students had already covered the content that I was to deliver, so my lessons were taught with revision and reinforcement in mind, but employing the same resources as in the ADL class, all the while observing students' class participation, interaction with, and understanding of each resource.

Findings

The use of resources

Observations of both groups and feedback from the ADL class suggest that most resources created for Dhurga language learning were appropriate and effective to use with each group. Adults and school-aged students alike were positively engaged in each lesson; their participation was, more commonly than not, voluntary. The theme of each lesson was recurrent in every resource created for each lesson and incorporated each of the macro-skills, thus increasing the likelihood of new language retention. This approach seemed to be successful for each group because language retention and recognition from week to week was quite high, based on oral and written revision.

The use of metalanguage

At the onset of this investigation my hypothesis was that identical resources could be used to teach youth and adults alike. I believed that the same pedagogical resources could be used, but with adaptations to the teaching practice.

One of those adaptations might be the use of metalanguage. I thought that it would be best not to introduce metalanguage to the youth, as it may be too confusing. However, after doing so with some Stage 2 and 3 students I was surprised to find that these students were much more accepting of new terms, for example *interrogatives*, *labial*, *ablative*. Possibly the YDL had come in contact with these terms sometime within the past five years of their Dhurga lessons.

The adults, on the other hand, found the introduction of metalanguage quite daunting, and preferred not to make use of it. For example I thought that the ADL would prefer to learn about place and manner of articulation, but most found it to be 'too scary' (ADL participant, pers. comm., 14 December 2008). Most of the ADL wanted to use simple terms, such as *question words, lip sounds, from endings*. It seems that the YDL were more open to new and unfamiliar things while the ADL found it difficult and wanted information to be more accessible.

The influence of age

I had imagined that the ADL would be more likely to participate in class or group activities and that they might be less likely to be affected by the shame factor. However, the adult students tended to work in isolation not wanting to work in pairs or groups. It seemed the YDL were far more willing to volunteer, to have a go. The YDL were also more likely to ask for assistance when needed. Usually the assistance sought by the YDL was in relation to literacy, not about the Dhurga language itself, and particularly English words that they were unable to decode to complete class activities. I noticed that the YDL had a little more difficultly spelling Dhurga words than saying them. Maybe they had not actually mastered the relation between the spelling and the sounds. It was very hard to determine the differences in acquisition as the YDL had been exposed to the sounds, vocabulary and grammar of the language for much longer than the ADL class. What was noticeable was that the YDL classes were able to apply the rules of Dhurga grammar with a little more ease. After the six ADL classes some of the participants were reluctant to verbalise vocabulary at all, especially on an individual basis.

Conclusion

Since the development of the NSW Aboriginal languages syllabus in 2003 many NSW schools have introduced Aboriginal languages programs. Some have been put in place to help close the gap between Aboriginal and non-Aboriginal students' education levels after the review of Aboriginal education found that Aboriginal students lag behind their non-Aboriginal counterparts (NSW Aboriginal Education Consultative Group Inc. & NSW Department of Education and Training 2004). These schools have found that there are many other significant benefits to these languages programs within their curriculum.

Many communities have supported the introduction of Indigenous languages in schools. Bringing Aboriginal languages into schools is crucial to all students as a way of learning about and practising reconciliation and fostering awareness of cultural difference. For Indigenous students it is all the more important because learning an Indigenous language can increase their self esteem, improve decoding skills in literacy (BOS NSW 2000) and may positively influence attendance and retention rates of Aboriginal students.

Many Indigenous language programs in NSW schools are carried out only through successful applications for funding to various bodies. This research project is important because large amounts of Indigenous language funding are committed to developing pedagogical resources. When costs are reduced, language programs might be able to continue over longer periods with more funds to pay community language teachers, and to carry out research, development and production of grammars and dictionaries to aid our teachers in the revival process.

Teaching these two groups was an enlightening experience. Theories, methods and resources ultimately were tested, and all proved very different than I had anticipated.

As a matter of fact, there was very little need for the modification of my pedagogical resources. It was my teaching methods that needed to be changed more. My preconceived ideas about how to teach adults and youth Dhurga needed to change to be able to accommodate the needs of each group.

I suggest that we, as teachers, need to be capable of examining ourselves, our methods, our practices and preconceptions, and be receptive to change to better suit the needs of our students. I also firmly believe that we, as Aboriginal people, should work together sharing what we know. Let's form language teams that consist of whole language areas or boundaries, rather than individual school language teams. By doing so we will have a wealth of knowledge, skills, experience and resources that can be shared. Sharing is a vital part of our Aboriginal culture; let's not lose that along with our languages. 'One of the important lessons that's been learnt over the years, however, is that if experiences, resources and successful teaching techniques are shared, then Aboriginal language courses can continually improve to benefit everyone, but particularly our Aboriginal students' (BOS NSW n.d.). By sharing what we have learnt we will provide better opportunities for our youth, communities and languages to succeed.

Acknowledgements

I would like to acknowledge and thank wholeheartedly all those people who supported me throughout my study - family, friends and particularly the staff and my fellow students from the Koori Centre at the University of Sydney. Also much thanks to both Mogo Public School and Broulee Public School, the two schools that allowed me to carry out this research, and the youth and community members for their positive participation and allowing me to carry out my project, either through observation or through sharing their valuable feedback and knowledge. I would also like to thank the two Dhurga language teachers who gave me the opportunity to fulfil requirements needed to complete my study. And, finally, a big thank you to Susan Poetsch and John Hobson who worked very patiently with me on drafting and re-drafting this paper. Without these people's input, participation and cooperation I would not have been able to share this with you.

References

Board of Studies New South Wales (2000). *Teaching Aboriginal language: case studies*. Sydney: Board of Studies New South Wales.

Board of Studies New South Wales (n.d.). *Aboriginal languages*. Sydney: Board of Studies New South Wales [Online]. Available: ab-ed.boardofstudies.nsw.edu.au/go/aboriginal-languages [Accessed 6 January 2009].

Board of Studies New South Wales (2001). *Working with Aboriginal communities: a guide to community consultation and protocols*. Sydney: Board of Studies New South Wales.

Board of Studies New South Wales (2003). *Aboriginal languages K–10 syllabus*. Sydney: Board of Studies New South Wales.

Dick B & Swepson P (1997). *Action research faq (frequently asked questions file)* [Online]. Available: www.scu.edu.au/schools/gcm/ar/arp/arfaq.html [Accessed 12 September 2008].

Eades DK (1976). *The Dharawal and Dhurga languages of the south coast*. Canberra: Australian Institute for Aboriginal Studies.

Federation of Aboriginal & Torres Strait Islanders Languages (2004). *FATSIL guide to community protocols for Indigenous languages projects*. Melbourne: Federation of Aboriginal & Torres Strait Islanders Languages [Online]. Available: www.fatsil.org.au/FATSILCommunityProtocolsGuide/FATSILProtocolGuide/ [Accessed 21 November 2008].

New South Wales Aboriginal Education Consultative Group Inc & New South Department of Education and Training (2004). *Report of the review of Aboriginal education*. Darlinghurst, NSW: New South Wales Department of Education and Training.

Rhydwen M, Munro J, Parolin E & Poetsch S (2007). *Report on school-based Aboriginal language program activity in NSW during 2006*. Sydney: Board of Studies New South Wales [Online]. Available: ab-ed.boardofstudies.nsw.edu.au/go/resources/languages [Accessed 5 January 2009].

Smith LT (1999). *Decolonising methodologies: research and indigenous peoples*. Zed Books: London.

Technical & Further Education New South Wales (n.d.). *NSW Certificate I in Aboriginal Language/s* [Online]. Available: www.nci.tafensw.edu.au/courses/general%20education/17411-cert-i-aboriginal-languages.htm [Accessed 1 January 2009].

14
Aboriginal languages programs in TAFE NSW: delivery initiatives and strategies

Jackie Cipollone[1]

Abstract

There is a recognised link between culture and language and each is dependent on the other. Language orders and makes sense of a group's culture, and a group's culture is bounded by language. Aboriginal language skills, then, can play a critical role in developing Aboriginal cultural identity. The recognition of the language-culture relationship forms a valuable part of the 'broader Indigenous development agenda that seeks to strengthen individuals and promote sustainable communities' (Aboriginal & Torres Strait Islander Commission 2004, p. 1). Consistent with this the *Report of the Review of Aboriginal Education* notes:

Students' knowledge and use of Aboriginal languages are fundamental to the development of their identity and enhance their self esteem. Since the teaching and learning of languages provide an important gateway to Aboriginal culture, this process also ensures that the school staff and community understand and respect their students' heritage. It is important that students are increasingly given access to the study of Aboriginal languages... (New South Wales Aboriginal Education Consultative Group Inc. & New South Wales Department of Education & Training 2004, p. 113).

The first part of this paper will outline a Technical and Further Education New South Wales (TAFE NSW) response to The Aboriginal and Torres Strait Islander Commission Training Policy Statement 2004–06, which led to the development of three nationally accredited Aboriginal language qualifications. The second part of this paper will present three case studies that show how Aboriginal languages programs are being delivered in TAFE NSW, and report on some of the successes and challenges experienced in doing so.

---

1 Social Inclusion & Vocational Access Skills Unit, TAFE NSW in partnership with Aboriginal Education & Training Directorate, NSW Department of Education and Training.

Development of the Certificates in Aboriginal Language/s

Investigating need and demand

The NSW Department of Education and Training's (DET) Aboriginal Education and Training Directorate (AETD), in partnership with the TAFE NSW Social Inclusion and Vocational Access (SI&VA) Skills Unit, set about investigating the need and demand for the development of Aboriginal languages qualifications. Information was gathered by way of a series of focus group questions and follow-up consultation. TAFE NSW institutes and members of Aboriginal communities in NSW identified that there was a need to provide an opportunity for Aboriginal people to learn an Aboriginal language at an introductory level.

Findings

Existing practice

In NSW, according to research, there are around 70 different Aboriginal languages that have survived colonisation, although many have been lost. In NSW all the current language programs are associated with revival or reclamation. Indeed, many Aboriginal Elders in NSW believe that the languages are not dead, but are sleeping and waiting to be revived.

Workshops in some of these languages: Dunghutti, Gamilaraay (Kamilaroi), and Gumbaynggirr, were being delivered in NSW as part of General and Vocational Education and Training (VET) courses in response to local demand. The programs were being delivered in Armidale, Coffs Harbour, Coonabarabran, Dubbo, Kempsey, Nambucca Heads, Narrandera, Narrabri and Walgett. In addition, a Statement of Attainment in Indigenous Language (under licence from TAFE Queensland) was used to deliver Wiradjuri. Future delivery of Aboriginal language programs was being planned in Moree and Tamworth.

Identified needs

The information gathered indicated that there was sufficient widespread demand to develop a short course or entry level Certificate I qualification in local Aboriginal languages, with the permission of the relevant Elders and traditional owners. It was thought that such a course would help to rejuvenate and increase the use of the languages. The following languages were identified for delivery: Anaiwan, Awabakal, Biripi, Bundjalung, Dharug, Dunghutti, Eora, Gamilaraay, Gumbayngirr, Guringai, Onerwal, Wangkumarra, Wailwan, Wiradjuri, and Yuwaalaraay. The members of each language group expressed an interest in undertaking a course in their own language. It was noted that cultural obligations had to be considered for those Aboriginal people who, due to their background, come from two language groups.

There was a range of potential target groups identified for the new course: school students, young people, and adults – in particular, members of both Aboriginal and non-Aboriginal communities such as Aboriginal education assistants and teachers and other school staff. It was estimated – based on expression of interest, programs already running and anecdotal reports – that initial enrolment would exceed 100 across NSW. The spread of enrolments was expected to vary depending on the number of language groups in the regions.

Demand for higher-level courses at Australian Qualifications Framework (AQF) Levels 2 and 3 was also identified. It was thought that such courses, in addition to revitalising Aboriginal languages, would provide formal recognition of Aboriginal people's knowledge and skills and could provide an accredited vocational pathway for graduates of the entry level programs. People with the higher-level qualifications, for instance, could go on to become teachers of their languages.

First steps to development

With the need and demand for certificates in Aboriginal languages firmly established, stakeholders turned their attention to specifics: what content such courses might cover, where and how they might be delivered, and who would deliver and assess them.

Content

There was widespread agreement that each of the four language macro-skills – listening, speaking, reading and writing – should be an integral part of the course, and that development of speaking and listening should be given priority. In addition to communication skills three specific knowledge areas were considered relevant to include: Aboriginal cultural protocols, the use of basic technology, and an understanding of school structures and environments. It was also felt that such a course would enable participants to extend their knowledge about and protect their cultures, and to further instil Aboriginal cultural values.

Delivery

Flexibility was the overriding concept that characterised most of the discussion about course delivery in recognition of individual circumstances and learning styles. Options discussed regarding flexible location included that any site should be negotiated with the community before delivery, and the local Aboriginal land council venue should be considered. It was also suggested that courses should be offered in both part-time and full-time modes, of short duration, with achievable outcomes possible in one semester. Each course should flow into the next one to allow continual learning momentum, but the length could vary. The preferred assessment method should be spoken with options for written assessment according to the needs, abilities, requests and commitment of students.

Teacher qualifications

An Aboriginal language course should be delivered by an Aboriginal person with language knowledge or teaching skills assessed by Aboriginal Elders. If, in exceptional circumstances, the course were to be delivered by a non-Aboriginal teacher, then an Aboriginal person should be employed as a team teacher.

Other

The general consensus was that there should be no formal entry requirements, only an interest and a desire to learn. Entry to the course should be limited to Aboriginal people only, if that is the decision of the local Aboriginal community. Ongoing support would be essential for people who may need assistance with literacy and numeracy. Allowances should be made and support provided for people who may have hearing disabilities and who may need sign language interpreters.

Accreditation and beyond

The Certificates I, II and III in Aboriginal Language/s were duly developed and accredited in 2007. As nationally recognised accredited courses the three qualifications are listed on the National Training Information Service (NTIS) database.

The Certificate I was first delivered in NSW in the second half of 2007, and the Certificates II and III were first delivered in 2008. In that short time there have been approximately 450 student enrolments in NSW with the bulk of these at Certificate I level.

There are advanced standing arrangements among the Certificate courses and units offered by the Koori Centre at the University of Sydney as part of the Bachelor of Arts, Graduate Diploma of Indigenous Languages Education, and Master of Indigenous Languages Education programs.

In November 2008 the TAFE NSW Keeping Aboriginal Languages Strong workshop was held in Sydney, and attended by people from across NSW. Participants shared their experiences about aspects of course delivery including community consultation, course promotion, challenges faced, and successful outcomes. Talking about what has worked is a good way to help get further language revitalisation happening.

Initiatives and strategies to deliver Aboriginal languages programs

Dhurga Buradja – Speaking Dhurga Tomorrow

Context and implementation

Following the introduction of the NSW Government's Draft Aboriginal Languages Policy in 2001–02 the chair of the Cobowra Local Aboriginal Land Council applied for funding through the Department of Communication Information Technology and the Arts' Maintaining Indigenous Language and Records program. The application was successful on the basis of the language's endangered status.

In 2007 the TAFE NSW Illawarra Institute's Aboriginal Development Manager (ADM) identified that there was a need and demand for the delivery of Dhurga language in

Moruya. The ADM liaised with the local community and sought its members' support to establish the teaching and learning of Dhurga in Moruya.

A language program had already been established at Broulee Public School taught by two experienced Aboriginal teachers, and Vincentia High School was offering a 100-hour course to Year 8 students taught by another Aboriginal community member (see also Lane in this volume). A doctoral student in linguistics from the Australian National University supported both programs. These teachers and the PhD student, together with the TAFE ADM, were the driving force behind the success of the Dhurga Buradja – Speaking Dhurga Tomorrow (Certificate I) course. They all felt that speaking, reading and writing a language is important and that the Dhurga language needed to go back to the people that own it.

The eight-week course was initially offered to 20 students. Preference was given to community Elders, the Yuin community and then the general community. The two teachers and the linguist were invited to teach Dhurga. A partnership was formed.

A professional development and information day was held at the Moruya TAFE campus. People from the TAFE AETD and the SI&VA Skills Unit were invited to provide professional development to teachers and staff involved in the delivery of the Certificate I. Participants were given an overview of the curriculum content and resources. The day concluded with a barbeque, which allowed teachers, students and community members to mingle and network.

Dhurga Buradja – Speaking Dhurga Tomorrow was ultimately delivered to 18 students at Moruya TAFE between October and December 2007, with 100% attendance. All 18 completed the course and both students and teachers looked forward to attending each Saturday; 13 graduated with Certificate I in Aboriginal Language/s, and five students completed at various levels of proficiency. Those five were given the opportunity to complete the course in Semester 1, 2008.

In April 2008 the students were invited to the *Dhurga Buradja* book launch, where each was presented with a copy of the book. The Cobowra Land Council provided a spectacular evening and feast at the Moruya Golf Club, where the Council's chief executive officer spoke highly of the Institute ADM's achievement in establishing an historical community partnership.

Resources used

All resources used in delivering the course were designed and made by the two class teachers and were based on the resources they had made and used at Broulee Primary School. The afternoon sessions each Saturday were devoted to the students producing their own resources to use when teaching the language to their own children or other community members. They were also intended to assist the students with their short projects, which were part of the course assessment requirements.

Keys to success

A vital component in the success of the Dhurga Buradja course was that it was underpinned by a community partnership. The real driving force were community members of the Cobowra Local Aboriginal Land Council (LALC) and the ADM from Illawarra Institute. The ADM had always felt strongly that language belongs to community, and she had waited for an opportunity to partner with the community.

Another partnership developed around funding arrangements. Moruya TAFE campus agreed to supply the venue and facilities, and the Cobowra LALC agreed to supply the teachers, meals and resources.

Community partnership also developed through community presence in the classroom and was seen as the biggest benefit of the program. Community presence allowed language to be shared, and it encouraged young and old to learn together. The social interaction during the course played a big part in the attendance of all of the students and the sharing that occurred also encouraged enthusiastic participation. Involving Aboriginal language speakers in running the program was also crucial to its success.

The two teachers delivering the Dhurga Buradja program worked very closely with the linguist and this specialist involvement was another key to the program's success. The linguist was able to use the recordings of Elders held at the Australian Institute of Aboriginal and Torres Strait Islander Studies in order to 'know' language and teach it to others. In addition to her expertise the linguist was 100% committed to the establishment and success of the program and travelled between Canberra and the Moruya campus every week (a 350-kilometre, five-hour round trip).

The course has been a huge success with the grandchildren, children and Elders now incorporating basic language into their daily activities and communication. This has been very important for the Dhurga language revitalisation. The community was excited not only about reclaiming its language but to obtain a nationally accredited qualification as well. Many of the participants were already working in schools so an opportunity to promote language within the school sector was strengthened. For many of the Elders returning to education it was an opportunity for them to bring *their* language back into the classroom, where they felt comfortable having qualified teachers and a linguist supporting them with spelling and grammar.

Challenges and issues

Adequate funding is required to ensure that this successful program is ongoing. To deliver and assess the TAFE NSW certificates requires a minimum educational qualification of Certificate IV in Training and Assessment as well as knowledge of and skills in the relevant Aboriginal language. Language teachers who do not have the Certificate IV need to be supervised and mentored by TAFE teachers. The involvement of a linguist is a valuable human resource. Funding is also required for the purchase of existing resources and the development of new ones.

Community disagreement can be an issue in cases where there are some divisions in the Aboriginal community about language. For example, community members may have different views about the 'right' and 'wrong' language being used to describe things.

Student confidence is another matter that needs to be recognised and addressed. Sometimes local speakers lack confidence in their use of language – because of shame related to representations of Aboriginality or the banning of the use of Aboriginal language in policy and practices governing Aboriginal peoples – and need to believe in their own credibility as language speakers and users.

Experience showed that support of community was central to the ongoing success of the program. This could also indicate that the opposite might occur, with enrolment numbers declining if there are negative attitudes in the community concerning the program.

Outcomes and future directions

The recording and reclamation of cultural and language knowledge was considered paramount during the delivery of the course. Course outcomes included the intention to collect language information from the students to complement and reinforce language that the linguist had collated from her research.

As a result of the TAFE course delivery, three of the students ensured that a Dhurga language program was established at Batemans Bay Public School in 2008.

The college is in the process of delivering community workshops to four different communities within the Dhurga language area in an effort to encourage future participation in the TAFE courses.

It is anticipated that a community language centre will eventually be set up to collect, collate and store language material as a part of the reclamation process.

Gamilaraay in New England

Context and implementation

The Aboriginal Education and Training Unit (AETU) in New England Institute of TAFE has run several Gamilaraay (Kamilaroi) language workshops over a number of years in Tamworth and Moree. These were facilitated by a linguist who has studied and taught the language extensively. Workshop participants who mostly work in the health and education sectors came from a wide geographical area including Coonabarabran, Caroona, Coonamble, Dirranbandi, Tingha and Tamworth.

In the absence of an accredited course, workshops had been delivered under generic courses such as Statements of Attainment in Outreach and Workskills. The AETU team leader had keenly promoted these workshops and was subsequently able to assist in the development of the new Certificate I in Aboriginal Language/s. The accreditation of a nationally recognised course was welcomed as a vehicle for enabling recognition of the existing skills of a number of Aboriginal people in the region.

The director General Education and Equity Services (GE&ES) in TAFE NSW New England Institute was keen to have a bank of Aboriginal people qualified to deliver training in Aboriginal languages in the region, and to assist with the promotion of the Certificate I in Aboriginal Language/s. The director's support has enabled this to occur, as well as the production of resources.

Resources used

Funding was provided to develop resources to support course delivery and learning. In addition, three Aboriginal languages assessment tasks and accompanying marking guides were produced. These can be used to assess the proficiency of course participants and can also be used as part of skills recognition.

Keys to success

Involving Aboriginal language speakers in running the program was a great asset. The Aboriginal teachers had studied Gamilaraay at the University of Sydney, and one had also worked extensively in teaching that language to children. They worked closely with the linguist and this co-facilitation of the workshops enhanced the program's success.

Good language pedagogy has a basis in theories about how language is acquired that inform teaching methodology. Access to information about widely accepted principles of language teaching and learning helps to ensure success. The use of a dictionary on its own is not enough!

The support of the GE&ES director for the promotion and delivery of Aboriginal language in the region also assisted in the program's success. Funding was provided for a small resource development project to produce songbooks, CDs demonstrating pronunciation and online resources. It has been identified that more resources need to be made available.

Challenges and issues

Providing adequate recognition of students' existing skills was seen as being very important, as there were a number of former students who had previously completed language courses that had been delivered under generic course titles. In acknowledgement of this a two-day recognition of prior learning workshop was run. Workshop participants sought to have their prior learning recognised by undertaking challenge tests that were based on the learning materials developed for the Certificate I in Aboriginal Language/s. The challenge test items were devised by the teachers of the Certificate I and were validated by TAFE NSW teachers of English for speakers of other languages, who hold specialist applied linguistics qualifications.

Ways of maintaining student attendance need to be investigated. Tamworth was the site for course delivery, but participants came from a wide geographical area. As a consequence attendance declined in the face-to-face mode, so a shift was made to distance learning and 12 online lessons were developed. To try to manage this issue in the future it was decided to run the full Certificate I course at Tamworth with a more localised group able to attend the campus on a regular basis.

Outcomes and future directions

There is a sense in the community that the program and resource production protect the language and make it available to the community. Support and continued training is essential for course graduates so that delivery of the Certificates in Aboriginal Language/s by Aboriginal facilitators becomes an essential component in the development of cultural pride and identity for the whole Aboriginal community.

Dharawal in South Western Sydney

Context

Dharawal language (Biddigal dialect) had already been taught in some south-western Sydney schools for two years with funding from DET. The south-western Sydney region Aboriginal support officer had been instrumental in working with the schools and with the local community to gain its support for that work to occur. An initial question had been, 'Where do you start?' The schools had decided that teaching the language of the land, the traditional local language, was a good starting point and that other languages could be taught further down the track.

Community people expressed a wish to learn language too. In response to that local need and demand there was a series of community consultations with Aboriginal community Elders, Aboriginal groups and the local Aboriginal Education Consultative Group. The language program offered through TAFE builds on that work.

The program was jointly funded by one of the South Western Sydney Institute of TAFE faculties and by the Institute's Aboriginal Unit. The Certificate I in Aboriginal Language/s was delivered by two teachers: a teacher of the Aboriginal language with the support of a literacy and language teacher.

Twenty-one students enrolled in the Dharawal language course. They ranged in age from young teenagers to older people and ranged in experience from school students to a senior of the Dharawal people. The class was conducted on a Wednesday evening as that was usually the night set aside for community meetings. This meant that attendance varied because community members had a raft of other obligations. However, classes averaged 12 to 15 students on any evening. Four members never missed a class, whilst others missed classes only once a month. To manage this, all teaching and learning material was printed and handed to members in a special folder with relevant instructions. The students completed the course at the end of Semester 2, 2008.

Resources used

The resources available for delivery of the course were a dictionary of the Dharawal language and a CD of common phrases.

Keys to success

The success of the program was a result of the participation and commitment of a range of people. The teacher was a local language speaker but did not have the formal qualifications required to deliver the Certificate I course so the faculty decided to offer support from a specialist language and literacy teacher. This was a way of ensuring a quality program that satisfied the requirements of the Australian Quality Training Framework. The specialist teacher appeared to play a low-key role in delivery of the course by not entering the classroom, but supported the language teacher through collaboration on assessment and administration tasks. This collaborative partnership approach to delivery was underpinned by the community consultations that had already been established.

The design of the program also helped to make it a success. It was decided to package the core units so that the course could be completed in a semester. This approach helped to provide learners with a strong sense of achievement.

Challenges and issues

It was possible to deliver the program successfully by way of a mentoring and team-teaching approach. While this was satisfactory, it is likely to be an interim measure only. People who graduate from the TAFE courses will qualify to teach them by going on to gain the Certificate IV in Training and Assessment. With the required experience in teaching language they will then be fully qualified to deliver and assess the TAFE Aboriginal language/s certificates in their own right.

Technology can support language acquisition but, of course, this requires funds. For instance, access to portable digital audio equipment would enhance outcomes by enabling learners to hear the spoken language at any time.

Outcomes and future directions

One of the most positive outcomes of the program has been the strengthening of culture and extension in knowledge of Country[2] through learning language.

Learning the local language has also helped those Aboriginal people who had been displaced or dispossessed to relate to the Country in which they now live. It awakened their sensitivity to the influence of Country on their lives, for example the connections created through placenames. This has made them feel more welcome and comfortable in a place that is not their homeland, but has become their adopted home.

Several of the class members have children who are attending the Dharawal language classes at school, and an unexpected outcome has been parents and children helping each other in their language learning thereby establishing an additional cultural bond.

---

2 Contributors to this report required that the word 'country' be capitalised when used in specifically Aboriginal contexts [Eds].

It is hoped that the courses will continue, enabling several of the class members to go on to be able to teach Dharawal in schools. For the present there is only the one teacher and many schools are also demanding the right to have their children taught.

Conclusion

The most crucial key to success to date appears to have been the contributions of the people who know (quite literally) what they're talking about – the speakers of Aboriginal language and their communities. Where those contributions inform all aspects of course delivery, there are successful outcomes for learners.

The development of the TAFE NSW Certificates I, II and III in Aboriginal Language/s has been a recent and significant contribution to language revitalisation in NSW. It has also helped develop new partnerships, added another dimension to existing community participation, and established a new vocational pathway for Aboriginal people.

References

Aboriginal & Torres Strait Islander Commission (2004). *Training policy statement 2004 to 2006*. Canberra, Australia: Aboriginal & Torres Strait Islander Commission [Online]. Available: svc003.wic001g.server-web.com/issues/education/training/default.asp [Accessed 4 November 2005].

New South Wales Aboriginal Education Consultative Group, Inc & New South Wales Department of Education and Training (2004). *The report of the review of Aboriginal education*. Darlinghurst, NSW: NSW Department of Education.

15
Reclamation process for Dharug in Sydney using song

Richard Green[1]

Abstract

I have been learning my language, the Dharug *dalang*, since my youth and have accessed linguistic work on the grammar and pronunciation of the language. Because of my efforts with reclamation I have been given permission from prominent members of the Darug[2] clan and community to reclaim and implement paradigms suitable for teaching in classroom settings.

I have used a variety of approaches to bring the language alive. I have linked the students' learning to their local community through looking at the Dharug root of many Australian placenames. Also I have taken modern English words and translated their root into Dharug to enable students to talk about their present life. Finally I have made their learning highly interactive with games, songs and weather reports.

Games such as Bingo are used to reinforce learning the words for animals. 'Simon says … ' and the song 'Head, shoulders, knees and toes' provide reinforcement of the names of body parts. In particular, in songs the melody provides a reference point for remembering words and their pronunciation. Weather reports provide a practical exercise that is carried out purely in language. Teachers can also implement report making in classes when I am not there.

This work has now extended to classes with community Elders. The participants include speakers from other nations as well as fluent Dharug speakers. The result is that those who come are starting to agree on a common pronunciation and semantics for the languages in the greater Sydney area. They are also looking at how different these languages may really be, in terms of reclamation for Sydney.

---

1 Chifley College Dunheved Campus, St Marys.

2 The preferred spelling for references to the people is currently Darug, while the language is more commonly spelt Dharug.

History of the language

The Dharug language was spoken around Sydney for thousands of years BC (before Cook). It is similar to the languages now studied as Dharawal and Eora, and they may have all been forms of the same language. As such it is an important language for the people of Sydney, whether they moved here or were originally from the area. It is the language in which the land around Sydney was described and in which the care of country was carried out. The culture of the Darug nation also has other unique forms, such as X-ray art where an animal's bone structures and internal organs are displayed, which is now popular throughout Australia. This heritage is an important part of the present culture for Aboriginal people and for all Australians.

As it has become safer for people to speak their language and openly practise their culture, there is now opportunity for those who have carried knowledge to stand up and contribute to the reclamation process. This will include a long period of establishment where the different knowledge parts fit together, as well as the role of those who have been told these parts, in a larger framework of cultural practice. This will be verified in the environment of a long oral history of descent and cultural relations that will constitute an extended process. This is the story of the reclamation of the Dharug language from what has been remembered and recorded and the story of the Dharug courses now being run in Sydney schools for children and adults.

The heritage of the tutor

Due to the long period of occupation of Sydney there is much debate as to the heritage of the language of the area and of the people now living here. While many people have been moved here by force or looking for work, there are families who are descended from the original people around Sydney. Also, as most Darug men were killed early in the settlement period, the Aboriginal men who came to work here married the Darug women. One family recorded as from this area was the Webbs. The Webbs were pushed to the mountains from Parramatta then went north to Bundjalung country. I am descended from this family and live in Sydney.

I learnt the language as a child in Parramatta by listening to the stories told by the men, as the women were not speaking it then. I lived among Elders, including my great grandmother, who were still speaking around Parramatta when I was born in 1963 in Katoomba. My contact with the language had begun and I was acknowledged as a storyteller from a young age by my people. I was relocated to Parramatta then later to Queensland and Aotearoa (New Zealand). This common dislocation of Aboriginal people from their community is one issue in trying to track peoples' place and identity.

When I was 20 I tracked down my dad who was impressed by my use of Dharug words and encouraged me to speak in full sentences. My father died in 1997 and I continued an interest in languages in general and mixed with the Bundjalung, Dhanggati, Gamilaraay and Wiradjuri speakers around Redfern who, while pronouncing their own languages, provided the different sound patterns for me to learn my own *dalang* or tongue. In particular the Australian coastal languages such as Bundjalung, Dhanggati and Dharug have long been known to be similar and thus can support each other in their reclamation or revival.

The Aboriginal linguist Jakelyn Troy researched the archives and existing speakers of Dharug for her book *The Sydney language* (Troy 1994). This work provided me with a systematic spelling and grammar, as it is a complete study of the Sydney language. It is now being recognised by some community members that what was called Eora, which means people in Dharug, is in fact the same language as Dharug.

I have proven to be a very quick learner of many languages including Arabic, Greek, Turkish, Japanese and Chinese. It has been this unique skill with languages, and my love and knowledge of music and musical patterns, which has enabled me to produce a spoken Dharug for teaching which is fluent and poetic, enabling me to teach in song. I have been working with the Elders of the Darug nation to secure their permission to teach their language and to provide a consistent form of Dharug for teaching to all students. Most importantly for the reclamation process is that I am acknowledged as a songman, a man able to revive the songs of the culture and land around Sydney.

History of the language program

I initiated the Dharug language program when I started teaching it in the community and taking it to the schools. Through my work, consultations were held among Chifley College Dunheved Campus and the Darug and community Elders. From this an agreement was developed among the Elders, the College and the Department of Education and Training to run the program. These school programs, however, are only part of a broader community re-awakening.

The next stage involved aligning my teaching with the Aboriginal language syllabus from the Board of Studies. The linguist Amanda Oppliger wrote the program that was accepted for use in the schools. At present the program is 15 hours for all students in Years 7 and 8 at the College. This provides the students with enough word and language structure to start talking language and using it in their daily lives. However this needs to be extended, particularly with the training and accreditation of more Aboriginal languages teachers.

Chifley College is located on Darug land, and the staff members are aware that they are surrounded by the many artefacts and past experiences of the Darug people. While much of this is not visible to many people today the language is alive and present, and it is vital to bring this awareness back to all people living in this land. The College has incorporated in its strategic plan the statement, 'Our journey with the Dharug Language program is teaching us that we must listen to the Land as it speaks to us of Darug ways of knowing, learning and teaching.' (Chifley College 2005, p. 2).

I have now been teaching the Dharug *dalang* for three years at Chifley College Dunheved Campus, which has a 23% Aboriginal enrolment. The success of the program has been acknowledged in the western Sydney region and I have also been employed by Doonside Technology High School for the past two years.

Teaching Dharug as a familiar language

I have developed the language program over many years, finding what will motivate students and what they need to learn to be able to use the language. As with all unfamiliar languages the first step is to teach the new sounds of the language. Most of the students laugh when they first hear the language spoken. Yet I am able to explain that Dharug is the language used on most of their local street signs and for some suburb names of western Sydney, as this is the original language of the area. That is, they are living where the language still exists, even if dormant. This brings the language to life for the students and shows that it is a more appropriate source of a youth language than the Pig Latin they are already speaking. After the very first class at Dunheved the pupils begin using *yuin* as yes instead of the *eshay* they used previously.

The next step for me is to bring the language up to date. Words such as the days of the week were not found in Dharug. However, these words have a history or root in their English form, and that root can be translated from the ancient stories into similar Dharug words. The days of the week are a great tool to help students practise using the tongue in their everyday life. Even the front office staff at the College and School can use these words for the calendar.

This process involves teaching students the history of the English words, the equivalent Darug stories, and the new words. This provides a link between the old cultures of Australia and Europe in a way that is ignored in many presentations of ancient 'mythologies'. It suggests that the Aboriginal people in Australia have retained a history and knowledge which many Europeans have lost, particularly in coming to other lands, establishing colonies and claiming some advanced 'civilised' status.

Talking Dharug as relevant

The days of the week are presented as part of the cycle of time, rather than just a time-keeping measure. Therefore the seasons are also described: not the four seasons of Europe, but those of the central eastern coast of Australia. Also the weather is described in Dharug. This is important as Australia has unique seasons and weather patterns and, as the effect of climate change increases, it important our children understand what are the long-term cycles of Australia, and what are the changes to which they and the environment will have to adapt.

The lesson in weather is then followed by the students giving weekly weather reports from the morning paper in Dharug. The compass directions are also introduced for this reporting. This is both topical and a regular exercise that the teacher can continue with on the days that I am not in that class. This process enables the students to think and listen in Dharug each day, encouraging fluency and the use of Dharug for entire parts of the lesson, rather than needing to mix with English.

Teaching Dharug as fun

The next step is to enforce and increase vocabulary to improve pronunciation and extend this into singing. I use a process of interchanging between games and revision for this process. Games such as 'Simon says ... ' for the body parts, and Bingo for the words for animals, are good for repetition. Similar to Bingo is the game *Ngan diya giyara?* (What's its name?), with the Dharug word on the card and the names called out in English, or vice versa.

Then the words can also be used in songs that repeat around a thematic structure, introducing new words each verse, such as 'Head, Shoulders, Knees and Toes'. I have taught the children to sing this for all parts of the body, even down to the fingernails.

These songs introduce the ergative form in the repeated sections; a characteristic of many Australian languages – as well as some other Oceania languages – that is different to English (Lynch 1998, p. 199; Senior Secondary Assessment Board of South Australia 1996, p. 140). It is also an important first step in terms of learning to construct Dharug sentences, and move on from the wordlist approach to language revival that has been followed for many years.

Once students have reached Year 8 they are able to form grammatical sentences and have an understanding of what is being said in Dharug by the teacher and their peers. Every lesson is practised using song for two reasons. Firstly, the language was a sung language. Its flexible form and loose structure, compared to English, enable the generation of a poetic form and the maintenance of rhythm throughout a long story. Secondly, the stories were always sung, as the song format is important for memorising words and sounds, and otherwise young learners would forget the stories. Once students have sung a lesson they seem to find that point of melody that can enable them to recall at will.

With singing it is possible to teach students the different parts of words; the tenses, the different forms of nouns and the various endings to do with time and location. They can first learn new constructions in song, with repetition, and then this can be explained as they become familiar with the form. At the same time as I teach language I am teaching music to the students, the scales they are using in the Dharug songs and the intervals they need to learn.

Tricks of the trade

I have found that perhaps the most rewarding aspect of teaching is not just the passing on of the language, but also the amount of understanding of the language and language learning that I have gained through this.

The most important aspect is to make the language relevant, and accessible. For example, in modern culture singing is not a strong point for many boys. However, Aboriginal stories are traditionally sung in a high-pitched voice. This makes the songs more accessible to young men, and less confronting.

I have realised that there are many tricks to teaching and learning languages. Firstly is the strength of song as a teaching tool; secondly is how the structure of the music supports the learning of particular words or language structures. Also I have learnt to study my own learning and convey these tricks to the students, such as how you learn to see a word on the back of your eyelid when you want to remember how to pronounce it.

What has been most important to the strength of the language reclamation has been the fact that it is being taught on the land which it describes and that it has been taught under the control of, and in the manner specified by, the Dharug speakers. By teaching the students Dharug I am teaching them about where they live and who they are as residents of Darug land. I also set up the program in consultation with the community and Dharug speakers. As a result the method of teaching has been much more fluid and derived more from telling the story of the culture, than from syllabus or linguistic requirements. It is this method of teaching that is an integral part of Aboriginal ways of knowing.

Community involvement

The students speak Dharug every day at Dunheved and it has carried over into the community. What started with ten adult students at Dunheved is a class that has grown to 60 men, women and children including Uncle Wes Marne, a Bidgambul man, Greg Simms and the accomplished Dharug speaker Auntie Edna Watson. These people come from many different backgrounds yet are all very respectful of my knowledge in the area of language reclamation. By working with people who have maintained the language orally I have been able to introduce the work of linguists such as Jakelyn Troy to them. This is leading to a consistent pronunciation of words across the region and recognition of the unity of the Sydney languages, while acknowledging local variations if they exist.

Also, while people such as Edna Watson speak the language and readily understand most of what is being said, she acknowledges that she doesn't have the skills to teach in a formal classroom setting. I have been able to both learn the language and to explain the language to others. The adult program at Chifley College Dunheved Campus has unearthed at least six Aboriginal people who could teach if there was some way of them gaining accreditation. With the support of the federal government we are building a Dharug language centre next year at Chifley College to continue this work.

Modern communication tools

Another feature of my approach to language, which is common among Aboriginal people, is my interest in using modern technology. The linguist working with the Dharug and Dharawal languages, Amanda Oppliger, has put about 100 of my words onto a phone database (see Wilson, this volume). This means that I can SMS Dharug to others learning the language. Stuart Marshal, who has been given permission to speak Dharug in Queensland, is learning with support from me using phone calls and texting. Chris and Jacinta Tobin in the Blue Mountains are also using this medium.

I have also just been approached by the National Parks and Wildlife Service to set up a website to share sound bites in language. This will be an interactive site where speakers can add their own material. It is important we hear our language again, as the words have always remained in the names of places and in our children's slang. We need to build on this and bring back the full meaning of the language as the sound of this land.

Conclusion

In teaching Dharug, grammar is covered with comparisons to both English and the Kriol spoken by many of the students. By providing a holistic approach to their studies the classes are engaging the students as never before. This has been linked to a great improvement in attendance at the schools and has resulted in increased support for Aboriginal languages in Sydney. As the next step we are organising children's choirs in schools in western Sydney to learn songs about the land where they live.

Through classes run at Dunheved College I have also trained many adult speakers to reclaim their language. We now need more of their people to be trained and employed as language teachers. There have been many dictionaries and grammars produced by linguists over the years and many people have studied our language to try to speak it again. Now we need to have access to these resources and bring together these people to use this knowledge in reconstructing our speech.

This process has involved confronting the many attempts to discredit me as a language speaker, and to discredit the language I speak – saying it is not correct, or is a combination of many neighbouring languages. I have been learning my language since very young, from those who still spoke it then, and have stood by my right to speak and teach it, as granted me by my Elders. It is only through the strength of this backing from the knowledge holders of our community that I have succeeded in reclaiming a language that was called 'dead'. Yet there are still people who would rather criticise the efforts of my and others' learning than value the language which we have, and with which me must move forward.

References

Chifley College (2005). Dunheved College annual strategic plan. Unpublished internal document.

Lynch J (1998). *Pacific languages: an introduction*. Honolulu, Hawaii: University of Hawaii Press.

Senior Secondary Assessment Board of South Australia (1996) *Australia's Indigenous languages*. Wayville, South Australia: Senior Secondary Assessment Board of South Australia.

Troy J (1994). *The Sydney language*. Flynn, ACT: J. Troy.

16
Developing the Dhurga Program at Vincentia High School: the language teacher's perspective

Karen Lane[1]

Abstract

This paper describes the introduction and teaching of Dhurga at Vincentia High School on the south coast of New South Wales. It begins with an explanation of who was involved in the initial research and planning phase and the rationale for implementing the local language in the school curriculum. It describes the relationship among community members, school staff, the linguist and the Board of Studies and focuses on the team teaching approach taken by the Aboriginal community language teacher and myself (an experienced teacher of Indonesian). The paper outlines how we overcame some practical challenges and describes the types of activities that we have found successful with the students, and which are supportive of learning through a communicative language teaching approach.

Vincentia High School is a comprehensive state high school on the south coast of New South Wales (NSW). It is within walking distance of Jervis Bay and a short bus ride to Booderee National Park, managed by the traditional owners of this land, the Wadi Wadi people. Of the 1100 students who attend Vincentia High School, approximately ten percent identify as Aboriginal. These students come from the surrounding towns and villages including Huskisson, Vincentia, Sanctuary Point, Erowal Bay, Old Erowal Bay, Wrights Beach, Hyams Beach, St Georges Basin, Basin View, Tomerong, Wandandian, Sussex Inlet, Woollamia, Jervis Bay Village and the Aboriginal community of Wreck Bay.

Since the opening of the school in 1993 Aboriginal students have featured prominently in its success in a variety of areas. Among these, there are students who have been school leaders, sports stars, those talented in the creative and performing arts and those who have achieved outstanding academic results. With the development of

---

1 Vincentia High School.

the *NSW Aboriginal Languages K–10 Syllabus* (Board of Studies NSW 2003) it seemed only natural that Vincentia High School would include an Aboriginal language in its curriculum.

The idea was the beginning of many hours of hard work for a dedicated group of people, whose dream was finally to become a reality with the trial introduction of a Dhurga language program to all Year 8 students in 2006. The journey to reach this point was at times both frustrating and exciting as many obstacles were encountered and overcome along the way.

Walawaani, ngayaga Karen Lane. You guessed it! I've just greeted you and introduced myself in Dhurga. I did not become involved in the Dhurga language program at Vincentia High School until after much of the preliminary research had been done. I have therefore relied heavily on information given to me by Gary Worthy, Head teacher of technology and applied studies at Vincentia High School, who has played a major role in developing Aboriginal education programs there. This is how the journey started.

Planning the journey

Interest in developing a program for an Aboriginal language at Vincentia High School began in 1995. Gary came to Vincentia High School having been involved with an Aboriginal languages program at another school at which he had taught. He was strongly aware that involvement with Aboriginal languages evokes emotional responses from people and that the language belongs to the community, not one individual. When he came to Vincentia, Gary built vital links between the school and the community, through his contact with Elders and community leaders who were researching local languages.

Between 1999 and 2000, Helen Pussell, the Aboriginal education officer (AEO) at Vincentia High School, together with the AEO at Jervis Bay Public School joined Gary and they were successful in obtaining funding from the then Aboriginal and Torres Strait Islander Commission to develop the Dhurga language program. A cultural heritage submission was made on behalf of the Wreck Bay Community Council.

In 2001, Helen and Gary spoke about the possibility of developing a language course for Vincentia High School with staff at the Board of Studies NSW (BOS), who suggested seeking linguistic support from and making contact with established language programs in other schools. Helen and Gary were joined by another teacher at Vincentia High School, Helen Ford, and another local Aboriginal community member, Colleen Brown. Together they visited two schools – the Gumbaynggirr language program at Bowraville Central School on the mid-north coast of NSW and the Kaurna language program at Kaurna Plains School in Adelaide. They observed then that Aboriginal students at Bowraville Central School learnt their language outside school, rather than the program being a formal part of the school curriculum. They were impressed by the programs at both schools, which included songs and games to motivate the students.

Jaky Troy, then manager of the Department of Aboriginal Affairs NSW Aboriginal Languages Research and Resource Centre, facilitated some helpful meetings and, in 2003, the group travelled to Canberra where they spent three days receiving valuable guidance from the research and technical staff at the Australian Institute of Aboriginal and Torres Strait Islander Studies (AIATSIS). The group was joined by a number of other community members including Waine Donovan and Kerry Boyenga – both teachers at Broulee Public School – as well as Ursula Brown, Mary Duroux and Danielle Towers. AIATSIS staff provided advice on how to access and use the relevant resources. The wheels were well and truly in motion for the Dhurga language program now.

In 2004, Jutta Besold, a PhD candidate in the School of Language Studies at the Australian National University became involved with the project. She began researching the available archival materials and making connections with Aboriginal community leaders and members. Through collecting and analysing the language material for her thesis Jutta has been able to support the Dhurga language programs at both Vincentia High School and nearby Broulee Public School, as well as a number of community-based language programs.

This is when I joined the team. I had been teaching Indonesian for many years and have always been interested in other languages and cultures. Although in the beginning I did not know much about Aboriginal languages in general, or Dhurga in particular, I have been able to learn the language alongside the community members and work closely with the Aboriginal community language teacher, Mitch Martin. As a member of the program team I have been able to contribute my skills in effective language teaching methods and strategies suitable for high school students.

The journey begins

During 2004 and 2005, Pip Dundon and Dr Jennifer Munro, curriculum officers at BOS, coordinated a series of workshops with community members, school staff and the linguist. These meetings were an opportunity for us all to work together as a team to write a teaching and learning program. They were also an opportunity for Mitch to work on both his teaching and language skills. Although Mitch did not grow up speaking his language, through this program he has been committed to learning and preparing to teach it.

By 2006 the language was ready to teach at an elementary level. Mitch and I approached this initial stage with trepidation and excitement, as finally an idea was about to become a reality, even though it was only to be delivered to Year 8 classes for one 56-minute period per fortnight. Much hinged on this year.

In the beginning we faced some criticism from a few members of the school and community who questioned the value of teaching a language that was largely not in use and had little relevance. However, the supportive staff and community members constantly defended and promoted the benefits of its inclusion in the Year 8 curriculum.

Fortunately the school's principal, Steve Glenday, provided ongoing support and dealt with opposition in a very diplomatic but forthright manner, explaining that this subject was an extremely important and integral part of the school's focus and future plans. This strong leadership certainly helped to instil confidence and optimism in the program team.

In these early days Mitch and I travelled from one end of the school to the other wherever there was a vacant room, sometimes a science laboratory, an art room or a design and technology room. All resources had to be carried from room to room and occasionally a few were lost in transit. One day a Year 8 student in the Dhurga class commented that one of the particularly big, tough rugby league boys in Year 11 was walking around the school with one such resource stuck to his chest. The laminated Dhurga word read *minga* (mother). This did not really suit his image and the Year 8 students had a bit of a laugh.

With only an hour a fortnight set aside for the Dhurga language class, topics were limited in that first year. As a matter of fact, Mitch and I were only just keeping one step ahead of the kids. Jutta passed on new vocabulary and grammatical information as it came to hand as part of her research, almost on a daily basis. Sometimes she would discover that a particular word actually had a different spelling or meaning to what we had previously believed so there were often changes. An example of such a change was with the words *njin* (this) and *djin* (that). These words seemed to change meaning from one year to the next over the next three years, and both Mitch and I had to constantly remind each other which was which. Although this was sometimes frustrating, at the same time the changes and clarifications provided rich learning opportunities for the students allowing them to discuss the intricacies and difficulties involved in the process of revitalising a language. This is also consistent with the syllabus, which recognises that Aboriginal languages in NSW are being learned and taught in the context of language revival.

The topics covered initially included basic greetings, family members, animals and body parts. Of course, in conjunction with these topics we taught relevant cultural aspects, since language and culture are interdependent. For example, when students learnt Dhurga words for family members they also learnt about the traditional Aboriginal family structures and drew comparisons with other indigenous cultures around the world.

Learning vocabulary was based around games such as memory, snap cards and charades. Charades was great fun for learning Dhurga vocabulary for animals. This game was often used at conferences in demonstration lessons and was always enjoyed by all. One of the funniest moments was watching the principal of a south coast high school acting as a *burnaaga* (tree goanna). His team members were stumped, as he appeared to be trying to climb a wall! The value of games and songs should never be underestimated – in language classrooms it is often the case that the more noise, the more productive the lesson.

All in all this first year ended on a positive note. The students had responded well to the new course and morale among those involved in its development was high. After much consultation among community members, Aboriginal staff, the principal and I, it was decided that Dhurga would be the language taught for the mandatory 100 hours[2] for Year 8 students beginning in 2007.

Even though this was a wonderful opportunity, it was a daunting task, and now the hard work had really begun. Instead of just one period per fortnight students would study Dhurga for five periods a fortnight, which had to be allocated into an already tight timetable. None of this would have been possible without the ongoing support of BOS staff who worked with us on writing a full teaching program, including scope and sequence and eight units of work. Neither could we have done it without linguistic support from Jutta who taught us about the language and its structures. Mitch and I faced the challenge of presenting this material (which sometimes looked quite dry) to our students in creative and fun ways, and in ways that would facilitate use *of* the language rather than just discussion *about* the language.

Next steps

With the introduction of the 100-hour course in 2007 came much excitement. The lack of a homeroom was still the major issue but we were promised one for 2008, so we soldiered on carrying an ever-growing box of resources from one end of the school to another. It was a small price to pay for the chance to expand the language and have greater exposure throughout the school. The Year 8 students were more enthusiastic and there was a more serious approach towards Dhurga as it was now a subject that would be assessed and included in their school report.

Throughout the year students really began to extend their vocabulary, and they now could write more complex sentences and create short spoken and written texts on a broader range of themes and topics. An integral part of the program was an excursion to Booderee National Park guided by the park's Indigenous rangers. Students were able to learn about food sources, plants and their medicinal uses. This was a huge step forward as tangible connections were being made among the language, cultural knowledge and country.

These connections were also made through cross-curriculum content. A local artist visited all classes and her beautiful artwork truly inspired the students to tell stories in conjunction with their own paintings. Many previously disengaged students who struggled with learning vocabulary and grammar excelled in their explanations of visual representations of stories. Mitch and I helped them write their stories. They were extremely proud and felt a strong sense of personal achievement.

We launched in 2008 confident that we were teaching something of great value, which involved not only language skills but also increased understanding in the unique local

---

2 In NSW all students must complete a minimum of one 100-hour language course as part of their School Certificate.

Aboriginal people, land and culture. We finally secured our own Dhurga classroom, somewhere to hang our posters and display students' work. This was a fantastic year. Classes displayed their skills to various dignitaries and visitors to the school and were also featured on Triple J Radio's 'Hack' program.

The classroom now has alphabet stepping-stones on the floor and the windows are adorned with Aboriginal print curtains. There are large cushions, kindly made by Helen Pussell, which students use when working in groups. Mitch has used his artistic skills to paint and stencil the walls. Posters around the room help to reinforce new vocabulary. Everyone loves coming to this room and laughter, singing and chanting can often be heard as the students engage in communicative activities. A garden of native plants has recently been designed which makes the room more inviting. Dhurga is now firmly embedded in the curriculum at Vincentia High School.

While my experience has predominantly been with the program at Vincentia High School, our efforts link to other schools in the area who are already teaching, or plan to establish, a Dhurga program. We are able to share resources and ideas for teaching and learning through workshops organised by BOS and the NSW Department of Education and Training. Further, there is a local Technical and Further Education program, which means that adult community members such as Mitch can continue to learn their language.

The journey continues

One of the great benefits of teaching Dhurga for me has been co-teaching with Mitch. He is strongly committed to both learning and sharing his language and culture with all Year 8 students. He views the team-teaching approach positively and as an opportunity to pass on his expertise in other areas such as art. This experience has also increased his appetite to continue to develop his language skills. His links to the community are strong and he is well respected, which adds credibility to the program. The Year 8 Aboriginal boys relate particularly well to Mitch and he provides a great role model for these students. This program could not exist without Mitch and much of its success is due to him.

By the end of 2009 all students in Years 9, 10 and 11 will have had the opportunity to learn Dhurga. This is a great achievement for those hardworking people who had a vision so many years ago. I acknowledge these wonderful people and their efforts for the Dhurga language. I feel privileged and proud to be part of the incredible journey. *Walawaani*!

References

Board of Studies NSW (2003) *Aboriginal languages K–10 syllabus.* Sydney, Australia: Board of Studies NSW [Online]. Available: www.boardofstudies.nsw.edu.au/syllabus_sc [Accessed 5 May 2009].

17
So you want to work with the community? Principles and strategies for school leaders affecting the establishment of Aboriginal language programs

Kevin Lowe[1] and Peter Howard[2]

Abstract

The inclusion of Aboriginal language programs within a school's mainstream curriculum has long been the aspiration of many New South Wales Aboriginal communities. In implementing language programs schools may encounter Aboriginal community resistance to a number of educational, social and political issues. This chapter provides an exemplar for schools to engage with Aboriginal communities when establishing authentic curriculum programs that positively privilege Aboriginal cultural knowledge, languages and histories. It explores the views of eight Aboriginal educators in a central school in remote New South Wales who sought to establish a local Aboriginal community language program. Issues such as contemporary Aboriginal cultural identity, trust, reciprocity and the essential importance of Aboriginal language revitalisation to Aboriginal communities are identified. What clearly emerges from this case study is the critical role of the principal, shared and community leadership in establishing educational relationships to address such issues and concerns, and the capacity of Aboriginal people to challenge ingrained curriculum and pedagogical practices.[3]

The adoption by the New South Wales (NSW) government of the *Aboriginal Languages K–10 Syllabus* (Board of Studies NSW 2003), strengthened by the *NSW Aboriginal Languages Policy* (Department of Aboriginal Affairs 2004), has provided school curriculum and teaching and learning support for the revitalisation of Aboriginal

---

1 Aboriginal Curriculum Unit, Office of the Board of Studies NSW.

2 Faculty of Education, Australian Catholic University.

3 This chapter is based on Lowe and Howard (2009) but revised, expanded and updated.

languages in the state. Based on key commitments made by the NSW government, Aboriginal communities have sought support from schools, educational systems and higher education institutions in establishing strategies that will assist in the revitalisation of local Aboriginal languages. Indicative outcomes from the early stages of language revitalisation have shown schools to be potent sites for collaborative action between Aboriginal communities and government agencies. Such collaboration both nationally and internationally has shown that effective and sustained school-based language teaching and learning contributes significantly to language revitalisation (Hinton 2001, p. 7; Amery 2003, pp. 153–77).

The successful implementation of Aboriginal language programs in NSW has shown that they are highly dependent on the role of the school-based Aboriginal educators. One of their primary tasks across each phase of the project is forging community–school partnerships among key Aboriginal community members, principals and teachers. Underpinning the success of this relationship is an essential recognition by the school that within the language program there is deep but often fragmented cultural knowledge that embeds powerful links to traditional life. The quality of these relationships, based upon levels of trust, respect and reciprocity, has been identified as an essential element in establishing the tenuous foothold that the language program may have within the school's curriculum (Lowe & Ash 2006). The desirability of establishing school–community partnerships has long been recognised as a way of overcoming the unacceptably high levels of social and cultural disjuncture between schools and Aboriginal communities (Mellor & Corrigan 2004), and improving the educational outcomes of Aboriginal students (Erebus 2005). The Review of Aboriginal Education (NSW Aboriginal Education Consultative Group [AECG] & NSW Department of Education & Training [DET] 2004) explicitly cited genuine partnerships between schools and Aboriginal communities as a major reason for higher rates of school attendance, deeper engagement and better learning outcomes for Aboriginal students, as well as 'significantly improving the quality and scope of services provided by government agencies' (pp. 205–06).

This chapter, based on the initial year of the establishment of an Aboriginal language program, reports on collaborative research gathered in the establishment of a school program that in itself was a major shift in the direction of the school's curriculum. It focuses on *school leadership*, exploring its meanings and attributes, as identified through interviews with Aboriginal personnel, to better understand the key concerns and attributes that underpin Aboriginal community–school teaching and learning collaboration.

Building social capital, unleashing community capacity

Recent commonwealth and state policy developments have sought to embed educational program outcomes around social capital in order to empower stronger and more engaged families and communities in the wider Australian community. (Johnson 2003; Keele 2007). There has been a growing acknowledgement that governments and social agencies need to look at both program delivery and the nature and resilience of the community in which they work if significant disadvantage is to be addressed. The greater the degree of disadvantage of people, the greater the likelihood that program clients would be unable to affect the conceptualisation of project outcomes and strategies, resource allocation and the government expectations on participant roles and responsibilities (Makuwira 2007).

Such tensions are highlighted as governments have sought to impose programs on often-sceptical Aboriginal communities who have awaited the heralded improvements in their social, economic and political worlds. While governments of all persuasions continue to define community capacity in narrow economic development, managerial and welfare terms (Makuwira 2007, p. 130), Aboriginal communities have argued for programs to be receptive to their diverse cultural identities providing Aboriginal people with the confidence to interact across all operational domains and the skills to challenge program goals strategies and outcomes.

Ah Met's (2001) opening address to the Cape York Partnerships Conference raised the paternalistic construct of deficit thinking:

> I want to say some words of caution about the concept of 'capacity building' which has become the new buzzword of Aboriginal policy and social policy in general. The problem is that the concept of capacity building comes to be based on the idea that Aboriginal people are inherently incapable or somehow lacking. There is a danger of fostering a hidden bureaucratic racism and prejudice against our people. (cited in Tedmanson 2005, p. 2)

The failure of countless government programs to make any substantial improvement to social and economic realities for Aboriginal communities across Australia has cast a pall over the latest Council of Australian Governments (COAG) review, and has again seen policy makers identifying the need for service deliverers to engage with Aboriginal communities (COAG 2009, p. A.24). The initiation of authentic community capacity projects between agencies and Aboriginal communities within a school has reshaped their focus from economic development to deep collaborations and sustainable policy partnerships. Such partnerships have been seen to enable both schools and communities to better address significant social, political, governance and economic matters. The gaze of these programs has turned from the 'problem' community to the 'problematic' agency, where policies and practices are scrutinised for their ability to engage and empower policy clients.

Howard and Perry (2007), reporting on community capacity programs in NSW schools, noted the positive impact in developing and implementing community capacity building on teachers, students, community leaders and community members alike. However, as noted by Lowe (2007), from an Indigenous perspective, the efficacy of these programs is clearly linked to the degree to which government agencies develop a sustained capacity to engage openly with Aboriginal people to deliver high quality services that suit their needs.

A sojourn: A study of culture and identity

The story of this investigation grew out of an ongoing project with one school in a NSW rural community, remote in distance from cities, resources and infrastructure. The community worked in partnership with the support of the NSW Board of Studies, Aboriginal education workers and a local language teacher in implementing the *Aboriginal languages K–10 Syllabus*.

Since 2000, attempts to establish an Aboriginal language program in the school had proven to be unsuccessful. Negotiations between the school and John,[4] the Aboriginal language tutor took place over several years before he was willing to participate. His concerns centred on:

- the school's willingness to negotiate with him and the local community
- the need to broaden the base of community language teachers
- the proper provision of funds to support his employment
- his anxiety about upsetting the delicate balance between competing clans and languages in the town.

The language program, which commenced in earnest in 2006, began with discussions between the school, language teacher, Aboriginal teachers and education workers. The critical importance of establishing school teams committed to viable and sustainable community-driven Aboriginal language programs is well documented (Amery 2002, 2003; Lowe 2007; Green & Oppliger 2007). Initial school–community discussions looked to address the complex mix of issues and questions that surround language revitalisation programs, including:

- Which Aboriginal languages would be taught?
- What would be the initial focus of the program (which stage of learning)?
- What was the community expectation of the school? How was the school going to demonstrate its support?
- What role did the Aboriginal teachers have in advocating and driving the program?
- How were the Aboriginal education workers to be involved?
- How was the school going to fund the program, in particular the employment of the language tutor?

Areas of investigation

This project focused on the processes adopted by its Aboriginal educators and their school in establishing a sustainable partnership that would support the implementation of the syllabus. The focused interviews held with Aboriginal teachers, school workers and Aboriginal language teacher reported on the initial phase of this language revitalisation project. This study investigated the views and feelings of those Aboriginal people who were most closely involved in the establishment of the language school-based Aboriginal program in four broad areas (Table 1).

---

4 All personal names used in this paper are fictitious.

Area of investigation	Key focus questions
Respectful relationships	What do Aboriginal people identify as the key elements within respectful relationships between communities and schools?
Valuing Indigenous knowledge	How do schools represent Aboriginal knowledge within the school curriculum? How is the inclusion of this knowledge negotiated with Aboriginal communities? To what degree is the authenticity of this knowledge linked to the school and community negotiation?
Community/parent perceptions of school	What impact would the inclusion of Aboriginal knowledge within the school's educational programs have on the community's perception of the school?
Aboriginal programs in mainstream curriculum	Does the inclusion of Indigenous programs within the school's curriculum positively impact on the community's valuing of the school?

Table 1. Areas of investigation.

Interviewing the Aboriginal educators

Interviews were conducted in early Term 2 and Term 4 of 2007, though there were other opportunities to observe the unfolding language project and to discuss issues of the development and implementation of the program. One issue of concern centred on gaining the trust of the school and the community alike. The research participants changed over the course of the three interviews, with the Aboriginal language tutor being part of each interview and one of the two Aboriginal primary teachers participating in two of the interviews.

The direction of each interview was informed by a series of broad questions (Table 1), developed from a review of national and international literature on community–school partnerships. The interviews followed the broad direction of the key focus questions, laced with conversational comment and counterpoints between the interviewees and the researcher. Each interview was transcribed with copies provided to the interviewees. These were discussed informally with the Aboriginal educators over the year and in some cases participants asked that clarifications or additional reflections be added to the transcript. An agreed text was constructed and substituted into the interviews.

The school site

The field site was a K–12 central school located in a small rural town in NSW that draws its enrolment from the immediate township and nearby settlements. A small number of children travel by bus from several very small settlements within a 50-kilometre radius. The school population fluctuated around 200 students in 2007, with about 120 Kindergarten to Year 6 students and 80 in the secondary school. The overwhelming majority of students (99%) identify as Aboriginal. The town's Aboriginal population is drawn from a number of language groups. At various times there have been tensions within and across these different language groups that has challenged community cohesion.

> There's a generalised misconception that all of these Aboriginal communities are the same and they're not. But you see we know that they are somewhat different … not factions but there are some people with different perceptions. (Rhonda)

The historical relocation of Aboriginal people from diverse language groups was the result of policies of forced removal of Aboriginal people from their country and relocation to Aboriginal reserves or missions across NSW. People from communities as far away as south-west Queensland and the Northern Territory, as well as nearby towns, had been relocated to the town mission. A Shared Responsibility Agreement established in 2003[5] has forged a significant role for itself within the community. One area of ongoing interest has seen it advocate strongly for the importance of cultural awareness and community involvement in being about sustainable improvements to Aboriginal student outcomes (Jeffries 2006).

Since 1990, as with many rural Australian communities, the township has suffered the consequences of the rationalisation and loss of significant community services such as banking, legal, health, an Aboriginal cultural centre and Aboriginal medical service. During the early 1970s the school's enrolment was approximately 50% Aboriginal. In 2007 the school's Aboriginal enrolment had almost reached 100%, as many of the non-Aboriginal families had left the surrounding area seeking long-term employment stability. This significant change in student demographic is not reflected in strategic curriculum development, with particular regard to the recognition of the role of Aboriginal languages in improving learning outcomes for Aboriginal students, an enhanced view of self identity, and broader school–community engagement.

> You look at when we were at school, all the teachers' kids and all the ambulance officers' kids, all the police officers' kids, all the public servants' kids went here. Not only kids from the rest of the town all came here too, and the property owners' kids too and principal's kids went to the school as well. All of a sudden through the 70s and 80s the whole society swung the other way so all these service providers became positions for young up and coming single people … who don't have the attachment through their children to the school, to the community or to their kids' friends. (John)

---

5 A joint agreement between the regional council, the Commonwealth and NSW State Governments (signed on August 22, 2003) to establish partnerships and share responsibility for achieving measurable and sustainable improvements for Indigenous people living in the region.

Aboriginal educators

The Aboriginal language tutor

John, in his late 30s, has lived in the town from birth other than when he went travelling to look for work in his early 20s. Since his return John has spent time working with the Aboriginal Elders in the community, learning language, culture and connectedness. He has also worked closely with a well-known non-Aboriginal linguist who had learnt and documented the language from elderly speakers during the 1960s. This information and ongoing access to the linguist has been a significant source of language and cultural knowledge.

Aboriginal teachers

There were two Aboriginal teachers at the school, Rhonda, the assistant principal and Susan, the Year 3 teacher. Both teachers were born in the community and have strong familial links to many students and other Aboriginal workers in the school. Rhonda has strong views concerning broad social issues that impact on the town, the impact of the current school curriculum on Aboriginal student learning and the positive influences of an Aboriginal language program on Aboriginal students and their community. Susan proved to be more circumspect in her views, especially in regard to her role in the development and implementation of the school Aboriginal language program. She was aware of the efforts made by the principal to establish the program, and provided advice on John's employment and on providing the other Aboriginal education workers with opportunities to be actively involved in the program. Both Rhonda and Susan spoke of the levels of disconnection among their teaching colleagues, themselves and the other Aboriginal educators on staff. This accentuated what they saw as an unenviable position of being Aboriginal teachers in the school with the recent history of disconnection between the school and the Aboriginal community.

The Aboriginal education officers and in-school tutors

There were seven Aboriginal educators employed in the school. While the Aboriginal Education Officers (AEOs) were permanent employees, the in-class tutors were employed on part-time contracts. The AEOs and in-class tutors were employed to support teachers in the classroom. Differences in their employment status and access to benefits such as holiday pay, training and development appeared to cause friction among Aboriginal staff. The principal had hoped that their collective involvement in the Aboriginal language program would assist in moulding them into a more cohesive group as well as supporting John in his role as a language tutor. It was within this staff context that data was collected.

Voices: key themes emerge

The interview transcriptions were initially coded into four key themes that had been drawn from the literature. These themes were further analysed to identify consistent elements used to describe and illuminate issues raised by the Aboriginal educators. These elements described the Aboriginal educators' relations with Aboriginal parents and the wider town Aboriginal community, their personal and professional relationships, the school's educational programs, the aspirations they had for the successful development of the Aboriginal language program, and their accepted roles in its development and implementation. These were then aggregated for closer content analysis. The identified themes and related elements are described in Table 2.

Themes	Elements (elucidated from interviews)
School leadership	Openness, positive roles and impact, trust, understanding, resources, programs
Aboriginal community school partnerships	History, purpose, respect, challenges, purposeful action, commitment, openness, access
Local Aboriginal language program	Connection, relevance, identity, enjoyment, engagement, community building, ownership, training
Teacher preparedness and engagement	Local cultural understanding, diversity, openness, student and community expectations, resistance, engagement, community connections

Table 2. Themes and Elements.

School leadership

While the full study identified four main themes and elements, the remainder of this chapter will focus on just the first of these, the role of the principal in facilitating, leading, resourcing and opening the school to the establishment of the school-based Aboriginal language program.

Positive role model and effective staff leadership

In a small and increasingly introspective community struck by the long economic downturn brought on by drought, corporate rationalisation and closure of public and private services, the significance of the school principal is as one of the most senior representatives of government in the town, presiding over the largest single enterprise other than the shire council. The influence of this position is extensive and goes well beyond the school. The Aboriginal educators noted the role of principal as being critical to the way in which the town perceived and interacted with the school and the teachers.

Mulford and Johns (2004) reviewed multi-site research on the nature and effectiveness of school leadership. While their findings go beyond this investigation, one of their research questions was pivotal in identifying the capacity of school leaders to positively impact on the in-school learning environment of students, through being responsive to the needs and aspirations of the broader community within which the students resided.

> Many successful leaders in schools serving highly diverse student populations enact practices to promote school quality, equity, and social justice. These practices include building powerful forms of teaching and learning, creating strong communities in school, nurturing the development of educational cultures in families, and expanding the amount of students' social capital valued by the schools. (Mulford & Johns 2004, p. 2)

A key responsibility of the principal is to act as mentor and role model, not just to the school staff, but also to the wider parent and community body (Hughes 2007; Mulford & Johns 2004). Schools have a central role in ensuring parents from low socio-economic communities are actively involved in student learning if they are looking to improve educational outcomes for Aboriginal students (Lareau & Horvat 1999; Mulford & Johns 2004). This is in line with other research that emphasises the wide range of educational, cultural and social variables that impact on student achievement (Cuttance, Angus, Crowther & Hill 2001)

The Aboriginal educators recognised the pivotal role played by the principal in initiating and managing significant changes, but bemoaned the school's poor management of the substantial human and cultural resources that resided within the group, and the lack of capacity from previous principals to openly engage with the Aboriginal parents. However, both Aboriginal teachers identified a shift in commitment with the new principal's public assurances of changing the entrenched school practices:

> but the positive things so far would be the fact that we do have a principal, a principal after so many years who's willing to drive this program, the language program, that's the most positive thing that's come out of it. (Rhonda)

The Aboriginal teachers in particular had quickly developed high expectations of the new principal, seeing in him a capacity to make the types of changes that they believed were necessary to embed the establishment of the languages program. In their eyes the principal had appeared to take a positive position and support community aspirations in supporting the initiation of the language program. Central to this perception was a view that his support demonstrated a level of cultural engagement that had hitherto not been apparent from previous principals. Evidence of this change in support was the increased level of resourcing and the fact that the school had taken steps to timetable the course for inclusion in both the secondary and primary curriculum. However, while this effort was acknowledged, the Aboriginal educators were keenly aware of the levels of negative comment that had emerged from the non-Aboriginal teaching staff. The comment concerning driving the program was also squarely focused on his leadership in securing acceptance of the program from the other teaching staff.

The question of teacher engagement was an issue that became the focus of significant comment from all the Aboriginal educators. They questioned whether the principal understood the vision and particular leadership required to develop authentic community participation. The Aboriginal staff that were interviewed focused clearly on many teachers' lack of cultural understanding and the need to challenge the school's teaching staff to open their classrooms to parents so that educational partnerships could be established. Several saw that it was only through the development of such relationships that the Aboriginal community could see that the school was seeking an understanding and being responsive to local aspirations by acknowledging local Aboriginal culture and language knowledge.

> you'd see the principal more engaged then, then the staff more engaged in what's happening in the school and then the students are more engaged and it needs to trickle throughout the engagement process. It comes with improving their relationships with the community. (Rhonda)

Clearly the Aboriginal staff saw a strong correlation between the actions of the principal in actively supporting Aboriginal community aspirations for the language program, and staff and student engagement. For Rhonda, as one of the Aboriginal teachers, there was a clear link between leadership and improved student engagement and performance.

Many interviewees reported the issue of needing to overcome teacher resistance. The principal was seen to be key in encouraging school staff to establish effective dialogue with Aboriginal parents. They identified a lack of commitment from the class teachers in supporting the language program as symptomatic of a wider divide between the school teaching staff and the town. The establishment of the Aboriginal language program was personal as it spoke of who the staff, students and community were, and how they wanted to be addressed as an Aboriginal community.

The issues of respect and trust figured prominently in many of the conversations with the Aboriginal educators. These were seen as key elements in the establishment of successful relationships with themselves and the wider community. Underpinning these elements were issues of cultural respect for both the language and the culture that was embedded within it. This was manifested in how the school was seen to treat the Aboriginal language tutor. John was held in high regard and any slight on him was seen to reflect on the whole town community. Unequal treatment such as his level of pay, teaching hours and access to employment rights had been the cause of deep concern for John and the other Aboriginal staff.

> ... It has to be reciprocal – reciprocal respect, reciprocal faith, reciprocal trust. (Rhonda)

> ... you have to be addressed the same as everybody else, on the same level, so you don't have anybody in the school talking down to you or addressing you and giving you directions as a lesser person; and they speak to you and deal with you on a level that they wish to be dealt with.

> ... when they respect your knowledge (John)

> ... value your knowledge (Joan)
>
> ... definitely ... recognition (Rhonda)

John acutely felt the impact of these issues and he spoke of them as exposing deeper concerns about the school, its lack of cultural respect and its larger incapacity to engage with the broader community on issues that the Aboriginal educators saw as critical to the establishment of the language program.

An effective attribute of school leadership is the necessity to develop a range of strategies that are seen as genuinely indicating a long-term commitment to work collaboratively to effect changes in the schooling experiences of Aboriginal students. For the participants, these attributes centred on both the personal and institutional, and were captured by comments on the level of real engagement, commitment and trust that the community had in the school's ability or willingness to deliver on the many promises to improve Aboriginal student learning outcomes. Key ideas such as two-way engagement, reciprocity, collaboration, trust and a commitment to work together were used to describe the professional and personal relationships that the Aboriginal educators sought.

Elucidating meanings

The findings of this study indicate a keen understanding of the key role that the principal has in developing and sustaining a positive role model for both the community and school staff. The Aboriginal educators articulated an acute awareness of the importance of the principal in challenging past policies and practices. The hope of the community, as articulated by the Aboriginal education workers, was that the principal's strong support for the Aboriginal language program would provide tangible evidence to others of the importance of the human, social and cultural capital of the local community. Indeed, the findings indicate that effective leadership should be built on the concerted efforts of the school principal to:

- foster a culture-building environment in which students and the community see tangible evidence of the recognition of Aboriginal culture
- facilitate a clear articulation of the school's vision for the development of an educational environment that challenges staff to engage positively with the Aboriginal students, parents and community.

Trust, respect and reciprocity

Notions of trust, respect and reciprocity figured significantly in defining the role of the principal, his own relationships with the non-Aboriginal teaching staff, and the relationship that the teachers had with the Aboriginal community. The interrelated notions of trust, respect and reciprocity are critical in social capital research as they are seen to underpin both the depth and quality of civic connectedness (Putnam 1993).

The issue of leadership and the connection to trust and respect were identified by all the Aboriginal educators as critical to the sustainable advancement of Aboriginal education in their school. 'Initiatives focused on creating or strengthening the internal school community often involve approaches to "moral education" and strive to build trust, respect and a sense of engagement among students and staff' (Schwab & Sutherland 2001, p. 2).

Rhonda and Susan spoke of the need for the principal to engender trusting relationships with the community by following through on the promises made when establishing the school Aboriginal language program. The histories of partially implemented programs, alongside the failure to develop sustainable and culturally engaging ones, has littered Aboriginal education and have often been the cause for the low levels of respect and trust that some schools are held in by Aboriginal parents and communities (NSW AECG & NSW DET 2004).

Trust has been identified as being a key indicator of social cohesion and community wellbeing. Putnam (1993), in his work on social capital, isolated the concept of trust underpinning strong communities and the strength of connections among individuals that are formed and supported by networks; norms of reciprocity. 'Trust is an essential building material which social groups are able to marshal to support their collective civic life to enable them to engage with the wider community' (Beem, cited in Smith 2007, p. 2). It is accepted that schools must develop a capacity to establish relationships with disconnected communities and to challenge the teaching and learning practices that underpin the low levels of social and educational engagement for Aboriginal students.

Those interviewed spoke of the distance that they felt existed between themselves and the rest of the staff, and the isolation between teachers and the Aboriginal community. Van Deth (2003) linked trust, respect and reciprocity within schools to both the personal and social domains of students, staff and parents and, in turn, tied these norms of reciprocity to personal and collective confidence. The capacity for the development of shared values and higher degrees of trust is unlikely to be achieved without significant intervention by effective school leaders. Difficulties in establishing and maintaining trusting relationships between schools and Aboriginal communities are evident by high levels of social disconnection among the values and experiences of many non-Aboriginal teachers and Aboriginal people. This disconnection can be challenged when greater bodies of shared trust and values underpin the relationship.

For Rhonda, the potential of the new relationship evidenced in the principal's actions was that it would affect other school staff and influence their willingness to reach out and seek closer links to the town community. Achieving such links would require the development of linking ties between the local Aboriginal community and school. From Rhonda's perspective, an underpinning assumption for the development of these partnerships was that it would expose deeply flawed school structures and non-responsive school-delivered curriculum. By providing a structure and a focused purpose, a partnership would give teachers and the Aboriginal community the capacity to challenge those impediments that have deeply separated schools from Aboriginal people. Underpinning these new and purposeful partnerships was a relationship based on increased levels of trust between key stakeholders and government institutions (Stone & Hughes 2001, pp. 3-4). When these conditions are met, effective and reciprocal school–community relationships can be established (NSW DET 1999).

> As a teacher I envisage the students learning the language and then teaching their parents and, then hopefully, that will permeate throughout and then you have sort of closeness and everyone has a commonality. (Rhonda)

This case study witnessed a developing synergy of shared values and growing trust among the Aboriginal education workers themselves, and between them and the school, as they collaborated to establish a common program that was valued and respected by both parties. However, issues such as the rates of pay for the tutor had to be addressed before the program could move forward. Though a short-term solution was found, this issue remained unresolved and continued to impact on the capacity of the program.

The partnership provided a mechanism through which these matters could be raised and their importance vented between the language team and the principal. In genuinely seeking sustainable solutions to these key concerns, the school provided stronger evidence that the establishment of the partnership had a real purpose, and was worthy of deeper engagement. The partnership provided a legitimacy and space where serious issues could be raised within a developing framework of openness and genuine trust among team members. This was the new interface of common purpose that could meld school curriculum and community capacity into a powerful force for sustainable educational change.

Recommendations for effective school leadership

This chapter has focused on school leadership, one of the four key themes identified by Aboriginal educators as significant in the meaningful educational engagement required for the establishment of school and Aboriginal community partnerships. This research project has indicated the potential of sustained partnerships to positively impact on the levels of engagement of Aboriginal educators within the teaching and learning domain of schools. The project has found that in developing sustainable community change:

- principals need to be provided with explicit advice and support in the development of real and sustainable school–community educational partnerships that focus on trust building and two-way respect
- schools must be given the highest systemic support to build and sustain effective partnerships with the Aboriginal community
- action plans and strategies should be centred on learning
- professional development should be shaped around the learning needs of Aboriginal students

- systemic advice in protocols and cultural norms in developing purposeful relationships should be available to schools.

A second clear outcome of this study was how strongly committed the Aboriginal educators had become to the establishment of the language program at the school. The clear commitment by the school principal to commence teaching their language had the effect, in their eyes, of compensating for the historical role of schools in enforcing the loss of so many Aboriginal languages. The support of the principal in facilitating the establishment of this cultural program was highly significant, as it had the capacity to draw strong community acclaim for its acknowledgement of long-held aspirations. Schools can play a key role in supporting the revitalisation of Aboriginal community languages through their unambiguous commitment to providing ongoing support for the program. This should include:

- a clear and unequivocal commitment by the school to work with the community on the establishment of culturally appropriate programs
- the development of partnerships with Aboriginal parents and community as high value programs are being developed
- an acknowledgement of the key role of Aboriginal languages and cultural inclusion in curriculum
- strategic development of language, and teaching and learning support to the Aboriginal language teachers which should be built into larger community planning
- co-developing a strategic plan to support integration of negotiated language and cultural programs, including matters such as sustainable funding, teaching, professional support and resourcing.

References

Amery R (2002). *Indigenous language programs in South Australian schools: issues, dilemmas & solutions* [Online]. Available: ab-ed.boardofstudies.nsw.edu.au/go/resources/languages [Accessed 16 September 2007].

Amery R (2003). *Warrabarna Kaurna! reclaiming an Australian language.* Lisse, The Netherlands: Swets & Zeitlinger.

Board of Studies, New South Wales (2003). *Aboriginal languages K–10 syllabus.* Sydney, NSW: Board of Studies, New South Wales.

Council of Australian Governments (2009). *Overcoming Indigenous disadvantage: key indicators.* Melbourne: Productivity Commission.

Cuttance P, Angus M, Crowther F & Hill P (2001). Preface. In Cuttance P (Ed). *School innovation: pathway to the knowledge society.* Canberra: Department of Education, Employment & Workplace Relations [Online]. Available: www.dest.gov.au/sectors/school_education/publications_resources/school_innovation/preface.htm [Accessed 25 May 2008].

Department of Aboriginal Affairs New South Wales (2004). *NSW Aboriginal languages policy* [Online]. Available: www.daa.nsw.gov.au/policies/langpolicy.html [Accessed 25 May 2008].

Department of Education & Training New South Wales (1999). *School community partnerships: case studies of congruence*. Sydney: New South Wales Department of Education & Training.

Erebus (2005). *Review of the recent literature on socio-economic statues and learning*. Sydney: New South Wales Department of Education & Training.

Green R & Oppliger A (2007). The interface between Indigenous and non-Indigenous systems of knowing and learning: a report on a Dharug language programme. *The Australian Journal of Indigenous Education*, 36S: 81–87.

Hinton L (2001). Language revitalization: an overview. In L Hinton & K Hale (Eds). *The green book of language revilization in practice* (pp. 3–18). San Diego: Academic Press.

Howard P & Perry B (2007). Enhancing mathematics learning through effective community capacity building. In LC Sam, F Saleh, M Ghazali, H Sulaiman, HM Yunus, GW Ling & HT Yong (Eds). *East Asia Regional Conference in Mathematics Education: meeting the challenges of developing a quality mathematics education culture* (pp. 404–10). Penang: Universiti Sains Malaysia.

Hughes P, Khan G & Matthews S (2007). *Leaders: acting to improve outcomes for Indigenous students*. Paper presented at the Australian Council for Educational Research Conference 2007. The Leadership Challenge – Improving learning in schools, 12–14 August, Sebel Albert Park, Melbourne [Online]. Available: www.acer.edu.au/documents/RC2007_HughesKhanMatthews-ImproveOutcomesForIndigenous.pdf [Accessed 23 March 2009].

Jeffries S (2006). *Rhetoric and reverse gear: Indigenous policy as a strategic afterthought*. Paper presented at the 4th National Indigenous Education Conference: getting on with the job: Indigenous engagement in education, 27–29 November, Civic Precinct, Newcastle, NSW.

Johnson D, Headey B & Jensen B (2003). *Communities, social capital and public policy: literature review*. Melbourne Institute Working paper 26/03 [Online]. Available: www.melbourneinstitute.com/wp/wp2003n26.pdf [Accessed 23 March 2009].

Keele L (2004). Social capital and the dynamics of trust in government. *American Journal of Political Science*. 51(2): 241–54 [Online]. Available: www.jstor.org/pss/4620063 [Accessed 10 March 2008].

Lareau A & Horvat E (1999). Moments of social inclusion and exclusion: race, class and cultural capital in family–school relationships. *Sociology of Education*, 72(1): 37–53.

Lowe K & Ash A (2006). *Talking each other's lingo: the Aboriginal languages K–10 Syllabus and its role in language revival in NSW* [Online]. Available: ab-ed.boardofstudies.nsw.edu.au/files/talking_each_others_lingo.pdf [Accessed 10 March 2008].

Lowe K & Howard P (2009). *The impact of educational leadership in the implementation of a community–school Aboriginal language program in western NSW*. Paper presented at the Australian Association For Research In Education International Education Research Conference, 29 November–3 December 2009, Canberra, Australia.

Makuwira J (2007). The politics of community capacity-building: contestations, contradictions, tensions and ambivalences in the discourse in Indigenous communities in Australia. *The Australian Journal of Indigenous Education*, 36S: 129–35.

Mellor S & Corrigan M (2004). *The case for change: a review of contemporary research in Indigenous educational outcomes*. Camberwell, Victoria: Australian Council for Educational Research.

Mulford B & Johns S (2004). *A preliminary model of successful school leadership*. Paper presented at the Australian Association for Research in Education International Education Research Conference, 29 November–2 December, Melbourne [Online]. Available: www.aare.edu.au/04pap/mul04848.pdf [Accessed 23 April 2008].

New South Wales Aboriginal Education Consultative Group & New South Wales Department of Education & Training (2004). *The Report of the Review of Aboriginal Education: Yanigurra Muya: Ganggurrinyma Yarri Guurulaw Yirringin.gurray. Freeing the spirit: dreaming an equal future*. Sydney: New South Wales Department of Education & Training.

Putnam RD (1993). *Making democracy work: civic transitions in modern Italy*. Princeton: University of Princeton Press.

Schwab RG & Sutherland D (2001). *Building Indigenous learning communities*. Canberra, ACT: Centre for Aboriginal Economic Policy Research.

Smith MK (2007a). Robert Putnam, social capital and civic community. *The Encyclopedia of Informal Education* [Online]. Available: www.infed.org/thinkers/putnam.htm [Accessed 4 May 2008].

Smith MK (2007b). Social Capital. *The Encyclopedia of Informal Education* [Online]. Available: www.infed.org/biblio/social_capital.htm [Accessed 23 April 2008].

Stone W & Hughes J (2001). *Social capital: linking family and community*. Paper presented at Family Strengths: Everybody's Business, Everybody's Gain: The Second Australian Conference on Building Family Strengths, December 2001, University of Newcastle [Online]. Available: April 23, 2008 from www.aifs.gov.au/institute/pubs/papers/stone5.html

Tedmanson D (2005). *Whose capacity needs building? Open hearts and empty hands. Reflections on 'capacity building' in remote communities*. Paper presented at Critique and Inclusivity: Opening the Agenda. The 4th International Critical Management Studies Conference, 4–6 July 2005, University of Cambridge [Online]. Available: merlin.mngt.waikato.ac.nz/ejrot/cmsconference/2005/abstracts/postcolonialism/Tedmanson.pdf [Accessed 14 September 2007].

Tonkiss F (2004). Trust and social capital. In J Franklin (Ed). *Politics, trust and networks: social capital in critical perspective* (pp. 17–22). London: Families & Social Capital Economic & Social Research Council Research Group [Online]. Available: www1.lsbu.ac.uk/families/workingpapers/familieswp7.pdf [Accessed 23 April 2008].

Van Deth JW (2003). Measuring social capital. *Social Research Methodology*, 6(1): 79–92.

18
Establishing a school language program: the Parkes High School experience

Stephen Maier[1]

Abstract

This paper details the introduction and development of the Wiradjuri Aboriginal language into Parkes High School. It covers the process undertaken to initiate the program and its subsequent developments; the support received from various people along the way; the roles of those involved in the program; the material taught; the positive outcomes for students, the school and the community; critical success factors; hopes for the future; and areas in need of further development.

Initial interest and community consultation

I first became exposed to Wiradjuri language toward the end of 2005. A community and schools language meeting in Dubbo, where some ideas were floated and discussed by the New South Wales (NSW) Board of Studies (BOS), gave us the initial impetus. Participants were then very fortunate to have several days of intense Wiradjuri instruction from elder Stan Grant Snr and Dr John Rudder, sponsored by a nearby school establishing their own Wiradjuri program. This instruction was delivered to teachers and community members from Parkes, Forbes and Condobolin. Hearing the language spoken and being part of the positive experiences of others, who recalled words and phrases from their childhood, convinced us to set things in motion for introducing Wiradjuri language into Parkes High School.

Parkes High School is a co-educational public high school with around ten percent of the 700 students being Aboriginal. There are also three public primary schools, a Catholic primary school and a small Christian independent school in the town. Parkes Shire is a rural area of around 15,000 people, 10,000 of whom live in the Parkes township.

---

1 Parkes High School.

An essential element of an Aboriginal language program, emphasised strongly by Stan Grant, other community leaders and BOS, is the need for community consultation and endorsement. We advertised a community meeting to discuss the introduction of Wiradjuri language for the end of 2005, with a view to introducing it at Parkes High in 2006. We were privileged to have Stan and John attend the meeting, with Stan giving his support to the revival and teaching of Wiradjuri in schools.

Around 18 people attended the meeting, including a few teachers from the high school. Initially I was a bit disappointed with the turnout, until another perspective was put to me. Proportionately more parents turned up representing the Aboriginal students in the school than parents who attend parent and citizen meetings representing all students in the school. Considering this, it was a positive response and, as I was also reminded, small steps can lead to big things.

Stan Grant spoke about the revival of the Wiradjuri language, the benefits he saw for young people in learning the language, the fostering of pride and identity, and the turnaround from times past when speaking the language and practising culture were forbidden. He emphasised the importance of the local community's wishes and views. I outlined the plans for introducing Wiradjuri language into Parkes High School. The meeting endorsed the proposal and a Parkes Wiradjuri language team was formed to oversee the introduction of the language into the school.

The team consisted of Wiradjuri community members, the school's Aboriginal Education Officer (AEO), language teacher, Aboriginal studies teacher and myself (a teacher of social sciences). As co-ordinator of the Wiradjuri language program at Parkes High I was to liaise with the BOS, the school principal and executive, organise language team meetings and prepare funding submissions. Meeting fortnightly the group practised language, learnt new words and phrases and prepared material for use in the school. The Aboriginal members of the group gave cultural input and provided an important link to the broader Aboriginal community (see also Anderson in this volume).

Wiradjuri language comes to Parkes High School

Beginning in 2006 the language was taught to mostly Aboriginal students across all year groups, 20 minutes each morning during RATS time (Reading Across The School). When the rest of the school read books or magazines, we listened to, read, spoke and sang Wiradjuri. This time was chosen as it allowed students from several year groups to be involved, maximised the participation of Aboriginal students who showed the most initial interest, and didn't compromise other established subjects in the students' timetables. Across the school the RATS time aims to improve literacy by encouraging reading. Students' literacy was not disadvantaged by giving up the general reading opportunity and replacing it with Wiradjuri language learning. Rather, as language teachers already know, the learning of another language assists literacy development. Pronouncing unfamiliar words, identifying nouns, verbs and pronouns, using suffixes, and comparing English and Wiradjuri grammatical structures all improve literacy.

We were very fortunate to have become a BOS project school in 2005–06. They arranged four two-day workshops each year and assisted our language team to write a program for a Stage 4 Wiradjuri language course based around the *NSW Aboriginal Language K–10 Syllabus* (BOS 2003). Chris Kirkbright, a Wiradjuri man who had been teaching the language in Sydney, attended the workshops and helped us with our language development. Stan Grant also came and shared his invaluable knowledge and expertise. At various times throughout the year our emerging language course was shown to and discussed with Wiradjuri community members for feedback and ideas.

At these workshops and other BOS seminars I was exposed to invaluable linguistic knowledge. I had never thought much about linguistic patterns and structures before in my life and now I was suddenly confronted with locative suffixes, transitive and intransitive verbs, ergative markers and the like. I had to hear it several times before things started making sense, and still not all of it does. However that linguistic instruction is very helpful when learning and using an unfamiliar language and these workshops really gave us the incentive to launch the language as a fully fledged course into Parkes High.

A recognised Stage 4 language course

Toward the end of 2006, Year 7 students were surveyed to see who would like to study Wiradjuri language the following year. From this we were able to create two classes that included 20 Aboriginal students. We were about to launch the Stage 4 program we had worked on in 2006. The school played a significant and commendable role here by freeing up timetable space for the two Year 8 classes. This was additional language above the mandatory 100 hours. Wiradjuri was also going to be taught to a Year 7 language class.[2]

A milestone was achieved when the school successfully applied for a grant from the Aboriginal Education and Training Directorate of the NSW Department of Education and Training to employ a community language tutor, Ron Wardrop. He was able to come in to the school ten hours a week and work with the classes. This obviously is an important element of the program. For Aboriginal languages to have integrity, relevance and authenticity, they need to be taught by Aboriginal people. Funding to sustain real jobs for Aboriginal men and women in these educational roles is critical for the success of Aboriginal language programs.[3]

The students responded extremely well to the language tutor. They were interested in what he had to say and he also brought cultural expertise to the classroom with his art and music. As the teacher in the classroom my primary role is to write the program in

---

2 In NSW all students must complete a minimum of one 100-hour language course as part of their School Certificate.

3 Unfortunately the funding to employ a community language tutor is not guaranteed year to year and is subject to budget constraints.

consultation with the language team, provide resources and manage the class, leaving most of the cultural and language instruction to our tutor. We come up with teaching ideas and language activities together with the help of the school's language teacher who is a teacher of French and German, and now also team-teaching Wiradjuri. Having a trained language teacher involved really helps with the development of language activities and resources.

One of the exciting aspects of the language revitalisation is not only seeing kids learn language and culture, which fosters identity, pride and respect; but also to realise that Aboriginal languages have the potential to create job opportunities, not only in education but also in cultural tourism and land management. Our tutor's work at the school has provided the students with an excellent role model.

2008 saw the continuation of the Stage 4 program taught to a new group of students. This year, however, all of Year 8 studied Wiradjuri language for three hours a fortnight. Select Year 7 classes again studied Wiradjuri as part of their mandatory language component. An exciting development in 2008 was that after being offered since 2007, Wiradjuri language could now run in 2009 as a Stage 5, Year 9 elective for the first time. Enough students in Year 8 embraced the Wiradjuri language and culture to choose further study in this area.

The material taught at Parkes High in Stage 4 has included basic greetings, animals common to the central western region of NSW, people and family names, body parts, numbers and natural features. Students are taught that locative and other nominal suffixes are used on nouns, with past, present, future and command suffixes used on verbs. By combining noun (actor), verb and noun (object) with appropriate suffixes a variety of sentences can be created. Incorporating pronouns and interrogatives further expands vocabulary and basic conversations can be held. An important aim of the BOS syllabus and the Parkes High teaching program is to move beyond wordlists into communication in the language.

At this stage students (and teachers) are still slow when speaking the language and take time processing sentences heard. A challenge for everyone is to use the language more frequently to increase familiarity and improve fluency. Songs have been an excellent way to learn language. One of the current Year 8 classes has relatively low levels of literacy, with some in the group experiencing learning difficulties. This class has really embraced the songs and sing with gusto, more so than any other group I have had.

Cultural relevance

A significant part of the language program is Wiradjuri culture. Stan Grant stressed from the beginning that language and culture must go together. Indeed, learning words without cultural connection is hollow. Our language tutor has contributed greatly here, again highlighting the need to have Aboriginal community members involved for the integrity and authenticity of the course. His didgeridoo and clap sticks enliven songs and his artwork has brightened the room and given inspiration to students. We use the book *Windradyne, A Wiradjuri Koorie* by Mary Coe (1989) as a prime source of material on Wiradjuri traditional life. The first chapter of this book is excellent and describes Wiradjuri country, traditional foods, hunting and gathering practices, tools and weapons, roles of men, women and children, clothing and body adornments, and the significance and relationship with the land. A group of girls from various years have formed an Indigenous dance group at the school. They have been taught some traditional dances by an Aboriginal teacher at a nearby primary school. These girls have performed dances and traditional story telling at NAIDOC (National Aboriginal and Islander Day Observance Committee) celebrations in town and at school.

Despite the above, cultural relevance and knowledge is an area of the course that needs further development. Whilst we have canvassed some community members there is still much local knowledge we have yet to tap into. Stories, songs, words, significant sites, customs and traditions, if passed on and recorded, should be used in the language program. The school can play an important role in preserving and reviving this knowledge. Of course the school does not own the knowledge, that will always belong to the communities, but the school can help facilitate its transfer to new generations, both Indigenous and non-Indigenous.

An exciting development here is the establishment of an adult community language group that has met weekly for the past two years. Led by community Elder Geoff Anderson, this group of Aboriginal and non-Aboriginal adults practise and learn Wiradjuri language, share knowledge and ideas, and prepare teaching resources. It requires teamwork, commitment and effort for a language to be revived. And, while we are a relatively small group at the moment (8–12 people), we are putting language out into the community, raising interest and awareness, and providing a link with the school language programs. In time it is hoped that more people will become involved, not only spreading the language further throughout the community, but also bringing out community members' cultural knowledge and ideas.

Overall the language program has had a very positive effect on the school and wider community. It has raised awareness of Wiradjuri language and culture among the general school population and the town more broadly. Other classes in our homeroom read the Wiradjuri terms for animals and people painted on the wall and often have discussions around these. A Welcome to Country is now given in Wiradjuri language at all formal functions. This is increasingly common at community functions as well. Classes have sung and danced at school assemblies and community events.

For Aboriginal students, we believe the language program helps strengthen pride and identity and supports them to reconnect with their culture. For non-Aboriginal students, we believe the language opens their eyes to new ways of seeing a different culture, where the land is sacred and relationships between people and the earth carry special significance. For all, learning Wiradjuri is helping improve student literacy and promoting respect and reconciliation.

References

Board of Studies NSW (2003). *Aboriginal Languages K–10 Syllabus*. Sydney: Board of Studies NSW.

Coe M (1989). *Windradyne: a Wiradjuri Koorie*. Canberra: Aboriginal Studies Press.

19
Language revitalisation: community and school programs working together

Diane McNaboe[1] and Susan Poetsch[2]

Abstract

Since it was published in 2003 the New South Wales *Aboriginal Languages K–10 Syllabus* has led to a substantial increase in the number of school programs operating in the state. It has supported the quality of those programs, and the status and recognition given to Aboriginal languages and cultures in the curriculum. School programs also complement community initiatives to revitalise, strengthen and share Aboriginal languages in New South Wales. As linguistic and cultural knowledge increases among adult community members, school programs provide a channel for them to continue to develop their own skills and knowledge and to pass on this heritage. This paper takes Wiradjuri as an example of language revitalisation, and describes achievements in adult language learning and the process of developing a school program with strong input from community.

A brief history of Wiradjuri language revitalisation

Wiradjuri is one of the central inland New South Wales (NSW) languages (Wafer & Lissarrague 2008, pp. 215–25). In recent decades various language teams have investigated and analysed archival sources for Wiradjuri and collected information from both written and oral sources (Büchli 2006, pp. 58–60). These teams include Grant and Rudder (2001a, b, c, d; 2005), Hosking and McNicol (1993), McNicol and Hosking (1994) and Donaldson (1984), as well as Christopher Kirkbright, George Fisher and Cheryl Riley, who have been working with Wiradjuri people in and near Sydney. Stan Grant Snr has been a key figure in Wiradjuri language revitalisation

---

1 Dubbo West Public School.
2 Aboriginal Curriculum Unit, Office of the Board of Studies NSW.

since 1992 when he initiated a Wiradjuri language reclamation project guided by the Wiradjuri Council of Elders and assisted by Dr John Rudder. As part of the project a dictionary and language learning materials suitable for community members have been developed. Grant has spent many years travelling around Wiradjuri country teaching adult learners, giving the materials wide currency and strong credibility in communities throughout the region.

In more recent years some of Grant's students have gained sufficient skills and confidence to become teachers of Wiradjuri themselves. Diane McNaboe is one of these people, the next generation of Wiradjuri language developers, learners and teachers. While Grant works mostly in the southern area of Wiradjuri country, McNaboe works with colleagues and communities in the northern area. McNaboe holds a Master of Indigenous Languages Education and is a community leader who supports less experienced learners and teachers of Wiradjuri. She explains the context of language revitalisation this way:

> Traditionally Aboriginal people of NSW were multi-lingual, and my old grannies, uncles and aunties from Dubbo could speak several Aboriginal languages. The main languages they spoke were Wiradjuri, Gamilaroi, Ngiyampaa and Murawari. These languages were almost lost within one or two generations due to the strict laws of the time with Aboriginal people not being allowed to speak their languages. My dad, Keith Riley, used to say that the old fellas would protect us by speaking in whispers and would go quiet if we came around so we wouldn't learn the language and get punished for it. My dad's older brother, Tommy Riley, could speak Wiradjuri and Ngiyampaa. He told me that when he was a little fella and got comfortable with the teachers at school he would drop into speaking in language. He said that he was punished for using 'bad' language. He didn't think he was swearing, and it wasn't until he was older that he understood that they meant his Aboriginal languages. So he learnt to keep quiet. This situation was still in place in my time, so my family protected us by not using language, to keep us safe from the *gandyibuls* (constables) or the *gandyiwas* (government men).

> I've been very lucky to be born into two of the biggest family groups and also belong to two of the largest Aboriginal nations in NSW. While growing up I have been able to make comparisons among the languages and cultures of these two groups. I have made a point of chasing language and cultural knowledge from an early age. I feel the old people have been watching over me and helping me, as I have had knowledge and experiences shared with me for as long as I can remember by people from other parts of NSW (including Elders and other people throughout Wiradjuri, Gamilaroi and Ngiyampaa country), as well as Aboriginal people in Victoria and the Torres Strait Islands, and Kathy Marika my sister under kinship from north-east Arnhem Land in the Northern Territory. I have also learned from people in the National Aboriginal and Islander Skills Development Association and Bangarra dance group. I am only where I am today because of

the willingness of these people to share their language and culture knowledge with me. They have given me the understanding to appreciate other people's culture and the guidance to do my best for the Wiradjuri language programs. I am striving to get the sharing process happening across NSW language groups.

In recent years McNaboe and other adults in the Wiradjuri community have been involved in a growing range of language learning opportunities including the following:

- Weekend workshops and informal classes have been held in a number of towns in Wiradjuri country, for example Dubbo, Orange, Bathurst, Kelso, Narromine and Parkes. These gatherings often involve community members of all ages coming together to socialise as well as to learn and share their language and culture. Some of these language learning opportunities are held infrequently depending on the time and resources of the participants, for example Wiradjuri language weekend camps. Others may be regular local events which occur on a weekly, fortnightly or monthly basis.

- The Aboriginal languages summer school held annually at the University of Sydney's Koori Centre, and co-ordinated by the Muurrbay Aboriginal Language and Culture Co-operative, offers intensive two-week courses. It was established in January 2008 with a Gumbaynggirr and a Gamilaraay-Yuwaalaraay language class; Wiradjuri joined the program in January 2009.

- Certificates I, II and III in Aboriginal Language/s, developed by Technical and Further Education (TAFE) NSW and available since 2007, provide Aboriginal people with formal qualifications and educational pathways (see Cipollone, this volume). The Riverina and Western Institutes of TAFE NSW have been notably proactive in making the certificates available at a number of campuses in Wiradjuri country, including Bathurst, Dubbo, Forbes, Narrandera, Orange, Parkes and Wagga Wagga. Grant reports (pers. comm., 10 March 2009) that the Wiradjuri Council of Elders values these courses as a means of supporting the quality of school programs and ensuring that Wiradjuri teachers have the necessary skills and knowledge.

The demand for, and participation in, language learning opportunities such as these indicates community interest in revitalising language and culture, and the importance that this holds for them (see Anderson, this volume, for example). Further, whether they lead to formal qualifications or not, language and culture programs for adults are a key to skills development and a potential source of Aboriginal community language teachers for the school programs. While Grant has been working for many years to meet with Wiradjuri people and teach language and culture, he reports that revitalisation efforts have flourished in the past couple of years through school, TAFE and community initiatives and the interaction among these programs (pers. comm., 10 March 2009). The NSW *Aboriginal Languages K–10 Syllabus* (Board of Studies NSW 2003a) has contributed to this growth in Wiradjuri revitalisation through school programs that add to and complement the adult learning in the community.

Syllabus overview

The syllabus and support materials (Board of Studies NSW 2003b, 2004) were developed in order to assist communities in the task of language revitalisation.

> The Board of Studies intends, through this syllabus, to support the aspirations of Aboriginal communities in the revitalisation of their languages ... In order to arrest [the] decline in world languages it is necessary, among other strategies, for language-owning communities to have supportive educational contexts to assist in the process of reviving their languages ... School-based language programs are one part of the larger process of language revival. While local communities provide the primary impetus and are the main drivers, the place of schools in this larger process is significant; they can play a critical role in the revitalisation of languages across the state. (Board of Studies NSW 2003a, pp. 5–7)

The syllabus is generic, rather than language-specific; potentially any Aboriginal community in NSW can work with staff of a local school to use the syllabus to develop a teaching and learning program for their language. The syllabus incrementally builds the language and cultural knowledge and skills that the students acquire from kindergarten through to Year 10. It is similar to other language syllabuses, and is part of the languages key learning area in the NSW curriculum. The three objectives of the syllabus (2003a, p. 5) – using language (UL), making linguistic connections (MLC) and moving between cultures (MBC) – are interwoven.

Through UL students gain proficiency in one language across the four macro-skills of listening, speaking, reading and writing in the target language. This objective is a challenge for languages in the context of revitalisation as it relies on the developing language proficiency of the teachers. Through MLC students gain grammatical knowledge and metalanguage, and compare and contrast the target language with other languages. Through MBC students build on their knowledge of Aboriginal cultures and relationships among those cultures. This objective acknowledges that language and culture are deeply intertwined and are learned and taught together. It provides valuable opportunities for learning and teaching about cultural practices and a broad range of Aboriginal knowledge, including knowledge of land, sea, rivers, flora, fauna, food and medicinal sources, seasonal relationships, constellations, kinship and family. For more detail on the development of the syllabus see Lowe & Ash (2006) and Lowe & Walsh (2008).

Syllabus implementation

The Board of Studies (BOS) advocates taking a team approach and setting up local partnerships to develop programs:

> This syllabus encourages the development of long-term partnerships between communities, schools and those with linguistic knowledge of Aboriginal languages. These partnerships, which primarily support the community's efforts to revitalise language, will be enhanced when appropriate consultation processes and protocols are undertaken. (Board of Studies NSW 2003b, p. 5)

Each year the BOS works with a small number of local school–community teams to develop programs. This collaboration takes the form of regular workshops throughout the school year, over a two-year period, in order to establish a program. These are intensive workshops for a particular local school, community and language. Other workshops include a much larger number of school–community teams networking with each other, and are arranged in collaboration with colleagues in school systems[3] and their regional or diocesan offices (see also Rhydwen, this volume). Content of the workshops includes team-building, linguistics and language revitalisation, local language and culture knowledge, effective teaching methods and strategies, and program writing, as well as opportunities for sharing resources and ideas for teaching, learning and assessment activities.

Prior to the development of the syllabus in 2003 a small number of school programs operated in NSW however these programs were extra-curricular; classes were often for Aboriginal students only and were held outside of the formal school timetable. At the end of 2006 the BOS NSW and NSW Department of Education and Training (DET) collected some initial indicative data (Rhydwen, Munro, Parolin & Poetsch 2007). By that time the number of schools offering Aboriginal languages programs had grown to 46. These programs were in both government (41) and non-government (5) schools for 1356 Aboriginal and 3553 non-Aboriginal primary and secondary school students. Across the 46 programs, ten languages were being taught.

Community input is essential for the integrity of any Aboriginal languages program. Communities decide if and when they want a program in their local schools, which languages will be taught and who will teach. It is the intention of the syllabus to support significant community involvement in program development and delivery:

> In seeking the guidance of Aboriginal communities through their language custodians, schools can ensure that key decisions in the implementation of a school-based program are made in the community's interests and with their approval. It is a clear aim of this syllabus to empower communities to take a substantial role in the implementation of this syllabus and to assert their co-ownership of resultant programs and materials. (BOS NSW 2003b, p. 5)

A number of local Aboriginal people need to invest in the school program and feel their knowledge is respected and valued. In this way they give direction to the program as part of the process of maintaining and rebuilding their knowledge of culture and country, unique worldviews and ways of communicating. Much of this identity has survived not only in what is known and remembered of the languages but also in the way people speak English.

A school program cannot begin without an Aboriginal community language teacher, who needs to be committed to improving their language skills and knowledge, as well as developing their language teaching skills, either through gaining appropriate

---

3 In NSW the school systems are the NSW Department of Education and Training, NSW Catholic Education Commission, and the Association of Independent Schools.

qualifications or through team-teaching with a qualified teacher of languages.[4] While the Aboriginal community language teacher is a key to ensuring respected community participation in program development and implementation, other community members can have input into the content. Elders may not want to teach on a daily basis but still provide advice to the teachers. Others with specialised knowledge and expertise may bring their skills to particular lessons or units of work.

Dubbo College Wiradjuri program

Dubbo College provides an example of the process of developing a program which values community views and input, makes the most of current language skills in the community and builds on those skills. Dubbo College is one of the schools the BOS worked with in 2008–09 to develop a 100-hour Stage 4 course[5] for which McNaboe is the teacher. The course is based on the following text:

Widyunggalu-ndhu wi-gi?	How are you going to live?
Gariya yaambul yala dhulubul ya-la.	Do not tell lies. Speak the truth.
Ya-l-mambi-ya mayiny-galang. Marun-bunmi-la-dha.	Teach the people. Love each other.
Marraga-la-dha. Walan-ma-ya mayiny-galang.	Hold together and empower the people.
Marun-bunmi-ya mayiny-guwal-bang-gu.	Be kind and gracious to strangers.
Winhanga-gi-gila-dha. Ngu-ng-gi-la-dha.	Care for each other. Share with each other.
Yindyama-la Mayiny-galang-gu.	Give honour and respect to all people.
Bangga-ya-la.	Cause quarrelling to stop.

---

4 Aboriginal community languages teachers in schools in NSW have a range of backgrounds and experience. The majority do not hold formal teaching qualifications so they are supported by a staff member in the school who assists with lesson preparation and classroom management. Some are qualified primary or secondary teachers, and are full-time members of the school staff. A small cohort holds the Master of Indigenous Languages Education, a course available at the Koori Centre at the University of Sydney since 2006.

5 In NSW schools it is mandatory for students to complete a 100-hour course of language study. The course must be in one language, in one 12-month continuous period, preferably in Stage 4, which is one of the first two years of high school (Years 7 and 8). It is not compulsory for the language to be an Aboriginal language. The syllabus also includes the possibility of 100-hour and 200-hour elective courses in Stage 5 (Years 9 and 10).

Gulbala-dha murraya-la marrum-bang-gu.	Speak up for justice and peace without fighting.
Nga-nga-dha garray-gu bila galang-gu.	Look after the land and the rivers.
Yandhu garray-bu bila-galang-bu nga-nga-girri nginyalgir.	Then the land and the rivers will look after you all.

(Wiradjuri Council of Elders, cited in Dubbo College and Wiradjuri community 2009)

The concepts in this text were divided into four themes that provide the focus for teaching and learning during each of the four terms of the school year. Relevant vocabulary (relating to a broad range of domains including kinship, country, health and wellbeing, relationships within Aboriginal communities and between Aboriginal and non-Aboriginal Australians) and grammatical structures (including making statements, asking questions, a range of nominal suffixes, verb forms and pronouns) are taught as part of each theme, and the language content of the course becomes increasingly challenging throughout the year.

The program for Dubbo College was prepared during a series of planning meetings and writing workshops. The writing team was comprised of the Wiradjuri teacher, two Aboriginal education consultants for the NSW DET western region, an Aboriginal studies teacher (who was also studying to be an Aboriginal languages teacher at the time of writing) and two teachers of French.

After each meeting of the program-writing team, progress checks were made by the steering committee, which consisted of the school principals, Elders, local community members and the president of the Dubbo Aboriginal Education Consultative Group. This committee's advice ensured both school and community input into the program. Community input was also facilitated through many of the teaching, learning and assessment activities for the course being written in ways that required the students to make contact with community members and families. For example, local community guest speakers are a part of some lessons; for other lessons students showcase, display and perform their work for parents and families. This type of school–community interaction, with student learning at the centre, is a key feature of the program and keeps community members informed and involved in the program.[6]

Many languages undergoing revitalisation have used song as an effective way to teach both child and adult learners (see also Green; Sometimes & Kelly, this volume). Often the songs have been translations of English nursery rhymes, children's songs, folk, pop or country and western songs, all of which entail the risk of applying English stress and tone patterns to Aboriginal languages. McNaboe has begun to take what is considered by the community as a more authentic approach starting with a reworked version

---

[6] For more detail on teaching and learning activities and examples of programs written by a number school–community Aboriginal languages teams, see the BOS NSW website at ab-ed.boardofstudies.nsw.edu.au/go/aboriginal-languages

of 'Gulambali', a song that many Wiradjuri learners already know. The version they have learned teaches aspects of Wiradjuri grammatical patterns, word construction and related vocabulary. The song was created deliberately for this purpose and, in this sense, has an important place in the learning and teaching of Wiradjuri language structures. However the English melodic style is in stark contrast to McNaboe's version of the song, which carries not only the grammatical and vocabulary lessons but also musical patterns and gestures derived from Aboriginal languages and cultures. McNaboe believes that this song came to her through country and is also informed by her knowledge of and connections with other Aboriginal people and cultures and stronger languages. Her students respond to it very positively and believe it is more true to the language and a meaningful contribution to its revitalisation. Grant and the Wiradjuri Elders have encouraged McNaboe's approach. She plans to create more songs in this way as part of reconnecting with language, culture and ways of doing things that affirm and build on Wiradjuri identity. Wiradjuri people are mindful of decisions involved in learning their language again. They are open to hearing and being influenced by voices from the past. Older people and earlier generations still speak today and give their wisdom to language workers such as McNaboe.

Conclusion

School programs in NSW both support and are supported by the revitalisation work that has been undertaken by community leaders and others for a number of years. In the revitalisation of Aboriginal languages, school programs also play an important role in complementing adult learning. Aboriginal community language teachers are the link between the two. The development of their language skills and effective teaching strategies are keys to successful school programs. Whether in adult learning or schools, programs must have strong credibility in the community. Aboriginal people must be active agents in the process, participating in the full range of language learning, teaching and revitalisation activities and tasks.

References

Board of Studies New South Wales (2003a). *Aboriginal languages K–10 syllabus*. Sydney: Board of Studies New South Wales [Online]. Available: www.boardofstudies.nsw.edu.au/syllabus_sc [Accessed 30 April 2009].

Board of Studies New South Wales (2003b). *Aboriginal languages: advice on programming and assessment for Stages 4 and 5*. Sydney: Board of Studies New South Wales [Online]. Available: www.boardofstudies.nsw.edu.au/syllabus_sc [Accessed 30 April 2009].

Board of Studies New South Wales (2004). *Winangaylanha dhayn-gu gaay: understanding Aboriginal languages* [CD-ROM]. Sydney: Board of Studies New South Wales.

Büchli C (2006). Reversing language shift in New South Wales: reclaiming and teaching

Wiradjuri. Unpublished mémoire, Department of Linguistics, Faculty of Philosophy, University of Fribourg, Switzerland.

Donaldson T (1981). Wiradjuri words remembered by participants in the Back to Warangesda Week, July 1980. Unpublished typescript. PMS 3471, Australian Institute of Aboriginal & Torres Strait Islander Studies.

Dubbo College and Wiradjuri community (2009). Stage 4 Wiradjuri program. Sydney: Board of Studies New South Wales [Online] Available ab-ed.boardofstudies.nsw.edu.au/go/aboriginal-languages [Accessed 30 June 2010]

Grant S & Rudder J (2001a). *Wiradjuri language – how it works*. Canberra: Restoration House.

Grant S & Rudder J (2001b). *Learning Wiradjuri book 1 (place and direction) & book 2 (about actions)* [with audio CD]. Canberra: Restoration House.

Grant S & Rudder J (2001c). *Wiradjuri language song book 1 & book 2* [with audio CD]. Canberra: Restoration House.

Grant S & Rudder J (2001d). *Introducing Wiradjuri sentences*. Canberra: Restoration House.

Grant S & Rudder J (2005). *Wiradjuri dictionary*. 2nd ed. Canberra: Restoration House.

Hosking D & McNicol S (1993). *Wiradjuri*. Canberra: Australian Institute of Aboriginal & Torres Strait Islander Studies.

Lowe K & Ash A (2006). *Talking each other's lingo: the Aboriginal languages K–10 syllabus and its role in language revitalisation in NSW*. Sydney: Board of Studies New South Wales [Online]. Available: ab-ed.boardofstudies.nsw.edu.au/files/talking_each_others_lingo.pdf [Accessed 30 April 2009].

Lowe K & Walsh M (2008). California down under: Indigenous language revitalization in New South Wales, Australia. In W Leonard & SEB Gardner (Eds). *Language is life.* Proceedings of the 11th Stabilizing Indigenous Languages conference (pp. 100–15). University of California at Berkeley, 10–13 June 2004. Berkeley: Survey of California & Other Indian Languages.

McNicol S & Hosking D (1994). Wiradjuri. In N Thieberger & W McGregor (Eds). *Macquarie Aboriginal words: a dictionary of words from Australian Aboriginal & Torres Strait Islander languages* (pp. 23–40). North Ryde, NSW: Macquarie Library.

Rhydwen M, Munro J, Parolin E & Poetsch S (2007). *Report on school-based Aboriginal language program activity in NSW during 2006*. Sydney: Board of Studies New South Wales and New South Wales Department of Education [Online]. Available: ab-ed.boardofstudies.nsw.edu.au/go/resources/languages [Accessed 30 April 2009].

Wafer J & Lissarrague A (2008). *A handbook of Aboriginal languages of New South Wales & the Australian Capital Territory*. Nambucca Heads, NSW: Muurrbay Aboriginal Language & Culture Co-operative.

20
The importance of understanding language ecologies for revitalisation

Felicity Meakins[1]

Abstract

Most language revitalisation models are pitched at people who are either monolingual or who are multilingual but separate languages according to different functional domains, such as home, school, church, or public functions like opening ceremonies. Yet many children and adults in northern Australia do not speak one language, nor do they use only one language in single utterances. For example in the Victoria River District of the Northern Territory code-switching between a traditional language and Kriol is a pervasive and longstanding practice. McConvell (1988) documented code-switching between Gurindji and Kriol at Kalkaringi in the 1970s. These code-switching practices continue, and younger people in the Victoria River District now speak youth languages which are fossilised forms of code-switching (Meakins 2008b; McConvell & Meakins 2005). These mixing practices represent grassroots and informal forms of language maintenance (Meakins 2008a). Understanding these kinds of language ecologies is essential to tailoring an effective language revitalisation program. If language mixing is a common practice even of older people then the goal of fluent monolingualism in the target language requires not only language learning but also changing communicative conventions. This is an unfortunate goal if it means undermining the mixing practices that have been successfully maintaining aspects of the traditional language. The approach I present works within the framework of the speakers' own mixing practices. Language programs that take into account these informal language maintenance practices can augment them with the staged introduction of new words and grammar (see Amery 2000).

1 School of Languages, Linguistics and Cultures, University of Manchester.

The aim of language revitalisation is to breathe life back into a language in danger of no longer being spoken. Typically the language only has older speakers and no child language learners (Amery 2000, p. 18). Such degrees of language endangerment have many causes but are most broadly the result of the profound domination of one group over another. This degree of power imbalance has been shown to have a detrimental effect on languages all over the world. In this paper I focus on the southern Victoria River District (VRD) in Australia and the communities of Kalkaringi, Yarralin and Pigeon Hole. The VRD consists of the land surrounding the Victoria River that is bounded by the Victoria and Buntine Highways (Figure 1). The languages associated with this area are Ngarinyman, Bilinarra, Karrangpurru, Mudbura and Gurindji, however all of them are highly endangered. Indeed Karrangpurru has not been spoken for some time and Bilinarra has no full speakers remaining. Instead Kriol is gaining currency with younger generations. Generally speaking, the younger the person the less they speak of their traditional language and the more Kriol they use.

Although this situation represents a devastating loss of traditional languages, informal maintenance practices are the norm. Among older people these maintenance practices involve switching between a traditional language and Kriol. Youth languages have also formed from these mixing strategies as the result of systematically combining a traditional language with Kriol. In this respect younger generations are demonstrating a commitment to the maintenance of their language. Formal language revitalisation programs have also existed in a number of schools in the VRD including Pigeon Hole (2000–present) and Kalkaringi (1980s, 1996–99), most recently structured under the Indigenous Languages and Culture (ILC) component of the Northern Territory Curriculum Framework (2002). Although the suggested structure of ILC programs includes the development of aural, oral, reading and writing skills, typically most programs are reduced to wordlist learning via English or the vernacular language, usually Kriol. This type of language teaching strategy has faced much criticism, which can be summed up by the question: What's the point of only learning words? Indeed no child can learn a language from an hour a week of wordlist learning. Immersion models that expose children to greater amounts of language have been proposed as better alternatives.

In this paper I discuss the language situation at Kalkaringi, Pigeon Hole and Yarralin, characterising these communities as fluid bilingual speech communities where language mixing is the unmarked and customary language practice. I also examine how the school-based language revitalisation programs work within this language ecology. I then present some immersion models such as language nests and the master–apprentice model which have been used in similar situations of language loss, and therefore may be considered to have some potential for the VRD. The reason for my focus on immersion models is that they are constantly being toyed with by linguists and education department people in the Northern Territory (NT) as a better alternative to current language learning models. Yet I show that, while these immersion models have some advantages, they have two problems: (a) they are based on the idea of monolingualism and language purity, and (b) they are top-down models which do not take account of already-present informal language maintenance strategies. In communities such as those in the VRD where monolingualism is not the norm I claim that these immersion models are unlikely to be effective. Instead I suggest rather than disregarding ILC programs and opting for a completely new model,[2] ILC programs can provide an effective framework for language revitalisation if they are tailored to suit existing language ecologies and take into account already existing informal community language maintenance strategies. I argue that ILC programs should only be designed after an initial survey of community language practices. In places where language mixing is common, teaching strategies such as wordlist learning can be used to augment existing maintenance strategies by introducing a greater repertoire of language material to community mixing practices. Wordlist learning can be viewed as a beginning point for introducing new material and can be further supplemented by the gradual inclusion of phrases and structural material. In this respect I follow Amery (2000) in arguing for a staged introduction of traditional language material. The focus of such a language revitalisation program is not full monolingual control of the traditional language but rather supporting existing community maintenance practices.

Language mixing in the Victoria River District

As in other parts of Australia the colonisation of the VRD had devastating consequences for the Aboriginal people and their traditional language and culture. In late 1855 the first party of European explorers, led by Francis and Henry Gregory, arrived from the north. They followed the Victoria River and its tributaries and came upon the VRD (Makin 1999, p. 43 onwards). The area is mostly a black soil plain, which made it attractive cattle country for the European colonists. Bilinarra, Ngarinyman and Karrangpurru country were the first to be stocked with cattle in 1883. In the process the colonists brought with them diseases that Aboriginal immune systems and traditional bush medicines could not cope with (Rose 1991, p. 75 onwards). The settlers further decimated the Aboriginal population of the VRD in a series of massacres in an attempt to gain control of the land (Wavehill 2000). The aim of the killing sprees probably would have been complete genocide had the settlers not realised that Aboriginal people would make an excellent source of cheap labour. As a result they survived and were put to work as stockman and kitchen hands on the cattle stations, where they also lived in fringe camps. By the 1960s discontent was running high among the Aboriginal workers. On August 23rd, 1966 a Gurindji elder called Lingiari gathered his people and they walked 16 kilometres to Jurnani (Gordy Creek) and later another ten kilometres to Daguragu, which is eight kilometres from Kalkaringi and now an established Gurindji settlement (Hardy 1968). In 1975, after nine years of persistent campaigning and a change to a more liberal federal

---

2 See Hobson (2008) for some arguments for working with existing language learning syllabuses that have government support, rather than being drawn to new quick-fix solutions to language loss which require diverting funds and retraining language practitioners.

government, Prime Minister Gough Whitlam flew to Daguragu to grant the Gurindji a lease for 3236 square kilometres of land around Daguragu. Twenty years later, in 1986, they were granted the security of inalienable freehold title under the *Aboriginal Land Rights [Northern Territory] Act*. Further small claims followed around Pigeon Hole and Yarralin. Nonetheless much of the land in the VRD remains privately owned cattle stations with the Gurindji, Bilinarra, Ngarinyman and Mudbura people living in a small number of Aboriginal communities including Yarralin, Pigeon Hole, Kalkaringi and Daguragu (Figure 1).

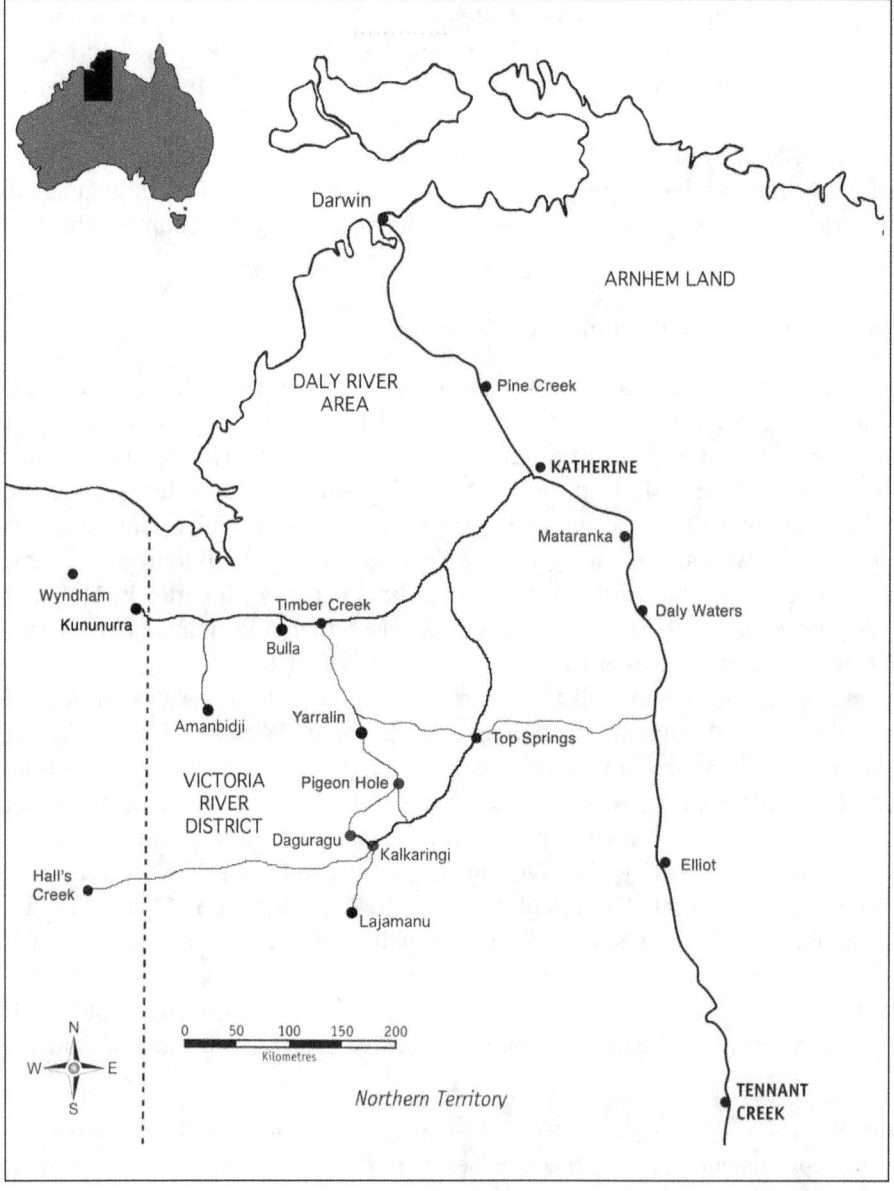

Figure 1. Victoria River District (NT).

The colonisation of this area has had a significant impact on the traditional languages. The language of Kalkaringi and the surrounding area, Gurindji is now highly endangered with approximately 70 full speakers remaining (Lee & Dickson 2002). Most middle-aged Gurindji people have a good knowledge of the language, but they are only partial speakers. Gurindji people below the age of 35 understand Gurindji but do not speak it in its traditional form. Instead they speak a youth variety which has been called Gurindji Kriol (Charola 2002; McConvell & Meakins 2005; Meakins 2008b). The situation for Pigeon Hole and Yarralin is very similar. Pigeon Hole lies in Bilinarra country and Yarralin in Ngarinyman country. No full Bilinarra speakers remain in Pigeon Hole, however many middle-aged people speak some Bilinarra. Elderly Ngarinyman speakers can be found in Yarralin and the middle-aged people also speak some Ngarinyman. As in Kalkaringi, younger Bilinarra and Ngarinyman people speak a youth version of their language that has a large Kriol component. It does not differ much from Gurindji Kriol, which is not surprising given that Gurindji, Bilinarra and Ngarinyman share a lot of grammar and vocabulary.

Despite the different languages, what is characteristic of these three communities is the language practice of mixing. Although it is common to hear some monolingual sentences in traditional language, Gurindji, Bilinarra and Ngarinyman are rarely found in longer stretches of speech without some mixing with Kriol. This language mixing occurs in two different ways: *code-switching* among older people and a *youth language* used by younger people (Meakins 2008b). First, code-switching involves changing languages within one speaker's sentence. Often a speaker inserts a word from one language into the sentence of another language. Some examples from Kalkaringi are given below. In (1) the speaker inserts a Kriol verb *jouim* (show) into a Gurindji sentence.[3] In the second example, the Gurindji noun *kartiya-lu* (whitefella-ERG) is inserted into a Kriol sentence. In other cases of code-switching, an utterance begins with a clause in one language and finishes in another. This is shown in (3) where the speaker alternates between languages. She begins in Gurindji and finishes in Kriol, as indicated by the slash.

(1)

nyawa-ma	*mangarri*	*na*	*ngu-ngantipa*	*ngu-rnalu-rla*	jouim	*jayingana.*
this-DIS	veg.food	FOC	CAT-our	CAT-we-to.her	show	give.PRS

This is our food. We're showing it to her.

(2)

laika	*kartiya-lu*	wen	jei	putim	tar	yu	nou	langa	bityumin.
like	whitefella-ERG	when	they	put	tar	you	know	on	bitumen

Like the roadworks mob when they put tar, you know, on the bitumen.

---

3 Note that in all of these sentences the Kriol and English elements are in plain font and the language words and suffixes are italicised.

(3)

nama-ngku	kangarni	ngu	wuyarnani	ngu	/laika	weya	wi	kilim
bee-ERG	take.PST	it	throw.PST	it	/like	where	we	hit

The bees took it and put it the wax there /like here where we knock it off.

Code-switching is not a new language practice in the VRD. Code-switching between Gurindji and Kriol was observed in the mid-1970s (McConvell 1988). Code-switching was regularised by new generations of Gurindji people and led to the youth language, Gurindji Kriol (McConvell & Meakins 2005). An example is given below. The degree of mixing can be seen from the alternation of italicised words (Gurindji) and words in plain font (Kriol).

(4)

nyila	jinek	im	gon	yapart	la	im	kajirri-yu.
that	snake	it	go	sneak	to	her	woman-DAT

That snake sneaks up on the old woman.

In this youth language a large amount of Gurindji is preserved including nouns, verbs, demonstratives (such as *this* and *that*) and many other parts of the grammar. Although this form of mixing looks like code-switching, it is different because it is very regular; and many words, although they are derived from Gurindji and Kriol, are used in different ways in the youth language (Meakins 2007). These kinds of mixing practices can also be seen at Pigeon Hole and Yarralin.

In many respects these code-switching practices and the youth language can be considered an informal way that traditional languages are being maintained by the communities, despite immense functional pressure from both Kriol and English (Meakins 2008a). Despite these maintenance practices, both young and old people in these communities are aware and acutely concerned about the rapid shift away from traditional languages. For example Biddy Wavehill, a Gurindji elder from Kalkaringi, is unhappy with the children's use of particular word stems and endings.

> *Ngurnayinangkulu kurru karrinyana karu* yu nou *kula-lu marnana* jutup. *Ngulu marnani 'Nyawa-ngkirri'. Nyawangkirri-ma, nyampayila ngulu marnana 'Murlangkurra'. 'Kawayi murlangkurra,'* kuya yu nou. An *'Pinka-kirri,'* jei tok rong jarran. *'Pinka-kurra,' kuya. 'Pinka-kurra kanyjurra'. 'Nyawangkirri,'* dat not rait word *jaru. Ngurnayinangkulu kurru karrinyana kuya* laik *ngurnayinangkulu jutuk kuya-rnangku jarrakap* brobli-wei.
>
> We listen to the kids, you know, and they don't talk properly. For example, they are always saying *nyawangkirri* for 'that way'. They always say *nyawangkirri* not *murlangkurra* which is wrong. You should say *murlangkurra*. And they also say *pinka-kirri* for 'to the river' which is wrong. They should say *pinka-kurra*. *Nyawangkirri* is not proper Gurindji. We listen to the kids and they don't talk as well as I am talking to you. (pers. comm., 20 August 2008)

Due to concerns about language loss, informal maintenance practices such as code-switching and youth languages have also been supplemented by formal school-based language revitalisation programs. Kalkaringi has had the longest history of school language programs, though it has been sporadic. Missionaries ran a Gurindji school program in the 1980s. Gurindji also figured very strongly in church life at that time. Many hymns were translated into Gurindji as was the Eucharist and other church sacraments. Diwurruwurru-jaru Aboriginal Corporation (DAC) started the school language program again in 1996 and it ran until the end of 1999 when the principal discontinued it. The community's desire to reinstate the Gurindji language program has been hindered by the English-only policy of subsequent principals. Pigeon Hole School has had a shorter but more consistent Bilinarra language program supported by DAC linguists. This language program was set up in 2000 and has been running since then, albeit with a number of short breaks, for example due to the death of a senior Bilinarra woman. Yarralin has not had a formal Ngarinyman program at the school though various attempts have been made to set one up. Stronger and more consistent language programs are desired in these communities. For example Violet Donald, a Gurindji elder, says:

> School-*jirri ngurnayinangulu yanangku. Jarrakap ngurnayinangulu marnangku. Jarrakap ngurnayinangulu marnangku, jaru-yawung. Ngulu pinarri too karrinyana nyarralu-ngan.* Tumaji *kula-lu marnana jaru-ma punyu. Nyatparrak*-wei *ngulu marnana.*
>
> We want to go to school. We want to be talking to them there. We want to talk to them in Gurindji. They have to learn Gurindji as well as English because they don't speak Gurindji well. They are talking any which way. (pers. comm., 20 August 2008)

These language programs are run by a language team minimally consisting of a speaker and a language worker who are supported by a DAC linguist. The language worker is a younger person who is not a full speaker of the language, but is often literate in English and has some teacher training or at least an understanding of formal learning strategies. The structure of the classes largely follows the ILC component of the NT Curriculum Framework (2002). The classes are based on themes such as body parts, bush medicine and fishing and they aim to develop listening, speaking and writing skills in the children's traditional language. Though the aural parts of the classes involve listening to stretches of traditional language, for example stories, the speaking and writing components have only focused on individual words, usually nouns and verbs, and short phrases.

These school-based language programs have faced a number of problems including the lack of commitment from principals; the sporadic nature of funding; the lack of language resources; the mobile nature of the community, including students and the language team; the lack of commitment by the language team; and the distance from DAC which supports the language programs from Katherine approximately 500 kilometres away. Children are also rarely assessed for their language abilities. In fact they are often judged by new teachers and linguists as knowing less than they do know; as a result lessons such as body part names are often repeated unnecessarily and new material is slow to be introduced. These problems are common to these types of programs (Schmidt 1990, p. 88 onwards). With regard to the lack of commitment, the main reason has often been given as a frustration with the teaching strategy. The focus on wordlists is rightly seen as not being the way back to language competence. Indeed children are not immersed in the language for long enough to develop their language competency. As a result these language programs can appear to be no more than tokenistic. The solution may be to seek out alternatives to ILC programs suitable for the language situation in the VRD. The next section will present some models and assess their appropriateness. What I will ultimately demonstrate is that ILC programs which have been tailored to the specific linguistic practices of the community, and which include wordlist learning as a teaching strategy, can prove valuable in tapping into the already existing language maintenance practices of younger generations.

Models of language immersion

Many different methods have been proposed for revitalising endangered languages. The appropriateness of these methods depends on the health of the language. The health of a language can be measured by a number of factors including the absolute number of speakers, whether the language is still being learnt by children, the isolation of the language community, the economic and political status of the speaker community, the institutional status of the language (whether or not it is used in government, religion, schools), and the attitudes of the speakers themselves to their language and the dominant language of the region (see McKay 1996, p. 226 for the Australian situation). Fishman (1991, p. 87 onwards) uses these indicators of language health to set up an eight point scale which grades language disruption. It ranges from languages that are strong, that is languages which are still learnt by children and are used in government and universities, to languages which have only a few elderly speakers and have no institutional status. Fishman also provides suggestions for revitalisation models for each of these levels of language viability. The languages of the VRD fall into Fishman's Stage 7 because only adults beyond child-bearing age such as grandparents are full speakers. Fishman recommends language immersion as a method for reversing this language shift. Language immersion involves providing an environment where learners will hear and speak only the endangered language. A number of immersion models exist, including language nests and the master–apprentice scheme. These models are appropriate for revitalising languages that only have speakers in the grandparent generation.

Language nests

Language nests have been one of the most successful examples of immersion programs used in the school context. These programs have been operating in New Zealand and Hawai'i since the early 1980s and are based on Canadian French immersion schools. For example *Te Kōhanga Reo* are early childhood language immersion programs developed by Māori communities to reverse the continuing loss of the Māori language. The model was born out of two observations: (a) most Māori speakers were often beyond child-rearing age and (b) children are the best language learners. Te Kōhanga Reo aimed to close this generational gap by teaming up older speakers with young children, thereby providing Māori children with the input they needed to acquire the language (Biggs 1968; Irwin 1991; King 2001). The Hawaiian story is similar; the model was replicated as *Pūnana Leo*, with the first centre opened in 1982. In 1987 these preschool immersion programs were extended through to Grade 12 (Huebner 1985; No'eau Warner 2001; Reinecke 1969; Wilson & Kamana 2001).

Both New Zealand and Hawai'i had the capacity to set up these language nests partly due to the presence of a good number of speakers who were young and trained in teaching methodology, and partly due to structural and institutional support. New Zealand and Hawai'i also both have one main traditional language that is enshrined in the constitution. The governments are therefore compelled to symbolically recognise these languages, for example in signage; and provide funding for education, interpreting, translation and media services. Other areas in the world suffering severe language loss do not have the same numbers of speakers or the institutional support for language nests, at least not within official institutions such as schools. Smaller scale projects have been designed, however.

The master–apprentice model

The master–apprentice model was developed in California in 1992. It aims to reverse the devastating language loss of native languages by pairing young Native Americans with older native speakers thereby crossing the generation gap in much the same way as the language nests. One important difference is the context of learning. Where language nests are school-based immersion programs, the master–apprentice model operates in everyday situations such as cooking, washing, as well as more traditional activities. The focus of the master–apprentice model is oral transmission and developing conversational skills. Both the speaker and learner are not allowed to use English, even for translations. Context and other non-verbal forms of communication such as gesturing help the learner understand utterances. The end aim is slightly different from the language nests. Where the language nests have aimed to create a whole new generation of Māori or Hawaiian speakers, the master–apprentice model can only hope to keep language alive within a small group of people over successive generations (Hinton 1994; 1997; 2001).

Problems with immersion models in language mixing contexts

The language nest model is the most appropriate language immersion program appropriate to school-based learning. The master–apprentice model is geared towards the individual language learner which is not possible in the school context. While language nests can operate within schools, they require enormous time and commitment. In the NT this time and commitment is not available within the education system. The

ILC component of the NT Curriculum Framework is the only non-compulsory part of the curriculum which has translated into sporadic government funding. Of course immersion can be achieved outside of the school system as the master–apprentice model demonstrates; however, it must be noted that school already occupies six hours of a child's waking hours, making this difficult. Pressing social issues also hinder the implementation of immersion models (and indeed all community development programs) in the Australian situation. For example, overcrowding, substance abuse and poor health in communities all contribute to low energy levels in language teams and child learners. This means that language revitalisation can have a low priority in the life of the community (Schmidt 1990, p. 90).

Even with time and commitment from the community for language revitalisation work, these immersion models present two related problems for language revitalisation in the context of the VRD: (a) the 'purity' of the input, and (b) the lack of acknowledgement of existing maintenance practices.

With regard to the first problem, even if language nests were set up for children in schools, it is unlikely that the end result would be fluent monolingual speakers of Gurindji, Bilinarra or Ngarinyman. The reason is that older speakers themselves generally do not speak the language without some mixing with Kriol. Language purity cannot be an expectation of learners if it is not a practice of the teachers. Yet insisting that speakers speak only their traditional language would result in stifling natural interaction and discouraging learning. Similar problems were noted by Hinton in the master–apprentice model when speakers were expected not to use any English (Hinton 1994, p. 243).

Secondly the immersion models take a top-down approach, imposing a model on a language situation without sensitivities to the language ecology. They do not take account of the way a community may already be maintaining languages, through language mixing. For example the language mixing practices found in the VRD can be viewed as a sign of language decay. Indeed this is the belief of older community members. Yet they can also be seen as language maintenance. Young Gurindji people believe that their youth language represents a new Gurindji identity, which cannot be achieved through the sole use of Kriol. The maintenance of Gurindji is important to this, though the use of the full language is not required. In fact the Kriol component of the youth language is necessary as it evokes a *modern* Gurindji identity which is connected with other north Australian Aboriginal people (Meakins 2008a). A good revitalisation program should tap into these grass-roots maintenance practices and aim to augment these practices rather than change them. A whole-language approach that is purist and imposes itself on an existing language ecology which is characterised by mixing is unlikely to achieve any discernable results.

Given these concerns, it is worth looking again to the framework that ILC programs can offer, particularly because these programs have the advantage of some institutional support within the NT Department of Education and Training. Unlike immersion models, ILC programs can be tailored to take account of community mixing practices. They can be used to supplement the traditional language content of children's everyday talk by identifying what children know and don't know and targeting the gaps. Unlike immersion models, ILC programs allow lesson delivery in the vernacular language. This means that new content can be introduced into the children's reportoire through the mixed structures already used by the children. Indeed this is not a new concept. One method that promotes language mixing as a teaching methodology is the formulaic method (Amery 2000, pp. 209–15). The formulaic method is aimed at language reclamation, that is reviving a language that has not been spoken for at least a generation. This approach was developed for Kaurna, an Adelaide language which no longer has full speakers. The method introduces language back into the community by the 'staged introduction of well-formed utterances' (Amery 2000, p. 209). This begins with one-word utterances such as commands, questions and interjections. Longer and more complex expressions are gradually introduced with the aim of slowly replacing dominant language. In this respect the dominant language, English in the case of Kaurna reclamation, is not banned or discouraged and what emerges is code-switching between English and Kaurna. The code-switching is encouraged if it promotes natural language use. So naturalistic conversation is promoted over language purism. This methodology is not at all at odds with the ILC structure.

Language teaching through language mixing

Amery's formulaic method may have some applicability to language revitalisation work in the VRD where the traditional languages are more vital and language mixing is a practice already widespread. Children are already being immersed in language at home, albeit largely mixed with Kriol, and this practice can be supported by a well-designed staged learning model based on the already familiar wordlist learning models. Such an approach would build on knowledge children already have. Following the formulaic method, the ILC program would begin with individual utterances and gradually introduce more grammatical material while using the children's own language, Gurindji Kriol, as a base. The much-maligned practice of wordlist learning provides a strong place to begin. To give an example, children from Kalkaringi, Pigeon Hole and Yarralin know many verbs of body posture such as *makin* (lie, sleep) and *kutij* (stand). They use them within their own language, Gurindji Kriol:

(5)

dat	*warlaku*	im	*makin*	tri-*ngka*.
the	dog	it	lie	tree-LOC

The dog lies under the tree.

Yet there are many words where they will use the Kriol form such as *jidan* (sit) instead of a Gurindji word. A staged introduction approach would use the general Gurindji Kriol frame, as in (5) and add new words such as *lurlu* (sit), *wulujurr* (sit with legs out), *jarrap* (sit cross-legged) and so on. This vocabulary building can extend to all areas of a child's lexicon including developing their knowledge of animal and plant names, which contain more cultural content than postural verbs. While children are still speaking Gurindji Kriol, they are using more and more Gurindji content and gradually replacing Kriol words with Gurindji words.

This staged introduction of traditional language material can also be extended to the grammar. In the VRD there are some parts of traditional language grammar that children do not use such as pronouns and the inflected part of a two-part verb that contains tense, mood and aspect information. There are other parts that they do know and use, but which show signs of Kriol influence. For example children generally use Gurindji case markers to indicate spatial relations, but are beginning to use Kriol prepositions more than their parents (Meakins 2008a, p. 90). In (5) the Gurindji locative case marker {-ngka} is used to indicate where the dog is in relation to the tree, however in (6) the Kriol preposition *langa* (LOC) is used instead.

(6)

dat	*warlaku*	im	*makin*	langa tri.
the	dog	it	lie	LOC tree

The dog lies under the tree.

Language lessons structured within the ILC program can be used to reinforce the traditional language grammar where children are beginning to use Kriol elements such as prepositions. This can strengthen the language component of Gurindji Kriol and help prevent the shift to Kriol. Gradually a stepped program would reintroduce language structures which children no longer use such as pronouns and inflecting verbs. By this stage the language classes would have buttressed the knowledge that children already have of their traditional language and added items to word classes that children already use such as nouns and verbs. This technique builds on the knowledge that children already have and values this knowledge by operating within the language maintenance practices that they have already developed themselves.

This type of teaching technique can be applied to many other situations in northern Australia. Youth languages such as Gurindji Kriol have also been observed in Lajamanu where a new form of Warlpiri which includes large amounts of Kriol and English is spoken (O'Shannessy 2008). Other forms of language mixing such as code-switching can be found among younger people in the north. One of the characteristics of Wumpurrarni English spoken in Tennant Creek is the insertion of Warumungu words, particularly nouns, into sentences which use a contact form of English (Disbray 2008). Another example comes from Timber Creek where young people use Jaminjung or Ngarinyman verbs and nouns in Kriol sentences (Schultze-Berndt 2007). See Figure 1 for the location of these places.

Conclusion

This paper has discussed the pitfalls of ILC language programs in the VRD. However it does not consider immersion models such as language nests and master–apprentice as appropriate alternatives. Instead I advocate ways of improving ILC programs using Amery's formulaic method. It is worth noting that, except in a very long-term application of this model of staged learning, full fluency in a traditional language is an unlikely outcome. Thus such a model requires clarification of aims by the language community about what can be reasonably achieved in the limited time given over to traditional language teaching in the schools. I have been witness to many moments in language classes where children are rebuked for not speaking properly. These outbursts from language teachers are largely the result of disappointment at the rate of learning and a lack of understanding of the mechanisms involved in second language learning. Unfortunately these comments usually act to silence children further. Indeed this view has also been held by some academics who have been disparaging about revitalisation programs which aim for anything less than complete fluency (see, for example, Fishman 1991, p. 397). Yet, as Amery (2000, p. 207) argues, all forms of revival in situations of language loss should be valued. Students should not be blamed for something they have no control over, that is their lack of rich language input, and should be encouraged within an environment that nurtures learning. All participants in such a program including the language team and students need to have a good understanding of the mechanisms of second language learning. Additionally they need to know what can be reasonably achieved at the various stages of such a stepped program. In this way, the language maintenance strategies already present in a language community can be built on with more formal teaching approaches.

Acknowledgements

I first started thinking about the issues raised in this paper during my work as a community linguist at DAC where my job was to support language programs in Pigeon Hole, Bulla and Amanbidji. My thanks to the people I worked with on these programs: Ivy Hector,† Mildred Hector and Barbara Bobby (Pigeon Hole), Annie Packsaddle† and Christine Ahwon (Amanbidji), Eileen Roberts† and Noelene Nemit (Bulla). Also thanks to other DAC linguists, past and present, for the many thoughtful discussions about these issues: Erika Charola, Sarah Cutfield, Eleonora Deak, Greg Dickson, Lauren Campbell, Eugenie Collyer and Salome Harris.

References

Amery R (2000). *Warrabarna Kaurna! reclaiming an Australian language.* Lisse: Swets & Zeitlinger.

Biggs B (1968). The Maori language past and present. In E Schwimmer (Ed). *The Maori people in the 1960s* (pp. 65–84). Auckland: Blackwood & Janet Paul.

Charola E (2002). The verb phrase structure of Gurindji Kriol. Unpublished honours thesis, School of Languages & Linguistics, Melbourne University, Melbourne.

Department of Education & Training Northern Territory (2002) *Northern Territory curriculum framework* [Online]. Available: www.det.nt.gov.au/teachers-educators/curriculum-ntbos/ntcf [Accessed 30 March 2009].

Disbray S (2008). Story-telling styles: a study of adult-child interactions in narrations of a picture book in Tennant Creek. In J Simpson & G Wigglesworth (Eds). *Children's language and multilingualism: Indigenous language use at home and school* (pp. 56–78). New Jersey: Continuum.

Fishman J (1991). *Reversing language shift: theoretical and empirical foundations of assistance to threatened languages.* Clevedon: Multilingual Matters.

Hardy F (1968). *The unlucky Australians.* Melbourne: Nelson.

Hinton L (1994). *Flutes of fire: essays on Californian Indian languages.* Berkeley: Heyday Books.

Hinton L (1997). Survival of endangered languages: the California Master–Apprentice Program. *International Journal of the Sociology of Language,* 123: 177–91.

Hinton L (2001). The master–apprentice language learning program. In L Hinton & K Hale (Eds). *The green book of language revitalization in practice* (pp. 217–26). San Diego: Academic Press.

Hobson J (2008). Training teachers for indigenous languages education: what's happening overseas? In R Amery & J Nash (Eds). *Warra wiltaniappendi: strengthening languages.* Proceedings of the inaugural Indigenous languages conference (ILC) 2007 (pp. 97–105). University of Adelaide, South Australia, 25–27 September 2007. Adelaide: University of Adelaide.

Huebner T (1985). Language education policy in Hawaii: two case studies and some current issues. *International Journal of the Sociology of Language,* 56: 29–49.

Irwin K (1991). Maori education in 1991: a review and discussion. *New Zealand Annual Review of Education,* 1: 77–112.

King J (2001). Te kōhanga reo: Māori language revitalisation. In L Hinton & K Hale (Eds). *The green book of language revitalization in practice* (pp. 118–28). San Diego: Academic Press.

Lee J & Dickson G (2002). *State of Indigenous languages of the Katherine region.* Katherine: Diwurruwurru-jaru Aboriginal Corporation.

Makin J (1999). *The big run: the story of Victoria River Downs Station.* Adelaide, SA: J. B. Books.

McConvell P (1988). Mix-im-up: Aboriginal codeswitching old and new (pp. 97–150). In M Heller (Ed). *Codeswitching: anthropological and sociolinguistic perspectives.* Berlin: Mouton de Gruyter.

McConvell P & Meakins F (2005). Gurindji Kriol: a mixed language emerges from code-switching. *Australian Journal of Linguistics*, 25(1): 9–30.

McKay G (1996). *The land still speaks: review of Aboriginal and Torres Strait Islander language maintenance and development needs and activities*. Canberra: National Board of Employment, Education & Training.

Meakins F (2007). Case marking in contact: the development and function of case morphology in Gurindji Kriol, an Australian mixed language. Unpublished doctoral thesis, School of Languages & Linguistics, University of Melbourne, Melbourne.

Meakins F (2008a). Land, language and identity: the socio-political origins of Gurindji Kriol. In M Meyerhoff & N Nagy (Eds). *Social lives in language* (pp. 69–94). Amsterdam: John Benjamins.

Meakins F (2008b). Unravelling languages: multilingualism and language contact in Kalkaringi. In J Simpson & G Wigglesworth (Eds). *Children's language and multilingualism: Indigenous language use at home and school* (pp. 247–64). New York: Continuum.

No'eau Warner SL (2001). The movement to revitalize Hawaiian language and culture. In L Hinton & K Hale (Eds). *The green book of language revitalization in practice* (pp. 133–44). San Diego: Academic Press.

O'Shannessy C (2008). Children's production of their heritage language and a new mixed language. In J Simpson & G Wigglesworth (Eds). *Children's language and multilingualism: Indigenous language use at home and school* (pp. 261–82). New York: Continuum.

Reinecke J (1969). *Language and dialect in Hawaii: a sociolinguistic history to 1935*. Honolulu: University of Hawai'i Press.

Rose DB (1991). *Hidden histories: black stories from Victoria River Downs, Humbert River and Wavehill stations*. Canberra: Aboriginal Studies Press.

Schmidt A (1990). *The loss of Australia's Aboriginal language heritage*. Canberra: Aboriginal Studies Press.

Schultze-Berndt E (2007). Recent grammatical borrowing into an Australian Aboriginal language: the case of Jaminjung and Kriol. In Y Matras & J Sakel (Eds). *Grammatical borrowing in cross-linguistic perspective* (pp. 363–86). Berlin: Mouton de Gruyter.

Wavehill RJ (2000). *Nyawuyinangkulu larrpa kujilirli yuwanani ngumpit-ma kartiyarlu* (E Charola, Trans). Katherine, NT: Diwurruwurru-jaru Aboriginal Corporation.

Wilson W & Kamana K (2001). 'Mai loko mai o ka 'i'ini: Proceeding from a dream': The 'aha pūnana leo connection in Hawaiian language revitalization. In L Hinton & K Hale (Eds). *The green book of language revitalization in practice* (pp. 146–76). San Diego: Academic Press.

21
The rebirth of Wergaia: a collaborative effort

Julie Reid[1]

Abstract

This paper describes the methodology used in the reconstruction of the Wergaia language and its renaissance in the classroom from the perspective of the linguist involved, with additional comments from the group of Wotjobaluk students who learned their heritage language. I was asked to assist in the revitalisation of the language by the Wotjobaluk people of the Wimmera region. Some members of this group expressed their desire to learn the language via the Victorian Certificate of Education study design, *Indigenous languages of Victoria, revival and reclamation: Victorian Certificate of Education study design* (Victorian Curriculum and Assessment Authority 2004) with me as their teacher. This enabled them to actively collaborate in the reconstruction of Wergaia, documented in the consultation copy of the *Wergaia Community Grammar and Dictionary* (Reid 2007). They are now able to write simple Wergaia sentences, translate Dreaming stories into their heritage language, and teach Wergaia to other community members.

The transmission of Victorian Aboriginal languages ceased abruptly after the establishment of government and church missions where Aboriginal people were forbidden to speak their language, or practise their culture, under threat of having their children removed. Victorian Aboriginal languages are no longer spoken as the primary means of communication though people are familiar with some words or phrases from their heritage language, often without realising it.

> What meant the most to me was the start, when a fellow worker [Peter Shaw-Truex] came to me and asked about language in the Wimmera, and how we went about following the (cultural) protocols to LAECG [Local Aboriginal Education Consultative Group] and Land Council. That's what people forget. (Marjorie Pickford)[2]

---

1 School of Languages, Cultures and Linguistics, Monash University.

2 The student comments in this paper are the result of a survey instrument designed for this

In 2005 members of the Wotjobaluk community invited Dr Heather Bowe and me, two linguists from Monash University, to participate in a workshop to discuss the possible reclamation and revival of their language, Wergaia. Representatives from the Victorian Aboriginal Corporation for Languages (VACL), the Victorian Curriculum and Assessment Authority (VCAA), the Victorian School of Languages (VSL), and the Victorian Department of Education and Early Childhood Development (DEECD) also attended the workshop. At the end of the two days the community decided that they would like to reclaim their language and asked me if I would assist them. This was to be the beginning of one of the most rewarding experiences of a lifetime for all involved.

Getting started

Once the decision to undertake the reclamation and revival of Wergaia had been made the community appointed volunteer Jennifer Beer, a Wotjobaluk woman living in Horsham, as the project coordinator and a workshop was held in Horsham to which all Wotjobaluk community members were invited. One of the primary aims of the workshop was to decide on a spelling system to be used by the linguist when compiling the Wergaia wordlist. There was much discussion about when and how to begin both work on the language and the Wergaia language class. The optimum situation would be for the community to be involved in the development of the wordlist and the proposed grammar. Several people attending the workshop expressed their desire to learn Wergaia as soon as possible, but a language class could not begin without further work being carried out by the linguist and funding was needed to undertake this work. The community applied for and received funding from VACL to develop a Wergaia wordlist. It was agreed that workshops would be held in Horsham when there was sufficient material to warrant feedback from the community.

However there were practical problems to be dealt with before any language learning could take place. The prospective students lived in Horsham and Ballarat, and the linguist lived in Melbourne, and they needed a way to conduct regular, weekly language classes necessary for successful language learning. Many people wanted to learn the language in a community setting but with the linguist in Melbourne, more than 300 kilometres away, it was not possible to hold such classes on a weekly basis. There was also the question of an appropriate curriculum to ensure that the students received the highest standard of education available. The first issue was solved through the generous assistance of the VSL, a state government secondary school specialising in languages and distance education. It was decided that the most appropriate method of delivery would be video-conferencing, with a classroom in Horsham, another in Ballarat, and the teacher–linguist in Melbourne. The weekly two-hour classes were supplemented by regular, one-day workshops held in Ballarat,

---

purpose by Kylie Kennedy, a member of the class. Once I had finished the paper, Kylie chose and inserted the comments where she felt they were most appropriate, to allow readers some insight into the students' experience.

which is midway between Horsham and Melbourne. Although this form of delivery was not always ideal, particularly during thunderstorms that caused the video conferencing link to drop out, it proved successful.

In 2004 the VCAA accredited the *Indigenous languages of Victoria, revival and reclamation: Victorian Certificate of Education study design*, specifically designed to teach Aboriginal people the fundamentals of language reclamation. It was developed by a group of educators, linguists and Aboriginal people to include the production of language resources for future students. However the proposed course's status as a VCE subject caused some consternation among those wishing to learn the language. It was eventually decided to use the study design, acknowledging that those finding it unsuitable would be able to withdraw at will. The study design proved to be successful, in fact, far more than ever envisaged by any of those involved.

> There is no other system that supports revival and reclamation of languages except the VCE units ... We just wanted the skills to be able to speak and write our language. VCE was a barrier for some people who didn't want to attend something that formal; the classroom environment wasn't a culturally appropriate setting. However it did give us a framework and because it was a formal setting we were able to get funding for tutors, teachers and resources. (Jennifer Beer)

> Using the VCE system meant we could begin immediately and resulted in the publication of the *Wergaia Community Grammar and Dictionary*. Although this method was hard on some of our community members ... we had to push ourselves and I don't think another course would have achieved so much. Without this we would not have speakers now. (Richard Kennedy)

> The VCE system was so structured that it didn't leave time to spend on any one thing. (Marjorie Pickford)

> We were able to explore all aspects of language revival and reclamation ... [the barrier was] meeting the timeline requirements versus working full time. (Bronwyn Pickford)

> To start with I wondered why we spent so much time learning about other Australian Indigenous Languages (AIL) rather than Wergaia. However, by understanding theories about the origins of AIL, learning about grammatical structures, and even vocabulary of other AIL, we understood Wergaia much better. It helped us to be able to create new words for the modern world, by understanding the connections Wergaia has to neighbouring languages and how inter-related most AIL are. (Kylie Kennedy)

> The VCE system was actually one of the best ways that I can think of to have learnt our language. Not only did we learn the basics and the process of revival and reclamation, but also how to recognise and break down words that are similar and create new words using the correct processes. Very rewarding! (Natasha Kennedy)

At the commencement of the project I had a list of words believed to be Wergaia compiled as part of an earlier project (see Blake and Reid 1998), and a copy of Hercus' (1986) grammar and vocabulary of the language based on her 1960s audio recordings of individuals. These two factors greatly reduced the time taken to reconstruct the language. Before work on the wordlist could begin all sources needed to be carefully re-examined and compared to ensure that they were indeed Wergaia sources. This process saw a few, small sources removed from the list. Once this was completed the sources were combined in a database and individual words were reconstructed using the historical sources, information from surrounding languages and general knowledge of Australian languages.

As the study design began with information about Australian languages in general, it was decided to begin the classes during the word reconstruction phase to allow the class to participate in the process. It was agreed at the outset of the course that any decisions made by the class were for the class and not for the community at large. It was up to the community to make their own decisions in relation to the language. Each week a list of words was presented for comment. Sometimes there were words that were familiar, particularly to an Elder participating in the class, who remembered some words that her mother had used. However it took a great deal of work for me to keep the reconstruction process ahead of the class. The students were keen to begin using more than just individual words and it quickly became obvious that this would be necessary to keep them motivated.

Funding had been sought to develop a grammar to be used in conjunction with the wordlist, and this was provided by the Australian Institute of Aboriginal and Torres Strait Islander Studies (AIATSIS). The grammar written by Hercus (1986) was used as a starting point to begin teaching the class the structure of words and sentences in Wergaia. At the same time I compared all of the grammatical information in the sources, to ascertain as much information as possible about the language. When there were issues where a choice needed to be made these were discussed with the class, and it was the latter that decided which path to take. For example there is evidence for two possessive constructions, probably dialectal. The class chose to learn both constructions.

After the language reclamation project commenced there were disputes in the community and, despite several requests, no workshops were permitted to allow feedback from the entire community. However there was continuous community feedback through the students in the class, several of whom were Elders. In March 2008 consultation copies of the *Wergaia Community Grammar and Dictionary* (Reid 2007) were printed and distributed to the many community members who attended an open workshop in Horsham. It was hoped that this would elicit feedback from those at the meeting.

A successful collaboration

Languages can be reclaimed and revived. The extent to which this is successful directly relates to the quality and quantity of the historical records of the language; the grammatical information that can be retrieved via the language reconstitution work carried out by linguists using the rigorous, academic techniques of language reconstruction on the available data; and the commitment of the Aboriginal community undertaking the process.

Source material

The historical sources used in language reclamation are generally books, articles and notebooks written in the 18th and early 19th centuries in which government officials and private citizens recorded words they had learnt from local Aboriginal people, with each recorder using their own spelling system, not the standardised International Phonetic Alphabet (IPA) used by linguists today. While some of this material was published at the time it was collected and is available in the reference collections of major libraries, manuscript material is generally only available in research libraries or on microfiche. This makes accessing source material a difficult and expensive process.[3]

Modern studies of some of this material have been undertaken by linguists, including Hercus (1986), Dixon (1980, 2002), and Blake and Reid (1998), all of whom have classified Victorian languages into groups. For example the Kulin language group covers much of central and western Victoria and is, in fact, so named because these languages all use a form of the word *kulin* for man or people. In some instances linguists have analysed the material for a particular language and written sketch grammars and wordlists for that language. Many of these are now available in published books and journals including work on Woiwurrung (Blake 1991), the language of the Warrnambool area (Blake 2003a), Bunganditj (Buwandik) (Blake 2003b), Pallanganmiddang (Blake and Reid 1999), Dhudhuroa (Blake and Reid 2002), the Colac language (Blake, Clark & Reid 1998), Wathawurrung (Blake, Clark & Krishna-Pillay 1998), Yorta Yorta, Bangerang and Yabula Yabula (Bowe, Peeler & Atkinson 1997: Bowe & Morey 1999), and Ganai (Fesl 1985). Although most of the linguistic descriptions of these languages are available, non-linguists often find them difficult to understand because they are written in an academic style. Indeed, community members are often not aware of their existence.

> Before we started I had absolutely no idea that our language even existed. Now I can look at other languages and see similarities. (Natasha Kennedy)
>
> I didn't know information existed (on Wergaia) or how to access it. (Katrina Beer)
>
> I remember growing up hearing Uncle Walter and others speak language as a small child, but I didn't know he had been recorded. When I heard his voice

---

3 See Bowe, Reid & Lynch, this volume for a discussion of how this problem has been addressed.

on the tapes, I had a deep sense of pride and it brought back lots of memories.
(Jennifer Beer)

The Wotjobaluk people have several advantages in relation to the sources for Wergaia. Firstly there is Hercus' (1986) work, which includes Wergaia. The people she interviewed did not use the language everyday but recalled what they could from their childhood. Hercus was able to write a comprehensive sketch grammar of Wergaia based on the material she recorded. Both Hercus (1986) and Blake & Reid (1998) found that Wergaia, a Western Kulin language, is closely related to Wemba Wemba, another Western Kulin language for which Hercus (1986) wrote a detailed sketch grammar. Traditionally Australian Aboriginal languages borrow extensively from neighbouring languages, particularly after a person dies and their name becomes taboo, so Wemba Wemba provides evidence to substantiate some of the words recorded as Wergaia words. Indeed other Kulin languages also provide a good reference point when sorting through the various *tokens*, a name that indicates that the word is spelt as it was in its original source. For example the Wergaia word *wutyu* (man) was recorded by many people using the following tokens: *wootyoo, wudju, woot-cha, wootye, wootcha, wood tehoo, watye,* and *wut-yo*. This does not mean that only recognised Kulin words are correct, nor that they are the same in all Kulin languages. If this were the case then all Kulin languages would be the same. Linguists see resemblances that non-linguists often do not. For example the word for eat in various Kulin languages takes the forms *thaka, tjakili, tjawa, tjakela, tjika, thawa, tjaka, tjaki,* and *thanga* (Blake & Reid 1998, p. 36). We call words like these *cognates* which means they are related somewhere in the history of their languages. Languages also have to have words that differentiate them from related languages and we call these *shibboleths*. The Wergaia word for a stone tomahawk is *badyik,* but in Wemba Wemba it is *dir*. This is one of many words that indicate which language a source belongs to. Grammatical information found in the various sources is also compared when determining which sources belong to a language. Hercus' work provided a benchmark against which the other sources could be compared, saving possibly years of work in the reconstruction of Wergaia.

Blake & Reid (1998) compared over 200 sources to develop their classification of the languages of central and western Victoria and, of these, 35 sources are Wergaia. Unfortunately some languages have only a couple of sources, which means their traditional owners have much less material to work with when reconstructing their language. Although most of the comparative work was done by me the Wergaia class did learn about, and participate in, this process particularly when there was any doubt about a source. For example the class compared three unnamed sources and, unknowingly, came to the same conclusion that I had. They decided that source A belonged with source C, not source B. Source A was Mathews' Wuttyabullak Language (Mathews 1902–03), source B was Wergaia and source C was Djab Wurrung, another Western Kulin language.

> I picked up a book a few years ago which said it had Wotjobaluk language in it. I copied all the words out to take home and practise. I realise now that

> you can't just pick up a source and trust that it will be correct, or that it's the language it says it is as people often recorded things incorrectly, or used people as resources who spoke a totally different AIL, a visitor! Julie has taught us to critically analyse the sources we read and hear; how to check if it's Wergaia or not. I have confidence that in the future I will know how to recognise my own language. (Kylie Kennedy)

Many of the sources for Wergaia were of a relatively high standard, having been written by experienced amateur anthropologists like R.H. Mathews and missionaries who had lived with the Wotjobaluk and learned their language. Some of these contained grammatical as well as lexical (vocabulary) information. Even at the level of single words the class had much to discover. For example the concepts of one language do not translate directly to another language. The kinship system used by Europeans is quite different to that of traditional Australians. Your biological mother and her sisters are all addressed as *bap* in Wergaia, only your father's sisters are addressed as *ngaluk* (aunt).

> One of the first things I remember learning is about kinship; I remember sitting in Horsham with Auntie Jenni figuring out how to call her Auntie and Auntie Jenni trying to figure out niece. And having Uncle Peter there and realising that traditionally he is also my dad definitely made me feel more connected. (Natasha Kennedy)

Grammatical information

The grammar of Australian languages is very different to that of English, the first language of the Wergaia students. For example in English when we use the word *we* it means the speaker plus others, but we do not know who the others are, which can lead to some embarrassing situations. Wergaia, like most Australian languages, makes it very clear who *we* includes. Consider the various Wergaia interpretations of the English sentence: 'We slept in Ballarat'.

Gumb-in- angul   *Ballarat- ata.*
Sleep-past-1.du.in   Ballarat-loc.
You and I slept in Ballarat.

Gumb-in- angulung   *Ballarat- ata.*
Sleep- past-1.du.ex   Ballarat-loc.
She and I slept in Ballarat.

Gumb-in-angu gulik   *Ballarat-ata.*
Sleep-past-1.tri.in   Ballarat-loc.
You two and I slept in Ballarat.

Gumb-in-andang gulik   *Ballarat-ata.*
Sleep-past-1.tri.ex   Ballarat-loc.
Those two and I slept in Ballarat.

Gumb-in-angu   *Ballarat-ata.*
Sleep-past-1.pl.in   Ballarat-loc.
You all and I slept in Ballarat.

Gumb-in-andang   *Ballarat-ata.*
Sleep-past-1.pl.ex   Ballarat-loc.
They all and I slept in Ballarat.

By the end of the first unit, the class understood the importance of learning about Australian languages in general as part of trying to reclaim their own language.

> I found the pronoun system very difficult to understand because I did not have a great understanding of the English system, although I could use pronouns competently. The use of bound and free pronouns is still confusing but the distinctions (between subjects and objects) are a lot clearer in Wergaia than in English. (Richard Kennedy)

Community commitment

The third requirement for successful language reclamation is the motivation and commitment of the language learners, in this case the Wotjobaluk people in the Wergaia class. To say that the task they had undertaken was hard is an understatement. They were faced with new concepts in both English and Wergaia; grammatical terminology most had never encountered; words that were difficult to say because they contained sounds the students had never heard before; sentences that did not resemble anything they had ever heard or read; and a linguist who warned them that she would, as the knowledge gleaned from the sources grew, need to change things like the recommended spelling or word meanings. The class found themselves in an alien world – a language class.

The class were all adult members of the community. At the original workshop the Elders had decided that it was important for the adults to learn the language first. This was a very wise decision as this was no ordinary language class. Unlike people learning French there were no dictionaries, movies, books, or even speakers to aid their learning. The members of the class are the modern pioneers of the language. They grappled with many strange and unexpected problems in order to participate in the reconstruction of the language, to learn Wergaia, and to create resources as they learned so that other community members would have an easier task when they learned Wergaia. It required determination, self-discipline, and the ability to keep moving forward despite the difficulties encountered both inside and outside the classroom.

> I feel pride and greater confidence. I discovered an untapped talent – my linguistic skills. (Bronwyn Pickford)

> Learning Wergaia has increased my self-esteem, strengthened my pride, health, wellbeing and confidence in myself; it enabled a stronger identity and recreated a strong bond within my family. (Richard Kennedy)

> I was able to add a giant piece of the puzzle regarding my history, culture, community and identity. (Katrina Beer)

One of the most difficult tasks of all was learning how to compose a sentence in Wergaia. Not only is the order of the words different but most words have one or more suffixes attached to them. Suffixes are additions that are used repeatedly on words of one particular category, to give more information. For instance in English we have a suffix {-s} that we add to words of the noun category (names of things) which speakers recognise as meaning plural (more than one), for example one cat, two cats. This is the plural suffix in English. Reconstructed Wergaia has over 80 suffixes at the present time. There would have been more in traditional Wergaia but they have been lost. These suffixes have to be added in a specific order and used only in specific situations. The simple English sentence: 'A big man threw a boomerang from a redgum tree' looks like this in Wergaia:

Yungg-in	*gurrung-u*	*wutyu-ku*	*gatim-gatim*	*bial-ang*
Throw-past	big-erg.	man-erg.	boomerang	red gum tree-abl.

A big man threw a boomerang from a redgum tree.

The past tense (time) suffix {–in} indicates that the action took place before the sentence was spoken, and erg. stands for ergative, a suffix used in most Australian languages to indicate who carried out the action. It is on both gurrung (big) and wutyu (man) to show that it was the man who was big, not the boomerang or the tree. The ablative suffix {-ang} (from) tells us that the boomerang came from a tree; it did not go towards it or into it. From is not a separate word in Wergaia as it is in English. You will also notice that the English indefinite article 'a' does not occur in Wergaia, nor does the definite article 'the'. If we wrote the sentence in English, but using Wergaia word order, it would be: 'Threw big man boomerang red gum tree from'.

The class wrote and translated countless Wergaia sentences. They would email their first draft to me and I would let them know that, say, the word order was not right or that they needed a case suffix. They would then try again and the process would be repeated many times, as the students were determined to get it right.

> One of the defining moments for our class was a visit to the Brambuk visitor centre in Gariwerd. We spotted a sign written in an Indigenous language, a

neighbouring language to our own, and began interpreting it. The spelling was different to the agreed-upon spelling we've used in class and in the Grammar and Dictionary, but we were able to see past that to find the meaning of the word. This was a proud moment for us as a class and as part of the wider community.
(Kylie Kennedy)

When the class began to write stories they realised how limited the language information they had was, and were concerned about the authenticity of the reconstructed language. They asked whether traditional Wotjobaluk people would be able to understand them. Linguists know that a reconstructed language will never be exactly the same as the original but, with good sources and lots of hard work, it should be a good approximation. It could be likened to someone with basic school French communicating with French speakers in Paris. It might not be quite right but the message should still get across. Also communities need to keep in mind that all living languages change, constantly. Even within our own lifetime the meaning of English words like gay has changed; we have borrowed words like *yum cha* from other languages, and we have created new words such as 'googling', 'skyping', and 'texted', using common processes for word creation. This was, and still is, the next big challenge for the Wergaia students who have created all of the new words needed in the classroom to date.

The words and sentences recorded in the sources for Wergaia are mostly simple sentences using traditional words for traditional concepts. The class has several methods of word creation available to them when they need new words. The simplest is the traditional practice of borrowing words from neighbouring languages, or even unrelated languages. While borrowing from a neighbouring language is easy because they are already able to communicate with their neighbours, borrowing from a completely different language requires some adaptations. For example if the class chose to borrow the English word 'flash' they would need to make several changes before it would fit into the Wergaia sound system. There is no /f/ in Wergaia, so you would need to find the closest existing sound which would be /p/ or /b/. Wergaia words only begin with voiced sounds which means you would probably choose /b/. The sequence of sounds /bl/ does not occur in Wergaia so you would need to insert a vowel between them. The vowel sound in flash is not found in Wergaia but the /a/ sound in car is, so you could use that. Unfortunately the sound represented by sh is also not found in Wergaia so you would need to use the closest Wergaia sound which is spelt *ty*. Therefore the word flash, when borrowed into Wergaia, would look something like *balaty, bulaty,* or *bilaty*, depending on what the class decided to use for the first vowel. A check of the Wergaia dictionary shows that *balaty* is already the word for a cherry tree so the choice would be narrowed down to either *bulaty* or *bilaty*.

Words can also be created by extending the meaning of an existing word to include another meaning, in cases where there can be no confusion, such as using *gurrak* (sand) to refer to sugar. After all you would never put sand in your tea! Compounding is another popular way of creating words like babysit, which puts the words baby and sit (with) together to create a word with a new but similar meaning. Finally the suffixes referred to above can be used to create new words as the ancestors did. The word for echidna in Wergaia is *yulawil*, which is literally *yula* (spike) plus {*-wil*}, a suffix that means having. The class carefully examined the recorded words for examples of this last type so that they could use the same suffixes when creating new words. At times this required a great deal of mental gymnastics.

An area yet to be explored in the renaissance of Wergaia is complex sentences. Sentences such as: 'I told you to tell her that we could not go with her' are currently too difficult for reconstructed Wergaia. Work needs to be done on the meagre material available for complex sentences in Wergaia. This is also a good example of where a thorough knowledge of Australian languages is essential. If you know what to look for when examining these sentences you will have a better chance of getting it right.

The effort the Wergaia class put into the reconstruction of their language is nothing short of amazing. These people, some of whom did not finish school, have gone from knowing almost nothing about the language to being able to write simple sentences, translate Dreaming stories and teach other community members their heritage language in just two and a half years. There were times when they wanted to quit, when they felt they would never understand and that it was all just too difficult, but they continued anyway supporting each other throughout the course. They have achieved something that is worth recording in the history books. When the class began there were 13 students some of whom chose not to continue within the first few weeks. Sadly two very valuable class members were forced to discontinue for health reasons. In December 2008 nine people completed the *Indigenous languages of Victoria, revival and reclamation: Victorian Certificate of Education study design* with Wergaia as the community language for the first time. Several class members are also VCE top scorers. This is an outstanding feat by anyone's standards and one that will not be easy to replicate. However the journey for other Wotjobaluk people wanting to learn Wergaia will be much easier as, thanks to the dedication and sheer hard work of this group, there are now resources that new students can use, and community members able to explain and teach the difficult concepts underlying their heritage language.

> I would like Wergaia to be documented as a 'strong' language; a journey of many Wotjobaluk traditional owners to restore pride amongst our people by further awakening a language that slept for so long. (Bronwyn Pickford)

> I wish that [the community] were all learning and sharing Wergaia; to one day hopefully be able to teach this to our people. (Marjorie Pickford)

Conclusion

The current outcomes of the Wergaia reclamation and revival project are, firstly, a consultation copy of the *Wergaia Community Grammar and Dictionary* (Reid 2007) funded by VACL and AIATSIS; and, secondly, a group of Wotjobaluk people who are now able to write simple sentences, translate Dreaming stories and teach other community members their heritage language. They have produced resources for teaching the language that they intend to publish. This is clearly an excellent result, made possible by the availability of good historical and academic resources and the collaboration of members of the Wotjobaluk community and a linguist, all of whom share a passion for the language and the commitment and determination to bring that language into the modern world. The revival of Wergaia has a long way to go before it can claim to be successful but, if there are other community members willing to show the same commitment as their predecessors to the reclamation and revival of Wergaia, the language has a bright future.

> Learning Wergaia has not been a commitment but a necessity, as though there is some kind of force propelling me to learn Wergaia, like I'm in a desert and Wergaia is my water. The classes and the Wergaia language brought me closer to my family – a friend of mine commented that Wergaia has brought my extended family together in a way that the English language never could. (Kylie Kennedy)

> Learning Wergaia has meant everything to me! Having been involved in the native title process it sparked my interest to do more ... the language program didn't grab me right away, when I saw how much it was doing in terms of confidence for *mamek* (my father) I thought maybe I could give it a go. And now I feel like our family is so much closer and I have skills that I never thought would be possible! And I am keen to share the knowledge as I am so proud of our language being reclaimed. I want to get the language into the community, to share it with everybody, to create resources so that it never dies! (Natasha Kennedy)

Acknowledgements

The author and the class would like to thank VACL who funded the Wergaia wordlist; AIATSIS for providing the funds for the development of the grammar; Pandora Petrovska, Angelo Capraro and Antonella Cicero from the VSL for their munificence; Dr Heather Bowe for her unending assistance and support; and Maree Dellora who encouraged and supported us. I would particularly like to thank class members Auntie Nancy Harrison, Jennifer Beer, Richard Kennedy, Marjorie Pickford, Kaylene Clarke, Gloria Clarke, Peter Kennedy, Katrina Beer, Bronwyn Pickford, Natasha Kennedy, Belinda Marks; and especially Kylie Kennedy who organised the class responses in this paper.

References

Blake BJ (1991). Woiwurrung, the Melbourne language. In RMW Dixon & BJ Blake (Eds). *The handbook of Australian languages, volume 4* (pp. 31–122). Melbourne: Oxford University Press.

Blake BJ (2003a). *The Warrnambool language: A consolidated account of the Aboriginal language of the Warrnambool area of the western district of Victoria based on nineteenth century sources.* Canberra: Pacific Linguistics.

Blake BJ (2003b). *The Bunganditj (Buwandik) language of the Mount Gambier region.* Canberra: Pacific Linguistics.

Blake BJ, Clark ID & Reid J (1998). The Colac language. In BJ Blake (Ed). *Wathawurrung and the Colac language of southern Victoria* (pp. 155–77). Canberra: Pacific Linguistics.

Blake BJ, Clark ID & Krishna-Pillay S (1998). Wathawurrung: the language of the Geelong-Ballarat area. In BJ Blake (Ed). *Wathawurrung and the Colac language of southern Victoria* (pp. 59–154). Canberra: Pacific Linguistics.

Blake BJ & Reid J (1998). Classifying Victorian languages. In BJ Blake (Ed). *Wathawurrung and the Colac language of southern Victoria* (pp. 1–58). Canberra: Pacific Linguistics.

Blake BJ & Reid J (1999). Pallanganmiddang: a language of the upper Murray. *Aboriginal History*, 23: 15–31.

Blake BJ & Reid J (2002). The Dhudhuroa language of northeastern Victoria: A new description based on historical sources. *Aboriginal History*, 26: 177–210.

Bowe H & Morey S (1999). *Yorta Yorta (Bangerang) language of the Murray-Goulburn including Yabula Yabula.* Canberra: Pacific Linguistics.

Bowe H, Peeler L & Atkinson S (1997). *Yorta Yorta language heritage.* Clayton: Monash University, Department of Linguistics.

Dixon RMW (1980). *The languages of Australia.* Cambridge: Cambridge University Press.

Dixon RMW (2002). *Australian languages: their nature and development.* Cambridge: Cambridge University Press.

Fesl E (1985). Ganai – a study of the Aboriginal language of Gippsland based on 19th century materials. Unpublished masters thesis, Linguistics Department, Monash University.

Hercus LA (1986). *Victorian languages: a late survey.* Canberra: Pacific Linguistics

Mathews RH (1902–03). The Wuttyabullak language. *Queensland Geographical Journal*, 18: 52–68.

Reid J (2007). *Wergaia community grammar and dictionary: consultation copy.* Melbourne Linguistics Program, Monash University.

Victorian Curriculum & Assessment Authority (2004). *Indigenous languages of Victoria: revival and reclamation. Victorian Certificate of Education study design.* East Melbourne: Victorian Curriculum & Assessment Authority [Online]. Available: www.vcaa.vic.edu.au/vce/studies/lote/ausindigenous/ausindigindex.html [Accessed 17 March 2009].

22
Strategies for doing the possible: supporting school Aboriginal language programs in NSW

Mari Rhydwen[1]

Abstract

Echoing the title of an earlier paper published ten years ago, 'Strategies for doing the impossible', this paper examines the role of school programs in language revival and reclamation. Since 2005 the Languages Unit of the New South Wales Department of Education and Training has employed a consultant to support the implementation of the Aboriginal languages syllabus in government schools. This paper describes and discusses the issues and challenges involved in supporting the teaching of languages that are incompletely documented and for which there are few published teaching resources.

What is possible?

Soon after I started working as consultant, Aboriginal languages, I was asked by a senior Aboriginal educator how long it would be before the languages were revived and were spoken fluently again by communities. Undeterred by my hedging admission that this would not be achieved quickly or easily he demanded a definite answer, suggesting '30 years?' It is hard to be the bearer of bad news but I felt obliged to tell him what I really believed. The only language that I knew of that had been successfully revived was Hebrew. And that was a very special case, bolstered by being already widely spoken by Jewish men (albeit for limited religious purposes), then promulgated as policy by leaders of the Zionist nationalist movement in Palestine in the early twentieth century and, finally, by being adopted as one of the two official languages at the establishment of Israel in 1948 (Spolksy & Shohamy 2001). I was forced to admit that I did not think New South Wales (NSW) Aboriginal languages would once again be spoken fluently and regularly as the first languages of NSW

---

1 Languages Unit, Curriculum K–12 Directorate, NSW Department of Education and Training.

Aboriginal people *in the forms in which they had existed prior to settlement*. However I explained that this was no reason not to teach them in NSW schools, for reasons which will be clarified here.

The sorry state of languages in NSW

NSW was where the first settlement took place in Australia and, within just over a year of the arrival of the First Fleet, the Aboriginal population around Sydney and inland along rivers had been decimated by smallpox. Ongoing disease and displacement ensured that, around the most settled areas of NSW, many language varieties were lost without known trace early in the history of settlement. Of those which have survived, Bundjalung is the only NSW language appearing on the United Nations Educational, Scientific and Cultural Organization (UNESCO) list of endangered languages which is defined as severely endangered, all the rest being defined as critically endangered (UNESCO 2003). The *National Indigenous Languages Survey (NILS) Report* of 2005, which is far more comprehensive, similarly indicates that no NSW languages are spoken fluently.

Despite this history, NSW is the only state or federal jurisdiction in Australia with an Aboriginal languages policy (NSW Department of Aboriginal Affairs 2004). According to an undated pamphlet produced by the Department of Aboriginal Affairs (DAA) to advertise its launch, the policy was developed ' … to preserve and rekindle languages' with strategies to support its implementation, including the development of an Aboriginal languages syllabus (Board of Studies NSW 2003). Furthermore there is no evidence of any other jurisdiction in the world where *all* the indigenous languages are in need of revival[2] and yet are still formally recognised as meeting a mandatory language requirement for graduation from high school. It was an act of extraordinary optimism to create a Kindergarten to Year 10 syllabus, comparable in every way to the other languages syllabuses used in the state, for a group of languages that are all only partially documented.

Yet students who begin the study of the other languages such as French or Japanese for the 100 hours of mandatory language learning required in order to fulfil the School Certificate requirements, do not become anywhere near fully fluent speakers of those languages after just 100 hours of study. Indeed even for languages that are regarded as easy to learn for English speakers (and Aboriginal languages do not fall into this category!) achieving professional proficiency[3] on the Foreign Service Institute (FSI) scale would take around 600 hours of study whereas, for difficult ones, the estimated time needed to achieve proficiency jumps to 2200 hours (American Educational Research Association 2006) (see also Hobson, this volume). I was confident that

---

2 In other states in Australia where languages can be studied at this level, at least some of the languages are under maintenance rather than in revival.

3 Sufficient structural accuracy and vocabulary to participate effectively in most formal and informal conversations.

many NSW Aboriginal languages could be learned to a level commensurate with that achieved by students of other languages in NSW schools. Even a limited knowledge of, and facility in, the languages that are sparsely documented can be enough to allow students to learn something of their complexity and their role in maintaining relationship to country.

There are currently programs in ten languages in NSW government schools. The extent of published resources available for each language varies, but is generally very limited compared to that available for other languages taught in Australian schools. In some cases language programs began in areas where there was not even a published sketch grammar or dictionary, although there may have been local people with some knowledge of vocabulary and expressions. Undeterred by the difficulty of the task some community organisations have employed linguists to help remedy the problem. For example the Darkinyung Language Group, chaired by Bronwen Chambers, worked with a linguist to produce a grammar and dictionary (Jones 2008). There are now plans to find a way for community members to receive training in the language so that there will be a pool of people available to teach Darkinyung in school language programs. Other communities too have worked with linguists through Many Rivers Aboriginal Language Centre to develop grammars and dictionaries (See Ash et al., this volume). The lack of well-analysed, professionally researched and accessible language resources is perhaps the greatest gap to be overcome in order to establish viable school language programs.

It is very recent in the history of humanity that any languages have been written and only 106 of the 7000 or so known languages ever developed their own written literature (Ong 1982, p. 7). Aboriginal languages remained unwritten until Europeans, often missionaries or government officials, attempted to represent them in written form. Orthographies, specially designed writing systems based on a careful analysis of the sounds of each Aboriginal language, are developed in order to accurately analyse and document the languages. Such orthographies usually form the basis of practical writing systems necessary to meet the demands of modern education. It has long been hypothesised that, as a consequence of new media technology, the written form may be bypassed completely (Postman 1970). Certainly there is technology available that could allow people to learn and be assessed on their proficiency in oral languages without the use of writing. However at this stage reading and writing form part of the curriculum and indeed, in the case of NSW languages, much of the data (the corpus on which language learning is based) comprises only written records produced before the advent of sound recording equipment. An example of one such language is Awabakal, recorded by the Reverend Lancelot Threlkeld in the mid-19th century, when the language spoken in the Hunter and Lake Macquarie region was 'all but *extinct*'(Threlkeld 1850, preface). It is not the role of the education system to undertake the linguistic research necessary to develop the language content that underpins languages education. It is made very clear too, in the guide published by the NSW Board of Studies (2001) that the role of the education system is to respond to community demand for language programs, not to initiate it. However it is clear that the requirements of the NSW Aboriginal languages syllabus are one of a number of factors contributing to the perceived need for more good quality publications in and about NSW Aboriginal languages and may, indirectly, have contributed to the spate of publications from the Muurrbay Aboriginal Language and Cultural Co-operative in recent years.

While the NSW Department of Education and Training (DET) does not undertake the development of language resources such as dictionaries and grammars, it does produce resources directly related to the classroom. The NSW DET Curriculum Directorate's Languages Unit and the Centre for Learning Innovation worked together to produce an interactive web-based Aboriginal languages resource for Stage 4 students. As well as introducing students to some of the common features of NSW Aboriginal languages, the resource also includes interviews with Elders and community language teachers across the state talking about their experiences, to help explain why and how Aboriginal people were discouraged or prevented from speaking their languages.

Working with the community

No Aboriginal language programs in NSW DET schools may be taught without the support of the local Aboriginal community. In order to obtain funding for a program in a government school,[4] the school is required to demonstrate that it has consulted with the community, and that the teacher is an Aboriginal person who is teaching the local language[5] with the support of that community. When the syllabus began to be implemented in 2005 the general pattern was that members of the local community would teach the language in the presence of a classroom teacher whose presence was necessary to ensure that legal duty-of-care requirements were being met. In the best cases there was genuine collaboration among the members of the school languages team, so that classroom teachers, members of the school executive and community members would work supportively together. Often the school staff would be learning the language themselves as well as helping with programming and classroom management. In other cases the community teacher was expected to teach the class with minimal support and the classroom teachers would simply be physically present.

In schools with a vibrant and ongoing language program there is generally a real commitment and interest shown by the principal or another senior member of the school executive. While schools are neither expected nor encouraged to push the establishment of language programs, which should be a response to community demand, the reality is that if the people with the authority or influence to make things happen in a school context do not give their support, nothing is likely to happen.

---

4 Funding for programs comes from the NSW DET Aboriginal Education and Training Directorate and must be applied for annually.

5 In rare cases the language is not the local language, but this is not encouraged, and protocols to obtain permission from both the community where the school is located and the donor community are necessary.

Community members or Aboriginal Education Officers who want to start a language program, without the support of someone with authority within the school system to help advocate on their behalf, tend to experience disappointment (see Lowe & Howard, this volume).

It can seem as if the requirement that there be a school language committee, bringing school personnel and community together to plan and develop a school language program, is simply another bureaucratic hurdle for educators. Seen from another perspective it can be viewed as an opportunity, a perfect excuse to bring community and school together. The experience of many schools is that when they genuinely involve the community in decision-making there is more likely to be community support, with parents coming to school events where the students are going to be performing in the local language. In a report on a joint presentation at the Rights, Reconciliation, Respect and Responsibility conference at the University of Technology Sydney,

> Geoff Anderson (Member of the Wiradjuri Elders Council) … asked some students what they thought about the Wiradjuri program at their school. He described a moving moment in which a seven-year-old Wiradjuri girl replied, 'I learn my language and my culture then I teach my parents'. Geoff believes Aboriginal languages have healing powers for both children and adults. He said, 'The languages each belong in that country, in the hearts of the people that learn, speak and teach them; but most importantly in the schools and in the mouths of our future of this country.'
>
> Gary Worthy, a teacher at Vincentia High School, described how, as a non-Aboriginal person, he felt that he needed to earn the right to be involved in the Dhurga program. He feels privileged to be involved in this work and is honoured to work with Aboriginal community members to revive their languages. He does not assume it is his right to do this. He feels the responsibility of supporting their rights to their languages.
>
> Gary also talked about the background research done by school and community members to set up the school programs. This research was a collaborative effort and took a number of years. This time was a worthwhile investment for setting up strong and successful programs. (Poetsch 2008 p. 3–4)

One decision that must be made by the community is whether the language should be taught to all students in the school, or only those who are Aboriginal. There was initial concern in some communities about the possible negative effect on the confidence of Aboriginal students if the local language was taught to all the students, but this was not borne out. In Parkes East Public School, where all students have the opportunity to learn the local language, it was reported by community members (at a workshop in Dubbo in 2008) to be a really powerful tool in breaking down racism (see also Anderson, this volume).

Another factor in the decision is that it is generally much easier to timetable classes if they are open to all students. Formerly, Indigenous students at Nambucca Heads High

School studying Aboriginal languages had to attend classes during sport time and this discouraged participation. Following a community decision the local language, Gumbaynggirr is now taught to non-Indigenous students too and can be timetabled at the same time as other language classes. Two Stage 4 classes of 25 students are running in the school in 2009 and the qualified Aboriginal teacher at the school attributes this directly to the changed timetable.

Teacher training and careers

Until 2006 there was no career pathway to enable anyone to become a qualified Aboriginal languages teacher nationally. To be a teacher of any language in a NSW school it is generally necessary to meet certain requirements, including two years of post-secondary education in the language being taught, but there was no tertiary institution offering such a course in any NSW Aboriginal languages. However, in 2006, the Master of Indigenous Languages Education offered by the Koori Centre at the University of Sydney sought recognition for providing qualifications that would allow someone to be designated as an Aboriginal languages teacher in NSW and, after extensive discussion and negotiation with all the parties involved, this was granted (see also Hobson, this volume).

While this is evidence of progress, and meets the needs of many, the reality is that the people who currently have the best language skills are often senior community members who are understandably unwilling or unable to undertake professional teacher training, and there is no other way for their unique expertise to be recognised. Currently community language teachers are paid at an hourly rate of between $19.95 and $25.25 per hour depending upon experience. However this pay scale does not reflect the difference between the skills and experience demonstrated by a young community language tutor who has just started to learn their language and a respected community Elder who learned their language as a young child at a time when it was still habitually spoken in the community.

There is some discrepancy between what would appear to be the most efficient system of delivering a school language program from an education system provider's perspective and the most effective way of delivering it from a community perspective. While it is commonly envisaged that, within a relatively short time frame, Aboriginal languages will be taught by qualified Aboriginal languages teachers who will be regular members of the fulltime school teaching staff, there are a number of reasons why this is unlikely to happen, at least in all schools, in the near future. Many of the middle-aged and older people who currently have the greatest degree of language skill are not inclined to undertake teacher training. Yet they are essential to the viability of developing school language programs in the communities and they need to be supported financially and otherwise to fulfil this role. In the longer term they will undoubtedly train up younger people in the language and these people will be the ones to subsequently undertake teacher training.

However, if the older people with language skills are not adequately recompensed at this stage, they are likely to walk away and no one will be able to learn the language. Secondly, even if languages are generally taught by an Aboriginal languages teacher, there will always be a need to involve other community members. A significant aspect of Aboriginal culture is the emphasis on community, as opposed to the individual, and to teach an Aboriginal language without being able to reflect the community context in which it is embedded would be to divorce it from its vital roots. Thirdly, working with the community is a wonderful channel for communication between school and community. Time and again Elders have expressed their sense of pride and delight at being able to participate in school language programs. This is part of the healing that one community language teacher, Murray Butcher was referring to when he said, 'People are starting to look for that language for a revival I suppose, for medicine for the soul, to start repairing the soul' (NSW DET 2009).

Professional development is provided to all NSW teachers in government schools and, in 2005, a team at the Languages Unit completed a package funded by the Australian Government Quality Teaching Project, entitled *Teaching Methodology for Aboriginal Languages*. This package drew on years of expertise in training languages teachers, particularly teachers of community languages.[6] The package consists of resources for a two-day workshop that introduces Aboriginal community language teachers, and classroom teachers with no language-teaching experience, to the fundamentals of language teaching methodology. It also covers some basic aspects of the linguistic features of Aboriginal languages for teachers with no previous knowledge of the topic. In 2005 approximately sixty people from around the state attended the workshops. Since then a variety of further professional development workshops have been run in venues across the state.

Networks

Right from the start of working to support schools with Aboriginal language programs it was evident that it was going to be necessary for schools and communities in the same language area to work together. Because of the lack of resources to support language teaching of the kind available for other languages it would be beneficial for schools to share their ideas and expertise. It was also evident that those involved in the provision of support to the programs needed to work together. In two areas of NSW, which had some of the most developed language resources for use in schools, much of the linguistic work on which the programs depended had been done by Catholic clergy working in conjunction with teachers in the Catholic school system. In other language areas pioneering work was being done in the government system. Overall the numbers of people involved are small; there is usually only one linguist at most deeply familiar with any particular language, and only a handful of people

---

6 Community language teachers, in the context of the NSW DET, refers to teachers of the thirty-one non-Aboriginal languages spoken in the community and taught as a school subject such as Arabic, Hindi, Vietnamese and Spanish.

with language skills sufficient to teach in a school program in each language. For this reason those involved in supporting language programs in the NSW DET and the Office of the Board of Studies have often worked together, jointly convening workshops that brought together both government and private school personnel, staff from the regional education offices and diocesan offices, and the linguists and community Elders involved in those programs. Increasingly members of established school language teams from the local language area are encouraged to act as mentors to schools that are initiating programs and to form local language networks, both at the workshops and throughout the year. In addition, working in conjunction with other institutions like DAA and the Koori Centre, we have co-organised conferences such as Bayabangun Ngurrawa, the 2007 NSW Aboriginal Languages Forum and the Indigenous Languages Institute in 2008. These events brought members of Aboriginal language teams from across the state together with Indigenous languages experts from around Australia and overseas. Gary Williams, a Gumbaynggirr teacher speaking in an interview said, 'I do feel like language now has built New South Wales up into a community. We have something in common to talk about and you can recognise differences, you can recognise you know what's identical and all that kind of thing and you can talk about it ... I think it's opened up New South Wales' (NSW DET 2009).

Even in areas where there are currently no language programs, schools, regional offices and community personnel are encouraged to work together. However in some instances there are no programs because, even though many people would like one and there are some resources available, there is a lack of community agreement about the use of a standard orthography, who should be appointed as a teacher, or even which language to teach.

Conclusion

In September 1998 I bade farewell to Australia and to academia with a swansong paper called 'Strategies for Doing the Impossible' at the Foundation for Endangered Languages conference in Edinburgh. The title of the paper reflected a frustration bordering on despair with the difficulty of working to support endangered languages at a time when there was a strong tide of opinion against such activity in Australia. Core funding for Language Australia,[7] a vestigial remnant of the 1987 *National Policy on Languages*, had been withdrawn, One Nation[8] had risen to prominence and, according to Lo Bianco & Rhydwen, 'all considerations of language policy were sublimated to literacy' (2001, p. 418). At the time I had run out of any strategy other than tactical retreat. Returning some years later, and despite an overall diminution in activities to support Australia's endangered languages such as the continued erosion of bilingual education programs in the Northern Territory, I took up the newly-established position of Aboriginal languages consultant to support Aboriginal languages programs in NSW

---

7 The National Language and Literacy Institute of Australia under the directorship of Jo Lo Bianco.

8 A political party led by Pauline Hanson and committed to a policy of one language.

schools. To continue to do this I myself had to be convinced that implementing an Aboriginal languages syllabus in a place where every language taught was in need of revival, was possible. This paper explains both why it is, and what makes it so.

References

American Educational Research Association (2006). *Research Points*. (4)1 [Online]. Available: www.aera.net/uploadedFiles/Journals_and_Publications/Research_Points/AERA_RP_Spring06.pdf [Accessed 25 March 2009].

Australian Institute of Aboriginal & Torres Strait Islander Studies (2005). *National Indigenous Languages Survey report 2005*. Canberra: Department of Communications, Information Technology and the Arts.

Board of Studies New South Wales (2001). *Working with Aboriginal communities* [Online]. Available: ab-ed.boardofstudies.nsw.edu.au/files/working-with-aboriginal-communities.pdf [Accessed 14 March 2009].

Board of Studies New South Wales (2003). *Aboriginal languages K–10 syllabus*. Sydney: Board of Studies New South Wales [Online]. Available: www.boardofstudies.nsw.edu.au/syllabus_sc [Accessed 25 March 2009].

Jones C (2008). *Darkinyung grammar and dictionary: revitalising a language from historical sources* Nambucca Heads, NSW: Muurrbay Aboriginal Language and Culture Co-operative.

Lo Bianco J & Rhydwen M (2001). Is the extinction of Australia's Indigenous languages inevitable? In J Fishman (Ed). *Can threatened languages be saved?* (pp. 391–422). Clevedon, UK: Multilingual Matters.

New South Wales Department of Aboriginal Affairs (2004). *New South Wales Aboriginal languages policy*. Sydney; New South Wales Department of Aboriginal Affairs.

New South Wales Department of Education and Training (2009). *Campfire* [DVD-ROM]. Sydney: New South Wales Department of Education & Training.

Ong WJ (1982). *Orality and literacy: the technologizing of the word*. London: Methuen.

Poetsch S (2008). Rights, reconciliation, respect and responsibility. *Aboriginal Languages Newsletter*, Term 4, 2008: 13.

Postman N (1970). The politics of reading. *Harvard Educational Review*, 40: 244–52.

Rhydwen M (1998). Strategies for doing the impossible. In N Ostler (Ed). *Endangered languages: what role for the specialist?* Proceedings of the Second FEL Conference, Edinburgh, 1998 (pp. 101–06). Bath: Foundation for Endangered Languages.

Spolsky B & Shohamy E (2001). Hebrew after a century of RLS efforts. In J Fishman (Ed). *Can threatened languages be saved?* (pp. 350–63). Clevedon, UK: Multilingual Matters.

Threlkeld LE (1850). *A key to the structure of the Aboriginal language; being an analysis of the particles used as affixes, to form the various modifications of the verbs; shewing the essential powers, abstract roots, and other peculiarities of the language spoken by the Aborigines in the vicinity of Hunter River, Lake Macquarie etc, New South Wales; together with comparisons of Polynesian and other dialects* [Online]. Available: www.newcastle.edu.au/service/archives/aboriginalstudies/pdf/threlkeld1850.pdf [Accessed 28 August 2009].

United Nations Educational Scientific & Cultural Organization Ad Hoc Expert Group on Endangered Languages (2003). *Language vitality and endangerment.* Document submitted to the International Expert Meeting on UNESCO Programme Safeguarding of Endangered Languages Paris, 10–12 March 2003 [Online]. Available: www.unesco.org/culture/ich/doc/src/00120-EN.pdf [Accessed 14 March 2009].

United Nations Educational Scientific & Cultural Organization (n.d.). *Interactive atlas of the world's languages in danger.* (2009) [Online]. Available: www.unesco.org/culture/ich/index.php?pg=00206 [Accessed 14 March 2009].

Part Five
Literacy and oracy

Introduction
Literacy and oracy

Michael Walsh[1]

Given their importance it is actually quite surprising that relatively little has been written on literacy and oracy in the context of the revitalisation of Australian Aboriginal languages. Many of us have been present when a prepared speech in some Aboriginal language is read out very slowly and haltingly by a person not very familiar with the language in its oral form, let alone its written representation. This can be awkward for the person attempting to perform in a public setting and may trigger some unease among members of the Aboriginal group as they monitor audience reactions. Aboriginal people who are fluent in an Aboriginal language as well as non-Aboriginal people may judge the performance to be a poor reflection of the ancestral language. They may question the authenticity of such modern renditions of a re-awakened language and even suggest that the enterprise is fundamentally flawed.

This section is therefore a welcome contribution to a little researched area. Jones, Chandler and Lowe surveyed some 114 children from Aboriginal as well as non-Aboriginal backgrounds across four primary schools. Although they stress that the research is very preliminary they were able to gain some evidence that there might be a positive relationship between learning a re-awakened language and learning to read in English. English spelling of course is notorious for its poor correlation between sound and symbol, whereas the spelling adopted for re-awakened languages typically is much closer to a one-to-one correlation. It is this greater consistency that may assist students in that initial hurdle of acquiring literacy.

However, as is pointed out by Reid, the pronunciation of re-awakened languages may be strongly influenced by English spelling. Particularly where people first encounter their re-awakened language as adults, they already have a lifetime of familiarity with English spelling. For non-Aboriginal people it is scarcely surprising that an encounter with a word like Tabidgi (the Aboriginal name of the maternal uncle of Jimmy Blacksmith in the Thomas Keneally novel) produces a pronunciation which is not very faithful to Aboriginal languages of the region in question: stress on the second

---

1 Department of Linguistics, University of Sydney.

syllable; the reduction of the first vowel to schwa[2]; the equation of the first consonant with the apico-alveolar t of English (although it is much more likely that the sound should be lamino-dental) and the rendering of dg as in English jug rather than as a lamino-palatal. Of the six sounds represented by Tabidgi only two (the b and the final vowel) are pronounced 'accurately'. And this is an instance where one has no oral source to fall back on.

But even when we encounter the name of the famed singer from north-east Arnhem Land, Gurrumul Yunupingu, it is quite common for most of the vowels to be mispronounced as well as two of the consonants, even when there is immediate oral feedback. As Reid points out we need to consider the aspirations of the community whose heritage the re-awakened language is. It may be that a phonemic orthography is suitable for one group but not for another. And sometimes the purpose for which the particular spelling system has been devised will determine its shape. Troy and Walsh (2009), for instance, developed a spelling system for reinstated Aboriginal placenames in the Sydney Harbour area which seeks to use English spelling conventions to approximate what the original pronunciation might have been. This is a practical approach in which the intention is to have the majority of readers getting the pronunciation about right rather than a slightly improved accuracy being limited to a tiny minority of academic specialists. In this and other situations future generations of relevant Aboriginal people may choose to coincide more strongly with 'authentic' pronunciations, but the choice should be theirs and evolve in concert with community aspirations.

This leads to the important paper by Hobson, which addresses questions of fluency in relation to re-awakened languages. As foreshadowed in the opening paragraph of this introduction there are plenty enough people who are skeptical about the whole enterprise of revitalising languages. Such people are apt to comment, 'They don't *really* speak it, do they?' And some of the people involved in regaining their ancestral language(s) are ambivalent about their abilities. This ambivalence is fuelled not just by skeptical non-Aboriginal people but also by Aboriginal people from northern Australia who have acquired their language(s) as children. Hobson stresses that this is a sensitive issue but one that needs to be addressed, not only to underpin the validity of revitalising languages, but also to add credibility to Aboriginal language teaching and learning. He predicts that education and funding bodies will insist on some form of appropriate certification and encourages us to consider models that have already been tried elsewhere.

References

Troy J & Walsh M (2009). Reinstating Aboriginal placenames around Port Jackson and Botany Bay. In H Koch & L Hercus (Eds). *The land is a map*. Vol 2 (pp. 55–70). Canberra, Australia: Pacific Linguistics.

---

2 The final vowel in the rapid pronunciation of English word, the.

23
Questions of fluency in Australian languages revitalisation

John Hobson[1]

Abstract

Fluency is a concept that can be interpreted in different ways, from the simple capacity to produce speech clearly, to a measure of someone's overall ability to speak a specific language. It is also often used impressionistically based on very little evidence, and the description of someone as fluent sometimes just seems to mean, 'speaks it better than me'. How relevant and useful are ideas of fluency to revitalising languages which may only be spoken partially by a few speakers? How fluent does a language educator need to be? How can or should fluency in these languages be measured, and who should do the measuring? Is it a task for government, schools, universities or community agencies? This paper canvasses possible answers to some of these questions. It will also review some examples of how other decolonising peoples are attempting to address these issues to see if their experience can help us deal with issues of fluency in Indigenous Australian languages revitalisation.

My interest in fluency originates from some different experiences. When I lived in Alice Springs among several of this country's strongest languages I had the privilege of working with some extraordinarily patient and persistent teachers. Any positive outcomes I had in learning their languages were, I am quite sure, far more due to their ability than mine. Nevertheless our mutual success was such that I was eventually able to function across at least two languages in some very limited and highly predictable social settings. Included in these, at one stage, was a role coordinating the delivery of beginner classes in those languages for the Institute for Aboriginal Development (IAD).

---

1 Koori Centre, University of Sydney.

Although my primary responsibilities in this operation were logistic we always worked as a team delivering lessons in the classroom, probably because my teachers also saw this as an economical way of continuing my apprenticeship. And, on those occasions when unforeseen circumstances caused the real teachers to be absent, I knew I had their confidence, if not always my own, to keep the customers satisfied and pursue the scheduled activities until their return. One of the things I learned from this experience was, like the teacher who stays only one lesson ahead of their students, as long as your fluency is greater than someone else's they really have very limited capacity to accurately assess yours and will often significantly overestimate it, especially when you're the one standing in front of the class!

Continuing to work and socialise with my teachers and their friends and families over several years greatly improved my speaking and listening abilities and exposed me to a range of everyday expressions and interactions that were rarely touched upon in classes. Their close attention to my pronunciation also helped me minimise my English-speaker accent as much as I was able. A consequence of their persistence and my still quite limited capacity to hold a conversation was that native speakers, or local multilinguals, would sometimes mistakenly assume that I could speak a language *right through*. My teachers' very flattering tendency to also assert this on my behalf, while no doubt largely intended to offer me encouragement, contributed significantly to creating that illusion. I knew I still had the language skills of a learner. But moderately better pronunciation than the average whitefella and the capacity to understand and make simple jokes, for example, meant that speakers could be misled about my fluency for a short time at least. This taught me not only the importance of a good accent and authentic expression, but that non-expert speakers can easily make inflated assessments of someone's fluency in a language based on only a slight amount of evidence.

Subsequent travel in non-English-speaking countries has reinforced this awareness. I now understand only too well how a reasonable accent and a few memorised phrases can quickly get me into or out of some very difficult situations. And the effect operates in both directions; when local people are taught stock English dialogues for use with foreign visitors it can take a while for the traveller to realise that any unexpected answers or deviation from the script are largely incomprehensible to their new friend. While many bilinguals and linguists might consider these ideas self-evident they are, however, not at all obvious to those who dwell in a monolingual environment.

Now operating in Indigenous languages education in south-eastern Australia[2] my contact is mostly with people who are engaged in a quest to develop fluency in their ancestral languages and supporting others to achieve similar goals. I am also directly involved in training and assessing those people who wish to be professionally recognised as teachers of those languages. In such contexts fluency is a central concern.

---

2 As the coordinator of graduate programs in Indigenous languages education at the Koori Centre, University of Sydney.

While the majority of the owners of most languages in southern Australia are currently also non-speakers it can be especially difficult for them to establish who is fluent and to what extent. Most people, apart from a few elder speakers, are at an early stage of their journey towards fluency and therefore have limited capacity to accurately assess the fluency of others. There are also people who are taking matters into their own hands and endeavouring to teach themselves their language from learners' guides, dictionaries and wordlists.[3] While this is an admirable ambition, unaware of the sound and grammatical systems of their language they can end up making simple statements, but without the necessary detail to make clear who did what to whom and whether it happened yesterday, today, or is yet to occur. Coupled with a convincing accent and rapid delivery this can be very impressive to non-speakers, but any fluent speakers probably wouldn't regard it as real fluency, or even real language, assuming they could recognise it at all. And this is clearly a concern for those who can tell and have an interest in revitalising their languages as faithfully as possible.[4]

Of course in languages education, teachers are required to constantly assess their students' language abilities and the concept of fluency is directly relevant here. But even more importantly, in languages teacher training there is a justifiable assumption that accreditation has some connection to language ability. And learners of languages usually have an expectation that their teachers have an appropriate level of ability to perform the task, as do those who employ them.

So my interest in fluency stems from several positions – outsider and insider, language learner, speaker and teacher, linguist and trainer of languages teachers. It is definitely not as a gatekeeper with a desire to apply set standards, although I am required to deal with authorities that would very much like me to. Mostly it is as someone who is interested in seeing Australian languages survive and flourish and supporting individuals and communities to attain that goal.

What is fluency?

Fluency is an unfortunately vague term. It can be used to refer to both the ability to speak a language smoothly and a person's overall capacity to communicate in a language as indicated by speaking it; two measures that have an obvious connection. Thus we can identify someone as a fluent speaker based on the lack of hesitation or interruption in their speech and the absence of particular disturbances such as stuttering. We can similarly identify someone as a fluent reader or even writer. To avoid confusion and focus particularly on the ability of a person to communicate meaningfully in a language through speech, linguists and language educators usually prefer to use the term *oral proficiency*.

---

3 Sometimes compiled by English speakers who may have had limited ability to accurately recognise, record or understand what they were hearing.

4 See also Giacon and, for an alternative view, N. Reid, this volume.

Of course a person's total language abilities consist of more than just oral proficiency, and languages teachers are accustomed to dealing in terms of the macro-skills of speaking, listening (understanding), writing and reading. It is also widely recognised that learners' abilities in listening typically precede those in speaking. However in everyday contexts the primary indicator of overall language ability is normally taken to be speaking, which is commonly discussed in terms of fluency, and I have chosen to follow that use.

Is fluency relevant to revitalising languages?

Clearly many people believe otherwise. Simply raising fluency as a topic of discussion with those involved in language revitalisation in Australia can bring a rapid halt to conversation or suspicion of gatekeeper motivation. In the context of a recent conference presentation that was, rather tellingly, quite poorly attended my audience reached their own consensus that it was simply too far removed from their circumstances to warrant consideration. Such reactions continue to provide me with concern and motivate my persistence.

Surely if the ability to speak a language is irrelevant, we are not discussing revitalisation so much as awareness. If a language is to be re-awoken to live again then a principal goal must be to have people speak it (Fishman 1991; Hinton 2002). And, if people begin to speak a language, then they must be expected to improve that ability to some extent, or we are only talking about language maintenance. Of course, for some languages that have little recorded information and no surviving speakers, the ultimate goal of revitalisation may be simply speechmaking or the mastery of a few fixed phrases. Even so the change from non-speaker to speaker in such contexts represents a positive change in fluency that we can at least observe and discuss, and assist people to achieve.

Where language revitalisation efforts are in their early stages and not many people have significant fluency, to focus on it might seem disheartening, even embarrassing, for some. Especially where claims for recognition and possibly even funding are involved, there might also be fears of negative outcomes if the truth about current levels of fluency in the community were known. Those concerns are understandable and not without some justification. However, in the long term, I believe they are also likely to be counter-productive. The assumption that progress is being made as long as some teaching-like activity is taking place and people are engaged and feeling good, may be quite reassuring. But unless people are actually developing greater fluency, it seems to me that revitalisation is not really happening.

To make a language vital again requires its speakers to progress from less to more fluent, both individually and as speech communities, even if the ultimate goal is not as lofty as restoring a first language speaker population (see Meakins, this volume). While such outcomes might conceivably occur naturally they are far more likely to be successful if they involve some language planning, and to plan for an increase in fluency requires some measure of both starting and end points as well as strategies to effect change. This is not to suggest that at either the individual or community level the measurement of fluency should be arbitrarily imposed. However, for those individuals and speech communities that can see benefit in knowing where their current skill level lies, it would certainly be useful to have the option and an appropriate mechanism available.

How is fluency measured?

Linguists and language educators have been measuring speakers' fluency in many languages for many years and there is a wide range of highly developed testing methods available.[5] Essentially all of them require the performance of some speaking task, the result of which is measured against some scale based on observation by someone with training and experience in the area. Tests of oral proficiency are also often married with tests of listening and, for written languages, with tests of literacy skills. Because test output at higher levels of fluency is more likely to be unique, its measurement is less likely to require specific words or strings to be uttered so much a judgement made regarding its overall communicative adequacy – is it only sufficient to perform basic fixed tasks like introduce oneself, enough to perform in a workplace, or sufficient to freely converse with native speakers on any topic?[6]

While the exact nature of the tasks may vary, the scales of measurement tend to be fairly consistent, although variously proposing finer or coarser grades of measurement. Usually each point on a particular scale is given a descriptive title, possibly a number, and an extended description of the functional indicators for assessment at that level. Some internationally popular and electronically accessible scales include the Canadian *New Brunswick second-language oral proficiency scale* (Government of New Brunswick, n.d.), the American Council on the Teaching of Foreign Languages (ACTFL) *Proficiency guidelines: speaking* (1999), and the Stanford Foreign Language Oral Skills Evaluation Matrix (FLOSEM) (Padilla & Sung 1999) that measures comprehension, fluency, vocabulary, pronunciation and grammar. The dominant scale in Australian settings, however, remains the *Australian second language proficiency ratings (ASLPR)* (Wylie & Ingram 1995a; 1995b)[7] that provides the following developmental series:

---

5 English fluency is routinely measured as a core component of the education of every child in Australia.

6 It is also possible to give measurements in terms of some gain having taken place without reference to set levels. This can be useful to indicate that learners are improving and provide them with encouragement to persist. However it ultimately does not reveal what they can or cannot do.

7 No longer published and renamed the International Second Language Proficiency Ratings (ISLPR) in 1997.

Proficiency level	Descriptive title
5	Native-like Proficiency
4+	Advanced 'Vocational' Proficiency
4	'Vocational' Proficiency
3+	Basic 'Vocational' Proficiency Plus
3	Basic 'Vocational' Proficiency
2+	Social Proficiency
2	Basic Social Proficiency
1+	Transactional Proficiency
1	Basic Transactional Proficiency
1-	Minimum 'Creative' Proficiency
0+	Formulaic Proficiency
0	Zero Proficiency

Table 1. ASLPR numbers and names of levels (Wylie & Ingram 1995a, p. iv).

But these are not the only means of assessing fluency. For example in languages education in schools, teachers should be familiar users of a range of assessment activities and measurable speaking objectives that derive from syllabus documents such as the *New South Wales* [NSW] *K–10 Aboriginal Languages Syllabus* (Board of Studies NSW 2003) and its associated support materials, although these may themselves have originally had some basis in scales like the ASLPR. Colleges, universities and community agencies are similarly providing courses that are generally recognised as indicating, at least, implied levels of fluency among other language skills.[8] So the measurement and certification of fluency in revitalising Australian languages is already actively being undertaken both by government and community agencies. And that, rightly or wrongly, intentionally or not, affords them a considerable level of control.

---

8 In NSW these currently include the University of Sydney's Speaking Gamilaraay I & II, Muurrbay Aboriginal Language & Culture Co-operative's Certificate II in Gumbaynggirr Language and Culture Maintenance and Certificate IV in Teaching Language & Cultural Maintenance, and the generic NSW Technical and Further Education Certificates I, II and III in Aboriginal Language/s. Purdie et al. (2008) provide a comprehensive survey of offerings nationally.

Of course scales such as the ASPLR have been principally designed for vital languages from around the world with the assumption that near-native fluency is achievable for second language learners. They are also clearly based in a modern Western worldview, a fact that raises questions of cross-cultural appropriatness. Some may also assert that the notion of formal testing itself is inherently non-traditional for Indigenous Australians. This may be true, but no more so than the idea of formal second language classes to learn one's ancestral language, language centres, dictionaries or literacy.

McConvell (1994) addresses some of these concerns and provides a sample alternative testing instrument for one Australian language, Kija. Although the material discussed is specific to that language it provides an excellent model from which other language-specific tests could readily be developed. In the North American context the Ganöhsesge:kha:': Hë:nödeyë:stha (Faithkeeper's School) that teaches in the Seneca language has undertaken a comprehensive adaptation of the standard FLOSEM instrument to produce a culturally sensitive and appropriate scale for their own use (Borgia 2009).

How fluent do teachers need to be?

While the measurement of fluency can be construed as at least useful and relevant for individuals and communities engaged in revitalising their languages, it becomes critical for those who are required to use a language professionally. This is nowhere more so than for languages teachers. Both students and providers would normally have a justifiable expectation that someone working as a teacher of any language would have a reasonable level of fluency as well as being competent to foster its development in learners. Although in the early stages of revitalisation it is conceivable that the teacher might be literally only one lesson ahead of the class, or even on the same page, after languages education has been in effect for some time those who have a history of participation in the process would hopefully have significantly higher levels of fluency than beginners, and be able to feed their skills growth back into the community revitalisation cycle.

Australian primary (elementary) teaching qualifications do not normally require a languages component. However for secondary teaching the NSW Institute of Teachers (NSWIT), for example, currently specifies a minimum standard of a language major to qualify as a designated languages teacher; a major being, 'a defined program of study in a designated area, generally comprising 3 years of degree level study of 6 semester long specified units of study or equivalent, including 4 units from later stages of the program (level 2 or above)' (2008, p. 3), in addition to languages pedagogy requirements.

During initial discussions with the NSW Department of Education and Training's Teaching Qualifications Advisory Panel (TQAP), a precursor to NSWIT, regarding recognition of the University of Sydney's Master of Indigenous Languages Education (MILE),[9] a figure of 200 hours post-secondary study in an Aboriginal language or

---

9 The MILE (MIndigLangEd) is currently recognised as a professional development qualification

languages was suggested as a minimum standard of fluency.[10] Equally telling, but more functionally defined, the ASLPR scale for second language teachers does not commence until Level 2, Basic Social Proficiency, for regular modes of teaching with a minimum standard of Level 4, 'Vocational' Proficiency, for immersion or bilingual programs (Wylie & Ingram 1995b, p. iii).

In many Australian languages currently undergoing revitalisation such standards are unlikely to be achievable for even the most fluent teachers. If, for instance, a language is not yet offered to the final year of high school or in any university it is simply not possible for any teacher to have achieved to such levels themselves. And if there has been a breakdown in transmission over several generations and only a few elder speakers exist, or none at all, similarly skilled candidates are unlikely to exist in the community. Sadly this situation describes most, if not all, the languages of southern Australia and there would be few, if any, teachers who could realistically satisfy requirements for the lowest ASPLR teaching standard of Basic Social Proficiency. Given that each revitalising language is probably at a different point to every other, a standard to be applied across all, even within a single state, would be impossible to determine. And, if the process of revitalisation produces improved fluency across whole speech communities, both minimum and maximum standards must necessarily be expected to change over time.

Fortunately the various education authorities that permit Australian languages to be taught in schools have largely responded pragmatically to date and allowed languages to be taught by those who simply have some knowledge of the language and a preparedness to engage in school classrooms. These may be qualified Indigenous teachers but not normally with languages teaching accreditation (or training) or any certification of fluency. They may also be Indigenous community members without teaching qualifications but 'some' knowledge of the language working alongside a qualified teacher, who may or may not have languages education training themselves. In some cases they may even be non-Indigenous. The dedication and commitment of these people is not in question here, but their potential to continue without further fluency development as the languages are revitalised warrants consideration.

This situation is not likely to persist indefinitely and, as revitalisation and particularly school-based languages programs develop, it is increasingly likely that educational authorities will move to pursue a goal of parity for Indigenous Australian languages taught in schools with those originating from outside Australia. The limited accreditation of the MILE to 2010 is telling in this regard:

---

for graduate teachers who wish to add Aboriginal Languages as a designated teaching subject in NSW schools.

10 The possibility of offering three languages arbitrarily chosen from the state's strongest together with some appropriate linguistic concepts as set content was also raised, as was the potential for the University to act as a fluency testing and accreditation authority for Aboriginal languages teachers across the state. Both were ultimately rejected by the Koori Centre as impractical and inappropriate.

> The NSW Department of Education & Training acknowledges the availability of the Master of Indigenous Languages Education offered at the University of Sydney and accepts this program as providing appropriate training for qualified Aboriginal teachers seeking additional approval to teach an Aboriginal language. Aboriginal teachers completing the Master of Indigenous Languages Education up to the end of 2010 will be eligible for approval to teach Aboriginal languages. In 2009 the Department will reconsider the Master of Indigenous Languages Education and any other available Aboriginal languages programs in terms of the requirements for Aboriginal languages teachers after 2010. (Koori Centre, n.d.)

Such measures suggest that the imperative for government to apply 'standards' to Indigenous languages educators is looming large on the horizon, and the push for professionalisation should be anticipated, especially in states like NSW where a standardised state syllabus and expanding implementation is rapidly normalising them in the languages key learning area.[11]

What's happening overseas?

Questions of fluency are not restricted to the Australian languages revitalisation process and it is of value to consider some of the responses from commonly compared situations overseas.[12]

The example of Aotearoa (New Zealand) is typically sophisticated and inspiring, but equally removed from the realm of possibility in Australia today. It nonetheless is worth considering as a possibly ideal goal. A single language and single state government together with legislative recognition of *te reo Māori* permits a formal testing regime applied by the Māori Language Commission (MLC):

> Whakamātauria Tō Reo Māori is the new Māori language proficiency examination system developed by Te Taura Whiri i te Reo Māori [MLC] in conjunction with local and international specialists in Māori language and language testing. The system comprises a general Māori language knowledge test, a set of sector-related Māori language proficiency tests and a proficiency test framework.
>
> ...
>
> The framework identifies five progressive levels of Māori language proficiency. Each sector-related proficiency test fits within one of these levels. (Te Taura Whiri i te Reo Māori, n.d.)

Candidates initially sit a one-hour Level Finder Examination to assess general ability across all language macro-skills and may then undertake either of the two-

---

11 National curriculum standards are not currently being applied to languages in Australia, but they are scheduled for inclusion in the next wave (Australian Curriculum, Assessment and Reporting Authority, n.d.).

12 Further discussion of teacher training for Indigenous languages revitalisation in each of these jurisdictions is available in Hobson (2008a, 2008b).

hour Public Sector Māori or Teaching Sector Māori examinations. The standard for teachers is the highest. Accreditation of fluency for teachers and others is also possible through the university and college systems, much as for (non-Indigenous) languages education qualifications in Australia. The MLC exams provide an alternative means of certification for those who have not completed coursework, or who have increased their fluency by other means and wish to obtain a revised measure, or would just like to know how their current abilities rate.

The situation in the United States of America entails substantially greater diversity than here based on the sheer number of state jurisdictions and the considerable autonomy of local school boards, but has some similarities to both Australia and New Zealand at its extremes. Strong revitalising languages, especially those that have access to a substantial resource base, may implement their own fluency certification regime or have access to accredited university or college coursework options, as well as school-based programs. Thus for the Navajo (Diné) language, 'Individuals seeking the Navajo Language Endorsement in New Mexico or Arizona are required to take the Navajo Language Proficiency Test. Diné College is authorised by the Navajo Nation to administer this test.' (Diné College 2008, p. 32). Although, as Dean of Humanities and Social/Behavioral Sciences, Wesley Thomas pointed out, other community agencies operating in the Diné language offer fluency certification for teachers acceptable in some schools based on only a brief interview (pers. comm., 10 August 2007). Anecdotally, for smaller languages in the USA the situation is mostly similar to that in Australia; those who say they can, and are prepared to, can participate in teaching revitalising languages as long as the school community permits.

In Canada, self- or community-selection of languages teachers is also possible as is course-based certification through universities, colleges and seasonal institutes. However of greatest interest is an initiative from British Columbia (BC), a province that entails some linguistic situations directly comparable to many in Australia. Here the BC College of Teachers (BCCT) has developed in collaboration with Aboriginal community interests a system for the accreditation of First Nations language authorities recommended by a tribal council or other body acceptable to the College. These authorities may issue Interim First Nations Language Teacher Certificates to ' ... proficient First Nations language speakers ... [whose] proficiency is determined by the recognized Language Authority, and the Language Authority recommends ... for certification.' (BCCT n.d., p. 1). Remarkably, as Beverley Maxwell, the BCCT director of certification advised, how the authorities determine proficiency is entirely their concern as *it is their language* (pers. comm., 16 July 2007). There is also a clear assumption that standards and certification methods will vary over time according to the current health of each language.

These certificates only permit the holder to teach classes in a specific language, and have potential to be made permanent. But the preferred outcome is for students to undertake formal teacher education through a program such as the laddered model auspiced by the University of Victoria. Through this program, certificate holders may take further training to obtain a Certificate in Aboriginal Language Revitalisation offered in partnership with the University's Division of Continuing Studies, Department of Linguistics and the En'owkin Centre, an accredited First Nations language authority. Further study in languages and education leads to the award of the Developmental Standard Term Certificate issued by BCCT that allows the holder to teach in BC elementary (primary) schools, but has a standard term of four years within which a full teaching degree must be obtained. An additional two years full-time education coursework at the University of Victoria leads to the award of a Bachelor of Education (University of Victoria, Faculty of Education, n.d.)

Could community certification of fluency work here?

Devolving the certification of fluency to autonomous indigenous agencies might seem extraordinary viewed from within the current Australian environment. Yet it does not appear to have caused the downfall of Canadian Aboriginal education, or Navajo or Māori, and has much to recommend it. In fact, to a limited extent, community-controlled certification of fluency *does* already exist here. Indigenous language centres such as Muurrbay and the IAD have, through the provision of their accredited language courses, been acting as de facto certifying agencies for many years without apparent harm.

Acknowledging the right of Indigenous Australian communities to decide the standards for their languages and those who teach them would afford the potential for self-determination, in language revitalisation at least. It would put government authorities at arm's length and give communities the status of ultimate judges of a cultural expression that should be undeniably theirs. It would relieve government, linguists and the rest of non-Indigenous Australia of any illusion that they need to be controlling the future of Australian languages and allow the transfer of responsibility back to community hands.

To broadly implement such a strategy would require a number of major steps, each requiring much consultation and negotiation. Existing community language agencies would need to develop language-specific materials and procedures for the local administration of testing. Where no such agency existed one would need to be established, possibly auspiced by other Indigenous bodies with a resource base and cultural role such as land councils, and with assistance from government or other interested institutions like universities. The potential to act as certifying authorities would, of itself, lend weight to the need for such agencies to be established and provide them with an immediate role in addition to the great deal of other valuable language work they could potentially undertake.

A system of accreditation for certifying agencies would need to be implemented together with a mechanism for meaningful and practical recognition of their authority. The BC example suggests that state-based professional teacher registration bodies would be suitable candidates, but school education boards of studies, vocational education and training authorities, and similar agencies could also be involved. Indigenous language authorities could then be given a place at the table in the accreditation of courses offered by those providers, further consolidating their role as well as determining how fluent a teacher of their language currently needs to be.

Mechanisms for articulation with training opportunities in languages education and other forms of language work could be developed, as in BC. Fishman (2001) has identified the critical role of sociocultural reward in motivating individuals to learn their language. If employment opportunities were aligned with the certification process the benefit of achieving fluency would be very clearly defined. But, for many, achieving a level of fluency in their language that was certified by their community would be reward enough, as it should be.

Of course such a system would need to allow for considerable variability by language and over time to take account of the dynamic nature of revitalisation. The optimum level for fluency in a specific language at a particular point in time would necessarily be different to another language and as community levels of fluency rose. For that reason the application of limited term certification might also be considered.

Conclusion

The measurement of fluency in Indigenous Australian languages is possible and is already being undertaken by schools, colleges, universities and community agencies. Culturally appropriate materials, methods and scales have been developed. As languages revitalise, assessing the fluency of individuals and communities has potential to assist in planning the future of that process.

Indigenous communities can pursue their current activity in revitalisation without regard to fluency or seek to exercise control. If they don't it is probable that governments, particularly through education and teacher training, will increasingly do so.

Other indigenous populations have developed their own systems to deal with questions of fluency in their languages. A model that seems particularly appropriate is that applied in British Columbia where community-based language bodies have been established and exercise authority recognised by government for the measurement and certification of fluency in a framework of articulated qualifications for teachers and other language workers. Consideration of a similar model for the Australian context by language owners and other interested parties is suggested.

Postscript

As this volume was going to press, the NSW DET advised that continued recognition of the University of Sydney's MILE as an acceptable qualification for Aboriginal languages teachers beyond 2012 would require the inclusion of 'at least two units of study (or equivalent) in the Aboriginal language the applicant intends to teach' (pers. comm., 21 September 2009). Fortunately, after several meetings where the Koori

Centre asserted the current impossibility of compliance for any Aboriginal language in NSW, a practical way forward was found and the combination of linguistics and research units within the degree were deemed to satisfy this requirement (pers. comm., 28 January 2010).

References

American Council on the Teaching of Foreign Languages (1999). *ACTFL Proficiency Guidelines – Speaking (revised 1999)* [Online]. Available: www.actfl.org/files/public/Guidelinesspeak.pdf [Accessed 6 April 2009].

Australian Curriculum Assessment & Reporting Authority (n.d.). *Australian curriculum* [Online]. Available: www.acara.edu.au/curriculum.html [Accessed 25 September 2009].

Board of Studies New South Wales (2003). *New South Wales K–10 Aboriginal languages syllabus*. Sydney: Board of Studies, NSW.

Borgia M (2009). Modifying assessment tools for Ganöhsesge:kha:' Hë:nödeyë:stha – a Seneca culture-language school. In J Reyhner & L Lockard (Eds). *Indigenous language revitalization: encouragement, guidance & lessons learned* (pp. 191–210). Flagstaff, Arizona: Northern Arizona University.

British Columbia College of Teachers (n.d.). *Application for First Nations Language Teacher's Certificate of Qualification*. Vancouver: British Columbia College of Teachers [Online]. Available: www.bcct.ca/Newsroom/FormsAndPublicationsOverview.aspx [Accessed 6 April 2009].

Diné College (2008). *2008–09 general catalog*. Tsaile, Arizona: Diné College [Online]. Available: www.dinecollege.edu/catalog/catalog.php [Accessed 6 April 2009].

Fishman JA (1991). *Reversing language shift: theoretical and empirical foundations of assistance to threatened languages*. Clevedon, Philadelphia: Multilingual Matters.

Fishman JA (2001). If threatened languages can be saved, then can dead languages be revived? *Current Issues in Language Planning*, 2(2–3): 222–30.

Government of New Brunswick (n.d.). *New Brunswick second-language oral proficiency scale* [Online]. Available: www.gnb.ca/0000/publications/eval/oralprofgr12.pdf [Accessed 6 April 2009].

Hinton L (2002). *How to keep your language alive: a commonsense approach to one-on-one language learning*. Berkeley: Heyday Books.

Hobson J (2008a). Training teachers for Indigenous languages education: what's happening overseas? In R Amery & J Nash (Eds). *Warra wiltaniappendi – strengthening languages: Proceedings of the inaugural Indigenous languages conference (ILC) 2007* (pp. 97–105), University of Adelaide, South Australia, 25–27 September 2007. Adelaide: University of Adelaide.

Hobson J (2008b). *Towards a model for training Indigenous languages educators in Australia* [video file]. Koori Centre Lecture, April 11, 2008. Sydney: University of Sydney [Online]. Available: hdl.handle.net/2123/2323 [Accessed 6 April 2009].

Koori Centre University of Sydney (n.d.). *Master of Indigenous Languages Education, Graduate Certificate & Graduate Diploma of Indigenous Languages Education* [brochure] [Online]. Available: www.koori.usyd.edu.au/studying/postgrad.shtml [Accessed 6 April 2009].

McConvell P (1994). Oral proficiency assessment for Aboriginal languages. In J Henderson & D Hartman (Eds). *Aboriginal languages in education* (pp. 301–15). Alice Springs: Institute for Aboriginal Development.

New South Wales Institute of Teachers (2008). *Graduate teacher standards 1.1.1-1.1.3 subject content requirements – June 2008*. Sydney: NSW Institute of Teachers [Online]. Available: www.nswteachers.nsw.edu.au/ITE_Program-Requirements.html [Accessed 6 April 2009].

Padilla A & Sung H (1999). *The Stanford foreign language oral skills evaluation matrix (FLOSEM): a rating scale for assessing communicative proficiency*. Palo Alto, CA: Stanford University Press [Online]. Available: www.asdk12.org/depts/ELL/SpEd/FLOSEM_Eng.pdf [Accessed 6 April 2009].

Purdie N, Frigo T, Ozolins C, Noblett G, Thieberger N & Sharp J (2008). *Indigenous languages programmes in Australian schools: a way forward*. Camberwell: Australian Council for Educational Research [Online]. Available: www.dest.gov.au/NR/rdonlyres/FBEAC65B-3A11-41F0-B836-1A480FDD82F9/25487/LPfinal130109NP.pdf [Accessed 25 March 2009].

Te Taura Whiri i te Reo Māori (Māori Language Commission) (n.d.). *Whakamātauria tō reo Māori – Māori language proficiency examination system* [Online]. Available: www.tetaurawhiri.govt.nz/english/services_e/language_proficiency.shtml [Accessed 6 April 2009].

University of Victoria Faculty of Education (n.d.). *Aboriginal teacher education* [Online]. Available: www.educ.uvic.ca/become/programs/aboriginal/aboriginal.php#ate [Accessed 6 April 2009].

Wylie E & Ingram DE (1995a). *Australian second language proficiency ratings (ASLPR): master general proficiency version (English examples)*. Nathan, Qld: Centre for Applied Linguistics and Languages, Griffith University.

Wylie E & Ingram DE (1995b). *Australian second language proficiency ratings (ASLPR): version for second language teachers*. Nathan, Qld: Centre for Applied Linguistics and Languages, Griffith University.

24
Sounds, spelling and learning to read an Aboriginal language

Caroline Jones,[1] Paul Chandler[2] and Kevin Lowe[3]

Abstract

Children who are in Australian Aboriginal language programs in revitalisation settings in New South Wales are learning an Aboriginal language at the same time as learning to read in English. Aboriginal languages and English have alphabetic writing systems and Aboriginal language spelling systems are usually more consistent than English. This means it is possible that learning an Aboriginal language spelling system might influence a child learning to read in English. We report on a pilot study where we explored whether learning an Aboriginal language in a revitalisation program at school is related to skill in decoding in English. We worked with 114 English-speaking children from Aboriginal and non-Aboriginal backgrounds in four public primary schools in two areas of regional New South Wales. Two of these schools were running a whole-of-school program in a local Aboriginal language in accordance with the *Aboriginal Languages K–10 Syllabus* (Board of Studies New South Wales 2003). We found some evidence to support a positive relationship between learning an Aboriginal language in a revitalisation setting and learning to decode in English. We also discuss limitations to our study and the need for further research.

Writing systems and learning to read

The writing systems used in Aboriginal language revitalisation programs in Australia use an alphabet to write words. Spelling systems (also called orthographies) in revitalisation programs have usually been established fairly recently. In addition

---

[1] Faculty of Education, University of Wollongong.
[2] Faculty of Education, University of Wollongong.
[3] Aboriginal Curriculum Unit, Office of the Board of Studies NSW.

spelling systems for revitalisation are often supported by a linguistic analysis of what are (likely to be) the distinctive speech sounds in the language. These sounds are called phonemes.

What are phonemes?

Phonemes play an important job in making sure that words with different meanings sound different. All languages have phonemes, including Aboriginal languages. As just one example, in the Gamilaraay language of north-west New South Wales (NSW), the word for eye is *mil* and the word for one is *maal* (Yuwaalaraay Language Program 2003). So the words mean different things. The only pronunciation difference is a short 'i' in *mil* and a long 'aa' in *maal*. There are other word pairs like this, too. We say these two vowel sounds we spell with the vowel letters *i* and *aa* are different phonemes in Gamilaraay.

Types of spelling systems

Compared with some other languages of the world the spelling systems used in Australian Aboriginal language revitalisation programs are regular systems. This means they are consistent, in that each letter or group of letters always stands for the same sound. In the Gamilaraay spelling system each letter or group of letters always stands for the same phoneme. This is called a phonemic system. There are also allophonic systems which indicate if there is more than one pronunciation of a phoneme, for example when the letter 'k' is between two vowels it sounds like an English 'g', but it sounds more like English 'k' when it occurs at the start or end of a word.

As an example of phonemic spelling here is the first line of the song '*Burrulaa Birralii*' (Lots of Children) in Yuwaalaraay language. We could have chosen any other group of words from any other Aboriginal language that uses phonemic spelling to illustrate this point:

> *Milan, bulaarr, gulibaa birralii*
>
> One, two, three children (Yuwaalaraay Language Program 2003, p. 4)

In this line of song the letter b always indicates a /b/ sound. The letter l always indicates the same /l/ sound, and so on. The same is true for vowels: there are three short vowel sounds spelled i, a, and u, and two long vowel sounds spelled aa and ii.

English spelling, language revitalisation, and learning to read

English works differently from the regular system described above. English does not have a regular spelling system to the same extent as Aboriginal languages. In English some words are spelled so that each letter stands for its usual phoneme, for example dog or dig. But it is well known there are also words which contain irregular or unusual spellings that are exceptions to the usual patterns. For example in yacht the 'y' stands for its usual phoneme, but the rest of the spelling (except the 't') does not.

This situation in English is part of the reason why it is recommended that children learning to read are taught to recognise some words instantly as wholes or *sight words*, as well as how to decode (*sound out*) words letter by letter, sound by sound, so that children can independently use alphabetic reading to read words that they know from spoken language but have not read before. Modern theories of reading and a large body of research evidence support the inclusion of phonics instruction in this way in Australian schools (see Coltheart & Prior 2007).

In current Aboriginal language revitalisation programs for young school-aged children or for adults, the spelling system is typically taught early in the program and literacy is a major focus of teaching activities and resources. In this situation the teacher is often learning the language too and, as written language has status for many people, it is common practice to base lessons around printed words and the spelling system together with some songs, conversational words, and other culture.

For children in language revitalisation programs in the community or at school, learning language is something they are doing alongside learning to read in English. This situation raises a question: What is the relationship between learning an Aboriginal language, especially its spelling system in a revitalisation context, and learning to read in English?

In recent pilot research we collected some data to try to start to answer that question. We considered that some of the relationships might be positive, based on theories of reading in English and existing research that others have done. But we wanted to see if that was true for Aboriginal languages in revitalisation contexts as well.

Learning to read in English is an intrinsically hard and seemingly unnatural thing. Many of the reasons relate to the cognitive demands of the spelling system: the choice of an alphabet (rather than a syllable or word based writing system) and the mix of regular and irregular spelling patterns. Much research evidence (see Rayner et al. 2001) indicates that an early challenge for all children is realising that English spelling is a writing system where letters represent phonemes. This is called the Alphabetic Principle. The Alphabetic Principle is difficult for many children to grasp probably because, until taught to read, children's memories for words are more likely to be based on larger units such as syllables and words. The task is probably made harder by the irregular patterns in English spelling. A related skill that children need and develop in learning to read with an alphabet is phonological awareness: being able to reflect on the sounds in words, rather than their meanings. Teaching activities designed to foster phonological awareness in pre-readers and early readers include syllable games (tapping, counting); rhyming, alliteration and phoneme-based activities; and explicit exploration of how speech sounds are made (using the mouth, tongue, nose, voicebox and lungs). It is recognised that learning to sound out and spell probably promotes phonological awareness too (see Castles & Coltheart 2004).

It seems possible that teaching a child a language in a revitalisation or heritage language situation, using written and spoken forms of the language, could potentially help children learn the Alphabetic Principle and phonological awareness, and consequently improve their decoding skills. Alternatively, or in addition, children who learn consistent letter-sound relationships in a second language might simply be able to transfer them across directly into reading English. This seems most likely to happen if the letter-sound relationships are the same or very similar in the two languages, as in the letter i in English pin compared with i in Gamilaraay/Yuwaalaraay *gulibaa* (three), for example. Either way we might expect positive impacts on English reading from learning an Aboriginal language in a well taught revitalisation program with a typical emphasis on reading and spelling.

Previous research on learning to read in two languages

There is an increasing amount of research on children learning to read in two languages, which is the normal situation around the world. This research compares children's phonological (sound-related) and orthographic (spelling-knowledge related) skills in one language with their word reading skills in a second language (Bialystok et al. 2005; Chiappe & Siegel 1999; Cisero & Royer 1995; Comeau et al.1999; D'Angiulli et al. 2001; DaFountoura & Siegel 1995; Durgunoglu et al. 1993; Geva et al. 1993; Gomez & Reason 2002; Gottardo et al. 2001; Luk & Bialystok 2008; Wang et al. 2005). For example Gomez and Reason (2002) looked at English reading skills in 69 seven–eight-year-old Malaysian children who spoke Bahasa Malaysia, which has a regular spelling system like most Aboriginal languages in Australia. Compared with children of the same age and reading experience who only spoke English the Malaysian children were better at reading aloud nonwords (for example blif, nug), which indicates stronger decoding skills.

Research which is especially relevant as a basis for our research in language revitalisation settings looks at children learning a second language but with quite limited hours of instruction, for example after-school or in-school heritage programs in Italian for English-speaking children (D'Angiulli et al. 2001; Yelland et al. 1993). This kind of program differs in important ways from a school-based revitalisation program but in its relatively limited hours of instruction it is similar. Both these studies found positive relationships; students who were learning Italian in this context had stronger decoding and word reading skills in English compared to students of the same age and school year who were not learning Italian.

Details about the study

We compared decoding skills in English in children who were learning a NSW Aboriginal language at school and children of the same age and school year who were not learning an Aboriginal language (or any other second language). Because of the observational nature of the study the data we collect are correlational. The data do not let us make conclusions about any specific or direct effect or impact of learning an Aboriginal language on English decoding skills. In this study we research the relationships or associations between learning an Aboriginal language and English decoding skills, and acknowledge that many factors may be acting causally in this relationship.

Spelling systems of the Aboriginal languages in the study

This study involved two Aboriginal language programs for two different languages. The spelling system for these languages is shown in Table 1. These systems are phonemic. The only spelling difference between the languages is that the same sounds are spelled dj, nj in one language, and dy, ny in the other. Many of the consonant letters indicate consonant sounds which are similar in English for the same letter, for example n, d, l. Consonant sounds which aren't in English are written with letter groups, for example rr, dh. Some vowel letters indicate sounds similar to English vowel sounds, for example i, but some consistently have unusual values from an English perspective, for example a and u. The linguistic terms in the table are provided for accuracy and full information but it is not necessary to understand these terms to follow the rest of the chapter.

Spelling of consonant phonemes					
	Bilabial	Dental	Alveolar	Palatal	Velar
Stops	b	dh	d	dy / dj	g
Nasals	m	nh	n	ny / nj	ng
Laterals			l		
Rhotics			rr		
Approximants	w		r	y	

Spelling of vowel phonemes			
		Front	Central
Short / Long	High	i / ii	
	Low		a / aa

Table 1. Spelling system for the two Aboriginal languages in the study.

Children in the study

The child participants in our study were 114 Aboriginal and non-Aboriginal children who were in Year 1 (51 children) or Year 2 (63). We worked with those children who brought in signed parent/guardian consent forms and wanted to participate on the day (just one student did not want to participate). The children who participated were a mix of girls (56) and boys (58). They were typically seven- and eight-year-olds. A total of 18 children were described by parents as Aboriginal, 90 as non-Indigenous, and for 6 no information was provided. Four different Aboriginal language group backgrounds were represented among children according to parents and guardians. Full details about the participants are in Table 2.

Region	Condition	Year	No.	Mean age in years (range)	% Male participants (no.)	% Aboriginal participants (no.)
A	Language program	1	9	7.1 (6.5-7.6)	67 (6)	33 (3)
		2	20	8.4 (7.8-8.9)	45 (9)	40 (8)
	No language program	1	7	6.8 (6.3-7.4)	43 (3)	28 (2)
		2	17	8.1 (7.8-8.8)	65 (11)	6 (1)
B	Language program	1	20	7.2 (6.5-7.6)	55 (11)	0
		2	14	8.5 (7.8-9.2)	43 (6)	21 (3)
	No language program	1	15	7.4 (6.7-7.8)	40 (6)	7 (1)
		2	12	8.4 (7.9-8.7)	50 (6)	0

Table 2. Participant details.

Location of the study

We ran our study in four public primary schools. The schools are anonymous here to preserve confidentiality as required by the NSW Department of Education and Training. The schools were in two geographically separate, non-metropolitan areas

(Region A and Region B). Two schools were in one region (Region A – 53 children) and two in another (Region B – 61 children). In both regions the language program school was teaching a local Aboriginal language for all children in the primary school from Kindergarten to Year 6 in accordance with the *Aboriginal Languages K–10 Syllabus* (Board of Studies NSW 2003).

The comparison school was chosen for not having a language program, but having children from a similar mix of socioeconomic backgrounds to the language program school. Tables 2 and 3 below show that, socioeconomically, the backgrounds of students in the language program schools were similar to, and in some cases slightly lower, than in the comparison schools.

The numbers in Table 3 are the percentage of parents in each occupation or job category (Australian Bureau of Statistics ANZSCO [Australian and New Zealand Standard Classification of Occupations] categories). Each category is marked by a number beneath the table, and in brackets are the raw numbers.

		ANZSCO Category								
		1	2	3	4	5	6	7	8	Not employed
Region A	Language program	5 (2)	5 (2)	8 (3)	53 (4)	5 (2)	3 (1)	20 (8)	3 (1)	(9)
	No language program	16 (5)	23 (7)	19 (6)	16 (5)	13 (4)	3 (1)	6 (2)	3 (1)	(10)
Region B	Language program	2 (1)	17 (9)	35 (18)	21 (11)	12 (6)	4 (2)	6 (3)	4 (2)	(11)
	No language program	3 (1)	29 (10)	9 (3)	15 (5)	12 (4)	12 (4)	12 (4)	9 (3)	(6)

Key: 1 Managers, 2 Professionals, 3 Technicians and Trades Workers, 4 Community and Personal Service Workers, 5 Clerical and Administrative Workers, 6 Sales Workers, 7 Machinery Operators and Drivers, 8 Labourers.

Table 3. Background information: occupation of parent(s).

In Table 4 are percentages (and raw numbers in brackets) of parents reporting their highest level of education as primary, secondary, technical college or university.

	Primary	Secondary	TAFE	University
Region A, language program	0	58 (28)	40 (19)	2 (1)
Region A, no language program	0	30 (13)	51 (22)	19 (8)
Region B, language program	3 (2)	36 (23)	39 (25)	22 (14)
Region B, no language program	0	33 (14)	35 (15)	33 (14)

Table 4. Background information: education of parent(s).

What we researched?

We had a 10–15 minute individual session with each child. The child completed two activities with verbal encouragement and general praise throughout. At the end each child received a sticker or hand stamp for participating. They were told they could stop if they wanted but all the children finished the full session.

In the first activity the child was shown pictures of familiar things (big and little) and asked if its name was big or little (for example the word caterpillar is a 'big', that is to say long name for a little thing). If a child can do this it tells us they can reflect on the sound of a word separate from its meaning, an early reading-related skill called word awareness. In using this task, we followed Yelland, Pollard & Mercuri (1993) who found stronger word awareness among English speaking Kindergarten children learning Italian after school. Most children, who were in Year 1 or 2, did very well in this task whether they were in a language program or not, so we do not discuss this activity further in this paper.

The second activity was to find out each child's level of decoding skills in English to see if that was related to learning an Aboriginal language. Each child completed the Martin and Pratt Nonword Reading Test (Martin & Pratt 2001); a standardised, five–ten minute individual test of decoding in English. The test uses nonsense words (for example yil, juf) so that it does not discriminate against children on the basis of vocabulary size (how many words they know in English). As nonwords all items are similarly unfamiliar to all children.

We administered the nonword reading test according to the test manual instructions. After the session we counted up an accuracy score for each child. We converted the accuracy score to a standardised score to take into account the child's age. Then we compared the groups to see if decoding scores were higher for children in a language program.

Results

We found some evidence that there is a relationship between children's decoding skill and whether or not they are learning an Aboriginal language in a revitalisation setting. In particular we found that while children's decoding skills in Year 1 did not differ depending on whether they were in a language program or not, in Year 2 there was a difference. In Year 2, children who were in a language program had stronger decoding skills in English than children who were not in a language program. Figure 1 shows the mean (average) scores for students in the different groups.

This was a statistically significant effect, meaning that it was unlikely (less than five chances out of 100) to have occurred by chance. We used a 2 x 2 x 2 ANOVA (analysis of variance) to see if standard scores for decoding were related to Program (whether or not the child was in a language program), Region (A versus B) and Year of School (Year 1 versus Year 2). There was a Program by Year interaction, $F(1,106) = 11.09$, $p = 0.001$ ($\eta_p^2 = 0.095$, that is a medium-sized effect). This means that the effect of being in a language program depended on the year of school the child was in.

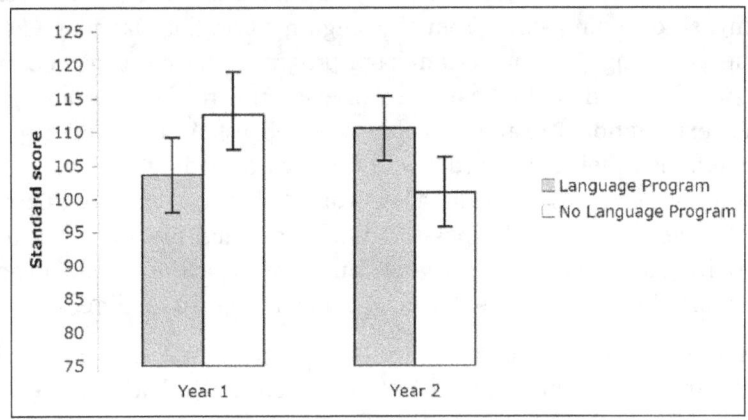

Figure 1. Relationships among school year, being in a language program, and decoding skill in English.

To explain the pattern in Figure 1 we did follow-up comparisons (that is post-hoc tests using Tukey-Kramer test for unequal n, critical value of $q_{3, 106, 0.05} / \sqrt{2} = 2.38$). These comparisons indicated that, statistically, decoding scores were the same in Year 1 for children in a language program versus children who were not, ($t = 1.90$). But, in Year 2, there is a difference: decoding scores are higher for children in a language program than for children who were not, ($t = 2.54$).

Decoding skills in our sample of children who were not in a language program were lower in Year 2 than in Year 1 ($t = 2.58$). All other differences among the average group scores in Figure 1 were not statistically different from each other.

Discussion

There are a number of limitations in our study that mean that we cannot draw strong conclusions from the data about any effect of Aboriginal language programs in revitalisation settings. We were restricted in the scope of our study by limitations including funding. We simply sampled groups of students from different years of schooling; we were not following the same students as they go from Year 1 to Year 2 (ours is a cross-sectional study, not a longitudinal one). Not all students in the schools participated; we simply worked with volunteers. We also knew which schools had a language program, and which did not, when we worked with the children. Our data collection methods were relatively protected from bias and expectations, but not completely. We also do not have detailed data about the nature of the English literacy programs in the different schools, and many other school factors that might also explain the results.

Given these limitations the pattern of results is suggestive of a positive relationship between English decoding skills from learning an Aboriginal language at school in a revitalisation setting. Without a language program, the performance of students in Year 2 was lower than in Year 1 relative to the reference norms (age-based performance expectations) of the nonword reading test. With a language program, students maintained their age-based level of nonword reading skill from Year 1 into Year 2, that is no decline in performance occurred. This is true in both geographical regions we studied. It is at least possible that additional practice with the regular phonemic writing system of the Aboriginal language as part of the language program acted to support children learning decoding skills in English reading.

This research is preliminary research; we have made a first step only. We need to do more research to be sure about our findings so far and to know exactly what is causing the differences in decoding skill. We also need to do more research to answer the broader question: What is the relationship between learning an Aboriginal language and students' reading (and writing) in English? This is a big question, but one which we think is well worth researching further.

Acknowledgements

We acknowledge the considerable contributions of Dr Jennifer Munro to the research project described here, and thank her for all her work. We thank the students who participated, the research assistant Caroline Haid who helped the students walk to and from class, the students' families and schools, principals, teachers and support staff at the participating schools, local and regional Aboriginal Education Consultative Groups, and the NSW Department of Education and Training. This project was supported by funds from the NSW Office of the Board of Studies and the Faculty of Education, University of Wollongong. The project received human ethics approval from the University of Wollongong (HREC 07/351).

References

Bialystok E, McBride-Chang C & Luk G (2005). Bilingualism, language proficiency, and learning to read in two writing systems. *Journal of Educational Psychology*, 97(4): 580–90.

Board of Studies New South Wales (2003). *Aboriginal Languages K–10 syllabus*. Sydney: Board of Studies New South Wales.

Castles A & Coltheart M (2004). Is there a causal link from phonological awareness to success in learning to read? *Cognition*, 91: 77–111.

Chiappe P & Siegel LS (1999). Phonological awareness and reading acquisition in English- and Punjabi-speaking Canadian children. *Journal of Educational Psychology*, 91: 20–28.

Cisero CA & Royer J (1995). The development and cross-language transfer of phonological awareness. *Contemporary Educational Psychology*, 20: 275–303.

Coltheart M & Prior M (2007). *Learning to read in Australia*. Occasional Paper 1/2007 Policy Paper 6. Canberra: The Academy of Social Sciences in Australia. Available: www.assa.edu.au/Publications/op/op12007.pdf [Accessed March 19, 2009].

Comeau L, Cormier P, Grandmaison E & Lacroix D (1999). A longitudinal study of phonological processing skills in children learning to read in a second language. *Journal of Educational Psychology*, 91(1): 29–43.

D'Angiulli A, Siegel LS & Serra E (2001). The development of reading in English and Italian bilingual children. *Applied Psycholinguistics*, 22: 479–507.

DaFountoura HA & Siegel LS (1995). Reading, syntactic and working memory skills of bilingual Portuguese-English Canadian children. *Reading and Writing: An Interdisciplinary Journal*, 7: 139–53.

Durgunoglu AY, Nagy WE & Hancin-Bhatt BJ (1993). Cross-language transfer of phonological awareness. *Journal of Educational Psychology*, 85(3): 453–65.

Geva E, Wade-Woolley L & Shany M (1993). The concurrent development of spelling and decoding in two different orthographies. *Journal of Reading Behavior*, 25(4): 383–406.

Gomez C & Reason R (2002). Cross-linguistic transfer of phonological skills: a Malaysian perspective. *Dyslexia*, (8): 22–33.

Gottardo A, Yan B, Siegel LS & Wade-Woolley L (2001). Factors related to English reading performance in children with Chinese as a first language: more evidence of cross-language transfer of phonological processing. *Journal of Educational Psychology*, 93(3): 530–42.

Luk G & Bialystok E (2008). Common and distinct cognitive bases for reading in English-Cantonese bilinguals. *Applied Psycholinguistics*, 29: 269–89.

Martin F & Pratt C (2001). *Martin and Pratt nonword teading test*. Camberwell, Vic.: Australian Council for Educational Research.

Rayner K, Foorman BR, Perfetti CA, Pesetsky D & Seidenberg MS (2001). How psychological science informs the teaching of reading. *Psychological Science in the Public Interest*, 2(2): 31–74.

Wang M, Perfetti CA & Liu Y (2005). Chinese-English biliteracy acquisition: cross-language and writing system transfer. *Cognition*, 97: 67–88.

Yelland G, Pollard J & Mercuri A (1993). The metalinguistic benefits of limited contact with a second language. *Applied Psycholinguistics*, 14: 423–44.

Yuwaalaraay Language Program (2003). *Yugal: Gamilaraay & Yuwaalaraay songs*. Tamworth, NSW: Coolabah Publishing.

25
English influence on the pronunciation of re-awakened Aboriginal languages

Nicholas Reid[1]

Abstract

This chapter explores the influence of literacy and teaching, by first language speakers of English, on the pronunciation of Aboriginal languages in the context of language re-awakening in New South Wales (NSW). Wherever languages are learned in the absence of a generation of first language speakers we find that the learners' first language will have a major impact – the linguistic resources that you have to build on play a strong role in shaping the new language that you acquire. This paper canvasses some pronunciation changes currently taking place in NSW in the context of learning revitalised languages. It raises the need for open discussion about the authenticity of re-created languages and argues that, for re-created languages, phonemic orthographies might not be the best choice. While this paper focuses on New South Wales its arguments may be relevant to other parts of the country where re-creation-type programs are underway.

What is being learned in revitalisation programs

Language re-awakening work undertaken in NSW typically involves learners whose first language is Australian English (from standard to Aboriginal English varieties) engaged in the learning of Aboriginal languages. The input that learners receive is generally either written language in the form of wordlists, learner guides or other pedagogical materials, or spoken language samples modeled by someone else who also learned pronunciation from written sources. In some lucky cases there are still Elders with enough speaking knowledge to record words as pronunciation guides, however the usual scenario involves careful decision-making about how words should be pronounced and sentences constructed, under two serious restrictions: the absence

---

1 School of Behavioural, Cognitive & Social Science, University of New England.

of any community of first language speakers of the target language, and the paucity of the materials available.

Such learning is fundamentally different from normal second language learning. When you learn a second language you can access information to answer any questions that arise, and you have the option of immersion among first language speakers. In NSW these options are not available. The paucity of materials available for even the best documented languages (probably Awabakal, Bundjalung, Gumbaynggirr, Paakantji and Wiradjuri), provide us with basic grammatical descriptions, but tell us little about such simple things as how to have a conversation.

Learning a language under these restrictions inevitably induces changes in that language. Some changes, such as creating new vocabulary, result from deliberate language engineering. Others, such as changes to pronunciation and grammar, are likely to be less deliberate and may largely result from the inherent difficulties of learning a language in the absence of native speaker models.

For these reasons, although the goals of revitalisation programs are often worded in terms of 'getting our old language back', the outcomes of many are likely to be quite different from the traditional languages that they are based on. This is no criticism, just a statement of the inevitable. No language has ever ceased to be spoken and then later revived in a way that is the *same* as the earlier form. Even the much-cited example of Israeli (Zuckermann 2005) turns out to now be, although healthy, a Germanic/Hebrew hybrid language, vastly different from Hebrew as it was last spoken. We understand now that, because any language reflects the communicative needs and social world of its speakers, the same language cannot do that for two groups of people displaced in time, society and culture. With respect to pronunciation in particular, wherever a generation of learners revitalises a language in the absence of first language speakers, the learners' first language will have a major impact on the sound system of the target language.

Details of the changes taking place

Here we consider some of the ways that changes are taking place in NSW languages in the context of revitalisation learning. We can find examples of induced change in all areas of language. Sometimes we find that verb suffixes become simplified, so that a single form of a verb is used in a non-inflecting way for all tense categories, for example in Paakantji the use of the present participle ending {-*ana*} on all remembered verb forms regardless of their actual tense (Thieberger 2002, p. 322). In other cases we find case marking on nouns either simplified or avoided, and even case suffixes detached and used like prepositions. Syntactically we can hear the development of simplified or fixed word order, often based on English. We also find many changes taking place in sound systems, and here we'll focus on just four types of pronunciation change.

Neutralisation of rhotic contrasts

Most NSW languages have traditional phonemic contrasts among more than one r sound – usually a flap or trill written as rr, contrasting with a continuant (more like the English r) often written as r. Some of the northern NSW coastal languages appear to have a third r sound. Many early written sources failed to distinguish among these sounds so, in many cases, it is difficult to know which pronunciation is right. In the context of language revitalisation programs many learners have circumvented the question by adopting various simplification strategies. Some pronounce the continuant r in all cases, a quite natural conflation for anyone whose first language is a variety of English. A few learners go the other way (what's known as *hyper-correction*) and pronounce the trill rr in all cases. Other people might adopt the strategy of using only one sound mostly, but being careful to distinguish between them for just those important minimal pairs, for example being careful to pronounce *wirri* and *wiri* differently, but otherwise just using a single r sound where it doesn't really affect the meaning.

Loss of variation in stop

Most NSW languages have just a single series of phonemic stops (sounds that block off airflow completely). Orthographies for these languages usually use a single series of symbols, either b, dh, d, dj, g or alternatively p, th, t, tj, k. In NSW the voiced symbols happen to have predominated, though there are some exceptions like Paakantji.

Being phonemes means that these stops function as contrasting sounds in the minds of their first language speakers. But choosing to write them with either b, dh, d, dj, g or with p, th, t, tj, k tells us nothing about how they would have been traditionally pronounced. In any given language it was likely that both voiced and unvoiced stop sounds could be heard, depending on what part of the word they appeared in and what other sounds surrounded them. To use a made-up example, a word [pabap] with unvoiced stops initially and finally but voiced stops medially, could be written phonemically as *babab* in one language but as *papap* in another, even though it is pronounced identically.

In NSW revitalisation programs, phonemic orthographies have been widely adopted under considered input from linguists who tend to promote them as being the best linguistic practice. They *are* best practice for first language and second language literacy, however phonemic orthographies tempt Aboriginal people trying to re-awaken a language in the absence of first language speakers, falling back on their knowledge of English orthography, to pronounce such words 'as they are spelled'. So *babab* tends to be pronounced as [babab], and *papap* tends to be pronounced as [papap].

This is happening quite widely in NSW, so we tend to now hear that Paakantji begins with a [p], and Gamilaraay with a [g], regardless of how they might have once been pronounced. Where previously in each language the phonetic realisation of stops depended on word position and preceding or following sounds, now that pattern is being replaced by one where stop sounds, at all places in a word, are more likely to be either all voiced or all voiceless. Because the voiced symbols have predominated in NSW, we are currently hearing an escalation of voiced stop pronunciations; that is, orthography is driving change in pronunciation.

Affricated realisation of palatal stops

While the finer articulatory details of the realisation of palatal stops can vary considerably across Aboriginal languages (see Butcher 1995), it is likely that when most NSW languages were spoken as first languages their palatal stops were unaffricated stops made with tongue tip down and blade raised. Now it is increasingly common to hear palatal stops (International Phonetic Alphabet [IPA] symbol [ɟ] and [c]) realised as palato-alveolar affricates (the j of English jam, IPA symbol [dʒ], or the ch of English chew, IPA symbol [tʃ]), so putative word *badjanu* is pronounced [bʌdʒʌnu] rather than [bʌɟʌnu]. This is phonetically a fairly natural shift, so a link to English is not necessary. However the influence of English is the likely explanation here. A contributing factor is the many, well-intended, learner pronunciation guides (see Reid 2008, p. 5 for an example) that casually describe palatal stops as being 'like ch in English 'chew''.

Neutralisation of unstressed vowels

Vowel inventories differ in only small ways across NSW with typically three vowel places and often also a short/long vowel contrast, yielding systems of six phonemic vowels, typically written as a, aa, i, ii, u, uu. As is fairly typical of small vowel systems (Butcher 1994) in NSW languages we find the traditional pattern of some minor allophony, but generally vowel phonemes are quite discrete. There is little evidence of any vowel sound being an allophone of more than one phoneme. Nor is there widespread evidence of the centralisation of unstressed vowels. This can be contrasted with English where schwa [ə] is an allophone of most vowel phonemes, and the common realisation of vowels in unstressed syllables.

The traditional patterns of word stress also varied, but there is evidence that stress on either the first syllable of a word or on long vowels were the most common patterns. This can be seen in the following Gamilaraay examples, where the length contrast between short i and long ii distinguishes two words with distinct meanings, and stress (indicated by bolding) is on the first syllable except where a non-first syllable is long:

yili	lip
yiili	savage
gunii	mother

Under contemporary language revitalisation it is common to hear schwa-like vowels and English-like stress patterns in the pronunciation of words in the languages of

NSW. English is the likely source of this. Of course it is not a new phenomenon that has just arisen in the context of language revitalisation, as all loanwords from Aboriginal languages into Australian English have long been pronounced this way. So, for example, well-known loanwords such as placenames assume typical English-like patterns of vowel neutralisation and primary and secondary stress, for example [pæ̀ɹəmǽtə] Parramatta, [jəgúnə] Yagoona, and [wəláɹə] Woollahra. It is no surprise then that the pronunciations arising in revitalisation classes have often followed the pattern of loanwords into English, dovetailed with learners' first language patterns, and resulted in new significantly different pronunciations of words where they are used as Aboriginal language words, for example [əwʌ́bəgal] Awabakal for what was probably once [ʌ́wʌbʌgʌl].

Vowel length contrasts are also changing under interference from English, although the picture here is complex. English vowels do not *systematically* involve length contrasts, and a quick look at the typical quadrilateral of Australian English vowels in a standard linguistics textbook suggests that each vowel occupies a unique space. The implication here, that all vowels involve different tongue configurations, is a simplification of the facts and in reality pairs like [i] and [ɪ], [u] and [ʊ], and especially [ʌ] and [a], do involve quasi-systematic differences in length. In language revitalisation contexts we can hear the traditional length contrast being reinterpreted in various ways. In some cases it is largely neutralised, in other cases it is being reinterpreted to align with the [i]/[ɪ], [u]/[ʊ], and [ʌ]/[a] vowel pairs in Australian English.

The four changes discussed above are just a small sample of some of the ways in which NSW languages are being re-created. Let's briefly touch on why these kinds of changes can happen, before considering how we might deal with them.

Why sound changes happen

The kinds of differences discussed in the section above arise for a variety of reasons, which range from unconscious influences to (semi-)conscious decisions.

All languages change all the time

All languages change naturally, so no healthy language is pronounced the same way across any significant span of time. If there were first language speakers of Dhurga alive today who'd miraculously remained unaffected by contact with English, their Dhurga would sound distinctly different to how Dhurga was in 1788.

Internal and external forces

Sometimes languages change because of the external influence of other languages; sometimes they change because of internal forces. We can illustrate both these processes with examples from contemporary Māori. In Māori the front vowels [e] and [ɛ] are raising, and the back vowels [u] and [ū] are fronting (King, Harlow, Watson, Keegan & Maclagan 2009). While it is possible that these changes are internally driven, the same sound changes have been taking place in New Zealand English over the same time period. As all Māori speakers also speak New Zealand English, it is likely that these changes have been either triggered, or at least strengthened, by one language affecting the other.

Conversely in contemporary Māori we find the sound [t] becoming palatalised before the vowel [i], so the names Matiu and Hineiti have shifted from [mætiu] to [mætʃiu], and from [hıneıti] to [hıneıtʃi]. These changes are naturally occurring ones. They are *not* also occurring in New Zealand English but they are phonetically plausible. There is a straightforward articulatory explanation for this change and unrelated examples of it have taken place in many languages around the world.

Substratum influence

Anyone learning a second language struggles with the influence of their first language. Our first language puts such a strong stamp on our mental conceptualisation of sounds that we are naturally poor at hearing sounds 'as they are'. To learn a second language we have to learn to hear differences among some sounds that our first language made us deaf to, and unhear contrasts to which our first language attuned us. Acquiring a second language phonology is difficult. Surprisingly few people acquire a second language without some accent, and that difficulty is compounded for learners in any revitalising scenario by limited source materials, and having no community of first language speakers to listen to. It is inevitable under such conditions that the learners' first language will have a major impact on the sound system of the revitalised language (Flege, Schirru & Mackay 2003).

Choosing a substratum-friendly system

Second language learners might choose to, or be content to, acquire a form of a language that is different from the first language speaker model. Such choices might be dictated by the learners' desire, in the face of practical constraints like time, to set as their goal something do-able. I recently met Australian expats in Vietnam who learned Vietnamese, baulked at the complexity of phonemic tone, and resolved the all-or-nothing nature of the tone system in favour of nothing. They carried on and learned to speak the language, but without engaging with tone at all. They'll never be great speakers, but their Vietnamese interlocutors accommodate to this, and they are functionally communicative in Vietnamese.

Similar examples abound in language maintenance contexts. Goodfellow (2003) describes how the youngest generation of Kwak'wala speakers have rephonologised their ancestral language in ways that mostly maintain contrasts found in English, but abandon contrasts not found in English. So their modern Kwak'wala phonology has lost glottalised consonants altogether, neutralised the distinction between velar and uvular consonants, and is further losing the velar fricative.

Language revitalisers can also make these kinds of deliberate choices. Consider the following hypothetical scenario:

- One Wiradjuri learning group aim to learn a form of Wiradjuri as close as possible to its traditional form, making careful effort to maintain a distinction between r and rr, have just three vowels without neutralised forms, and maintain the noun case system.
- A second Wiradjuri learning group aim instead to learn a form of Wiradjuri which employs largely English word order, abandons the case system but keeps the locative case suffix as a general preposition meaning in and on, and conflates r and rr to just r. They decide to write the language with an orthography best intended to help English speakers pronounce words.

This Wiradjuri scenario is hypothetical, but not far-fetched. The explosion in language revitalisation work around the world over the last decade is throwing up increasing numbers of cases where language revitalisers deliberately choose to acquire heavily substratum-influenced varieties. Let's briefly consider two North American examples.

The Esselen language from the mid-Californian coast is currently being revitalised by two sisters who each approach the task in very different ways. Deborah Miranda is motivated to revive Esselen in a manner most faithful to its earlier recorded form. Louise Miranda-Ramirez is less interested in the 'purity' of the form she acquires, and is happy to learn an English-influenced variety on the grounds that it provides her with a realistically achievable goal that satisfies her desire for a language of identity. Louise's Esselen reinterprets case suffixes as prepositions, and employs largely Subject-Verb-Object word order. In writing she detaches prefixes and writes them as separate words, where that parallels the English structure. So, for example, she writes *nish welel* (my language), where Deborah writes *nishwelel*. (L. Hinton, pers. comm., 28 March 2009). Louise's thoughts about this deliberately chosen stance are worth quoting here:

> The structure of our language is subject, object, and verb, but in my own Esselen writing, I also use our words in the typical English structure of subject, verb, and object ... After much intensive study of my language, I believe that it might be easier to create new prayers, stories, and other pieces using Esselen words in an English sentence structure ... I believe that using the words differently from our ancestors doesn't change the language. Do we choose not to change our own language for the satisfaction of a linguist to return an 'extinct' language? Hasn't the English language changed from all the 'thee-s and thou-s'? All languages change throughout the years: new words are created, and definition and usage change. (Miranda-Ramirez 2008–09, pp. 11–12).

Powell (1973, in Thieberger 2002) describes a language program in Quileute from west Washington state, which has highly complex word morphology with lots of inflections, making it hard to learn in the absence of a fluent first language speech community. The Quileute revivers' highest priority was to acquire a link with their heritage, and a salient badge of their Quileuteness. Faced with the complexity of the language they chose to learn a substrate-influenced form of Quileute. They employed the learning strategy of taking an English sentence and, by doing a word-for-word substitution, created a sentence using Quileute words but English word order, as in the following example:

> Give me half that candy,
>
> Give me half that lape',
>
> Hes me half sa' lape',
>
> Hes me tala'a sa' lape'. (Powell 1973, p. 6)

Linguistics as a discipline does not have a generally agreed-upon label for the kinds of deliberate choice exemplified here by Esselen and Quileute learners. Powell used the term *pidgin*, but this is an unfortunate choice for a second language learning strategy. Nor is *mixed language* a good option as it describes an outcome of bilingualism. Sandefur (1983) describes the use of Ngandi words with Kriol word order as *relexification*, but this label explicitly focuses on vocabulary. A better term might be *substratum influence* although it is mostly used in the literature to refer to the result of language shift, not second language learning. Thieberger (2002) recommends *re-creation* as an alternative. In the remainder of this paper to avoid further coinage I'll adopt re-creation.

Coming back to NSW it is clear that revitalisers have a choice – to aim for outcomes most like the traditional language, or to choose a re-created language as their goal. Re-created languages may be the only viable outcome for some revitalisation projects because of lack of sources. In other cases they may simply be chosen for more pragmatic reasons. In all cases they are at risk of being viewed as cases of 'insufficient learning', so let's turn our attention to attitudes about re-created language, the need for open discussion of the choices available, and the importance of identified goals in choosing how to write a language.

Re-created languages and conflicting views about authenticity

The unavoidable modernisation and induced change that are inherent in language revitalisation efforts can give rise to contestation within any revitalising community about issues of authenticity. Some will take a more conservative position and allow only revitalised language closest to the oldest remembered form to be viewed as authentic. Others will take a more change-friendly position and view a newly emergent variety of a language as being equally legitimate. Such contestations over authenticity have been discussed in the language revitalisation literature with respect to Hawai'ian (Wong 1999), Californian languages (Hinton & Ahlers 1999), and Māori (Crombie & Houia-Roberts 2001), but have received little discussion in Australia to date. With respect to pronunciation, claims about authenticity typically draw on the active ability of older speakers, as was possible for Māori in recent decades, so the pronunciation and vocabulary of revitalised Māori could still be anchored to the older remembered forms. In NSW however, for most languages there have now been several generations of no first language speakers, and thus there simply are no models that can provide definitive answers to the questions that modern revivalists need to ask.

This lack of anchoring to the past forms of the language licenses the *creat-* in language re-creation, and facilitates new hooks on which claims about authenticity might be hung.

Some of the potential tensions inherent in revitalisation work in NSW include the following.

Aboriginal language revitalisers have to negotiate potential mismatches between the rhetoric of getting the old language back, and the reality of the acquisition of a variety that is quite different to the old language, and in some obvious ways English-influenced. This difficulty can be heightened by comparison with, or criticism from, those who either speak 'more traditional' languages or are in a stronger position to revive a 'more traditional-sounding' variety. When the different outcomes of revitalisation projects with very different aims are not subject to open discourse, then issues of authenticity become harder to negotiate.

Linguists are usually trained for description of stable languages, and can be unprepared for the creativity of language re-creation. Regarding the authenticity of new languages, the same linguist can boldly counter misguided assertions about 'bastardised languages' by pointing out that creoles are indeed full rich languages deserving of recognition in their own right, but at the same time struggle to sanction language creation in process. This at least partly reflects the evolution of the discipline which arose around backwards-looking interests in the history of languages, and which has only become interested in language contact phenomena relatively recently.

Aboriginal people engaged in language re-awakening felt caught in a 'powerful educated academic' versus 'powerless Indigenous revitaliser' paradigm and have struggled to persuade linguists that language revitalisation does not have the same goals or methods as descriptive or historical linguistics, but that nevertheless it is a serious form of contact linguistics. A clear articulation of this view can be found on the Victorian Aboriginal Corporation for Languages website:

> Linguists who work with communities in this area sometimes find we have to reinvent our own discipline as we go. Linguistics has mostly developed in terms of languages that develop continuously over time, that are passed down to children in their natural home learning environments and used by a large community in lots of different contexts. The discipline doesn't yet have established ways of understanding about languages that have been silenced and then begin to re-emerge, languages that rely heavily on written sources, languages that involve a lot of planning and decision-making by their communities, languages that change because there are words missing or knowledge lost, or because their communities want to bring the needs of the new century into their language ... thorough description of what revival languages are like will greatly assist in: getting revival languages recognised and understood in the linguistics community, reducing the battle that people have in getting the ways they use their languages taken seriously, helping communities to have a clearer view of

the pathways of language revival, and including the needs of revival languages in the training of student linguists. (n.d.)

The last decade has seen this paradigm partly eroded, and increasing evidence that revitalisers in NSW are quietly and busily doing their own thing. The formal context of revitalisation programs with input from linguists focusing very heavily on normalised historical data, phonemic orthographies, adhering to the 'the rules' of revitalisation, and treating as 'right language' those texts produced and sanctioned by the project, often succeeds in producing outcomes consistent with the rules. But outside those formal contexts, when Aboriginal people are simply enjoying using their language among themselves in insider-only settings, they tend to be much more creative and their output less closely aligned to patterns learned in the classroom (J. Troy, pers. comm., 9 March 2009).

In the Australian context we need to move beyond these tensions and generate increased discussion of these issues for two good reasons. Revitalisers are out there doing great things, some aiming for more traditional language goals, others pushing further into re-created language goals. We need ways of understanding that re-created language outcomes are legitimate in their own right. We require the vocabulary to make these different types of outcome more discussable. And we need clear identification of goal types in order to make smart choices about orthographies.

These discussions would be helped by pointing out a limitation of the Australian Indigenous Languages Framework (AILF) descriptions of language program types – what can thought of as the *re-* words (revitalisation, revival, renewal, reclamation). These labels are all redolent, by virtue of the again sense of the prefix, of some kind of return to the old form of a language. Because these classifications are concerned with resources, not outcomes, they do not distinguish those projects that deliberately aim for a variety that is not the same as the traditional language. We can illustrate this with reference to the hypothetical Wiradjuri scenario discussed earlier. In AILF descriptor terms these two very different types of project would both fall under 3.1 Language Renewal because they involve the same situational/resource characteristics such as the absence of 'right through' speakers, the 'presence of active language identification', and the 'significant amount of linguistic heritage' (Senior Secondary Assessment Board of South Australia 1996, p. 22). Our lack of labelling for projects with such different outcomes has probably contributed to the tensions alluded to above and made it more difficult for re-created language work to be acknowledged as a legitimate activity in its own right.

Outcome-focus and its implications for pronouncing and writing language

A focus on type of outcome holds implications for the way in which we develop curriculum resources. Here we'll focus on the phonology of the revitalised language and show how identifying type of outcome has major implications for how we pronounce the language we are learning, and how we choose to write it.

Where the intention is to relearn a traditional variety of a language, the smart writing system will be one that is maximally phonemic. This means that learners make the effort to learn to pronounce words as they were spoken by native speakers and write words in the way native speakers would have found sensible. In effect this is like second language learning where the deliberate aim is to acquire the ability to speak like a native speaker. Of course like all second language learners, you may never be fully fluent, you may always have an accent, and your vocabulary might be limited. The important thing is not the level of attainment, but that the variety of language you are aiming for is pronounced as the last of the first language speakers pronounced it. In the case of a NSW language this would involve aiming to learn a new phonology that is different from English. In real terms this would involve such things as learning to hear and pronounce:

- stops and nasals at different places of articulation – so that *yadhu*, *yadu* and *yardu* all sound different
- the difference between rr and r
- vowel sounds as i and a and u without neutralising them to [ə]
- vowel length contrasts among i and ii, u and uu, and a and aa
- words with the stress patterns of the target language, and so on.

Learning a new phonology is not easy. However, where there is enough known about how the language used to be pronounced, this can and should be done – this is the normal goal of second language learning. When adopting this approach to language revitalisation you'll want a phonemic orthography, that is one that employs an unchanging symbol to uniquely represent each phoneme of the target language.

However revitalisers also face the option of aiming for a very different type of outcome, deliberately choosing to learn a re-created variety of a language that is quite different from its traditional form. There are many reasons this might be an appropriate choice: the language might have too-limited resources; the learner might know from experience that they aren't very good at learning second languages; or might be a good second language learner but know that learning without access to a native speaker community is too difficult. Like the Quileute speakers discussed above, they might decide that a re-created, English-influenced Aboriginal language still serves as a means of cultural connection, provides a link with their heritage, and constitutes a public emblem of their Aboriginal identity.

This means that you choose to speak the language in a way that is strongly influenced by your actual mother tongue, which is likely to be somewhere in the range between Standard Australian and Aboriginal English. With respect to the sounds in particular, this strategy involves a rephonologised approach whereby you would pronounce words with an English-like set of phonemes. Note that this is not like second language learning where your deliberate aim is to acquire the ability to speak like a native speaker. In real terms this would involve such choices as:

- distinguishing stops and nasals at just bilabial, alveolar, palatal and velar places of articulation, and neutralise the contrast among dental, alveolar and retroflex. So *yadhu*, *yadu* and *yardu* all would be pronounced [yadu]
- pronouncing all r sounds the same way (which could all be the continuant r, as in English red, or all be the trill/flap rr)
- pronouncing vowels in unstressed syllables as schwa [ə]
- stressing words following English stress patterns, as though they were loanwords into English.

There will be some negative consequences of these decisions. Neutralising the contrast among *yadhu*, *yadu* and *yardu* would have the effect of creating homophones; sets of words that sound the same but have different meanings. This is not necessarily a huge problem. Most languages cope with a certain amount of homophony and context generally disambiguates them. However you might have to develop other strategies where a particular pair of homophones creates a real problem.

Most importantly, if you adopt a rephonologised strategy as your approach, when it comes to spelling you will not want to try and represent this language with a traditional phonemic orthography. If you did you would be spelling words unlike the way you say them, and this will create difficulties in learning to spell. In cases like this the smart writing system might well be one that is non-phonemic. The benefits of a non-phonemic orthography can already be seen operating in the very languages for which not much modern phonemic orthographic work has yet been done.

To take Dharug as an example, the earlier wordlists from Dawes (1790–91) and King (1790/2006) right through to Ridley (1875) spelled words in non-phonemic ways, using both voiced and voiceless stop symbols. These words were recorded by people who, by virtue of being native English speakers and thus hearing voicing contrasts, faithfully recorded allophonic detail of Dharug speakers' pronunciations that those speakers themselves were deaf to. It follows then that the more 'phonetic' writing system for Dharug could now help modern relearners to pronounce these words in a manner even more consistent with old Dharug than a phonemic orthography might. Such wordlists could of course be cleaned up and made phonemic, but under a language re-creation scenario sensible arguments could be made for maintaining a non-phonemic writing system.

There has been some work undertaken already which can serve as a model for what non-phonemic writing systems for NSW languages might look like. Troy & Walsh (2009) and Reid (2002) discuss applied philology projects involving placenames, where decisions about spellings for Aboriginal words are approached specifically and deliberately from the perspective of how English speakers might pronounce them most faithfully. Where language revitalisers make deliberate choices to learn re-created languages with rephonologised pronunciations, such models might offer orthographic choices that make more sense to readers, and which, in some cases at least, might lead to pronunciations surprisingly faithful to the earlier form of the language.

Acknowledgements

This paper benefitted from useful suggestions, observations, and examples from Rob Amery, Tamsin Donaldson, Christine Eira, Mary-Anne Gale, John Giacon, Richard Green, John Hobson, Harold Koch, Cat Kutay, Amanda Lissarrague, Amanda Oppliger, Susan Poetsch, Mari Rhydwen, Nick Thieberger, Jaky Troy, Michael Walsh, and Greg Wilson. I am grateful to each of these people for their helpful input, but they would not all be in full agreement with my argument, for which I take sole responsibility.

References

Butcher AR (1994). On the phonetics of small vowel systems: evidence from Australian languages. In R Togneri (Ed). *Proceedings of the 5th Australian International Conference on Speech Science and Technology.* Vol 1 (pp. 28–33). Canberra, Australia: Australian Speech Science and Technology Association.

Butcher AR (1995). The phonetics of neutralisation: the case of Australian coronals. In J Windsor Lewis (Ed). *Studies in general and English phonetics. essays in honour of Professor J. D. O'Connor* (pp. 10–38). London, UK: Routledge.

Crombie W & Houia-Roberts N (2001). The rhetorical organisation of discourse: language revitalisation and the question of authenticity. *He Puna Kōrero: Journal of Māori and Pacific Development,* 2(2): 57–68.

Dawes W (1790–91). Vocabulary of the language of N.S. Wales, in the neighbourhood of Sydney. (native and English). ms. Marsden Collection, School of Oriental and African Studies, London.

Flege JE, Schirru C & MacKay IRA (2003). Interaction between the native and second language phonetic subsystems. *Speech Communication,* 40(4): 467–91.

Goodfellow A (2003). The development of 'new' languages in Native American communities. *American Indian Culture & Research Journal,* 27(2): 41–59.

Hinton L & Ahlers J (1999). The issue of 'authenticity' in California language restoration. *Anthropology & Education Quarterly.* 30(1): Authenticity and Identity: Lessons from Indigenous Language Education, 56–67.

King J, Harlow R, Watson C, Keegan P & Maclagan M (2009). Changing pronunciation of the Māori language: implications for revitalization. In J Reyhner & L Lockhead (Eds). *Indigenous language revitalization: encouragement, guidance & lessons learned* (pp. 75–86). Flagstaff, Arizona: Northern Arizona University.

King PG (2006). Eora: a Sydney vocabulary 1790 [facsimile edition]. Sydney: State Library of New South Wales. (Extract from the journal of PG King, April 1790 and from John Hunter's An historical journal of the transactions at Port Jackson and Norfolk Island 1793 published in conjunction with the exhibition Eora: Mapping Aboriginal Sydney 1770–1850, 5 June to 13 August 2006.

Miranda-Ramirez LJ (2008). Breathing language. *News from Native California*, 22(2): 8–12.

Powell JV (1973). Raising pidgins for fun and profit: a new departure in language teaching. In *Proceedings of the Pacific Northwest Conference on Foreign Languages*, 17, (pp. 40–43), Kingston, Ontario: Pacific Northwest Council for Languages.

Reid N (2002). Creating Aboriginal placenames: applied philology in Armidale city. In J Simpson & F Hodges (Eds). *The land is a map: placenames of Indigenous origin in Australia*, (pp. 241–54), Canberra, Australia: Pacific Linguistics.

Reid N (2008). *Ngan'gi dictionary*. Armidale, NSW: Australian Linguistics Press.

Ridley W (1875). *Kámilarói and other Australian languages*. 2nd Ed. Sydney: Thomas Richards, Government Printer.

Sandefur J (1983). The Quileute approach to language revival programs. *The Aboriginal Child at School*, 11(5): 3–16.

Senior Secondary Assessment Board of South Australia (1996) *Australia's Indigenous languages framework*. Wayville, SA: Senior Secondary Assessment Board of South Australia.

Thieberger N (2002). Extinction in whose terms? which parts of a language constitute a target for language maintenance programmes? In D Bradley & M Bradley (Eds). *Language endangerment and language maintenance* (pp. 310–28). New York: Routledge Curzon.

Troy J & Walsh M (2009). Reinstating Aboriginal placenames around Port Jackson and Botany Bay. In H Koch & L Hercus (Eds). *Aboriginal placenames: naming and re-naming the Australian landscape*. Aboriginal History Monograph 19 (pp. 55–69) Canberra: Aboriginal History Inc and ANU E Press.

Victorian Aboriginal Corporation for Languages (n.d.) *Typology project* [Online]. Available: www.vaclang.org.au/project-detail.aspx?ID=26 [Accessed 18 April 2009].

Wong L (1999). Authenticity and the revitalization of Hawaiian. *Anthropology & Education Quarterly*. 30(1): Authenticity and Identity: Lessons from Indigenous Language Education, 94–115.

Zuckermann G (2005). The Israeli language. *The Mendele Review: Yiddish Literature and Language*. 9(3) [Online]. Available: yiddish.haifa.ac.il/tmr/tmr09/tmr09013.htm [Accessed 1 April 2009].

Part Six
Language and technology

Introduction
Language and technology

John Hobson[1]

Technology or, more particularly, information (and communication) technology has become a pervasive element of language revitalisation work over recent decades, and it can be difficult to think of current language activities where some form of technology is not used to record, analyse or transmit the language, increasingly in integrated forms that support sound, images and text. Linguists and language workers have often been among the first to access each innovation as it comes along and test its potential to capture and present rich language data for preservation, future investigation or learning purposes. Some significant contemporary Australian examples not represented in this volume include the Ara Irititja project,[2] Miromaa database,[3] Gayarragi, Winangali CD-ROM[4] and the Ninti language learning site[5] attached to the Ngapartji Ngapartji project (Sometimes & Kelly, this volume), as well as initiatives still under development to use video-conferencing and networked facilities to teach languages to their distributed owner populations.

However, while many are justifiably attracted to high-tech solutions for language revitalisation needs because of their high profile, apparent potential as a quick fix, and ease to fund as short-term, self-contained projects, it can also sometimes seem that otherwise successful initiatives not deemed to be cutting edge are not considered as valid. This enthusiasm for the new needs to be balanced against the apparent limitations of technology and the usefulness of its application. Witness, for example, the number of high-cost CD-ROMs that were going to 'save' a language but sadly collect dust on shelves because they failed to stimulate more than one viewing or no longer run under this year's software, as well as the ongoing crisis of salvaging audio- and videotape recordings of language 'preserved' only a decade or so past.

---

1 Koori Centre, University of Sydney.

2 See www.irititja.com

3 See www.miromaa.com.au

4 See www.yuwaalaraay.org

5 See ninti.ngapartji.org

Ostler (1999, cited in Hinton 2001, p. 267) has identified computer-based technologies as anti-traditional and deskilling in their nature, arguing that they often alienate Elders, are unnecessarily expensive and subject to rapid obsolescence, while Kroskrity & Reynolds observe that, 'the most important thing in language revitalization is to increase the opportunities for speakers to use and learn their ancestral language in interpersonal exchange ... [and that] multimedia technology will never replace this as the highest order priority' (2001, p. 328). Similarly Zhao (2005) provides a very telling meta-analysis of the broader use of technology in language learning, suggesting that, despite its widely assumed effectiveness, there is currently only limited evidence 'that technology-based language instruction can be as effective as teacher-delivered instruction' (p. 31).

Clearly technology in language revitalisation can be a double-edged sword, and it behoves us to think carefully before assuming it will always provide the best answer to our needs. In this regard Bird & Simons (2003), while primarily discussing the portability of data for language documentation and description, comprehensively articulate standards of good and bad practice that warrant wider application in this field, and should perhaps be compulsory reading.

Notwithstanding these issues the applications of technology to language revitalisation reported in this volume provide us with some exciting examples of what is being attempted and can be achieved locally.

Wilson's discussion of the use of the increasingly ubiquitous mobile (cell) phone to provide access to electronic dictionaries explicitly responds to key issues of best practice for data storage, while documenting a creative and effective way of bypassing the limitations of computer and network access for remote and mobile Indigenous Australian communities. Utilising the computing potential of these hand-held devices, speakers and learners of an increasing number of languages can have ready access to a significant complementary resource regardless of their location; they can always keep the language with them. This is an example of innovative elegance in the Australian revitalisation context that seems clearly destined for export to the rest of the world.

Bowe, Reid & Lynch report on the successful collaboration among linguists and technologists to retrieve archival records and sketch grammars of multiple Victorian languages from obscure locations and place them directly into the hands of revitalising communities and academic linguists through the medium of the internet. The *Aboriginal Languages of Victoria Resource Portal* is strongly based in open source software and has undergone substantial useability testing and development in terms of both its architecture and interface which the authors document at length, providing an excellent script for others to follow. Community consultation and user-centred design have been cornerstones of the project that combines static, reference content coupled with the dynamic facility for community members to contribute their own in multiple formats. It is clearly a profound leap forward in accessibility for Victorian language communities and has potential to be a significant locus of revitalisation activity for the region.

Similarly located in the application of open source software, Kutay, Fisher & Green document a series of bold attempts by technologist and community members to develop a generic set of utilities to assist in the documentation and teaching of NSW languages. Canvassing a broad range of possibilities, including speech synthesis and recognition as well as machine translation, they have sought to create computer resources that will generate teaching materials and directly support people learning their own languages. Their paper documents their journey, some of the pitfalls they have encountered and the outcomes to date.

Elsewhere in this volume Amery (Chapter 4), Gale & Sparrow (Chapter 32) and Giacon (Chapter 34) offer further discussion of the use of technology in revitalisation activities, particularly the application of FileMaker Pro to database management and, in the case of Amery, the addition of a web interface that affords integration with Google Earth allowing the virtual mapping of language onto the land. Eira & Solomon-Dent (Chapter 31) also discuss the application of recorded interactions in virtual classroom environments as a way to inform communities about the developmental processes being applied to their languages. Collectively these papers provide an encouraging, indicative snapshot of current directions in the application of technology to Indigenous Australian languages revitalisation.

References:

Bird S & Simons G (2003). Seven dimensions of portability for language documentation and description. *Language*, 79: 557–82.

Hinton L (2001). Audio-video documentations. Chapter 21 in L Hinton & K Hale (Eds). *The green book of language revitalization in practice*, (pp. 265–71). San Diego: Academic Press.

Kroskrity PV & Reynolds JF (2001). On using multimedia in language renewal: observations from making the CD-ROM 'Tataduhaan'. Chapter 25 in L Hinton & K Hale (Eds). *The green book of language revitalization in practice*, (pp. 317–29). San Diego: Academic Press.

Zhao Y (2005). Recent developments in technology and language learning: a literature review and meta-analysis. Chapter 2 in Y Zhao (Ed). *Research in technology and second language learning education*, (pp. 17–37). Greenwich, Conn.: Information Age Publishing.

26
Increasing the accessibility of information on the Indigenous languages of Victoria

Heather Bowe[1], Julie Reid,[2] and Kathy Lynch[3]

Abstract

The authors have developed a web resource portal that allows easy access to information about the Aboriginal languages of Victoria. Written records of Victorian Aboriginal languages include language resources gathered in the 18th and early 19th centuries by government officials and interested private citizens. Some material was published at the time of collection, and is available in the reference collections of major libraries. Other material is only available in manuscript sources in research libraries or on microfiche. In the last 50 years linguists have analysed such material producing overview classifications of the languages of Victoria and, in some instances, complex linguistic descriptions of a particular language. These descriptions, called sketch grammars, are not easy to understand without linguistic training. The portal will enable non-linguists to access this vital language information via the web and provides a comprehensive list of sources for all of the major Victorian languages arranged according to the linguistic classification developed by Hercus (1969, 1986), Dixon (1980, 2002), and Blake & Reid (1998).

The resource portal is presented according to geographical regions and languages. It provides a window to information on the languages, their relationship to each other, lists of academic and historical resources, comparative wordlists, simplified grammars with examples, and comprehensive lists of the words collected for each language. It also allows for the uploading of community created resources, such as stories and images, together with an online discussion area. The site has the capability to be expanded to add comprehensive detail for all languages of Victoria, subject to funding constraints.

---

1 School of Languages, Cultures and Linguistics, Monash University.
2 School of Languages, Cultures and Linguistics, Monash University.
3 ICT Research and Development, University of the Sunshine Coast.

Accessing the information provided by the portal may save communities years of preparatory work when they undertake their language revitalisation programs.

Over the last 20 years Victorian Aboriginal people have demonstrated a resurgence of interest in their language heritage as they assert their Aboriginal identity as emerging writers, playwrights, educators and scholars (for example McKay 1996; James 2003; Gascoigne 2004; Walsh & Troy 2005). Aboriginal community initiatives have been undertaken by the Worawa Independent Aboriginal College, the Lodjba Koori Language Centre and, subsequently, the Victorian Aboriginal Corporation for Languages (VACL). The native title process has also made interest in Victorian language heritage more visible. The Yorta Yorta claim, although not successful, involved significant research by Aboriginal and non-Aboriginal people on the Aboriginal history of the Murray-Goulburn area. In 2005 the success of the land claim negotiated with the Government of Victoria by the Wotjobulak people of the western district of Victoria involved important academic and community research, and has also resulted in community-initiated language reclamation research. Other Aboriginal community language reclamation activities have been initiated by interested individuals, such as the introduction of the Gunnai language into early childhood centres in Gippsland by Lynnette Solomon-Dent.

In 1992 the Victorian Curriculum and Assessment Authority (VCAA) developed an *Indigenous languages of Victoria, revival and reclamation: Victorian Certificate of Education study design* in response to a request from Worawa Aboriginal College. The study ran as a pilot VCE study from 1995 to 2003 and was fully accredited in 2004. It has been successfully completed by members of several communities, most recently by a group of Wotjobaluk people in 2008 (see J. Reid, this volume). In all over 30 Indigenous students have successfully completed these studies. The study process requires students to learn to locate historical sources for Victorian Aboriginal languages and to acquire the skills necessary to analyse this material as part of the language reclamation process. Access to key historical and academic resources for Victorian Aboriginal languages is a crucial part of the implementation of this VCE study. In addition individual schools and the VCAA are working on the development of a P–10 curriculum for the Aboriginal languages of Victoria, so access to historical and academic resources for primary school teachers and Koori educators will also be crucial in the future.

Sources

Written records of Victorian Aboriginal languages include language resources gathered in the 18th and early 19th centuries by government officials and interested private citizens. Some material was published at the time it was collected and is available in the reference collections of major libraries. Other material is only available in manuscript sources in research libraries or on microfiche. More recently linguists, including Hercus (1969, 1986), Dixon (1980, 2002), and Blake and Reid (1998), have provided significant classifications of Victorian languages and the classification used in this web portal is based on their research. This classification was also followed by Clark (1990). The languages are presented in linguistic groupings using spellings recommended by VACL, where available:

1. Kulin Languages

    Western Kulin (North Western Victoria)

        Wemba Wemba (Swan Hill and Lake Boga)

        Barababaraba (Gunbower area)

        Madhi Madhi (Balranald area)

        Ladji Ladji (Mildura area)

        Wadi Wadi (Swan Hill)

        Wadi Wadi (Piangil)

        Wergaia (Wimmera)

        Djab Wurrung (Grampians)

        Dja Dja Wurrung (Loddon Valley)

        Jardwadjali (Upper Glenelg River)

    Eastern Kulin (Melbourne and surrounds)

        Taungurung (Goulburn Valley - southern)

        Woiwurrung (Yarra Valley)

        Boon Wurrung (Coastal Melbourne and Westernport)

    Wathaurong (Geelong/Barwon Valley area)

    Gulidjan (Lake Colac area)

2. Warrnambool Language (Warrnambool-Portland)

    Dhauwurd Wurrung

    Keeray Woorroong

    Tyakoort Wooroong

3. Buandig (Mt Gambier area)

4. Yorta Yorta and Jabulajabula/Bangerang (Murray Goulburn)

5. Dhudhuroa (High Country)

6. Pallanganmiddang (Kiewa Valley area)

7. Gunnai/Kurnai (Gippsland area)

      Brataualung (Corner Inlet area)

      Krautungalung (Lake Tyers area)

      Brabralung (Mitchell River)

      Tatungalung (Gippsland Lakes)

      Braikaulung (Latrobe River)

8. Ngarigu (Monaro/Snowy)

Linguists, including Hercus (1969, 1986), Blake (1991, 2003a, 2003b), Blake & Reid (1998, 1999, 2002), Blake, Clark & Reid (1998), Blake, Clark & Krishna-Pillay (1998), Bowe (2002), Bowe & Morey (1999), and Fesl (1985) have analysed the available material for particular languages, and much of this work is now available in published books and journals. In addition some linguists (for example Krishna-Pillay 1996) have been sponsored by local Aboriginal groups to write dictionaries and grammars of their heritage language, funded by Aboriginal organisations such as VACL. Bowe, Peeler & Atkinson (1997) is the result of collaborative research that involved Aboriginal collaborators and a linguist, and connected the contemporary language heritage of the Yorta Yorta people with historic sources. This research was initially funded by the Lodjba Koori Language Centre, and its publication was funded by the Aboriginal and Torres Strait Islander Commission, Victoria. Furthermore, work on Aboriginal languages is a routine part of linguistic research in many universities.

Although most of the recently published linguistic descriptions are relatively widely available, those engaged in language research often find these academic works difficult to interpret and wish to have access to the original source material, the bulk of which is not held in Victoria. Linguists working in this area of research have each needed to acquire their own collection of photocopies of historical material by personally visiting interstate libraries and photocopying material, ordering photocopies where possible, and inspecting original documents for clarification purposes.

The resource portal

The portal incorporates multi-layered access to primary source data and primary linguistic research, thus providing a crucial resource for members of the wider community interested in the Aboriginal languages of Victoria. At the same time the level of detail contained in the repository, and the online access to primary resources, is of value to academic researchers. It incorporates a repository containing references to primary (historical) and secondary (academic) resources for each language featured on the site.

The languages of the Murray-Goulburn (Yorta Yorta, Bangerang, Jabulajabula), Melbourne and surrounds (Woiwurrung, Boon Wurrung, Taungurung), Gippsland (Gunnai/Kurnai), and Western Victoria (Wergaia only) have individual vocabulary modules some of which include pronunciation (audio) and a proposed spelling for each word. Within these modules all source material for each vocabulary entry is linked to that entry. Other material, such as archival audiotapes of the language, can be included in the repository subject to access conditions. A simplified grammar describing the various linguistic elements of the language, with relevant examples where available, is included for each of these languages along with instructions on sentence construction for that language. General information on the location of the heritage language speakers, their social organisation, and their relationship to other languages in the area is also provided.

A particularly useful feature of the site is the Victorian Word Finder, which allows users to select a word in English, and view its equivalent in all languages that have recordings for this word on the site. In addition the site has some basic information on Australian Aboriginal languages in general.

Significantly the portal addresses the problem of access to crucial resources relating to the Aboriginal languages of Victoria. As most of the archival and historical resources are held in research libraries in Melbourne, Sydney and Canberra they are, in practical terms, not easily accessible. Furthermore because of the disparate backgrounds of the early writers and the academic terminology of modern linguistic research much of the information, when it can be accessed, is very difficult for a non-linguist to process. The site uses a database and layered report system to present language information in an accessible format backgrounding analytic reference and explanation for individual extension.

Behind the portal

Web portal growth began in the late 1990s in the domain of large companies. A portal is an entry point or a gateway to something. It provides access to a number of sources of information and facilities such as a directory of links to other websites, search engines, or email. Web portals commonly have a diverse target audience, therefore their design needs to be intuitive and informative.

When developing a portal it is important to build a site knowing, if not using, all the success factors of user acceptance of a portal. Winkler (2001) has identified a number of these factors. They are:

- **search and navigation** functionality, through presenting to the user appropriate information, suggesting additional information resources or services, allowing the user to search the contents of the portal, and perhaps giving users the ability to personalise resources and tools. However, not all web portals have these functions, as it depends on the prime purpose of the portal itself;
- **information integration**, to provide users with the ability to integrate information from disparate sources, through the use of a news service, wiki or blog;
- **personalisation**, through customisable content or services, or content based on user group or user preferences;
- **notification**, through push technology or email services;

- **tools and services** to improve the flow of the site, through customisation of personal preferences, or tutorial or help;
- **collaboration** among users of the portal, through the use of services such as discussion lists, wikis, messaging systems, and common workspaces (adapted from Winkler 2001).

Portal architecture

There are numerous approaches that can be used when developing web-based systems. For the *Aboriginal Languages of Victoria Resource Portal* (ALV-RP) the method used was a combination of the Web Site Design Method (WSDM) developed by De Troyer and Leune (1998) and the engineering approach developed by Lowe and Hall (1999). Both models have a focus on user-centred design in the development of the look and feel of the site and its navigation. WSDM relies on input from use-cases (or scenarios) to determine the requirements of each user type to define the information objects based on the information requirements of the users. The Lowe and Hall approach, among other requirements, suggests that the development is done in incremental steps.

The ALV-RP development team comprised an overall project manager, two sub-teams (information and communication technology [ICT] and linguistics) and two industry groups of stakeholders (government educators and Aboriginal organisations). The ICT team was located in Queensland and comprised a leader, programmers, graphic artist, and a research assistant. The linguistic team, located in Victoria, was composed of a leader, linguist, and research assistant.

During the development process the portal underwent three major iterations, each serving the dual purpose of testing the software development platform, content layout and content (or artefact in the form of text, images, and audio). Each iteration was tested for usability and user acceptance with the feedback used to inform the next stage (Lynch & Bowe 2006).

The development of the portal underwent continual content, programming and interface refinement and development. The choice of the programming language to be used for the site changed during each iteration until the most suitable language (and platform) was found, as the requirements for the site were complex.

The first version of the site was developed quickly to demonstrate the initial proof of concept, and thus used HTML (Hypertext Markup Language) as it is the rudimentary programming language used for presenting content on a web page, is quick and easy to use, and would produce a basic prototype without over-extending the limited resources of the team. This version contained limited content with very little capability for user interaction other than clicking through a few pages of content.

The next version of the site was developed using PHP (which originally stood for Personal Home Page, but has long since lost this meaning). PHP is a widely used, general purpose, open source (that is, free) programming language that is especially suited to web sites that are integrated with a database (in this case, Microsoft Access).

This version also had limited content and allowed little user interaction. However, page design templates were developed that enabled multiple pages to be presented using the same layout without them having to be individually marked up as was done with the first version using HTML. The content was more developed insofar as there was more of it and its display was controlled by database queries. Having the content in a database made the maintenance of the content much more streamlined, efficient and consistent. Most of the content obtained from the linguists was uploaded into the system using spreadsheet data and manually checked for inconsistencies and omissions. The remaining content was manually uploaded via online forms. This version was labour intensive with regard to programming, restrictive in developing a community space, and susceptible to content inconsistencies and omissions.

The final version of the site was developed using Drupal, an open source content management framework and social networking system written in PHP, integrated with a MySQL (Structured Query Language) database. Drupal was selected as the final platform for the development of the portal because it is open source (free and written in PHP) and is in wide use. It also has the flexibility to add characteristics to content type, for example defining access permissions for a particular language (a content type) or a particular piece of content such as an image; has free off-the-shelf applications, such as calendars that can be integrated into the application; in-built functionality, such as searching; and social networking capabilities, such as adding friends.

MySQL was selected as the database platform as it is robust, has advanced in-built security, and is an industry standard.

One of the advantages of using Drupal is that it contains a broad range of relevant features that are continuously developed by a large community of open source developers. The use of this platform enables this project to leverage knowledge and ideas in the ICT community to enhance the architecture and construction of this web portal.[4] Drupal enables the consistent collection and template-based presentation of content by defining content types with custom field names that are meaningful to programmers and linguists alike.

Content is of two types. Project content has been placed on the site during the development process by the project team. This includes general information about the portal, languages addressed in the project, references, language sources, a glossary, and biographies of recorders and researchers. The richness of the portal is through the presentation of wordlists from a wide range of historical sources and sketch grammars for each of the languages represented, a word finder enabling a comparison of Aboriginal words among languages, and a generic search on any word in the portal. This content is static in the sense that it cannot be edited by anyone other than the project team.

---

4 Our current implementation leverages the following key Drupal modules: CCK, Views, Biblio, TinyMCE, MCE and Organic groups. In addition we have developed custom code and templates as needed, where there is not already a community-developed solution for the features required.

On the other hand, the social or community content is dynamic as it can be constantly changing. It is placed on the site by the community, which is any individual who wishes to share their content, information or knowledge with others as a whole, or within a specific group. Community content is open for editing, comment, and discussion. It can be categorised according to *tags* decided upon by the person who provides them. Through the use of these tags the community content can be displayed in a number of places in the resource. For example when a person registers as one who is interested in Yorta Yorta, all content and user profiles that have been posted with the tag Yorta Yorta will be displayed. The community content facility has significant potential as a means of engaging all users in the ongoing development of the portal as it benefits from additions, edits, and discussion.

During the development process, standards were refined with others defined, for example, file name and type conventions, citation word order and presentation, English words, headers and footers for downloadable documents, and source naming conventions. As the portal's development progressed, requirements were more clearly defined in regard to the hierarchy of menus, linking, content, artefact type (text, audio, or video), access permissions and community-posted content.

Portal interface design

The aim of the interface design for the ALV-RP is to be intuitive, engaging, easy to navigate, and to have a look that is acceptable to the Aboriginal communities of Victoria. Alongside the iterative development of the portal's architecture and content, its interface was incrementally developed. Initial artwork and the site theme was basic with little artwork to give it an Australian Aboriginal feel. The second version employed the assistance of a graphic artist, therefore the imagery and colours were richer. However it was not suitable for a Victorian Aboriginal website which needs to reflect the heritage of its content. The current version is based on artwork by a Victorian Aboriginal artist, Vicki Couzens. This artwork is vibrant and suits the portal well. The artwork has been used to develop a theme for use throughout the portal giving it a true and legitimate Victorian Aboriginal feel.

During early usability evaluations of the site's navigation it was found that moving around the site was not intuitive, nor complete, as the users missed important content leaving them with a very basic understanding, not only of the portal itself, but of the value of the content held within it. A number of users indicated that they were lost in the portal not knowing for certain which language or region they were reading about. This feedback, together with further trials and demonstrations, has led to a change in the interface design to one that is more intuitive and engaging. This has been achieved through the use of 'breadcrumbs', highlighted menu items, themes for individual geographic regions, and a rearrangement of the menu items.

Furthermore, the social or community content needed to be presented with impact to encourage or initiate engagement with the site, and to differentiate it from the more static content. To this end a small video introduction to the social content has been embedded and is programmed to play automatically when the user enters this component of the site.

Conclusion

The ALV-RP provides information on Victorian languages that has been carefully examined, analysed and synthesised by linguists, thereby providing a reliable source of information to Victorian Aboriginal communities researching their heritage language. It also allows for the language reclamation process to be fast-tracked as the data has already undergone rigorous, academic processes that otherwise would need to be carried out prior to revitalisation of the language. The input of the partner organisations has contributed to the design of the site and has helped make the portal more accessible to educators and relevant to Aboriginal community members. One significant change made as a result of the input of Aboriginal partner organisations was the decision that the web portal should use the term Aboriginal rather than Indigenous. This work is still in progress at the time of writing.

The portal design has been developed using a combination of the web site design method proposed by De Troyer and Leune (1998) and the engineering approach suggested by Lowe and Hall (1999), as both of these models focus on user-centred design. While the linguistic content of the site is undoubtedly of enormous value to those investigating Victorian Aboriginal languages, it is the community content that makes the portal more than just a repository, as it is no longer looking outward but is a place where Victorian Aboriginal languages can be revitalised. Language reclamation can only occur when the language is embraced by its heritage community.

Acknowledgements

The authors would like to thank the Australian Research Council for funding the Reclamation of Victorian Indigenous Languages: Using ICT to enable effective exchange among academics, educators and the Indigenous community project, grant number LP0775283. This ARC Linkage Grant, shared by Heather Bowe at Monash and Kathy Lynch at the University of the Sunshine Coast is benefitting from the input of collaborating partners the Victorian Department of Education and Training, the Victorian Curriculum and Assessment Authority, the Victorian School of Languages, Worawa Independent Aboriginal College, the Victorian Aboriginal Corporation for Languages, the Federation of Aboriginal & Torres Strait Islander Languages, Mirrimbeena Aboriginal Education Group, and Cyberdreaming Pty Ltd.

References

Blake BJ (1991). Woiwurrung, the Melbourne language. In RMW Dixon & BJ Blake (Eds). *The handbook of Australian languages*. Vol. 4 (pp. 30–122). Melbourne: Oxford University Press.

Blake BJ (2003a). *The Warrnambool language: a consolidated account of the Aboriginal language of the Warrnambool area of the western district of Victoria based on nineteenth century sources.* Canberra: Pacific Linguistics.

Blake BJ (2003b). *The Bunganditj (Buwandik) language of the Mount Gambier region.* Canberra: Pacific Linguistics.

Blake BJ, Clark ID & Reid J (1998). The Colac language. In BJ Blake (Ed). *Wathawurrung and the Colac language of southern Victoria* (pp. 155–77). Canberra: Pacific Linguistics.

Blake BJ, Clark ID & Krishna-Pillay S (1998). Wathawurrung: the language of the Geelong-Ballarat area. In BJ Blake (Ed). *Wathawurrung and the Colac language of southern Victoria* (pp. 59–154). Canberra: Pacific Linguistics.

Blake BJ & Reid J (1998). Classifying Victorian languages. In BJ Blake (Ed). *Wathawurrung and the Colac language of southern Victoria* (pp. 1–58). Canberra: Pacific Linguistics.

Blake BJ & Reid J (1999). Pallanganmiddang: a language of the upper Murray. *Aboriginal History*, 23: 15–31.

Blake BJ & Reid J (2002). The Dhudhuroa language of northeastern Victoria: a new description based on historical sources. *Aboriginal History*, 26: 177–210.

Bowe H (2002). Linguistics and the Yorta Yorta native title claim. In J Henderson & D Nash (Eds). *Language in native title* (pp. 101–59). Canberra: Aboriginal Studies Press.

Bowe H & Morey S (1999). *Yorta Yorta (Bangerang) language of the Murray-Goulburn including Yabula Yabula.* Canberra: Pacific Linguistics.

Bowe H, Peeler L & Atkinson S (1997). *Yorta Yorta language heritage.* Clayton: Monash University, Department of Linguistics.

Clark ID (1990). *Aboriginal languages and clans: an historical atlas of Western and Central Victoria, 1800–1900.* Clayton, Victoria: Department of Geography and Environmental Science, Monash University.

De Troyer O & Leune C (1998). WSDM: a user-centered design method for web sites. Proceedings of the 7th International World Wide Web Conference, Brisbane, 14–18 April. In *Computer Networks and ISDN Systems*, 30(1–7): 85–94.

Dixon RMW (1980). *The languages of Australia.* Cambridge: Cambridge University Press.

Dixon RMW (2002). *Australian languages: their nature and development.* Cambridge: Cambridge University Press.

Fesl E (1985). Ganai: a study of the Aboriginal language of Gippsland based on 19th Century materials. Unpublished masters thesis. Linguistics Department, Monash University.

Gascgoine J (25 August 2004). Thunder in the court: land claim provided the inspiration for play about the Yorta Yorta's fight with the system. *The Age.* Section A3, pp. 2–3.

Hercus L (1969). *The languages of Victoria: a late survey.* Canberra: Australian Institute of Aboriginal Studies.

Hercus L (1986). *Victorian languages: a late survey*. Canberra: Pacific Linguistics.

James A (2003). *Yanagai Yanagai*. Strawberry Hills, NSW: Currency Press.

Krishna-Pillay S (Ed). (1996). *Dictionary of Keerraywoorrong and related dialects*. Warrnambool: Gunditjmara Aboriginal Co-operative.

Lowe D & Hall W (1999). *Hypermedia & the web: an engineering approach*. West Sussex, England: John Wiley & Sons.

Lynch K & Bowe H (2006). *One site – multiple users: designing a portal for multiple user groups*. Paper presented at Ausweb06: The Twelfth Australasian World Wide Web Conference, Australis, Noosa Lakes, 1–5 July 2006 [Online]. Available: ausweb.scu.edu.au/aw06/papers/refereed/lynch2/index.html [Accessed 17 March 2009].

McKay G (1996). *The land still speaks: review of Aboriginal & Torres Strait Islander language development needs and activities*. Canberra: Australian Government Publishing Service.

Victorian Curriculum and Assessment Authority (2004). *Indigenous languages of Victoria: revival and reclamation* [Online]. Available: www.vcaa.vic.edu.au/vce/studies/lote/ausindigenous/ausindigindex.html [Accessed 17 March 2009].

Walsh M & Troy J (2005). *A linguistic renaissance in the south east of Australia*. Paper presented at the Australian Linguistics Society Meeting, 28 September 2005, Monash City Campus, 30 Collins Street Melbourne.

Winkler R (2001). *Portals: the all-in-one web supersites: features, functions, definitions, taxonomy* [Online]. Available: www.sapdesignguild.org/editions/edition3/print_portal_definition.asp [Accessed 29 February 2006].

27
Flexible IT resources for community language reclamation: using culturally appropriate contexts

Cat Kutay[1], George Fisher[2] and Richard Green[3]

Abstract

This paper describes work utilising information technology developed by Cat Kutay and computing students at the University of New South Wales to support two different Aboriginal language programs in Sydney under the guidance of community tutors – George Fisher who teaches Wiradjuri and Richard Green who teaches Dharug. These languages are in the process of being reclaimed from archival resources, supported by the remaining speakers. Each language presents unique challenges. While the New South Wales Department of Education, Department of Aboriginal Affairs and Board of Studies have supported these languages in schools, it is also important to develop programs where the parents and community are involved in reclaiming the languages to ensure the process is ongoing. This work is located in both contexts. We discuss our experience using computing resources to promote the sharing of language, situating it in the field of research into computer-mediated human interaction.

The aim of language reclamation is to provide the original speakers of a language with the opportunity to once again express themselves in their language. This requires more than knowledge of a word list or dictionary, or even the language structure. Without deep knowledge of their language it is difficult for Indigenous people today to express their culture and the related knowledge. This paper looks at a variety of fairly simple information technology (IT) resources that are being used or developed to increase the depth of language teaching and sharing within the Sydney community.

---

1 Computer Science and Engineering, UNSW.

2 Bankstown Elders Group.

3 Chifley College, Dunheved Campus.

Firstly, we discuss why it is important we reclaim languages in Sydney. Then we look at some of the different situations in which this is occurring using IT. In particular we look at the role and suitability of existing or proposed IT to support this work – the main criterion being the reduction of the impact of the computer in the process of sharing language resources, by providing seamless communication among speakers or between teacher and student.

We look at the difficulties encountered in developing software resources, many of which remain the same as for developing any Aboriginal language teaching material: the lack of historical data and authentic modern examples of a vibrant language. However there is, in addition, the nature of the technology, which is viewed as difficult by most of the language community.

Finally we end with a request for more such resources to be developed. This is a critical area where computing can support human communication in an under-resourced area. Dr Kutay is researching how the computer can mediate among the human users who provide the innovation and creativity within a framework afforded by applications on the web or on a local computer. In particular we look to the open source community as, while the resultant products tend to be designed by developers for developers, these can provide appropriate support for the process of language reclamation in a domain where funding for technology support is restricted.

Language for knowledge

Indigenous languages developed over centuries to enable the expression of a particular culture or worldview. In reclaiming Indigenous languages we seek to provide the original vocabulary and syntactic structure that is required for this expression. The significant difference between Indigenous languages and European languages is often the former's ability to describe detailed landscapes and interrelations as required for story telling. These descriptions are of interactions which are often spiritual in nature and which are human-to-human, and human-to-nature, with all relations presented as between equals. The language is highly contextualised in a continuum of time (Dreamtime stories) or place (songlines) (Groome 1995; Harkins 1994). European languages tend to be more focused on the expression of an individual negotiating with an external world, such as the use of dyads in teaching and the use of the impersonal form for many living beings, as well as a segmented view of time and place in describing events as located at one point (Christie 1985; Harris 1991).

Indigenous languages have developed to express Indigenous knowledge. Indigenous cultures in Australia have a very different focus on knowledge management to European cultures. The main differences are summarised in Nakata et al. (2008) and these apply similarly to the language used for the transmission of this knowledge. Much of the difference in requirements of a language stems from the fact that Indigenous knowledge is generally conveyed orally rather than by being written. The sharing of knowledge involves a thorough teaching of that knowledge, within a framework of poetry and singing, for ongoing recollection. Furthermore if information was freely shared without the experience and background context required to enable understanding, the oral record would become jumbled and incoherent. This background context is the story in which the knowledge is conveyed. Thus when we teach Indigenous languages we need to retain the background context at all times.

Language information

We are working to promote the sharing of Indigenous cultural knowledge through language while incorporating IT to provide flexible language learning resources. These resources are intended to assist language teachers and students in learning the reclaimed languages and are not developed specifically for a single language or for linguists, but designed to support community workers in many languages. Examples of such resources are Miromaa database developed by the Arwarbukarl Cultural Resource Association[4] in Newcastle and LanguageWiki developed by the Sydney Aboriginal Language and Computing Centre (SALC)[5] in Sydney.

To develop online shareable IT resources we first consider the issues relating to enabling Indigenous use of them and what may alleviate any problems. In relation to the language information from which we develop the computer resources, we need to consider security issues versus the need for public access. We have to ensure the security of data, both for storage and sharing, so that information can be updated only by those with the rights to access it, while maintaining as open as possible access to the data for knowledge sharing; and we need to look at the validity of the information that we present as authoritative language resources on the computer, or the *accountability* of the data (Bird & Simons 2003).

When collecting the first wordlist for teaching a language we have to verify that each word is actually from that language. In the case of Dharug we are working mainly with an oral record so this may include material common to neighbouring languages from people now living in Sydney. We have tried to overcome this difficulty by providing each language with a wordlist in online databases on the SALC website that are available for editing within a content management system, with the facility to upload waveform audio format (wav) files and images. For Wiradjuri, three speakers started to enter the information into the language database (Figure 1) and upload teaching resources developed at community workshops. This ensures that the resources are not static but able to be updated as our knowledge increases. To ensure that these databases are not corrupted they can only be altered by people who are allowed to register and create a password-protected account.

The important issue then was how to use the language data we collected. As Christie (2004, p. 1) noted, 'databases do not contain knowledge, they contain information. Education is not the transmission of information from one head to another ... it is the negotiated production of knowledge in context'. Information must be presented

---

4 See www.miromaa.com.au

5 See www.salc.org.au

and shared in a manner that retains the context of that information. For instance in recording words from a language we want to link this to the pronunciation and an example of the use of the word. This is important, as any translation to English will not be an exact transfer of meaning, and much knowledge is lost by removing the words from their original context. Noting Nakata et al.'s (2008) concerns relating to the oral transmission of knowledge, we wanted to provide access for many users to upload their information including oral recordings, and enable these users to link this information to learning resources such as worksheets or games.

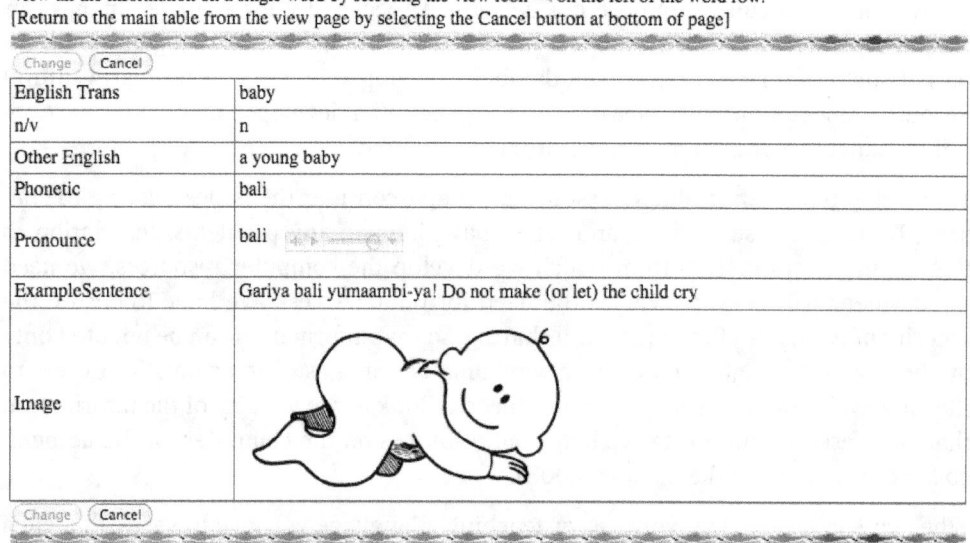

Figure 1: Web page view of data for a Wiradjuri word.

Learning environment

While much Indigenous knowledge is already shared online (Dyson et al. 2007; Kutay & Mooney 2008), the domain is still limited. In fact the need for the IT in this project arose from the language teaching environment. Most importantly the inclusion of technology was to enable a small number of language speakers to support a larger number of in-school tutors. We also saw the use of computers in language teaching as an opportunity for promoting computer literacy together with providing applications that go beyond word learning, to support grammatical literacy.

Aboriginal language teaching is rapidly expanding in Sydney schools, faster than tutors can be trained. These programs were originally seen as a way to promote Indigenous culture, however it is also believed to increase the participation of Indigenous students at school. The Dharug courses in Sydney have already gained support for their perceived effect on attendance rates, although this has not been formally studied. In the schools teaching Wiradjuri there have also been reports from teachers that students have become more involved in English classes as a result of their own language studies.

The number of languages we would like to support is very large. In the schools where this work is based we are dealing with students who identify with a range of different languages, all of which are near dormant; most students' parents cannot speak their ancestral language, although they may occasionally use words from a variety of languages. This situation was invariably arrived at through involuntary relocation or removal from family, however commitment to and interest in language reclamation is still very strong.

Computer-mediated human interaction

The development of software support for teaching Aboriginal languages in school adopts the approach that the computer tools need to be as ubiquitous as possible, and assist the Aboriginal tutors and student users to work with the language knowledge that can be stored on computer in the form of a database, or basic grammar in a language parser. The initial applications were kept simple and, as the users became more ambitious with what they wanted to achieve, the software was developed to keep pace, where it could.

While such software resources will always provide only a partial knowledge base for a language, they can support the existing courses in schools that focus on wordlists with simple sentence construction exercises, sometimes with example songs and stories. Also by having speakers provide audio for the database, we now have suitable expressions for English terms, such as greetings, rather than direct translations.

In order to support the in-school tutors we intended to build up a body of IT resource templates and applications that provided a learning environment that could be used for similar languages. Then, by linking these applications to databases for the different languages and providing grammatical parsing rules for simple translation, we hoped to provide support for each language. The goal was to assist tutors to provide different practical exercises in a cultural context and link these to feedback to be provided to the students' activities within the learning software. One difficulty is that this feedback should preferably be in the spoken language.

The first step in this process was to assist the present speakers of the main languages represented in Sydney to store their language knowledge through a simple database structure. We then combined one language database with the resources, such as recordings presented by other speakers and sentences, to provide a rich learning environment. The steps in this process are described below. At the same time we needed to carry out this process with the many different languages, to verify if the applications could be generic enough to support the basic language structures and, where there were differences, to see whether these required specific grammar rules or a different construction of the database.

With our present work focusing on providing subject lists of words with simple linking words and some tense variation, the applications so far developed have proved useful. However we are wary of how far we will be able to support any in-depth teaching of languages. While the Sydney languages are all closely located (being from coastal and central inland NSW) there is much variation even within these languages (see Dixon & Blake 1979). In particular, we will need to collect more example sentences for the system to interpret these variations among languages.

Collecting the language data

In the reclamation of languages in Sydney the collection of oral resources has been hard. This is partly because most languages currently used here are not from this area originally. Many people have moved and lived here for generations. In Wiradjuri we are working with archival resources and a handful of language speakers who live far apart. Most speakers are not in the Sydney region where we are working. While people have now started to relearn their language it remains very time consuming to gather spoken examples.

To collect resources in the spoken language we also needed to go back to archival material held at the Australian Institute of Aboriginal and Torres Strait Islander Studies (AIATSIS).[6] Much of the audio material is in the form of linguists' field recordings of wordlists or single sentences with some complete songs or stories, but little in the middle range suitable for beginning learners. Linguists are recorded asking, 'What is the word for … ' with a speaker's response. Long responses may not be transcribed or translated and longer recordings are often not described or analysed in any way. This results in long searches of archives to find material to support different lesson topics.

On the other hand, Dharug is a language of the Sydney area and many speakers live in western Sydney and the Blue Mountains to which we have ready access. To collect Dharug resources we work with the local speakers as well as including language structure and vocabulary described by the linguist Jakelyn Troy (1994). In Dharug we are also using song as the teaching medium (see Green, this volume). Song has always been recognised as a means of assisting retention of the words in a story and Aboriginal languages are ideal for singing, with a flexible phrase order that can permit re-arranging words to fit a rhythm or rhyme.

The next task was to store the wordlists electronically. Some short electronic wordlists have been published on CD by the Department of Aboriginal Affairs through the NSW Aboriginal Language Research and Resource Centre and more examples are available at SALC. The SALC wordlist database was designed to be used with different languages and built as a publicly accessible online site. The database has been modified in some cases, where language users wish to store alternative data (such as the archival source of a word definition) as part of their data. An image to portray

---

6 A large portion of text resources for Wiradjuri recorded by James Günther in the 1800s, and only recently discovered, has just been presented to the AIATSIS library for public use.

the meaning was added for words where possible. The Wiradjuri list was entered by scanning archival resources, then running text recognition software, which had to be checked by hand. The words were put into a table. Unfortunately it was only later that the words were linked back to their source sentence, kept in a separate database. The use of a computer made it easier to develop English to Wiradjuri and Wiradjuri to English lists, check for repetition, and so on. Then a sound file of a modern speaker saying the word and a text example of the word in a sentence were added. The sound was retrieved from different sources. We had some Central Australian Aboriginal Media Association recordings of recent speakers, as well as George Fisher who was equipped with good quality recording instruments and motivated to do this work for minimal funds. All resources could be uploaded at home by the language users, gradually in their own time.

The database was formatted as a flat table that uses web references to files for accessing non-text data. A single English word translation is used as one search field to enable the database to be more usable in parsing, and an alternative more explanatory meaning is included, however any word could be entered many times for its different meanings. Also the more complex meaning was included as an alternative translation. The web system is coded in PHP, a server-side scripting language, to read from the database using MySQL (Structured Query Language). This enables the database to be transmitted as a CSV (comma separated values) text file compatible with Microsoft Excel, including descriptors for each column. When users wish to find a word, variations can be provided based on all search fields, but for simplicity we used the single English word search only. This word can also be used to search the database of sentences for relevant examples.

This process has also been incremental. While the database was initially fairly simple, as we learnt of the growing needs both for tutors and students, more information has been linked to the table. Also while the table was designed for providing words lists, we wanted to join this to example sentences and include more grammatical constructions, which requires steadily more information be inserted. This approach was used as the initial users were very unclear as to the potential of computers to help their work, so the project developed as this understanding increased with further requirements. For example, we recoded the parser to search the example sentences first, then the alternative, then the single word search fields to provide a more reliable translator based on the extra information in the sentences and particular cultural expressions entered in the examples database.

The final task that we have completed on the word data at this stage was to collect grammatical information to teach how the words can be used correctly in sentences. However our understanding of the grammar is still developing as we continue teaching, so we are only learning a few steps ahead of the students. We initially worked in lessons with single words as the students were still at this level. Then we started to edit the example sentence we already had, replacing one or two words to change the context of the story and provide alternate examples. While some errors will be

330 Re-awakening languages

introduced due to the significant linguistic differences among Aboriginal languages and between them and English, this formulaic method is an approach to reclamation promoted by some Australian linguists, such as Rob Amery (2000) and Christina Eira (2008). It was only later that we added in the language parser that is discussed below, based on the grammatical structure as we learnt it.

Structure of the learning environment

To design the learning environment, we collected existing text-based resources that had already been published in various New South Wales Aboriginal languages, including Gamilaraay and Gumbaynggirr, and we are grateful to the authors of these resources for sharing them. These worksheets have exercises involving placing words on drawings, finding words, and answering questions with words. These exercises gradually move from wordlists into writing sentences. Much of this structure can be repeated in the software environment (Figure 2).

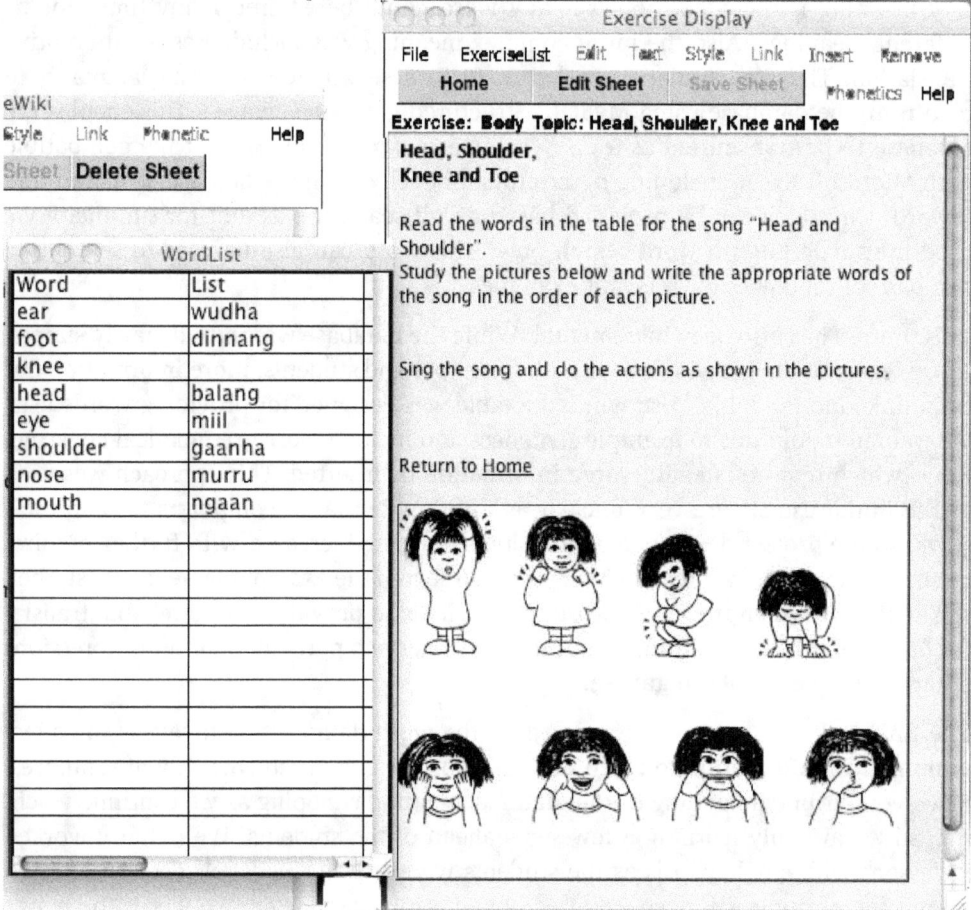

Figure 2: Example exercise with wordlist to assist students.

There are various ways in which IT can assist teachers to develop such worksheets in their language. An interface was developed in Runtime Revolution[7] that uses the language database as a back end, and provides tools for teachers to develop documents that are displayed as worksheets for the students to complete. The first step is to create a wordlists for each lesson or set of lessons. This wordlist window is retained through the set of lessons in each file. We also went back and updated the online database to enable all words to be sorted into topics. Tutors can then select a topic list for each exercise set. This ensured that students were dealing with a smaller, more manageable vocabulary list, yet using these words in a wider range of exercises, such as use of location and verb tense.

The worksheets that are written by tutors are interactive and provide feedback on the sound of words, as well as a translation of the sentences students enter in answer to a question. If a group of words is selected by the tutor for more information, each sound file is concatenated to form the sentence to be played, which provides a simple example of the spoken phrase, although lacking expression. Thus it was important that we supply a simple sound file for every word. This information on words and sentences can be selected with links, which are created in a similar manner to Wiki pages. That is, when a tutor wishes to create a new exercise, they enter the title as a link, and a new page is created as a worksheet with the ability to add text, image and audio resources. Also the idea of linking words to a page providing their translation and sound file is similar to links on Wiki pages. Users can select different pages or worksheets in the exercise file, and do the exercises on each one. Hence the software is called LanguageWiki.

The exercises the software supports include diagram labelling and word selection exercises as well as audio practice and sentence construction. Tutors are supported in making the exercise sheets with a database search that is automatically activated when they select a word for translation. All the versions of the word from the database are displayed for tutors to select one per example and tutors can add new information to the data including sound files, alternative meanings, or a new word. At present the school version of the database is localised to each school, although regularly updated, initially due to firewall issues in accessing the database outside the Department of Education network, but also due to the need to maintain integrity of the original online database.

There was an added advantage of having the tutors develop the worksheets rather than using published material and possibly translating this material to a different language. The tutors appreciate that the work done by linguists provides a grammatical structure for their language, but they wanted to have a role in contributing the cultural context to their lessons. Also, where there was interesting material available illustrating cultural differences (such as stories recorded and stored at AIATSIS), the stories are someone else's and the tutor felt they would not necessarily do them justice by using them in their course. LanguageWiki is designed for each tutor or group of tutors to author their own exercises using the database as support for their work.

---

7 See www.runrev.com/home/product-family/

Electronic recording of words

While some tutors are fluent we have many who are still learning their language. Because the process of recording speakers usually requires some technical assistance it was initially difficult to encourage speakers to do this on their own. As we needed a sound file for every word we initially looked at speech synthesis technologies, in particular the Festival[8] system but realised this could not readily be utilised for these languages.

Many of the resources used in teaching are literacy based, and hence rely on a written representation of the language. We were using a phonetic script (ITRANS-3) to assist students to learn the new sounds of the language. Some sounds are unfamiliar to the ears and tongues of the learners, such as the palatal sound written as dj or j in some Aboriginal languages (often anglicised to approximate the first and final sounds in judge). We used this unfamiliar script as a way to encourage learners to try to approximate as closely as possible the way sounds like this were pronounced at the time when there was a large community of active speakers. This script has already been used in speech synthesis projects for Hindi (Kishore & Black 2003).

Also Wiradjuri literacy was being taught in Sydney at the time by analysing words into their component two- or three-sound syllables. We considered the use of syllables as units to be concatenated in speech synthesis. However the available software was designed for the smaller unit of language diphones, not syllables, and the dynamic nature of spoken language is much more complex than such a system would allow. Schultz and Black (2007) identified the need for large amounts of spoken data for analysis as one of the major difficulties in building up computer support for language processing. While tools such as Shoebox[9] can provide support for collection of such a corpus of language resources, we were working with the mostly text-based resources we had. We did not have such a large body of spoken, let alone translated, language so relied on collecting a series of simple word recordings from three speakers. As mentioned, these words were combined to form phrases using the software, which is simpler than trying to combine syllables with varying stress to form words. However we still had the problem that the voices used often varied across the group of words.

The concern we have with the re-created form of speech, is similar to the experience of language speakers supplying the pronunciation of words for the phonetic description used in text-based dictionaries. Attempts by non-speakers to repeat the pronunciation have often been incorrect and the speakers who supplied the pronunciation have come to distrust dictionaries as a result (Simpson 2003). Audio recordings of text resources are still necessary to develop these kinds of learning resources, and human speech should always be preferred over computer output.

Given the above problems with the phonetically generated sounds, and since another teaching program was being devised at the same time by Wiradjuri speakers on country, we changed to their phonemically designed orthography for consistency.

---

8 See www.cstr.ed.ac.uk/projects/festival/

9 See www.ethnologue.com/tools_docs/shoebox.asp

Grammatical parser

When students are translating from English to language in class exercises they need accurate feedback on their translation or expression attempts. For this purpose we built a text parser using the existing grammatical information to try and translate their entries in the answer box provided on worksheets. While the software Shoebox is used by linguists to gloss transcribed text, we were working from a wordlist without grammatical information so had to attempt to derive the grammar ourselves from the sentence examples and other documents. The parser was written in Python using the Natural Language Toolkit,[10] which extends the principles used in Shoebox parsing.

In developing a language parser for Wiradjuri we had hoped to create a system that was fairly generic and could also be applied, then adjusted, to the local Sydney language which is even less well resourced. At the same time we wanted to be careful that, if a student entered alternative but correct forms, this would be translated correctly. The wordlist we started with was in the form of a simple corpus with words tagged for eight parts of speech: verb, noun, pronoun, adjective, adverb, preposition, conjunction, and interjection. This was a classification understood by the Aboriginal speakers setting up the data. However, while some flexibility was built into the parser, because it was based in the grammar of English it was not ideal for the purposes of automatically parsing Aboriginal languages.

Of course all our goals could not be achieved. In particular there are limits to the number of words in the wordlist, and so the parser may not 'know' a word even though it may have been introduced by the teacher in class. Thus a student may be given feedback that they are wrong when they are actually correct in their attempt. The software learning tool was therefore designed so that when tutors create worksheet resources, if they enter a language word not already in the database, they are invited to update it.

Aboriginal languages make extensive use of suffixes to show tense in verbs and case in nouns, or as shortened forms of pronouns. The same suffix form can also have different meanings depending on whether it is affixed to a noun or a verb and the kind of relationships among nouns in a sentence. As in English the same form can be the root of both a noun or adjective and a verb. There is also a high degree of systematic variation of form in suffixes in most languages. To add to these difficulties, when we go back to the archives to verify the wordlist, there are a number of words, or parts of words, which are not translated in the simple sentence examples. These may be repetitions for emphasis, colloquial use or simply undocumented uses of words.

Another issue for translation that came up was the absence of an equivalent to the English verb 'to be' in Wiradjuri, as in most Australian languages. This meant that when the parser attempted translation from English it would have to ignore this, and to translate into English it would have to insert it at required points. But this would usually not match the original sentence the students were translating – an impossible

---

10 See www.nltk.org

task. Again we returned to the people working on the project to assist by providing more examples for students of known correct sentences. Different users can edit these examples online and can upload audio recordings of these examples.

Sound comparison

The final software application we wanted to include was to support students improving their sound to match the existing language speakers. However there is much more to learning good pronunciation than simply hearing a word or sentence spoken. An example of the sort of open source support which can be provided for sound development is the software Fluency.[11] However this system uses a text-based interface relying on knowledge of linguistic terms and is currently available only for English. Hence it would not be suitable for either school students or the adult tutors in this context.

The approach we have taken is to link the words which have a recording included in the database with an option for the student to record themselves, and then compare the two versions using Audacity sound editing software.[12] The result is very simplistic, in that it only displays a graph that corresponds to variations in volume and frequency, allowing users to infer syllable divisions. Audacity offers students the option of playing back the sounds separately by muting each channel alternatively so they can compare the movement of pitch and intonation in their speech to the saved form, as recommended by Anderson-Hsieh (1992).

There were a lot of issues with such a crude method. When comparing sentences, rather than single words, the pauses between words by the speaker differed from the concatenated file provided by the software. If the student spoke softly or slowly, it was hard for them to match this with the original recording. Also both significant and insignificant differences in the sound were equally visually noticeable to the students.

However, this does provide visual and audio feedback to the student that they can practise with in their own time. Generally the students tend to mimic well, so the speed of the word tends to match that of the recording for single words. The initial response has been positive. The main limitation to enabling this feature is that it requires that the school computers possess a microphone for students to record themselves.

Speech and song-writing

The need for more extended texts for learning suggested we use existing technology for innovative purposes. One of the most used resources in Indigenous language teaching has been Microsoft PowerPoint slides with embedded sound files to present stories for the classroom. In providing material for the Bankstown Elders' Group, George Fisher used Microsoft Word files with embedded sound files. In Dharug, linguist Amanda Oppliger and Richard Green worked together with researchers at the University of

---

11 See www.lti.cs.cmu.edu/Research/Fluency

12 See audacity.sourceforge.net

Sydney to establish a dictionary accessible using mobile phones (see Wilson, this volume), and now some speakers share knowledge about Dharug words and language through SMS (see Green, this volume).

We also needed a robust song learning tool, so we purchased Finale Songwriter.[13] This has been used to provide Dharug songs for children to sing in schools. This work was possible as Richard Green is fluent in the language, and has an understanding of the poetic nature of the constructions. Students learning Aboriginal languages as part of their IT work were inspired by witnessing Richard develop the translation for the song 'O Come All Ye Faithful' in a day, scanning the new song correctly to the original tune.

A recent performance in Dharug involved students from schools around Sydney, including children from the Dharawal program in south-east Sydney. They responded to the new language with great enthusiasm, showing that in the process of teaching one Indigenous language we open our children to the knowledge and skills to communicate in many related languages. This also suggests opportunities to share resources among tutors of these languages. This similarity between the languages needs to be further researched, as students in Sydney schools will often be learning a language that is not that of their parents or grandparents, but is similar enough for them to use this knowledge later to reclaim their own language.

Extensions

The focus of the next stage of development is to enable the functionality of such programs directly on the web, rather than simply using local versions on single computers. This will enable wordlist updates and new features to be installed without having to distribute new versions to the users, or to bypass a firewall for remote access.

In developing media-rich environments for learning language we need access to more resources that are relevant to particular themes and topics. Developing standard tagging of sound and video files in the future would help this process. The next feature needed for the website is to enable users to upload and share detailed material in language. Audio resources can be recorded using internet telephony software such as Skype, or locally on a home computer. There is a need for video and sound annotation applications such as an online version of Elan[14] to encourage the speaker to provide some text information or translation while uploading, even if just a description of the topic. Speech-to-text tools exist, but require training to the individual speaker and are only available for major world languages, hence are not realistic at present. Then programs such as LanguageWiki or games software with a database back end, could integrate these resources into a learning environment based on a series of topics.

---

13 See www.finalemusic.com/SongWriter/

14 See www.lat-mpi.eu/tools/elan/

The transcriptions will need to come from language users, as well as linguists,[15] and hence the interface for such tools will need to consider various knowledge and cultural aspects, such as who has the authority to hear the information, and in what context it may be repeated. For instance some explanations may relate to images of kinship, or specific locations on land, so need to be presented in that context only. In particular there is hesitance by language speakers to share their material in an open context as this may risk losing control of the information residing in the language. What we are proposing is the development of easy-to-run software that provides a suitable learning environment, like the *Mayalambala: Let's Move It*[16] posters and cut-outs developed by Muurrbay Aboriginal Language and Culture Co-operative. Within such a framework, exercises from different languages, using a small selected vocabulary, could all be linked to relevant pictures or videos.

While language resource sharing sites such as that developed by Ngapartji Ngapartji[17] have been around for a few years (see Sometimes & Kelly, this volume), these could be enhanced by becoming more conversational in form (perhaps like Facebook or MySpace) and using audio more than text. This would allow the creation of interactive sites to share language resources and will enable learners to keep up to date with what has been created. The cultural and technical aspects to be considered in the interface requirements include: a focus on sound rather than text; the need to reduce complexity particularly for people to upload; and providing a rich environment where users feel they are contributing to a large body of work, rather than only adding a small drop to an diminishing pool of resources.

Conclusion

The market for computing support of language recording and teaching is growing to include members of Indigenous communities. There is a desire by community members to have direct access to recording and storage equipment which ensures they control how it is presented to the public, and how it can be used in learning. This will bypass, at least for the present, the challenge of developing sophisticated algorithms to support partially documented languages with few speakers and a small electronic corpus, and where few linguists have the time to provide full annotation for existing or future resources.

At the same time there is a growing interest in Aboriginal communities for IT products which support their use of their own language. It has been encouraging to see tutors who are often wary of computers become interested in taking up the opportunity to use these resources and tailor them to their teaching needs. And, while many

---

15 Thieberger discussed the difficulty of getting linguists to create reusable records of the languages they record in 'Does language technology offer anything to small languages?' (Australasian Language Technology Association, 2007).

16 See www.muurrbay.org.au/publications.html

17 See ninti.ngapartji.org

students are already familiar with computers and use them regularly, it is good to see the response of Indigenous students to discovering their culture and language is also being supported by IT.

Finally, this work has provided the opportunity to look at the similar needs across Australian Aboriginal languages undergoing revitalisation, which suggests that work on technology developed to support one language may in fact provide support for others, so the gains could be substantial.

Acknowledgements

The authors would like to acknowledge the resources used in the project. Christopher Kirkbright provided some of the grammatical analysis used to build the parser. Christopher Kirkbright and Cheryl Riley provided and checked the wordlist and some of the sound files used for the website. Diane McNaboe edited the worksheets. We are grateful to John Giacon and Muurrbay Aboriginal Language and Culture Co-operative for allowing us to use their worksheet resources in this work. The rest of the material was provided by the authors. We also wish to acknowledge the many students who helped develop the resources, including Alistair McLeod who developed the parser and Xinran Wu who developed the speech synthesis tool.

References

Amery R (2000). *Warrabarna Kaurna! reclaiming an Australian language.* Lisse: Swets & Zeitlinger.

Anderson-Hsieh J (1992). Using electronic visual feedback to teach suprasegmentals. *System*, 20(1): 51–62.

Australasian Language Technology Association (2007). *Australasian Language Technology Workshop 2007: invited Speakers* [Online]. Available: www.alta.asn.au/events/altw2007/alta-2007-speaker.html [Accessed 12 September 2008].

Bird S & Simons G (2003). Seven dimensions of portability for language documentation and description. *Language*, 79: 557–82.

Christie M (1985). *Aboriginal perspectives on experience and learning: the role of language in Aboriginal education.* Waurn Ponds, Victoria: Deakin University Press.

Christie M (2004). Computer databases and Aboriginal knowledge. *Learning Communities: International Journal of Learning in Social Contexts*, 1: 4–12.

Dixon RMW & Blake BJ (1979). *Handbook of Australian languages.* Canberra: Australian National University Press.

Dyson LE, Hendriks M & Grant S (2007). *Information technology and indigenous people.* Hershey, PA: Information Science Publishing.

Eira C (2008). *Language development on the ground: three practical sessions*. Paper presented at the Indigenous Languages Institute '08: Bayala ngarala. 10 July 2008, University of Sydney, NSW.

Groome H (1995). *Working purposefully with Aboriginal students*. Wentworth, NSW: Social Science Press.

Harkins J (1994). *Bridging two worlds: Aboriginal English and cross cultural understanding*. St Lucia, Qld: University of Queensland Press.

Harris P (1991). *Mathematics in a cultural context: Aboriginal perspectives on space, time and money*. Geelong, Victoria: Deakin University Press.

Kishore SP & Black AW (2003). Unit size in unit selection speech synthesis. In *Eurospeech 2003* (pp. 1317–20). The 8th European Conference on Speech Communication & Technology, 1–4 September 2003, Geneva, Switzerland [Online]. Available: www.isca-speech.org/archive/eurospeech_2003 [Accessed 9 June 2007].

Kutay C & Mooney J (2008). Linking learning to community for Indigenous computing courses. *Australian Journal of Indigenous Education*, 37S: 90–95.

Nakata M, Nakata V, Byrne A, McKeough J, Gardiner G & Gibson J (2008). *Australian Indigenous digital collections: first generation issues*. Sydney, NSW: University of Technology Sydney ePress [Online]. Available: epress.lib.uts.edu.au/dspace/bitstream/2100/809/1/Aug%2023%20Final%20Report.pdf [Accessed 10 January 2009].

Schultz T & Black AW (2006). *Challenges with rapid adaptation of speech translation systems to new language pairs*. Paper presented at the International Conference on Acoustics, Speech, and Signal Processing. 14–19 May 2006, Toulouse, France [Online]. Available: www.cs.cmu.edu/~awb/papers/ICASSP2006/0501213.pdf [Accessed 11 June 2008].

Simpson J (2003). Representing information about words digitally. In L Barwick, A Marett, J Simpson & A Harris (Eds). *Researchers, communities, institutions, sound recordings*. Proceedings of the Digital Audio Archiving Workshop, Sydney, October 2003. Sydney: University of Sydney [Online]. Available: www.paradisec.org.au/Simpson_paper_rev1.html#Abstract [Accessed 10 July 2008].

Troy J (1994). *The Sydney language*. Flynn, ACT: J. Troy.

28
Electronic dictionaries for language reclamation

Aidan Wilson[1]

Abstract

Owing to the disproportionately low level of literacy in remote Indigenous communities, especially in Indigenous languages, printed books are perhaps not the most appropriate form of delivering language-learning materials such as dictionaries. Electronic versions based on computers are more useful. However the availability of computers, and consequently computer literacy, in remote Australian communities is still very low. Mobile phones are a much more common form of technology. Unfortunately mobile phones generally only allow small applications, meaning that most content expected in a reasonable language learners' dictionary must be jettisoned. This paper proposes and documents a method of dictionary delivery that takes advantage of the flexibility and usability of computer-based dictionaries, as well as the portability of mobile phones. This process entails maintaining a single dictionary file that can be exported to dictionary visualisation programs and applications that can be installed on a mobile phone, as well as a number of other formats in various media. Computer-based resources may contain as much information as is necessary in a format that can be navigated easily, while a mobile phone-based version will contain only a reduced range of the original content, although it will be available to the user without the need of a computer.

Dictionaries are invaluable resources for language revitalisation; they aid linguists, language workers and teachers and, most importantly, provide critical access to information for the language learner. Several studies (Corris et al. 2000, 2004; Nesi 1999) have shown that electronic dictionaries can be much more accessible and engaging for users than traditional printed dictionaries, and suggest that they tend to be used much more frequently and for longer periods of time than paper dictionaries. Electronic dictionaries can offer ways of organising content and finding

---

1 Department of Linguistics and Applied Linguistics, University of Melbourne.

entries beyond the traditional method of searching through an alphabetically sorted list of headwords. They can also include multimedia content such as sound, images and video. With traditional printed dictionary materials however, it is only possible to include images.[2]

Not all electronic dictionaries, however, are so useful. An electronic dictionary consisting of formatted text is only as useful to the user as a printed dictionary, perhaps with the added benefits of being searchable and vastly more portable. Dictionaries consisting of marked-up text that is properly machine-readable allow for more electronic functionality than raw text; fields can be searched independently and content can be linked together through hyperlinking, allowing the user many more ways of navigating the content. Traditional dictionaries by contrast force the user into a reduced set of methods.

There are further considerations regarding the representation of data and the method by which dictionaries are delivered. Electronic dictionaries can be presented in a number of ways: online using a Hypertext Markup Language document; in a specialised electronic dictionary viewer such as Kirrkirr (Manning et al. 2001); or using mobile phones (McElvenny & Wilson 2009). As discussed below the optimal way to compile and deliver dictionaries in the remote Australian context, and possibly in other areas of extreme language endangerment, is probably a combination of computer-based resources for use within the classroom and smaller mobile phone-based resources to which the user has continual access.

The purpose here is to recognise and take advantage of a technological niche to aid the potential reclamation of Indigenous languages alongside other language revitalisation efforts.

Master dictionary file

The key to delivering dictionaries in multiple formats without having to independently maintain a number of different versions is to preserve a master copy of the dictionary in a format that is completely machine-readable, from which the other versions can be derived as needed. It is important for the longevity of the content of the dictionary that the format chosen for this be stable and not become obsolete in the future.

This master dictionary file is virtually unlimited as to size; it can contain high-resolution images, high-quality audio recordings of individual words or example sentences, and perhaps even videos. It is also able to contain lexicographic and metalinguistic information well beyond the actual needs of most learners' dictionaries.

The purpose of the master dictionary file is in fact not to be a dictionary in itself; it is not intended to be used by anyone apart from the linguist or lexicographer. Instead its purpose is to serve as the centrally maintained file from which other purpose-

---

[2] The ideas discussed here are a result of an ongoing project in collaboration with James McElvenny to produce free electronic dictionaries for minority languages.

built dictionaries will be derived. A dictionary intended for linguists working on the language, for instance, may contain grammatical information, pronoun paradigms, scientific classificatory names for flora and fauna, and recording numbers and time-codes for example sentences so that the researcher can check the source data. A learners' dictionary will likely include none of these but will include sounds to aid the learners' pronunciation of new words and images to identify particular plants and animals. Each of the dictionaries will be exported from the master dictionary file retaining or ignoring specific content and formatting it as required.

In maintaining master dictionary files we have adopted a markup language that is commonly used, is very well documented and will remain, in principle, readable well into the future. Extensible Markup Language (XML) is essentially text that contains tags or codes that inform the reader, human or machine, of the content's structure, how specific content is related, and what each piece of content is; whether it is a headword, a gloss, an example and so on (World Wide Web Consortium 2008).

Field-oriented standard format

Currently the most common markup language used for creating electronic dictionaries is Field-Oriented Standard Format (FOSF), more commonly known as *backslash codes*.[3] FOSF is the syntax used in programs such as Shoebox or Toolbox[4] and Lexique Pro[5] which remain the most common dictionary creation and display tools available to linguists and language workers. As a result many electronic lexical databases in existence – possibly the vast majority – are encoded in FOSF. Backslash codes are highly human readable as long as the alphanumeric codes are easy enough to interpret or are clearly documented, but the only programs that can computationally interpret FOSF are the programs mentioned above. Apart from this there are a number of disadvantages to FOSF that encouraged us to employ a more sophisticated and standard markup language.

The syntax of FOSF consists of a backslash \, an arbitrary alphanumeric code and a space, all followed by the actual content. For instance the headword content of a backslash-coded dictionary may look like \lx *headword* and a gloss will be \ge *gloss*. The content of the code, be it headword, example or gloss, is tacitly assumed to continue until the next carriage return; the start of the next line. Thus an example sentence in FOSF will look like \xv *this is an example*. The syntactic fact that a carriage return is the indicator for the end of one piece of content and the start of another has a serious corollary for the formatting of dictionaries: content cannot be embedded inside other pieces of content nor be grouped, which is important for distinguishing among different senses of a particular word or explicitly grouping a vernacular example and its gloss.

---

3 The acronym FOSF and the term backslash codes are used here interchangeably.

4 See www.sil.org/computing/toolbox/

5 See www.lexiquepro.com/

It must be said though, that FOSF had a number of benefits for which dictionary writers can be grateful. Firstly it is exceedingly easy to read and manipulate even without a program such as Toolbox, as the structure is entirely transparent and can be written with a mere text editor. Secondly using a program like Toolbox to create and manage dictionaries encourages a level of machine-readable consistency that other formats do not, although human error in selecting and using the correct codes can be common. Another benefit is that backslash codes enjoy a level of institutional support from the major source of field software, the Summer Institute of Linguistics, such that software is available that can quite easily convert backslash-coded text into formatted dictionaries ready for print. The Multi-Dictionary Formatter (MDF) for example, only requires that the alphanumeric code chosen be consistent with their specifications (Coward & Grimes 1995).[6]

Extensible markup language

XML differs significantly from FOSF in the way that data is structured. Rather than carriage returns marking the boundaries of content, information is delimited on either side by explicit tags. Data can also be embedded recursively by placing tags inside other tags, which is especially useful for lexical databases in that certain information can be explicitly grouped. An example and its gloss, for instance, can each be structured hierarchically within another dedicated tag to ensure that they stay together.

Despite the benefits of using such a structured and flexible markup language, XML has its distinct disadvantages. In particular it is nearly impossible for the untrained person to read, and editing XML without software that interprets the structure can have devastating consequences for the validity of the document. Although XML-editing software is readily available with varying degrees of quality, it generally amounts to highlighting – colour coding the machine-readable tags so the user can safely avoid them. Adding or removing tags or any other form of structural editing generally requires a more sophisticated XML editor or a knowledge of XML syntax sufficient to avoid any errors that would invalidate the document.

Although the disadvantages of XML would appear fatal to its use, the flexibilities of the more sophisticated structure make it a superior format and most suitable for our purposes. This however does not mean that linguists and language workers should stop using backslash codes; indeed, using FOSF is relatively easy as compared with XML and ensures a level of machine-readable consistency from which the lexicographer will benefit further downstream. In any case, any machine-readable format has enormous computation benefits over raw, untagged text.

Computer presentation

While there are a number of programs that have been developed to interactively display dictionaries, Kirrkirr (Manning 2003; Manning et al. 2001) utilises an intuitive

---

6 The FOSF codes given as examples are all MDF compliant.

and engaging user interface and is most suitable for children. Kirrkirr was originally developed as a means of electronically displaying the Warlpiri dictionary (Laughren et al., in preparation; Laughren & Nash 1983). It is open source, cross-platform and free. Kirrkirr allows the user to navigate content using a variety of methods and supports multimedia content such as images, audio files and video files, although the latter has yet to be explored as an option within the scope of this project. Users can search for words using the target or the source language, travel among words in a network by their links to one another, or move through a collection of semantic domains to find related words. Most importantly with respect to language revitalisation projects in Australia and elsewhere, Kirrkirr is designed specifically to be accessible to dictionary novices.

Using a program such as Kirrkirr takes full advantage of the hierarchical structure of XML. For instance elements (contiguous chunks of information) can be hidden, meaning that while they are still present in the master dictionary file they are not shown on the display. This key feature is very important for the ideology that informs much of the project described here. An important principle in creating digital versions of information is to preserve everything, lest that version be the last record in existence at some point in the future. So all information (internal comments, tape references of example sentences, scientific names of flora and fauna and so on) is retained in the underlying dictionary structure: the master dictionary file. Using XML stylesheets to render surface realisations enables the lexicographer to decide which elements are displayed. A potentially limitless number of stylesheets can be specified for different versions of the dictionary and users can easily switch among the various stylesheets within the Kirrkirr user interface.

The Kaurna electronic dictionary

In 2008 a team at the University of Sydney was commissioned[7] to create an electronic dictionary of Kaurna based on two original documents from the 19th century (Teichelmann 1857; Teichelmann & Schürmann 1840) that had been typed into backslash-coded text. An important concern for this project was that the text from the original documents be displayed alongside any modern interpretation, both for the inquisitive user and for the digital preservation of the originals. In effect the electronic version was to serve as a digital archival copy of both Teichelmann (1857) and Teichelmann and Schürmann (1840).

We decided then that Kirrkirr would be a suitable application as it allows for the display of multiple versions at once and for the option to hide everything apart from the modern interpretation showing only the lexical information. Furthermore it allows for the insertion of sound files so that learner users can access information regarding pronunciation.

---

7 The Department of Communications, Information Technology and the Arts is owed a debt of gratitude for funding the Kaurna electronic dictionary project.

During the Kaurna electronic dictionary project McElvenny (2008) devised a method of displaying the content of the dictionary on a mobile phone, as it would be more accessible to the younger Kaurna community members. After reducing the size of the sound files that had been recorded by Kaurna learners for the electronic dictionary we were able to include them in the mobile phone version, thus enabling the learner immediate access to pronunciation. Exploring the possibilities of mobile phone dictionaries has since become an important aspect of our larger project.

Mobile phone presentation

While delivering dictionaries electronically using computers is more intuitive than traditional printed materials in the remote and Indigenous Australian context, using mobile phones as a method of presentation is the most appropriate. Computers are still rare in remote communities and only schools are adequately equipped with them.

Several recent studies have shown that mobile phones are very common among Indigenous people in various regions around Australia. In Cape York for instance, mobile phones are the dominant form of information and communications technology (Brady, Dyson & Asela 2008; Dyson & Brady 2009). The rate of mobile phone ownership among Indigenous people in Central Australia is around half, and is highest among younger people (Tangentyere Council & Central Land Council 2007). Mobile phone ownership is moderate even in communities that still lack coverage (Australian Communications and Media Authority 2008).

Furthermore an informal survey of researchers active in remote communities around Australia suggests that mobile phones are far more common than computers and that many people either own mobile phones or can access one without difficulty. Consequently, young adults are generally more phone-literate than they are computer-literate. With all this in mind, mobile phones should be carefully considered for the effective delivery of language learning materials such as dictionaries.[8]

Naturally there are a number of drawbacks to mobile phones as a means of dictionary delivery. Most obviously there are tight restrictions as to the amount of data they can contain, and any further information – which may include example sentences, grammar and usage information, comments and notes – is unfortunately jettisoned. However the purpose of mobile phone dictionaries as proposed here is not to compete with or usurp the status of computer-based electronic dictionaries, but instead to complement them; to provide continued access to users even when the computer with the full version of the dictionary is no longer available for use. Computer dictionaries and mobile phone dictionaries are intended to work together to reinforce language learners' efforts.

---

8 For a more full discussion of individual mobile phone dictionary projects, or for information about the software and how to produce mobile phone dictionaries, please see the website for the Project for Free Electronic Dictionaries pfed.info/ .

Given the observable trajectory with respect to technological development it is entirely plausible that mobile phones in several years will be closer to hand-held computers, with higher capacity for memory and the ability to run software designed for a computer, such as Kirrkirr or other dictionary visualisation programs. It will then be possible to create dictionaries for mobile phones that do not sacrifice any content. Until then it is more important to make use of the multitude of electronic dictionaries of Indigenous languages by delivering them in a form that people can utilise effectively.

The Wagiman dictionary

Kybrook Farm, about 90 kilometres north of Katherine, is the home of around 100 people, roughly half of whom are ethnically Wagiman (S. Wilson 1999a). The Wagiman language is now only natively spoken by less than five individuals all of whom are aged in their sixties. Without a concerted effort to revitalise it Wagiman is expected to disappear within ten years (A. Wilson 2006).

Kybrook Farm is a typical remote Aboriginal community in that computers are rare; while the community office has a small number of computers they are generally not available for community members to use freely. Furthermore individuals do not have their own computers. Mobile phones though, are ubiquitous; almost all community members have mobile phones and all are technologically proficient in using them. For these reasons Wagiman was one language chosen for a trial run of an early incarnation of a mobile phone dictionary.

While an electronic dictionary had been created for Wagiman by S. Wilson (1999b), a revision of the dictionary contents was necessary. This provided an opportunity to port the Wagiman dictionary into Kirrkirr and moreover, to produce a mobile phone version. A demonstration version using the content from the online dictionary was produced and shown to the Wagiman community during a fieldtrip in February 2009. The response to the dictionaries was very positive, both from the younger members of the community and the adults and Elders. The consensus was that the portability of the mobile phone meant that the children, and indeed the adults, could always keep the dictionary with them. After subsequent work to complete the dictionary, a first edition was released in September 2009.

Conclusion

Computers are still rare in areas that are enduring language endangerment although mobile phone ownership is relatively high; most people high school age and above either own, or are in close proximity to, a mobile phone at all times. Mobile phones, though continually evolving closer to miniaturised computers, are still unable to contain a large amount of information. As a result dictionaries developed for mobile phones must sacrifice a large amount of content that is usually critical for language learners' dictionaries. Resources based on computers on the other hand are not subject to the same space constraints as today's mobile phones; they are able to contain huge amounts of data including images, sounds and movies. The disadvantage of computers is that they are not portable and their price still restricts their availability, meaning they are relatively rare in remote Australia and Aboriginal Australia. However these constraints on computers and mobiles phones may soon diminish, as recent history shows that computers are becoming smaller and less expensive, while mobile phones are becoming more powerful and, in fact, closer to computers in their capacity for multimedia content and functionality.

One potentially effective way to take advantage of the technological infrastructure of remote Australia is to create and disseminate both computer- and mobile phone-based language materials such as dictionaries. The computer-based resources would be of considerable use in classrooms – which are in fact well equipped with computers – and the mobile phone-based resources would be available to everyone at any time.

This is not to suggest that mobile phone- and computer-based dictionaries are in themselves sufficient to stave off language endangerment; they are merely tools and should be utilised in conjunction with other initiatives, such as bilingual education and Indigenous language education, in an attempt to strengthen Indigenous languages in Australia.

Acknowledgements

The project owes much to many people, most notably Jane Simpson for her unceasing mentorship, but also Peter Austin, Steven Bird, Sarah Cutfield, David Nash and others who attended the 2009 Australian Languages Workshop at Kioloa in March for their helpful comments, discussions and willingness to test and show off some of our dictionaries. We would also like to thank the linguists of Katherine: Lauren Campbell, Greg Dickson, Salome Harris and Colleen McQuay for their enthusiasm and support.

Most of this project would not be possible without the financial support of the Hoffman Foundation, whose donation has already enabled us to produce a number of dictionaries for minority languages.

References

Australian Communications & Media Authority (2008). *Telecommunications in remote Indigenous communities.* Canberra: Australian Communications & Media Authority.

Brady F, Dyson LE & Asela T (2008), Indigenous adoption of mobile phones and oral culture. In F Sudweeks, H Hrachovec & C Ess (Eds). *Proceedings: Cultural attitudes towards communication and technology 2008*, (pp. 384–98). Perth: Murdoch University.

Corris M, Manning C, Poetsch S & Simpson J (2000). Bilingual dictionaries for Australian Aboriginal langauges: user studies on the place of paper and electronic dictionaries. In U Heid, S Evert, E Lehmann & C Rohrer (Eds). *Proceedings of the Ninth EURALEX International Congress, EURALEX 2000* (pp. 169–81). Stuttgart: Universität Stuttgart.

Corris M, Manning C, Poetsch S & Simpson J (2004). How useful and usable are dictionaries for speakers of Australian Indigenous languages? *International Journal of Lexicography*, 17(1): 33–68.

Coward DF & Grimes CE (1995). *Making dictionaries: a guide to lexicography and the Multi-Dictionary Formatter*. Waxhaw, NC: Summer Institute of Linguistics.

Dyson LE & Brady F (2009). Mobile phone adoption and use in Lockhart River Aboriginal community. In X Hu, E Scornavacca & Q Hu (Eds). *2009 International Conference on Mobile Business* (pp. 170–75). Dalian: Dalian University of Technology.

Laughren M, Hale K & Hoogenraad R (forthcoming). Warlpiri dictionary. Unpublished electronic datafiles. Brisbane: University of Queensland.

Laughren M & Nash D (1983). Warlpiri dictionary project: aims, method, organization and problems of definition. In P Austin (Ed). *Papers in Australian linguistics No. 15: Australian Aboriginal lexicography*. Series A-66 (pp. 109–33). Canberra: Pacific Linguistics.

Manning CD (2003). *Kirrkirr: software for the exploration of indigenous language dictionaries*. [Online]. Available: nlp.stanford.edu/kirrkirr/ [Accessed 26 March 2009].

Manning CD, Jansz K & Indurkhya N (2001). Kirrkirr: software for browsing and visual exploration of a structured Warlpiri dictionary. *Literary and Linguistic Computing*, 16(2): 135–51.

McElvenny J (2008). *Mobile phone dictionaries* [Online]. Available: blogs.usyd.edu.au/elac/2008/07/mobile_phone_dictionaries.html [Accessed ?].

McElvenny J & Wilson A (2009). *Electronic dictionaries for language reclamation*. Paper presented at Supporting Small Languages Together: The First International Conference on Language Documentation and Conservation, University of Hawai'i at Manoa, 16–17 March 2009.

Nesi H (1999). A user's guide to electronic dictionaries for language leaners. *International Journal of Lexicography*, 12(1): 55–66.

Tangentyere Council & Central Land Council (2007). *Ingerrekenhe antirrkweme: mobile phone use among low income Aboriginal people – a Central Australian snapshot*. Alice Springs: Tangentyere Council & Central Land Council.

Teichelmann CG (1857). Dictionary of the Adelaide dialect. ms. No. 59 Bleek's catalogue of Sir George Grey's library dealing with Australian languages, South African Public Library.

Teichelmann CG & Schürmann CW (1840/1962). *Outlines of a grammar, vocabulary, and phraseology, of the Aboriginal language of South Australia, spoken by the natives in and for some distance around Adelaide*. Adelaide: Published by the authors at the native location. Facsimile edition 1962 State Library of South Australia. Facsimile edition 1982, Adelaide: Tjintu Books.

Wilson A (2006). Negative evidence in linguistics: the case of Wagiman complex predicates. Unpublished honours thesis, Department of Linguistics, University of Sydney, Sydney, NSW.

Wilson S (1999a). *Coverbs and complex predicates in Wagiman*. Stanford, CA: Center for the Study of Language & Information.

Wilson S (1999b). *The Wagiman online dictionary* [Online]. Available: www.arts.usyd.edu.au/departs/linguistics/research/wagiman/ [Accessed 26 March 2009].

World Wide Web Consortium (2008). *Extensible Markup Language (XML) 1.0*. 5th Ed. [Online]. Available: www.w3.org/TR/2008/REC-xml-20081126/ [Accessed 26 March 2009].

Part Seven
Language documentation

Introduction
Language documentation

Michael Walsh[1]

The issue of the value of documentation and its role in language revitalisation has occupied greater attention in recent years (for example Amery 2009; Himmelmann 2006, 2009; Woodbury 2003). Amery raises this important question in the context of language revitalisation of the motivation for language documentation: 'Phoenix or Relic?' In other words, are the results to be deployed for bringing a language back, or relegating the language to some archive? More broadly, Grinevald (2003, pp. 60–62) warns that sometimes it might be better not to proceed with fieldwork on an endangered language. And Wilkins, with considerable experience in Australian situations, observes (2000, p. 61):

> in fragile, embattled, minority indigenous communities, good intentions are not sufficient for good and useful results, and we must be self-reflective and self-critical about the sorts of practices we engage in that unwittingly will exacerbate rather than alleviate the problem.

The contributions in this section emphasise the urgency for language documentation but remain conscious of the need for caution, care and consultation.

Himmelmann is generally credited with distinguishing descriptive linguistics from documentary linguistics. Briefly put, the latter is 'a lasting, multipurpose record of the language' (Himmelmann 2006, p. 1) and is in contrast to the grammar–dictionary format of language description for which the primary goal is to explore the language as an abstract system. Much of the documentation on Australian Indigenous languages in the past has had this focus and, while it has the limitations inherent in the descriptive approach, it has underpinned many of the revitalisation efforts. Woodbury (2003, pp. 46–47) sets out the ideal requirements for a corpus in the documentary approach: diverse, large, ongoing, distributed and opportunistic, transparent, preservable and portable, ethical. The diversity includes examples of everyday interaction: talk between infant and adult; swapping jokes and anecdotes; service encounters; political disputes – most of which are absent in the descriptive approach. Obviously the corpora for Australia's Indigenous languages vary considerably and the documentation efforts set out in this section also show diversity.

---

1 Department of Linguistics, University of Sydney.

Baisden's project is paradoxically at once small scale and broad in scope. It is small scale in the sense that it does not attempt to carry out a multitude of tasks but is broad in that it potentially covers the entire state of Queensland: from Weipa in the north to the settled south-east corner. The project relies on the commitment of the State Library of Queensland, tapping the potential within an existing but under-utilised repository of documentation but also providing infrastructure through its network of some 330 library branches and 16 Indigenous knowledge centres. This gave rise to training workshops enabling consciousness raising, confidence building and opportunities for Indigenous people to become much more closely involved in the documentation process. It seems apparent that the Indigenous researcher, Faith Baisden, was instrumental in ensuring appropriate community consultation, the crucial ingredient for the success of this process.

The account by Bowern & James contrasts with other situations in this section and indeed in the entire volume. It is an instance of one language variety falling victim to language shift in the midst of otherwise strong language vitality. In fact one could see this group as subject to language prejudice where more prestigious varieties in the region have stigmatised the group's language. Interestingly, the project seems unlikely to have created any additional speakers but, according to Bowern & James, it has still produced positive outcomes: a hitherto poorly documented language is now much better documented; people have greater confidence in their language and its profile in the region has been lifted; and there have been positive effects in areas that are not strictly linguistic, like the intergenerational transmission of cultural and ecological knowledge. They argue that judgements of the success or otherwise of revitalisation projects should not be confined to purely linguistic considerations.

The title of the contribution by Eira & Solomon-Dent evocatively captures the recurring problem in language revitalisation of shoring up the linguistic foundations of a language while it is already in use. The renovation of a house already lived in can be not only inconvenient for its inhabitants but raise strong passions about what is to be done. One point of cleavage is the extent to which the new additions are compatible. This account emphasises the need to fill in gaps and exemplifies the process in some detail. It also presents a use of technology to alleviate the tyranny of distance that bedevils language revitalisation where typically the re-emerging speech community is widely dispersed.

The account by Gale & Sparrow is one of two projects describing the process of compiling a dictionary for an endangered language. In this case a primary need arose from school-based teaching of Ngarrindjeri where teachers and Aboriginal education workers required a contemporary, consolidated and authoritative resource for the word-stock of the language. They describe the process through collaborations with two universities, the take up of relevant technologies and the evolution of involvement by Aboriginal people. Intriguingly Ngarrindjeri students at Batchelor College from the 1980s have contributed to this recent upsurge in the documentation of the language. This is particularly through their teacher there, the late Steve Johnson, who built on the contribution of these students and collected material from people who have since become Elders. Another source of documentation goes back to the 1930s when the ethnographers, Ronald and Catherine Berndt, gathered material from an earlier generation. So it is a good example of material from the archive being re-deployed in a modern context.

Giacon's focus is on the development of the *Gamilaraay, Yuwaalaraay & Yuwaalayaay Dictionary* and sets out principles for dictionary development (see also Corris, Manning, Poetsch & Simpson 2002, 2004). He amply exemplifies the tension between standardisation and variation – the former being a less faithful reflection of the original language situation and the latter having the potential to interfere with language revitalisation. The solution in this situation has been to acknowledge variation but frame the dictionary in such a way that a common language can emerge across a wide area. In the future there is the possibility that regional varieties might separate but at this early stage of language revitalisation a pragmatic approach has been adopted after suitable community consultation.

In outlining their Cape York project Hill & McConvell stress the complementarity of endangered language documentation and language revitalisation. They also emphasise the *two-way* approach whereby there is a genuine exchange between Indigenous and non-Indigenous participants; ten languages in all were supported involving five researcher–community partnerships. An important feature of such collaborations was training in basic documentation tasks so that Indigenous language workers could evolve into co-researchers in their project. However some projects fared better than others and, interestingly, there was more success – particularly with regard to training – where local government and community organisations were strong. Although the results were mixed the overall outcomes were mostly quite positive and the documentation portion of the project yielded rich and varied results including not just audio- but also video-recording across a wide range of contexts and genres, including site recording, songs and cultural events and practices. This goes well beyond more traditional approaches to language documentation, the purpose of which has mainly been seen as an understanding of word formation and grammar. Whatever the merits of such approaches the richer range of documentation sought for in the Cape York project is not only more readily applicable to pedagogical requirements but also seems to be preferred by members of the Indigenous communities.

Obviously only some of the issues that might arise in language documentation for revitalisation have been canvassed in this section. Nevertheless we are presented with a varied array of case studies each with particular benefits and problems. Hopefully they will contribute to an emerging literature that speaks not just to academic theorists and practitioners but also to the wider community.

References

Amery R (2009). Phoenix or relic? Documentation of languages with revitalization in mind. *Language Documentation & Conservation.* 3(2): 138–48 [Online]. Available: hdl.handle.net/10125/4436 [Accessed 24 November 2009].

Corris M, Manning C, Poetsch S & Simpson J (2002). Dictionaries and endangered languages. In D Bradley & M Bradley (Eds). *Language endangerment and language maintenance* (pp. 329–47). London: Curzon Press.

Corris M, Manning C, Poetsch S & Simpson J (2004). How useful and usable are dictionaries for speakers of Australian Indigenous languages? *International Journal of Lexicography*, 17(1): 33–68.

Grinevald C (2003). Speakers and documentation of endangered languages. In P Austin (Ed). *Language documentation and description.* Volume 1 (pp. 52–72). London: School of Oriental & African Studies.

Himmelmann N (2006). Language documentation: what is it and what is it good for? In J Gippert, N Himmelmann & U Mosel (Eds). *Essentials of language documentation* (pp. 1–30). Berlin: Mouton de Gruyter.

Himmelmann N (2008). Reproduction and preservation of linguistic knowledge: linguistics' response to language endangerment. *Annual Review of Anthropology*, 37: 337–50.

Wilkins D (2000). Even with the best of intentions … : some pitfalls in the fight for linguistic and cultural survival (one view of the Australian experience)'. In F Queixalos & O Renault-Lescure (Eds). *As linguas amazonicas hoje: the Amazonian languages today* (pp. 61–83). Belem, Brazil: Museu Paraense Emilio Goeldi.

Woodbury A (2003). Defining documentary linguistics. In P Austin (Ed). *Language documentation and description.* Volume 1 (pp. 35–51). London: School of Oriental & African Studies.

29
Libraries, languages and linking up

Faith Baisden[1]

Abstract

There are many large organisations that have within their charter an expressed commitment to provide services to Aboriginal and Torres Strait Islander people. The challenge for these institutions is to find a way to meet such a pledge, and to do this in ways that have meaning for the people with whom they aim to connect. This paper describes the process by which the State Library of Queensland extended its services to Aboriginal and Torres Strait Islander people through offering support for language programs. It covers the development of the project from the initial consultation processes through to the organisation and delivery of training workshops and creation of resources, in a collaboration between the State Library of Queensland, the communities and partner organisations. It provides an example to other institutions of the outcomes that can be achieved when services are effectively and appropriately adapted to support the initiatives of Aboriginal and Torres Strait Islander clients.

With a charter to support Indigenous cultural heritage and a bent for innovation, the State Library of Queensland embarked on a visionary project to link its considerable resources with the needs of even the smallest community projects, giving welcome support to the revitalisation of Indigenous languages in Queensland.

> These places are filled with volumes written about Indigenous people and not nearly enough, by them. This is where Indigenous people can be telling the real stories, recording their own histories, and in their own languages. These are very much your libraries. (Queensland State Librarian Lea Giles Peters to members of the Queensland Indigenous Languages Advisory Committee 2007.)

The commitment of the State Library of Queensland would encourage Aboriginal and Torres Strait Islander people to actively record their stories, to be stored and shared

---

[1] State Library of Queensland.

with others as they deemed suitable. It would help bring together people in all parts of the state, many with no prior involvement in language programs, and it would support people to learn to record languages and create resources for the sharing of their language knowledge.

The question

The Queensland Indigenous Languages Project was initiated by the State Library of Queensland (SLQ) in 2006 in response to some of the recommendations from the *National Indigenous Languages Survey Report* from the year before. This survey, which had been commissioned by the Commonwealth government to document the status of languages in Australia, contained disturbing statistics pointing to the rapid decline in the use of traditional languages in Queensland and the imminent loss of many of them. It was within the charter of the SLQ to support the preservation and promotion of Indigenous culture and the organisation was recognised already for the depth of its Indigenous library services. These included the network of 16 Indigenous Knowledge Centres (IKCs) in the more remote areas of the state, and projects to support the delivery of information technology to these communities.

The concept underpinning this project was: with such a critical situation in terms of language preservation occurring, how could the SLQ make a difference? What resources do libraries have that could be of help to people working in Aboriginal and Torres Strait Islander language programs? To find the answer to this open-ended question the SLQ project team began consulting with community representatives around Queensland. The group most directly involved was the Queensland Indigenous Languages Advisory Committee, with members holding a breadth of experience over many years in the development of programs aimed at revitalising and preserving their traditional languages.

So began a process to list the resources that could be accessed through libraries and had potential to be of use. This was interesting, because it required a new way of thinking about the resources that are taken for granted by people who work in such a large system, looking with new eyes to see what value they could have for people who had been working with very limited resources.

The possibilities

Bringing together SLQ staff and the Indigenous language consultants, ideas soon began to flow as to how best to form a productive partnership. People saw the potential benefits of using the library spaces for meetings where there was no language centre available to fill this role. Helping language workers with access to computer equipment and internet were also considered, as well as the fact that some of the libraries were equipped with listening post facilities with multiple headsets for shared learning.

The network of over 330 libraries in key locations were considered as possible venues for the promotion of Indigenous languages through special exhibitions, and through the display and promotion of the books and resources that have been created through local projects. The public libraries were seen to represent an excellent distribution channel for language materials and, where desired by the community, public library services could be approached to purchase and distribute these published materials.

Website promotion was also considered, and the potential to include in the SLQ website some pages specifically devoted to Aboriginal and Torres Strait Islander languages. These would also be used to direct people to online access of the library resources catalogues.

In terms of the research that is integral to any of the language projects, the discussions highlighted the potential benefits of promoting greater connection between library staff and community users, to offer support to people as they attempt to manoeuvre their way through historical records and catalogue systems. But the point that came out most strongly through these consultations was that people wanted to learn to make their own language recordings. The SLQ could contribute immediately to the revitalisation of languages by teaching community workers how to record their own people and to show how computers and technology could be used with these recordings to make teaching resources. With the race against time that many people now acknowledge they are engaged in, the language workers were ready and willing to put the time into recording the sounds of the remaining speakers, given the appropriate training.

More than just a wish to see recordings being made, there was also a strong drive to reclaim control over the processes of linguistic documentation and recording which was seen to have been so firmly in the hands of non-Indigenous academics to this point in time. The sentiment expressed in these talks was that for too long people had been coming into communities and recording, writing and leaving with the outcome of their research. The books and recordings were acquired by visitors to the communities through the gifting of knowledge, time and effort generously afforded them by their hosts. People in many cases were then left with a challenge to gain access to recordings made of their own family members and were not credited as being custodians of the knowledge they had shared. This was, of course, not the case in all instances and was acknowledged to be a practice that is changing for the better. However the impact from those negative experiences was a key issue reflected in these talks.

With this background as added incentive one of the first tasks of the Queensland Indigenous Languages Project became the coordination of training workshops to provide the skills people wanted in order to take control of their own language revitalisation.

The workshop

The first of these training workshops took place in Townsville, north Queensland. It was coordinated with the North Queensland Region Aboriginal Corporation Language

Centre (NQRACLC) with people from six different language groups from around the Townsville area taking part. The number of participants was more than expected and it was seen from the outset that the program needed to be adaptable to cater for the unexpected.

In this first workshop people from the Girramay, Nyawaygi, Gudjal, Djirrbal, Ngadjan and Warrgamay groups worked together. Beginning with the basics of using audio and video recording equipment, participants worked in pairs or small teams to record each other demonstrating the sounds of the languages. They were able to produce videos that could teach correct tongue and mouth positions for forming the words. They recorded each other's oral histories and in interview settings. There were mistakes and laughter, embarrassment and pride as people struggled with and mastered unfamiliar sounds and skills. There was also a wonderful bonding between the older and younger students. Where some of the older people were short of computer confidence, they had the younger ones to help them. In turn the Elders shared their language knowledge and stories. As one of the teenage students later said:

> I was always so ashamed to try to use language because I thought I would say it all wrong. But being here and hearing our Elders make mistakes too sometimes makes me feel really OK about trying. That's what I'll do from now and start to learn and speak it.

The project has highlighted the need for adaptability and innovation at times from people who are involved in capturing language. The primary aim is to teach people to make recordings on quality audio and video equipment, with appropriate microphones and attention to the immediate surroundings to produce best results. Digitising standards are taught for scanning and photography. However, as valuable opportunities for recording cultural information, stories and snippets of language may occur at any unplanned moment, the workshops have been helping to prepare the students in the use of whatever equipment is available to capture a recording. So, while best practice and archival quality recording remains the primary aim, participants are also shown how to record information on mobile phones, take video on small digital cameras and to record directly into a laptop without an available microphone. New ways are mixed with old in finding ways to teach language to community. These range from the use of podcasts and social networking sites to putting lessons on cassette tapes to be played in car stereos.

The project also covers some photography basics. While everyone knows how to point and shoot, the tricks to resizing for email, basic retouching of photographs and importing images to other applications are popular inclusions in the workshops. Also pivotal to the training is learning to transfer collected data to computers and to organise the information in retrievable, logical systems for future reference.

Partnerships

This first workshop set a pattern of creating partnerships that has continued as the project moves around the state. Taking part in the Townsville meeting with SLQ and the NQRACLC were the local Indigenous radio station 4KIG and the Arwarbukarl Cultural Resource Association (ACRA) from Newcastle, which has played a key role in a number of the training workshops conducted since. The staff at 4KIG provided a number of rooms to cater for over 20 participants with access to recording studio spaces, helpful links to local media and on-air promotion of the project.

ACRA is a recognised Aboriginal training agency that has provided major input to the recording workshops. ACRA has helped train people in the use of the most suitable computer programs and technologies for the work they want to undertake, and trains in effective practices for data collection and storage which are key aspects of the workshops. ACRA's Miromaa Language Program[2] is a community-focused computer program for the collection, collation and storage of language data. Miromaa has proven to be a valuable inclusion in the training workshops empowering people to begin hands-on work on their language projects while learning a range of skills to support their desired outcomes. Having a place on the computer to input wordlists, audio, video and relevant research data, with the ability to easily export to dictionary and document creation tools, has proven to offer both incentive and encouragement for people to be involved in language projects.

Accessing suitable equipment for the workshops is important to their success. A starting point is always to establish what people already have available to them and, from there, decide what needs to be brought in. In some cases there is equipment available which has had little or no previous use due to a lack of training for the staff. Providing this training has been a useful outcome from the workshops. SLQ has a number of portable minilabs with audiovisual recording and computer equipment. ACRA also provides an extensive range of transportable equipment. For the Townsville workshop the materials needed were contributed by ACRA, SLQ and 4KIG, again reflecting the collaborative nature that has extended as the project continued.

A key aspect of the project has been listening to the needs of the community group involved to determine their particular focus. This varies all the time according to whether people are just starting to work on languages or whether they are connected to a language centre with well-established programs.

The broader picture

Although the training workshops are a major part of the project there are many other suggestions from the initial recommendations that have been taken on and are now expanding the reach of the project.

Through the SLQ website, pages have been made available to promote the language centres, their work and publications. This has been useful for the majority of Queensland language centres who don't as yet have an individual web presence. The SLQ website also displays a number of Indigenous language children's books

---

2 See www.miromaa.com.au

in an easy to read and hear virtual format, and will soon be expanding its links to educational resources and research materials.

The Library is encouraging people to use its facilities for the safe storage of language materials, giving due recognition to issues of limited and appropriate access to the materials as determined by the depositor. This complements the work of the Australian Institute for Aboriginal and Torres Strait Islander Studies in Canberra and, it is hoped, will eventually provide people in this state with more ready access to copies of records also held there.

Supporting the growing network of communities who are becoming involved in language revitalisation is another of the project's roles. This takes the form of information-sharing using email networks and blogsites. Community outreach meetings are being held in areas where no established language centres are operating as well. These are jointly coordinated with nearby language programs or centres. They involve bringing people from established programs into a community to give presentations about their work and their achievements to date, and to offer encouragement to people who may consider starting work in their own communities. These meetings are also a way of linking communities with the staff and services of their local regional libraries.

The identification and digitisation of old language recordings is taking place, as is the reformatting and reproduction of language teaching materials and the creation of new resources. Issues of ownership of the materials are discussed with each community, with permission sought for copies of items produced to be held in the SLQ.

The project extends from Weipa and the far north Cape York communities to the southern border towns and western Queensland, with ongoing outreach planned. The web of contacts grows and the number of people who are willing to share their knowledge, and support new communities in their endeavours, is inspiring.

It is also inspiring to see the commitment of the SLQ to support Aboriginal people and Torres Strait Islanders in creating their own records of history and culture in this state; the message and the hope to tell your own story, and be heard in your own voice.

References

Australian Institute of Aboriginal & Torres Strait Islander Studies (2005). *National Indigenous Languages Survey report 2005*. Canberra: Department of Communications, Information Technology & the Arts.

30
Yan-nhaŋu language documentation and revitalisation

Claire Bowern[1] *and Bentley James*[2]

Abstract

The purpose of this paper is to discuss revitalisation prospects for the Yan-nhaŋu language of Eastern Arnhem Land, northern Australia. We review previous work on the language and outline some issues to consider for language revitalisation. We tackle the difficult question of evaluating 'success' in revitalisation. We argue that language revitalisation projects should not be judged successful or otherwise purely on the basis of linguistic outcomes; as such programs may produce valuable outcomes in the socio-cultural context of language use even if they do not increase the number of speakers of the language.

Linguistic, social and geographical background

Yan-nhaŋu is a Yolŋu (Pama-Nyungan) language of the Crocodile Islands of North-Eastern Arnhem Land. It is a member of the Nhaŋu dialect cluster spoken from the Crocodile Islands in the west to the Wessel Islands in the east.[3] The language name literally means this language; *yän* (tongue or language), *nhaŋu* (this). This naming convention is common to most Yolŋu language varieties.[4]

---

1 Linguistics, Yale University.

2 Anthropology, Australian National University.

3 Information on the classification of Yolŋu (Yolngu, Yuulngu) languages can be found in Bowern (2005), Schebeck (2001) and the references therein.

4 This paper contains the names of people who have passed away. These names should not be spoken aloud in the presence of family members. In this paper we quote all Yan-nhaŋu and Yolŋu words in the widely used Yolŋu Matha orthography (used, for example, in Zorc, 1986). Underlining indicates retroflection, ŋ has the same value as its IPA value, ä is IPA /a:/. Nh and

Many Yan-nhaŋu people now live at the ex-mission settlements on their homelands at Milingimbi and Galiwin'ku, although some also live at Maningrida (the next community to the west) and surrounding outstations. The founding of the Milingimbi Mission in 1922 brought extensive changes to the Yan-nhaŋu traditional lifestyle, not least because it involved the permanent settlement of a large number of people on Yan-nhaŋu clan lands from other Yolŋu groups. Much of the day-to-day business of Milingimbi community is run by groups other than the Yan-nhaŋu. Nonetheless Yan-nhaŋu proper names are still used by the *Yolŋu* (Aboriginal people) of Milingimbi to refer to sites on the Islands and in the sea. Yolŋu living at Milingimbi acknowledge the sacred links among Yan-nhaŋu and the seas of the Crocodile Islands, although the Yan-nhaŋu are one of the least politically powerful groups in the area. Migrations of larger clans from the east and a legacy of marginalisation from the day to day running of the missions provide a background to the diminution of Yan-nhaŋu language use.

There is also a Yan-nhaŋu outstation settlement on the largest of the outer Crocodile Islands of Murruŋga, some 50 kilometres from the northern Australian coast. During the period of intense inter-clan fighting immediately following the Mission settlement many Yan-nhaŋu withdrew to this island. More recently the North-Eastern Arnhem Land homelands movement of the 1970s made it possible for Yan-nhaŋu people to return more permanently to their customary outer island home, as well as to travel more easily among Murruŋga outstations and the larger settlements on their other island homelands. Murruŋga Island is these days a focal point of Yan-nhaŋu identity and a large part of language work has involved recording subject matter related to this place (Yan-nhaŋu Language Team, forthcoming; James, forthcoming; Bagshaw 1998).

Historically Yan-nhaŋu speakers have had extensive ceremonial, cultural and economic links with other Yolŋu groups as well as with speakers of genetically unrelated languages further west. They are active participants in the extensive social networks that crisscross the whole of the Arnhem Land region. For example, Yan-nhaŋu women marry into other language groups including Dhuwal and Dhuwala speaking groups in the east, Djinaŋ and Djinba language groups to the south, and Burarra to the west (Keen 1978, pp. 130, 138; Bagshaw 1998 pp. 156–77).

The linguistic situation at Milingimbi is complex and many people are bi- or multilingual. Yan-nhaŋu people now generally speak Dhuwal (also known as Djambarrpuyŋu) in day-to-day interaction. Prestige languages in the area include local variants of Dhuwala (Gupapuyŋu) and Dhuwal at Milingimbi, Ganalbiŋu (Djinba) at the nearby community of Ramingining, and those residing at Maningrida regularly speak Burarra (Gun-nartpa) and English; all of these languages are exerting pressure on Yan-nhaŋu. Many Yan-nhaŋu people speak some English and most also know something of other more distant languages in the region, including Rembarrŋa and Gunwinygu.

---

dh are lamino-dental consonants; ny, dj and tj are palatal consonants. This paper is based on Bowern and James (2006) but revised, expanded and updated.

Yan-nhaŋu itself is not a homogeneous language (Bowern 2008). There are six patrilectal or *clan* varieties; three are Dhuwa, three Yirritja.[5] Not all the varieties are still spoken and most of the speakers involved in language work come from the Mäḻarra and Gamalaŋga clans. In addition to the small number of fluent speakers between the ages of 40 and 80 there are approximately 150 heritage owners with patrilineal ancestral connections to Yan-nhaŋu language, land, sea and *maḏayin* (sacred paraphernalia), and a further 120 Yirritja Burrara/Yan-nhaŋu (Gamal, Gidjingali, and Anbarra) people with language ownership rights. Table 1 provides information on the Yan-nhaŋu groups, their moiety, and the number of people belonging to each (see also Bagshaw 1998, p. 157).

Name	Patri-moiety	Linguistic affiliation(s)	Full speakers	Partial speakers	Total
Walamaŋu Gamal	Yirrchinga	Burarra/Yan-nhaŋu	27	89	116
Ŋurruwulu	Yirritja	Yan-nhaŋu	2	4	6
Bindararr	Yirrchinga	Burarra/Yan-nhaŋu	5	10	15
Gorryindi	Dhuwa	Yan-nhaŋu	8	30	38
Mäḻarra	Dhuwa	Yan-nhaŋu	10	36	46
Gamalaŋga	Dhuwa	Yan-nhaŋu	9	35	44

Table 1: Yan-nhaŋu language groups.

The complex relationships among groups are mapped through the idiom of kinship. Marriage in this area is exogamous so husband and wife will always be from different moieties and different clans. The Yan-nhaŋu groups signify their identities as separate from more distant groups primarily through reference to language rather than any distinct cultural practices. This linguistic identification includes groups speaking languages other than Yan-nhaŋu, so that purely linguistic classifications are not without ambiguities. The Gamal and Bindararr are referred to with the Ŋurruwulu as the Walamaŋu *bäpurru* (patrigroups) consistent with the logic of their ritual linkages (James, forthcoming, p. 92). Gamal people identify as Yan-nhaŋu but speak Burarra as 'their' language. This is relevant in a revitalisation program when part of the target group for language revitalisation expresses intellectual property of the language and

---

5 The Dhuwa or Yirritja moiety categories fundamentally divide and classify every aspect of the Yolŋu universe. Everything is either one or the other, so that every person or animal is Dhuwa or Yirritja and belongs to a Dhuwa or a Yirritja clan.

wish to have a say in the revitalisation and description process, but have no intention of shifting towards speaking the language themselves.[6]

Dhuwa Yan-nhaŋu patri-groups may also call themselves Märinga based on ritual associations. The three clans refer to each other as *yapa-manydji* (sister-dyad).[7] That is, kinship terms are used to denote the relationship among the clan groups. In certain contexts they may also refer to each other as *märi-manydji* (grandchild/grandparent-dyad). We include this information about the way that the patri-groups talk about their relationships to one another because it shows the cohesiveness of the Yan-nhaŋu speech community, despite evident patri-linguistic differences. The same type of cohesion exists among the Yirritja Yan-nhaŋu groups, which are known collectively as Malkurra. Myths and stories, shared country and secular ceremonial and marital links further strengthen alliances among these groups who also refer to each other as sister or company in Aboriginal English.

Despite the small number of Yan-nhaŋu speakers in each patri-group there is a great degree of cooperation among the Yan-nhaŋu-speaking patri-groups and the different varieties can be treated as a single language for the purposes of linguistic description. We leave aside for the moment the problems involved in deciding how much of the variation among speakers should be attributed to idiolects and how much to differences in clan language, although we note the considerable technical problems in providing a coherent description of a language where each variety is spoken by perhaps only a few family members.

Previous research on Yan-nhaŋu

Almost all of what has been recorded for Yan-nhaŋu before the last few years comes from incidental notes in ethnographic descriptions. Between 1926 and 1929 Lloyd Warner carried out fieldwork at Milingimbi Mission. In 1937 he published his ethnography, *A Black Civilization*. His account of Yolŋu life is primarily concerned with Yolŋu groups that in-migrated to Milingimbi Mission from the east. He produced extensive discussion of local social organisation, material culture, technology and warfare. Despite living on the Yan-nhaŋu island of Milingimbi, his focus on the whole *Murngin* (Yolŋu) culture bloc largely obscures the differences between Yan-nhaŋu and the more numerous speakers of Central Yolŋu varieties such as Dhuwal and Dhuwala. Later ethnographers – among them Thomson (1939, 1949), Berndt (1951), and Keen (1978, 1994) – also describe the characteristics of the larger terrestrial group which they call the Yolŋu, touching only briefly on the Yan-nhaŋu and again glossing over the linguistic peculiarities of the most western of the North East Arnhem Land Yolŋu. Each of these works contains some pan-Yolŋu terminology and some vocabulary peculiar to Yan-nhaŋu, but no detailed linguistic information.

---

6 Bowern (2008) studied linguistic variation within Yan-nhaŋu and found that variation indexes primarily age and clan; gender was not studied.

7 *-manydji* is the dyadic suffix, thus *märi-manydji* denotes a pair of people who are in the grandchild-grandparent relationship to each other.

There has been some desultory descriptive work on the Yan-nhaŋu language but very little before the work of the current Yan-nhaŋu language team, a collaboration among the authors of this paper, Salome Harris and six Yan-nhaŋu speakers; Laurie Baymarrwaŋa, Allison Warrŋayun (dec.), Laurie Milinḏitj, Rayba Nyaŋbal, Rita Gularrbanga and Margaret Nyuŋunyuŋu. Ray Wood and Barry Alpher both made brief recordings with Buthugurrulil (dec.) in the 1970s and Joy Kinslow Harris wrote down some words and a few short stories with Miḻmiḻpini (dec.) and Djarrga (dec.). The Milingimbi Literature Production Centre made a few storybooks with traditional stories. Gamaḻaŋga clan songs have been recorded by Alice Moyle (1962, 1974) and Ian Keen (1974).

The current phase of Yan-nhaŋu language work began in 1993 with the training of three of the Yan-nhaŋu language team at Batchelor College's School of Australian Linguistics. Rita Gularrbanga produced almost single-handedly a preliminary dictionary of about 350 items, arranged by initial syllable and with equivalents in Djambarrpuyŋu and English. This formed the basis for later dictionary work by the Yan-nhaŋu language team. In 1994 James in collaboration with senior Yan-nhaŋu initiated the Yan-nhaŋu dictionary team. In 1997 he intitiated bilingual classes recording the outcomes in his masters thesis (1999). In 2003 James et-al published the draft Yan-nhaŋu dictionary of 1800 forms.

James' PhD work focuses on the cosmological, sociological, ecological and economic dimensions of Yan-nhaŋu marine identity based on extensive work in species identification, site mapping and recording mythological narratives starting in 1993. The draft dictionary (James 2003) is being edited, revised and expanded in work by Harris and Bowern with the rest of the Yan-nhaŋu language team. Emphasis has been placed on illustrative example sentences, translation equivalents among Yan-nhaŋu, Djambarrpuyŋu and English, and the English–Yan-nhaŋu section has been greatly expanded. Thirdly, Bowern has completed a draft learners' guide that has been circulated at Milingimbi (Bowern et al. 2005) and has gathered the materials for a grammatical description of the language. She has also been working with the Yan-nhaŋu teachers at Murruŋga outstation school to build a small collection of language resources and activity ideas for school lessons as part of a language revitalisation project. Furthermore, she has been involved in language training work designed to help Yan-nhaŋu speakers produce their own resource materials. In a recent collaboration James has set up a project enhancing the intergenerational transmission of Yan-nhaŋu language and Yan-nhaŋu Ecological Knowledge (YEK) through an online (talking) pictorial encyclopedia. The online database will be linked to preschool Yan-nhaŋu 'Language Nests' and a Sea Ranger Program on the islands.

In summary there was no detailed work on the language before the 1990s, but in the last few years activity has steadily increased and at present there are several approaches to revitalisation and description.

The linguistic prospects for language revitalisation

The Yan-nhaŋu language team was formed with the twin aims of language description and revitalisation. On the one hand it comprises the Yan-nhaŋu speakers who are interested in working with linguists to describe and document the language. The team has the further aim of facilitating the use of Yan-nhaŋu in a wider sphere than its current use, including its introduction at Murruŋga school where all the children have ownership rights to the Yan-nhaŋu language through one or other parent. Yan-nhaŋu speakers have frequently expressed their desire to see their language more widely used and the language team is a collaborative effort to see this realised. Another strong focus has been the documentation of as much of the language as possible. Speakers are very aware of the fragile state of the language and wish to make use of linguists and technology to record as much Yan-nhaŋu as possible.

On the face of it, however, revitalisation programs are doomed to failure. Yan-nhaŋu language learning is not a high priority for heritage owners. As is often the case in such projects, the impetus for language documentation and for increasing the use of the language comes from those who already speak it, not from those who do not.[8]

Entrenched patterns of language use are also against adding to the number of speakers. Even those who speak Yan-nhaŋu fluently are in the habit of speaking to their children and grandchildren in Djambarrpuyŋu; they also frequently use Djambarrpuyŋu or Burarra with each other, even when all parties are fluent in Yan-nhaŋu. Language revitalisation in this case would mean not only teaching the language to those who do not speak it; it would also involve changing the linguistic habits of remaining speakers.

In the public domain Djambarrpuyŋu is the lingua franca among Yolŋu at Milingimbi, and English is used with the non-Indigenous school and government service providers, such as store managers, teachers and nurses. Church services are conducted in a mixture of Djambarrpuyŋu, Gupapuyŋu, and English as well as a fourth, hybrid language of Gupapuyŋu and English. Yan-nhaŋu is not spoken at all outside the clan groups who own it – unlike Djambarrpuyŋu/Dhuwal, for example, which is a lingua franca, or Djinaŋ or Gumatj, which are known to some extent by people without primary ties to these languages (see further Amery 1993). Therefore the linguistic ecology of Milingimbi is already well divided into areas where English, Djambarrpuyŋu, Burarra and other languages are used, and Yan-nhaŋu people, who are already fluent in these other languages have no need to redistribute these patterns of language use other than as a political or social statement. Yan-nhaŋu has very low prestige at Milingimbi outside the Yan-nhaŋu clans. Yan-nhaŋu is sometimes said by other people to be a worthless, simple language spoken by intellectually inferior people. That is, Yan-

---

8 It should be noted, however, that some other aspects of traditional culture are much more attractive to heritage owners. For example, Anita, a 14-year-old Yan-nhaŋu heritage owner said, 'I like going to Murruŋga because there's lots to do there. At Miliŋinbi it's boring, there's only TV' (pers. comm., 22 June 2004).

nhaŋu people are subject to all the usual unimaginative prejudices that are often held against speakers of endangered languages.

Finally, within the sphere of education, Djambarrpuyŋu and Burarra, along with other Indigenous languages of the Northern Territory, are themselves under threat from English-only or English-dominant policies. At the time of writing the proposal to mandate at least four hours of English instruction per day for all schools was being held over, but more general pressure against bilingual programs continues. Ironically, just at the time there is an increase in language materials for a school program, there is a decrease in the possibilities for utilising those materials in the formal curriculum.

What, therefore, is the point in running a revitalisation project when it is almost guaranteed not to produce any more Yan-nhaŋu speakers?

Successes

We argue that the revitalisation project has brought considerable positive outcomes for Yan-nhaŋu people at Milingimbi, even if it has not produced any more speakers of the language.

First there has been the raising of the profile of the Yan-nhaŋu language within the Milingimbi community. The presence of a linguist has raised Yan-nhaŋu self-confidence, particularly in using Yan-nhaŋu in public. For example, at the funeral of a Yan-nhaŋu woman in July 2004, several people spoke publicly in Yan-nhaŋu and one speaker, who began her speech in Djambarrpuyŋu, was heckled and told to speak in Yan-nhaŋu (Bowern, field tapes 14–17, 2004).

This increase in language profile is also manifested in increased confidence in asserting authenticity/efficacy of linguistic links to traditional sites, practices and experiences in Yan-nhaŋu country. Based largely on James' linguistic and ethnographic work meetings to determine land rights' management (as part of the *Aboriginal Land Rights [Northern Territory] Act*) with the Northern Land Council (NLC) have also resulted in the public reassertion of Yan-nhaŋu rights to country and marine estates. There has been considerable progress towards setting up a turtle management program and breeding sanctuary on Gurriba Island in the north of Yan-nhaŋu country. These combined projects have been instrumental in further supporting the continuation of links with marine sites and in the intergenerational transmission of cultural and ecological knowledge; for example, marine pharmacopoeia, turtle management, and ancestor spirit consultation. Thus the language project has been beneficial in promoting the transmission of cultural knowledge (although primarily through Dhuwal, not Yan-nhaŋu); this transmission places Yan-nhaŋu people in a better position to defend their rights to country in future. This in turn places them in a better position to negotiate for division of things like royalties. Importantly, these projects have been conducted primarily by Yolŋu themselves, and not by outsiders.

A further result of this research has been the increased profile of Yan-nhaŋu as a distinct group in relation to sites, sea country and marine resources in academic research. For example, the Northern Territory museum is investigating their sea country, the NLC is researching their sites and genealogies, and the North Australian Indigenous Land and Sea Management Alliance is investigating their turtle management strategies. The Aboriginal Areas Protection Authority has launched an investigation of Yan-nhaŋu sacred and archaeological sites. All of these projects employ Yan-nhaŋu people and promote exchanges of knowledge between Yan-nhaŋu people and researchers.

The presence of a linguist in the community has increased the use of Yan-nhaŋu among speakers and part-speakers and has, at least temporarily, altered the dynamic of language use in favour of Yan-nhaŋu. Bowern does not speak Djambarrpuyŋu fluently and frequently the only language that all members of the language team had in common is Yan-nhaŋu since not all Yan-nhaŋu speakers speak English. This ruled out Djambarrpuyŋu and English as lingua francas in such circumstances and increased the use of Yan-nhaŋu. It also increased the use of Yan-nhaŋu by part speakers who had someone else of similar ability to talk to. It remains to be seen whether this will have any longer term implications.

The project has been highly collaborative and has resulted in the transfer of literacy skills from Gupapuyŋu and Djambarrpuyŋu to Yan-nhaŋu. Yan-nhaŋu speakers had a great deal of control over what went into the documentation and the format of the end result. They proof-read the draft of the dictionary and have had editorial control over content from the beginning.

Positive experiences working with linguists have led the Yan-nhaŋu speakers to go to extraordinary lengths in working on the documentation program. This has resulted in large amounts of material being recorded. Bowern has been at Milingimbi for a total of 19 weeks over three years. A six-week field trip resulted in (among other things) the recording of all the material for the learners' guide, extensive dictionary expansion (approximately another 1500 items, doubling the number of headwords), and textual recording and transcription. The second, eight-week trip was focused on extensive elicitation and narrative recording, proof-reading the entire Yan-nhaŋu dictionary for publication, and checking of previous materials. The third trip included the creation of Djambarrpuyŋu–Yan-nhaŋu parallel translations for the dictionary, further grammatical materials, sociolinguistic interviews, and conversation data to record language in use. If and when heritage learners want to learn Yan-nhaŋu in future, they will have much more material to work from than they would otherwise have had.

A further corollary of this increase in publications is the increased awareness of the existence of the Yan-nhaŋu group in the anthropological and linguistic literature. The NLC had thought the Bindarra were extinct and the Gorryindi comprised of only one living person. This is of some importance to the Yan-nhaŋu patri-groups, who are worried about their knowledge being passed over and assigned to other groups. For example, Margaret Nyuŋunyuŋu related a conversation she had had with an anthropologist who told her that he had thought that the Gamalaŋga patri-group had been absorbed into another clan and its members had all passed away, and how disenfranchised it made her feel.

Conclusion

Endangered language reporting is often accompanied by gloom and doom and so we have emphasised the positive outcomes of recent Yan-nhaŋu language work. The difficulties in reversing a shift in language use are enormous and are not ultimately up to the linguist, although the linguist can be a help where the community itself is willing. We do not think that the linguistic work here will result in any more speakers of Yan-nhaŋu, even though we have been working with the central aim of linguistic revitalisation, but these projects are creating opportunities for the use of language on country where it counts.

However language revitalisation projects can do good even if they don't achieve the 'rebirth' of a language. We have shown here that language projects are not simply about language; they encompass issues of language use, culture, society and politics as well, and they can have a positive effect on non-linguistic spheres of culture and society. Therefore, importantly, we should not measure a revitalisation program's success or failure solely by the number of speakers recruited (see Amery 2000). By that yardstick the Yan-nhaŋu program was a failure. It is highly unlikely that the Yan-nhaŋu-owning communities will suddenly change entrenched patterns of language use. But equally clearly, the Yan-nhaŋu project was not a failure on any objective scale as it continues to build and encourage opportunities for the use of Yan-nhaŋu language in practical projects for Yan-nhaŋu people on their traditional homelands.

Another important point is the relationship between language documentation and language revitalisation. There is a theme in the literature that documentation should play second fiddle to revitalisation materials such as children's readers or alphabet books, and that salvage work (recording as much of a language as possible before the last speakers pass away) is in essence a type of media migration; transferring knowledge from a speaker's head to an archive which fossilises the language (Reyhner et al. 1999) and renders speakers almost unnecessary. In the Yan-nhaŋu case, intensive documentation has not relegated the language to a 'museum piece' (see Dauenhauer 2005 for further discussion of this). On the contrary, enthusiasm for the documentation project remains high and speakers have articulated a sense of relief that aspects of their language are now safely preserved for future generations. Yan-nhaŋu knowledge (both *in* the language and *of* the language) is valuable to its owners, who want to take care of it. Therefore we prefer the metaphor of 'backup creation' rather than media migration or the creation of a museum piece.

In short, the result of the Yan-nhaŋu language team's work has been to change Yan-nhaŋu from a very fragile language in the extremely endangered category with almost no documentation, to a somewhat less fragile language with good basic documentation whose speakers are now better off than they were before, and in a number of ways. Further, language revitalisation projects contribute in an important way to the future prospects of Yan-nhaŋu children and the use of their language in the Crocodile Islands. By all accounts this is a relatively happy result.

Acknowledgements

Claire Bowern gratefully acknowledges the support of the Hans Rausing Foundation's Endangered Language Documentation Project who provided a field trip grant (FTG0010) to cover her expenses in the 2004 and 2005 field seasons, and National Science Foundation BCS-844550 for the 2007 trip.

Bentley James would like to thank the Yan-nhaŋu for the ongoing privilege of working on their language and living on their sea country.

References

Alpher B (1977). Yanhangu field notes. Unpublished manuscript [PMS 2933]. Canberra: Australian Institute of Aboriginal & Torres Strait Islander Studies.

Amery R (1993). An Australian koine: Dhuwaya, a variety of Yolnu Matha spoken at Yirrkala in North East Arnhemland. *International Journal of the Sociology of Language*, 99: 44–65

Amery R (2000). *Warrabarna Kaurna! reclaiming an Australian language*. Exton, PA: Swets & Zeitlinger.

Bagshaw G (1998). Gapu Dhulway, Gapu Maramba: conceptualization and ownership of saltwater among Burarra and Yan-nhangu peoples of Northeast Arnhemland. In N Peterson & B Rigsby (Eds). *Customary marine tenure in Australia*. Oceania Monograph 48 (pp. 154–77). Sydney: Oceania Publications, University of Sydney.

Berndt R (1951). Ceremonial exchange in Western Arnhem Land. *Southwestern Journal of Anthropology*, 7(2): 156–76.

Bowern C (2005). *Yan-nhaŋu and Yolŋu Matha*. Invited Seminar, 19 July. Department of Linguistics, Australian National University, Canberra.

Bowern C (2008). *Seven speakers, eight varieties: variation in an Arnhem Land clan language.* Paper presented at the New Ways of Analyzing Variation conference: NWAV37, Rice University, Houston, Texas, 6–9 November 2008.

Bowern C, Baymarrwaŋa L, Gularrbanga R, Milinditj L, Nyaŋbal R, Nyuŋunyuŋu M & Warrŋayun A (2005). *Yan-nhaŋu learner's guide*. Milingimbi: Milingimbi Literature Production Centre.

Bowern C & James B (2006). Yan-nhaŋu documentation: aims and accomplishments. *Proceedings of the Chicago Linguistic Society*, 41(2): 61–69.

Capell A (1942). Languages of Arnhem Land. *Oceania*, 12(13): 24–51, 364–92.

Dauenhauer R (2005). Seven hundred million to one: personal action in reversing language shift. *Études/Inuit/Studies*, 29(1–2): 267–84.

James B (1999). The implications of Djambarrpuyŋu at Murruŋga. Unpublished masters thesis. Department of Linguistics, Northern Territory University, Darwin.

James B (Ed) (2003). *Yan-nhaŋu dictionary*. Milingimbi, NT: Northern Territory University.

James B (2009). Time and tide in the Crocodile Islands: change and continuity in Yan-nhangu marine identity. Unpublished doctoral thesis, Department of Archaeology & Anthropology, Australian National University, Canberra.

Keen I (1974). *Traditional songs from Arnhem Land*. [cassette recording]. Australian Institute of Aboriginal & Torres Strait Islander Studies, Canberra, Archive 006501-006609.

Keen I (1978). One ceremony,one song: an economy of religious knowledge among the Yolngu of North-East Arnhem Land. Unpublished doctoral thesis. Department of Archaeology & Anthropology, Australian National University, Canberra.

Keen I (1994). *Knowledge and secrecy in Aboriginal religion*. Oxford: Oxford University Press.

Moyle A (1962–63). *Songs and documentation from Arnhem Land and other northern parts of the Northern Territory*. [Sound tape reels]. Australian Institute of Aboriginal & Torres Strait Islander Studies, Canberra, Archive 001370-001389.

Moyle A (1974). North Australian music. Unpublished doctoral thesis, Department of Music, Monash University, Melbourne.

Reyhner J, Cantoni G, St Clair RN & Yazzie EP (Eds) (1999). *Revitalizing indigenous languages*. Flagstaff, AZ: Northern Arizona University.

Schebeck B (2001). *Dialect and social groupings in North-East Arnhem Land*. Munich: Lincom Europa.

Thomson D (1939). Notes on the smoking-pipes of north Queensland and the Northern Territory of Australia, *Man*, 39: 81–91.

Thomson D (1949). *Economic structure and the ceremonial exchange cycle in Arnhem Land*. London: Macmillan.

Warner L (1937). *A black civilization.* Harper: New York.

Zorc RD (1986). *Yolŋu-matha dictionary*. Batchelor, NT: School of Australian Linguistics.

31
A house already lived in

Christina Eira and Lynnette Solomon-Dent[1]

Abstract

In Victoria the urgency of language reclamation has motivated communities to focus on using their languages as much and as soon as possible. The analysis of historical sources and its incorporation into community language programs has tended to lag behind. This creates a very particular situation for language research, in that research findings must be used to firm up the linguistic foundations of 'a house already lived in'.

The Gunnai language program in Gippsland, Victoria has been active for some 20 years. Language teaching, interpretive signage and teaching materials are all well established in the community. As an example a range of pronouns sourced from Elders has been in active use for some years. On investigating the historical sources for the language it was found that the full range of pronouns was once more extensive, offering the expected range of meanings and distinctions.

During 2008 we – a Gunnai language worker and teacher (Lynnette) and Victorian Aboriginal Corporation for Languages community linguist (Christina) – worked together with the twin goals of: (a) reclaiming the full range of Gunnai meanings for pronouns while simultaneously (b) fully supporting the already existing language knowledge and use in the community. We compared the findings of an analysis of historical sources with the existing contemporary pronoun system, using the former not to replace the latter, but to expand it. The revised system will be introduced into teaching and resources, and the process has been recorded for training purposes.

This chapter presents a summary of the most salient material from historical sources, a comparison between this and the pronouns already available to the community, and the collaborative process of developing the revised system. The process raises key issues of deeper concepts of collaborative research, contemporary versus historical representations of language, priorities in

---

[1] Both authors are from Victorian Aboriginal Corporation for Languages.

language revival, and authenticity and change in contemporary Aboriginal revival languages.

Ngaju dhuna, Werna dhuna, dala, parrewatti, Werna dhuna. Wariga il nambur thooloo Werna. [I speak, we speak, a little or a lot, but we speak, so listen to us and talk with us].

It is important to speak language as our languages have been and are passed on orally still today; the written is just one way of documenting our language but not the only way, so firstly and foremostly listen to us and our Elders and don't correct the oral words with the way the language has been written. (L Solomon-Dent 9 April 2009)

Communities and linguists working in language revival face a common and constant challenge: how to balance the possibilities of linguistic analysis and the knowledge latent in archive sources with contemporary knowledge, usage and priorities for the language. The working solutions range (at various stages, with different groups of people, and from different starting knowledge bases) from ratifying the remaining orally transmitted knowledge exclusively, through to referring to linguistic advice on authentic grammar as an ongoing primary strategy.

In Victoria, while different language programs have taken divergent paths, the tendency is for communities to prioritise community knowledge and to reclaim their languages step-by-step as understanding develops. Community knowledge may start from the memories of Elders, words and meanings embedded in local varieties of Aboriginal English, and particular records of the language valued by individuals. As language awareness increases the knowledge broadly held in the community may expand to greetings and other set phrases, relatively fixed speeches, and sets of words such as the names of animals or elements of a traditional practice such as eel trapping. The emphasis is on rapid release of what is available into community use, community control of language products and processes, accessibility of the language to community members, maintaining cultural appropriacy of teaching content and approaches, and authoritative lines of transmission (see Eira & Stebbins 2008 for a detailed exploration of this last element). Linguists work closely with very few programs, but are more generally available as a support resource for training and consultancy on specific projects. Grammatical and phonological sketches are available for a number of languages, and wordlists or dictionaries produced by communities, linguists or both.

The emphases indicated above give rise to languages which have great value for Aboriginal people and high importance for identity and community strengthening. They are also languages-in-process, being expanded and revised at each new stage of development and each time information from an archival source or a linguist gains acceptance by language workers, Elders, and others. For example initial research by

Taungurung community language workers resulted in a wordlist widely distributed among the community, generating some language use at community events and in public arenas. While some understanding of the phonology of the language was gained through community workshops, for the most part people simply pronounced the words as the written form suggested to them. The importance of this stage was access to the words as such, as a means to reconnect with language, identity and culture. It was a few years later that a new language worker, Lee Healy, began a painstaking reconstruction of the pronunciation of each word from a comparison of all available sources, proposing an orthographic system as part of the process. The greatest challenge here will be to bring the results to the community in a way that promotes their acceptance, without undermining the achievements of the first stages of language reclamation (L. Healy, pers. comm., 14 August 2009). Here is an example of a house already lived in. Any new stage of development must be carefully grafted in without loss to the pride and confidence in their reclaimed knowledge and connection to their heritage that people have already gained. Because the house is lived in it is used – the fundamental groundwork, the framework, the roof, the rooms are there, but it needs renovations and new rooms added as it is expanding and growing.

How do we do this and stay true to the look of the house?

First and foremost is to work with that fundamental groundwork which is the Elders past and present, and the community still living who know these words and speak these words, sometimes without even noticing that they are speaking the language.

Gunnai/Kŭrnai language reclamation[2]

The Gunnai language program is a case in point. It is a strongly community-based program often held up as a model for other Victorian programs due to its continuation over 20 years and its establishment throughout the education system in the region. The initial materials for teaching arose from an Elders' workshop in 1991 focused on plants and their uses. From here a community wordlist (Dent 1997) was eventually developed which remains the basis of teaching in community and formal education to the present. Formal language teaching began at Gippsland Institute of Advanced Education (later Monash University, Gippsland campus) before the community language program was established in 1996 through the Gippsland and East Gippsland Aboriginal Cooperative. Teaching gradually expanded to schools including Woolum Bellum Koorie Open Door Education, and then preschools. In 2004 Gunnai was introduced into the Victorian Certificate of Education (*Indigenous languages of Victoria, revival and reclamation: Victorian Certificate of Education study design*), and

---

2 The term Gunnai/Kŭrnai is the formal designation of the Gippsland peoples and often used for the language as well. It recognises the two main variants on the name used by different groups in the community. Kŭrnai is the spelling used in, for example, Fison & Howitt (1880), now pronounced [kɜːnaɪ]. Gunnai is the preferred spelling of the Community Language Program, pronounced [ganaɪ]. In this chapter we will use Gunnai and Gunnai/Kŭrnai interchangeably.

into certificate programs at the Central Gippsland Institute of Technical and Further Education (TAFE) Koorie Unit in 2006. Informal language teaching is also developing, for instance in a Sunday school class. Gunnai/Kŭrnai speaker/learners range in age from three to 77 years old and live across the full extent of south-east Victoria.

The presence of Gunnai language is now evident in forms including public signboards (some quite extensive), speeches given by various Gunnai/Kŭrnai people, casual use by people who have been through the teaching programs, and an expanding range of language resources including illustrated books, a CD and accompanying learning guides. As teachers of the language are largely graduates of one or more of the above programs their teaching is quite homogenous and uses the same basic set of materials as a reference and resource kit.

The central principle underlying teaching and development of Gunnai is the value of oral transmission. This is the way Lynnette was taught. We need to use that oral information that we have; then we look at the oral documentation of our Elders, such as tapes. Next we look at written documentation approved by the Elders. Lastly, and only when we need to get further help or support, we use additional material documented by non-Aboriginal early recorders and linguists, but only when it has been talked about with Elders and community learners to see if it fits with our way of using language. The principle is that the written supports the oral language knowledge of plants, medicines and so forth, the stories passed down, and the speaking knowledge of sounds and the way those words were said before written documentation. This often causes problems and divisions in the community because the sound appears changed in the writing. Relying on the archive and academic sources can mean that the written takes away the oral.

This system of priorities establishes the lines of authority in language as firmly within the community, and maintains a traditional practice of learning from your own Elders according to their decisions about what is available to be learned, who by and how. There are obvious benefits here for identity and community strength and cohesion, as well as the maintenance of values such as respect, patience, deep rather than fast learning, and the role of Elders in directing and mentoring the community. While Elders freely acknowledge that their language has changed from various influences including English, many in this community have a view of living languages that can accommodate change. What is most crucial here is that the knowledge and views of Elders remain central to decisions and practice, and the community is in control of their language. The downplaying of archival records does mean however that, aside from those sources which some Elders appear to draw on as part of their own knowledge base, additional storehouses of Gunnai/Kŭrnai language records have remained largely unutilised to this point.

Gunnai/Kŭrnai pronouns: A case study

In this chapter we describe the process by which Lynnette (language worker and Gunnai teacher) and Christina (Victorian Aboriginal Corporation for Languages

[VACL] community linguist) recently reviewed the current pronoun system by incorporating an analysis of archival sources into current knowledge. This differs radically from an approach whereby analysis of archival sources together with cross-linguistic comparison and reconstruction are considered primary. In this system a much higher value is placed on current community knowledge and practice, and oral transmission principles as described above, with archival sources brought in to support and expand the language to its next stage of development.

Pronouns in current use

Tables 1 and 2 set out the pronouns as listed in the current community wordlist (Dent 1997). The core set of words most commonly taught and used at present is highlighted in bold.

	Singular	Dual	Plural or unspecified non-singular
1st person	**ngaju** (I) ngio (me)	nalloo, nalu (us two) ngallu, nanangoo (we two)	**werna** (we plural, us)
2nd person	**njinde** (you) nungoo, ngowo (you)[3]	limbaook (you two)	
3rd person	noonga (he, him) noong (her) jilly, gindi, mali, ngal (he)[4]		thana, mandha (they)

Table 1. Current personal pronouns.

	Singular	Dual	Plural or unspecified non-singular
1st person	ngetal (my, mine)[5]		**nindethana**, warulung (ours) wurnalung (our)
2nd person	**ngingal** (yours) ngawana thanal (your singular) koothoula (yours singular)	limbaulung (yours dual)	
3rd person	nungal (his)	thanal (theirs dual)	**ninde thana** (theirs plural) booloonga, kandha (their plural)

Table 2. Current possessive pronouns.

All the core teaching set are glossed with meanings parallel to those of English. However the wider set of pronouns here reveals some indications of the possibilities latent in the list. A distinction among one, two and more is evident. There is an apparent possessive suffix {-lung}, sometimes {-l }. This is confirmed by the names of subgroups and/or dialects within Gunnai/Kŭrnai such as Braiakaulung or Tatungalung (approximately, of the men of the west and of the sea, respectively). There are apparent choices of word for a number of English meanings such as you, suggesting that more detailed meanings might be buried in this listing. In this regard the implied distinction between *ngaju* as I and *ngio* as me is significant.

These indications within what is already familiar open a door to expanding the system for greater reclamation of the breadth of meaning and complexity latent in the language.

Analysing the historical sources

Historical collections and recent analyses

Nineteenth century Gunnai speakers were recorded anonymously in over 30 documents, some of which are revisions and publications of earlier notes. The most important of these for our present purposes are those with texts, sentences and paradigms: the sections in Smyth (1878) contributed by Bulmer (pp. 24–39, 96–97), Hagenauer (pp. 97–98) and Howitt (pp. 48–49), an additional manuscript by Hagenauer (n.d.), and the extensive work of R.H. Mathews (1902, n.d.a & n.d.b). Some wordlists also include individual pronouns, such as Crouch (1863) and the survey response by Miss Henry, collated by J. Mathew (n.d.).

Little analysis of this material has been carried out, and still less published. A masters thesis by Fesl (1985) collates and discusses some of the grammatical information evident in historical sources. The chapter on pronouns draws almost exclusively on various work by R.H. Mathews (including 1902, n.d.a & n.d.b) and, while this certainly achieves some inroad into the complexities represented by the full range of documentation, it necessarily leaves a considerable amount of data, and hence questions and possibilities, unconsidered. Information in the cross-linguistic tables in Blake & Reid (1998) follows Fesl, though more cautiously. In an unpublished analysis of the textual sources for Gunnai/Kŭrnai, focused primarily on case and verbal morphology, Morey contributes some more complex consideration of both free and bound pronouns, but states wisely that ' … a comprehensive discussion of Gippsland pronouns is beyond the scope of this paper' (n.d., p. 55).[6]

---

3 Number unspecified for all three.

4 Also glossed as by themselves.

5 *Also nheetall* (myself).

6 Thanks to Stephen Morey for provision of both this paper and a large folder of his meticulous working notes on the language.

Analysing the pronouns: the next stage

Due to the status of research on pronouns in Gunnai we decided to start from scratch. Christina compiled a list of all tokens glossed with pronominal meanings in the historical sources, parsing all sentences, phrases and texts in Toolbox. This resulted in a ridiculous 120 putative pronouns, counting possible bound, inflected or derived forms separately, but not counting obvious spelling variants. A few possible additional tokens may also be embedded in currently analysable phrases. Clearly it is beyond the scope of this chapter (to echo Morey) to discuss the analytical process involved in considering all of these candidates. Instead we restrict ourselves to exploring the issues posed by first person singular (1sg) forms to give a general picture of what was involved, then summarise the least problematic choices for the whole paradigm as one of the bases for our proposal for a new contemporary paradigm. Forms recorded only as clitics or bound forms are not included in this paper.

The following forms are recorded for 1sg:

Pronominal forms recorded	Sources	Position (stated or implied contextually)
ngaiu, ngio, ngaju	Bulmer; R.H. Mathews (RHM); Hagenauer	subject & object (Bulmer), subject & agent (RHM)
ngi	Bulmer	subject and agent
ngioma	Bulmer	causative
ngan	Bulmer	object (including [hit] me [head])
ngat, nat, ngaty	Bulmer; R.H. Mathews; Howitt; Hagenauer	subject, object, agent (Bulmer), subject & agent (RHM), agent (Howitt), subject (Hagenauer)
watha	Bulmer	object

Table 3. First person singular pronoun tokens in the historical sources.

R.H. Mathews also glosses *ngal* as 1sg, but this is surely a misunderstanding of first person dual (1du) *ngalo* or *nalloo*. Both Mathews and Bulmer also record *ngal* as 1du, Mathews listing it as inclusive.[7] It is easy to understand a 19th-century speaker of English struggling with a lexicalised concept of I and you.

---

7 For those unfamiliar with this concept, this is a way of specifying the meaning of we. In English we can mean either me and you, or me and someone else, possibly including some

We have assumed *ngaiu*, *ngio* and *ngaju* to be alternative spellings for the same form. *Ngi* can also be added to this set, interpreting i as /aɪ/ or /ajɪ/ and assuming the last sound was quiet or dropped in the speech context. *Ngioma* appears to display the Gunnai clitic {-ma}. The functional range of {-ma} includes, but is not limited to, possessive marking. It would not be expected to cliticise to a pronoun. Without a context it is hard to understand Bulmer's analysis of *ngioma* as causative. He also includes *nindoma* as second person singular (2sg) causative (by thee). Causative is a common 19th century description of the ergative function, but *ngioma* and *nindoma* do not match easily with other tokens for the ergative singular forms.[8] Regardless of the final analysis of {-ma} it seems clear that it can be treated as a suffix or clitic, rather than an integral part of the pronouns themselves. This brings *ngio(ma)* also into line with the *ngaiu* set. *Ngan* and *watha*, listed by Bulmer as having object function, also remain a little mysterious at this point suggesting that further cross-linguistic comparison may be needed. *Watha* may related to *wert*, a form collected as first person plural (1pl). *Ngat*, *nat* and *ngaty* (Fesl /ŋaḍ/) match well with the apparent clitic *ngadha* (Bulmer; Hagenauer and Mathews), recorded in both subject and agent contexts. (A possible reduced form {-ndha} also appears in Mathews.)

Historical sources suggest an ergative/absolutive or possibly nominative/accusative distinction in at least 1sg and 2sg with (inconsistently) different forms listed for S(ubject), A(gent) and O(bject) by R.H. Mathews and especially Bulmer. (From this point we will use terms employed in teaching; active for ergative, and non-active for absolutive). Cross-linguistically, forms cognate to the Gunnai candidates *ngaiu* and *ngaty* suggest the former as non-active and the latter as active, which is at least compatible with the Gunnai evidence.

Following the kind of investigation indicated above for all tokens in the sources, we made a heavily reduced summary of the most useful and likely pronoun forms recorded, to discuss in relation to the contemporary list (Tables 4 and 5):

---

other people besides. In most Aboriginal languages these meanings are two different words. Inclusive we *includes* the person I am speaking to (me and you). Exclusive we *excludes* the person I am speaking to (me and someone else).

8 An *ergative* (or active) pronoun is used when one person is actively doing something to another. Nineteenth-century collectors explored this by the use of sentences such as He killed the possum, where he is clearly doing something active to someone else (in this case, the possum). Other possibilities could include She lifted the child or, I hugged my grandfather. Conversely the *absolutive* (or non-active) pronoun can show either that: (a) someone else is doing something *to this person* (Mother lifted *him*, my grandfather hugged *me*), or (b) the person is doing something *not* particularly active in the direction of another, such as sleeping or thinking. The easiest way to think of it is that the nonactive pronoun is the ordinary one, used most of the time, while the active one is *only* used if the person is directly acting on someone/something else. Most Aboriginal languages make the distinction between these two meanings in some form or other.

	Singular	Dual	Plural
1st person	ngaiu, ngadju, ngadha, ngaty Active and non-active meanings evident, but not clearly identified.	nalla, nalloo, nangoo Inclusive and exclusive meanings evident, but not clearly identified.	wurroo (inclusive) werna (exclusive)
2nd person	nginna, ngingu, njinde, nindo, nginda As above.	limbaook, ngowo	ngoortana (non-singular)
3rd person	ngunga, jilly	bulla	thana, thinana, mandha

Table 4. Personal pronouns from historical sources – summary selection.

	Singular	Dual	Plural
1st person	ngetal, ngeethaloong	nanalaloong, nalanaloong (exclusive)	warulung, wurnalung, nindethanal
2nd person	ngingal, nginalung, koothoula	limbaulung	ngooradhanaloong, ngwana thanal
3rd person	ngungal, nungalung, ngungowa (feminine)	booloonga	dhinaloong

Table 5. Possessive pronouns from historical sources – summary selection.

While even this reduced paradigm is clearly not without discrepancies, it highlights for present-day speakers and learners some of the extended meanings possible in Gunnai. The distinction among singular, dual and plural is partly clarified. An inclusive/exclusive distinction is clearly evident and there are indications of a partial active/non-active distinction. Importantly one or more candidates are now available for every expected slot in the paradigm.

For accessibility to the contemporary community it is at least as important that there is a significant degree of overlap between this list and Dent (1997). Some words are identical in probable pronunciation, if not also spelling; others are similar such as 1du *nangoo* (current list *nanangoo*). The suffix {-*lung*} apparent in Dent (1997) is attested here for more of the pronouns, offering regular alternatives for all members of the paradigm.

The next step forward

With a relatively clear picture both of contemporary usage and the contribution of historical sources, it was now possible to develop an expanded set of pronouns to propose to the Elders who formed the reference group. We designed a set of working principles to support the knowledge and confidence already built up in the community while also providing people with a new level of access to the richness of their language:

1. Keep what's familiar
2. Reclaim the full range of Gunnai meanings for pronouns
3. When there's more than one word in the current wordlist, choose the one that matches the historical sources
4. Select just one spelling for each word (or morpheme) each time it appears
5. Fill in 'missing' pronouns by using the patterns we can see, then from the historical sources.

Tables 6 and 7 list the newly expanded pronoun paradigm developed on this basis.

	Singular	Dual	Plural
1st person	*ngaju* (active) *ngaiu* (non-active)	*ngallu* (inclusive) *nangoo* (exclusive)	*waru* (inclusive) *werna* (exclusive)
2nd person	*njinde* (active) *ngingoo* (non-active)	*limbau*	*ngurtana*
3rd person	*noonga*	*boola*	*thana*

Table 6. The expanded personal pronouns.

	Singular	Dual	Plural
1st person	*ngetal*	*ngalluloong* (inclusive) *nangaloong* (exclusive)	*waruloong* (inclusive) *wernaloong* (exclusive)
2nd person	*ngingal*	*limbauloong*	*ngurtanaloong*
3rd person	*noongal*	*booloong*	*thanaloong*

Table 7. The expanded possessive pronouns

First it is important to note the degree to which we have been able to affirm pronouns already in use (Principle 1). *Ngaju, ngaiu* (respelt from *ngio*), *ngallu* (subsuming *nalloo* and *nalu*), *werna, njinde, noonga* (subsuming *noong*), *thana, ngetal, ngingal, noongal, limbauloong, waruloong* and *wernaloong* (spelling adjusted to match *werna*), are all present and accounted for. Slight adjustments adapt *nanangoo* to *nangoo* as the simplest option in a set of apparent variants, and *limbaook* to *limbau* as a solution to inconsistencies in the historical evidence. *Ngurtana* is added from archival sources but was found in Dent (1997) as every (every one of you). We have also made a couple of adjustments for consistency: we can safely assume that *booloonga* (their plural) should be specifically dual as it relates directly to *boolaman* (two),[9] a common strategy in other languages, while *thanal* seems misplaced as theirs dual as this morpheme is associated everywhere else in the wordlist with plural.

We have consistently applied the possessive {*–loong*}, evident in Dent (1997) and further attested in the archival sources, across all dual and plural pronouns (Principle 5 extended). It is also offered as an optional alternative for the singular paradigm, retaining the more familiar *ngetal, ngingal, noongal* as primary. 'Missing' pronouns can be backformed by removing this suffix, yielding *boola* and *waru* (supported also by the archival sources), as well as supporting our choice of *limbau* (Principle 5).

Spellings have been regularised such as {*-loong*} and *noongal* (Principle 4). Note that this is done at lexical or morphological level, not at phonological level as in a standard orthography.

We have been able to account for the apparent choices in the current wordlist for both I/me and you. *Ngaju* and *ngio* match well with both historical sources for Gunnai and active/non-active pronouns in languages across the continent, as discussed.[10.] Looking at the options for you, we have a slightly more complex problem. None of the sources shed much light on the multiplicity of words given or their possible shades of meaning. *Njinde* is already very established in community use, being part of the standard greeting *Wunman njinde?*, and so has to be retained. Comparison with other Aboriginal languages indicates that a *nginda*-like word is more likely as the active pronoun, while a *nginna*-like word is more likely as the non-active. All things considered, we have opted for *njinde* as the active pronoun and *ngingu* as the non-active. In its contemporary pronunciation /nɪndʒɪ/, the former approximates the expected form of an active 2sg – although in the 19th-century spelling nj is probably intended to represent, not an n followed by English j, but a palatal nasal (as in Spanish *señor*). *Ngingu* is a compromise between Dent (1997) and a historical/comparative representation of the word. In practice, since *njinde* is so thoroughly established as the general word for you (extending also to dual and plural by analogy with English), this will probably be the slowest pronoun to shift to the proposed meaning. Current usage may, in the end, override the revision in this case.

---

9 Or *bullung* (dispreferred).

10 Ironically these two forms probably did not originate as active and non-active pronouns respectively. In our analysis of the historical sources we represent *ngaju* as a variant spelling of *ngaiu/ngio*, with the j representing a /y/ sound as in yes. Given the default English pronunciation of j, it is easy to see how these variant spellings could have diverged into two different words. As it happens, the end results fortunately do match reasonably well with what we can expect to find in an Aboriginal language.

Similar procedures were applied to identify the inclusive and exclusive pronouns. All four words for we (and their possessive counterparts) are apparent in both community wordlist and historical sources with minor adaptations as above. Historical sources are fairly clear about which is which for the plural pronouns. While they are less clear about the duals, discussions by R. H. Mathews result in slightly better evidence in favour of *ngallu* as inclusive and *nango* as exclusive. Data analysis for language revival has a particular purpose: it has to result in a workable decision that people can use now. Where the available evidence leaves issues in doubt, in many cases a best guess or even simply a choice has to be made. In this sense, as well as in the sense of community processes, language revival is necessarily an ongoing phenomenon.

Where additional pronouns in Dent (1997) are unexplained by this process of expanding the range of meanings, we have not included them in the basic pronoun paradigm (Principle 3). This does not entail their removal from the wordlist, as they are easily explained as alternative means of referring to someone. That one, or similar, is commonly used even in Aboriginal English to refer to a third person, which makes sense of the many words given for he and they. Some of these demonstratives, such as *gindi*, also match well with forms found in other languages. Lynnette suggests that other possible explanations may account for other forms, such as *nindethana*, misunderstood as a core pronoun, which may be simply you and they.

This completes the basic singular, dual and plural paradigms for all three persons. As some readers may have noticed our proposal is not completely finished. For example it is not clear how to spell *thana* when it appears as part of another pronoun, {-*tana*}. *Noonga* may be better represented as *ngoonga*, as this form does appear in the historical sources, and it is well known that ng at the start of a word was commonly overlooked by collectors. We have not even touched on pronouns as suffixes on the verb though these abound in the historical sources. These and other questions will serve to raise discussion topics for the next generation of language students and a way for them to participate actively in the development of their own language.

Aboriginal people have been told over nearly two centuries that they and their languages are 'primitive'. While people today may know at some level that their language is as rich and complex as any other, this fact is usually talked about with considerable emotion indicating that the wound is far from healed, and the indictment of both language and people is still in need of strong resistance. The tangible evidence of this richness in the form of complex distinctions between exclusive and inclusive, singular/dual/plural and so on, is an important contribution to finally overturning the power of this label.

The Elluminate session

As a linguist and language worker in partnership we have had many discussions about the words of the language – what's available, what's missing, what's clear from the historical sources and what's tentative – but these discussions and the language development process which results is generally unavailable to others. For this reason we decided to record an interactive session in Elluminate Live![11] targeted to advanced students and language workers. Elluminate provides a virtual classroom environment with interactive whiteboards, breakout rooms and so on. Lynnette has already been using Elluminate for distance education through the Central Gippsland Institute of TAFE, so it seemed a logical next step to record a staged conversation between ourselves complete with PowerPoint slides and tables of the proposed revisions at various stages. The one-and-a-half-hour session documents our discussions about historical sources, how to match them with the knowledge already in circulation, and the issues which are raised by the process. Viewers can observe the process and apply what they understand to their own language, in terms of possible gaps and how to fill them, in ways which are readily traceable to the language as recorded by 19th century speakers, while at the same time supporting contemporary knowledge and practices. The session can be pulled apart to form digestible pieces for students and intertwined with additional training material as relevant. For example, at a VACL language workers' workshop in 2009, we used a framework of about half the session to raise issues of ongoing language development, interpretation of historical sources, and identification of morphological patterns.

Conclusion

Our case study illustrates how it might be possible to continue developing the house already lived in with minimal cost to the 'residents'. The fact that the language is known and in use in the community means that current community knowledge and usage has to be privileged if any further development is to be successful. In the Gunnai context an important principle for this is to value the oral above the written. Written or archival sources are viewed as supporting knowledge that has been transmitted orally, and for seeking words and meanings missing from current knowledge. All language decisions are referred to Elders. The principles we followed in developing the pronouns aim to ensure that: (a) the confidence of learner-speakers in their current knowledge can be maintained, (b) community authority in their language is maintained, and (c) the contemporary language is validated as a 21st-century living language, regardless of the completeness of that language and the theoretical challenges this presents for notions such as authenticity and language change.

For the linguist in this partnership the point of the collaborative process is that it allows me to gain a better understanding of what the community knows they need to do. It helps me to work *with* what's happening, thereby smoothing out potential blocks to collaborative productivity as we go. When this is working well the collaboration also gives the community good access to the kinds of interpretations that linguistics can bring to historical sources, returning more of the ancientness of the language's structures and meanings to the language of the present.

In addition the way of working trialled here has potential to take the principle of collaborative research to a deeper level. We are not simply proposing a partnership

---

11 See www.elluminate.com/products/live/

model, which has been suggested and implemented many times before, but a *merging of the principles by which we determine what is correct*. For Christina as linguist, correctness can be determined by careful analysis of data. For Lynnette as language worker, correctness can be determined by listening to those with the authority to know. We see no benefit in pitting these principles against each other. Instead, in the interests of accessibility and acceptability of the research to its end users, we simply prioritise as data what is already validated and in use in the contemporary community. In all probability we will need to reconcile ourselves to a separation between the methods, goals, and validation systems for reconstructing a historical language, and those targeted to a functional analysis for a contemporary emerging language.

To include contemporary usage and knowledge in assessing what is correct challenges the assumption often held by both linguists and communities, that the only correct or authentic form of the language is what was spoken at the time of colonisation. For linguists this represents a theoretical shift in our understandings of language loss and change. For communities it represents a process of recognising and then coming to terms with that loss and change – what Jeanie Bell (2009) has called 'the grieving phase of research'. This research also underlines the need to accept the staged nature of language revival – again, an issue faced continually by both communities and linguists. It is clearly neither feasible nor desirable to wait until language analysis and language decisions are final before using what is accessible. Thus both analysis and language planning decisions are necessarily a work in progress. The solution we propose is to embrace what is known and accepted now, and use it loudly and proudly, while also understanding that if change is an intrinsic part of living languages, it is even more a part of living reclaimed languages.

References

Bell J (2009). Address given at Puliima 2009: National Indigenous Language & Information Communication Technology Forum, 31 March, Koori Heritage Trust, Melbourne.

Blake B & Reid J (1998). Classifying Victorian languages. In B Blake (Ed). *Wathawurrung and the Colac language of Southern Victoria* (pp. 1–58). Series C, 147. Canberra: Pacific Linguistics.

Crouch JWC (1863). An enquiry into the etymological construction of the Australian Aboriginal tongue with analytical remarks on languages generally. Unpublished manuscript held at La Trobe Library, State Library of Victoria, Box 46, Item 1(2).

Dent L (1997). Ganai dictionary: English – Ganai. Unpublished manuscript.

Eira C & Stebbins TN (2008). Authenticities and lineages: revisiting concepts of continuity and change in language. *International Journal for the Sociology of Language*, 189: 1–30.

Fesl E (1985). Ganai: a study of the Aboriginal language of Gippsland based on 19th century materials. Unpublished masters thesis, Monash University, Melbourne.

Fison L & Howitt AW (1880/1991). *Kamilaroi and Kŭrnai: group marriage and relationship, and marriage by elopement; also the Kŭrnai tribe: their customs in peace and war*. Melbourne, George Robertson. Facsimile edition published in 1991 by Aboriginal Studies Press, Canberra.

Hagenauer FA (n.d.). *Lakes Wellington, Gippsland.* (Recopied with notes apparently by RH Mathews and held in the RH Mathews collection.) National Library of Australia, MS 3179, Item 14.

Mathew J (Comp) (n.d.). Language word lists: Krauatungalung, Maap, Ngarigu. (Questionnaire responses compiled by Mathew. Collector: Miss Henry). In Papers of John Mathew. Unpublished manuscript held at Australian Institute of Aboriginal & Torres Strait Islander Studies, MS 950, Item 67/2.

Mathews RH (1902). The Aboriginal languages of Victoria: the Brabirrawulung language. *Journal and Proceedings of the Royal Society of New South Wales*, 37: 92–106.

Mathews RH (n.d.a). Notebook 5: Thurga and Jirringan. Unpublished manuscript held at National Library of Australia, MS 8006, Box 3, Series 3, Folder 5.

Mathews RH (n.d.b). The Kurnai language. Unpublished manuscript held at National Library of Australia, MS 3179, Item 52.

Morey S (n.d.). Texts in the Gippsland language: new insights into an Aboriginal language of southeastern Australia. Unpublished manuscript.

Smyth R Brough (Ed) (1878). *Aborigines of Victoria and other parts of Australia and Tasmania*. Vol II. Melbourne: Victorian Government Printer.

32
Bringing the Language home: the Ngarrindjeri dictionary project

Mary-Anne Gale and Syd Sparrow[1]

Abstract

This paper reflects on the long, collaborative process of compiling a contemporary Ngarrindjeri dictionary of the language belonging to the people of the Lower Murray, Lakes and Coorong region of South Australia. The project began in 2003 with a small wordlist of a couple of hundred words still remembered by a few Ngarrindjeri Elders, but it soon grew into a much bigger project involving many more community members, and countless hours spent poring over old books and numerous card files held in museum archives. The latest edition includes nearly 3700 entries, including both written and oral sources, which have all been inserted into an electronic database transportable into Toolbox (a versatile software program for dictionary-making). The aim has been to compile a dictionary that makes some logical sense of the many words that have been recorded and spelt in a multiple of ways by a variety of recorders over a period of nearly 170 years. This variety is not just because of the different spelling systems employed, but also due to the many dialects that make up the diverse Ngarrindjeri language bloc (Rev George Taplin recorded 18 clans or *laklinyerar*, while the anthropologists Ronald and Catherine Berndt listed 74 clan dialects). In compiling this dictionary priority has been given to the words remembered by the Elders, using their present day pronunciation, knowing that Ngarrindjeri is a language that never 'went to sleep'. Over a period of six years the making of the dictionary has given the community a renewed sense of hope about what is possible for the Ngarrindjeri language, and a growing sense of pride in a collective cultural identity.

---

[1] Both authors are from David Unaipon College of Indigenous Education and Research, University of South Australia.

There are many long-felt consequences that exist for Aboriginal people caused by the colonisation of their land and their subsequent dispossession. Perhaps the most devastating of these consequences has been the widespread denial of their primary medium of communication – their mother tongue or traditional languages. For the Ngarrindjeri people of the Lower Murray, Lakes and Coorong region of South Australia the burden of not allowing our heritage to perish is carried by the people and researchers alike, as we embark upon a revival of languages and cultural practices that place the original people of this country in their rightful place in education and the public environment of Australia. This chapter discusses an important dictionary project for the Ngarrindjeri people that will impact on future generations, and is a labour of love for the writers.

Our research on this project has become a way for young and old to work together on the revival of our linguistic and cultural heritage. The impacts of this work are both personal and uplifting for the authors: Syd Sparrow is a Ngarrindjeri person and lecturer at the University of South Australia (UniSA), and Mary-Anne Gale is an adjunct research fellow at the University of South Australia and a member of the Mobile Language Team at the University of Adelaide. She is a linguist and teacher who grew up on the colonised lands of the Ngarrindjeri people. For both of them there is a very strong personal motivation for the development of the dictionary and deep satisfaction in the way that so many Ngarrindjeri people have become involved in the research.

The Ngarrindjeri Dictionary Project evolved out of a need among teachers and Aboriginal Education Workers (AEWs) teaching the language in schools for a reliable contemporary dictionary. Although language teachers had access to a number of wordlists, which had been compiled by people working in the school sector, these lists adopted a variety of spelling systems and didn't name the sources of their Ngarrindjeri words.[2] Teachers were confused about which spellings of words they should be using and whether these alternative spellings represented the pronunciation used by Ngarrindjeri Elders today.

Hence, in 2003 the Ngarrindjeri Dictionary Project was born. It strives to record a comprehensive listing of words in the Ngarrindjeri language still known and used by Elders, plus additional words recorded by missionaries, linguists, ethnologists and anthropologists in the past. The thing that makes this project different to past attempts is that it draws together all the written and oral recordings of each Ngarrindjeri word under one entry, so that every representation of that word can be easily compared. This means that alternative spellings and pronunciations are not listed as separate entries and therefore do not confuse. The aim is to make searches for words in the Ngarrindjeri language and their English meanings a relatively painless

---

2 A couple of dedicated teachers such as Greg Albrecht, working with Paul Kropinyeri, Agnes Rigney, Bessie Rigney, Ashley Couzens and Oscar Abdulla at Glossop, and Dave Roe-Simons working with Connie Love at Murray Bridge High, produced Ngarrindjeri wordlists that greatly assisted students in their high school programs in the 1990s.

and straightforward exercise and, in the process, demystify the Ngarrindjeri spelling system and the way individual Ngarrindjeri words are pronounced.

Early beginnings in schools

In 2002 Mary-Anne was approached by the principal of a primary school in Murray Bridge to write a Ngarrindjeri language curriculum for use in a cluster of local public schools. It soon became apparent, however, that these schools needed much more than a curriculum. There was a very real shortage of quality language teaching and learning resources. Teachers could only look on enviously at other Languages Other Than English programs, which had several choices of quality dictionaries with consistent standardised spelling. So Mary-Anne embarked on producing a comprehensive listing of Ngarrindjeri words to accompany the curriculum.

Initially she began by making tables of words drawing from old missionary sources, and crosschecking them with Elders to see if they used or remembered the words. She utilised the standard Microsoft Word program listing the words alphabetically under categories. These categories were largely based on the topics the schools had decided to cover in the language curriculum, for example birds, animals, body parts, kinship terms, action words, and emotion words. However, as the tables grew and the list reached hundreds of words, it became apparent that by continuing with Word there were limits on what could be done with the wordlist. Word does not allow one to sort items alphabetically, nor does it allow one to sort words by topic. It was soon realised that it was time to transfer the wordlist to a program that is designed to manage large databases.

The University of South Australia's involvement

Up until the end of 2003 the project had been directed at schools, but it would be wrong to say that there was little Ngarrindjeri community involvement. What was striking about the Murray Bridge cluster schools was the determined manner in which they involved the Elders in their Indigenous language and cultural programs.

Being an adjunct staff member of the UniSA Mary-Anne was aware that there were five Ngarrindjeri people on the staff, so she showed several of them the early stages of the draft dictionary. Syd Sparrow took an immediate interest in the project and together we decided to apply for an internal university grant to take the project further. We knew we had to do more community consultations beyond Murray Bridge and Adelaide, and we also knew there was a lot more work to be done on the dictionary if it was to be a comprehensive listing of all the major sources. With more time and funding we felt we could make this dictionary a resource that would benefit the survival and revival of the language within the broader Ngarrindjeri community.

We were successful in gaining a small UniSA grant in November 2003. So under Syd's leadership we embarked on a process of community consultation whereby various focus group meetings were held for those Ngarrindjeri people interested in the production of a community-owned dictionary. The UniSA funding allowed this consultation process to proceed. In 2004 the members of the UniSA team included Sydney Sparrow (team leader), Howard Sumner, Bevin Wilson, Sharon Gollan, Kizze Rankine and the late Maria Lane. We held focus group meetings in the city (at the UniSA and the Nunkuwarrin Yunti community centre), at Raukkan (formerly Point MacLeay mission), Camp Coorong (near Meningie), at the Lower Murray Nungas Club in Murray Bridge and at Port Ellliot. In 2005 we were successful in gaining another internal university grant to allow the project to expand and the consultation process to continue.

Choosing Filemaker Pro for the dictionary

With funding from the UniSA we were also able to spend time transferring the dictionary to a more suitable database program, which opened up the opportunity to expand the file. Easy-to-use options were limited in 2003. Mary-Anne had heard of the dictionary-making software Shoebox (developed by the Summer Institute of Linguistics and now known as Toolbox),[3] and knew it had been used for dictionaries for Australian languages such as Yolngu Matha in Arnhem Land, but was wary of the possibly unjustified reputation it had developed for not being user-friendly. Contemporary dictionary-making software, such as Miromaa[4] was just not available at that time. Mary-Anne was already familiar with FileMaker Pro and was impressed with its possibilities when she saw what had been done in the neighbouring Narungga language. Because FileMaker Pro seemed to be more user-friendly than Shoebox, we embarked on transferring the Ngarrindjeri wordlist from Word to FileMaker Pro, despite the understanding that schools and the Ngarrindjeri community would have to purchase FileMaker Pro software if they wished to access the electronic version of the dictionary. It was however reasonably inexpensive to buy two sets of licences for the school cluster and for computers at the University for keen team members.

Establishing a template and layout for the dictionary

With the assistance of others more familiar with the potential of FileMaker Pro, Mary-Anne established a template for the dictionary. Each entry was given a full page with the Ngarrindjeri headword being spelt in a standardised form. The orthography and spelling system adopted was that already being used in most Department of Education Aboriginal Studies materials, originally developed by Brian Kirke in collaboration

---

3 See www.sil.org/computing/toolbox/. Since the writing of this paper, a core group of Ngarrindjeri people have undertaken training through the TAFE sector, and started working with the Ngarrindjeri dictionary in Toolbox. The software is free off the web, and with their own laptops they now do searches via the Filter function, and have been analysing long Dreaming texts using the Interlinearizing function. In October 2010 we had 3860 Ngarrindjeri lexemes.

4 This was developed as a language database system by the Arwarbukarl Cultural Resource Association specifically for Aboriginal languages.

with the Ngarrindjeri community for a language kit produced in the mid-1980s. It is similar to that used by Steve Johnson with Ngarrindjeri students at Batchelor College around the same time.

The information for each entry included: the head word in Ngarrindjeri, the English meaning or meanings, any dialect variations for that same word (again spelt with the standardised spelling), the written sources of the word (with the exact spellings used by those sources), any oral source (using a code derived from their initials, for example VB = Veronica Brodie), notes on the use of that word or any culturally interesting associations, any synonyms, the date the word entry was made, the origin or etymology of the word, the word class (noun, verb, pronoun, and so forth), plus the search categories for each word by topic (animal, bird, emotion, kin term, and so forth). There have been a couple of versions of the template over the years, particularly to make it compatible with Toolbox for future transfer and printing purposes. Figure 1 shows the latest version of the screen in FileMaker Pro with the single page template used for each word entry:

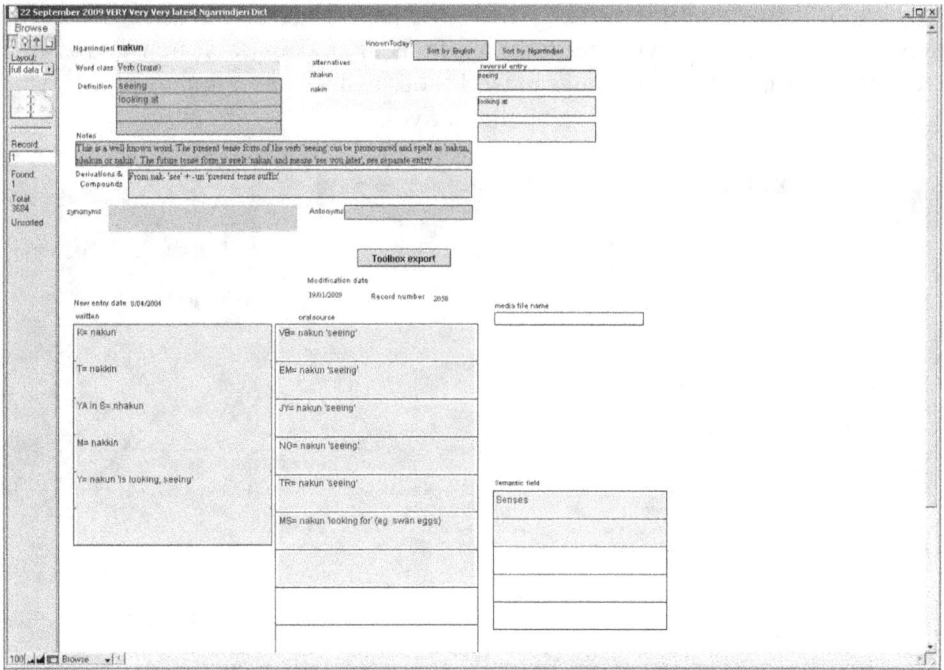

Figure 1. A single page word entry *nakun* from the Ngarrindjeri dictionary in FileMaker Pro.

Over the years we have changed and improved some aspects of the FileMaker Pro template with the generous help of linguist Nick Thieberger. In the early stages of the dictionary project, schools requested that a field be added to the template which indicated whether or not the Ngarrindjeri word is known by the Elders. If it was known, an asterisk was added so that it was possible to do a search for them all. In March 2005 there were 2818 Ngarrindjeri word entries in the database, with at least 300 words known by the Elders. Teachers in the schools preferred to use these words in their lessons knowing that they could ask an Elder to assist them with the pronunciation. They also asked for an asterisk to be added to the known words listed in the Ngarrindjeri language curriculum document. In fact initially some of the Ngarrindjeri teachers were very reticent to use any words in their classrooms that were not marked with an asterisk, but, as their confidence grew and the needs of their students expanded (particularly in Years 10 to 12), they realised they were limiting their programs by restricting themselves to only the known words. By 2006 we had compiled a separate booklet, *Ngarrindjeri Picture Dictionary for Older Students*, containing 470 Ngarrindjeri words known by the Elders. All these words have been added to the database.

The electronic dictionary has been set up with several different layouts. In the Full Data layout there is a whole page per entry (Figure 1, above). A second layout is designed for listing multiple entries on the one page (Figure 2, below). This layout offers the opportunity of viewing multiple finds after doing a search and is often used when translating texts or songs in workshops and we are trying to choose which Ngarrindjeri word to use from several alternatives.

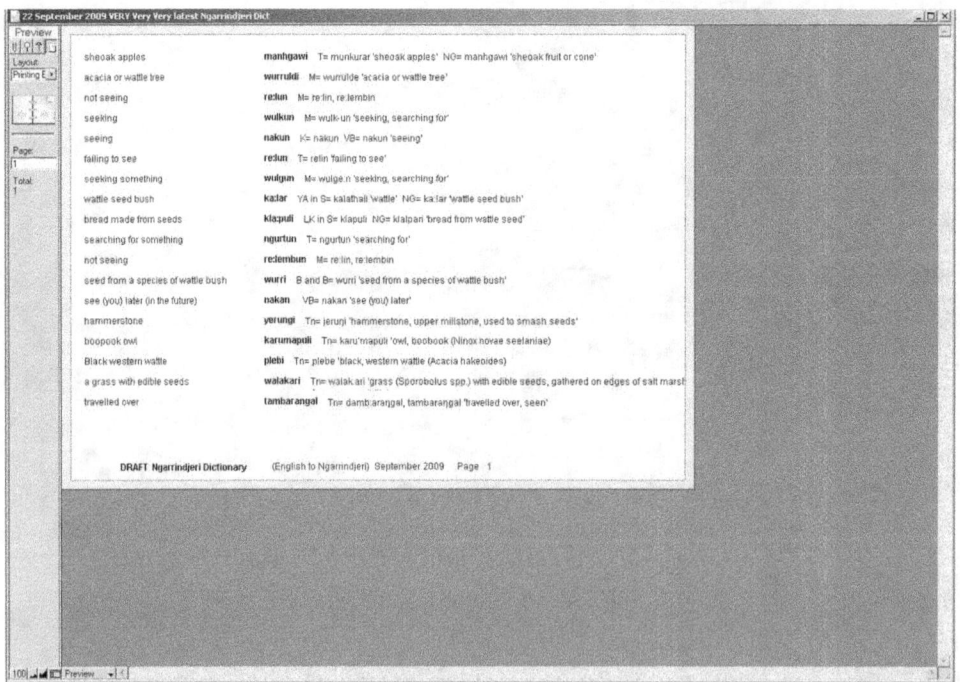

Figure 2. A sample search result for English 'see'.

University of Adelaide involvement

Since 2004 the University of Adelaide, which offers courses in linguistics, has been successful in gaining Commonwealth grants to conduct research on various Indigenous languages of South Australia, originally through DCITA (Department of Communications, Technology and the Arts) and later through DEWHA (Department of Environment, Water, Heritage and the Arts). Meanwhile 2004 draft editions of the Ngarrindjeri dictionary were being distributed in the community and schools by Syd Sparrow's team from UniSA. Feedback from focus group meetings in the community however was that, although the dictionary project was a much appreciated endeavour, some were finding the printed document indecipherable. This was a response in particular from young men who were not involved in the school language programs, so did not participate in the regular discussions we had on spelling during professional development workshops held in schools. They simply did not know how to read the words unless they were words they already knew, and even then they disagreed with the standardised spelling. Indeed even Syd himself once preferred an English system for spelling Ngarrindjeri words and said to Mary-Anne in the early days of the project, 'I've been spelling *nakan* as 'nukkin' all my life, and I'm not about to change now!' It only took an hour of explaining the inconsistencies of using English spelling for Syd to become a born-again speller!

Such responses triggered Mary-Anne and another Ngarrindjeri colleague Dorothy French (who worked as an AEW in the schools) to apply in 2005 through the University of Adelaide for a grant from DCITA, to produce an alphabet book and picture dictionary containing known words that clearly explained the sound and contemporary spelling system chosen and ratified by the community in 1989. These small booklets are accompanied by a compact disk with recordings of the familiar words. To make the CDs Dorothy and Mary-Anne spent two years consulting and recording Elders, such as Julia Yandell, Totty Rankine and the late Veronica Brodie and Neville Gollan, using Audacity sound editing software.[5] They also had to learn a great deal about PowerPoint, inserting sound files, photography, layout and design, and making books using Publisher. In the meantime the dictionary project continued through the UniSA under Syd Sparrow's leadership as feedback was sought on the draft version circulating in the community. Down the track we knew that each entry needed to be checked, more words had to be added, and the format demanded a rework so that the printed version looked more like a 'proper dictionary'.

The dictionary project enters stage two

Because there was a group of supportive Ngarrindjeri staff working at the David Unaipon College of Indigenous Education and Research within UniSA, and no Aboriginal staff in linguistics at the University of Adelaide, it was decided that any further applications for funding from DCITA to develop further Ngarrindjeri language

---

5 See audacity.sourceforge.net/

materials should be made through UniSA. With Syd Sparrow as the project manager we were successful in 2006–07 in gaining another grant to employ Mary-Anne and Dorothy French to write the *Ngarrindjeri Learners' Guide* (2007b). So their efforts in developing the dictionary further were put on hold for 12 months as they wrote an accessible guide to the grammar of the Ngarrindjeri language, drawn in particular from the old grammars written by the missionaries Meyer and Taplin.[6]

In 2007–08 we were successful at the UniSA in receiving further funds, this time from DEWHA, to work on stage two of the dictionary project. Supplemented with the second internal grant received from the UniSA, Syd once again headed up a team to produce the next edition of the dictionary. This project also aimed to produce revised editions of the alphabet book (Gale & French 2009a), picture dictionary (Gale & French 2009b) and accompanying CDs, plus an update on the picture dictionary for older students (Gale & French 2007a) that listed all the Ngarrindjeri words still known by the Elders. We quickly produced the latter booklet and gave copies out at the launch of the learners' guide, so community members could start checking if there were more words they remembered which could be added to the next edition of the bigger dictionary.

The main aim of stage two of the project was to produce a printed edition of the dictionary that looked more professional in its layout and contained a lot more entries from sources we had not had time to include in the earlier draft. We also wanted to improve the template and layout of the electronic version of the dictionary. Unfortunately we underestimated how much more work would be involved in accessing some of the remaining written sources. Toward the end the project became a real labour of love especially for Mary-Anne and one of the Elders, Auntie Eileen McHughes. This was particularly so when incorporating the Ronald and Catherine Berndt materials and the Norman Tindale card files, discussed below. With the improved print layout the entry for the word *nakun* (to see) now appears in the print version of the dictionary as:

> **nakun**   *Verb (trans).* **seeing; looking at.** *Variant*: nhakun; nakin. *Written source*: K= nakun; T= nakkin; YA in S= nhakun; M= nakkin; Y= nakun 'is looking, seeing' *Etym*: From nak- 'see' + -un 'present tense suffix'. [*Note*: This is a well known word. The present tense form of the verb 'seeing' can be pronounced and spelt as 'nakun, nhakun or nakin'. The future tense form is spelt 'nakan' and means 'see you later', see separate entry] [*Oral source*: VB= nakun 'seeing' EM= nakun 'seeing' JY= nakun 'seeing' NG= nakun 'seeing' TR= nakun 'seeing' MS= nakun 'looking for' (eg. swan eggs)].

---

6 This guide was launched amongst much community celebration at Raukkan in May 2008. Members of the community commented on how good it felt to be returning to that lovely little old church to commemorate the coming-back-to-life of the Ngarrindjeri language, rather than coming back to mourn the death of yet another community member.

The sources

As mentioned already a key source of words for the contemporary Ngarrindjeri dictionary was the Elders, as Ngarrindjeri was a language that never went to sleep, unlike the neighbouring Kaurna language of the Adelaide Plains. Even though the grammar of the language has been lost from everyday speech, at least 470 words still remain which we have managed to record from the Elders over a period of years. But the main source of words for the dictionary, numerically, has undeniably been the old written sources that were recorded by various researchers over a period of 170 years. In the database these words are listed in the written sources field using the exact spelling of the original, particularly if it contrasts with the contemporary standardised spelling used for the headword. This makes it clear in the dictionary that the many alternative spellings listed from the different recorders are not different words, but are just spelling variations or alternate dialect pronunciations.

The first list of Ngarrindjeri words to be systematically entered into the database was in fact the first comprehensive list of Ngarrindjeri words ever recorded. These were collected in the early 1840s by Heinrich A. E. Meyer, a German missionary to the Aboriginal people of the Encounter Bay region. Meyer worked with people such as Encounter Bay Bob who spoke the Ramindjeri (or Raminyeri) dialect of the Ngarrindjeri language. Meyer published his wordlist of about 1750 words (from Raminyeri to English) in 1843. His words are listed with the code M in the database. Meyer also provided many sample sentences demonstrating the contextualised use of words, plus a remarkably insightful grammar which was invaluable in writing the learners' guide 165 years later.

In 1859, 16 years after Meyer's publication, George Taplin established the Point McLeay mission on Lake Alexandrina[7] and one of the first tasks he undertook was to reverse Meyer's wordlist from English to Ramindjeri. Twenty years later, having worked with people who spoke different dialects of Ngarrindjeri, including Yaraldi and Portawalun, such as James Unaipon (the father of David Unaipon), Taplin published this list with additional words from Point McLeay, resulting in 1668 English entries (Taplin 1879). Taplin's wordlist, listed with the code T, was the next to be included in the electronic dictionary.

Following Taplin's list, more recent written sources were added including the words provided by the Elder, the late Rhonda Agius (n.d.) who had built up a collection of worksheets and booklets through her teaching of the Ngarrindjeri language at Mansfield Park Primary school in Adelaide over a period of ten years. Again Rhonda's spelling was retained and listed with the code RA.

Another important and more contemporary wordlist entered into the dictionary was that compiled by the late Steve Johnson, mentioned earlier, who taught linguistics at the School of Australian Linguistics at Batchelor College in the 1980s. He compiled

---

[7] This community is now known as Raukkan and is considered the homeland of the Ngarrindjeri people.

two wordlists of Ngarrindjeri, the first being a printed list produced with the assistance of three different groups of adult Ngarrindjeri students who studied with him from 1985 to 1986, including people who are now key Elders working on the contemporary dictionary, such as Auntie Eileen McHughes. Steve later compiled an electronic wordlist, which is now available from the Aboriginal Studies Electronic Data Archive (ASEDA) held at the Australian Institute for Aboriginal and Torres Strait Islander Studies in Canberra. Unlike the first, this second wordlist included a number of written sources along with a code that identified each of Steve's various sources.

Unravelling Steve's code has been a challenging exercise for all those working on the dictionary for the past five years, but we think we have now finally cracked it. Steve used the initials of the people he taught at Batchelor for his oral sources including Kevin Kropinyeri (KK), Lorraine Kartinyeri (LK), Eileen McHughes (EM) and Totty (Harriet) Rankine (TR),[8] but the codes used for his written sources are less straightforward. Two major sources, YA and SA were a complete mystery for quite some time. Eventually we established that YA stands for Yaraldi, the dialect spoken by James Brooksie Kartinyeri and other sources whose recordings were transcribed by Maryalyce McDonald during her mid-1970s research on Ngarrindjeri phonetics, and accessed by Steve (see McDonald 2001).[9] We then noticed that the many SA entries were fairly commonly known words, so assume it stands for the words that were collectively known by the group from South Australia who worked with him. Other codes were less common, but were equally hard to crack.

We eventually noticed that YH, YM, NH and EW only provided bird names so, when a colleague alerted us to a couple of issues of the *South Australian Ornithologist* which listed different bird names from Aboriginal languages, Mary-Anne did an immediate cross-check to excitedly find that the ornithologist H. T. Condon (1955) was Steve Johnson's source. Hence YH stands for Yaraldi bird words from A. Harvey (1943), YM stands for Yaraldi words collected by the Protector M. Moorhouse (1846), NH stands for Narrinyeri words collected by A. W. Howitt (1904), and EW stands for W. Wyatt who collected words from Encounter Bay (1879). All entries from Steve Johnson's wordlist are included in the dictionary under written sources with the coded initials he used, for example KK in S means Kevin Kropinyeri in Steve Johnson.

Yet another important source for our dictionary was the 1975 publication by the linguist Colin Yallop who, like McDonald, drew from the recordings made in the 1960s

---

8 Others to attend courses at Batchelor in either 1985 or 1986 included Mary Ellul (née Smith), Sylvia (Nordy) Rigney, Stella Campbell, Vicki Kropinyeri (Hartman), Bernice Karpany, Heather Aspel (née Smith), Dennis Aspel (Jnr), Patty Kropinyeri, Richard Kropinyeri, Sharon Gollan, Myo Doug Milera, Flossy Rigney, George (Muddy) McHughes, Les Talbot, Sharon Gollan (née Webster), Greg (Rauli) Rankine, Shirley Gollan, Aileen Talbot, Gail Multa, Glenys Multa, Ellen Williams, Janice Rigney, Wayne Rigney, Richard Goldsmith, Phyllis Williams, Doris Synett, Jean Smith and Lawrence Ellul.

9 We assume Steve Johnson worked from McDonald's 1977 thesis rather than from the original tapes recorded by Luise Hercus, Catherine Ellis and Elaine Treagus in the mid-1960s.

of James Brooksie Kartinyeri. Yallop's work compares the grammatical structures used by Taplin in his translation of the New Testament with the Kartinyeri phrases recorded by Catherine Ellis and Luise Hercus. Yallop provides a list of Kartinyeri's words in the back of his study, and it is these words that have been included in the contemporary dictionary under the code Y.

Some entries have also been entered directly from the body of Maryalyce McDonald's 1977 thesis but to list all entries in her appendix would be duplicating Steve Johnson's or Yallop's lists. In addition to James Kartinyeri's words McDonald includes words recorded by Elaine Treagus in Adelaide in 1964–65 from people such as Mike Gollan, David Unaipon, Rebecca Wilson (the late Veronica Brodie's mother), Walter McHughes, Alison Lovegrove, Mrs S. Harrison, M. Karpany and Mrs Anne Rankin (sic) (McDonald 2001, pp. 24–25).

In the 1980s the linguist Brian Kirke from the South Australian College of Advanced Education worked with the Ngarrindjeri people Marj Koolmatrie, Mark Koolmatrie, Marlene Stewart and Jillian Sumner to produce a language kit, mentioned earlier, called *Ngarrindjeri Yanun* (Speaking Ngarrindjeri). This kit included resources such as word cards and a booklet of comic strips and narrative texts. All the words in the kit are included in our dictionary under the code K.

In 1993 the long-awaited book by Ronald and Catherine Berndt was published, entitled *A World That Was: The Yaraldi of the Murray River and the Lakes, South Australia*. It includes prolific texts in Ngarrindjeri of Dreaming narratives and ethnographic accounts collected by the Berndts in Murray Bridge between 1939 and 1942. They worked with Yaraldi speakers, particularly Albert Karloan, Pinkie Mack and Mark Wilson. This book contains a huge amount of remembered information about traditional cultural and social practices, the various plants, birds, fish and animal totems, placenames and clan names. Attempts have been made to include many of the words and associated information from this major resource in the dictionary, at the insistence of Auntie Eileen McHughes. Anyone who has been involved in compiling a dictionary will know that it is an enormous and very tedious job, and can be very exhausting when time and money is limited. But with Auntie Eileen's encouragement and tireless help Mary-Anne completed the task of including a very large portion of the words from the main body of Berndt and Berndt (1993). It must be said that there is quite a bit of information in this book of a sexual nature which Auntie Eileen decided to censor, as the final dictionary is to be used as a resource in schools. Such decisions could only be made by an Elder. We still haven't included material from the huge appendices as this is largely text-based material and needs much further analysis.[10]

---

10 Linguist, Barry Alpher (2001) produced an electronic wordlist on Word that includes much of the Berndt material, including the appendices. He also includes the Maryalyce McDonald wordlist plus Meyer's and Johnson's wordlists. However Alpher's list does not conflate the multiple entries of the same words under the one head word, nor are the compound and

One major set of entries added during stage two of the dictionary project was words from the card files compiled by Norman Tindale, now held in the archives of the South Australian Museum. The Tindale collection (SA Museum reference AA338/7/1) has an enormous number of card files with four sets relating to Ngarrindjeri, filed under four different dialect names: Jaraldekald,[11] Ramindjeri, Potaruwutj and Tangane. This project has only attempted to include the words from the Tangane (or Tangani, AA338/7/1/23) collection, mainly because no other Ngarrindjeri wordlists have included this southernmost dialect of the Ngarrindjeri language. These words were given to Tindale by Clarence Long (also known as Milerum) who worked closely with Tindale over a long period of time until Milerum's death in 1941. Milerum's knowledge added 530 new words to our database which were not known by any other sources, including words for some extinct mammals such as *maikari* (eastern hare wallaby, *Lagorchestes leporides*), *rtulatji* (toolache wallaby, *Macropus greyi*) and *wi:kwai* (pig-footed bandicoot, *Chaeropus ecaudatus*). Again any information in these card files that looked remotely unsuitable for the dictionary was censored. All Milerum's words are listed with the code Tn in the dictionary.[12]

If time and money permitted it would have been insightful to go through Tindale's other Ngarrindjeri dialect card files. However the Jaraldekald cards were based on Taplin's (1879) wordlist and crosschecked with the Yaraldi man Albert Karloan (the Berndt's main informant). The Ramindjeri files were repeats of Meyer's wordlist, but with Tindale's spelling. The Potaruwutj cards were largely compiled with Milerum 'as from his mother', but Tindale has a note on one card saying he will later incorporate these cards into his Jaraldekald file. It should be noted that Tindale was a fluent speaker of Japanese, which seems to have influenced the way he heard Ngarrindjeri words pronounced by his informants. Ngarrindjeri has some very unusual consonant clusters compared to other Aboriginal languages, with words like *tloperi* (ibis), *throkeri* (seagull) and *pargi* (wallaby). But Tindale tended to insert vowels where they didn't belong, hence lists these same words as *tolopori, torokori* and *paragi* respectively. He also missed most interdental sounds, represented by th, dh, nh and lh, which is particularly problematic for Ngarrindjeri, as they are used prolifically (note Tindale's use of the regular /t/ sound in *torokori*).

One final written source to be added to the dictionary was the list recorded by the medical doctor and Aborigines Protector, William Wyatt, provided by Encounter Bay Bob between 1837 and 1839 but not published until 1879. Wyatt actually collected these words prior to missionary Meyer's arrival, but most are Kaurna words. Effort

---

inflected words from the Berndt appendix analysed into their component parts. Alpher himself used the two electronic wordlists from ASEDA.

11 Today this clan name is spelt Yaraldi, as Tindale used the letter j for the /y/ sound. Note {-kald} means 'tongue language'.

12 There are well over a thousand words listed from the Tindale source in the dictionary, with half likely cognate with those from other sources.

was made to distinguish the two with the help of linguist Rob Amery, so that just the Ramindjeri words were included in our dictionary. The code used for Wyatt's collection is W, and we have retained Wyatt's very anglicised spelling.

At the eleventh hour a further list of 70 words came to light that were collected from Billy Koo.e.cum.mung in 1845 by the government protector in Victoria, George Robinson. Billy was apprehended by police in Victoria but heralded from Lake Alexandrina in SA. His words appear as K in R in the dictionary.

Conclusion

When Mary-Anne first sat down with the late Doug Wilson and his sister Veronica Brodie back in May 2003 compiling that first list of Ngarrindjeri words for schools, she had no idea it would lead to a contemporary dictionary of nearly 3700 entries six years later. With Mary-Anne and Syd teaming up at UniSA the dictionary project became real community research in action. The way the Ngarrindjeri community of all ages have actively involved themselves has been an inspiration the likes of which has seldom been felt by the authors of this chapter. We have been privileged in this project because we have witnessed the best of both worlds, the best of how universities can engage Aboriginal people, and Aboriginal people displaying their pride at the best our culture provides.

The great thing about our dictionary is the way young Ngarrindjeri have received it and how they have participated in its development. This is absolutely vital for the future, as they will be handed the legacy of keeping the language going in much the same way that Syd was given this responsibility by his Elders. There is cause for great optimism that our young people will take the Ngarrindjeri language to places it has never been before. The long-term goal must now be for the language, in some form, to be spoken fluently and this will come from the continued use of language and the entrenchment of linguistic study within the education system. Some of this is happening already in schools and now in the Technical and Further Education sector (Gale with Mickan 2008). More needs to be done at other levels of education and this is another of our long-term goals.

Just as the Ngarrindjeri word *molotulun* explains how the waves of Lake Alexandrina ebb and flow, so has the Ngarrindjeri language ebbed and flowed. We trust the fresh waters of the threatened lake will never dry out and hopefully the Ngarrindjeri language will never cease to be spoken. The *Ngarrindjeri Dictionary* was launched to great celebration in the newly renovated church at Raukkan in October 2009, 150 years after the establishment of the mission on the lake's shores. This dictionary will help ensure that more people will continue to speak some form of the language in the future. The Ngarrindjeri language has come home and we are honoured to have been a part of bringing it back!

Figure 3. The Ngarrindjeri Language Choir singing hymns in Ngarrindjeri at the launch.

References

Agius R (n.d.). Wordlists, booklets and worksheets prepared for students. Unpublished manuscript.

Alpher B (2001). Ngarrindjeri lexicon, preliminary draft. Unpublished manuscript.

Berndt RM & Berndt CH (1993). *A world that was: The Yaraldi of the Murray River and the Lakes, South Australia.* Carlton, Victoria: Melbourne University Press.

Condon HT (1955). Aboriginal bird names: South Australia. *South Australian Ornithologist*, 21: 74–88, 91–98.

Gale M & French D with the Ngarrindjeri community (2009a). *Ngarrindjeri alphabet book*. Raukkan, SA: Raukkan Council on behalf of the Ngarrindjeri community.

Gale M & French D with the Ngarrindjeri community (2009b). *Ngarrindjeri picture dictionary*. Raukkan, SA: Raukkan Council on behalf of the Ngarrindjeri community.

Gale M & French D with the Ngarrindjeri Elders (2007a). *Ngarrindjeri picture dictionary for older students: Ngarrindjeri words known by the Elders*. Trial edition. Raukkan, SA: Raukkan Council on behalf of the Ngarrindjeri community.

Gale M with French D (2007). *Ngarrindjeri learners' guide*. Trial edition. Raukkan, SA: Raukkan Community Council.

Gale M with Mickan P (2008). Nripun your ko:pi: we want more than body parts, but how? In R Amery & J Nash (Eds). *Warra wiltaniappendi: strengthening languages* (pp. 81–88). Proceedings of the inaugural Indigenous Languages Conference, 24–27 September 2007 Adelaide. South Australia: University of Adelaide.

Gale M with Sparrow S & the Ngarrindjeri community (2009). *Ngarrindjeri dictionary*. First edition. Raukkan, SA: Raukkan Community Council.

Gale M (2003–04). *Draft Ngarrindjeri dictionary*. Adelaide. SA: University of South Australia.

Harvey A (1943). Untitled. *Mankind*, 3: 108–12.

Howitt AW (1904). *The native tribes of south-east Australia*. London: Macmillan.

Johnson S (1985–86). *Ngarrindjeri wordlist*. Batchelor, NT: School of Australian Linguistics.

Kirke B, Koolmatrie M & Stewart M (1986). *Ngarrindjeri yanun* [Language kit]. Adelaide, SA: South Australian College of Advanced Education.

McDonald M (2001). *A study of the phonetics and phonology of Yaraldi and associated dialects*. Lincom Studies in Australian Linguistics 6. Munich, Germany: Lincom Europa.

Meyer HAE (1843). *Vocabulary of the language spoken by the Aborigines of the southern and eastern portions of the settled districts of South Australia, preceded by a grammar*. Adelaide, SA: James Allen.

Moorhouse M (1846). *A vocabulary and outlines of the grammatical structure of the Murray River language spoken by the natives of South Australia from Wellington on the Murray as far as the Rufus*. Adelaide, SA: Andrew Murray.

Robinson G (1998–2000). *The Journals of George Augustus Robinson, chief protector, Port Phillip Aboriginal protectorate*. Vol 4, 1 January 1844–24 October 1845. ID Clark (Ed). Melbourne: Heritage matters.

Taplin G (1859–79). Unpublished journal of Rev. George Taplin. State Library of South Australia, PRG 186 – 1/3.

Taplin G (1879). The 'Narrinyeri' tribe. vocabulary of the 'Narrinyeri' language. the grammar of the 'Narrinyeri' tribe of Australian Aborigines. In G Taplin (Ed). *The folklore, manner, customs, and language of the South Australian Aborigines*. Adelaide, SA: E. Spiller.

Wyatt W (1879). Vocabulary of the Adelaide and Encounter Bay tribes. In JD Woods (Ed). *The native tribes of South Australia* (pp. 169–82). Adelaide, SA: Wiggs & Son.

Yallop C (1975). *Narinjari: an outline of the language studied by George Taplin, with Taplin's notes and comparative table*. Oceania Linguistic Monograph, 17. Sydney, NSW: University of Sydney.

33
The development of the Gamilaraay, Yuwaalaraay & Yuwaalayaay Dictionary

John Giacon[1]

Abstract

The *Gamilaraay, Yuwaalaraay & Yuwaalayaay Dictionary* was published in 2003, one of a series of publications produced as part of Gamilaraay-Yuwaalaraay language revival. This paper outlines the context in which the Dictionary was developed, beginning with the Gamilaraay-Yuwaalaraay area and the decline and current situation of the languages. Then it considers the revival programs beginning around 1990 and the production of the Dictionary, with a major discussion on the range and quality of the sources of information. A number of principles of dictionary development are considered. It concludes with some thoughts on the role of the Dictionary as one resource in the evolution and revival of the languages.

Gamilaraay, Yuwaalaraay and Yuwaalayaay country and languages

Gamilaraay, Yuwaalaraay and Yuwaalayaay[2] are languages from the inland north of New South Wales (NSW). The Gamilaraay area includes towns such as Tamworth, Gunnedah, Coonabarabran, Narrabri, Moree, Pilliga, Toomelah-Boggabilla and Collarenebri. The Yuwaalaraay area is further west including Goodooga, Lightning Ridge, and Walgett. These languages are closely related and also share many features with other Central NSW languages (Austin, Williams & Wurm, 1980) – Wangaaybuwan and Wayilwan (these two are also known as Ngiyambaa) and Wiradjuri. Their use declined rapidly after colonisation.[3] The Gamilaraay language declined much more

---

1 Australian National University.

2 In the rest of this article Yuwaalaraay will be used to refer to both Yuwaalaraay and Yuwaalayaay since there is very little difference between these dialects.

3 See Buckhorn (1997) for details of the early contact history.

rapidly than Yuwaalaraay further west. So, the Gamilaraay records begin earlier, but there are few records of fluent Gamilaraay on tape or recorded by experienced linguists, whereas there are around 60 hours of Yuwaalaraay tapes held at the Australian Institute of Aboriginal and Torres Strait Islander Studies (AIATSIS) which have provided most of the information for revival. Peter Austin has worked extensively on Gamilaraay and his recent article (2008) provides further background to that language and an extensive bibliography. More information about the Gamilaraay area can be found in O'Rourke (1997) and the *Gamilaraay, Yuwaalaraay & Yuwaalayaay Dictionary* (*GYYD*) (Ash et al. 2003) has information on the whole area.[4]

Gamilaraay-Yuwaalaraay language revival

The *GYYD* was produced as part of the increased revival work on Gamilaraay–Yuwaalaraay (GY) that began around 1990. Peter Austin, a native of Tamworth and, at that time professor of linguistics at La Trobe University, published short Gamilaraay dictionaries (1992, 1994) and with David Nathan produced an online Gamilaraay dictionary (1996). It is difficult to find information about community language activity in those years.

Uncle Ted Fields in Walgett and Auntie Rose Fernando in Collarenebri had also been working on language and I worked with Uncle Ted from 1994. In 1996, after consultation with Aboriginal people at the school, a Yuwaalaraay language program began at St Joseph's Primary, supported by the school and the Catholic Schools Office with funding initially from the Department of Employment, Education, Training and Youth Affairs and later from Aboriginal and Torres Strait Islander Commission (ATSIC) (Cavanagh 2005). After further community meetings the NSW Department of Education and Training (DET) funded resource production and training as part of setting up a Year 7 GY program at Walgett High School. A language program also began in Goodooga around 1998. The model employed in the school programs included a linguist (myself) with Uncle Ted generally teaching the teachers. I used Williams (1980) as my basic grammar source and the Yuwaalaraay tapes from AIATSIS for other information, particularly pronunciation.

It was clear that there was a hunger for language among many GY people. Most knew a few words but few knew many. And no-one knew how to put words into sentences and to string sentences together as people like Arthur Dodd and Fred Reece had been known to in the 1970s.

Between 1999 and 2001 there were a number of language meetings around the GY area, with GY people and others coming from many towns. Largely because of the

---

4 The website *www.yuwaalaraay.org* provides information on developments in GY. It lists resources, including the *Gaay Garay Dhadhin* (Picture Dictionary) (Yuwaalaraay and Gamilaraay Language Program, 2006) and has a link to *Gayarragi, Winangali,* a GY multimedia language resource launched in March 2009. This includes a searchable dictionary with sound, many Yuwaalaraay sentences, stories, songs and games.

existence of the tapes there is much more Yuwaalaraay information than Gamilaraay. There are some 1600 Yuwaalaraay words (more than double the Gamilaraay recorded) and considerable grammatical information. Over 70% of the words and much of the grammar are the same (Austin, Williams & Wurm 1980, p. 170). The meetings recognised that Gamilaraay revival would be severely limited by this lack of information and decided that, where one language lacked a word or grammatical information, it would use what was known from the other language.

Earlier publications

1998 saw a flurry of language work in Walgett. DET provided funding for development of resources and inservicing of prospective language teachers, specifically Aboriginal education workers from Walgett and nearby towns. Marianne Betts (a teacher at Walgett High School) and I prepared a 100-hour high school GY course, with Marianne designing the program and going through the time-consuming process of getting Board of Studies approval for the course. One result was *Yaama Maliyaa*[5] (Giacon & Betts 1999), a text for the Walgett High School program. *Yuwaalayaay – Language of the Narran River* (Giacon 1998) contains material collected by Ian Sim at Goodooga in the 1950s and edited by me.

In 1999, I produced a Yuwaalaraay–Gamilaraay wordlist based on the Austin dictionaries and the wordlist in Williams (Giacon 1999). This, like its sources, generally gave a one word equivalent to the headword. It included the source for each word (Williams [CW] or Austin [PA]), the part of speech and whether each verb was transitive or intransitive. It included an introductory section and three lists of words; GY to English, English to GY, and semantic fields (word groups like fish, and so on). A sample is given below.

bundaa-ng	V-INT	fall	CW, PA
bundaama-l	V-TR	knock down	CW
bundabunda	N	poison	CW

The spelling system was largely borrowed from Austin's earlier dictionaries. There were also some minor changes to entries based mainly on information from the tapes.

Users of the list need to know that N means noun and need to know how nouns are used in GY – it is not the same as English. Similarly the ng in *bundaa-ng* tells you which group of verbs it belongs to, but you then need to know how to use the verb. There is no word *bundaang* in GY but there are *bundaagi* (will fall), *bundaanhi*

---

5 For a brief introduction to pronunciation of the Gamilaraay–Yuwaalaraay words see yuwaalaraay.org/pronunciation.html, and for a longer explanation, yuwaalaraay.org/lessons/pron.html

(fell) and many others formed by adding suffixes to bundaa-. The difference between transitive verbs (TR) and intransitive verbs (INT) is crucial to GY and Aboriginal languages in general. A dictionary requires prior knowledge on the part of the reader if it is to be properly used.[6]

The first publication that included sound appeared in 2001. *Gaay Yuwaalaraay* (Giacon 2001) included a CD of Yuwaalaraay words and phrases which had been extracted from the tapes and, for the first time, it was possible for people to learn directly from the pronunciation of the older traditional speakers. Originally the publications were distributed by the Walgett language program, but it became clear that commercial distribution had many advantages. It was also clear that there was a need for a more complete dictionary and a grammar. The latter is still in progress.[7]

Production of the Gamilaraay, Yuwaalaraay & Yuwaalayaay Dictionary

By 1998 the need for a comprehensive dictionary to provide a firm basis for the revival work was clear. There was also new information available from the tape transcripts. There was some funding available – part of a NSW DET grant and contributions from local clubs. Anna Ash had linguistic qualifications and experience and was available, and I was able to work on the project part time. However it was also something very new we were taking on and we knew that more funding would be needed, so it was with some trepidation that work began. Fortunately more funding was provided by ATSIC and the overall expenditure was something over $150 000. Anna Ash gathered material from the old sources and tapes to include in the database, Amanda Lissarrague worked on verbs, and we all worked on the final entries, mostly in telephone meetings. As well there was ongoing consultation with members of the Walgett, Goodooga and Toomelah–Boggabilla programs and others. This covered many areas – layout, wording, design, readability, sale price and more. The final consultation concerned words that might be excluded. There were strong and differing opinions among the Elders and a number of words were excluded from the published dictionary. The final stage included production of the grammar section, proof-reading by the authors and friends, and negotiations with the publishers.

What is a dictionary?

Typically a dictionary includes many sections. Generally there is an introduction then a list of words and their meanings. Often there is other information for each word; perhaps part of speech, pronunciation, where the word came from and if there are any special rules for its use. There will often be example sentences. In bilingual dictionaries, such as the *GYYD*, the headword (the first word in an entry) and

---

6 When producing the published wordlist I wondered if anyone would ever use it. In fact it was widely used and I was delighted one day, when visiting a school, to see a very worn, well-used copy of the book.

7 For a list of currently available publications see yuwaalaraay.org/gypublications.html

explanation are in different languages. The process of making a dictionary involves collecting examples of a word then trying to succinctly and unambiguously describe its form (what the word sounds like and how it is written), its meaning and how it is used. The information to be included depends on the audiences the dictionary is aimed at. The *GYYD* would be used by people from a wide variety of backgrounds, from people looking for information about their language, to school and tertiary students, and academics that would be looking for specialised information.

The process

The main aspects of the production of the *GYYD* were establishing the team and administrative structure, community consultation, information gathering and processing, data entry, writing the definitions and overall entries, and design and production. Three linguists worked on the project. Anna Ash did most of the data entry, I co-ordinated the work, and Amanda Lissarrague was part of the team for a shorter time. The administration of the funds was initially provided by Walgett High School and later by the Catholic Schools Office, Armidale.

Previous publications had included Gamilaraay and Yuwaalaraay words. However there are differences between Yuwaalaraay and Yuwaalayaay, albeit minor, and it was decided to distinguish three languages, Gamilaraay, Yuwaalaraay and Yuwaalayaay. It is worth noting that there are several dialects of Gamilaraay (Austin, Williams & Wurm 1980, p. 168) but that so little of them has been recorded that it was not practical to set up separate sections for them in the Dictionary.

Another major decision was how to input data and output the text for the Dictionary: that is, which computer program to use. It was decided to use FileMaker Pro. This was satisfactory in producing the Dictionary but has had some disadvantages subsequently. Users need the (expensive) FileMaker Pro program to read the data. The program is also relatively complicated, so a consultant was employed to design the input screens and manage the output. This at times led to delays. It is difficult to update the material and output new versions of the Dictionary. At the moment we are working on producing a version of the database using Toolbox, a program with specific capacity for dictionary prodution.

Figure 1 and 2 below provide examples of the FileMaker Pro version of the Dictionary. They show sections of the database to do with the Yuwaalaraay word *guwaali*. Figure 1 shows the main Yuwaalaraay screen. There are similar Gamilaraay and Yuwaalayaay screens. Sources of information are shown at the bottom, (Williams' grammar, Uncle Ted Fields, Arthur Dodd, Stephen Wurm). Other information includes four definitions, the part of speech and a record of decisions about the word. Figure 2 is associated with the meaning tell. It contains an example sentence and a linguistic comment.

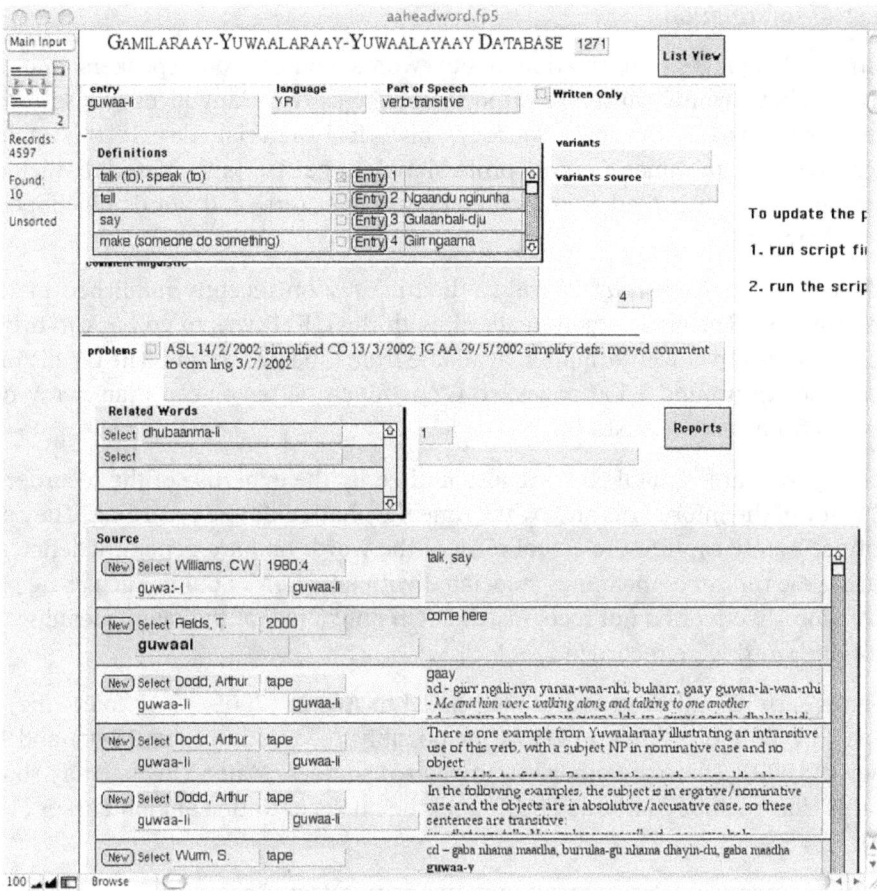

Figure 1. The main database page for Yuwaalaraay *guwaali*.

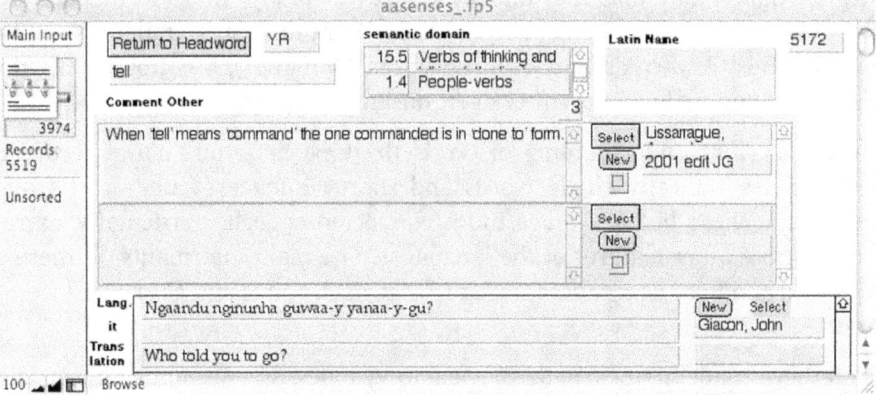

Figure 2. The database page for tell.

Sources of information

For strong languages, information about words comes from speakers and text. Questions about words can be referred to speakers. With languages whose use has declined, such as GY, the main source is historical material. For GY this includes written material by amateur and professional linguists; tape material, including transcripts; words recorded from contemporary speakers, and words developed by language programs.

The *Yuwaalaraay Gamilaraay Wordlist* relied mainly on recently published material for information. The aim, largely realised, with the *GYYD* was to go back to original sources and use the new information available from tape transcripts. The GY historical records contain around 1500 pages, so GY is much better placed than many other languages from eastern Australia.

Written sources are valuable but are also limited by the expertise of the recorder and the fluency of the informants and by the time they had to do the recording. They often do not accurately capture the actual form of the words and are generally deficient in capturing the full set of meanings associated with any word. Sounds such as ng at the start of words were often not recognised. Often only a few of the many meanings and uses of one word were recorded.

The main early Gamilaraay sources are listed in Austin (2008, p. 48 following) and include Rev William Ridley (1875) (but possibly recorded around 1840) and R.H. Mathews (1903). There are other less important sources. Major Yuwaalaraay sources from this time include Mathews (1902) and the books of Katie Langloh Parker (1896, 1905).

In 1938 Norman Tindale recorded material from Harry Doolan and George Murray (Austin & Tindale 1986). In the 1950s Ian Sim, working with Dr Arthur Cappell, collected Yuwaalaraay material at Goodooga from Mrs G. Rose, Willy Willis, Greg Fields and Mrs West (Giacon 1998). Gerhardt Laves (1929–32) worked with George Murray on Gamilaraay and Ada Murray on Yuwaalaraay. In 1955 Stephen Wurm worked with Burt Draper, Peter Lang and Mrs F. Munro on Gamilaraay, and with Harry Hippi (also known as Harry Murray, from Mungindi), Mrs Rose of Goodooga, Charley Dodd and Arthur Dodd of Walgett on Yuwaalaraay.

Key to our current understanding of GY is the tape material. Wurm recorded 20 packed minutes – mostly single words and short sentences. Later tapes from the 1970s include these but also have more connected speech, particularly narrative, and so illustrate other features of the languages. The main informants for these were Arthur Dodd and Fred Reece, both born in 1890. Jack Sands and Harry Hall were also recorded.

Janet Mathews made some 50 of the Yuwaalaraay tapes. She was not a linguist and the speakers mostly translate the words, sentences or stories that Mathews provides. The final tapes were made by Corrine Williams as part of her linguistics honours research. They have the great advantage that Williams knew much about the language and so was aware of interesting features that emerged in elicitation and was able to follow up some of these. Williams' thesis was published in 1980 and has since been the key reference for GY work. By the time the current GY revival began there was no-one left with anything like the knowledge of Yuwaalaraay that Dodd and Reece had, and knowledge of Gamilaraay was even less.

The great value of tapes is that they record the actual speaker, not the interviewer's understanding of the speaker. It is possible to re-listen to the tapes to check the sound and language structures and the more experienced listener will also hear more. In addition tapes often have many examples of the one word in different sentences, allowing a better understanding of its meaning or meanings than that given by the one English word typically found in wordlists. Transcription is the first step in using the tapes. There are some 600 pages of Yuwaalaraay transcriptions, which have taken thousands of hours to produce.

There were also some relatively recent sources. Peter Thompson (n.d.) collected words in Toomelah–Boggabilla in the 1980s and I collected around one thousand words from Uncle Ted Fields. Some were already in the records. Others – such as *gadjigadji* (tree regrowth) – were not recorded elsewhere. At other times Uncle Ted was not certain about a word. When pressed for a word for welcome he came up with a number of words that he remembered that might be appropriate but that he was not sure of. The word *gulbiyaay* is now used for welcome, but Ted was uncertain of the precise meaning and form, with options for the latter including *galbiyay, gulbiyaanha,* and *gulbiyay*. Finally there are words, including numbers, developed by the language programs.

Gathering and interpreting the information

The production of the entries for each word involved gathering information and then composing sections of the entry.

It was often difficult to decide on the form of a word. Written sources need to be interpreted – they often do not capture the difference between long and short vowels or the difference between r sounds.

Figure 3 shows the Gamilaraay sources entered for *gagil* (bad). Austin had given the modern spelling as *gagil.* Mathews had *kuggil* (bad) and *kugil* (wet). It was decided that wet was not an appropriate translation. In the current orthography both k and gg would be rendered as g. It is common for sources to follow the English pattern and use u for both the sounds in put and putt – these sounds are represented by u and a respectively in current GY. Where there is tape evidence, as there is for *gagil*, it is easy to decide what the actual sound is. In general the information about a word in one language would be similar to that in the other languages, so the final entry, given below, drew on information from all three languages:

gagil **(YR, YY, GR)** *adjective, adverb, placename*

1 bad, no good (YR, YY, GR). •**Gagil-wan.gaan ngaama dhadha-y-la-nhi.** (YR)

That tasted really bad. •**Gagil nhama gungan.** (YR) That's bad water.

2 Coghill (a placename) (GR). Ridley said 'bad, nasty (water)'. *Gagil* has a wide range of meanings, including 'naughty, horrible, sore, sick, jealous and stale'. Sometimes occurs in *gagil-dhuul* (bad - little, one) meaning 'unhappy' or 'bad one, bad person'.

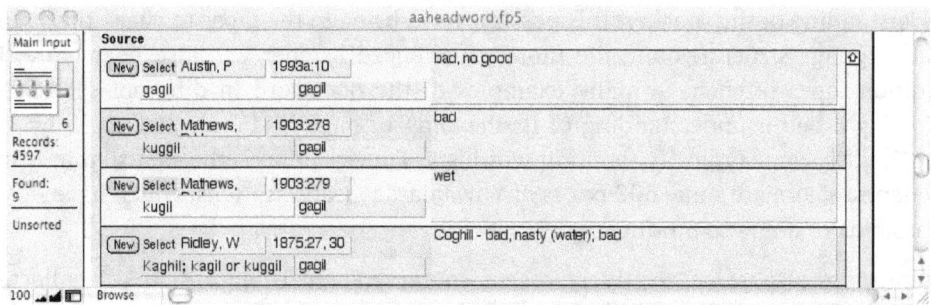

Figure 3. Gamilaraay sources in the database for *gagil* (bad).

A particular difficulty arose with words still being used. Often because of English influence the forms being used now are different from the traditional ones. For instance mother is *guni* in current usage with stress on the gu and the final vowel short but, on the tapes, it is *gunii* with *nii* containing a long vowel and being stressed. *Gabaa* was previously used for white man but it is now pronounced *gaba*. Uncle is traditionally *garruu* but now often said *garu*, with the final sound shortened, stress on the first syllable and the r not trilled. The traditional form of the word is used in the Dictionary.[8]

Generally GY words that have developed since colonisation, such as animal names, also have a range of forms. The words for horse include *yirraamaan* (Giacon 1998); *yarraamaan, yarraaman* (Fred Reece); *yarraaman* (Arthur Dodd); Williams (1980); Austin (1992) and *yaramun* (Milson c. 1840.). Contemporary use is *yaraaman* and *yaraman* showing the common tendency to lose the trilled rr and to shorten vowels. The Dictionary headword is *yarraaman* but I suspect that *yarraamaan* is the more traditional form.

The meanings of words are often much more complicated than their forms. Below I give a few examples to illustrate this complexity and the ease with which words can be misinterpreted, or have their meaning unintentionally modified.

It is relatively easy to get information about some words, such as the names of objects. The interviewer points at their hand and asks, 'What is that?' The informant says, '*Mara*' (Gamilaraay) or '*Maa*' (Yuwaalaraay). It would be very easy to miss the fact that those GY words are also used for finger. Similarly *dhaygal* (Yuwaalaraay) and

---

[8] See N. Reid, this volume, for an extended discussion of these issues.

gawugaa (Gamilaraay) mean head, but also hair of head – and not other hair. In these instances we are aware that the one Gamilaraay or Yuwaalaraay word has various translations in English and vice-versa. However it is also likely that for other GY words parts of their previous meaning have been lost and they are now used to represent exactly the same information as an English word. For instance the information on the GY words for left and right (hand) is quite limited and we cannot be sure of how these words were traditionally used.

The word *gaba* also illustrates the range of meanings a word can have and the ease with which these can be lost. There is no argument about the form of this word or about its main translation, good. However, it would be a major mistake to think that *gaba* is equivalent to English good. Other translations found include glad, happy, pleased, tender, right, all right, fresh, sweet, honest, pleasant, nice, wholesome, pretty, and kind. As well *gaba* combines with other words in GY in expressions such as *giirr gaba* (that's right), *gaba ngulu* (good looking; literally: good face) and *gaba guyaay* (happy, literally good spirit). It would be foolish to expect that all meanings of *gaba* have been recorded, and particularly foolish to expect that we have anything like a complete list of the common phrases in traditional GY that included *gaba*.

Gaba mostly functions an adjective but, at times on the tapes, it is also used as an adverb qualifying a verb. The Dictionary entry lists *gaba* as adjective and adverb, but I have some doubts. It may be that the use of *gaba* as an adverb is a misinterpretation of the tapes. It may be that the informant has been influenced by English, and that the use of *gaba* as an adverb does not represent traditional GY. It would be easier to make a decision if it were known whether related Aboriginal languages have words that are both adjectives and adverbs, but that is one of the many pieces of research that has not yet been done.

The Dictionary also gives information about the way to use a word in phrases and sentences. Giving the part of speech gives considerable information about usage. It is also critical to distinguish transitive and intransitive verbs in most Aboriginal languages, since this indicates major differences in the way they are used. It is particularly important to point out ways that a word is different from what an English speaker would expect. For example English speakers tend to interpret *guwaali* as equivalent to English talk in all situations. Some give other translations including tell and speak. Below are some examples of the use of *guwaali* in Yuwaalaraay. The word order of traditional GY sentences is variable and generally different from English word order.

(1)

I will talk.

Gaay	*guwaa-li*	*ngaya.*
word	will.tell	I

(2)

I will talk Yuwaalaraay.

Yuwaalaraay	*guwaa-li*	*ngaya*
Yuwaalaraay	will.tell	I

(3)

We will talk (converse).

Gaay	*guwaa-la-y*	*ngali*
word	will.tell-each.other	we (2 people)

(4)

Talk to me.

Gaay	*guwaa-la*	*nganunda.*
word	tell (*com*mand)	me.at

(5)

Tell me.

Guwaa-la	*nganha.*
tell (command)	me

The Dictionary entry for *guwaali* is quite long. It provides information about the word but also tries to give an indication of the complexity of the rules governing its use in GY. In the examples above, the one English word (talk) is translated as *gaay guwaa-li* (1), *guwaa-li* (2), *guwaa-la-y* (3) and *gaay guwaa-la* (4). It is part of the role of the Dictionary to inform readers about this sort of complexity in the use of GY words.

Another area where GY and English do things very differently is in the description of time. English speakers often use the words yesterday and tomorrow, and would look for equivalents in GY. In fact, as Arthur Dodd and Fred Reece point out clearly, GY did not have words for yesterday and tomorrow, but had other ways of conveying that information. There are a number of verb suffixes that are used to translate yesterday and tomorrow, but their meanings do not correspond totally with those of English words. Further research will help us to better understand the GY time system, and then the dictionary entries will change. In the meantime the dictionary has *ngurrugu* 'tomorrow' and *gimiyandi* (one source) 'yesterday' – words probably written down by someone who expected every language to have these words, but whose actual meanings are more like 'after the night' and 'when it happened a day or so ago'.

The entries often give indications about how sure we were about the information given. The annotation, one source, is found nearly 500 times in the Dictionary. It is an indication that there may be uncertainty about the form and meaning of the word. Uncertainty is also signalled in the entry for *guugaarr* (tree goanna, Varanus varius), which includes the text 'perhaps a Wangaaybuwan word', indicating that there is some question as to whether this is a GY word at all.

At times there are multiple entries with the same English translation. For instance both *balandharr* and *dhaygal* are translated head hair. However the entry for *balandharr* contains the text 'This is a rare word, the common word is *dhaygal*'. It is quite possible that *balandharr* has a slightly different meaning which has now been lost.

The work process

Production of the entries involved data entry and analysis followed by the actual writing of the definitions. Anna Ash worked for approximately two years on data entry and analysis. She and I would regularly have telephone conversations about the material. My tasks included to review the tape material and to work with Anna on any difficulties. Amanda Lissarrague also worked on the project for some months, entering material on verbs and writing many of those entries.

There was a plethora of small jobs such as checking scientific names, deciding what constituted sufficient evidence that a particular word was found in a language, assigning words to semantic domains and deciding on the cover photo. It was decided early on to include a sketch grammar in the Dictionary. This was necessary to give people some basic idea as to how the languages works; we were aware it would be some time before a comprehensive grammar was available.

The IAD (Institute for Aboriginal Development) in Alice Springs had published a number of impressive Aboriginal language dictionaries and agreed to publish the *GYYD*. A major strength of their dictionaries was the high quality design and editing by Christine Bruderlin and Mark MacLean. One role of the Dictionary is to provide information, but another is to make a clear statement of the existence and status of Gamilaraay and Yuwaalaraay. The marvellous design and high standard publishing have very much helped achieve those aims.

Principles

I am not clear at what stage the following principles became clear to me – some of them were explicit before the work on the Dictionary began.

The main aim of language revival is to help maintain and develop the pride and identity of the people of the language. A dictionary should be something that people can be proud of, both in appearance and in the quality of the work that it contains. Another aim was to provide information about the traditional languages. When a language is declining in use there is simplification and loss, and the language adopts many of the features of the dominant language. The aim of the *GYYD* was to document traditional

GY and words that have been adopted into GY. Some adopted words such as *gulbiyaay* (welcome), discussed above, are of uncertain form and meaning but do have some basis in the sources and are useful. Others have been specifically developed because there is a need and no existing word. Examples include the expanded number system, or *wiyayl*, traditionally an echidna quill and now extended to mean pen or pencil.

Standardisation of language is a major issue. We have at times tried to produce resources that incorporate local dialects. But to produce even one resource for the whole GY area is a major task – to produce a different resource for each town is impossible. At this stage of language revival, when there is virtually no one who can hold even a brief conversation in language, the emphasis will be on a common language. Local variation can co-exist with the common language but to focus on the variations could impede language revival. The Dictionary recognises variation, beginning with three languages, but it also provides the basis for a common language across a substantial area.

A dictionary is a record but it also includes many decisions that will influence the reviving language. It is the responsibility of dictionary creators to make sure that decisions are based on good information and appropriate research. The database contains notes on discussions that led to many of these decisions and is available for people who want to check the information and process used to arrive at any particular entry.

The Dictionary needs to honour the people whose knowledge and work it builds on, so the names of informants are included on numerous occasions. Many entries make reference to the source of information – often Arthur Dodd, Fred Reece, Uncle Ted Fields and others.

The Dictionary has multiple audiences. Some people might like to have it on their bookshelf and rarely open it. Others, such as people learning the language or students, could use it regularly. Professional linguists have used it as part of their work to compare languages or to find out information about kinship terms. An attempt was made to cater for a wide range of readership in the printed dictionary and the material is available in other forms. I often use the FileMaker Pro database or the text files of the Dictionary rather than the book itself. The database has been deposited in the Australian Institute of Aboriginal & Torres Strait Islander Studies and both it and the text files are available.

After consultation with the community it was decided to exclude some words, mostly with sexual reference, from the Dictionary and to clearly label words that had been recently developed.[9] Some words were excluded on the basis that they added little to the usable language. It is not clear which bird *guinarey* (*guwinaray?*) (light eagle hawk) refers to, and so it is not included in the printed dictionary but is in the database.

A constant principle in language revival is: Do the best you can do now. The Wordlist (Giacon 1999) was produced first, and later the Dictionary. I hope that there will be

---

9 See yuwaalaraay.org/gynew_words.html

an updated and corrected dictionary in future but the current one is what we could do with the personnel, knowledge and finance available at the time.

An important part of the production of the Dictionary was that a team was involved. Having three linguists working on this led to much better decisions and fewer mistakes. It was also good that the work was peer-reviewed, with Christina Eira's review appearing in the *Australian Journal of Linguistics* (2005). Having works well reviewed will only increase the effectiveness of language revival. More importantly the process of creating the Dictionary involved many GY people and was one factor in the ongoing development of a community of GY speakers.

Some errors have been found in the *GYYD*. One is *Gundhimayan* as the origin of the name Condamine. The word Condamine comes from English and is not a GY word. Placenames are a trap for players young and old.

Conclusion

Some 900 copies of the Dictionary have been sold and it is the main source of the languages for the vast majority of people. There is no doubt that both the process and the Dictionary have had a strong impact on GY revitalisation and current use.

The Dictionary is widely used in GY language work. However it is important to recognise that any language is extremely complex, and that learning a language is a long and demanding process that generally needs lots of assistance and feedback. There are people who are working together to develop their skills, and their GY is getting closer to the traditional languages. These people recognise the need to constantly revise their use of language and therefore to change some patterns they have adopted, often unconsciously. However there are also many people relearning GY on their own, generally without a background in languages or linguistics. In these situations many aspects of revived GY differ greatly from the traditional languages. Some aspects of pronunciation and rhythm can follow English, the structuring of words and sentences also often follows English patterns, and the choice of words can be inappropriate. These people will be developing different versions of GY. It is encouraging to see people who are so committed to relearning the languages. It is a great pity that there are not classes and appropriate resources which would help people to better learn the basics of the languages, nor is there ready access to someone who can advise whether new and creative language use conforms to the traditional language structure.

Appropriate planning, structures and resources are needed for the development of a revived language which is consistent with the original language, which does not split into multiple versions, which is a functional language and which has a chance of long-term survival. The *Gamilaraay, Yuwaalaraay & Yuwaalayaay Dictionary* is an authoritative work and provides one of the many resources and structures necessary for the rebuilding of Gamilaraay and Yuwaalaraay.

Acknowledgements

Thanks to Moy Hitchen, Anna Ash and Amanda Lissarrague for comments on earlier versions of this paper.

References

Ash A, Lissarrague A & Giacon J (Eds) (2003). *Gamilaraay, Yuwaalaraay & Yuwaalayaay dictionary*. Alice Springs, NT: IAD Press.

Austin P (1992). *A dictionary of Gamilaraay*. Melbourne: La Trobe University.

Austin P (1994). *A reference dictionary of Gamilaraay*. Melbourne: La Trobe University.

Austin P (2008). The Gamilaraay (Kamilaroi) language, northern New South Wales – a brief history of research. In W McGregor (Ed). *Encountering Aboriginal languages: studies in the history of Australian linguistics* (pp. 37–58). Canberra: Pacific Linguistics.

Austin P & Nathan D (1996). *Kamilaroi/Gamilaraay web dictionary* [Online]. Available: coombs.anu.edu/WWWVLPages/AborigPages/LANG/GAMDICT/GAMDICT.HTM [Accessed 15 April 2009].

Austin P & Tindale NB (1986). Emu and brolga, a Kamilaroi myth. *Aboriginal History*, 9: 8–21.

Austin P, Williams C & Wurm S (1980). The linguistic situation in north-central New South Wales. In B Rigsby & P Sutton (Eds). *Papers in Australian Linguistics No 13* (pp. 167–80). Canberra: Pacific Linguistics.

Buckhorn R (1997). *Boobera Lagoon, a focus for reconciliation*. Sydney: Australian Catholic Social Justice Council.

Cavanagh P (2005). *It makes you proud to be you: a report on the Yuwaalaraay language program at St Joseph's, Walgett.* Strathfield, NSW: Australian Catholic University [Online]. Available: www.arm.catholic.edu.au/documents/Pat%20Cavanagh%20Report.pdf [Accessed 15 April 2009].

Eira C (2005). Review of 'Gamilaraay, Yuwaalaraay & Yuwaalayaay Dictionary'. *Australian Journal of Linguistics*, 25(2): 281–88.

Giacon J (Ed) (1998). *Yuwaalayaay, the language of the Narran River*. [Information supplied by Mrs G. Rose, Willie Willis, Greg Fields and Mrs West, at Goodooga, collected and recorded by Ian Sim]. Walgett, NSW: Walgett High School.

Giacon J (Ed) (1999). *Yuwaalaraay /Gamilaraay wordlist*. Walgett, NSW: Yuwaalaraay – Gamilaraay Language Program, Walgett High School.

Giacon J (2001). *Gaay Yuwaalaraay*. [CD and booklet]. Walgett, NSW: J. Giacon.

Giacon J & Betts M (1999). *Yaama maliyaa, Yuwaalaraay – Gamilaraay: an Aboriginal languages textbook*. Walgett, NSW: Walgett High School, Yuwaalaraay Gamilaraay Program.

Laves G (1929–32). *Papers: field notebooks, correspondence and language cards*. Australian Institute of Aboriginal and Torres Strait Islander Studies MS2189.

Mathews RH (1902). Languages of some native tribes of Queensland, New South Wales and Victoria – Yualeai. *Journal of the Royal Society of New South Wales*, 36: 135–90.

Mathews RH (1903). Languages of the Kamilaroi and other Aboriginal tribes of New South Wales. *Journal of the Royal Anthropological Institute*, 33: 259–83.

Milson Mrs (c. 1840). *Kamilaroi vocabulary*. Mitchell Library, Sydney, NSW, MLA 1608.

O'Rourke MJ (1997). *The Kamilaroi lands*. Griffith, ACT: The author.

Parker KL (1896). *Australian legendary tales: folk-lore of the Noongahburrahs as told to the piccaninnies*. Melbourne: D. Nutt, Melville, Mullen & Slade.

Parker KL (1905). *The Euahlayi tribe. a study of Aboriginal life in Australia*. London: Archibald Constable.

Ridley W (1875). *Kamilaroi and other Australian Languages I*. Sydney: Government Printer

Thompson P (n.d.) Gamilaraay words. Unpublished manuscript.

Williams C (1980). *A grammar of Yuwaalaraay*. Canberra: Pacific Linguistics.

Wurm SA (1955). *Kamilaroi Language*. MS 2335 PMS 3658, 4380, 4381 & tape 2895a. Canberra: Australian Institute of Aboriginal and Torres Strait Islander Studies.

Yuwaalaraay & Gamilaraay Language Program (2006). *Gaay garay dhadhin – a Gamilaraay & Yuwaalaraay picture dictionary*. Alice Springs: IAD Press.

34
Emergency language documentation teams: the Cape York Peninsula experience

Clair Hill[1] and Patrick McConvell[2]

Abstract

Language revitalisation and endangered language documentation are complementary endeavours – they feed into each other and both benefit from the support of the other. This idea is at the heart of a community teams approach called Emergency Language Documentation Teams (McConvell et al. 2005). This paper will review the underpinnings of this idea and discuss the successes and difficulties encountered while applying it in the Cape York Peninsula region.

The findings of the Cape York Peninsula Language Documentation project pilot discussed in this paper include that informal approaches to both language worker training and language learning were, across the board, far more successful than more formal approaches (including one-on-one versions of master–apprentice schemes). We also found that the project approach was more difficult in situations where there were more social and linguistic divisions and heterogeneity. There is some irony in this given that often in the Australian context linguistic homogeneity within a speech community can itself be a result of language shift and language loss.

Project approach

Many of the original Cape York Peninsula (CYP) languages are no longer spoken, and many more are on the brink of loss. An amount of what would now be called endangered languages research in CYP was carried out in the 1970s under the rubric

---

1 Language and Cognition, Max Planck Institute for Psycholinguistics and Linguistics, University of Leuven.

2 School of Language Studies, Australian National University.

of 'Before it is Too Late' (BIITL) (Sutton 1992). This was not linked at the time to community language maintenance and revival. Today, a small number of languages on the west coast of CYP are still being learnt by children and have larger numbers of speakers, but most of the still-spoken CYP languages have only a handful of mainly elderly speakers, and many of these languages are only scantily documented and described. The project discussed in this paper, broadly referred to here as the Cape York Peninsula Language Documentation project (CYPLD),[3] was developed in response to a challenge that faces linguists and community members alike working in critically endangered language situations such as these. How do we adequately respond to requests to undertake urgently needed language documentation work and at the same time help establish language revitalisation initiatives? The project's aim was to tackle this dual challenge by piloting a community teams approach to language documentation.

This approach sets out to establish a three-way relationship among the linguist, proficient language speakers and younger community members (ideally semi-speakers or hearers). This is related to the visions of *two-way* research and education encountered by McConvell (1991, 1994) among Indigenous people in which there are two *two-way exchange* relationships combined: between the (usually non-Indigenous) researcher or educator and the community on the one hand; and on the other, between the older community generation and the younger generation. These exchanges are built on complementary skills and knowledge sets: the older generations with greater traditional knowledge, and the younger generations who wish to acquire this knowledge and who generally have better mainstream education and related skills, thus also contributing their own expertise to the exchange. In broad terms, the Emergency Language Documentation Teams model combines documentation work on endangered languages with community language worker training and, to a lesser extent, a master–apprentice approach to language revitalisation (Hinton 2002). As the title suggests this team works closely together to document an endangered language. This complementary approach to documentation and revitalisation came from strongly held community views about language work priorities. The predominant view in CYP speech communities is that revitalisation attempts must happen in conjunction with rich and comprehensive documentary work.

Speakers and Elders talk frequently about creating records that will preserve knowledge of the languages for when they pass away or are no longer able to pass on the knowledge in person. They feel that even if all parties within the community try their hardest, time is running very short for documentation and transmission. Thus, the project aimed to provide on-site language worker training to community members with the idea of increasing opportunities to document these languages, as

---

3 Discussion of this project and approaches to documentary and revitalisation work in CYP were presented in a paper by Clair Hill, Peter Sutton and Patrick McConvell titled 'Emergency Language Documentation in Cape York' at the Indigenous Languages Conference, University of Adelaide, 26 September 2007.

well as developing a skills base which would encourage the development of renewal programs. Here the line between language worker and language learner is somewhat blurred. Unsurprisingly, those who are interested in undertaking language work projects are also the ones who want to increase their knowledge of their heritage language. These two aims go hand-in-hand for many community members. Lastly, documentation is clearly crucial for development of tools and resources for language revitalisation work, both for current revitalisation work and also any language reclamation work future generations pursue.

Within this three-way team model all members have mutually beneficial roles and skills that contribute to the work unit. The linguist has technical and linguistic skills and is able to provide on-site community-specific training in recording, analysing and documenting the local language(s). The speakers provide language and cultural tuition to the linguist and, to a lesser extent, the language worker. The younger community members also often contribute invaluable cultural knowledge, and usually have literacy and computer skills that are important for their role as a community language worker. The speakers and language workers contribute an in-depth knowledge of community needs and priorities for the language work, and this assists in shaping strong language projects that are tapped directly into key community concerns.

The CYPLD project's aim was to pilot this approach in a variety of locations and language situations in CYP, and to assess the effectiveness of the approach, and the outcomes and issues that arose.

Some key parts of the Emergency Language Team Model

Participant roles

An important aspect in the growing body of literature theorising about language documentation, language maintenance and revitalisation (for example, Austin 2003–09; Bowern 2008; Hinton & Hale 2001) is the consideration of the roles, needs, expectations and relationships among project participants. The role of linguist is perhaps the most debated, and views vary widely on the scope and responsibilities the linguist's role should include (for a summary of various perspectives see Walsh 2005). We were also concerned with paying more attention to the human factor of fieldwork and to the multi-faceted nature of the relationship among the linguist(s), speakers and the wider community (Grinevald 2005; Nagy 2000). We kept the following questions in mind in project planning. What implications do participant roles (active versus passive speaker and language worker involvement) have for comprehensive and representative documentation (Himmelmann 1998)? What language records do speakers and community language workers think make for good comprehensive documentation? And, given the often multi-faceted nature of the linguist's work in endangered language situations, in what ways and situations can multiple goals be combined and achieved simultaneously?

Relationship between language documentation and language revitalisation

Language revitalisation intervention and endangered language documentation can be complementary endeavours but often they are seen as in competition or conflict. Views on the relative priority and validity of documentation and revitalisation efforts vary widely, some giving documentation work a secondary priority compared to revitalisation and others the inverse. A minority disfavour documentation in general, or at least have serious misgivings regarding use and access to documentary materials by non-Indigenous people, for example, at least one Indigenous language centre in the Kimberley region (Walsh 2005). In our view, both are urgent tasks in critical endangerment situations. Fluent speakers of the languages are pivotal to both and are usually old and few in number, especially with small languages such as in Australia. There is another element crucial for both undertakings – understanding of the language situation and language ecology so as to be able to plan intervention in ways which are likely to put a brake on language loss and in order to document the range of language knowledge and uses (contexts, registers, gender effects) in the community..

Criticism of 'pure' documentation work from community members often relates to the inaccessibility of the material produced. Products of documentation sometimes languish in archives unbeknownst to community members, or unfamiliarity with archive procedures can make applications for access difficult. Alternatively, documentation material may be physically available but inaccessible due the format in which it is written up. Long stretches of interlinearised transcriptions or untranscribed material are of limited use in a moribund language situation and can be difficult to readily transform into user-friendly resources. From the other perspective, some community projects redo basic work such as collecting basic wordlists often simply due to lack of knowledge of existing documentation or how to utilise such sources. Thus, it is also vital for Indigenous people and organisations to be aware of the importance of documentary work even given these difficult accessibility problems. In this way community initiatives can focus their own documentation and revitalisation efforts on the more important and detailed knowledge that has not been collected and is in more immediate danger of disappearing. As we describe in following discussion of the CYPLD project, active partnership with a wider range of community members, outside the usual linguist–speaker collaboration, can go a long way to making documentary materials and the documentary process more transparent. It also makes community members more aware of where to find existing material, types of documentation, and how to work with them in order to create new resources.

Project details

The CYPLD project work officially ran from December 2004 to the end of September 2005,[4] involved five researchers and associated collaborative community

---

4 Work started during this project with community language workers has been ongoing in some instances – particularly in the Lockhart River case. In Lockhart River, work of this type continues by David Thompson and Lucy Hobson as part of the Online Language Community Access Pilot

partnerships,[5] and supported ten languages in total. Each of these linguists undertook fieldwork, for the most part based in one community and supporting one or more languages: Barry Alpher worked on Kuuk Thaayorre and Kuuk Yak in Pormpuraaw; Alice Gaby worked on Kugu Muminh, Kugu Mu'inh, Kuuk Thaayorre and Wik Mungkan in Pormpuraaw; Clair Hill worked on Umpila and Kuuku Ya'u in Lockhart River, and Kaanju in Napranum, Cairns and Yarrabah; Erica Schmidt worked on Kuku Thaypan in Laura; and Jean-Christophe Verstraete worked on Mbarrumbathama (also known as Lamalama), Umbuygamu (also known as Morrobolam) and Umpithamu (also known as Umbindhamu) in Coen. On the ground project work ran from between two weeks and seven months in each of the community locations with overall fieldwork totalling about 12 months. The project was managed and coordinated by Hill. In addition to the five linguists, scientific and research guidance was given by two advisors, Patrick McConvell and Bruce Rigsby. Community collaboration in all participant communities totalled 85 people. This included language speakers, cultural experts (for example, singers and musicians), semi-speakers, hearers and younger interested community members as language worker participants. Throughout the project 23 people received language worker training.

Researchers' field trips varied in length, and thus, the extent and scope of both the documentation and time available to collaborate with language workers and incoprorate them into the work model also varied.[6] The longest time spent working on the project was by Hill at Lockhart River. Therefore, in this case there were more participants involved in the training, and there was the opportunity for a variety of approaches to the team model to be tried out. The bulk of the comments that follow in this paper are based on the Lockhart River experience.

The documentation element of the project was straightforward and produced good results. Ten languages were documented, resulting in just under 100 hours of audio-recording and a little less than 20 hours of video-recording, as well as collections of photographs and field notes, and ancillary materials like transcriptions. These documented a wide range of linguistic material: elicited lexical and grammatical data; narrative and interactional data from a variety of contexts and genres; song recordings;

---

project (coordinated by Australian Institute of Aboriginal and Torres Strait Islander Studies), and informally as part of continuing documentation work by Hill. Documentation work on many of the languages supported by the CYPLD team continued in 2006 till the present via a major documentation project, Documentation of Five Paman Languages, sponsored by the Hans Rausing Endangered Languages Project.

5 The nature of these partnerships and collaborative teams varied widely between locations. See following discussion.

6 The stage of the linguist's work with the community or language also impacted on the feasibility of the community teams approach. The work undertaken by Alpher (on Kuuk Yak) and Schmidt was preliminary and exploratory, and so a more traditional approach to documentation was taken.

video footage of important sites, cultural events and practices; and annotation of archival materials. This material has contributed to the ongoing production of a range of descriptive and community resources. For example, for Umpila, Kuuku Ya'u and Kaanju, lexical data contributed to ongoing work on a user-friendly dictionary, textual material to production of literacy booklets, and grammatical elicitation material to continuing work on a scientific grammar.

The bulk of the work undertaken within the linguist–language worker partnerships focused on building confidence and further developing the considerable linguistic skills the language workers already possessed. Most of the language workers were semi-speakers or hearers of the language being documented and had a lot of existing knowledge to contribute to the sessions. As a result they had more of a co-researcher role as opposed to a trainee/trainer relationship with the linguist. Much of the training centred on core documentation tasks like how to use a variety of recording equipment, elicitation and recording techniques, and transcription. Trainees were most keen to acquire transcription skills in all the participant communities. They repeatedly expressed a desire to be literate in their traditional language understanding the benefits this would generate for revitalisation work and the production of resources, thus ensuring permanent and accessible materials.

Successes and difficulties

Outcomes of the involvement of community language worker 'trainees' were highly variable depending on the community situations in which the work was undertaken. As is often the case, some of the elements contributing to the success of the training in one community were often not transferrable or relevant in a different situation. It is not possible in this space to outline all the combinations of timing, personnel and so forth that caused one situation to be more successful than another. Instead, we discuss some of the major factors in broad cross-community terms[7] that contributed to successes and difficulties.

A key contrast between the situations in which the training was successful and those where the training proved more difficult was the degree of homogeneity in both the linguistic situation and local government and community infrastructure.

Across the communities and language groups involved in the project, language workers[8] had to be of the appropriate linguistic and social group affiliation to work

---

7 We do not discuss these details in terms of specific communities or language groups. Difficulties noted as due to particular community situations do not mean, of course, that language programs will not work in such communities, just that they may need modification or a different approach.

8 For ease of reference, we will refer to the participants who were simultaneously community language workers, language consultants, and language learners in the teams as (community) language workers.

on a language. That is, they had to be viewed by the wider community as having the right to access linguistic and cultural knowledge on the language being documented. This has been widely cited as a factor in the organisation of Indigenous language programs of all types across Australia, and relates to the notions of inheritance rights in languages amounting to *ownership* in Australia generally, but more especially in CYP (Tsunoda 2005, p. 137, 211; Sutton 2001, p. 462).

Given this restriction on the community members who can legitimately engage in work on a specific language, a larger pool of potential and appropriate community members could generally be recruited as language workers in situations with fewer language differences (more linguistically homogeneous situations). However, involvement and training of language workers on minority languages in communities with a number of different languages (linguistically heterogeneous situations) was often difficult simply due to a lack of appropriate potential participants. Similarly, in such situations, much of the weight and demands of the project rested on just two or three elderly speakers – clearly a less than ideal scenario. The extra demands of this project on top of regular documentation work were sometimes too much, even given the strong commitment of all individuals. And, more often than not, it is this same small group of speakers who are the key traditional owners and target participants for many community initiatives. It was also more difficult to build up links with the school in linguistically more heterogeneous situations, widely viewed within communities as one of the most practical and important community applications of language worker skills. This would require serving several language groups at the same time, or dealing with cultural and political issues which can arise around a language program being provided in one language to groups of children of multiple language and social group affiliations.

The training component also proved more successful in situations and communities with strong local government and community organisational structures. The support offered by community councils led to a wide variety of benefits and generally assisted in promoting and validating the team approach. These ties played an important role in increasing the researchers' visibility and approachability. This was especially important for opening up the language work to younger community members who prior to this generally did not feel they had a place participating in traditional documentary work. Organisational support also facilitated access to community resources that contributed to the attractiveness of the initiative to potential language workers, for example, access to computers and use of vehicles for language work related excursions. This sort of access to resources can increase the perceived validity and prestige of the work in the eyes of the wider local community. Both linguistic and organisational homogeneity meant that there was less slicing up the pie of community resources. Additionally, it is quite natural that programs of all types have more chance of success when they are relevant to, and therefore supported by, a substantial portion of the population.

The other factor contributing to variation in success was simply the practicality and feasibility of being flexible with the timing, content, location and participants of a session. Informal on-the-job involvement of language workers generally achieved better outcomes than more formal approaches – that is, having language workers actively involved in the documentation sessions with the language speakers and linguist. With very few exceptions formal training/language-learning sessions and workshops proved inappropriate and ineffective. Coordination of language workers proved difficult and so room for flexibility in all regards increased chances of success and engagement. Unpredictability and the subsequent need for flexibility is a basic lesson of any fieldwork experience. Documentary plans adapted on-the-fly to suit the interests and talents of various combinations of speakers available at any one particular time is a daily event in most field situations. The addition of the language workers to the mix added another level of potential complication to this coordination, especially since the involvement, skills development, and language interests varied among language workers. While not being able to definitively plan the who, when or what of sessions was sometimes frustrating for all parties involved, it was far more productive than any of the more formal approaches attempted, such as workshops or language lessons.

In the same vain, being able to adapt the team format to suit evolving community situations and dynamics was important. Training and language learning was less team-like than planned, that is the language workers and speakers did not form master–apprentice style teams or work units in the way that was anticipated. The logistics and coordination involved in arranging for language workers to consistently work with one or two speakers in a team was generally difficult and problematic – for the same reasons that attempts at formal training sessions were also ineffective. Due to the more informal on-the-job training approach adopted, language workers worked with a range of speakers (often working with three or four speakers at once) in the same way the linguist did, as opposed to working in a concentrated one-on-one fashion. In most circumstances, the speakers preferred to work together in groups so they could assist each other. Apart from providing a cooperative and sociable working environment language speakers have a 'real' conversational partner for the language work – documentary material will be richer if it is also a genuine communicative act shared between interlocutors of comparable proficiency.

The group work option was particularly preferred in the more critically endangered language situations. Some speakers were not completely comfortable with taking sole responsibility for the language tuition of a language worker, and this would tend to rule out the one-on-one version of master–apprentice schemes. This may change over a longer period of time with an increase in speaker confidence, but within the project time frame the one-on-one model did not suit the majority of speakers.

It is easy to proclaim that flexibility is the key. However, in practice, there are complications. A small minority of speakers felt uncomfortable with the regular participation of language workers in documentation sessions. Some speakers, after trying out the various permutations of this approach, preferred a clearer division among the documentation endeavours, the language learning, and the linguist's general training of language workers. Once again the availability of human resources factor in here. In some situations there were just not enough speakers and language workers for on-the-fly arrangements to work. If there are only two or three speakers then sessions by default end up needing more organisation. Another factor is the accessibility of the linguist, often at a moment's notice. If the linguist did not have a readily available public workspace in which they were based then it was difficult for sessions to develop organically depending on the availability and interest of combinations of language workers and speakers. Availability of a good public workspace can often be a by-product of homogeneous local organisational infrastructure, as discussed above.

Lockhart River case study

In this section we discuss some of the project experiences in Lockhart River, in particular the positive effects the involvement of language workers had on the documentation and language work efforts in general. As described above, the most successful training and language learning approach involved on-the-job participation of language workers in run-of-the-mill documentation sessions.[9] The involvement of the language workers in everyday recording sessions also had positive effects on the documentation. This was most strongly the case in Lockhart River.

In Lockhart River, there were two main language workers who were involved in the project over a four to five month period in 2005. They usually participated in three or four sessions with speakers per week. Additionally, there were around a dozen other people intermittently involved in a language worker capacity, either in recording sessions or the more formal workshops. Here the target language for documentation was the Kuuku Ya'u and Umpila dialect group. This language is moribund with a micro-speech community of a handful of elderly speakers who use some language with each other. There are quite a number of younger semi-speakers or hearers, and in some circumstances, elderly speakers also use traditional language with them (replies are made in creole and mixed language varieties).

Both main language workers are semi-speakers and so were able to contribute considerable linguistic and cultural knowledge to the documentation. Because of their existing language knowledge and close family ties with speakers they were often able to elicit and document more culturally sensitive material than Hill could as an outsider. They were fluent in Lockhart River Creole (the community vernacular) and had received more of a mainstream education than the speakers, and so were able to translate between the linguist and speakers where necessary, explaining any unfamiliar and foreign concepts. This resulted in more informed discussion among all members of the team surrounding documentation issues, such as intellectual property rights, access conditions to archived materials, and use of materials in further research.

---

9 Though some one-off formal workshops had the benefit of drawing a number of people who did not have time or interest for regular involvement in the project.

The interests of the two language workers influenced the material documented and at times both broadened and restricted the scope of the data gathered. The documentation work under this project approach was determined by the key dual imperatives of: (a) supplementing existing records of the languages concerned in order to produce fuller documentation, and (b) practising elicitation, transcription and other documentary techniques appropriate to the learning stage and interests of the language workers. Where these aims came into conflict (for example, in the collection of already documented words) priority was given to the needs and interests of the language workers. It was hoped that maximising their documentation skills and confidence would result in a fuller documentary record in the long term.

In Lockhart River the documentation teams model generated feedback and positive effects between the documentary efforts and a variety of revitalisation related work . A good example of this was the traditional song documentation work:

- The project attracted the attention of local Aboriginal teachers, who were enthused by the potential applications of the language work and documentary material to their school activities and duties to their local culture program.
- One of these teachers participated in the project as one of two key language workers. This teacher used the skills learnt and support from the project to start working on establishing a small language program within the culture classes at the school.
- Hill became involved in wider cultural retention activities that are part of the school's culture program. Hill had increased contact with a group of traditional singers and musicians also involved in cultural tuition at the school.
- Singers asked Hill to assist them by documenting *malkari* (shake-a-leg style) and *thaypu* (Island style) songs. This lead to a series of recording sessions with a wide range of performers who had not previously been involved in language or cultural documentation activities.
- From these sessions a number of CDs were produced and widely distributed in the community.
- The enthusiasm generated both by the documentation process and tangible by-products lead to increased involvement in ongoing song recording work, which continued to increase the visibility of the project and open up language work to younger community members who were stimulated by the increased access to, and the rejuvenation of, cultural practices.
- These song sessions then stimulated further language documentation work with speakers on production of dance paraphernalia and associated material culture, paint designs used in dances, for example, recording descriptive and procedural texts on production of items and on the cultural import of designs.
- This documentation fed directly into language workers' training and production of lessons and pedagogical resources for the school culture program.

Some concluding remarks: language ecology and language intervention

One aim of the CYPLD project was to explore the interaction between documentation and capacity-building practices in a community teams approach. This interaction generally had substantial mutual benefits for both the language documentation and a range of applied goals. We found that documentary and revitalisation work can inspire and provide positive feedback to each other (see Ward 2003 for similar points). The project approach stimulated increased awareness of the language situation and documentary goals, increased community involvement in the documentation, widened the range of information and language phenomena recorded, and thus resulted in a more complete picture of the language community's ecology.

The main contrast between the more and less successful incorporation of language-worker training and language learning into the documentation work was the degree of linguistic and infrastructural homogeneity – the more languages and different groups and organisations, the less these aspects tended to come together well. This finding both parallels hypotheses about the conditions for language maintenance and shift, and reveals possible contradictions between the necessary conditions for language maintenance and the necessary conditions for language maintenance intervention.

There is evidence that linguistic homogeneity, at some stage(s) of obsolescence in threatened language situations, tends to favour retention and transmission of at least some of the old language, whereas linguistic heterogeneity favours rapid and complete language shift (McConvell 2008).[10] This is not to say that multilingualism and diversity in speech communities is necessarily a problem for language maintenance. It is well documented that multilingualism was the norm in Aboriginal Australia, and people often maintain languages precisely to maintain distinct identities in such heterogeneous situations (Brandl & Walsh 1982, p. 75). Multilingualism is still found in some speech communities, with English and creole being added to repertoires. However, in the situation of very small languages which have been historically embattled and are under even greater pressures today, heterogeneity tends to give way to monolingualism in the new language – a form of English or a creole in most cases, but a lingua franca based on a form of a regional traditional language in some cases.[11] So, often contemporary situations of increased linguistic homogeneity are a

---

10 Meakins (2008, p. 88) criticises the hypothesis on the basis that Kriol was not adopted at Wadeye, originally a highly multilingual community. However, just as Kriol was a lingua franca in other areas, at Wadeye the traditional language Murrinh Patha became the lingua franca and language shift to Murrinh Patha occurred. This is consistent with the hypothesis that a lingua franca becomes the first language in a linguistically heterogeneous community.

11 For instance, Wik Mungkan at Aurukun in Cape York Pensinsula, Djambarrpuyngu and Dhuwaya in North East Arnhem Land, and Murrinh Patha at Wadeye mentioned in the previous footnote. While these are lingua francas they are still to some extent associated with a particular ethnic group and are not 'neutral' in the same way that creole and English varieties are. While the strengthening of these languages by becoming a community's standard language may

stage in the process of linguistic and cultural shift being undergone by these speech communities. For example, groups isolated by sedentary mission or community-based life no longer learn each other's languages or, as above, a dominant traditional language in an imposed community setting becomes a lingua franca at the expense of other languages. Thus paradoxically, conditions for more successful project outcomes, such as less linguistic, social, political and infrastructural divisions to navigate, may be a result of the shift and loss process itself. This presents interesting questions about the nature of the interaction among forces contributing to language loss in the first instance and our ongoing revitalisation efforts through various stages of loss. Relatedly, one of the major challenges facing those working for language revitalisation is, how do we minimise the impact on our revitalisation efforts of the very pressures which contributed to the language loss situation we are trying to reverse? Another challenge these project findings highlight is how to create policy and infrastructure that supports practitioners and communities to work in organic and flexible ways. In our experience, room for flexible on-the-job involvement of the language worker was a key prerequisite for successfully integrating documentation, language learning and language worker training.

A wide range of benefits were generated by increased awareness and the opening up of language work to the wider community. However, for the linguist it was sometimes difficult to manage the increased community demands and the heavy documentation workload. At times the training needs, language maintenance and other applied work in the community overshadowed the documentation component of the work. The desire to respond to community needs and the desire to undertake quality language documentation tasks that include substantial elements of descriptive and analytical work can be difficult to balance.

This project was not straightforwardly a revitalisation project. It indirectly targeted increased language use while more directly responding to documentation needs and community requests to have younger community members engaged in language work. So, revitalisation in this case was not targeted through the standard approach of language classes in the local school or adult language tuition classes, or through one-to-one master–apprentice schemes, but was instead mediated through other project aims. This approach did not aim to generate new full speakers of the language but to generally increase language use and language awareness in the community. Aside from the obvious connections between documentation and revitalisation, the approach we adopted had quite a number of positive points as a model of revitalisation. Having language workers involved in the planning of a documentation session, elicitation of data, and then working on transcription skills via playback of session recordings, provides multiple reinforcement of language input spread across days or weeks. This involvement in the entire documentary process right through to resource production, results in more engagement and feelings of ownership of the language material than would be expected with a formal teacher–student language learning situation.

---

increase their survival chances, the loss of smaller local languages is also a cause for concern within these communities.

This approach makes it more possible to sustain documentation and language learning that is less reliant on the linguist. It also takes some pressure and focus off language learning and hence mitigates some of the difficult social dynamics that can go hand-in-hand with this (Dauenhauer & Dauenhauer 1998; Hill 2001). In a number of the participant communities language learners talked of finding the expectations of the speakers paralysing, while some speakers were frustrated and disappointed by the language worker/learners' 'slow' progress. The speakers feel pressure to be adequate teachers with enough knowledge to do justice to the language and *old people*,[12] and the language worker/learners in their ability to learn quickly and satisfy the speakers' (and wider community) expectations.

The community team design also gives much deserved credit to the language worker. Built on a three-way sharing of expertise the language worker/learners are able to contribute their already considerable language knowledge to the documentation process. Most language workers involved in the project were semi-speakers and so in this process they were simultaneously language expert and language learner. Many semi-speakers are reluctant to admit gaps in their knowledge and understanding but we found, in a more informal documentation setting, that some of these anxieties were put to rest when they realised their knowledge was more extensive than the outside language researcher, and that they could help the speaker with instruction of the linguist. These experiences help build a community network of language teams that have a life after the linguist has gone.

Acknowledgements

This project would never have gone ahead without the dedication and enthusiasm of numerous language speakers, language worker trainees, and the support of many community organisations. Many people were involved in this project throughout seven CYP communities, all of which deserve more recognition and acknowledgement than can be afforded in the space available in such a footnote. Hill would like to especially acknowledge Lockhart River language workers Lucy Hobson and Vincent Temple. The project team would like to acknowledge funding support from the Maintenance of Indigenous Languages and Records program at the Department of Communication, Information Technology and the Arts (now managed by the Department of the Environment, Water, Heritage and the Arts), and the administrative support of the Lockhart River Community Arts and Cultural Centre. The authors thank Barry Alpher, Alice Gaby, Bruce Rigsby, Erica Schmidt and Jean-Christophe Verstraete's invaluable discussion of the project's successes and difficulties. Many of their observations have made their way into this paper – here particular thanks go to Jean-Christophe. Thanks also to Nick Enfield and Mark Sicoli for their comments.

---

12 Speakers often invoke responsibilities to ancestral elder generations.

References

Austin P (Ed) (2003–09). *Language documentation and description.* Vols 1–6. London: Hans Rausing Endangered Languages Project.

Bowern C (2008). *Linguistic fieldwork: a practical guide.* New York: Palgrave Macmillan.

Brandl MM & Walsh M (1982). Speakers of many tongues: toward understanding multilingualism among Aboriginal Australians. *International Journal of the Sociology of Language*, 36: 71–81.

Dauenhauer NM & Dauenhauer R (1998). Technical, emotional and ideological issues in reversing language shift: examples from Southeast Alaska. In L Grenoble & L Whaley (Eds). *Endangered languages: current issues and future prospects* (pp. 57–98). Cambridge: Cambridge University Press.

Grinevald C (2005). Speakers and documentation of endangered languages. In P Austin (Ed). *Language documentation and description.* Vol 1 (pp. 52–72). London: Hans Rausing Endangered Languages Project.

Hill J (2001). Dimensions of attrition in language death. In L Maffi (Ed). *On biocultural diversity. linking language, knowledge, and the environment* (pp. 175–89). Washington, WA: Smithsonian Institute Press.

Himmelmann N (1998). Documentary and descriptive linguistics. *Linguistics*, 36(1): 161–95.

Hinton L & Hale K (Eds) (2001). *The green book of language revitalization in practice.* San Diego, CA: Academic.

Hinton L (2002). *How to keep your language alive: a commonsense approach to one-on-one language learning.* Berkeley, CA: Heyday.

McConvell P (1991). Cultural domain separation: two-way street or blind alley? Stephen Harris and the neo-Whorfians on Aboriginal education. *Australian Aboriginal Studies*, 1991(1): 13–24.

McConvell P (1994). Two-way exchange and language maintenance in Aboriginal schools. In J Henderson & D Hartman (Eds). *Aboriginal languages in education* (pp. 235–56). Alice Springs, NT: IAD Press.

McConvell P (2008). Language mixing and language shift in indigenous Australia. In G Wigglesworth & J Simpson (Eds). *Children's language and multilingualism: Indigenous language use at home and school* (pp. 205–25). London: Continuum International.

McConvell P, Marmion PD & McNicol S (2005). *National Indigenous Languages Survey (NILS) report.* Canberra: Australian Institute of Aboriginal and Torres Strait Islander Studies.

Meakins F (2008). Land, language and identity: the socio-political origins of Gurindji Kriol. In M Meyerhoff & N Nagy (Eds). *Social lives in language – sociolinguistics and multilingual speech communities* (pp. 70–92). Amsterdam: John Benjamins.

Nagy N (2000). What I didn't know about working in an endangered language community. *International Journal of the Sociology of Language*, 144: 143–60.

Sutton P (1992). Last chance operations: 'BIITL' research in far north Queensland in the 1970s. In T Dutton, M Ross & D Tryon (Eds). *The language game: papers in memory of Donald C. Laycock* (pp. 451–58). Canberra: Pacific Linguistics.

Sutton P (2001). Talking language. In J Simpson, D Nash, M Laughren, P Austin & B Alpher (Eds). *Forty years on: Ken Hale and Australian languages* (pp. 453–64). Canberra: Pacific Linguistics.

Tsunoda T (2005). *Language endangerment and language revitalization.* Berlin: Walter de Gruyter.

Walsh M (2005). Will Indigenous languages survive? *Annual Review of Anthropology*, 34: 293–315.

Ward M (2003). Language documentation and revitalization – is there really a conflict? In J Blythe & R McKenna Brown (Eds). *Maintaining the links: language, identity and the land* (pp. 158–64). Proceedings of the 7th Foundation for Endangered Languages Conference, Broome, Western Australia, 22–24 September. Bath, UK: Foundation for Endangered Languages.

Index

A

Aboriginal and Torres Strait Islander Commission (ATSIC) 107, 403, 405
  Training Policy Statement 2004–06 170
Aboriginal Education Consultative Group (AECG) xiii, xviii, 69, 178, 195, 205
  Dubbo 222
Aboriginal Education Officers (AEOs) 189, 200, 211, 257
Aboriginal English xix, 6, 9, 15–16, 76, 91, 147, 293, 303, 364, 373, 383. *See also* Kriol
Aboriginal Land Rights [Northern Territory] Act 228, 367
Aboriginal Languages of Victoria Resource Portal (ALV-RP) 310, 315, 317, 320
  portal architecture 317–319
  Victorian Word Finder 316
Aboriginal Languages Summer School 108, 218
Aboriginal Resource Development Services (ARDS) xxix
absolutive case 379
accusative case 379
adjectives
  Gamilaraay 409, 411
  Ngemba 46
  Wiradjuri 333
  Yuwaalaraay 411
Adnyamathanha (language) 57
  audio recordings of 57
  language program 30
adult language-learning xvi, xviii, xix, 72, 88, 97, 108, 110, 117, 123, 125, 127, 133–34, 138, 140, 158–59, 162–66, 168, 171, 193, 214, 218, 265, 283, 429.
  case studies 158
  Dharug 182, 186–87
  Miriwoong 149
  Ngarrindjeri 396
  Wergaia 247
  Wiradjuri 159, 214, 216–18, 222–23
adverbs 333, 409, 411
Alphabetic principle 283–84
Anaiwan (language) 171
  Certificate I qualification 171
Anangu Pitjantjatjara Yankunytjatjara (APY) 86. *See also* Pitjantjatjara (language)
Arabana (language) 30
  language program 30
archival records. *See* language source materials
Arrernte (language) 84–85
Arwarbukarl Cultural Resource Association (ACRA) 359. *See also* Miromaa Language Program
  Aboriginal training agency 359
  workshops 359
Audacity sound editing software 334, 393
audio recordings 29–30, 32, 56, 94, 96, 104, 109–11, 115–16, 121, 123–26, 128, 148, 175, 243–44, 309, 316, 327–28, 331–32, 334–35, 340, 353, 357–59, 368, 375, 388, 403, 405, 408, 422. *See also* CDs; Maintenance of Indigenous Languages and Records program (MILR); sound files
Audiamus (software) 114
digital audio equipment 179

audiovisual
  recording 359
  training 140
Australian English 6, 10, 15–16, 91, 94, 116, 133, 136, 138, 140, 153, 164, 167, 177, 181, 184–85, 187, 211, 223, 230, 233–35, 246–47, 268, 281–82, 284, 288–89, 293, 303, 362, 365–66, 368, 375, 377, 410–11, 428. *See also* translation
  Alphabetic Principle, and 283–84
  dominance 6, 8–9, 11, 15, 76, 92, 367
  fluency in, 13, 271
  grammar 333
  literacy. *See* literacy
  Northern Territory, in the 16
  orthography 265, 295, 393
  proficiency 14, 18
  vowels 285, 297
Australian Indigenous Languages Framework (AILF) 302
Australian Institute of Aboriginal and Torres Strait Islander Studies (AIATSIS) xvi, 108, 175, 190, 243, 250, 328, 331, 360, 403, 414, 422
  Aboriginal Studies Electronic Data Archive (ASEDA) 396
  National Indigenous Languages Survey Report 2005 108
Australian Labor Party 7, 11–13
Australian Language and Literacy Policy 8, 11
Australian National University 190
Australian Second Language Proficiency Ratings (ASLPR) 271–74. *See also* fluency
Awabakal-Wanarruwa (language) 110, 113, 255, 294, 297. *See also* Arwarbukarl Cultural Resource Association (ACRA); Miromaa Language Program
  Certificate I qualification 171

B

Bamay Possum's Party (book) 115
Barriyala: Let's Work (book) 115
Batchelor Institute of Indigenous Tertiary Education (BIITE) xvi, xix, xxi, 352, 365, 390, 395–96
  Centre for Australian Languages and Linguistics 120
Batemans Bay Public School (NSW)
  Dhurga language program xviii, 159, 162, 164–66, 173–76, 188–93, 257
Bayabangun Ngurrawa (conference) 260
Bayungu (language) xv, 104. *See also* Wangka Maya Pilbara Aboriginal Language Centre (Wangka Maya)
  audio recordings of 125
  dictionary 125–26, 128
  documentation, of 125–26
  language program 125
  Payungu Picture Dictionary 104, 125–28
  phrasebook 126
  sketch grammar 125, 128
Berndt, Ronald and Catherine 353, 387, 394, 397–98
  A World That Was: The Yaraldi of the Murray River and the Lakes, South Australia. 397
bicultural education 7, 13, 17, 24
Biddigal (dialect). *See* Dharawal (language)
Big hART 84, 87. *See also* Ngapartji Ngapartji (touring show)
Bilinarra (language) xix, 159, 226–28, 234. *See also* Pigeon Hole School (NT); Victoria River District (VRD) NT
  endangered 226, 229
  fluency in, 234
  grammar 229
  language program 231
  vocabulary 229
bilingual. *See also* language mixing
  dictionaries 405
  education xiv, xxiii, xxv, 3, 7, 9, 13, 16–18, 24, 31, 120, 123, 260, 274, 346, 367
  signs 28, 76–77, 83, 148, 150, 233, 372
  speech communities 226, 362
  touring theatre 84, 86
Biripi-Gathang (language) 112
  Certificate I qualification 171
Birrbay (language) 110, 114
Bonalbo Central School (NSW)

language program (Bundjalung) 113
Boon Wurrung (dialect). *See* Kulin (language family)
Brennan, Gloria 132
Broulee Public School (NSW) 163–68, 174, 190
Buandig (language) 314
Bundjalung-Yugambeh (language) 110–11, 113, 182–83, 294
  audio recordings 110
  Certificate I qualification 171
  endangered 254
  language program 113
  pronunciation 111
  vocabulary 111
Burarra (language) 362–63, 366

C

Canadian Assembly of First Nations
  language policy 3
Cape York Peninsula Language Documentation project (CYPLD) 418, 420–22, 424–25, 428. *See also* Lockhart River case study
Carnarvon Senior High School (WA)
  language program (Bayungu) 125
case
  absolutive 379
  accusative 379
  ergative 97, 185, 212, 248, 379, 382
  marking 236, 294
  morphology 377
  nominative 379
  suffixes 248, 294, 299
  system (noun) 299, 333
CD-ROMs
  Winangali 309
CDs 4, 85, 114–15, 125–26, 177–78, 328, 393–94, 405, 427
Centre for Australian Languages and Linguistics 120
certification. *See also* qualifications (Aboriginal Language Teaching)
  Aboriginal community, controlled by 277–78
Chifley College-Dunheved Campus (NSW) 183, 186–87. *See also* Dharug (language)
code-switching xix, 225, 229–31, 235–36
community-based language revitalisation 75, 80, 91, 93, 108, 110, 113, 115, 131, 190, 278, 374
community-driven language revitalisation 14, 55, 123, 128, 134, 197, 313
community linguist (Indigenous) xv, xix, xxi, 108, 139, 237, 372, 376
computers 107, 125, 148, 310, 323–24, 326–27, 329, 334–37, 339, 344–45, 356–59, 406. *See also* electronic dictionaries; information technology (IT); software
  access to 22, 345, 424
  computer-based resources 117, 311, 325, 339–40, 346
  disadvantages of 310, 346
  literacy, as aid to 30
  North Coast Computer Project 110
  presentation on 342
  support from 332
conjunctions 333
consonants 266, 285, 298, 362, 398
  consonant phonemes 285
  lamino-dental 266, 362
  Ngarrindjeri 398
  palatal 362
  pronunciation of 266, 285
  sounds of 285
courses (teaching). *See also* qualifications (Aboriginal Language Teaching)
  accreditation of, 158, 173, 177
  Certificate in Aboriginal Language Work (WA) 125–26
  Certificate (TAFE NSW) 115, 158, 165, 171, 173–80, 218
  content of, 172
  delivery of, 172, 178
  entry requirements 173
creoles 6, 16, 295, 301, 426, 428. *See also* Kriol
  Lockhart River Creole 426
cross-linguistic comparison 376–77, 379
curricula 6, 13, 41, 48, 68, 120, 158, 174, 189, 192, 194–95, 198, 200, 205–06, 367. *See also* Northern Territory Curriculum Framework (2002); *NSW Aboriginal Languages K-10 Syllabus*; Victorian Curriculum and Assessment Authority (VCAA)
  bilingual 31

development of 3, 47, 199, 302, 313, 392
Dhurga (language) 188, 193
inappropriate 136
Indigenous languages, for 3, 13, 158, 167, 189, 194, 198, 207, 216, 220
national standards (Aust) 275
Ngarrindjeri (language) 389, 392
NSW 112, 174, 190, 194, 219, 255
oral 140
primary schools, for 202
secondary schools, for 202
support with 120
Western Australian 140
Wiradjuri (language) 159

D

Darkinyung (language) 110, 113
   Darkinyung Language Group 110, 255
   grammar-dictionary 114, 255
Darug (people). *See* Dharug (language)
de facto language policy. *See* invisible language policy
Dhanggati (language) 110, 112–13, 182–83
   Certificate I qualification 171
   grammar-dictionary 114
   Thunghutti Tiddas Aboriginal Corporation 110, 112
   workshops in, 171
Dharawal (language) 158, 178–80, 182, 335. *See also* toponyms
   accredited teaching qualifications, in 158
   Biddigal (dialect) 178
   CD 178
   Certificate I qualification 178–79
   dictionary 178
   language program 178–180, 335
   Oppliger, Amanda (linguist) 186
Dharug (language) xvi, 181–84, 187, 328, 334–35. *See also* Chifley College-Dunheved Campus (NSW); toponyms
   Certificate I qualification 171
   Elders 183
   fluency in, 181, 183–84, 335
   grammar 183, 187
   language centre 186
   language program 159, 183–86, 326
   mobile phone dictionary 335
   nouns 185
   oral record 325
   orthography 183, 266
   pronunciation 181, 185–86, 304
   songs 181, 183, 185–87, 335
   sounds of 184–85
   translation 181, 184
   vocabulary 184–85, 328
   Watson, Edna 186
   website 187, 335
   wordlists 304, 325
Dhudhuroa (language) 314
Dhurga (language) 158–59, 162–63, 173, 188–193, 297. *See also* Broulee Public School (NSW); Mogo Public School (NSW); toponyms; Vincentia High School (NSW)
   accredited teaching qualifications, in 158
   audio recordings of 175
   Batemans Bay Public School. *See* Batemans Bay Public School (NSW)
   Cobowra Local Aboriginal Land Council 173–75
   curricula 188, 193
   Dhurga Buradja (book) 174
   Dhurga Buradja - Speaking Dhurga Tomorrow (Certificate I) 173–75
   Elders 189
   endangered 173
   grammar 163–64, 167, 191
   language program xviii, 159, 162, 164–66, 173–76, 188–193, 257
   metalanguage, use of 166
   orthography 167, 175, 191
   phonemes 165
   pronunciation 165
   songs 189, 191
   sounds of 163, 166–67, 297–98
   teaching resources 165–66
   vocabulary 163, 167, 185, 191–93
   workshops 176, 190, 193
   Wreck Bay Community Council 189
Dhuwala (language) 362, 364. *See also* Gupapuyŋu (language)
Dhuwal (language) 362, 364, 367. *See also* Djambarrpuyŋu (language)

dictionaries 86, 94, 110, 112, 114, 116, 124, 126–27, 133–35, 139, 147–49, 167, 177, 187, 256, 269, 273, 315, 373, 413, 423. *See also* electronic dictionaries; grammar-dictionaries; mobile phones; *Gamilaraay, Yuwaalaraay & Yuwaaalayaay Dictionary*; Ngarrindjeri Dictionary Project; software; wordlists
  Bayungu 125
  bilingual 405
  Darkinyung 255
  development of, 353
  Dharawal 178
  Gajirrabeng 147
  Gumbaynggirr 108, 116
  Miriwoong 147, 149
  Ngarluma 122–23, 128
  Payungu Picture Dictionary, (Bayungu) 104, 125–28
  talking 30
  Thalanyji 121
  Wergaia 160, 242–43, 249
  Wiradjuri 217
  Yan-nhaŋu 365, 368
Diwurruwurru-jaru Aboriginal Corporation (DAC) xv, xix, 109, 120, 231, 237. *See also* Gurindji (language)
  linguists 231
Djambarrpuyŋu (language) 366–68. *See also* Dhuwal (language)
  fluency in, 368
  Yan-nhaŋu, parallel translations 368
Djinaŋ (language) 362
Djinba (language) 362
Djirrbal (language) 93, 95–96
  workshops 93, 358
documentation of languages 5, 14, 79, 110, 120, 127, 131, 134, 137, 139–40, 142, 147, 200, 310, 351, 353, 356–57, 369, 375, 418, 420–22, 424–26, 429. *See also* audio recordings; Cape York Peninsula Language Documentation project; Emergency Language Documentation Teams; language source materials
  Awabakal-Wanarruwa 294
  Bayungu, of 125–26

  Bundjalung-Yugambeh 294
  endangered languages, of 353
  Gumbaynggirr 294
  Gunnai 375, 377
  incomplete 160, 253–55, 336, 352, 419
  Kaurna 56, 65
  Kimberley Language Resource Centre, by 133, 135–36, 140–41, 143
  Kuuku Ya'u 426
  language-centres, by 79, 108
  Mirima Dawang Woorlab-gerring Language and Culture Centre, by 148
  Miriwoong 76, 147–48, 150
  Ngarluma 122
  Nyangumarta 123
  Paakantji 294
  Pitjantjatjara 86
  Queensland, of 352
  Thalanyji 121
  Umpila (dialect group) 426
  Victorian, of 28
  Wangka Maya, by 126–27
  Wergaia 240, 250
  Wiradjuri 294
  Yan-nhaŋu 364, 366, 368–69
dual naming. *See* toponyms
Dubbo College (NSW) 222
  language program 48, 159, 221
Dulaybam Dunggiir (book) 115
Dunghutti (language). *See* Dhanggati (language)
DVDs 85, 104, 117, 122–24, 128
Dyirrbal (language) 93, 94. *See also* language revitalisation programs
  Djirrbal (language) 93
  Girramay (language) 93
  Ngadjan (language) 93

E

Eastern States Indigenous Languages Working Group xiii, 73
East Kimberley region (WA). *See* Mirima Dawang Woorlab-gerring Language and Culture Centre (MDWg); *See* Miriwoong (language)
education policy (languages) 3–10, 12–14, 16, 18, 76, 78, 82, 87, 99, 108, 119–20, 129, 133–34, 142–43, 176, 195, 204, 231, 260,

429. *See also* Australian Language and Literacy Policy; invisible language policy; language ideologies; Maintenance of Indigenous Languages and Records (MILR); National Aboriginal and Torres Strait Islander Education Policy; national Indigenous languages policy; *National Policy on Languages* (1987); visible language policy;
   bilingual education 16–17
   Canada, of 3–4
   Community Languages Assistance Program (NSW) 108
   defined 10
   development of xxix, 4, 10
   Draft Aboriginal Languages Policy (NSW, 2001–02) 173
   Indigenous control of 82
   National Aboriginal and Torres Strait Islander Education Policy 13–14
   New South Wales, of 108, 173, 194, 254
   New Zealand, of 3–4
   Northern Territory, of the 367
   Report on a National Language Policy (1984) 10
   Training Policy Statement 2004–06 170
   United States, of the 3
educators. *See* teachers
Elders' councils 4
   Wiradjuri xiii, 67, 73, 217–18, 222, 257
electronic
   databases 387
   technology 25
   wordlists 328, 396–98
   words, recording of 332
electronic dictionaries 310, 339, 341, 344–45, 390
   contents of 341
   Extensible Markup Language (XML) 341–42
   Field-Oriented Standard Format (FOSF) 341–42
   Gamilaraay 403
   Kaurna 343–44
   Kirrkirr (viewer) 340, 342–43, 345
   master dictionary file 340
   mobile phones, on 30, 123, 335, 339–40, 344–46
   Multi-Dictionary Formatter (MDF) 342
   Ngarluma 123
   Ngarrindjeri 392, 394–95
   Wagiman 345
   Warlpiri 343
Emergency Language Documentation Teams 419–20
endangered languages 23–25, 28–29, 76, 80–82, 85, 124, 126–27, 132, 226, 232, 254, 340, 345–46, 351, 353, 418–21, 425. *See also* Graded Intergenerational Disruption Scale for Threatened Languages (GIDS); National Indigenous Languages Survey (NILS) 2005; Reversing Language Shift model (RLS);
   Bilinarra 226, 229
   Bundjalung-Yugambeh 254
   Dhurga 173
   Gurindji 226, 229
   Karrangpurru 226
   Miriwoong 76, 147
   Mudbura 226
   Ngarinyman 226, 229
   Ngarluma 122
   Ngarrindjeri 352
   Nyangumarta 123
   Pitjantjatjara 85
   revitalisation of, guidelines for 25, 82
   Thalanyji 121
   Yan-nhaŋu 366, 369
   Yitha-Yitha/Dadi-Dadi 28
English. *See* Australian English
Eora (language) 182–83. *See also* Dharug (language)
   Certificate I qualification 171
Extensible Markup Language (XML) 341–43
   syntax 342

F

Federation of Aboriginal and Torres Strait Islander Languages (FATSIL) 87, 164
   Guide to Community Protocols for Indigenous Projects (2004) 164
Field-Oriented Standard Format (FOSF) 341–42

Index 439

fluency xxviii, 53, 99, 132, 134–35, 157, 225, 237, 253–54, 265–70, 273, 275, 408, 421, 426. *See also* Australian Second Language Proficiency Ratings (ASLPR); oral proficiency
    Bilinarra, in 234
    certification of, 272, 274, 276–78
    Dharug, in 181, 183–84, 335
    Djambarrpuyŋu, in 368
    Gamilaraay, in 403
    Gurindji 234
    measurement of, 271–72, 274, 278
    Miriwoong, in 76, 147, 149
    Ngarinyman, in 234
    Ngarrindjeri, in 399
    Standard Australian English, in 13, 271
    teachers, of 273–74, 278, 332
    Thalanyji, in 121
    Warrgamay, in 97
    Wiradjuri, in 68, 70, 213
    Yan-nhaŋu, in 363, 366

G

Gajirrabeng (language) 146, 148
    dictionary 147
Gamilaraay (language) xvi, 158, 182, 218, 284. *See also Gamilaraay, Yuwaalaraay & Yuwaalayaay Dictionary (GYYD)*; toponyms; Walgett High School (NSW); Yuwaalaraay (language)
    accredited teaching qualifications, in 158
    adjectives 409, 411
    audio recordings of 403, 408–09
    Certificate I qualification 171
    dictionary 403
    fluency in, 403
    New England Institute of TAFE 176
    orthography 282, 404, 409
    phonemes in, 282, 295
    pronunciation 282, 403–04
    songbooks 177
    sounds of 282–84, 403, 405–06, 408–10
    sources of words 408–10
    text-based resources 330
    verbs 404
    vocabulary 409–10, 412
    vowels 282, 296, 409–10
    website 403
    wordlist, Yuwaalaraay-Gamilaraay 404, 408, 413–14
    workshops 171, 176–77
Gamilaraay, Yuwaalaraay & Yuwaalayaay Dictionary (GYYD) xiii, 353, 402–04, 409–15
    Ash, Anna 405–06, 413
    production 405, 411, 413
    sketch grammar 413
    sources of words 404, 408–10
    Yuwaalaraay-Gamilaraay Wordlist 404, 408, 413–14
Ganalbiŋu (language) 362
Gardiner, William (Nyaparu) 124, 127
    biography 124, 127
Gathang (language) 110, 113–14
Geographical Names Board of NSW (GNB) 28. *See also* toponyms
Girramay (language) 93, 95
    language program 99
    workshops 93, 95, 358
Girringun Aboriginal Corporation 93
Graded Intergenerational Disruption Scale for Threatened Languages (GIDS) 75, 80–82, 147, 232
grammar-dictionaries 108, 110, 114, 351
    Darkinyung 114, 255
    Dhanggati 114
    Gumbaynggirr 114
    Wergaia Community Grammar and Dictionary 240, 242–43, 250
grammars 42, 45, 47, 92, 94, 110, 115–17, 133–35, 151, 160, 163, 167, 187, 191, 225, 246, 256, 269, 271, 294, 312, 315–16, 327, 329, 333–44, 353, 373, 423. *See also* grammar-dictionaries; parsers
    Australian English 333
    Bayungu 125
    Bilinarra 229
    Dharug 181, 183, 187
    Dhurga 163–64, 167, 175, 192
    Gumbaynggirr 108, 114, 116
    Gunnai 372, 376–80
    Gurindji 229–30, 236
    learners' grammar 122, 128
    Miriwoong 150–51

Ngarinyman 229
Ngarluma 122–23, 128
Ngarrindjeri 394–95, 397
Pitjantjatjara 86
sketch grammar 56, 122–23, 125, 128, 150, 244–45, 255, 310, 312, 318, 373, 413
Thalanyji 128
Wergaia 160, 241, 243, 246–48
Wiradjuri 212, 222–23
Yan-nhaŋu 365, 368
Yitha-Yitha/Dadi-Dadi 28
Yuwaalaraay 403–06
Grant (Snr), Stan 67, 210–13, 216–17, 223
Green book of language revitalization in practice, The xxvi, xxviii, 106
Gudjal (language) 93, 95–96
  Elders 96
  language program xxi, 90, 95–96
  workshops 94, 358
Gugu-Badhun (language) 93, 96
  Elders 96
  language awareness workshop 93
Guiwan (language) 110
Gumatj (language) 93, 100, 366
Gumbaynggirr (language) xxii, 27, 32, 103, 107–08, 110–12, 258, 260, 294. *See also* Muurrbay Aboriginal Language and Culture Co-operative; Nambucca Heads High School (NSW); St Mary's Public School (NSW); toponyms
  Aboriginal languages summer school 218
  audio recordings of 32, 111
  Bamay Possum's Party (book) 115
  Barriyala: Let's Work (book) 115
  Certificate II qualification 115
  Certificate I qualification 171
  dictionary 116
  Dulaybam Dunggiir (book) 115
  Elders 107
  grammar-dictionary 108, 114
  Gumbaynggirr Language Student Workbooks 115
  language program 25–26, 32, 115, 189
  manifesto 24, 32
  Mayalambala: Let's Move It (book) 115
  sound recordings of, 32
  suffixes 116
  teachers of, 26
  text-based resources 330
  translation 115
  vocabulary 116
  workshops in, 171
Gunnai (language) 313, 372–385. *See* documentation of languages
  CD 375
  grammar 372, 376–80
  illustrated books 375
  language program xxi, 372, 374
  language records 375
  learning guide 375
  orthography 374, 378–82
  pronouns 372, 375–84
  pronunciation 374, 380, 382
  sounds of 375, 379, 382
  suffixes 377, 379–80, 382–83
  verbs 383
  vocabulary 315, 376–81
  wordlists 374, 376–77, 381–83
  workshops 374
Gupapuyŋu (language) 362, 366, 368. *See also* Dhuwala (language)
Gurindji (language) xix, 159, 226–27, 229, 234. *See also* code-switching
  Diwurruwurru-jaru Aboriginal Corporation (DAC) 231
  endangered 226, 229
  fluency in, 234
  grammar 229–30, 236
  Kriol xx, 229–30, 234–36
  locative case marker 236
  nouns 229–31, 236
  pronouns 236
  translation 231
  verbs 230, 236
  vocabulary 229–31, 235
Guringai (language). *See* Guringay (language)
Guringay (language) 110, 114
  Certificate I qualification 171

H

Handbook of Aboriginal languages of NSW and the ACT, a 114
Hercus, Luise 243–44, 312
historical records. *See* language source materials

Howitt, A. W 374, 377–78, 396
Hypertext Markup Language (HTML)
    317–18, 340

I

Indigenous Community Volunteers 135
Indigenous Knowledge Centres (IKCs)
    352, 356
Indigenous language rights 3, 7–8, 11,
    16–18, 126, 136, 257, 363, 366
Indigenous Languages and Culture (ILC)
    program, NT 226–27, 231–34,
    236
Indigenous Languages Institute (conference 2008) 260
*Indigenous languages of Victoria, revival
    and reclamation: Victorian Certificate of Education study design* 160,
    240, 242, 247, 250, 313, 374
information technology (IT) 106, 323–
    27, 331, 335–37. *See also* Aboriginal Languages of Victoria Resource
    Portal (ALV-RP); computers; electronic dictionaries; software
  Extensible Markup Language (XML)
    341
  Hypertext Markup Language (HTML)
    317–18, 340
  Miromaa database 309, 325
  Ninti language learning site 309
  speech synthesis technology 311, 332,
    337
  worksheets 330–31
  workshops 107
Institute for Aboriginal Development
    (IAD) 267, 277, 413
International Phonetic Alphabet (IPA)
    96, 244, 296
internet 88, 310, 356
  telephony software 335
interrogatives 166, 213
intransitive verbs 212, 404–05, 411
invisible language policy 5–8, 10, 14–18.
    See also visible language policy
*It's a Hard Road to Hoe but You Gotta Start
    Somewhere: Designing a Community
    Language Project* (DVD) 117

J

Jaminjung (language) 148
Jarrakan (language family) 146. *See
    also* Gajirrabeng (language); Gija
    (language); Miriwoong (language)

K

Kalkaringi School (NT) 225–31, 235
  language program (Gurindji) 231
Kamilaroi (language). *See* Gamilaraay
    (language)
Karrangpurru (language) 226–27. *See
    also* Victoria River District (VRD)
    NT
  endangered 226
Katherine Regional Language Centre.
    See Diwurruwurru-jaru Aboriginal
    Corporation (DAC)
Kaurna (language) xiii, 235, 395, 398.
    See also Kaurna Plains School (SA);
    language revitalisation programs;
    toponyms
  code-switching 235
  documention of, 56, 65
  electronic dictionary 343–44
  grammar 56, 58
  Kaurna Aboriginal Community and
    Heritage Association Inc (KACHA)
    58
  Kaurna in the Public Arena Post 1980
    63–65
  Kaurna Placenames website 54, 56,
    61–62, 64–65
  Kaurna requests database 60–61, 65
  Kaurna Warra Pintyandi (KWP) xiii,
    54, 56, 59–60, 64
  language program xiii, 56–58, 189
  songs 57
  sound file 63, 65, 343–44
  translation 56–58, 60, 65
  vocabulary 57
  wordlist 56
  workshop 57, 59
Kaurna Plains School (SA) 57, 189. *See
    also* Kaurna (language)
Keeping Language Strong (report) 133
Kija (language) 273
Kimberley Language Resource Centre

(KLRC) xiv, xxviii, 79, 103, 131–32, 134, 137, 139, 141–43. *See also* documentation of languages
Business Plan 2008–11 136
dictionary 133, 139
draft policy 133
establishment of 131
Keeping Language Strong (report) xviii, 133
Kimberley Language Support Project 133
Language Continuation Continuum (LCC) 138–39
language policy 134
language revitalisation strategies 139–42
linguists 132, 137, 141
oral language transmission 136, 139
origins 132–33
project management model 137
Strategic Plan (2000 report) 134–35
Strategic Plan (2005 revision) 136
Teaching On Country (TOC) 139
teaching resources 134–35
Kirrkirr (electronic dictionary viewer) 340, 342–43, 345
Koori Centre (University of Sydney) xvi, xix, xxii, 31, 158, 163, 168, 173, 218, 221, 258, 260, 267–68, 274, 278. *See also* Master of Indigenous Languages Education (MILE)
Kriol xix, 76, 140, 147, 153, 160, 187, 225–26, 229–30, 234–36, 300. *See also* code-switching; creoles; language mixing
Gurindji xx, 229–30, 234–36
Kimberley Kriol xix, 147
Kulin (language family) 244. *See also* Wergaia (language)
Barababaraba 314
Boon Wurrung 314–15
Djab Wurrung 245, 314
Dja Dja Wurrung 314
Gulidjan 314
Jardwadjali 314
Ladji Ladji 314
Madhi Madhi 314
Taungurung 314–15, 374
Wadi Wadi 314

Wathaurong 314
Wemba Wemba 245, 314
Woiwurrung 314–15
Kŭrnai (language). *See* Gunnai (language)
Kuuku Ya'u (language). *See* Lockhart River case study

L

lamino-dental
 consonants 266, 362
lamino-palatal 266
land councils 4, 112, 172–74, 240, 277
 Central Land Council 344
 Cobowra Local Aboriginal Land Council 173–74
 Kimberley Land Council 143
 Northern Land Council (NLC) 367–68
language activists xxvii, 4, 10, 23, 29, 79, 104, 142, 152–53
language centres 4, 7, 12, 14, 17, 90, 103–04, 106–08, 111–14, 119–27, 129, 131, 148, 176, 273, 277, 356, 359–60, 421. *See also* Diwurruwurru-jaru Aboriginal Corporation (DAC); Kimberley Language Resource Centre (KLRC); language programs (Aboriginal); Lodjba Koori Language Centre-Many Rivers Aboriginal Language Centre (MRALC); Mirima Dawang Woorlab-gerring Language and Culture Centre (MDWg); Muurrbay Aboriginal Language and Culture Co-operative; North Queensland Regional Aboriginal Corporation Language Centre (NQRACLC); Wangka Maya Pilbara Aboriginal Language Centre (Wangka Maya)
activities 79, 103–04, 120, 127, 146
Dharug 186
establishment of 108–09, 119
funding from 113
funding of 14, 109, 120, 129, 148, 150
government support 120
language documentation, by. *See* documentation of languages
promotion of 359
role of 104, 108, 111–14, 119–20, 123, 126, 129, 148

vulnerability of 12
language continuation xxviii, 6–7, 11–14, 17–18, 24, 84, 87, 89, 98, 104, 107, 131–32, 136–37, 141–42, 160, 225–27, 230, 232, 234, 236–37, 254, 270, 298, 419–20, 428–29. *See also Green book of language revitalization in practice, The;* Maintenance of Indigenous Languages and Records program (MILR)
  community control 14, 17, 111, 127, 227
  informal strategies 225–27, 231
  Language Continuation Continuum (LCC) 138–39
  literacy-based approach to 133
  principle of, 14
  rights of, 17
  self-determination in 141
  strategies 136–37
language decline xxiii, xxv, 7, 76, 91, 219, 356, 402, 408
  reversal of 7
language documentation. *See* documentation of languages
language education policy. *See* education policy (languages)
Language Endangerment Status Indicator. *See* National Indigenous Languages Survey (NILS) 2005
language ideologies 6, 8–9, 14–18
  Australian Language and Literacy Policy 8
  defined 8
language immersion 149, 160, 226–27, 232–35, 274, 294. *See also* language nest model; master-apprentice model
  Australian English, in 15
  Canadian model (French) 232
  Māori model 232–33
  models of, 226–27, 232, 234–36
  one-on-one 149
  oral 140
language maintenance. *See* language continuation
language mixing 85, 159–60, 184, 225–27, 229–30, 233–36, 300, 366, 426. *See also* bilingual; code-switching; Kriol
  immersion models, and 233–34
  promotion of, 235
  youth language 226, 229–31
language nest model 132, 134–35, 139, 142, 226, 232–34, 236. *See also* language immersion
Yan-nhaŋu 'Language Nests' 365
Language Other Than English (LOTE) 95, 113, 389
language programs (Aboriginal) xi, xvi, xxvi, xxviii, 7, 13, 17, 22, 25–30, 32, 43–44, 46–47, 68–69, 80, 90, 95, 99, 104, 111–12, 120, 140, 142–43, 153, 157–60, 167, 171, 195, 200, 203, 206, 225–27, 234, 237, 260, 281, 283–90, 293–95, 299, 302, 313, 323, 326, 355–56, 358, 360, 363, 366, 369, 372–73, 392, 403. *See also* courses (teaching); language centres; Kalkaringi School (NT); qualifications (Aboriginal Language Teaching); school-community partnerships;
Aboriginal Education Consultative Group (AECG) 69
accredited teaching qualifications 170
bilingual 9, 16–17, 24
case study 194–207
community-based 41, 93, 108, 110, 190, 197, 220, 256, 374
Community Languages Assistance Program 108
community, support from 68, 256, 260
development of, 41, 95, 112, 158–59, 201, 219–20, 257–58, 323, 356, 404
establishment of, 54, 71, 117, 194–95, 197–98, 203–05
funding of, 13, 17, 31, 80, 99, 147, 163, 167, 197, 256
Indigenous concerns, regarding, 157, 196, 197
Indigenous input 54, 143, 159, 172, 222
Indigenous Languages and Culture (ILC) program, NT 226–27, 231–34, 236
linguists, role in 29, 302

Many Rivers Aboriginal Language Centre (MRALC) 113
Master-Apprentice Language Learning Program (MALLP) 79, 149, 153
methods used in, 79
Mirima Dawang Woorlab-gerring 146, 151
National Assessment Program – Literacy and Numeracy (NAPLaN) 16
NSW Department of Education and Training (DET) 112
Report on School-based Aboriginal Language Program Activity in NSW During 2006 162
school-based 25, 104, 140, 142, 159–60, 162–168, 194–95, 197, 200–01, 205, 207, 210–24, 226, 231, 233, 253–62, 274, 276, 281–93, 352, 367, 393
school principal, role in, 26, 69, 113, 191–92, 194–95, 200–02, 204–07, 211
structure of, 107
Technical and Further Education (TAFE) NSW 170–79
language publicity 77–83
language shift 6, 86, 122, 147, 153, 160, 230, 232, 236, 296, 300, 352, 364, 418, 428–29. *See also* Reversing Language Shift model (RLS)
language source materials 249. *See also* audio recordings; Australian Institute of Aboriginal and Torres Strait Islander Studies (AIATSIS); documentation of languages; wordlists
archival records 29, 57, 109–10, 125, 128, 183, 190, 216, 243, 310, 312–13, 316, 323, 328, 353, 373, 375–76, 382, 384, 387, 398, 423, 426
comparison of, 374
Elders 110, 375, 395
ethnographic accounts 353, 364, 397
historical records 94, 243–46, 250, 293, 295, 301–02, 312–13, 315–16, 318, 343, 353, 357, 372, 377–80, 382–84, 389, 391, 394–96, 398, 405, 408–09, 421
lack of, 56, 266, 298, 300, 324

libraries 29, 244, 312–13, 315–16, 328
linguistic 94, 96, 147, 181, 244, 259, 312, 422
oral histories 121, 182, 216, 325–26, 328, 355, 358, 375, 387–88, 391, 396, 409, 414
unreliability of, 245
language transfer 78–79, 148, 151, 153, 214
LanguageWiki 325, 331, 335
language workshops. *See* workshops
linguistic
analysis 116, 127, 134, 190, 244, 255, 259, 282, 309, 312–13, 315–16, 320, 372–73
assimilation 6
classification 76, 122, 146–47, 244–45, 302, 312, 314–15, 333, 363
comparison. *See* cross-linguistic comparison
diversity 8, 24, 129, 132, 139, 142, 330, 364, 366
divisions 418, 429
documentation. *See* documentation of languages
dominance 14
expertise 22, 29, 32
foundations 352, 372
heritage 9, 106, 136, 141, 232, 302, 388
heterogeneity 418, 424, 428
homogeneity 418, 423–24, 428
identity 7, 55, 75–76, 80, 82, 363
knowledge transfer 78
research 151, 255, 315–16
resources 96, 181, 293, 320
rights xxvi, 3, 136
scholarships 108
sources. *See* language source materials
support 29, 54, 110, 121, 127, 175, 177, 189, 192, 200, 255, 295, 302, 315, 317–18, 320, 331, 334, 336, 366–67, 369, 373, 391
terms 269, 282, 285, 300, 334
training 78, 108, 115–16, 141, 150, 152, 212, 301, 312, 393
linguists 8, 17, 29, 84, 87, 96, 99, 103–04, 108, 111–13, 116, 119–20, 122–25, 127, 131–32, 134–35, 137, 141–42, 147, 153, 174–76,

187–88, 200, 226, 231–32, 240–42, 244–45, 247, 249–50, 255, 259–60, 268, 271, 277, 295, 301–02, 309–10, 315, 317–18, 325, 328, 331, 333, 336, 339, 341–42, 366, 368–69, 373, 375, 383–85, 388, 403, 408, 414–15, 419–20, 422–23, 425–26, 429–30. *See also* community linguist (Indigenous)
Alpher, Barry 397
Amery, Rob 330, 399
Austin, Peter 403
Bowe, Dr Heather 241
Brennan, Gloria 132
Eira, Christina 330
Gale, Mary-Anne 388
Hale, Kenneth 122
Hercus, Luise 243–44, 313, 315, 396–97
Indigenous 17, 108, 111, 132, 139, 141
Kartinyeri, James Brooksie 396–97
Kirke, Brian 397
Kofod, Frances 147
language activists, interaction between 104
Morelli, Brother Steve 107
non-Indigenous 54, 108
O'Grady, Geoffrey 125
Oppliger, Amanda 183, 186, 334
Reid, Julie 241
Thieberger, Nick 391
Troy, Jakelyn 183, 186, 190, 328
von Brandenstein, Carl 122
Yallop, Colin 396
literacy 16, 25, 30, 32, 104, 124, 133, 135, 138, 148–49, 151, 163, 167, 173, 211, 213–14, 260, 265, 273, 283, 293, 295, 332, 368, 420. *See also* National Assessment Program-Literacy and Numeracy (NAPLaN); oral proficiency
Australian Language and Literacy Policy 8, 11
booklets 423
computer 326, 339, 344, 420
grammatical 326
low levels of 339
Nyangumarta, in 124
scaffolding programs 41, 45
skills, tests of 271
specialist teacher in, 178–79
Standard Australian English (SAE), in 7, 11, 13, 15–17, 149, 231, 290
Strelley Literacy Centre 123
loanwords 297, 304
locative case suffix 212–13, 299
Gurindji 236
Wiradjuri 299
Lockhart River case study 421, 426
CDs 427
documentation 426–27
Kuuku Ya'u (language) 426
Lockhart River Creole 426
song documentation 427
Umpila (language) 426
Lodjba Koori Language Centre 313, 315. *See also* Victorian Aboriginal Corporation for Languages (VACL)
Luritja (language) 85

M

Maintenance of Indigenous Languages and Records (MILR) xvi, 12, 14, 173, 430
Many Rivers Aboriginal Language Centre (MRALC) xiii, xxii, 26, 103, 106–07, 109–15, 255. *See also* Awabakal-Wanarruwa (language); Birrbay (language); Bundjalung-Yugambeh (language); Darkinyung (language); Dhanggati (language); Gathang (language); Gumbaynggir (language); Guringay (language); Muurrbay Aboriginal Language and Culture Co-operative; Warrimay (language); Yaygirr/Yaegl (language)
Gathang (Birrbay, Warrimay and Guringay) 110
Māori (language) xxvi, 31, 233, 275–77, 297–98, 300
Institute of Excellence in the Māori Language xxviii
language nest model 134, 232–33
Māori Language Act (1987) 3
Māori Language Commission (MLC) 275
pronunciation 300

vocabulary 300
vowels 297–98
markup language
  Extensible Markup Language (XML) 341–43
  Field-Oriented Standard Format (FOSF) 341
  Hypertext Markup Language (HTML) 317, 340
Master-Apprentice Language Learning Program (MALLP) 149
master-apprentice model 25, 79, 104, 146, 153, 226, 232–34, 236, 418–19, 425, 429
Master of Indigenous Languages Education (MILE) xiv, 31, 163, 173, 217, 221, 258, 273–75, 278. *See also* Koori Centre (University of Sydney)
Mathews, R.H. 245–46, 377–79, 383, 408–09
Mayalambala: Let's Move It (book) 115, 336
McNaboe, Diane 217–18, 221–22
metalanguage 163, 165–66, 219
Mirima Dawang Woorlab-gerring Language and Culture Centre (MDWg) xx, 76–78, 103–04, 146–49. *See also* Miriwoong (language)
  bush trips 149–53
  establishment 147
  language documentation, by 148
  language program 146, 151
  language-related employment 150, 152–53
  language revitalisation strategies 148, 150
  linguists 147
  Master-Apprentice Language Learning Program (MALLP) 149
  training and employment 150
Miriwoong (language) xx, 54, 75–78, 103–04, 146, 150, 152–53. *See also* documentation of languages; Mirima Dawang Woorlab-gerring Language and Culture Centre (MDWg); toponyms
  Action Plan for Miriwoong Language Survival 153

  audio recordings 148
  dictionary 147–49
  Elders 78, 146, 151
  endangered 76, 147
  fluency in, 76, 147, 149
  grammar 150–51
  Kofod, Frances 147, 150
  Kriol, shift to 147, 153
  language program 76, 78–79, 81–83, 149–50, 152–53
  master-apprentice program 146
  multimedia, use of 149
  orthography 78, 149
  public signage 150
  revitalisation strategies 148, 150–51
  sounds of 78
  sounds, of 149
  vocabulary 147, 149–50, 152
Miromaa Language Program 359, 390. *See also* Awabakal-Wanarruwa (language)
  database 309, 325
mobile phones 88, 122–23, 310, 344–46, 358
  Dharug dictionary 186, 335
  dictionary platform, as 30, 123, 339–40, 344–46
  Kaurna dictionary 344
  Ngarluma dictionary 123
  Wagiman dictionary 345
Mogo Public School (NSW) 162, 164–168
monolingualism 6, 9, 16, 18, 225–26, 229, 268, 428
  Aboriginal languages, in 234
  education, in 16
  English, in xxv, 9–10
Mudbura (language) 226, 228
  endangered 226
multilingualism 6, 8, 12, 46, 217, 225, 268, 362, 428
  policy and 11
multimedia 310
  learning materials 126, 149, 340, 343, 346, 403
  productions 128
Muurrbay Aboriginal Language and Culture Co-operative xiii, xvii, xxii, 24, 26, 32, 103, 106–15, 117, 218, 256, 272, 277, 336–37. *See*

also Gumbaynggirr (language); Many Rivers Aboriginal Language Centre (MRALC); *Mayalambala: Let's Move It* (book); Nambucca Heads High School (NSW)
MySQL (Structured Query Language) 318, 329

N

Nambucca Heads High School (NSW) xxii, 257. *See also* Muurrbay Aboriginal Language and Culture Co-operative
National Aboriginal and Torres Strait Islander Education Policy 12, 14
National Assessment Program-Literacy and Numeracy (NAPLaN) 16–17
national Indigenous languages policy 84, 87, 120
National Indigenous Languages Survey (NILS) 2005 108, 121–23, 147, 254, 356
   Language Endangerment Status Indicator 147
National Policy on Languages (1987) 8–11, 260
   Australian Language and Literacy Policy (1991) 8, 11
   Report on a National Language Policy (1984) 10
native title 4, 121, 127, 251, 313
   Buurabalayji-Thalanyji Association 121
   Ngarluma native title representative body 122–23
Navajo (language) 277
   language program xxviii
   Navajo Language Proficiency Test 276
Ndjébbana (language) 30
New Zealand English 298
Ngadjan (language) 93
   workshops 93, 358
Ngapartji Ngapartji (touring show) xxi, 55, 84–89, 336. *See also* Pitjantjatjara (language)
   Big hART 84, 87
   national tours, by 86
   Ninti language learning site 309
Ngarigu (language) 315
Ngarinyman (language) xix, 148, 159, 226–29, 231, 234. *See also* Victoria River District (VRD) NT; Yarralin School (NT)
   endangered 226, 229
   fluency in, 234
   grammar 229
   language program 231
   nouns 236
   verbs 236
   vocabulary 229
Ngarluma (language) 104, 122, 127. *See also* Wangka Maya Pilbara Aboriginal Language Centre (Wangka Maya)
   audio recordings of 128
   children's picture dictionary 122
   dictionary 122–23
   documentation 122
   endangered 122
   language-learning DVDs 122, 128
   mobile phone dictionary 123
   Ngarluma Language Project 122, 124, 129
   Ngarluma native title representative body 122
   sketch grammar 122–23, 128
   wordlist 122
Ngarralinyi Radio 110
Ngarrindjeri Dictionary Project 387–89, 391–96, 398–99. *See also* Ngarrindjeri (language)
   audio recordings 388
   electronic dictionary 392, 394–95
   Ngarrindjeri Dictionary 399
   Ngarrindjeri Learners' Guide 394
   Ngarrindjeri Picture Dictionary for Older Students 392
   Ngarrindjeri Yanun 397
   sources, of words 395–96, 398
Ngarrindjeri (language) xvi, 388. *See also* toponyms
   consonants 398
   curricula 389, 392
   dictionary. *See* Ngarrindjeri Dictionary Project
   endangered 352
   fluency in, 399
   grammar 394–95, 397
   orthography 387–88, 390–91, 393,

395, 398
  phonetics 396
  pronunciation 387–88, 392, 395
  Ramindjeri (dialect) 395, 398–99
  school-based teaching, of 352
  sounds of 393, 398
  vowels 398
  wordlist 387–91, 394–99
  workshops 392
Ngemba (language) 39, 42–47
  adjectives 46
  language program 42–47
  nouns 46
  pronouns 46
  pronunciation 46
nominative case 379
non-Pama-Nyungan (language family) 76, 146. See also Miriwoong (language)
North Coast Computer Project 110
Northern Territory Curriculum Framework (2002) 226
  Indigenous Languages and Culture (ILC) 226–27, 231, 233
North Queensland Regional Aboriginal Corporation Language Centre (NQRACLC) 93, 357, 359
nouns 391. See also object
  case system 299, 333
  Dharug 185
  Gurindji 229–30, 236
  Ngarinyman 236
  Ngemba 46
  Paakantji 294
  Wergaia 248
  Wiradjuri 211, 213, 299, 333
NSW Aboriginal Languages Forum (2007) 260
NSW Aboriginal Languages K-10 Syllabus xx, 112, 164–65, 167, 183, 189, 194, 197, 212–13, 216, 218–19, 254, 256, 272, 281, 287. See also curricula
  content 164
  development 254
  implementation 197, 219, 253, 275
  overview 219
NSW Department of Aboriginal Affairs (DAA) 108, 112, 115, 254, 260

Community Languages Assistance Program 108
Strong Language: Strong Culture 108
NSW Department of Education and Training (DET) xiv, xxi, 112, 178, 193, 195, 220, 222, 256, 259, 275, 278, 286, 403–05
  Aboriginal Education and Training Directorate (AETD) 171, 212
  Introducing an Aboriginal Languages Program 31
  Languages Unit 259
  Rhydwen, Mari 112, 160
  Teaching Qualifications Advisory Panel (TQAP) 273
NSW Office of the Board of Studies (BOS) xviii, xx, xxv, xxvii, 69, 71, 183, 189–90, 192–93, 197, 210–13, 219–22, 255, 259, 404. See also syllabus
Working with Aboriginal Communities; A Guide to Community Consultation and Protocols (2001) 164
Nukunu (language)
  audio recordings of 57
Nyangumarta (language) 104, 123–24. See also Wangka Maya Pilbara Aboriginal Language Centre (Wangka Maya)
  documentation, of 123
  endangered 123
  literacy in, 124
  Strelley Literacy Centre 123
  translation 124
  William (Nyaparu) Gardiner 124
Nyawaygi (language) 93, 95
  workshops 94, 358

O

object 213, 247, 299, 378. See also nouns
  function 379
  subject, and 378
  Subject-Verb-Object word order 299
Onerwal (language)
  Certificate I qualification 171
Oppliger, Amanda (linguist) 183, 186, 334
oracy. See oral proficiency

oral histories. *See* language source materials
oral language transmission 133–34, 136, 139, 140, 233, 326, 373, 375–76, 384. *See also* master-apprentice model
oral proficiency xxviii, 30, 32, 44, 135, 148, 165, 186, 226, 255, 265, 269–70. *See also* fluency; literacy
  Australian second language proficiency ratings (ASPLR) 271–74
  measurement of, 271–72
  New Brunswick second-language oral proficiency scale 271
  Proficiency guidelines: speaking 271
  Stanford Foreign Language Oral Skills Evaluation Matrix 271
orthography 30, 46, 58, 65, 94, 113–16, 123, 133, 149, 157, 181, 244, 247–48, 255, 260, 266, 281–85, 295, 302, 304, 314–15, 378–82
  Australian English, of 265, 393
  Dharug, of 183, 266
  Dhurga, of 167, 175, 191
  English, of 265–66, 281–83, 295
  Gamilaraay, of 282, 404, 409
  Gunnai, of 374, 378–82
  Miriwoong, of 78
  Ngarrindjeri, of 387–91, 393, 395, 398
  phonemic 266, 282, 295
  pronunciation, and 296
  training in, 127
  Warrgamay, of 96
  Wergaia, of 241, 247–48, 315
  Yuwaalaraay, of 404

P

Paakantji (language) 294–95
  nouns 294
  prepositions 294
  verb suffixes 294
palatal. *See also* lamino-palatal
  consonants 362
  nasal 382
  sounds 332
  stops 296
palato-alveolar affricates 296
Pallanganmiddang (language) 314
Pama-Nyungan (language family). *See* Yan-nhaŋu (language)
Parkes East Public School (NSW) 71–72, 74, 257
  language program (Wiradjuri) 71–72
Parkes High School (NSW) xix, 68, 70–71, 159
  language program (Wiradjuri) 71, 210–15
parsers 327, 329–30, 333, 337. *See also* grammars
Payungu Picture Dictionary 125–28
Pearson, Noel 142
phonemes 149, 283–85, 303, 374. *See also* phonemic orthographies; second language phonology; sounds
  consonant 285
  defined 282
  Dhurga 165
  Gamilaraay 282
  Ngarrindjeri 396
  palatal stops 296
  phonemic contrasts 295
  phonemic stops 295
  phonemic tone 298
  phonemic writing system 290
  pronunciation. *See also* pronunciation
  sound change 297
  vowel 285, 296
  Yuwaalaraay 282
phonemic orthographies 293, 295, 302–04, 332
phonetic script 304, 332. *See also* International Phonetic Alphabet (IPA)
phonology. *See* phonemes
Pigeon Hole School (NT) 226, 228–31, 235, 237
  language program (Bilinarra) 231
Pilbara Aboriginal Language Centre. *See* Wangka Maya Pilbara Aboriginal Language Centre (Wangka Maya)
Pitjantjatjara (language) xiv, xvi. *See also* Ngapartji Ngapartji (touring show)
  arts workshops 84
  Big hART 84, 87
  CDs 85
  documentation, of 86
  DVDs 85

Elders 84, 86
endangered 85
grammar 86
language program 84–89
linguists 84
Ninti Mulapa 86
translation 89
website 84–86, 89
workshops 85
placenames. *See* toponyms
policy. *See* education policy (languages)
possessive
 constructions 243
 marking 379
 pronouns 97, 376, 380–83
 suffixes 377
prefixes 299, 302
prepositions 116, 333
 Kriol 236
 Paakantji 294
 Wiradjuri 299
pronominal. *See also* pronouns
 forms 378
 meanings 378
pronouns 46, 341, 382, 384, 391
 absolutive (non-active) 379, 382
 dual 376, 381–82
 ergative (active) 379, 382
 Gunnai 372, 375–81, 383–84
 Gurindji 236
 missing 382
 Ngemba 46
 personal 97, 376, 381
 plural 376, 381–82
 possessive 97, 376, 380–83
 shortened forms 333
 singular 376, 378, 381
 Warrgamay 97
 Wergaia 247
 Wiradjuri 211, 213, 222, 333
pronunciation 43, 46, 56, 63, 65, 72, 94, 177, 182, 265–66, 268, 271, 294–96, 302, 304, 332, 334, 341, 343–44, 374, 382. *See also* sound files; sounds
 Bundjalung-Yugambeh, of 111
 consonants, of 266, 285
 Dharug, of 181, 185–86, 304
 Dhurga, of 165
 Gamilaraay, of 282, 403–04

guides 115, 293, 296
Gunnai, of 374, 380, 382
influence of English, on 265, 293–305
measurement of 271
Ngarrindjeri, of 387–88, 392, 395
Ngemba, of 46
orthography and, 296
Pilbara languages 124
voiced stop 296
vowels, of 266, 282, 304
Wergaia, of 315
Wiradjuri, of 299
Yorta Yorta, of 315
Yuwaalaraay, of 282, 403, 405, 415
public signage (bilingual) 28, 76–77, 83, 148, 150, 233, 372
Pundulmurra College (WA) 125–26
 Certificates in Aboriginal Language Work 125–26

Q

qualifications (Aboriginal Language Teaching) 158, 165, 170–73, 175, 178. *See also* courses (teaching); Master of Indigenous Languages Education (MILE); certification
 Advanced Certificate in Aboriginal Language Work 126
 Australian Qualifications Framework (AQF) 172
 Certificate III (TAFE NSW) 173, 180, 218, 272
 Certificate II (TAFE NSW) 115, 173, 180, 218, 272
 Certificate in Aboriginal Language Work 126
 Certificate I (TAFE NSW) 171, 173–74, 176–80, 218, 272
 Certificate IV (TAFE NSW) 115, 175, 179, 272
 demand for, 172
 development of, 171
 Graduate Diploma of Indigenous Languages Education 173
 National Training Information Service (NTIS) 173
 Statement of Attainment in Indigenous Language 171
 Teaching Qualifications Advisory Panel

(TQAP), NSW 403
Queensland Indigenous Languages Advisory Committee 356
Queensland Indigenous Languages Project 356–57
Queensland State Library. *See* State Library of Queensland (SLQ)

R

Ramindjeri (dialect). *See* Ngarrindjeri (language)
Raminyeri (dialect). *See* Ngarrindjeri (language)
reconciliation 18, 49, 61, 82, 167, 214
   Aboriginal languages, and 142, 214
Report on School-based Aboriginal Language Program Activity in NSW During 2006 162
Reversing Language Shift model (RLS) 79–80, 232, 369
Rhydwen, Mari 112, 160
Rudder, Dr John, 67, 210–11, 217

S

Samson & Delilah 88
school-community partnerships 7, 41, 47, 54, 159–60, 175–76, 178, 189, 194–03, 205–07, 210–11, 214, 216–224, 256–59
School of Australian Linguistics 120
second language phonology 298
sketch grammars. *See* grammars
software 112, 334, 336, 359. *See also* Miromaa Language Program
   Audacity (sound editing) 334, 393
   Audiamus 114
   development of 324, 327
   Drupal 318
   Elluminate Live! 384
   FileMaker Pro 60, 311, 390–91, 406, 414
   Finale Songwriter 335
   Fluency 334
   games 335
   internet telephony 335
   LanguageWiki 325, 331, 335
   Lexique Pro 341
   Microsoft PowerPoint 334
   Natural Language Toolkit 333
   open source 311
   Shoebox 332–33, 341, 390
   Skype 335
   Toolbox 114, 116, 341–42, 378, 387, 390–91, 406
   Transcriber 114, 116
songlines 38–39, 324
songs 37, 43, 45–47, 86, 89, 95, 97, 115, 117, 283, 327–28, 353, 392, 422, 427
   Dharug 181, 183, 185–87, 335
   Dhurga 189, 191
   documentation of 427
   Finale Songwriter 335
   Gamalaŋga 365
   Kaurna 57
   songbook (Gamilaraay) 177
   Warrgamay 98
   Wiradjuri 71, 213–14, 222
   Yuwaalaraay 282, 403
soundbooks 94
   Warrgamay 97
sound files 331–32, 334–35, 337, 393. *See also* audio recordings
   pronunciation of Kaurna, for 63, 65, 343–44
   pronunciation of Wiradjuri, for 329
sounds. *See also* Audacity sound editing software; audio recordings; phonemes; pronunciation
   Aboriginal languages, of 91–92, 94, 115–16, 183, 255, 266, 269, 282, 285, 288, 294–96, 301, 303–04, 331–32, 334, 336, 340–41, 346, 357–58. *See also* pronunciation
   Dharug, of 184–85
   Dhurga, of 163, 166–67, 297–98
   Gamilaraay, of 282–84, 403, 405–06, 408–10
   Gunnai, of 375, 379, 382
   Miriwoong, of 78, 149
   Ngarrindjeri, of 393, 398
   Wergaia, of 247, 249
source materials. *See* language source materials
speech synthesis technology 311, 332, 337
spelling systems. *See* orthography
Standard Australian English (SAE).

See Australian English
State Library of Queensland (SLQ) 352, 355, 356–60. See also Indigenous Knowledge Centres (IKCs)
website 357, 359
St Joseph's Primary School (NSW) Yuwaalaraay language program 403
St Mary's Public School (NSW). See also Gumbaynggirr (language)
Aboriginal language program 25–26
Stolen Generations 76, 91, 199, 240, 327
Strehlow, T.G.H xxv
Strelley Literacy Centre 123
Strong Language: Strong Culture (NSW report) 108
subject 247, 299, 379
agent, and 378
object, and 378
Subject-Verb-Object word order 299
suffixes 333
Gumbaynggirr 116
Gunnai 377, 379–80, 382–83
locative case 212–13, 299
nominal 213, 222
possessive 377
verb suffixes 294
Warrgamay 97
Wergaia 248–49
Wiradjuri 45, 211–13, 222, 299
Yan-nhaŋu 364
Sydney Aboriginal Language and Computing Centre (SALC)
LanguageWiki 325
website 325
wordlist database 328
syllables 266, 283, 332, 334, 365, 410
unstressed 296, 304
syllabus 69, 186, 227, 253. See also NSW Aboriginal Languages K-10 Syllabus
development of, xviii, 3, 220, 254
syntax 294, 324, 341
Extensible Markup Language (XML) 342
Field-Oriented Standard Format (FOSF) 341

T

Taungurung (dialect). See Kulin (language family)

teacher-linguists xxi, 111, 123, 241
Ingram, Andrew 113
teachers 7, 13, 16–17, 26–27, 30–31, 43–49, 53, 67–68, 70–71, 94–95, 98–99, 103, 106, 110–14, 119, 171–72, 267–70, 272, 276, 313, 324–25, 327, 331, 339, 352, 372, 388, 392, 403–04, 430. See also Master of Indigenous Languages Education (MILE); qualifications (Aboriginal Language Teaching)
Aboriginal people, as 24, 43, 49, 69, 73, 99, 108, 162–63, 167, 174, 188, 190, 197, 200–04, 206, 218, 220–21, 223, 256, 258–59, 274, 404, 427
cultural awareness of, 7, 27
Elders as, 30
fluency of, 273–74, 276, 278, 332
General and Vocational Education and Training (VET) courses 171
non-Aboriginal people, as, 99, 173, 202, 204–05
NSW Office of the Board of Studies (OBOS), support from 69
partnerships between, 48
professional development 259
training of, 31, 107–08, 115, 120, 151, 275, 278
teaching Aboriginal languages. See also language immersion; qualifications (Aboriginal Language Teaching); teaching resources
frameworks for, 48
programs 69
techniques 37–46, 71, 107, 149, 151
theoretical foundation for, 148
Western language models 141
Teaching Methodology for Aboriginal Languages 259
Teaching On Country (TOC) 139
teaching resources 94, 96, 108, 110, 112, 114–17, 122–23, 125, 128, 134, 148. See also Aboriginal Languages of Victoria Resource Portal (ALV-RP); dictionaries; grammars; information technology (IT); software; websites
A handbook of Aboriginal languages of

NSW and the ACT 114
Bamay Possum's Party (book) 115
Barriyala: Let's Work (book) 115
CDs 85, 114–15, 125–26, 177–78, 375
Dulaybam Dunggiir (book) 115
DVDs 85, 104, 117, 122, 124, 128
Gumbaynggirr Language Student Workbooks 115
illustrated books 110, 375
Mayalambala: Let's Move It (book) 115
Payungu Picture Dictionary 125–27
Teaching Methodology for Aboriginal Languages 259
Technical and Further Education (TAFE) NSW 158, 165, 170–71, 173–80, 218. *See also* courses (teaching); qualifications (Aboriginal Language Teaching)
General and Vocational Education and Training (VET) courses 171
Illawarra Institute 173, 175
Keeping Aboriginal Languages Strong workshop 173
Moruya campus 174–75
New England Institute 176
Social Inclusion and Vocational Access (SI&VA) Skills Unit 171, 174
South Western Sydney Institute 178
Ten canoes 88
Thalanyji (language) xv, 104, 121, 127. *See also* Wangka Maya Pilbara Aboriginal Language Centre (Wangka Maya)
Buurabalayji-Thalanyji Association 121
dictionary 121
documentation, of 121
endangered 121
ethnobotanical plant book 121, 128
fluency in, 121
language program 121
Ngambunyjarri 121
sketch grammar 128
Thunghutti Tiddas Aboriginal Corporation. *See* Dhanggati (language)
Tindale, Norman 394, 398, 408
toponyms 28, 54, 57–58, 61–62, 64–65, 76–77, 80, 82, 94, 98, 110, 115–16, 148, 266, 297, 304. *See also* public signage (bilingual)

Dharawal 179
Dharug 28, 181, 184, 187
Dhurga 164
Gamilaraay 409–10, 415
Geographical Names Board of NSW (GNB) 28
Gumbaynggirr 115–16
Kaurna xiii, 56–60
Kaurna Placenames website 54, 61–62, 64–65
Miriwoong 76–77, 80, 82
Ngarrindjeri 397
Warrgamay 98
Yaygirr/Yaegl 110
transcription 123–25, 127, 198, 200, 328, 333, 336, 368, 396, 405, 408–9, 421–22, 427, 429
Transcriber (software) 114, 116
transitive verbs 212, 404–05, 411
translation 86, 127, 233, 246, 327–29, 331–33, 335, 365, 368, 392, 408–09, 411–12, 426
Aboriginal languages to English 43–44, 56, 81, 124, 181, 326, 333, 395, 404, 413
Bible, of the 123, 397
Dharug, into 181, 184
English to Aboriginal languages 43, 222, 333, 395, 404
Gumbaynggirr, into 115
Gurindji, into 231
Kaurna, into 56–58, 60, 65
machine, by 311
Nyangumarta, from 124
Pitjantjatjara, into 89
songs, of 115, 222
speeches, of 115
Wergaia, from 248
Wergaia, into 240, 250
Wiradjuri, into 71, 222

U

Umpila (language). *See* Lockhart River case study

V

verbs 299, 331, 391, 411
Gamilaraay 404
Gunnai 383

Gurindji 230–31, 236
intransitive 212, 404–05, 411
morphology of 377
Ngarinyman 236
tense in 97, 333
transitive 212, 404–05, 411
verb suffixes 294
Wiradjuri 211–13, 222, 333
Yuwaalaraay 404
Victorian Aboriginal Corporation for Languages (VACL) xv, 241, 250, 301, 313–15, 372, 376, 384. *See also* Lodjba Koori Language Centre
website 301
workshop 384
Victorian Certificate of Education (VCE)
Indigenous Languages of Victoria, revival and reclamation: Victorian Certificate of Education study design 160, 240, 242, 247, 250, 313, 374
Victorian Curriculum and Assessment Authority (VCAA) 240–42, 313, 320.
Victorian Department of Education and Early Childhood Development (DEECD) 241
Victorian School of Languages (VSL) 241, 251, 320
Victoria River District (VRD) NT 225–28, 230, 232, 234–36. *See also* Bilinarra (language); Kalkaringi School (NT); Karrangpurru (language); language mixing; language programs (Aboriginal); Ngarinyman (language); Pigeon Hole School (NT); Yarralin School (NT)
Vincentia High School (NSW) xviii, 174, 188–93
Besold, Jutta 190–91
Brown, Colleen 189
Ford, Helen 189
Lane, Karen xviii, 189
Martin, Mitch xviii, 190–93
Pussell, Helen 189
Worthy, Gary 189, 257
visible language policy 10–12, 14, 18. *See also* invisible language policy; Maintenance of Indigenous Languages and Records program (MILR)

vocabulary 42, 46–48, 57, 94, 97, 111, 163, 184, 191, 242, 254–55, 288, 300, 302–03, 324, 331, 336. *See also* wordlists
Bilinarra 229
Dharug 328
Dhurga 163, 167, 185, 191–93
Gamilaraay 409–10, 412
Gunnai 376–81
Gurindji 229–31, 235
Kaurna 57
measurement of 271
Miriwoong 147, 149–50, 152
new, development of 294
Ngarinyman 229
Warrgamay 97
Wergaia 241–42, 245–46, 249–50, 315
Wiradjuri 213, 221–23
Yan-nhaŋu 364
Yitha-Yitha/Dadi-Dadi 28
Yuwaalaraay 410, 412
vowels 266, 285, 303–04, 398, 409
Australian English 285, 297
Gamilaraay 282, 296, 409–10
length contrasts, of 297, 303, 409–10
Māori 297–98
Ngarrindjeri 398
phonemes 285, 296
pronunciation of 266, 282, 304
sounds of 285, 303
unstressed, neutralisation of 296–97
Wergaia 249
Wiradjuri 299
Yolŋu Matha 266

W

Wadi Wadi (people) 188. *See also* Dhurga (language)
Wagiman (language) xxii, 345
mobile phone dictionary 345
Wailwan (language)
Certificate I qualification 171
Walgett High School (NSW)
Gamilaraay-Yuwaalaraay language program 403–05
Wanarruwa. *See* Awabakal-Wanarruwa (language)
Wangka Maya Pilbara Aboriginal Language Centre (Wangka Maya) xv,

103–04, 109, 119–20, 121–29. *See also* Bayungu (language); Ngarluma (language); Nyangumarta (language); *Payungu Picture Dictionary*; Thalanyji (language)
    administration 128
    audio recordings held by, 125
    language documentation, by 126–27
    language revitalisation strategy 119–20, 126–29
    linguists 124–25, 127–28
    specialist services 128–29
Wangkumarra (language)
    Certificate I qualification 171
Warlpiri (language) xvi
    dictionary 343
Warrgamay (language) 90, 93, 95–96. *See also* toponyms
    Elders 96–97
    fluency in 97
    language program xxi, 90, 93, 95–99
    orthography of, 96
    pronouns 97
    songs 98
    soundbook 97
    suffixes 97
    verbs 97
    vocabulary 97
    workshops 93, 97–98, 358
Warrimay (language) 110
Warrnambool (language) 314
Warrungu (language) 96
websites xvi, 4, 54, 61–62, 64–65, 83–86, 89, 316, 319, 337, 357. *See also* Aboriginal Languages of Victoria Resource Portal (ALVRP); information technology (IT); software
    Dharug 187, 335
    Gamilaraay 403
    Kaurna Placenames website 54, 61–62, 64–65
    Ngapartji Ngapartji (Pitjantjatjara) 84–86, 89
    Ninti 86
    State Library of Queensland (SLQ) 359
    Sydney Aboriginal Language and Computing Centre (SALC) 325
    Victorian Aboriginal Corporation for Languages 301
    Yuwaalaraay 403
Welcome to Country (ceremony) 4, 46, 56–57, 67, 70, 72, 77, 81, 83, 98, 113, 115, 214
Wergaia (language) 160, 245, 314. *See also* Wotjobaluk (people)
    audio-recordings of 243
    dictionary 160, 249
    grammar 160, 241, 243, 246, 248
    linguist 241
    nouns 248
    orthography 241, 247–48, 315
    pronouns 247
    pronunciation 315
    reconstruction 160, 240–51
    sketch grammar 245
    sounds of 247, 249
    suffixes 248–49
    translation 240, 246, 248, 250
    vocabulary 241–42, 245–46, 249, 315
    vowels 249
    Wergaia Community Grammar and Dictionary 240, 242–43, 250
    wordlist 241, 243, 251
    workshops 241, 243, 247
Western Australian Department of Environment and Conservation (DEC) 150
Wiradjuri (language) xix, 37–49, 67–74, 182, 216, 294, 327–28. *See also* Dubbo College (NSW); Grant (Snr), Stan; McNaboe, Diane; Parkes East Public School (NSW); Parkes High School (NSW)
    adjectives 333
    audio recordings 332
    Certificate I qualification 171
    curricula 159
    dictionary 217
    Elders' Council xiii, 67, 73, 217–18, 222–23, 257
    fluency in, 68, 70, 213
    grammar 212, 222–23
    language database 325
    language parser 333
    language program xix, 48, 210–13, 218, 257
    literacy 332
    locative case suffix 299
    nouns 211, 213, 299, 333

prepositions 299
pronouns 211, 213, 222, 333
pronunciation 299
songs 71, 213–14, 222
sound file 329
Statement of Attainment in Indigenous Language 171
suffixes 45, 213, 222, 299
verbs 211–13, 222, 333
vocabulary 213, 221–23
vowels 299
Windradyne, A Wiradjuri Koori (book) 214
wordlist 213
wordlist database 329
workshops 69–70, 212, 218, 222, 257, 325
Woiwurrung (dialect). *See* Kulin (language family)
Wonnarua (language) 113. *See* Awabakal-Wanarruwa (language)
Wonnarua Nation Aboriginal Corporation 110
Worawa Independent Aboriginal College (Victoria) xiv, 313, 320
wordlists 116, 244, 269, 293, 318, 325, 331, 333, 337, 373, 421. *See also* vocabulary; dictionaries
comparative 312
Dharug 304, 325
electronic 328, 333, 335, 359, 396–98
field recordings of 328
Gunnai 374, 376–77, 381–83
Kaurna 56
learning models, based on 160, 185, 226–27, 232, 235, 327, 330–31
Ngarluma 122
Ngarrindjeri 387–91, 394–99
Sydney Aboriginal Language and Computing Centre (SALC) database 325, 328
Taungurung 374
Wergaia 241, 243, 251
Wiradjuri 213
Wiradjuri database 329
Yuwaalaraay 404, 409
Yuwaalaraay-Gamilaraay 404–05, 408, 414
workshops xx, 94, 115, 136, 139, 220, 259–60, 325, 355, 374, 425–26

Arwarbukarl Cultural Resource Association (ACRA) 359
Australian Languages Workshop (2009) 346
community 176, 190, 218, 220, 325
Dhurga 176, 190, 193
Djirrbal 93, 358
Dunghutti 171
Gamilaraay 171, 176–77
Girramay 93, 358
Gudjal 94, 358
Gumbaynggirr 171
Gunnai 374
information and communication technology (ICT), on 107
Kaurna 57, 59
Keeping Aboriginal Languages Strong 173
language awareness xxi, 90, 93–95, 97–98, 176–77, 241, 243, 247, 358
Nambucca 113
Ngadjan 93, 358
Ngarrindjeri 392
Nyawaygi 94, 358
Pitjantjatjara 84–85
professional development 259, 393
Queensland Indigenous Languages Project, by 352, 355, 357–58
teaching techniques, on 107
training 59, 69–70, 84–85, 171, 193, 212, 220, 222, 241, 259–60, 352, 355, 357, 359
Victorian Aboriginal Corporation for Languages (VACL) 384
Warrgamay 93, 358
Wergaia 241, 243, 247
Wiradjuri 69–70, 212, 218, 222, 257, 325
Wotjobaluk (people) 160, 240, 244, 249–50. *See also* Wergaia (language)
Beer, Jennifer 241
native title claim 313
Pickford, Bronwyn 160
writing systems 255, 281, 283, 303–04
non-phonemic 304
phonemic 290, 304

X

XML. *See* Extensible Markup Language (XML)

Y

Yan-nhaŋu (language) 361–69
  audio recordings of 366, 368
  dictionary 365, 368
  Djambarrpuyŋu, parallel translations 368
  endangered 367, 369
  fluency in, 363, 366
  grammar 365, 368
  Language Nests 365
  learners' guide 368
  linguist, use of 368
  Milingimbi Literature Production Centre 365
  pictorial encyclopedia (talking) 365
  Sea Ranger Program 365
  suffixes 364
  vocabulary 364
  Yan-nhaŋu Ecological Knowledge (YEK) 365
Yan-nhaŋu (people) xiv, 366–67
  ethnographic descriptions 364
  kinship relationships 363–64
Yarralin School (NT) 226, 228–31, 235
Yaygirr/Yaegl (language) 110, 114. *See also* toponyms
  language program 110
Yindjibarndi (language) 122
Yitha-Yitha/Dadi-Dadi (language) 28
  grammar 28
  language program 28
  vocabulary 28
Yolŋu Matha (language family) xvi, 390. *See also* Burarra (language); Dhuwala (language); Djambarrpuyŋu (language); Gumatj (language); Yan-nhaŋu (language)
  Dhuwal. *See* Dhuwal (language)
  vowels 266
Yolŋu (people) xxix, 99–100, 142, 362
Yorta Yorta (language) 314–15
  pronunciation 315
  vocabulary 315
Yorta Yorta (people)
  native title claim 313
Yuin (community). *See* Dhurga (language)
Yuwaalaraay (language) xvi, 218. *See also Gamilaraay, Yuwaalaraay & Yuwaalayaay Dictionary (GYYD)*; Gamilaraay (language); Walgett High School (NSW); Yuwaalayaay (language)
  adjectives 411
  audio recordings of 403, 408–09
  CD 405
  Certificate I qualification 171
  Gaay Yuwaalaraay 405
  grammar 403–06
  language program 403–04
  orthography 404
  phonemes in, 282
  pronunciation 282, 403, 405, 415
  sketch grammar 413
  songs 282, 403
  sources of words 404, 408–10
  transcriptions 409
  verbs 404
  vocabulary 410, 412
  website 403
  wordlist 409
  wordlist, Yuwaalaraay-Gamilaraay 404–05, 408, 413–14
Yuwaalayaay (language) 402, 406. *See also Gamilaraay, Yuwaalaraay & Yuwaalayaay Dictionary (GYYD)*
Yaama Maliyaa 404
Yuwaalayaay-Language of the Narran River 404

www.ingramcontent.com/pod-product-compliance
Lightning Source LLC
Chambersburg PA
CBHW080117020526
44112CB00037B/2759